THE
ARLINGTON READER

Themes for Writers

THE
ARLINGTON READER

Themes for Writers

Fourth Edition

Lynn Z. Bloom
University of Connecticut

Louise Z. Smith

Bedford/St. Martin's
Boston ◆ New York

For Bedford/St. Martin's

Publisher for Composition: Leasa Burton
Executive Editor: John E. Sullivan III
Publishing Services Coordinator: Elizabeth M. Schaaf
Senior Production Supervisor: Jennifer Peterson
Marketing Manager: Emily Rowin
Editorial Assistant: Rachel Greenhaus
Project Management: Cenveo Publisher Services
Senior Art Director: Anna Palchik
Text Design: Jean Hammond
Cover Design: Billy Boardman
Cover Art: The Boardwalk courtesy of Michael Mao
Composition: Cenveo Publisher Services
Printing and Binding: RR Donnelley and Sons

President, Bedford/St. Martin's: Denise B. Wydra
Editorial Director, English and Music: Karen S. Henry
Director of Marketing: Karen R. Soeltz
Production Director: Susan W. Brown
Director of Rights and Permissions: Hilary Newman

Manufactured in the United States of America.

8   7   6   5   4

f   e   d   c   b

For information, write: Bedford/St. Martin's, 75 Arlington Street, Boston, MA 02116
   (617-399-4000)

ISBN 978-1-4576-4045-2

Acknowledgments
Acknowledgments and copyrights appear at the back of the book on pages 449–54, which constitute an extension of the copyright page. It is a violation of the law to reproduce these selections by any means whatsoever without the written permission of the copyright holder.

Preface for Instructors

WHY THIS BOOK?

This new edition of *The Arlington Reader* presents a mix of class-tested and cutting-edge essays designed not only to encourage discussion but also to provoke and address controversy. We hope to engage first-year composition students with topics that matter to them and to the world. *The Arlington Reader* is based on our extensive experience as researchers, writing teachers, and discriminating readers of contemporary writing. This blend of wide reading, theory, research, and practical expertise governs the book's philosophy and pedagogy. *The Arlington Reader* aims to

- teach students how to read, write, and think critically at the college level.
- help students respond actively to written texts and illustrations, with reflection, critique, dialogue, and debate.
- teach students to differentiate and make connections among important ideas.
- introduce students to a wide range of excellent modern and contemporary prose writers and major thinkers whose works are central to a liberal education.
- acquaint students with what professionals in various disciplines think, value, and argue about as critically important in our contemporary world.
- help newcomers to American culture respect their own traditions and values while they are learning new ones.
- enable all students, irrespective of birth and background, to share in America's ever-changing multicultural values and viewpoints.

CRITERIA FOR INCLUSION IN *THE ARLINGTON READER*

To be included in *The Arlington Reader*, an essay must first and foremost be teachable; it must contribute to the intellectual, political, and rhetorical balance of the whole book; and it must serve as a good illustration of professional or literary writing, in substance and in style.

An essay's *teachability* is determined in part by its *accessibility*. How much do teachers have to know or learn in order to teach the work? Will students understand its concepts and vocabulary, with or without much explanation in class? Is it intellectually appropriate for them? Is it too technical, too allusive, too arty for students to stick with it? Is the essay short enough to be discussed in one or two class periods?

An essay's *balance with the rest of the book* is reflected in the ways that its topic, point of view, and moral and ethical stance contribute to the kinds of dialogue, debate, and critical thinking *The Arlington Reader* hopes to engender. Will it enlarge the students' understanding of the world or of a particular issue? Does the essay represent views and values that students should consider, confront, and either challenge or adopt? Does the author's reputation, stand on issues, ethnicity, or gender contribute to the anthology's balanced perspective?

An essay's *aesthetic qualities* are related to form and style. Is its *form* a good example of narration or description or definition or comparison and contrast and the rest? Are these rhetorical patterns woven into an argument in a compelling way (since, it could be argued, every text is some kind of argument)? Is the essay clearly organized? Is its *style* rich in sentence rhythms, vocabulary, figurative language, tone, and even wit? Does the author "make it new," enabling readers to see the subject afresh?

FEATURES

Readings. *The Arlington Reader* includes a mix of class-tested and contemporary essays. Numerous *classic authors,* spanning the centuries but primarily from the twentieth and twenty-first centuries, provide continuity and intellectual solidity in this collection of significant writing. Among them are Henry David Thoreau, Alice Walker, Martin Luther King Jr., E. B. White, and Virginia Woolf. Distinguished fresh voices include Christine Overall, Lisa Miller, and Michael Oatman (online in the e-Pages). *The Arlington Reader* also includes many women and multicultural authors, among them Sherman Alexie, Gloria Anzaldúa, Leslie Silko, and Amy Tan, who bring alternative views and contemporary voices to the classroom.

Reflecting the needs of today's instructors and the interests of today's students, *The Arlington Reader* offers essays that are excellent models of good writing in style and technique and that illustrate one or more significant rhetorical concerns such as argument, comparison and contrast, and narrative. (See the Rhetorical Index on p. 455.) The essays range from three to fifteen pages long, so they're brief enough to be taught in one or two class periods but substantial enough to elicit serious discussion and writing.

Thematic orientation across disciplines. Seven thematic chapters address important areas of intellectual inquiry and controversy, intended to appeal to contemporary student writers. The chapters include Speaking, Reading, and Writing; Relationships and Life Choices; Education and the American Character; Gender; Technology; and Ethics. The chapters are broad and flexible enough to encompass a variety of topics, and the range of disciplines allows students to work across a number of academic subject areas.

Apparatus. Informative yet unobtrusive editorial commentary helps students move from critical reading to thoughtful writing and revising. Headnotes supply a substantial biographical note about the author of each essay and provide historical, cultural, and rhetorical contexts for essays. Questions for discussion and writing follow each essay. They include open-ended suggestions for discussion, interpretation, commentary, or dissent. These questions help students to read, think, and write about the essay's content, style, and rhetorical strategies and to make connections with other readings in the book and with issues outside the text as well.

A comprehensive Instructor's Manual. Available from our online catalog, the Instructor's Manual for *The Arlington Reader,* Fourth Edition, features answers to questions, alternative thematic clusters, and sample syllabi. See bedfordstmartins .com/arlington/catalog.

NEW TO THIS EDITION

An entirely new Part One provides coverage of critical reading, thinking, writing, and research. Three chapters introduce students to reading and writing in a practical way.

- **Chapter 1, Critical Reading,** helps students read thoughtfully and analytically. It includes instruction on active reading and note taking, plus help with analyzing visual and multimodal texts.
- **Chapter 2, Invention and Drafting,** takes students through the writing process. This chapter covers purpose, invention, rhetorical thinking, prewriting, thesis development, and organization, providing support for your students when they need it most.
- **Chapter 3, Using Sources, Revising, and Editing,** helps students enrich, re-see, edit, and format their papers. A sample student paper gives students a helpful model.

A more current collection, with 27 new, up-to-date selections. Among these exciting new readings, Malcolm Gladwell explores the relationships among the individual, culture, and alcohol in "Drinking Games." Tamara Winfrey Harris evaluates the cinematographic politics of race in "No Disrespect: Black Women and the Burden of Respectability." In "Liking Is for Cowards. Go for What Hurts.," Jonathan Frazen argues that we've confused consumer culture for what really matters, love.

Now with e-Pages. Students can do the work of the course online, with engaging readings that match the topics and approach of the book. In this edition, selections in *The Arlington Reader* now include a video presentation; audio interviews; and print, audio, and graphic essays available online, accompanied by helpful discussion and writing questions.

A chapter on gender. Based on instructor suggestions, we've added a chapter on the topic of gender. In it, students will read about how gender intersects with childhood, identity, politics, work, creativity, and stereotypes.

Popular culture throughout Part Two. Each thematic chapter now includes at least one reading that touches on an aspect of contemporary pop culture, which is sure to keep your students engaged. Examples include Barbara Ehrenreich's "Bonfire of the Disney Princesses" and Maria Konnikova's "Do You Think Like Sherlock Holmes? What the Detective Can Teach Us about Observation, Attention, and Happiness."

ACKNOWLEDGMENTS

We thank the following instructors who provided valuable feedback to help us improve *The Arlington Reader:* Alan Ainsworth, Houston Community College; Colleen Bakken, Bemidji State University; Alicia Beecher, University of Delaware; Cecilia Bonnor, Houston Community College; Cedric Burrows, University of Kansas; Tamy Chapman, Saddleback College; Elizabeth Cochrane, Harper College; Tommie Delaney, Columbus State University; Marina DelVecchio, Durham Technical Community College; Cheryl Easly, Central Texas College; Michael Edwards, United States Military Academy; Geri Harmon, Georgia Gwinnett College; Amy Handy, Austin Community College; Amy Heishman, Durham Technical Community College; Emily Hinnov, Boston University; Elizabeth Isaacs, University of Nebraska-Lincoln; Erica Johnson, San Diego State University; Lisa Drnec Kerr, Western New England University; Kelli MacCartey, University of Tennessee, Knoxville; Jared Magee, University of the Ozarks; Mary Rose Meade, Manchester Community College; Karen Meister, Ocean County College; Tomas Morin, Texas State University; Lyle Morgan, Pittsburg State University; Harry Newburn, University of Tennessee, Knoxville; Stacy Oberle, Lone Star College-Fairbanks Center; Lauren Petrino, College of Staten Island; Gina Rho, Fullerton College; Rene Scheys, Fullerton College; Jolly Sharp, University of the Cumberlands; Sandra Snow, Central Michigan University.

In the first edition, Chuck Christensen, Joan Feinberg, and Nancy Perry were instrumental in the conception and evolution of *The Arlington Reader.* Ning Yu brought his multicultural, Asian American scholar's perspective to a number of the headnotes and study questions and to the Instructor's Manual. Mark Gallaher and Matthew Simpson scrutinized our headnotes and questions and wrote some new ones, as did Kathrine Adeylott, crack researcher. George W. Smith gave quiet encouragement. For the second and third editions, Denise M. Lovett, a novelist of distinction, made significant revisions to the apparatus as well as prepared the new material for the Instructor's Manual. For this fourth edition, we are grateful to have had the assistance of Andrew Hoffman, who was instrumental in updating apparatus and the Instructor's Manual. Jenn Kennett oversaw permissions. Elizabeth Schaaf and Susan McIntyre supervised the book's production. Shannon Walsh helped develop this edition; we are grateful for her contributions. On all editions, John Sullivan coordinated the entire project, keeping track of details great and small, and keeping the work on target and on time with grace, good answers, and good will. Our students over the years have been emphatic about what works and what doesn't; their experiences reverberate throughout *The Arlington Reader.* Martin Bloom, philosopher and social psychologist, has contributed his expertise and a parodist's intolerance of the banal and trivial, an attitude he shares with our students.

YOU GET MORE CHOICES

Bedford/St. Martin's offers resources and format choices that help you and your students get even more out of the book and your course. To learn more about or order any of the following products, contact your Bedford/St. Martin's sales representative, e-mail sales support (sales_support@bfwpub.com), or visit the Web site at bedfordstmartins.com/readersguide/catalog.

Choose the flexible *Bedford e-Portfolio.* Students can collect, select, and reflect on their coursework and personalize and share their e-portfolios for any audience. Instructors can provide as much or as little structure as they see fit. Rubrics and learning outcomes can be aligned to student work, so instructors and programs can gather reliable and useful assessment data. Every *Bedford e-Portfolio* comes preloaded with *Portfolio Keeping* and *Portfolio Teaching,* by Nedra Reynolds and Elizabeth Davis. *Bedford e-Portfolio* can be purchased separately or packaged with the book at a significant discount. An activation code is required. To order *Bedford e-Portfolio* with the print book, use ISBN 978-1-4576-7822-6. Visit bedfordstmartins.com/eportfolio.

Watch peer review work. *Eli Review* lets instructors scaffold their assignments in a clearer, more effective way for students—making peer review more visible and teachable. *Eli Review* can be purchased separately or packaged with the book at a significant discount. An activation code is required. To order *Eli Review* with the print book, use ISBN 978-1-4576-7814-1. Visit bedfordstmartins.com/eli.

Select value packages. Add value to your course by packaging one of the following resources with *The Arlington Reader* at a significant discount. To learn more about package options, contact your Bedford/St. Martin's sales representative or visit bedfordstmartins.com/arlington/catalog.

- ***EasyWriter,* Fifth Edition, by Andrea Lunsford,** distills Andrea Lunsford's teaching and research into the essentials that today's writers need to make good choices in any rhetorical situation. To order *EasyWriter* packaged with *The Arlington Reader* use ISBN 978-1-4576-8368-8.
- ***A Pocket Style Manual,* Sixth Edition, by Diana Hacker and Nancy Sommers,** is a straightforward, inexpensive, quick reference, with content flexible enough to suit the needs of writers in the humanities, social sciences, sciences, health professions, business, fine arts, education, and beyond. To order *A Pocket Style Manual* with *The Arlington Reader,* use ISBN 978-1-4576-8369-5.
- ***LearningCurve for Readers and Writers,*** Bedford/St. Martin's adaptive quizzing program, quickly learns what students already know and helps them practice what they don't yet understand. Game-like quizzing motivates students to engage with their course, and reporting tools help teachers discern their students' needs. An activation code is required. To order *LearningCurve* packaged with the print book, use ISBN 978-1-4576-7817-2. For details, visit bedfordstmartins.com/englishlearningcurve.

Portfolio Keeping, **Third Edition, by Nedra Reynolds and Elizabeth Davis,** provides all the information students need to use the portfolio method successfully in a writing course. *Portfolio Teaching,* a companion guide for instructors, provides the practical information instructors and writing program administrators need to use the portfolio method successfully in a writing course. To order *Portfolio Keeping* packaged with the print book, use ISBN 978-1-4576-7815-8.

Try *Re:Writing 2* for Fun. What's the fun of teaching writing if you can't try something new? The best collection of free writing resources on the Web, *Re:Writing 2* gives you and your students even more ways to think, watch, practice, and learn about writing concepts. Listen to Nancy Sommers on using a teacher's comments to revise. Try a logic puzzle. Consult our resources for writing centers. All free for the fun of trying it. Visit bedfordstmartins.com/rewriting.

Instructor resources. You have a lot to do in your course. Bedford/St. Martin's wants to make it easy for you to find the support you need—and to get it quickly.

- *TeachingCentral* (bedfordstmartins.com/teachingcentral) offers the entire list of Bedford/St. Martin's print and online professional resources in one place. You'll find landmark reference works, sourcebooks on pedagogical issues, award-winning collections, and practical advice for the classroom— all free for instructors.
- *Bits* (bedfordbits.com) collects creative ideas for teaching a range of composition topics in an easily searchable blog format. A community of teachers— leading scholars, authors, and editors—discuss revision, research, grammar and style, technology, peer review, and much more.
- *Bedford Coursepacks* (bedfordstmartins.com/coursepacks) allow you to easily download digital materials from Bedford/St. Martin's for your course for the most common course management systems—Blackboard, Angel, Canvas, Desire2Learn, Moodle, or Sakai.

Brief Contents

Contents

For readings that go beyond the printed page, see
bedfordstmartins.com/arlington

3 Using Sources, Revising, and Editing   27

PART TWO   READINGS

4 Speaking, Reading, Writing: How Does Language Make Us Human?   47

5 Identity and Culture: Who Am I, and Why Does It Matter?   97

6 Relationships and Life Choices: How Should We Be with Ourselves, Others, and the World? 141

7   Education and the American Character: What Do We Teach? What Do We Learn? And Why Does This Matter?   196

8 Gender: What Makes Us Men and Women?   264

e-Pages at bedfordstmartins.com/arlington

9 Technology: What Are the Consequences of Life in a Connected World? 320

 e-Pages at **bedfordstmartins.com/arlington**

e-Pages at **bedfordstmartins.com/arlington**

THE
ARLINGTON READER

Themes for Writers

PART ONE

Critical Reading, Writing, and Research

CHAPTER 1

Critical Reading

WHAT IS CRITICAL READING?

In our everyday lives, we are often encouraged to be passive consumers, whether of products or television shows. Our culture also rewards speed, impatience, and superficiality—and for good reason: Clicking from Facebook to YouTube while text messaging a friend can be fun and exhilarating. But to engage with—and respond to—a piece of writing, you must cultivate the skill of **critical reading,** deliberate, careful reading that actively questions assumptions in the text. Moreover, to absorb ideas, develop critical thinking habits, and grow as a writer, you must do more than wait for something to happen as you run your eyes over sentences and paragraphs. You need to think about your purpose in reading a particular text. Will you be tested on the content of the material? Are you reading for class discussion? Will you be writing a response to the reading, or a journal entry? Are you reading to research an essay assignment? In every case, you should preview the text to gain a general sense of the writer's purpose, thesis, and supporting arguments. Along with reading the title and introduction, do not hesitate to read the last paragraph of the essay, which may contain a concise summary or restatement of the writer's main point. If you are reading to find a specific piece of information, skim the text (or even the book's index) to discover the section you need. Do not worry about "spoilers," particularly when reading for information and comprehension. You are not looking for a plot or a surprising, whodunit ending. Rather, you are reading to get as much from a text as possible to suit your purposes.

The text and your purposes may vary, but certain guidelines apply to all active reading. First, as you confront a text for the first time, try to avoid making reflexive and superficial judgments about what is "relatable." You may not have grown up on an Indian reservation in the 1970s–80s, but Sherman Alexie's "The Joy of Reading and Writing: Superman and Me" (p. 63) might speak to you about being an outsider or about the life-saving qualities of vicarious experience. You may have never been an Imperial Police officer in Burma, but that should not stop you from identifying with George Orwell's confusion, ambivalence, fear, and shame in "Shooting an Elephant" (p. 425). We may be a long way from the subterranean chamber in Plato's "The Allegory of the Cave" (p. 233), but we all struggle with problems of knowledge, perception, and truth.

Second, make sure to read what the author wrote, and not what you think he or she wrote. We all approach texts with biases and assumptions, but we must resist imposing our preconceptions preemptively—as when we assume we already know an author's thesis or interpret an essay looking for evidence that confirms what we already believe to be true (or what we think an instructor wants to hear). If we read Peter Singer's "The Singer Solution to World Poverty"(p. 400) with the assumption that poverty is "bad," but that a well-meaning individual can do little because the problem is so complex, and then seek evidence supporting our general view, we miss the most provocative aspects of Singer's "solution." The essays here should provoke strong responses and arguments, but those challenges must be grounded in an accurate comprehension of the writer's words. Slow down. Read deliberately. Reread.

PAYING ATTENTION TO FORM AND STRUCTURE

Perhaps the best place to understand the **structure** of writing—its plan, design, and arrangement—is at the point many writers find the most difficult: the beginning. Does an essay begin with a paradox? A specific example? A broad generalization? An unusual fact? In a way, every writing assignment is a puzzle or problem in need of a solution. So, notice how the writers in this anthology solve their problems—managing introductions, finding support for their arguments, addressing other points of view, taking readers beyond clichés and conventional wisdom, and concluding their essays without merely restating introductions.

The problems of writers are your problems, as well; and these are often matters of organization and design. In "The Joy of Reading and Writing: Superman and Me," Sherman Alexie confronts the structure of writing: "The words themselves were mostly foreign, but I still remember the exact moment when I first understood, with a sudden clarity, the purpose of a paragraph" (p. 64). Soon after, he "began to think of everything in terms of paragraphs." Although we may not have such a striking formative experience, good readers pay attention to the structural and formal building blocks of prose—words, sentences, paragraphs—as well as the way writing (in turn) structures thoughts and arguments. Consider paragraphs and their purposes. Does the paragraph begin with a generality, then move to specifics? Does the writer use it to explore and investigate one long example in support of a thesis? Does the writer use the paragraph to provide a series of short examples in succession? Does the paragraph provide background and context? Does it anticipate and refute an argument? Similarly, watch the way essays unfold and take shape in different patterns. Is the writer making a linear argument, moving from point to point? Is the writer structuring the essay by using contrasts and oppositions, or analogies? Does the writer move from personal observation and experience to a broader perspective—and more empirical research? How do writers incorporate specific evidence and quotation?

In many cases, writers will design their work so that the title, format, and even typography encourage comprehension and interpretation: numbered sections, topic headings, bullet points, and titles that indicate a thesis ("How

Computers Change the Way We Think," by Sherry Turkle, p. 325). Look for any visuals, such as graphs, charts, tables, and information set apart in boxes, placed in the margins or presented in a large or colored font. For many of the essays in this book, the structure and organization will be more subtle. But even in most nonfiction, you will find organization and design: titles that suggest subjects and themes; introductions that establish topic, context, purpose, and point of view; paragraphs with topic sentences that guide the reader from general assertions to specific examples; and sections that address counterarguments or establish qualifications.

Be mindful of words and phrases that reveal structure, as when writers enumerate reasons (*first, second, third*) or use **transitions** that indicate similarity and emphasis (*in addition, likewise, moreover*), as well as contrast (*but, however, in contrast*). Notice the shifts from generality to specificity, as when writers call attention to their illustrations with phrases like *for example*. As you get a sense of the author's larger structure and purpose, notice key terms and define any words that are unfamiliar to you. Look for connections between specific terms and the essay as a whole. For instance, some writers build their paragraphs—or even entire essays—around a single word. In "The Human Cost of an Illiterate Society" (p. 204), Jonathan Kozol's topic is illiteracy, but he also uses the noun "illiterates" in the topic sentences of his paragraphs. This repetition in the structure of the essay supports Kozol's main point; he uses that structural feature to illuminate the various implications and consequences of illiteracy.

ANNOTATING AS YOU READ

In most cases, you will want to mark up your book with a pen, pencil, highlighter, or even Post-it notes. That task encompasses underlining key terms, making marginal comments, and defining any words you do not know. But you should move beyond underlining and highlighting to **annotation,** which means asking questions in the margins, writing down key points so that you can refer to them later, looking for parallels with other readings, and engaging the text on all levels. Find and mark passages that capture the essence of the writer's argument or illustrate a point in an effective way; likewise, note places where you disagree with an essay, find it unclear, or see gaps in logic or evidence that weaken its argument. You can think of critical reading as a conversation with a text—and an essential part of the writing process. As a general rule, good writing comes from the active reading of *other good writing*. By noting key terms, capturing the writer's main points, and framing interpretive questions, you will be prepared for class discussion or journal entries that require you to summarize or respond to readings. More important, your initial responses and annotations will help enormously when you need to write your own assignment: You will already have writing prompts, ideas, arguments, and textual evidence to shape your own essays.

To show what active reading looks like, let's consider one student's annotation of two paragraphs from Martin Luther King Jr.'s "Letter from Birmingham Jail" (the full essay is on p. 406).

Oppressed people cannot remain oppressed forever. The yearning for freedom eventually manifests itself, and that is what has happened to the American Negro. Something within has reminded him of his birthright of freedom, and something without has reminded him that it can be gained. Consciously or unconsciously, he has been caught up by the *Zeitgeist,* and with his black brothers of Africa and his brown and yellow brothers of Asia, South America and the Caribbean, the United States Negro is moving with a sense of great urgency toward the promised land of racial justice. If one recognizes this vital urge that has engulfed the Negro community, one should readily understand why public demonstrations are taking place. The Negro has many pent up resentments and latent frustrations, and he must release them. So let him march; let him make prayer pilgrimages to the city hall; let him go on freedom rides—and try to understand why he must do so. If his repressed emotions are not released in nonviolent ways, they will seek expression through violence; this is not a threat but a fact of history. So I have not said to my people: "Get rid of your discontent." Rather, I have tried to say that this normal and healthy discontent can be channeled into the creative outlet of nonviolent direct action. And now this approach is being termed extremist.

But though I was initially disappointed at being categorized as an extremist, as I continued to think about the matter I gradually gained a measure of satisfaction from the label. Was not Jesus an extremist for love: "Love your enemies, bless them that curse you, do good to them that hate you, and pray for them which despitefully use you, and persecute you." Was not Amos an extremist for justice: "Let justice roll down like waters and righteousness like an ever flowing stream." Was not Paul an extremist for the Christian gospel: "I bear in my body the marks of the Lord Jesus." Was not Martin Luther an extremist: "Here I stand; I cannot do otherwise, so help me God." And John Bunyan: "I will stay in jail to the end of my days before I make a butchery of my conscience." And Abraham Lincoln: "This nation cannot survive half slave and half free." And Thomas Jefferson: "We hold these truths to be self-evident, that all men are created equal. . . ." So the question is not whether we will be extremists, but what kind of extremists we will be. Will we be extremists for hate or for love? Will we be extremists for the preservation of injustice or for the extension of justice? In that dramatic scene on Calvary's hill three men were crucified. We must never forget

Margin notes:

Topic sentence, supported with specific examples
"Manifests": "shows"

Parallelism and balance in sentence: forces within/ forces without
"Zeitgeist": defining ideas or mood of the age; spirit of a particular time
"Promised land": biblical connotation—inevitable, rightful, just
Examples of post-colonial movements of the time— "zeitgeist"

Importance of nonviolence and direct action as alternative to violent action and (implicitly) revolution (?)

Do words/writing/speeches count as "action," as well?

Connotation of "extremist"? Current meaning?
Jesus as "extremist" for love—tradition of extremists—biblical, historical, and (esp.) American traditions

Turns insulting label around—extremist for what?

that all three were crucified for the same crime—the crime of extremism. Two were extremists for immorality, and thus fell below their environment. The other, Jesus Christ, was an extremist for love, truth, and goodness, and thereby rose above his environment. <u>Perhaps the South, the nation, and the world are in dire need of creative extremists.</u>

What is a "creative extremist"? Other examples? Who gets to decide?

This student was required to write an analysis of King's "Letter from Birmingham Jail," highlighting one particular theme or aspect of the text that seemed especially important to understanding King's main point. The assignment was open-ended, and the student had a wide range of choices; such essays can be difficult for some writers. This student's notes, questions, and annotations in the text provided the material for her essay. Her active reading focused her attention on King's idea of "creative extremism"—his notion that discontent with injustice is "healthy," but that it must be "channeled into the creative outlet of nonviolent direct action." Although people often make a distinction between words and actions, the student argued that King does not: His powerful and persuasive rhetoric can itself be understood as a prime example of "creative extremism," a form of nonviolent action designed to motivate his readers to nonviolent action.

CHECKLIST: QUESTIONS FOR CRITICAL READING

- ☐ Have I previewed the text to get a sense of its purpose, topic, and thesis?
- ☐ Have I read slowly, carefully, and deliberately?
- ☐ How is the essay structured and organized?
- ☐ What formatting elements organize the essay: numbered sections, bullet points, boxed features, typographic elements?
- ☐ What new or unfamiliar words need to be defined?
- ☐ What key words or phrases are central to understanding the essay's main point?
- ☐ Have I annotated the essay thoughtfully and carefully?

FROM COMPREHENSION TO ANALYTICAL READING

Reading for **comprehension** is essential: We need to know the basic meaning of the words on the page, the thesis of the essay, the plot of the story, the difference between "mitosis" and "meiosis" in a biology text, and the dates of the Civil War in a history book. But **analytical reading** suggests a deeper and more lasting transaction between writer and reader. We can illustrate this contrast with Plato's "The Allegory of the Cave," a foundational text in Western thought (p. 233). When we read for comprehension, we follow what happens in the story. A group of people live chained in a "cavernous chamber underground." They watch the shadows of "artificial objects" on a wall, which flicker in a kind of puppet show. One of these individuals becomes free, escapes the cave, and sees the sun. He returns to share his experience but meets only scorn, ridicule, and the threat of death from his fellow cave-dwellers. If that was all there was to the story, no one would care about it, nor would it be republished thousands of years later in this anthology. Its meaning emerges only from analytical reading. Plato provides the keys to that analysis by explaining the tale's allegorical correspondences, which reveal the allegory's themes and thesis about false images, perception, knowledge, reality, human limitations, and the "Good" and the "True."

Martin Luther King Jr. absorbed this story, as well. His reading of Plato's works, including "The Allegory of the Cave," undergirds his understanding of "direct action," as well as his justifications for creating nonviolent conflict and "tension" in the cause of progress and equality. We see this at work in his "Letter from Birmingham Jail" (p. 406). Consider how he applies Plato's thought to his own argument:

> Just as Socrates felt that it was necessary to create a tension in the mind so that individuals could rise from the bondage of myths and half-truths to the unfettered realm of creative analysis and objective appraisal, so must we see the need for nonviolent gadflies to create the kind of tension in society that will help men rise from the dark depths of prejudice and racism to the majestic heights of understanding and brotherhood (p. 408).

So prejudice and inequality become the false images and myths; working toward justice, understanding, and truth becomes an ascent from the shadows toward Plato's "essential form of Goodness." But only through analytical reading—in the "unfettered realm of creative analysis"—can King express the cosmic stakes of the civil rights movement. The selections in this anthology not only reward analytical reading but also provide several models of what it means to be a great reader, from King to Eudora Welty and Sherman Alexie.

LOOKING FOR THEMES

Readers sometimes confuse a story's or essay's **subject**—"what happens" in a piece of writing, with its **theme,** the way it connects to events in the reader's life or the world in a larger sense. That crucial distinction reveals the difference between reading for comprehension (understanding subject) and analytical reading (understanding theme). Although this contrast is relatively obvious when we encounter a text like Plato's "Allegory," few of the essays here will have such self-evidently symbolic or figurative meanings. However, they still lend themselves to rigorous analytical reading. For instance, George Orwell's "Shooting an Elephant" (p. 425) recounts the writer's experience of shooting an elephant. He narrates the account, providing the plot, context, and details of the event. On one level, this narrative is "about" what the title indicates. When we read for comprehension, we might ask questions such as, *In what country does this story take place?* (Burma); or, *Did the narrator want to shoot the elephant?* (No). Analytical reading requires an accurate understanding of these facts and textual details, but the analytical reader also formulates different questions, ones designed to illuminate what a text is *really* "about": *What does this story reveal about the nature of imperialism and the relationship between colonizers and the colonized? How does shooting the elephant function as a metaphor for the paradoxes of English rule? In what way do the details of this essay support—or undermine—the writer's assertion that "when the white man turns tyrant it is his own freedom that he destroys"?* Notice that, unlike simple matters of recall and comprehension, these are questions to which well-informed readers might give differing answers. So, as you read and comprehend the details of a piece of writing, try to formulate questions that reveal more than its topic or "plot": Look for ways to understand and express what a text is really about.

PAYING ATTENTION TO STYLE, VOICE, AND TONE

The best writers pay as much attention to how they write as to what they write. When we communicate with language, we often seek clarity and transparency, as though words are an empty medium that we fill with "meaning." But the best writers do more than that. They pay attention to **tone,** which refers to a writer's attitude, and **style,** which encompasses tone, sound, connotation, diction, rhythm, irony, attitude, and other qualities of language that go beyond merely communicating literal meaning. In "Fighting Words," (p. 66), Richard Wright recalls responding to the texture and tone of writer H. L. Mencken's prose even before he notices Mencken's argument: "I was jarred and shocked by the style, the clear, clean, sweeping sentences. . . . Yes, this man was fighting, fighting with words. He was using words as a weapon, using them as one would use a club." Wright's close encounter with style is instructive: We read with our ears—and our guts—as well as with our eyes. Good writers, like good musicians, pay attention to sound, rhythm, and the visceral effects of language. As Eudora Welty writes in "Listening" (p. 47), the "cadence, whatever it is that asks you to believe, the feeling that resides in the printed word, reaches me through the reader-voice." When you read, consider that cadence, the sound, syntax, repetition, and connotation: the writer's choice of *this* word over *that* word, an active verb over a passive verb, a sentence with a long introductory subordinate clause over a series of short staccato statements.

It can be hard to define a prose stylist, but we know one when we read one: *"Summertime, oh, summertime, pattern of life indelible, the fade-proof lake, the woods unshatterable, the pasture with the sweetfern and the juniper forever and ever, summer without end. . . ."* (p. 158). So E. B. White writes in "Once More to the Lake," his writer's ear choosing the incantatory repetition of "summertime" (even though it's unnecessary to the passage's literal meaning); connecting the "f" in "life" with the "f" in "fade," as well as the echo of the "a" in "fade" in the long "a" in lake; giving a precise, tuneful chime in the unusual words "sweetfern" and "juniper" (how would the sentence be different had he just said "regional plant life" or resorted to a cliché like "splendors of nature" instead?). Like the summertime pattern of life, prose style is "indelible."

CHECKLIST: QUESTIONS FOR ANALYTICAL READING

☐ How can the themes of the essay be separated from its subject matter or general topic?

☐ Where in the essay does the writer use implication or suggestion instead of being explicit?

☐ What interpretive or analytical questions can be asked of this text? For example, what aspects of the essay might lead to disagreement between different readers?

☐ How would you characterize the tone of the essay? Is it sincere? Ironic? Angry? Exuberant? Detached? Urgent?

☐ How would you characterize the writer's style? Does he or she pay attention to sound, rhythm, connotation, figurative language, and aspects of words other than their literal meanings?

READING VISUAL TEXTS

Even though we may be used to passively viewing images and videos, they still require interpretive reading. Indeed, from cave paintings and tapestries to political propaganda posters, television advertisements, viral videos, and Internet memes, humans have always used visual media to express, inform, and persuade. Graphs and charts can inform us (or even mislead us). Images can evoke strong emotions. Movies can make us lose ourselves in the world of a filmmaker. Although we may be tempted to think of images like photographs, films, or realistic paintings as neutral representations of reality, they are themselves interpretations of reality. For example, a photographer will frame images in a certain way, choose an angle that emphasizes a particular aspect within the picture for effect, or stage a photograph deliberately.

When you read a visual image, consider its formal elements and its contexts, as well as the relationship between the two. As with written texts, you need to read for both comprehension (to determine what you are looking at) and interpretation (to discover the image's point, theme, or overall meaning). Some visual art can blur the distinction between comprehension and interpretation, or subvert them altogether—doing so may be the artist's, filmmaker's, or photographer's point. At other times, visual images will communicate clearly and present obvious messages, or even basic information (as in a pie chart).

Consider the following work by painter Norman Rockwell. We may view it as a kind of **visual rhetoric,** a term that refers to the way images can be designed to make an argument, suggest a specific theme, or illustrate a point for the viewer to interpret, rather than existing only as aesthetic objects of "art" or "beauty" (of course, these categories are not mutually exclusive).

"The Problem We All Live With" first appeared in a 1964 issue of *Look* magazine. Rockwell depicts a young girl—presumably six-year-old Ruby Bridges—on her way to an all-white public school in New Orleans as the city's schools underwent desegregation in 1960. We see an image of an African American girl walking under

Norman Rockwell, "The Problem We All Live With." Oil on canvas, 1964.

the apparent protection of four uniformed white men, whose armbands identify them as U.S. deputy marshals. Our eyes are drawn first to her and her white dress and shoes, which suggest her innocence. We also see the imposing figures of the marshals, which highlight the smallness of the girl, yet their heads are not included in the painting. In the background, we can see the letters "KKK" (in the upper left-hand corner of the painting), as well as the word "NIGGER" scrawled on the wall. The ugliness of these "texts" contrasts sharply with the image of the innocent child, as she is dwarfed by both people and the turmoil around her. A tomato, presumably thrown at the girl by a hostile-but-unseen crowd, lies at the lower right of the background, beneath its spatter on the wall. We might also notice some smaller details: that Ruby is slightly out of step with her escorts; that she carries books, pens, and a ruler; that she is left of the center in the painting. Even as the image conjures up sympathy for the girl and perhaps fear about the dislocations of social change, we should also consider that Rockwell forces the viewer to see the painting from the point of view of the hostile mob. The title implies that this painting represents or portrays "The Problem We All Live With"; although Rockwell does not explain the problem, the iconic image implies multiple themes (racism, intolerance, segregation, inequality) and a thesis (the inadequacy of public indifference in the face of injustice, the impossibility of ignoring a social problem, the importance of turning personal sympathy into political action), along with a suggestion that the viewers are complicit in the "problem."

If we are familiar with the artist, we might see a surprising image that contrasts with the themes and sensibility we associate with Norman Rockwell's sentimentalized, idealized, and nostalgic paintings of small-town America. We should consider the date of the painting's publication, 1964, in the middle of the civil rights era, as well as the fact that Rockwell produced several paintings depicting the country's racial strife. As noted previously, this image appeared in *Look* magazine, a publication aimed at primarily educated white readers. What effect do you think Rockwell was seeking? Do you see this as a realistic portrayal of the civil rights era? Do you see it as propaganda?

CHECKLIST: QUESTIONS FOR VISUAL ANALYSIS

☐ Who created the image? Does it include a title? What is the medium (photograph, painting, poster, advertisement, cartoon)? Where does the image appear?

☐ Who is the intended audience? Are they friendly? Skeptical? Hostile? Neutral? What values does the image assume in its audience?

☐ Is the visual representational? That is, does it show recognizable people or things? What, if any, specific images appear?

☐ Does the image use color? What within the image draws your eyes? What is in the foreground and what is in the background? What details does the image include? Does the visual use empty space? What is left out of the image that might have been included?

☐ What are the relative sizes of objects within the image? Is anything deliberately intensified or exaggerated?

☐ Does the image use words? If so, how do they contribute to its meaning?

☐ What is your overall impression of the image? Does the image suggest a theme, message, meaning, or thesis? Does it present a single, obvious meaning, or allow for different interpretations?

☐ What is the creator's apparent attitude toward the images within the visual? What is the image's purpose: to inform, express, persuade, entertain, shock, evoke emotion, tell a story, or some combination of these things?

☐ Is the image designed to encourage a particular action, such as voting or making a donation or purchase?

CHAPTER 2

Invention and Drafting

UNDERSTANDING PURPOSE, AUDIENCE, AND TOPIC

College coursework makes a wide range of demands on student writers. Some assignments will be informal and brief. In many cases, they will be directed by specific prompts, questions, or formats: An English professor may require you to write short, subjective responses to readings, keep a journal, or compose a personal narrative about an important event in your life; a business communications professor may have you write concise executive summaries of readings or brief memos; a political science professor might ask you to write a one-paragraph explanation of the "Take Care Clause" from Article II of the U.S. Constitution; or a biology instructor might have you prepare a written lab report explaining the process used to extract DNA from an onion.

Many college assignment prompts will require you to craft an analytical argument, take a stand on a topic, answer a question, or propose a solution:

- *Explain the role of irony in Edgar Allan Poe's story "The Cask of Amontillado."*
- *In what ways did the New Deal change the relationship between Americans and the federal government?*
- *Write an essay about the value of a liberal education in the global economy and the contemporary job market.*
- *How can the United States implement policies that encourage more students to pursue careers in science, technology, engineering, and mathematics?*

At other times—particularly in higher level classes—an instructor will give open-ended writing assignments that require students to generate their own topics based on their interests, reading, and research within the course material. But for all writing assignments, you will have to consider your **purpose**, your **audience**, and your **topic**.

PURPOSE: WHY ARE YOU WRITING?

Make sure you understand your assignment and your aims. Are you being asked to analyze? Summarize? Argue? Compare? Recommend? The aim of an essay will shape its form and content. Usually, your assignment will fit broadly into one or more of the following categories, but they often overlap:

Are you writing to inform? Informative writing seeks to communicate information to readers in forms such as summaries, research papers, investigative journalism, and status updates on projects in progress. These assignments may require you to be disinterested, objective, and impersonal in your approach.

Are you writing to persuade? When you write to persuade, you try to convince readers to agree with a specific point of view, support a proposal or policy, and think or act in a certain way. We see persuasive writing in editorials, Internet reviews, argumentative essays, position papers, policy proposals, and advertisements.

Are you writing to express yourself? When you write to express, you communicate emotions, perceptions, and thoughts to readers, often in forms such as personal narratives or descriptive essays. Expressive writing privileges subjectivity and originality, as well as individual insight, personal voice, and the first-person pronoun "I."

Again, most writing assignments—as well as many selections in this book—move among all three of these purposes. Richard Rodriguez's "Aria: A Memoir of a Bilingual Childhood" (p. 211) is a profoundly personal example of expressive, autobiographical writing, but the author also seeks to persuade the reader to adopt a particular view of bilingual education. In "Is Google Making Us Stupid?" (p. 331) Nicholas Carr offers a persuasive argument about the Internet's negative effects on deep reading and deep thinking, but he accomplishes this by informing: He presents findings on Internet research habits, brain science, and the history of technology. Your English professor may assign a formalist literary analysis requiring you to use textual evidence to support a particular reading of a short story or poem; as you make that argument, however, your interpretation may arise from highly subjective and expressive responses to the text.

CHECKLIST: UNDERSTANDING YOUR PURPOSE

☐ What key words in the directions identify the purpose of the essay (*explain, analyze, argue, compare, describe*)?

☐ How can I find a subject and focus that matter to me?

☐ Is this a major or minor assignment?

☐ What steps must I go through to write it? (When in doubt, ask your instructor.)

☐ How much time should I spend on it?

AUDIENCE: TO WHOM ARE YOU WRITING?

Your purpose will be intimately tied to your **audience,** that is, your presumed or intended readers. Usually, your immediate audience will be your instructor and perhaps your classmates, who expect clear, knowledgeable, and credible writing on your subject. The requirements—and quirks—of instructors will vary. Some will encourage writing in the first person ("I first looked at recent sources . . ."), while others will prohibit all first-person pronouns; some will forbid the use of contractions or deliberate sentence fragments, while others will allow them; some might emphasize clarity, correctness, and consistent formatting, while others might place greater value on ingenuity or even style. Part of your task as a writer is to understand who your readers are and write accordingly. In many cases (regarding the use of the first person, for example), you can ask about the assignment's requirements. At other times, however, you will have to respond to feedback and gauge responses to your writing. Carefully consider your instructor's written comments on your essays; they will be useful if you have the opportunity to turn in multiple drafts, but they will also help you understand his or her more subtle preferences and emphases. Similarly, if you participate in an in-class workshop or peer review, and readers are confused by your argument or put off by your tone, pay attention to their responses, even if you do not incorporate every suggestion.

As you tackle various writing assignments, keep in mind different readers for different writing occasions: skeptical newspaper readers for an opinion column; prospective employers for a cover letter; fellow cooks for a how-to recipe; music fans for a music review; or a community of scientists for a lab report. Your sense of audience should influence both the content and the style of your writing. For example, if you are writing about a specialized subculture (say, a particular genre of video games) for a general audience, you must provide more background information than would be required for an online review of a gaming Web site with a specialized audience. You will also have to find an approach that makes your subject accessible but that does not come across as condescending. If your task is a four-page formal analysis of Edgar Allan Poe's "The Cask of Amontillado" for an English class in which this story was an assigned reading, do not spend two pages summarizing the plot: Your teacher and classmates already know it. Different audiences will require different stylistic choices, as well. If you are writing the text of a speech or oral presentation, you may choose simpler words, use short sentences, and repeat certain key terms or points in ways that you would not in a written essay.

CHECKLIST: UNDERSTANDING YOUR AUDIENCE

- ☐ What effect do I want my writing to have on my audience? Do I want to teach them something? Convince them of my point of view? Change their minds? Move them to action? Entertain them?

- ☐ Do I have a specific reader or groups of readers in mind—instructors, classmates, scientists, churchgoers, teenagers, college administrators, hip hop fans?

- ☐ Do they know as much about the subject as I do? Do they know more? Do they know less?

- ☐ What opinions and values they probably share are relevant to my topic? Are they likely to agree with me? With one another?

- ☐ How simple or technical should my language be? What terms, concepts, and contexts will I need to define, explain, or illustrate?

DISCOVERING YOUR TOPIC

For college-level writing, you will often be responsible for generating your own topic and argument without a prompt from the instructor. For some writers, these essays are liberating and fun; for others, such assignments cause dread arising from what the existential philosopher Jean-Paul Sartre called "the terrible freedom." Open-ended paper topics can create a paradox of choice. With so many possibilities, where does a writer begin? Several **prewriting** techniques can help you find your topic and focus. Notice that several of these strategies share a common aim: to overcome your internal editing process. Remember, you will have time to organize, edit, and polish later. For now, you want to get as much raw material on paper or your computer screen as possible. Temporarily set aside your sense of audience, too. You prewrite for only one reader: yourself.

FREEWRITING

When you **freewrite,** take a set amount of time (say, five minutes) and write about your subject without stopping, letting your thoughts and associations flow onto the page. Do not stop typing or take your pen off the paper; keep your mind focused on the subject. The goal is exploration and invention. Forget proper spelling, syntax, grammar, or coherence. If you get stuck, keep repeating the same word or write out the question, *Why am I blocked?* Then freewrite an answer: *I am blocked because . . .* When the time period is up, look at your writing. Much of it will be chaotic, but if you give in to the process, you will often find a passage on the page, a cluster of words, a sentence, a phrase, or an emerging idea that leads you to a topic. Moreover, if you generally find it difficult to start writing assignments, make freewriting a habit. If you do it regularly, you will be able to generate your own topics much more easily. Although this exercise can seem like a fuzzy practice more related to therapy than writing, it is an eminently practical technique. Peter Elbow, an early champion of freewriting, developed his ideas about these exercises while working with students at the Massachusetts Institute of Technology. He understood that confronting a blank page or blinking cursor can be inhibiting rather than inviting, especially for graded assignments. Practices like freewriting break down inhibitions and allow access to sources of vital, powerful, and engaged prose. As Elbow notes in "Freewriting" (p. 80), the "main thing about freewriting is that it is nonediting. It is an exercise in bringing together the process of producing words and putting them down on the page. Practiced regularly, it undoes the ingrained habit of editing at the same time you are trying to produce." So, create now; structure and polish your prose later.

Here is a brief excerpt of freewriting from one student, Logan Block, who was beginning an assignment. The student was asked to write an argumentative essay in which he was to make a case for or against the value of pursuing a college education. His freewriting led him to questions about "values" as well as higher education:

Why do we need liberal arts education or a four-year degree? Can't buy food with "know thyself." Need jobs, jobs jobs jobs, need contacts and degree need to pay off loans but am I more than a job? Need a career and money is important and need to be able to support myself family so college is a hoop a hurdle expected to go sit through art spanish philosophy english anthropology american government history—why? Do I like being here? Yes and no. Could be working. Opportunity costs, but creating opportunities for myself. Well-rounded won't pay bills: What is this? What am I? thinker writer student intern employee worker. Need to buy house buy car / good for me good for economy need to be competitive country needs to be competitive economic growth = personal growth? Mom says priorities are: people then money then things. What values to apply? What does "value" mean? What are my values? Whose values? Happiness and family I need to think I need to speak and I need to read and I need to know need to be adaptable flexible social skeptical. Social skills. We read more than books, we read people. And I need skills understand critical thinking critical to me as worker, buyer, voter, citizen, person, boyfriend, human . . .

BRAINSTORMING

Brainstorming is even less formal than freewriting, but it seeks the same sources of inspiration. When you **brainstorm,** you take two, five, or ten minutes to list anything that comes to mind about your topic, including facts, associations, memories from your notes or class discussions, questions, and thoughts (even half-formed ones). Turn off your self-editing mechanisms and judgment. You are not trying to organize, establish logical connections, or distinguish between relevant and irrelevant information yet. Rather, you use brainstorming to unearth your topic, view it from new angles, and discover its importance to you as a writer. Do not worry about writing complete sentences; just use words, phrases, or fragments. Brainstorming is especially effective if you are already familiar with your prospective material and need to retrieve information and ideas. It is also useful when beginning group writing projects, as members can generate ideas, bat them around, and make new connections between them. As the American chemist Linus Pauling once said, "The best way to have good ideas is to have a lot of ideas." If you get one good idea for every ten bad ones while brainstorming, it will be worth the time and effort.

The student, Logan Block, also explored his topic with brainstorming, which suggested a focus for his essay:

Value of Liberal Arts

Useless? Useful? For all?	*Good for: talking,*	*Face to face*
For some?	*reading, writing,*	*Person to person*
Exceptional people	*thinking, listening,*	*Silence of reading*
never graduated	*seeing, voting,*	*Quietly think for myself*
from college: Gates,	*relating*	*Weigh words*
Branson, Zuckerberg	*Slow down*	*Know how to use words*
What do we value?	*Concentration*	*Look at evidence*

Know history	*Connects me to past*	*Know me*
Know people	*To people*	*Never knew I liked*
Know things	*To ideas, new ideas, old*	* economics until I took*
Perspective—big	* ideas*	* class*
* pictures, where things*	*Know bad ideas from*	*Know what I really want*
* fit, where I fit*	* good ideas*	

CLUSTERING

Clustering can be a powerful prewriting technique for visual learners. It uses graphic organizers like circles, arrows, and informal diagrams to translate ideas—and connections between ideas—into spacial relationships: a revealing map that may illustrate aspects of your topic you would not otherwise notice. Clustering begins with a single word, phrase, sentence, or subject in the middle of the page. Then, you connect related ideas, facts, notes, and associations around this phrase, placing smaller points, ideas, or details into smaller boxes or circles. Try to become more specific as you move outward, and look for links between the details or other associations that may become visible only when you perceive their relationship in space. In many cases, you will discover new connections between general aspects of the topic and specific examples within it, or between the whole topic and its particular components. Remember, prewriting techniques are not mutually exclusive. For example, you might use clustering to develop an idea that you discovered by freewriting or brainstorming.

This time, the student used clustering to consider the relationships between his ideas, along with ways of organizing the essay and using sources (see p. 19).

READING TO WRITE

If an essay assignment requires you to write about a specific piece of writing, recall the earlier section on annotation (p. 5). By reading critically, you should be able to find an aspect, theme, question, or problem to move from a general subject or text (Martin Luther King's "Letter from Birmingham Jail") to a more specific topic ("creative extremism" in Martin Luther King's "Letter from Birmingham Jail"). But reading has other practical uses as a prewriting technique, especially if you are unfamiliar with a subject or prospective topic. Reading accessible, general interest magazine or newspaper articles, as well as less specialized scholarly work in a field, can provide an overview and outline the shape of a subject, topic, or issue. More important, such reading will give you a sense of ongoing discussion about your topic: its history, its key figures, its points of disagreement, its most recent developments. For example, if you are embarking on an essay about online social networks, you might begin by reading a column about Facebook privacy policy on Slate.com or an article about the Internet's effects on the human brain in *Wired* magazine: What interests you, baffles you, bothers you, or suggests a space for your own insight? These sources may not be scholarly and you might not even cite them in your paper, but they might suggest an approach to a topic or light the spark for

- Bill Gates, Mark Zuckerberg, Richard Branson, Estée Lauder never graduated from college. But they are exceptional: Statistically, it's still worth it for most people.
- For some, their time is better spent doing something else, but it's probably best to play the odds.

These abilities are almost always useful: reading, writing, thinking, evaluating, judging, creating, improving. Not just what job I have, but who I am.

Is a college education and a four-year degree still worth it?

- Specialization and practical skills are necessary, but not mutually exclusive from liberal arts.
- Become too narrow and cannot adapt to changes

- More than an economy: We are a society, we make larger decisions, need to consider the big picture (socially, politically, nationally, globally) and see the forest as well as the trees.
- Want to know as much as possible, about the world and others
- Good citizenship and social life depend on these skills.
- Country needs an educated workforce to compete.

- Unemployment rate: significantly lower among college graduates
- Earning potential: higher for college graduates

an argument of your own. Good writing frequently comes from critically reading the work of other writers. When you assimilate and respond to their thoughts and prose rhythms, you make joining the conversation with them about a shared subject much easier. The eighteenth-century literary critic John Hughes advised poets to "prepare yourself, before you begin to write, by reading in some harmonious style, so that you may get your ear well in tune." For many prose writers, this advice will prove useful, so do not hesitate to "get your ear in tune." The essays in *The Arlington Reader* have been selected with this purpose in mind, and will serve as good models of fine writing.

Even if you are not writing about a text or reading for inspiration, you can use critical and analytical reading strategies to generate specific topics and angles for writing assignments. You can ask similar questions of a subject or topic that you ask of a piece of writing. You might start with a newspaper reporter's queries—who, what, when, where, how—and move to more complex questions. Of course, different subjects and topics will lend themselves to different questions. For example, if you are writing about a literary text, you might focus on finding paradoxes. If your essay is about a policy in a political science class, you might explore misunderstandings or sources of disagreement. If a personal essay or memoir is your goal, you might consider how your attitude toward an experience or person has changed over time. If you are writing about a marketing strategy in a business class, you might investigate cause-and-effect relationships.

CHECKLIST: UNDERSTANDING YOUR TOPIC

- ☐ What interests me about this topic?
- ☐ What do I already know about this topic? What don't I know?
- ☐ What are the key words and phrases associated with this topic?
- ☐ What are specific examples of this topic?
- ☐ What bothers me about this topic?
- ☐ Has this topic—or opinions about it—changed over time?
- ☐ Has my attitude about this topic changed and, if so, why?
- ☐ What do people misunderstand about this topic?
- ☐ What aspect of this topic seems unclear and in need of clarification?
- ☐ What caused my topic? Where did it come from?
- ☐ What is a source of disagreement over this topic?
- ☐ What components make up this topic?
- ☐ What cause-and-effect relationships can I find in this topic?
- ☐ How is this topic different from related topics?
- ☐ How can I define this topic?
- ☐ How can I classify this topic?
- ☐ Are there contradictions or paradoxes within—or about—this topic?

DEVELOPING AND REFINING YOUR THESIS

Coming up with an introductory paragraph can be the hardest part of writing and organizing an essay. Be aware, however, that you are not required to begin writing with an introduction. A working **thesis,** the claim you are making in your essay, is a helpful tool when composing a first draft, but if you do not have one, begin by focusing on another section of the essay: a specific example you want to discuss or some familiar background material or context. You may even want to begin with the **refutation of a counterargument**—your response to existing or anticipated objections to your thesis—that you wish to include in your essay. Once you have written other sections, you can work backwards and get a strong sense of what your essay is "about." On occasion, you may even find that your introductory paragraph is the last section that gets written.

Although most prewriting strategies aim to generate a broad range of material, the act of writing an effective essay is in many ways a narrowing and winnowing process. You might think of it as moving from generality to specificity: subject to topic to thesis. A **thesis statement** is a brief expression of the main argument and controlling idea of a piece of writing. It makes a claim that is debatable and supportable with evidence: facts, examples, statistics, research, observations, logical arguments, and personal experience. For most academic essays, you should be able to express your thesis in a sentence or two. This controlling statement will give shape and organization to your writing, as the thesis should suggest a logical series of related points and assertions that you will unify into one argument with the different elements of the essay. The following examples illustrate the differences among subject, topic, and thesis.

> *Subject:* Smartphones
> *Topic:* The use of smartphones in the college classroom
> *Thesis:* Rather than ban students from using their smartphones in class, college instructors should integrate these and other personal technological devices into their classroom teaching.

> *Subject:* Cheating in college (academic honesty)
> *Topic:* How so-called study drugs are affecting academic performance— and how colleges should respond
> *Thesis:* The university should institute a strict honor code to discourage and punish the use of study drugs.

The thesis also sets expectations for your readers, giving them a clear sense of both your topic and (just as important) your view of the topic. The thesis makes a commitment to the audience that the essay will fulfill. The thesis should also suggest your rationale and purpose in making your argument—the reason your essay is relevant, vital, timely, and significant. In other words, you need to answer the question often lurking in the minds of many readers: *So what?*

To that end, your thesis must be a claim about which reasonable individuals can disagree. If few or no people take another side of your argument, if you cannot imagine someone disagreeing with you, or if the general validity of your thesis has long been settled, then you probably need to revise it or come up with a new one. For example, most people already agree that *It is best to always get eight hours of sleep, Pollution is bad,* and *Education is good.* On their own, none of these claims are good theses; rather, they are vague statements of conventional wisdom. However, if you wanted to invert these claims and argue that pollution can be a *good* thing under certain conditions or that Americans overvalue formal education at the expense of other kinds of learning, then you may have the beginnings of a promising thesis.

Here are some other pitfalls to avoid. A thesis is not:

- A statement of fact

  Motorola invented an early handheld cellphone in 1973.

- A generalized announcement or statement of an essay topic

  In this paper, I will write about the history of cellphones.

- A brief summary of outside research or opinion

  People have many different opinions of mobile phones.

- A vague personal assertion or subjective judgment that cannot be proved or disproved

  I feel that the contemporary popularity of cellphones is a very interesting subject.

- A rhetorical question about a topic

  Have you ever wondered about the popularity of cellphones?

Although you should generally avoid using a question as a thesis, you may find that asking a specific question about a topic can lead you to a thesis:

- What can universities do about the prevalence of study drugs?

- How is technology affecting classroom learning, and are its effects mostly positive or mostly negative?

- Is the popularity of smartphones among college students damaging their social skills and making them less capable of real-time, face-to-face relationships?

None of these questions is a thesis statement. However, a thoughtful, supportable answer to each of them *will* be a thesis.

Make sure your thesis is narrow enough to cover within the length and research guidelines of an essay assignment. For example, if you are writing a four-page paper about an aspect of higher education in the United States, the following is too broad and vaguely worded to be an effective thesis:

American colleges and universities, along with all the country's public and private high schools that educate individuals, must get better at preparing people if America is to be a good country.

At the same time, you do not want your thesis to be too narrow:

A few of my professors do not use PowerPoint effectively in their classrooms.

This statement is too limited to function as the controlling idea for a college-level essay on higher education. However, elaborated with more detail and used as a representative example of a larger issue (e.g., the misuse of technology in the class-room), it might work as supporting evidence in the body of an essay.

You can find a thesis at different points in the writing process. On some occasions, you may begin with a preliminary hunch or tentative argument, particularly if you have already given the topic a lot of thought. For other assignments, you might need multiple freewriting and clustering exercises to generate a controlling idea or assertion. At times, you may even have to write a rough draft of an essay before you discover the thesis that works. Remember, do not hesitate to revise your thesis as you research and compose your essay. This principle suggests a contrast between high school–level and college-level essay assignments. For many high school students, longer writing assignments have meant a rigid procedure of note taking, outlining, and then composing from a detailed outline: a strict process that usually leads to a narrow, predetermined conclusion before they even begin writing. For college essays, especially in higher level classes, you will need to be more supple and sophisticated: assimilating new information, changing your mind in the face of new evidence, and adjusting your thesis in accord with your growing mastery of the topic.

Keep in mind that creating a thesis is not some sterile academic exercise, dreamed up by teachers and professors to burden students with busywork. Nearly every good piece of writing, from resumes and church sermons to music reviews and history textooks, has a thesis: an argument, a point of view, an assertion to prove or disprove. Indeed, novels, films, songs, and other works of art can have theses, too, even if those arguments are subtle or open to interpretation. Richard Rodriguez's "Aria: A Memoir of a Bilingual Childhood" (p. 211) is an introspective and lyrical autobiographical narrative of his childhood. Yet, it also contains a clearly stated thesis—and a sustained argument that supports his position on bilingual education. At times, the titles of essays will imply a thesis, such as Elie Wiesel's "Why I Write" (p. 91) and Nicholas Carr's "Is Google Making Us Stupid?" (p. 331). At other times, the thesis of an essay might be so subtle and implicit that we cannot paraphrase it exactly. In "Once More to the Lake," E. B. White suggests a view of childhood, technology, time, and mortality that is closer to poetry than to expository or academic writing, but a good analytical reader will sense the presence of a thesis, even if it cannot be precisely recaptured or summarized in other words.

CHECKLIST: CRAFTING YOUR THESIS

☐ Is the thesis debatable?

☐ Is there enough evidence to support the thesis?

☐ Is the thesis narrow enough to cover within the limits of the assignment?

☐ Is the thesis broad enough in its purpose to engage a general reader?

☐ Is the thesis an answer to a question?

☐ Does the thesis suggest a structure for the essay?

ORGANIZATION

You are likely familiar with the five-paragraph essay: an introduction with a thesis statement; three "body" paragraphs that support the thesis; and a concluding paragraph that restates the thesis or emphasizes key points. However, you will find no strict, five-paragraph essays in this book; you will rarely encounter them in scholarly journals, newspapers, or magazines, either. Although some instructors may assign the five-paragraph essay for specific purposes, college writing will require more sophisticated forms of organization. One way to think about it is this: In elementary school and high school, the structure often dictates the content or substance. That is, you had to write a five-paragraph essay, regardless of topic or purpose. Higher level academic writing reverses this relationship: Different topics, arguments, and purposes demand different forms of organization. This does not mean college assignments should be loose, disjointed, or formless. They still require introductions, body paragraphs, and conclusions. These elements just need to do a wider range of tasks than introducing a topic, elaborating on a list of examples, and summarizing in a conclusion.

Introductions Your **introductory paragraph** should probably include an explicit thesis, but you can use openers to perform additional functions as well, according to the needs of your assignment, topic, and purpose. Here are some examples of introductory paragraphs that perform various functions.

- Provide background or context for your topic.

  Gloria Anzaldúa, "Beyond Traditional Notions of Identity" (p. 135)

- Briefly narrate an anecdote, third-person narrative, or personal experience related to your topic.

  Malcolm Gladwell, "Drinking Games" (p. 166)

  Stephen King, "Write or Die" (p. 84)

- State an argument, misperception, or common error that your essay will clarify, refute, or correct.

  Andrea Cornwall, "Boys and Men Must Be Included in the Conversation on Equality" (p. 264)

  Linda Simon, "The Naked Source" (p. 250)

- Offer a curious or surprising paradox, fact, detail, assertion, or statistic to create interest for your reader.

  Eduardo Porter, "The New Mating Market" (p. 267)

  John Taylor Gatto, "Against School: How Public Education Cripples Our Kids, and Why" (p. 225)

- Give a general statement about your topic.

  Sherry Turkle, "How Computers Change the Way We Think" (p. 325)

  Jeffery Wattles, "The Golden Rule—One or Many, Gold or Glitter?" (p. 384)

- Provide or discuss a definition in a new or fresh way. (Avoid beginning with "Webster's defines" and presenting a standard definition for a familiar word.)

    Jhumpa Lahiri, "My Two Lives" (p. 97)

- Ask a question that your essay will try to answer.

    Elie Wiesel, "Why I Write" (p. 91)

    William Deresiewicz, "Faux Friendship" (p. 372)

Body paragraphs As in a five-paragraph essay, **body paragraphs**—which make up the main part of your argument between the introduction and conclusion—should succeed one another in a logical order that supports your main point. However, you often need these paragraphs to do more than elaborate on a single example or provide a list that supports an introductory statement. They may have to:

- Define a key term or concept for your reader
- Analyze a cause-and-effect relationship
- Summarize research or the opinions of others
- Explain an exception to your thesis
- Compare and contrast aspects of your topic
- Anticipate and refute counterarguments
- Narrate an anecdote that supports your thesis
- Interpret a statement, a quotation, an experience, or data
- Provide background information and context for your reader

Generally, a strict, five-paragraph essay will be too rigid to allow for these and all other functions of body paragraphs. Again, paragraphs must still follow logically and seamlessly, one to the next in the service of your thesis. But for longer assignments, you may need a range of logical and connective strategies beyond simply listing examples. One section of your essay may be structured by chronology (e.g., three narrative paragraphs about the history of an idea, from its origins through its development and current form), while another part may be organized using compare and contrast (e.g., two succeeding paragraphs that distinguish between two commonly confused words or ideas). Still another section might present a succession of three paragraphs to address and refute three counterarguments to your thesis.

Conclusions Five-paragraph essays typically end predictably and lifelessly, with a restatement of the thesis or introduction. That is probably why reading such essays is like going for a short, dreary car ride and then being dropped off at the original pickup spot. At times, you may want to restate or summarize the main idea of your essay in the **conclusion**—or final paragraph—especially if you are giving an oral presentation. More formal assignments will have strict guidelines about conclusions (as in a lab report). But while you should avoid introducing entirely new ideas in the closing paragraphs of an essay, try to move beyond conclusions that restate your thesis or summarize the points your reader has just read.

Here are some more sophisticated closing strategies:

- Close with a logical conclusion or causal relationship that follows from your argument.

  Sherry Turkle, "How Computers Change the Way We Think" (p. 325)

  Peter Elbow, "Freewriting" (p. 80)

- Use or discuss a quotation.

  Peg Tyre, "The Writing Revolution" (p. 254)

- Conclude with a resonant anecdote or narrative.

  Joan Didion, "On Keeping a Notebook" (p. 74)

- Conclude with speculation.

  Nicholas Carr, "Is Google Making Us Stupid?" (p. 331)

  William Deresiewicz, "Faux Friendship" (p. 372)

- Suggest a direction in your ideas, argument, or research, or make a recommendation.

  Michael Sandel, "What Isn't for Sale?" (p. 390)

  Jeffery Wattles, "The Golden Rule—One or Many, Gold or Glitter?" (p. 384)

- Ask a provocative question.

  Jonathan Franzen, "Liking Is for Cowards. Go for What Hurts." (p. 143)

  James Gleick, "How Google Dominates Us" (p. 350)

- Return to your introduction, after its meaning has been changed or given new insight by your essay.

  Elie Wiesel, "Why I Write" (p. 91)

  Sherman Alexie, "What Sacagawea Means to Me" (p. 106)

CHECKLIST: REVIEWING THE ORGANIZATION OF YOUR ESSAY

- ☐ Do you have an effective introduction? Does it include a clear thesis statement?
- ☐ Is your thesis supported with evidence in body paragraphs?
- ☐ Do the parts of your essay flow logically into one another? Are the parts of your essay distinct from one another? Does your essay clearly connect one section to another?
- ☐ Do you have an effective conclusion? Does it do more than simply restate the thesis?

CHAPTER 3

Using Sources, Revising, and Editing

EVALUATING SOURCES

For some assignments—particularly research papers or argumentative essays— you will need to read and incorporate outside sources into your work. This is not a formality. Good writers do not consult the work of others because doing so is a requirement (*"Your research paper is due on November 2 and must include at least three outside sources"*) or because writing a works-cited page is a pleasant exercise. Instead, scholars, researchers, journalists, college students, and other writers use research for specific purposes: to answer questions; to provide supporting evidence; to give background information and context; to help explain unfamiliar terms or ideas; to add credibility and authority by citing experts; and to use the striking, memorable language of other good writers (acknowledged through citation, of course) to further their own points. Most of all, they strive to engage with an ongoing conversation about their topics. Do not write your essay in a vacuum, as though you are the first person to consider your question or thesis. For example, if you are writing an argument about whether more Americans should earn college degrees, you would likely have to provide history and context for higher education in the United States, current statistics on college attendance, information about the social and economic consequences of a more highly educated population, employment data, and career trends. Given that many people have written about this topic, you would also need to familiarize yourself with various arguments regarding the advantages of college degrees—and then address them in your own essay.

When using a source in an essay, you must first make sure that it directly relates to your argument or topic: that it answers a question; lends expert opinion; presents pertinent facts and essential research; clarifies an idea; gives current, accurate, and representative views of your subject; suggests counterarguments or alternative points of view; supports a main point; and provides context, or grabs your reader with a key insight or a striking turn of phrase. Your sources should meet other, more general requirements as well.

Is the source up to date? Know when the source was published; verify that the material is still relevant. If you are writing about changes in immigration policy or the legal status of gay marriage, make sure you have the freshest information on those topics. Currency is especially important in an era of rapid technological and scientific change, but good writers know this principle applies beyond technology and the hard sciences. You do not want to write an essay lamenting the prevalence of violent crime in the United States that relies on research from the 1980s. Older sources can provide valuable historical context (such as anthropologist Elliot Liebow's *Tally's Corner*, a 1966 study of race and poverty in the United States), or enduring cultural insight (like poet and critic T. S. Eliot's famous 1921 essay on Shakespeare's *Hamlet*), but be aware that these are not current sources and that you must give your reader a clear understanding of why you are including dated material: to revisit an old controversy, to highlight a current issue with a historical contrast (or continuity), or to outline the history and development of a topic, question, or problem.

Is the source credible and authoritative? Who is the author, and how credible is he or she? Try to find experts on your topic—scholars, researchers, specialized scientists, preferably with matching professional or academic credentials. If you are writing about global climate change, a scientist who works in the field has more authority than an Oscar-winning actor or a newspaper columnist. If your essay addresses a controversial constitutional issue, a constitutional law scholar at an accredited university will probably be a better source than a former lawyer who now has a radio talk show. This does not mean that only academic figures and scientists provide useful information or make good arguments; nor does it follow that academics and experts are always correct and credible (especially when speaking or writing outside their specialties). However, you are usually better off giving more weight to experts who research and publish for others in their field than, say, television commentators who specialize in provocation and melodrama for a general audience, or anonymous bloggers seeking Internet clicks from online readers. Look for an author's background, experience, credentials, and reputation, as well as his or her institutional associations (such as universities, companies, or government organizations). Is his work cited by other scholars and researchers? What in her background gives her substantive authority on your topic? Does your source write primarily for a general audience, or for scholars and specialists?

Does the source provide broad and in-depth coverage? The best sources will give thorough and evenhanded accounts of a topic. If you are writing about federal funding for higher education and the issue of student debt, find sources that go beyond those offering narrow, polemical arguments based on a recent controversy. Instead, look for writers, journalists, scholars, and researchers who explore your topic in depth, give historical context, examine key issues, and provide fair accounts of different points of view. Some issues or questions *are* simple, and can be made needlessly complicated by bad, propagandistic, or dishonest writing. But college assignments frequently require you to wrestle with material that is many-sided and complex. Privilege sources who allow for such complexity—and who are not afraid to concede uncertainty. As the critic H. L. Mencken wrote, "There is always a solution to every human problem—neat, plausible, and wrong." Be wary of those who reduce and simplify, or who offer platitudes and facile answers about topics that demand deeper consideration or an acknowledgment of what remains unknown: Good scholars, researchers, and scientists are quick to admit the limits of their knowledge.

Is the source objective? Evaluate sources for objectivity and choose those that present honest and fair accounts of your topic. Look at the writer's thesis: Does it contain overstatement or make claims designed to disarm critical thought and appeal entirely to emotional responses? (*All gun-control laws will inevitably lead this country to become just like Hitler's Nazi Germany.*) Consider the source's language: Is it hostile, angry, dismissive, or mocking? Does the writer demonize or name-call (*right-wing nutjob, commie liberal, entitled trophy-kid, Rethuglican, redneck racist*) or pander to an audience that already agrees with his or her argument? Tone can be subtle and revealing. For example, does the writer put quotation marks around the word "marriage" in the phrase *gay marriage* to indicate sarcastic disapproval? Be skeptical of those who present only one side of an issue, mischaracterize counterarguments, or use statistics and research in manipulative or deceptive ways. You can often determine bias by considering the publication itself. Is it associated with an advocacy organization, political interest group, or commercial enterprise? Organizations and research institutes such as Focus on the Family, the Sierra Club, the American Enterprise Institute, the American Civil Liberties Union, and others have broad—and explicit—ideological and political goals. They will rarely, if ever, publish material that undercuts those broader aims. Similarly, if you are writing about organic food and you find a Web site sponsored by a commercial association of organic food growers, be aware that it is likely to be biased in favor of persuading consumers to buy organic products.

But remember: "Biased" is not synonymous with "dishonest" or "inaccurate." For example, political publications such as the *Nation,* the *New Republic,* and the *Weekly Standard* may include material that is honest and factually accurate, even if their writers' interpretations and editorial positions are shaped by ideological considerations. Indeed, you can use biased sources of many kinds in your research essays, as long as you fully acknowledge their slant and avoid passing them off as neutral, disinterested, or comprehensive. Likewise, be careful to avoid **confirmation bias** in your own work, especially when writing research and argumentative essays. Confirmation bias is our tendency to accept and agree with information that supports our point of view and dismiss evidence that contradicts it. We are all susceptible to this fallacy. The key to managing it is to remain skeptical of our own intuitions, arguments, and conclusions. Recall that scientists always test their theories and ideas by trying to *disprove* them. So when making your case in a written assignment, go out of your way to address the best counterarguments and account for the strongest evidence against your point of view. This point is doubly true for topics that are well known and often written about (abortion, the death penalty, the Vietnam War), but applies more broadly, as well. You will be able to find secondhand sources and evidence to back up *almost any argument you want* *to make* if you limit yourself to collecting the opinions of people who already agree with you. But if you minimize, mischaracterize, or avoid opposing points of view and inconvenient facts, you will not write effective, intellectually honest essays. You will write propaganda.

USING SOURCES FROM THE WEB

All of the previous guidelines apply to both Internet and print sources. However, take extra care when researching on the Web, as so much material is easily and quickly accessible online. Do not confuse "information" with "research" or "knowledge," because the Internet can create the illusion that a person is mastering a topic by hitting Google search. The Web is a boon to people who peddle urban legends and bad information—much of which is easy to spot. If a site offering prewritten academic essays for sale boasts about "THE ONE SECRET THAT YOUR PROFESSORS DON'T WANT YOU TO DISCOVER," or seems primarily designed to sell you a product or service, avoid using it as a source. If you stick to academic and scholarly databases available through your college's library (such as EBSCO and JSTOR), you will be far more likely to find authoritative, accurate, and current research, much of it peer-reviewed by experts in their fields. But the open Web can be a great source, too, as long as you keep in mind some questions and rules while evaluating sites.

Who are the site's authors? Much of what is published on the Web is anonymous, and bloggers often use nicknames. Try to identify the author and establish his or her credentials and area of expertise. Look for links and citations to sources: Is the author engaged with the work of other credible researchers, scholars, writers, and publications? If you cannot find any information about the writer or the writer's background and sources, then the site is probably not suitable for academic research. Also, be wary of Web authors who frequently cite themselves as authorities or link almost exclusively to their own work. Respectable and authoritative scholars do not generally rely much on overt self-promotion or give themselves titles like "America's foremost expert" (although another legitimate expert may compliment or recommend their work). Of course, many established academics and writers maintain personal Web sites and blogs in their fields, or in fields that interest them (e.g., Princeton neuroscientist and professor Sam Wang directs the online Princeton Election Consortium). These authorities may also use the Internet to publicize or promote their books and research. However, their Web sites will usually provide lists of their academic publications; their memberships in reputable, scholarly organizations; their curricula vitae (CV); their affiliation with well-known institutions; and, on occasion, praise from other respectable authorities in their fields.

Who sponsors the site? Is the site a well-known online publication (e.g., Slate .com)? Is it a site maintained by the academic department of a university (e.g., the Modern American Poetry site at the University of Illinois)? Does the federal government sponsor the site and provide its content (e.g., unemployment data at the U.S. Bureau of Labor Statistics)? Some sites are sponsored by political interest groups. Research their background so that you can understand—and compensate for—their biases. Other sites will be commercial, and therefore geared toward encouraging people to buy products or services (even indirectly). Assess whether the site's commercial interest influences its editorial content. Also, watch for advertising and whether it shapes the site's material, as well. Consider the URL ending, which can provide clues to the site's purposes. Educational sites will end in .edu, nonprofit organizations will end in .org, government sites will end in .gov, and commercial sites will end in .com. Be wary of sites that ask you to pay for information. Many legitimate organizations have paywalls (such as newspapers), but most scholarly databases are accessible through university and college libraries.

How accurate is the site? Just because a piece of information exists on the Internet does not mean that it is accurate or true. Keep a skeptical eye when evaluating a Web source. Does it contain factual errors, misinformation, or discredited research? You can test this by cross-referencing the site with sources you know are credible. Similarly, look for grammatical, spelling, and other errors. If a Web site's author gets small details wrong, he or she is likely to be careless about content as well. Also, make sure the site is current. If the author has not updated the page since 2009, you probably want to avoid citing it.

INTEGRATING SOURCES AND AVOIDING PLAGIARISM

Whether you are using a blog, a textbook, an online video, or any other outside source, you must give credit to the original author. If you do not, you will commit **plagiarism,** which means to steal the work of others and claim it as your own. Consult your university's handbook on plagiarism and academic honesty, as well as your professor's policies, which will likely be indicated on the course syllabus. In many cases, plagiarism may lead you to fail an assignment, or perhaps an entire course.

The guidelines and formats for incorporating the work of others into your essays will vary by subject and course. For example, an essay for an English class may require you to conform to the style rules of the Modern Language Association (MLA), while assignments in business or sociology may call for American Psychological Association (APA) style. But certain guidelines are more broadly applicable. Your goal is to ensure that your reader always knows which words and ideas are your own and which are from your sources. Try to make the transition between your own work and your sources as smooth and seamless as possible.

Summarizing When referring to the arguments, definitions, and ideas of other writers in your essay, you often need to summarize—that is, provide a highly condensed, but accurate and objective, account of your source. For example, you may need to briefly restate an article's thesis and concisely explain the writer's evidence and argument in a few sentences. You must still clearly indicate the source when you summarize, even if you do not quote the writer's words directly.

Paraphrasing A paraphrase is similar to a summary in that you present another writer's argument or idea in your own words, but your aim is not to shorten the passage. A good paraphrase may be as detailed and long, or longer, than the original writing. Paraphrasing is especially useful when you can present someone else's ideas more gracefully, clearly, or memorably in your own words. You might imagine a paraphrase beginning with an implied, *In other words*. . . . As with summaries, however, you need to cite the source.

Integrating quotations Use direct quotations to give authority to your argument, to provide precise language when it is essential, to include especially memorable or striking language, and to present a counterargument fairly. You must **integrate** quotations into your prose (make them flow into your writing and explain their purpose in supporting what you are trying to say), not "drop" them in without explanation. Use signal words (see below) to identify the author and speaker, and work the quotation into the syntax of your sentences.

Dropped

Certainly, students should think critically about their educations and career paths. Peter Thiel said, "Mark Zuckerberg from Facebook didn't complete Harvard. Steve Jobs dropped out of Reed College. Bill Gates dropped out of Harvard. When you do something entrepreneurial, the credentials are not what really matters" (Thiel, *60 Minutes*). Broader empirical evidence points to the enduring value of a college degree.

Integrated

Critics of higher education often tout the successes of exceptional individuals who dropped out of college, or never attended at all. As Peter Thiel told CBS's *60 Minutes* in 2011, "Mark Zuckerberg from Facebook didn't complete Harvard. Steve Jobs dropped out of Reed College. Bill Gates dropped out of Harvard. When you do something entrepreneurial, the credentials are not what really matters" (Thiel, *60 Minutes*). Such anecdotes are inspiring— especially for students who like to consider themselves exceptional. However, broader empirical evidence points to the enduring value of a college degree.

Signal words Whether you are summarizing, paraphrasing, or quoting directly, make sure you introduce and identify your source for the reader. Signal words help integrate sources into your own writing. Here is a list of common signal words you can use to introduce material drawn from your sources:

Acknowledges	Asserts	Denies	Observes
Adds	Believes	Disagrees	Points out
Admits	Claims	Implies	Responds
Agrees	Concurs	Insists	Suggests
Argues	Concedes	Mentions	Writes
Asks	Contends	Notes	

Be careful not to call unwanted attention to these signal phrases by varying them too often. In most cases, "writes," "argues," "suggests," or "asks" is suitable. But make sure the signal word fits the quotation and the context: Martin Luther King Jr. does not "mention" racial discrimination and segregation in "Letter from Birmingham Jail." Rather, they are his subjects.

Making sources work for you Remember to do something with the summaries, paraphrases, and quotations. Explain to your reader how a quotation, for example, is related to your argument. Make sure that you are using your sources—to provide support for your claims, present important context, clarify a point, offer counterexamples—and not letting them use you, or do the work of making your argument for you.

EXAMPLES OF MLA STYLE

When using the Modern Language Association system to cite material, include in parentheses the author's name and the page number of the quotation in the body of your essay. Then, in a list of works cited, include full publication information. Here is an example of a parenthetical citation in the body of an essay. The author's last name is Epstein and the source of the quotation is page 16.

The critic Joseph Epstein divides snobs into two categories: "those whose snobbery consists of looking down on others and those whose snobbery consists of looking up to, and being ready to abase themselves before, their supposed betters" (16).

The following are examples of entries in a list of works cited. Note that they provide the author's full name (last name first), the title of the publication (in italics), the location and name of the publisher, the year of publication, and the medium (such as print). Electronic sources also include the date of access.

Book with one author

Epstein, Joseph. *Snobbery: The American Version*. New York: Houghton Mifflin, 2002. Print.

Book with more than one author

Gilbert, Sandra M., and Susan Gubar. *The Madwoman in the Attic: The Woman Writer and the Nineteenth-Century Literary Imagination*. New Haven: Yale UP, 1979. Print.

Book with an editor

Damrosch, Leo, ed. *The Profession of Eighteenth-Century Literature: Reflections on an Institution*. Madison: U of Wisconsin P, 1992. Print.

An anthology

Benedikt, Michael. *The Poetry of Surrealism: An Anthology*. Boston: Little, Brown, 1974. Print.

Selection in an anthology

Cameron, Dana. "Femme Sole." *Boston Noir*. Ed. Dennis Lehane. New York:
    Akashic, 2009. 95-115. Print.

Magazine

Dean, Josh. "This Can't Be Happening." *Inc.* June 2012: 82-90. Print.

Magazine on the Web

Gallagher, Ryan. "The Threat of Silence." *Slate*. Slate, 4 Feb. 2013. Web.
    7 Feb. 2013.

Newspaper

Brooks, David. "The Nation of Futurity." *New York Times*. 17 Nov. 2009,
    natl. ed.: A33. Print.

Newspaper on the Web

McManus, Doyle. "Tax Reform That Hits Home." *Los Angeles Times*. Los
    Angeles Times, 6 Feb. 2013. Web. 7 Feb. 2013.

Periodical from an online database

Smith, Zadie. "Franz Kafka Versus the Novel." *The New Republic*. 3 Nov. 2003.
    Lexis Nexis Academic. Web. 15 Feb. 2013.

General Web site

Political Research Center. Suffolk University, 22 Oct. 2012. Web. 15 Feb. 2013.

Wikipedia

"Cesar Chavez." *Wikipedia*. Wikimedia, 26 Jan. 2013. Web. 20 Feb. 2013.

Blog post

Wolcott, James. "Bed Bath and Beyonce." *James Wolcott's Blog*. Vanity Fair,
    4 Feb. 2013. Web. 7 Feb. 2013.

Article in a scholarly journal

Kinugawa, Shosuke. "The Ring and the Gaze: Robert Browning's 'Love Among
    the Ruins.'" *The Explicator* 68:4 (2010): 235-38. Print.

CHECKLIST: USING SOURCES

- ☐ Have you evaluated your sources for currency, credibility, broadness of coverage, and objectivity?
- ☐ If your sources come from the Web, have you been particularly careful to make sure that they are appropriate sources? Have you examined the site's authors and sponsors and analyzed the site's objectivity?
- ☐ Have you smoothly integrated your sources into your paper, using appropriate signal words?
- ☐ Have you correctly documented your sources, providing full citation information?

REVISION

In 1924, after multiple false starts and rewrites, a novelist submitted a manu-script called *Trimalchio* to his editor, Maxwell Perkins. Perkins loved the story but suggested changes—mostly in the characterization and details: "You might here and there interpolate some phrases, and possibly incidents, little touches of various kinds. . . ." The author radically rewrote the novel, adding some parts, dropping others, adjusting the narrator's point of view, moving early sections of the story to its conclusion, and creating more mystery around the story's main character. Today, we are more familiar with F. Scott Fitzgerald's *Trimalchio* in its polished form and under its final title: *The Great Gatsby.* The novel did not spring, fully formed, from the mind of a solitary genius in a single writing session. Rather, the book's elegant contours and shapely identity became vis-ible only through the writer's elaborate revisions and his collaborations with an editor. The takeaway? Great prose rarely emerges from a clean transfer of prewriting—whether notes, an outline, or merely thoughts and intuitions—into sentences and paragraphs. Rather, it flows from the fluid process of writing, reacting to that writing, and revising: getting raw material on paper or on a computer screen, reading it, responding to it, shaping it, working with it, argu-ing with it, and soliciting the responses of others. That principle holds true for everything from novels and screenplays to business plans, your next academic essay assignment, and the prose you are reading right now. Revision requires you to read and listen to your early drafts carefully. They will help you discover what your essay really needs to be *about*—and revise it in the right direction. Here are some helpful strategies.

REVISING THESIS, EVIDENCE, AND ORGANIZATION

First, you might want to set your draft aside for a day or longer, if possible, before undertaking revision. This practice will give you a break—and fresh eyes when you read the draft again. Second, when you begin revising, focus on big-picture questions and issues, then slowly shift your attention to the details of your essay. Crossing "t's" and dotting "i's" is essential, but do not confuse "revision" with "proofreading," which comes later in the writing process. Like builders putting together a house, you want to get the foundation and structure in place before you paint the trim. Retest your thesis. Is it clear and debatable? Does it present a main point and indicate your purpose? Does it suggest the shape and organiza-tion of the essay as a whole? Consider the relationship between your thesis and the entire essay:

Does the thesis still fit the essay that follows? You may begin with a clear thesis statement, but as you proceed with making arguments, assembling evi-dence, and connecting paragraphs, the thesis may need to be adjusted, quali-fied, or even radically revised. Often, you do not realize this until you read the first draft. As a character in E. M. Forster's *Aspects of the Novel* asks, "How can I tell what I think till I see what I say?" "Thinking" does not precede the writing process; rather, thinking, understanding, and writing inform one another. So your best point or strongest organizing idea may not be clear to you until you have written a version of the essay. During the revision process, do not hesitate to qualify, reword, or rewrite your thesis entirely, no matter how much you think you like it. Nothing will be lost by doing so, as you can save earlier drafts and versions.

Do the supporting paragraphs, arguments, and evidence fit the thesis that begins the essay? For academic essays, your supporting paragraphs must be directly tied to your thesis. You may have a surprising fact, a compelling statistic, or a curious anecdote that, on its own, or in support of some *other* argument, may be relevant. But if it does not provide backing for your main point, you are probably better off removing it. When you read a draft, you will also perceive which of your arguments is the strongest and which evidence is the most persuasive and relevant. This may not be apparent when you are freewriting or researching your topic. Likewise, you might see that what you originally thought was a strong supporting example is weaker than you believed: You may choose to place less emphasis on it, or delete it altogether. As you begin revising, you may stumble across a new piece of evidence or source that changes your mind about your topic. Like thinking and writing, research and writing are overlapping activities, not exclusive ones. Do not hesitate to incorporate new information as you discover it.

Is the essay organized in the best possible way? As you work with a draft, you may discover that restructuring the paragraphs or changing the organization improves your essay. For example, in reading a paragraph that provides a key definition, you might realize that your point could be made clearer with two paragraphs offering a comparison and a contrast. Or, you may read a section in which you refute counterarguments and conclude that you could begin the essay by raising objections and refuting them. Sometimes, you will find that a better thesis statement emerges in your essay's conclusion, or even in the middle of a draft. Consider early versions as exercises in discovery: An argument that seemed fuzzy or secondary in your notes may appear sharp and gleaming once it takes paragraph form. When that happens, reorganize the essay around its strongest elements, even if that means changing your thesis or the overall design of the paper.

Is anything missing? Make sure your essay fulfills the promises it makes in its opening paragraphs. Does it raise any questions that remain conspicuously open, even though a reader should reasonably expect answers? Look for cracks in the argument that need reinforcement. For example, the essay may rely on missing background information or make implicit logical connections that are clear in your mind as a writer, but need to be made more explicit for your reader. Check for gaps in evidence, as well. Test generalizations and broad assertions with care, particularly in the topic sentences of paragraphs. Do not leave any room for a reader to ask, *According to whom?*—or, *What are you basing this statement on?*

Is everything necessary? Although college writers tend to labor under set page count requirements, always look for opportunities to remove words, sentences, paragraphs, or even entire sections of essays if these elements prove unnecessary. This is especially true regarding repetition. Do not repeat or restate sentences and paragraphs multiple times in an essay. Avoid reiterating the same example, quotation, fact, or statistic, unless you are doing so to make distinctive and separate points in support of your main argument. At a more detailed level, remove clunky phrases and unnecessarily wordy passages, which you might more easily recognize in reading the essay aloud.

Read the essay aloud. Reading your writing aloud can be one of the most helpful tools for revision. Listen for gaps and missing elements—an absent piece of evidence, an unanswered question, or a missing transitional phrase to guide a reader from one thought to the next. Additionally, you will hear stylistic problems: the long abstract grammatical subjects that lose readers, pretentious or tongue-twisting words and phrases that you'd never use while speaking, unnecessary technical jargon, too much passive voice, and repetitive sentence structures. Your prose must organize and communicate sophisticated ideas; although sentences might demand richness and complexity, make sure they are not needlessly complicated. Often, we can see problems in other people's writing more easily than we perceive them in our own. It is hard to be objective about our own prose, particularly after we spend a lot of time with a draft.

PEER REVIEW

Asking others—classmates and peers—to read your essay takes advantage of this gain in objectivity. Writing is not merely an academic exercise. Submitting a paper for peer evaluation highlights the need for clear communication with a real audience, not imaginary readers or an instructor's rubric. You wrote the paper; you know what you want to say, but you should not assume the same of your readers.

Encourage your responders to be concrete in their reactions and suggestions. *"Needs more details"* is less helpful than, *"In your fifth paragraph, you need to find a stronger example to make your counterargument more persuasive. The example in your conclusion might be better placed in paragraph 5."* Although you want peers to be specific, you should not expect them to rewrite the essay for you; similarly, while they should point out any glaring typos or proofreading errors, try to keep their attention focused on issues of content, organization, and clarity. These rules apply when you read their essays, too.

CHECKLIST: QUESTIONS FOR PEER REVIEW

☐ Can you identify and restate the thesis and main point of the essay?

☐ What are the strongest parts of the essay?

☐ What do you want to see more of?

☐ What are the weakest parts of the essay?

☐ What do you want to see less of?

☐ What questions need to be answered? What remains unclear?

☐ Are there any unsupported assertions or generalizations?

☐ What elements of the essay seem unnecessary?

☐ Where is the writing difficult? Unclear?

PROOFREADING

When you revise, you concentrate on global issues of structure, substance, and style; when you **proofread,** you narrow your vision to words, sentences, punctuation, formatting, and mechanics. These are not frivolous or minor aspects of the essay: A writer who is careless about small things is usually careless about big things, too. You may have an ingenious argument, well-chosen research, or a charming prose style, but if your paper is riddled with typos, run-on sentences, misspellings, and other errors, you will frustrate readers. Remember, fixing problems with issues like punctuation and spelling is the easy stuff, so reap the benefits of getting it right. Applications like spelling- and grammar-checkers on word-processing programs are helpful, but not perfect. Sometimes they miss ambiguous errors in punctuation or commonly confused words. So they are no substitute for reading your essay carefully. Be on the lookout for:

- Missing words and repeated words
- Minor typographical mistakes
- Spelling errors
- Run-on sentences and comma splices
- Unintentional sentence fragments
- Pronouns without antecedents, or pronouns that do not agree with antecedents in person and number
- Consistency of tenses
- Problems with mechanics and typography (words that need to be capitalized or italicized)
- Problems with formatting (e.g., making sure details of the essay match MLA guidelines)

Obviously, this list of errors is not exhaustive, but you can make proofreading easier and more effective if you are aware of problems that you already have (comma splices, for example) or if you pay attention to your professor's guidelines, comments, and preoccupations. For example, your instructor may have pointed out that you need to work harder on keeping pronoun agreement consistent, or avoiding sentence fragments. At the level of words and sentences, you may even want to read the essay *backwards,* a practice that enables you to read each sentence in isolation from the rhythm and flow of the argument, which can mask minor errors.

SAMPLE RESEARCH PAPER

Logan Block

Professor Patricia Cook

Composition 100

22 November 2015

Your name, your professor's name, the course, and the date

College Is Still Worth It: The Enduring Value
of a College Degree

Title of your essay, centered

In the wake of the economic problems of the last four years and the increasing concern over student-loan debt, many are questioning the value of a traditional college education. For example, Charles Murray, a conservative author and political scientist, argues that our society encourages too many students to pursue four-year degrees; in his view, America needs to "undermine the bachelor's degree as a job qualification" (Murray). Murray is just one voice among many. Peter Thiel, the billionaire creator of PayPal, has even started giving Thiel Fellowships, which offer candidates a "no-strings-attached" $100,000 grant to "skip college and focus on their work, their research, and their self-education" (Thielfellowship.org). Certainly, students should think critically about their educations and career paths. Some high school graduates can succeed without a college degree. But when critics like Murray and Thiel denigrate higher education, they obscure a simple truth: For a majority of high school graduates, a college degree remains a wise and responsible choice, economically, personally, and socially.

Introduction

Thesis statement

Economically, higher education is a safe bet. Critics often tout the successes of exceptional individuals who dropped out of college, or never attended at all. As Thiel told CBS's *60 Minutes* in 2011, "Mark Zuckerberg from Facebook didn't complete Harvard. Steve Jobs dropped out of Reed College. Bill Gates dropped out of Harvard. When you do something entrepreneurial, the credentials are not what really matters" (Thiel, *60 Minutes*). Such anecdotes are inspiring—especially for students who like to consider themselves exceptional. However, broader empirical evidence points to the enduring value of a college degree.

Parenthetical citation for source

Consider "The College Payoff: Education, Occupations, Lifetime Earnings," a comprehensive 2011 study by Georgetown's Center on Education and the Workforce. The research suggests that an individual with a high school diploma can expect lifetime earnings of $1.3 million; his or her counterpart with a college degree will earn (on average) $2.3 million over a lifetime (Carnevale et al. 2). That earning disparity seems to be growing wider: "In 2002, a Bachelor's degree holder could expect to earn 75 percent more over a lifetime than someone with a high school diploma. Today, that premium is 84 percent." (Carnevale et al. 2). Similarly, recent high unemployment and low economic growth have had much different effects on those with college degrees than they have on those without degrees. In the summer of 2012, the unemployment rate for all college graduates was 4.5% (Pope). For recent college graduates, it was higher: 6.8% (Pope). But for those with only a high school diploma, the unemployment rate was a staggering 24% (Pope). For college graduates, these figures will improve significantly as the economy recovers. That is less true for people without degrees. As Jordan Weissman writes in the *Atlantic Monthly*, "If the whole recovery had a job posting somewhere on Craigslist, it would say: 'Some college required, bachelor's preferred'" (Weissman).

Higher education does more than improve employability and lifetime earning potential. According to a 2012 Centers for Disease Control report on American health, higher levels of education correlate to higher levels of overall health and longer lifespans. Those lives will be fuller mentally, as well as physically. A good four-year degree program broadens students and provides them with strong healthy minds that will help them, regardless of their career choices. College training teaches them critical thinking skills and challenges their assumptions; it sharpens their writing skills, and makes them better readers of texts and people; it puts them into contact with history, literature, foreign languages, music, mathematics, and other disciplines that remind them of what they do not know, rather than affirming what they think they know or narrowing them for career specialization. Ideally, college is a means of discovery for students—of culture, of intellectual rigor, of other people, of themselves.

Of course, higher education has social and political benefits that go beyond a single individual's health, wealth, or happiness. A more educated population brings social and political rewards. For example, the United States system of government relies on informed people who can make intelligent decisions based on empirical evidence and good information. They need to know history, practice empathy, have a sense of perspective, communicate ideas, and adapt to changing circumstances in a dynamic world. They must be smart and skeptical, recognizing con artistry and propaganda, whether in television advertisements or in the policy proposals of politicians. Democracy cannot work effectively without education: A more educated and knowledgeable population will probably make better collective political and social decisions. This insight is hardly new, but we need to assert it again in response to those who evaluate higher education entirely in terms of individual financial self-interest. As the great Victorian clergyman and educational theorist John Henry Newman wrote in *The Idea of a University* (1852), the "practical end" of higher education is in "training good members of society": "Its art is the art of social life, and its end is fitness for the world" (Newman 1040). In our preoccupation with creating financially independent and employable individuals, we should keep in mind that higher education also helps produce the sociable and public-spirited citizens of a republic.

We can see the value of education in light of the domestic and global economy, as well. Higher education has long been a key to social and economic mobility. The rise of the American middle class after World War II coincided with a large increase in college students and college graduates. Internationally, America needs to remain competitive and innovative, but it cannot accomplish this by discouraging more of its citizens from pursuing college degrees. Emerging economic powers like China and India are graduating more students each year—and investing more public resources in higher education. These countries are not telling students to skip college. China overtook the United States in the number of college graduates in science, technology, engineering, and mathematics. By 2030, it will have 200 million college graduates overall (Cooper et al.). Universities are hotbeds of research, innovation, and patent creation. For decades, the United States has led the world in innovation. It is no coincidence that the United States has the most prestigious universities in the world. We should be skeptical of those who seek to undermine that status.

Critics of higher education usually qualify their criticism. For example, they reserve praise for college courses in STEM fields (science, technology, engineering, and mathematics) while scorning the liberal arts and other degree programs. Murray writes, "Readers who graduated with honors in English literature or Renaissance history should ask themselves if they could have gotten a B.S. in physics, no matter how hard they tried" (Murray). Thiel Fellow Dale Stephens concedes, "Of course some people want a formal education. I do not think everyone should leave college" (Stephens). But these critics are often disrespectful of both college students and higher education. Murray asserts that a "large majority of young people do not have the intellectual ability to do genuine college-level work" (Murray). Stephens sees colleges as merely factories for "conformity" and "regurgitation" (Stephens). Others are even more explicit in their disdain. "We can't deny it anymore," writes author and hedge fund manager James Altucher. "College is a scam and a bubble" (Altucher).

American higher education is far from perfect. Beneath   Conclusion
their disrespect and dismissal, these critics make some valid points. Murray is correct that many high school graduates should pursue vocational training instead of a traditional four-year degree. Higher education is enormously expensive, and students have a right to expect to be able to find a job when they graduate—especially those with big student-loan debts. College degrees do improve employability and lifetime earnings, but that return on investment can vary widely, depending on a student's major, the quality of the university, and the student's individual initiative. American universities, themselves, need to reflect on their own

practices and improve. In "Higher Education's Coming Crisis," Drexel University history professor Robert Zaller provides a critique of the corporatization and bureaucratization of American colleges, as higher education has become "a sweetheart racket for its beneficiaries" (Zaller). But Zaller writes with concern and hope for reform, not disrespect. He does not encourage students to drop out, or suggest that universities are deceptive and irredeemable factories of conformity for aimless, unprepared young people. He knows that democratic citizenship, social mobility, and economic growth require an educated populace, even if universities need some improvement. Educated people like Charles Murray (B.A., Harvard, Ph.D., MIT) and Peter Thiel (B.A., J.D., Stanford) should know that, too.

Works Cited

Altucher, James. "College Is a Scam—So Let's Make Money Off It." *Market Watch. Wall Street Journal.* 27 May 2011. Web. 7 Feb. 2013.

Carnevale, Anthony P., Stephen J. Rose, and Ban Cheah. "Executive Summary." *The College Payoff: Education, Occupations, Lifetime Earnings.* Georgetown University Center on Education and the Workforce. 5 Aug. 2011. Web. 7 Feb. 2013.

Centers for Disease Control. "Higher Education and Income Levels Keys to Better Health, According to Annual Report on Nation's Health." CDC. 16 May 2012. Web. 2 Feb. 2013.

Cooper, Donna, Adam Hersh, and Ann O'Leary. "The Competition That Really Matters." *Center for American Progress.* 12 Aug. 2012. Web. 8 Feb. 2013.

Murray, Charles. "Should the Obama Generation Drop Out?" *New York Times* 28 Dec. 2008 late ed.: WK09. Print.

Newman, John Henry. "From *The Idea of a University*." *The Norton Anthology of English Literature.* Gen ed. Stephen Greenblatt. 9th ed. Vol. 2. New York: Norton, 2006. 1035-42. Print.

Pope, Justin. "Studies Show You Are Better Off with College: But Middle Class Racks Up Most Debt." *Lewiston Morning Tribune* (Idaho) 21 Aug. 2012: All. Print.

List of sources used in the essay

Smith, Rodney K. "Yes, a College Education Is Worth the
    Costs." *USA Today* 6 Dec. 2011: 9A. Print.

Stephens, Dale. "College Is a Waste of Time." *cnn.com*. CNN.
    3 June 2011. Web. 9 Feb. 2013.

Thielfellowship.org. *About the Fellowship*. 8 Aug. 2012. Web.
    7 Feb. 2013.

Thiel, Peter. Interview by Morley Safer. *60 Minutes*. CBS.
    WBZ, Boston, 20 May 2012. Television.

Weissman, Jordan. "How the Great Recession Proved, Beyond
    a Doubt, the Value of a College Degree." *Atlantic Online*.
    Atlantic Monthly Group, 16 Aug. 2012. Web. 4 Feb. 2013.

Zaller, Robert. "Higher Education's Coming Crisis." *The
    Triangle* (Drexel University). 3 Feb. 2012. Web.
    7 Feb. 2013.

PART TWO

Readings

CHAPTER 4

Speaking, Reading, Writing: How Does Language Make Us Human?

EUDORA WELTY

Listening

Born in Jackson, Mississippi, Eudora Welty (1909–2001) devoted most of her life to reading, writing, and gardening in the house her parents built in the 1920s. Her one extended departure from the South took her to the University of Wisconsin (B.A., 1929) and then to Columbia University in New York. She soon returned, however, traveling through "Depression-worn" Mississippi towns as a part-time journalist and photographer for the Works Progress Administration. Her fiction—short stories such as "Why I Live at the P.O." and "Death of a Traveling Salesman" as well as novels such as Delta Wedding *(1946),* The Ponder Heart *(1952), and* The Optimist's Daughter *(1972)—reflects the rural and small-town southern life she came to know during the first half of the twentieth century. Her work has received a Pulitzer Prize (1972) and numerous other awards, including the Presidential Medal of Freedom. Welty died in Jackson on July 23, 2001.*

Welty's experience of language largely involved listening—even to the words she read. Welty reflects on her own literary skill in her autobiographical account of her development as a writer, One Writer's Beginnings *(1983). An excerpt from the chapter titled "Listening" follows, taking as its motif Welty's observation that "Ever since I was first read to, then started reading to myself, there has never been a line read that I didn't hear."*

I learned from the age of two or three that any room in our house, at any time of day, was there to read in, or to be read to. My mother read to me. She'd read to me in the big bedroom in the mornings, when we were in her rocker together, which ticked in rhythm as we rocked, as though we had a cricket accompanying the story. She'd read to me in the diningroom on winter afternoons in front of the coal fire, with our cuckoo clock ending the story with "Cuckoo," and at night when I'd got in my own bed. I must have given her no peace. Sometimes she read to me in the kitchen while she sat churning, and the churning sobbed along with *any* story. It was my ambition to have her read to me while I churned; once she granted my wish, but she read off my story before I brought her butter. She was an expressive reader. When she was reading "Puss in Boots," for instance, it was impossible not to know that she distrusted *all* cats.

It had been startling and disappointing to me to find out that story books had been written by *people*, that books were not natural wonders, coming up of themselves like grass. Yet regardless of where they came from, I cannot remember a time when I was not in love with them—with the books themselves, cover and binding and the paper they were printed on, with their smell and their weight and with their possession in my arms, captured and carried off to myself. Still illiterate, I was ready for them, committed to all the reading I could give them.

Neither of my parents had come from homes that could afford to buy many books, but though it must have been something of a strain on his salary, as the youngest officer in a young insurance company, my father was all the while carefully selecting and ordering away for what he and Mother thought we children should grow up with. They bought first for the future.

Besides the bookcase in the livingroom, which was always called "the library," there were the encyclopedia tables and dictionary stand under windows in our diningroom. Here to help us grow up arguing around the diningroom table were the Unabridged Webster, the Columbia Encyclopedia, Compton's Pictured Encyclopedia, the Lincoln Library of Information, and later the Book of Knowledge. And the year we moved into our new house, there was room to celebrate it with the new 1925 edition of the Britannica, which my father, his face always deliberately turned toward the future, was of course disposed to think better than any previous edition.

In "the library," inside the mission-style bookcase with its three diamond- 5 latticed glass doors, with my father's Morris chair and the glass-shaded lamp on its table beside it, were books I could soon begin on—and I did, reading them all alike and as they came, straight down their rows, top shelf to bottom. There was the set of Stoddard's Lectures, in all its late nineteenth-century vocabulary and vignettes of peasant life and quaint beliefs and customs, with matching halftone illustrations: Vesuvius erupting, Venice by moonlight, gypsies glimpsed by their campfires. I didn't know then the clue they were to my father's longing to see the rest of the world. I read straight through his other love-from-afar: the Victrola Book of the Opera, with opera after opera in synopsis, with portraits in costume of Melba, Caruso, Galli-Curci, and Geraldine Farrar, some of whose voices we could listen to on our Red Seal records.

My mother read secondarily for information; she sank as a hedonist into novels. She read Dickens in the spirit in which she would have eloped with him. The novels of her girlhood that had stayed on in her imagination, besides those of Dickens and Scott and Robert Louis Stevenson, were *Jane Eyre, Trilby, The Woman in White, Green Mansions, King Solomon's Mines*. Marie Corelli's name would crop up but I understood she had gone out of favor with my mother, who had only kept *Ardath* out of loyalty. In time she absorbed herself in Galsworthy, Edith Wharton, above all in Thomas Mann of the *Joseph* volumes.

St. Elmo was not in our house; I saw it often in other houses. This wildly popular Southern novel is where all the Edna Earles in our population started coming
from. They're all named for the heroine, who succeeded in bringing a dissolute,
sinning roué and atheist of a lover (St. Elmo) to his knees. My mother was able to
forgo it. But she remembered the classic advice given to rose growers on how to
water their bushes long enough: "Take a chair and *St. Elmo.*"

To both my parents I owe my early acquaintance with a beloved Mark Twain.
There was a full set of Mark Twain and a short set of Ring Lardner in our bookcase,
and those were the volumes that in time united us all, parents and children.

Reading everything that stood before me was how I came upon a worn old
book without a back that had belonged to my father as a child. It was called *Sanford
and Merton*. Is there anyone left who recognizes it, I wonder? It is the famous moral
tale written by Thomas Day in the 1780s, but of him no mention is made on the title
page of this book; here it is *Sanford and Merton in Words of One Syllable* by Mary
Godolphin. Here are the rich boy and the poor boy and Mr. Barlow, their teacher
and interlocutor, in long discourses alternating with dramatic scenes—danger and
rescue allotted to the rich and the poor respectively. It may have only words of
one syllable, but one of them is "quoth." It ends with not one but two morals, both
engraved on rings: "Do what you ought, come what may," and "If we would be great,
we must first learn to be good."

This book was lacking its front cover, the back held on by strips of pasted 10
paper, now turned golden, in several layers, and the pages stained, flecked, and
tattered around the edges; its garish illustrations had come unattached but were
preserved, laid in. I had the feeling even in my heedless childhood that this was
the only book my father as a little boy had had of his own. He had held onto it,
and might have gone to sleep on its coverless face: he had lost his mother when
he was seven. My father had never made any mention to his own children of the
book, but he had brought it along with him from Ohio to our house and shelved
it in our bookcase.

My mother had brought from West Virginia that set of Dickens; those books
looked sad, too—they had been through fire and water before I was born, she told
me, and there they were, lined up—as I later realized, waiting for *me*.

I was presented, from as early as I can remember, with books of my own, which
appeared on my birthday and Christmas morning. Indeed, my parents could not
give me books enough. They must have sacrificed to give me on my sixth or seventh birthday—it was after I became a reader for myself—the ten-volume set of
Our Wonder World. These were beautifully made, heavy books I would lie down
with on the floor in front of the diningroom hearth, and more often than the rest
volume 5, *Every Child's Story Book*, was under my eyes. There were the fairy tales—
Grimm, Andersen, the English, the French, "Ali Baba and the Forty Thieves"; and
there was Aesop and Reynard the Fox; there were the myths and legends, Robin
Hood, King Arthur, and St. George and the Dragon, even the history of Joan of
Arc; a whack of *Pilgrim's Progress* and a long piece of *Gulliver*. They all carried
their classic illustrations. I located myself in these pages and could go straight to

the stories and pictures I loved; very often "The Yellow Dwarf" was first choice, with Walter Crane's Yellow Dwarf in full color making his terrifying appearance flanked by turkeys. Now that volume is as worn and backless and hanging apart as my father's poor *Sanford and Merton*. The precious page with Edward Lear's "Jumblies" on it has been in danger of slipping out for all these years. One measure of my love for Our Wonder World was that for a long time I wondered if I would go through fire and water for it as my mother had done for Charles Dickens; and the only comfort was to think I could ask my mother to do it for me.

I believe I'm the only child I know of who grew up with this treasure in the house. I used to ask others, "Did you have Our Wonder World?" I'd have to tell them the Book of Knowledge could not hold a candle to it.

I live in gratitude to my parents for initiating me—and as early as I begged for it, without keeping me waiting—into knowledge of the word, into reading and spelling, by way of the alphabet. They taught it to me at home in time for me to begin to read before starting to school. I believe the alphabet is no longer considered an essential piece of equipment for traveling through life. In my day it was the keystone to knowledge. You learned the alphabet as you learned to count to ten, as you learned "Now I lay me" and the Lord's Prayer and your father's and mother's name and address and telephone number, all in case you were lost.

My love for the alphabet, which endures, grew out of reciting it but, before that, out of seeing the letters on the page. In my own story books, before I could read them for myself, I fell in love with various winding, enchanted-looking initials drawn by Walter Crane at the heads of fairy tales. In "Once upon a time," an "O" had a rabbit running it as a treadmill, his feet upon flowers. When the day came, years later, for me to see the Book of Kells, all the wizardry of letter, initial, and word swept over me a thousand times over, and the illumination, the gold, seemed a part of the word's beauty and holiness that had been there from the start.

My mother always sang to her children. Her voice came out just a little bit in the minor key. "Wee Willie Winkie's" song was wonderfully sad when she sang the lullabies.

"Oh, but now there's a record. She could have her own record to listen to," my father would have said. For there came a Victrola record of "Bobby Shafftoe" and "Rock-a-Bye Baby," all of Mother's lullabies, which could be played to take her place. Soon I was able to play her my own lullabies all day long.

Our Victrola stood in the diningroom. I was allowed to climb onto the seat of a diningroom chair to wind it, start the record turning, and set the needle playing. In a second I'd jumped to the floor, to spin or march around the table as the music called for—now there were all the other records I could play too. I skinned back onto the chair just in time to lift the needle at the end, stop the record and turn it over, then change the needle. That brass receptacle with a hole in the lid gave off a metallic smell like human sweat, from all the hot needles that were fed it. Winding up, dancing, being cocked to start and stop the record, was of course all in one the act of *listening*—to "Overture to *Daughter of the Regiment*," "Selections from *The Fortune Teller*," "Kiss Me Again," "Gypsy Dance from *Carmen*," "Stars and Stripes

Forever," "When the Midnight Choo-Choo Leaves for Alabam," or whatever came next. Movement must be at the very heart of listening.

Ever since I was first read to, then started reading to myself, there has never been a line read that I didn't *hear*. As my eyes followed the sentence, a voice was saying it silently to me. It isn't my mother's voice, or the voice of any person I can identify, certainly not my own. It is human, but inward, and it is inwardly that I listen to it. It is to me the voice of the story or the poem itself. The cadence, whatever it is that asks you to believe, the feeling that resides in the printed word, reaches me through the reader-voice. I have supposed, but never found out, that this is the case with all readers—to read as listeners—and with all writers, to write as listeners. It may be part of the desire to write. The sound of what falls on the page begins the process of testing it for truth, for me. Whether I am right to trust so far I don't know. By now I don't know whether I could do either one, reading or writing, without the other.

My own words, when I am at work on a story, I hear too as they go, in the 20 same voice that I hear when I read in books. When I write and the sound of it comes back to my ears, then I act to make my changes. I have always trusted this voice.

QUESTIONS FOR DISCUSSION AND WRITING

1. What connections does Welty make among listening, reading, and writing? Explain why Welty devotes so much space to her childhood *reading* in her essay on "Listening." Why are the people, places, and objects around which her reading took place so important?

2. With a partner, take turns reading aloud sentences or paragraphs from this essay or another essay of your choice. Notice where the emphasis in each sentence falls, where you have to pause for breath, the characteristic sounds of the words and cadence of the sentences. Repeat words, phrases, and whole sentences to understand their feeling and their meaning. Then try the same with your own writing and your partner's. What does your experience of close listening teach you about writing? What strikes you when you listen that you didn't notice when you read these silently?

3. Compare Welty's experiences as one who loves reading and books with Sherman Alexie's in "The Joy of Reading and Writing" (p. 63). Not every avid reader becomes a writer. What enabled these people to move from childhood reading to careers as writers?

4. Listen to Amy Walker perform in her video "21 Accents" (in the e-Pages at bedfordstmartins.com/arlington). In what ways does Welty's "Listening" inform your reception of that video? How is the spoken performance different from a written transcript? In other words, how do the various accents change the way you perceive what Walker says? What assumptions, other than geographic, might you make about each "character" Walker portrays? Be specific.

AMY TAN

Mother Tongue

Amy Tan's first novel, The Joy Luck Club *(1989), an integrated suite of stories about mothers and daughters, was a finalist for the National Book Award. Tan earned a bachelor's degree in English (1973) and a master's degree in linguistics (1974) at San Jose State University. Her second novel,* The Kitchen God's Wife *(1991), is based on her mother's life in China before she immigrated to the United States after World War II. Her third book,* The Hundred Secret Senses *(1995), examines marriage and the meanings of motherhood and sisterhood in two cultures. The* Bonesetter's Daughter *(2001) returns to the complex relationship of Chinese mothers and their American-born daughters. Her most recent novel,* Saving Fish from Drowning *(2005), departs from her usual themes depicting mother–daughter relationships to an adventure story that recounts the kidnapping of eleven American tourists in Burma by natives who mistake the fifteen-year-old among them for a "god."*

In "Mother Tongue," first published in the Threepenny Review *(Fall 1990), Tan discusses "all the Englishes I grew up with"—the "simple" English "I spoke to my mother," the "broken" English "she used with me," her "'watered down'" translation of her mother's Chinese, and "her internal language," or what Tan "imagined to be her translation of her Chinese if she could speak in perfect English."*

I am not a scholar of English or literature. I cannot give you much more than personal opinions on the English language and its variations in this country or others.

I am a writer. And by that definition, I am someone who has always loved language. I am fascinated by language in daily life. I spend a great deal of my time thinking about the power of language—the way it can evoke an emotion, a visual image, a complex idea, or a simple truth. Language is the tool of my trade. And I use them all—all the Englishes I grew up with.

Recently, I was made keenly aware of the different Englishes I do use. I was giving a talk to a large group of people, the same talk I had already given to half a dozen other groups. The nature of the talk was about my writing, my life, and my book, *The Joy Luck Club.* The talk was going along well enough, until I remembered one major difference that made the whole talk sound wrong. My mother was in the room. And it was perhaps the first time she had heard me give a lengthy speech, using the kind of English I have never used with her. I was saying things like, "The intersection of memory upon imagination" and "There is an aspect of my fiction that relates to thus-and-thus"—a speech filled with carefully wrought grammatical phrases, burdened, it suddenly seemed to me, with nominalized forms, past perfect tenses, conditional phrases, all the forms of standard English that I had learned in school and through books, the forms of English I did not use at home with my mother.

Just last week, I was walking down the street with my mother, and I again found myself conscious of the English I was using, the English I do use with her. We were talking about the price of new and used furniture and I heard myself saying this: "Not waste money that way." My husband was with us as well, and he didn't notice any switch in my English. And then I realized why. It's because over the twenty years we've been together I've often used that same kind of English with him, and sometimes he even uses it with me. It has become our language of intimacy, a different sort of English that relates to family talk, the language I grew up with.

So you'll have some idea of what this family talk I heard sounds like, I'll quote 5 what my mother said during a recent conversation which I videotaped and then transcribed. During this conversation, my mother was talking about a political gangster in Shanghai who had the same last name as her family's, Du, and how the gangster in his early years wanted to be adopted by her family, which was rich by comparison. Later, the gangster became more powerful, far richer than my mother's family, and one day showed up at my mother's wedding to pay his respects. Here's what she said in part:

"Du Yusong having business like fruit stand. Like off the street kind. He is Du like Du Zong—but not Tsung-ming Island people. The local people call putong, the river east side, he belong to that side local people. That man want to ask Du Zong father take him in like become own family. Du Zong father wasn't look down on him, but didn't take seriously, until that man big like become a mafia. Now important person, very hard to inviting him. Chinese way, came only to show respect, don't stay for dinner. Respect for making big celebration, he shows up. Mean give lots of respect. Chinese custom. Chinese social life that way. If too important won't have to stay too long. He come to my wedding. I didn't see, I heard it. I gone to boy's side, they have YMCA dinner. Chinese age I was nineteen."

You should know that my mother's expressive command of English belies how much she actually understands. She reads the *Forbes* report, listens to *Wall Street Week,* converses daily with her stockbroker, reads all of Shirley MacLaine's books with ease—all kinds of things I can't begin to understand. Yet some of my friends tell me they understand 50 percent of what my mother says. Some say they understand 80 to 90 percent. Some say they understand none of it, as if she were speaking pure Chinese. But to me, my mother's English is perfectly clear, perfectly natural. It's my mother tongue. Her language, as I hear it, is vivid, direct, full of observation and imagery. That was the language that helped shape the way I saw things, expressed things, made sense of the world.

Lately, I've been giving more thought to the kind of English my mother speaks. Like others, I have described it to people as "broken" or "fractured" English. But I wince when I say that. It has always bothered me that I can think of no way to describe it other than "broken," as if it were damaged and needed to be fixed, as if it lacked a certain wholeness and soundness. I've heard other terms used, "limited English," for example. But they seem just as bad, as if everything is limited, including people's perceptions of the limited English speaker.

I know this for a fact, because when I was growing up, my mother's "limited" English limited *my* perception of her. I was ashamed of her English. I believed that her English reflected the quality of what she had to say. That is, because she expressed them imperfectly her thoughts were imperfect. And I had plenty of empirical evidence to support me: the fact that people in department stores, at banks, and at restaurants did not take her seriously, did not give her good service, pretended not to understand her, or even acted as if they did not hear her.

My mother has long realized the limitations of her English as well. When I was   10
fifteen, she used to have me call people on the phone to pretend I was she. In this guise, I was forced to ask for information or even to complain and yell at people who had been rude to her. One time it was a call to her stockbroker in New York. She had cashed out her small portfolio and it just happened we were going to go to New York the next week, our very first trip outside California. I had to get on the phone and say in an adolescent voice that was not very convincing, "This is Mrs. Tan."

And my mother was standing in the back whispering loudly, "Why he don't send me check, already two weeks late. So mad he lie to me, losing me money."

And then I said in perfect English, "Yes, I'm getting rather concerned. You had agreed to send the check two weeks ago, but it hasn't arrived."

Then she began to talk more loudly. "What he want, I come to New York tell him front of his boss, you cheating me?" And I was trying to calm her down, make her be quiet, while telling the stockbroker, "I can't tolerate any more excuses. If I don't receive the check immediately, I am going to have to speak to your manager when I'm in New York next week." And sure enough, the following week there we were in front of this astonished stockbroker, and I was sitting there red-faced and quiet, and my mother, the real Mrs. Tan, was shouting at his boss in her impeccable broken English.

We used a similar routine just five days ago, for a situation that was far less humorous. My mother had gone to the hospital for an appointment, to find out about a benign brain tumor a CAT scan had revealed a month ago. She said she had spoken very good English, her best English, no mistakes. Still, she said, the hospital did not apologize when they said they had lost the CAT scan and she had come for nothing. She said they did not seem to have any sympathy when she told them she was anxious to know the exact diagnosis, since her husband and son had both died of brain tumors. She said they would not give her any more information until the next time and she would have to make another appointment for that. So she said she would not leave until the doctor called her daughter. She wouldn't budge. And when the doctor finally called her daughter, me, who spoke in perfect English—lo and behold—we had assurances the CAT scan would be found, promises that a conference call on Monday would be held, and apologies for any suffering my mother had gone through for a most regrettable mistake.

I think my mother's English almost had an effect on limiting my possibili-   15
ties in life as well. Sociologists and linguists probably will tell you that a person's developing language skills are more influenced by peers. But I do think that the language spoken in the family, especially in immigrant families which are more insular, plays a large role in shaping the language of the child. And I believe that it affected my results on achievement tests, IQ tests, and the SAT. While my English skills were never judged as poor, compared to math, English could not be considered my strong suit. In grade school I did moderately well, getting perhaps B's,

sometimes B-pluses, in English and scoring perhaps in the sixtieth or seventieth percentile on achievement tests. But those scores were not good enough to override the opinion that my true abilities lay in math and science, because in those areas I achieved A's and scored in the ninetieth percentile or higher.

This was understandable. Math is precise; there is only one correct answer. Whereas, for me at least, the answers on English tests were always a judgment call, a matter of opinion and personal experience. Those tests were constructed around items like fill-in-the-blank sentence completion, such as, "Even though Tom was _____, Mary thought he was _____." And the correct answer always seemed to be the most bland combinations of thoughts, for example "Even though Tom was shy, Mary thought he was charming," with the grammatical structure "even though" limiting the correct answer to some sort of semantic opposites, so you wouldn't get answers like, "Even though Tom was foolish, Mary thought he was ridiculous." Well, according to my mother, there were very few limitations as to what Tom could have been and what Mary might have thought of him. So I never did well on tests like that.

The same was true with word analogies, pairs of words in which you were supposed to find some sort of logical, semantic relationship—for example, "*Sunset* is to *nightfall* as _____ is to _____." And here you would be presented with a list of four possible pairs, one of which showed the same kind of relationship: *red* is to *spotlight, bus* is to *arrival, chills* is to *fever, yawn* is to *boring*. Well, I could never think that way. I knew what the tests were asking, but I could not block out of my mind the images already created by the first pair, "*sunset* is to *nightfall*"—and I would see a burst of colors against a darkening sky, the moon rising, the lowering of a curtain of stars. And all the other pairs of words—red, bus, spotlight, boring—just threw up a mass of confusing images, making it impossible for me to sort out something as logical as saying: "A sunset precedes nightfall" is the same as "a chill precedes a fever." The only way I would have gotten that answer right would have been to imagine an associative situation, for example, my being disobedient and staying out past sunset, catching a chill at night, which turns into feverish pneumonia as punishment, which indeed did happen to me.

I have been thinking about all this lately, about my mother's English, about achievement tests. Because lately I've been asked, as a writer, why there are not more Asian Americans represented in American literature. Why are there few Asian Americans enrolled in creative writing programs? Why do so many Chinese students go into engineering? Well, these are broad sociological questions I can't begin to answer. But I have noticed in surveys—in fact, just last week—that Asian students, as a whole, always do significantly better on math achievement tests than in English. And this makes me think that there are other Asian American students whose English spoken in the home might also be described as "broken" or "limited." And perhaps they also have teachers who are steering them away from writing and into math and science, which is what happened to me.

Fortunately, I happen to be rebellious in nature and enjoy the challenge of disproving assumptions made about me. I became an English major my first year in college, after being enrolled as pre-med. I started writing nonfiction as a freelancer the week after I was told by my former boss that writing was my worst skill and I should hone my talents toward account management.

But it wasn't until 1985 that I finally began to write fiction. And at first I wrote using what I thought to be wittily crafted sentences, sentences that would finally prove I had mastery over the English language. Here's an example from the first draft of a story that later made its way into *The Joy Luck Club*, but without this line: "That was my mental quandary in its nascent state." A terrible line, which I can barely pronounce.

Fortunately, for reasons I won't get into today, I later decided I should envision a reader for the stories I would write. And the reader I decided upon was my mother, because these were stories about mothers. So with this reader in mind— and in fact she did read my early drafts—I began to write stories using all the Englishes I grew up with: the English I spoke to my mother, which for lack of a better term might be described as "simple"; the English she used with me, which for lack of a better term might be described as "broken"; my translation of her Chinese, which could certainly be described as "watered down"; and what I imagined to be her translation of her Chinese if she could speak in perfect English, her internal language, and for that I sought to preserve the essence, but neither an English nor a Chinese structure. I wanted to capture what language ability tests can never reveal: her intent, her passion, her imagery, the rhythms of her speech, and the nature of her thoughts.

Apart from what any critic had to say about my writing, I knew I had succeeded where it counted when my mother finished reading my book and gave me her verdict: "So easy to read."

QUESTIONS FOR DISCUSSION AND WRITING

1. What connections does Tan make throughout the essay between speaking and writing? In which English has Tan written "Mother Tongue"? Why?

2. How do the "Englishes" spoken by Tan and her mother help them communicate their personalities, intelligence, and relationship with one another?

3. What differences are there between language used for family or home and language for public use?

4. With family, friends, teammates, or colleagues at school or work, record (video or audio) a conversation that involves more than one "language"— formal, informal, slang, specialized for the task at hand, or bilingual. Then analyze the recording and write a paper identifying the conspicuous features of the languages involved. How do the speakers know which language(s) to use under what circumstances?

5. Present to an audience of college-educated Americans an argument for or against the necessity of speaking (or writing) in Standard English. (What, in your estimation, are the conspicuous features of Standard English?) Are there times and places where you'd allow for exceptions?

6. Using Tan as a source, consider the various effects that Amy Walker achieves in her video "21 Accents" (in the e-Pages at bedfordstmartins.com/arlington). What might Tan say about this video? How is your understanding of what someone says influenced by the way he or she says it? What assumptions— positive or negative—might you have about the speech of someone whose dialect or accent is different from yours?

AMY WALKER

21 Accents   [VIDEO]

"Hello. My name is Amy Walker. I'm twenty-five years old, and I was born in London . . . Belfast . . . Berlin . . . Paris. . . ."

 In the e-Pages at bedfordstmartins.com/arlington

LESLIE MARMON SILKO

Language and Literature from a Pueblo Indian Perspective

Of Pueblo, Laguna, Mexican, and white ancestry, Leslie Marmon Silko (b. 1948) grew up on the Laguna Pueblo reservation before earning a bachelor's degree from the University of New Mexico in 1969. Her citation as the 2004 honoree of Women's History Month reads, "The family house sat on the fringe of Laguna Pueblo—not quite excluded, not quite included. It became a metaphor for Silko's life" and work, "anchored to the traditions and stories of Laguna Pueblo on one side with Anglo mainstream on the other." Silko writes fiction (Ceremony, 1977; Almanac of the Dead, 1991; and Gardens in the Dunes: A Novel, 1999), poetry (Laguna Woman: Poems, 1974), and nonfiction (Yellow Woman and the Beauty of the Spirit, 1997). In 2010 she released The Turquoise Ledge: A Memoir. She won a MacArthur "genius" fellowship (1983). Silko's concern for understanding and sharing Pueblo culture on its own terms pervades her work, leading her to examine the interaction between Native American and Western cultures.

For the Pueblo peoples, geographical, historical, and personal identities are bound up in a web of storytelling that appends tradition to modern reality. In "Language and Literature from a Pueblo Indian Perspective" (in Leslie A. Fiedler and Houston A. Baker, eds., English Literature: Opening Up the Canon, *Baltimore: Johns Hopkins UP, 1979), Silko explains how this oral tradition serves a unifying cultural function: Pueblo Indians learn and rehearse a vast repertoire of oral narratives covering everything from the creation of the world to family stories. Whereas Western anthropologists would create a hierarchy of Pueblo narratives, Silko explains that each Pueblo story—each word, in fact—is a passageway to another story in a seamless nonlinear unity.*

Where I come from, the words most highly valued are those spoken from the heart, unpremeditated and unrehearsed. Among the Pueblo people, a written speech or statement is highly suspect because the true feelings of the speaker remain hidden as she reads words that are detached from the occasion and the audience. I have intentionally not written a formal paper because I want you to *hear* and to experience English in a structure that follows patterns from the oral tradition. For those of you accustomed to being taken from point A to point B to point C, this presentation may be somewhat difficult to follow. Pueblo expression resembles something like a spider's web—with many little threads radiating from the center, crisscrossing each other. As with the web, the structure emerges as it is made and you must simply listen and trust, as the Pueblo people do, that meaning will be made.

My task is a formidable one: I ask you to set aside a number of basic approaches that you have been using, and probably will continue to use, and instead, to approach language from the Pueblo perspective, one that embraces the whole of creation and the whole of history and time.

What changes would Pueblo writers make to English as a language for literature? I have some examples of stories in English that I will use to address this question. At the same time, I would like to explain the importance of storytelling and how it relates to a Pueblo theory of language.

So, I will begin, appropriately enough, with the Pueblo Creation story, an all-inclusive story of how life began. In this story, Tséitsínako, Thought Woman, by thinking of her sisters, and together with her sisters, thought of everything that is. In this way, the world was created. Everything in this world was a part of the original creation; the people at home understood that far away there were other human beings, also a part of this world. The Creation story even includes a prophecy, which describes the origin of European and African peoples and also refers to Asians.

This story, I think, suggests something about why the Pueblo people are more 5 concerned with story and communication and less concerned with a particular language. There are at least six, possibly seven, distinct languages among the twenty pueblos of the southwestern United States, for example, Zuñi and Hopi. And from mesa to mesa there are subtle differences in language. But the particular language being spoken isn't as important as what a speaker is trying to say, and this emphasis on the story itself stems, I believe, from a view of narrative particular to the Pueblo and other Native American peoples—that is, that language *is* story.

I will try to clarify this statement. At Laguna Pueblo, for example, many individual words have their own stories. So when one is telling a story, and one is using words to tell the story, each word that one is speaking has a story of its own, too. Often the speakers or tellers will go into these word-stories, creating an elaborate structure of stories-within-stories. This structure, which becomes very apparent in the actual telling of a story, informs contemporary Pueblo writing and storytelling as well as the traditional narratives. This perspective on narrative—of story within story, the idea that one story is only the beginning of many stories, and the sense that stories never truly end—represents an important contribution of Native American cultures to the English language.

Many people think of storytelling as something that is done at bedtime, that it is something done for small children. But when I use the term *storytelling*, I'm talking about something much bigger than that. I'm talking about something that comes out of an experience and an understanding of that original view of creation—that we are all part of a whole; we do not differentiate or fragment stories and experiences. In the beginning, Tséitsínako, Thought Woman, thought of all things, and all of these things are held together as one holds many things together in a single thought.

So in the telling (and you will hear a few of the dimensions of this telling) first of all, as mentioned earlier, the storytelling always includes the audience, the listeners. In fact, a great deal of the story is believed to be inside the listener; the storyteller's role is to draw the story out of the listeners. The storytelling continues from generation to generation.

Basically, the origin story constructs our identity—within this story, we know who we are. We are the Lagunas. This is where we come from. We came this way. We came by this place. And so from the time we are very young, we hear these stories, so that when we go out into the world, when one asks who we are, or where we are from, we immediately know: we are the people who came from the north. We are the people of these stories.

In the Creation story, Antelope says that he will help knock a hole in the earth 10 so that the people can come up, out into the next world. Antelope tries and tries; he uses his hooves, but is unable to break through. It is then that Badger says, "Let me help you." And Badger very patiently uses his claws and digs a way through, bringing the people into the world. When the Badger clan people think of themselves, or when the Antelope people think of themselves, it is as people who are of *this* story, and this is *our* place, and we fit into the very beginning when the people first came, before we began our journey south.

Within the clans there are stories that identify the clan. One moves, then, from the idea of one's identity as a tribal person into clan identity, then to one's identity as a member of an extended family. And it is the notion of "extended family" that has produced a kind of story that some distinguish from other Pueblo stories, though Pueblo people do not. Anthropologists and ethnologists have, for a long time, differentiated the types of stories the Pueblos tell. They tended to elevate the old, sacred, and traditional stories and to brush aside family stories, the family's account of itself. But in Pueblo culture, these family stories are given equal recognition. There is no definite, present pattern for the way one will hear the stories of one's own family, but it is a very critical part of one's childhood, and the storytelling continues throughout one's life. One will hear stories of importance to the family—sometimes wonderful stories—stories about the time a maternal uncle got the biggest deer that was ever seen and brought it back from the mountains. And so an individual's identity will extend from the identity constructed around the family—"I am from the family of my uncle who brought in this wonderful deer and it was a wonderful hunt."

Family accounts include negative stories, too; perhaps an uncle did something unacceptable. It is very important that one keep track of all these stories—both positive and not so positive—about one's own family and other families. Because even when there is no way around it—old Uncle Pete *did* do a terrible thing—by knowing the stories that originate in other families, one is able to deal with terrible sorts of things that might happen within one's own family. If a member of the family does something that cannot be excused, one always knows stories about similar inexcusable things done by a member of another family. But this knowledge is not communicated for malicious reasons. It is very important to understand this. Keeping track of all the stories within the community gives us all a certain distance, a useful perspective, that brings incidents down to a level we can deal with. If others have done it before, it cannot be so terrible. If others have endured, so can we.

The stories are always bringing us together, keeping this whole together, keeping this family together, keeping this clan together. "Don't go away, don't isolate yourself, but come here, because we have all had these kinds of experiences." And so there is this constant pulling together to resist the tendency to run or hide or separate oneself during a traumatic emotional experience. This separation not only endangers the group but the individual as well—one does not recover by oneself.

Because storytelling lies at the heart of Pueblo culture, it is absurd to attempt to fix the stories in time. "When did they tell the stories?" or "What time of day does the storytelling take place?"—these questions are nonsensical from a Pueblo perspective, because our storytelling goes on constantly: as some old grandmother puts on the shoes of a child and tells her the story of a little girl who didn't wear her shoes, for instance, or someone comes into the house for coffee to talk with a teenage boy who has just been in a lot of trouble, to reassure him that someone else's son has been in that kind of trouble, too. Storytelling is an ongoing process, working on many different levels.

Here's one story that is often told at a time of individual crisis (and I want 15 to remind you that we make no distinctions between types of story—historical, sacred, plain gossip—because these distinctions are not useful when discussing the Pueblo *experience* of language). There was a young man who, when he came back from the war in Vietnam, had saved up his army pay and bought a beautiful red Volkswagen. He was very proud of it. One night he drove up to a place called the King's Bar right across the reservation line. The bar is notorious for many reasons, particularly for the deep *arroyo* located behind it. The young man ran in to pick up a cold six-pack, but he forgot to put on his emergency brake. And his little red Volkswagen rolled back into the *arroyo* and was all smashed up. He felt very bad about it, but within a few days everybody had come to him with stories about other people who had lost cars and family members to that *arroyo*, for instance, George Day's station wagon, with his mother-in-law and kids inside. So everybody was saying, "Well, at least your mother-in-law and kids weren't in the car when it rolled in," and one can't argue with that kind of story. The story of the young man and his smashed-up Volkswagen was now joined with all the other stories of cars that fell into that *arroyo*. . . .

There are a great many parallels between Pueblo experiences and those of African and Caribbean peoples—one is that we have all had the conqueror's language imposed on us. But our experience with English has been somewhat different in that the Bureau of Indian Affairs schools were not interested in teaching us the canon of Western classics. For instance, we never heard of Shakespeare. We were given Dick and Jane, and I can remember reading that the robins were heading south for the winter. It took me a long time to figure out what was going on. I worried for quite a while about our robins in Laguna because they didn't leave in the winter, until I finally realized that all the big textbook companies are up in Boston and *their* robins do go south in the winter. But in a way, this dreadful formal education freed us by encouraging us to maintain our narratives. Whatever literature we were exposed to at school (which was damn little), at home the storytelling, the special regard for telling and bringing together through the telling, was going on constantly.

And as the old people say, "If you can remember the stories, you will be all right. Just remember the stories." . . .

One of the other advantages that we Pueblos have enjoyed is that we have always been able to stay with the land. Our stories cannot be separated from their geographical locations, from actual physical places on the land. We were not relocated like so many Native American groups who were torn away from their ancestral land. And our stories are so much a part of these places that it is almost impossible for future generations to lose them—there is a story connected with every place, every object in the landscape.

Dennis Brutus has talked about the "yet unborn" as well as "those from the past," and how we are still *all* in *this* place, and language—the storytelling—is our way of passing through or being with them, or being together again. When Aunt Susie told her stories, she would tell a younger child to go open the door so that our esteemed predecessors might bring in their gifts to us. "They are out there," Aunt Susie would say. "Let them come in. They're here, they're here with us *within* the stories."

A few years ago, when Aunt Susie was 106, I paid her a visit, and while I was 20 there she said, "Well, I'll be leaving here soon. I think I'll be leaving here next week, and I will be going over to the Cliff House." She said, "It's going to be real good to get back over there." I was listening, and I was thinking that she must be talking about her house at Paguate Village, just north of Laguna. And she went on, "Well, my mother's sister (and she gave her Indian name) will be there. She has been living there. She will be there and we will be over there, and I will get a chance to write down these stories I've been telling you." Now you must understand, of course, that Aunt Susie's mother's sister, a great storyteller herself, has long since passed over into the land of the dead. But then I realized, too, that Aunt Susie wasn't talking about death the way most of us do. She was talking about "going over" as a journey, a journey that perhaps we can only begin to understand through an appreciation for the boundless capacity of language that, through storytelling, brings us together, despite great distances between cultures, despite great distances in time.

QUESTIONS FOR DISCUSSION AND WRITING

1. "Where I come from, the words most highly valued are those spoken from the heart, unpremeditated and unrehearsed. Among the Pueblo people, a written speech or statement is highly suspect because the true feelings of the speaker remain hidden as she reads words that are detached from the occasion and the audience" (paragraph 1). What is the relation between speaking and writing in the Pueblo culture, as Silko explains it?

2. What is the relation between speaking and writing in your own culture (or in the various subcultures to which you belong—for instance, your classes, your family, social or special interest groups of which you are a member)? Are there circumstances under which one is more important than the other? In your own communication, do speech and writing reinforce one another often? In what ways?

3. Why does a Pueblo story have many stories within it (see paragraphs 5–6)? Is there a sense of unity, common elements in a story that is so closely connected with many other stories? How so? When you're telling a true story—about your life, your family, your hometown, a life-changing experience or insight—are you ever cognizant of its relation to other people's stories? What connections do these have in common?

4. Why does Silko think that having been able to "stay with the land" (paragraph 18) is an advantage for the Pueblos in developing their unique views of language, literature, and life? Silko's argument about the close connection between the Pueblo stories and their "geographical locations" suggests that every life in every place is unique. If so, how can storytellers—orally or in writing—communicate meaningfully with people unfamiliar with the places their stories come from?

5. Silko says, "Within the clans there are stories that identify the clan" (paragraph 11). Examine the stories of two or three of the following authors to determine how they reflect on minority experience in the United States: Silko, Sherman Alexie (p. 63), Eric Liu (p. 100), James Baldwin (p. 118), Richard Rodriguez (p. 211), Lynda Barry (in the e-Pages). How do these stories handle issues such as exclusion, prejudice, stereotyping, culture clashes, and dual identity? What information do the writers have to include to ensure that a majority audience understands what they're saying? Do they have to write in Standard English rather than in another language or dialect in order to reinforce their points? If you identify with a particular racial, ethnic, or cultural heritage, incorporate your own story into your analysis.

SHERMAN ALEXIE

The Joy of Reading and Writing: Superman and Me

For author Sherman Alexie, Native American identity is a challenge to be met with imaginative writing. In over a dozen novels and collections of stories and poems, Alexie uses stories to deal with the tragic depression, stultifying normalcy, and quirky comedy of Indian life on and off the reservation. Unlike some authors, however, Alexie is impatient with mythical stereotypes. As he wryly informed a Cineaste *magazine interviewer, "I've never seen an Indian turn into a deer. I mean, I know thousands of Indians, I've been an Indian my whole life, and I've yet to see an Indian turn into an animal!" A descendent of Spokane and Coeur d'Alene tribal ancestors, Alexie was born in 1966 on the Spokane Indian Reservation in Wellpinit, Washington. He attended Gonzaga University and finished his degree at Washington State University (B.A., 1991). A year after graduation his first book,* The Business of Fancydancing: Stories and Poems, *appeared. Other work includes the screenplay for the film* Smoke Signals *(1998), based on his story collection* The Lone Ranger and Tonto Fistfight in Heaven *(1993). His story collection* Ten Little Indians *appeared in 2003. His first young adult novel,* The Absolutely True Diary of a Part-Time Indian *(2007), deals with disability in addition to Alexie's familiar themes of poverty and ethnicity; it captivates with its mixture of raucous humor and true grit. A collection of poems and stories,* War Dances, *won the PEN/Faulkner Award in 2010. His most recent book is* Blasphemy: New and Selected Stories *(2012).*

"The Joy of Reading and Writing: Superman and Me" (first published in The Most Wonderful Books, *1997) discloses the excitement, stimulation, and power that being immersed in books, literally and figuratively, can convey to readers, novice and sophisticated alike. As a child, Alexie understood their many messages, which together meant "I refused to fail."*

I learned to read with a *Superman* comic book. Simple enough, I suppose. I cannot recall which particular *Superman* comic book I read, nor can I remember which villain he fought in that issue. I cannot remember the plot, nor the means by which I obtained the comic book. What I can remember is this: I was three years old, a Spokane Indian boy living with his family on the Spokane Indian Reservation in eastern Washington state. We were poor by most standards, but one of my parents usually managed to find some minimum-wage job or another, which made us middle-class by reservation standards. I had a brother and three sisters. We lived on a combination of irregular paychecks, hope, fear, and government surplus food.

My father, who is one of the few Indians who went to Catholic school on purpose, was an avid reader of westerns, spy thrillers, murder mysteries, gangster epics, basketball player biographies, and anything else he could find. He bought his books by the pound at Dutch's Pawn Shop, Goodwill, Salvation Army, and Value Village. When he had extra money, he bought new novels at supermarkets, convenience stores, and hospital gift shops. Our house was filled with books. They were stacked in crazy piles in the bathroom, bedrooms, and living room. In a fit of unemployment-inspired creative energy, my father built a set of bookshelves and soon filled them with a random assortment of books about the Kennedy assassination, Watergate, the Vietnam War, and the entire twenty-three-book series of the Apache westerns. My father loved books, and since I loved my father with an aching devotion, I decided to love books as well.

I can remember picking up my father's books before I could read. The words themselves were mostly foreign, but I still remember the exact moment when I first understood, with a sudden clarity, the purpose of a paragraph. I didn't have the vocabulary to say "paragraph," but I realized that a paragraph was a fence that held words. The words inside a paragraph worked together for a common purpose. They had some specific reason for being inside the same fence. This knowledge delighted me. I began to think of everything in terms of paragraphs. Our reservation was a small paragraph within the United States. My family's house was a paragraph, distinct from the other paragraphs of the LeBrets to the north, the Fords to our south, and the Tribal School to the west. Inside our house, each family member existed as a separate paragraph but still had genetics and common experiences to link us. Now, using this logic, I can see my changed family as an essay of seven paragraphs: mother, father, older brother, the deceased sister, my younger twin sisters, and our adopted little brother.

At the same time I was seeing the world in paragraphs, I also picked up the *Superman* comic book. Each panel, complete with picture, dialogue, and narrative, was a three-dimensional paragraph. In one panel, Superman breaks through a door. His suit is red, blue, and yellow. The brown door shatters into many pieces. I look at the narrative above the picture. I cannot read the words, but I assume it tells me that "Superman is breaking down the door." Aloud, I pretend to read the words and say, "Superman is breaking down the door." Words, dialogue, also float out of Superman's mouth. Because he is breaking down the door, I assume he says, "I am breaking down the door." Once again, I pretend to read the words and say aloud, "I am breaking down the door." In this way, I learned to read.

This might be an interesting story all by itself. A little Indian boy teaches 5 himself to read at an early age and advances quickly. He reads *Grapes of Wrath* in kindergarten when other children are struggling through Dick and Jane. If he'd been anything but an Indian boy living on the reservation, he might have been called a prodigy. But he is an Indian boy living on the reservation and is simply an oddity. He grows into a man who often speaks of his childhood in the third-person, as if it will somehow dull the pain and make him sound more modest about his talents.

A smart Indian is a dangerous person, widely feared and ridiculed by Indians and non-Indians alike. I fought with my classmates on a daily basis. They wanted me to stay quiet when the non-Indian teacher asked for answers, for volunteers, for help. We were Indian children who were expected to be stupid. Most lived up to those expectations inside the classroom but subverted them on the outside. They struggled with basic reading in school but could remember how to sing a few dozen powwow songs. They were monosyllabic in front of their non-Indian teachers but could tell complicated stories and jokes at the dinner table. They submissively ducked their heads when confronted by a non-Indian adult but would slug it out with the Indian bully who was ten years older. As Indian children, we were expected to fail in the non-Indian world. Those who failed were ceremonially accepted by other Indians and appropriately pitied by non-Indians.

I refused to fail. I was smart. I was arrogant. I was lucky. I read books late into the night, until I could barely keep my eyes open. I read books at recess, then during lunch, and in the few minutes left after I had finished my classroom assignments. I read books in the car when my family traveled to powwows or basketball games. In shopping malls, I ran to the bookstores and read bits and pieces of as many books as I could. I read the books my father brought home from the pawnshops and secondhand. I read the books I borrowed from the library. I read the backs of cereal boxes. I read the newspaper. I read the bulletins posted on the walls of the school, the clinic, the tribal offices, the post office. I read junk mail. I read auto-repair manuals. I read magazines. I read anything that had words and paragraphs. I read with equal parts joy and desperation. I loved those books, but I also knew that love had only one purpose. I was trying to save my life.

Despite all the books I read, I am still surprised I became a writer. I was going to be a pediatrician. These days, I write novels, short stories, and poems. I visit schools and teach creative writing to Indian kids. In all my years in the reservation school system, I was never taught how to write poetry, short stories, or novels. I was certainly never taught that Indians wrote poetry, short stories, and novels. Writing was something beyond Indians. I cannot recall a single time that a guest teacher visited the reservation. There must have been visiting teachers. Who were they? Where are they now? Do they exist? I visit the schools as often as possible. The Indian kids crowd the classroom. Many are writing their own poems, short stories, and novels. They have read my books. They have read many other books. They look at me with bright eyes and arrogant wonder. They are trying to save their lives. Then there are the sullen and already defeated Indian kids who sit in the back rows and ignore me with theatrical precision. The pages of their notebooks are empty. They carry neither pencil nor pen. They stare out the window. They refuse and resist. "Books," I say to them. "Books," I say. I throw my weight against their locked doors. The door holds. I am smart. I am arrogant. I am lucky. I am trying to save our lives.

QUESTIONS FOR DISCUSSION AND WRITING

1. Elaborate—in discussion or in a paper—on Alexie's observations that "A smart Indian is a dangerous person" and "I refused to fail. I was smart. I was arrogant. I was lucky. I read books late into the night" (paragraphs 6 and 7). Why is a "smart Indian . . . widely feared and ridiculed by Indians and non-Indians alike" (paragraph 6)? What threats does an independent-minded Indian (or anyone) pose to complacent or powerful people or to society in general?

2. Compare and contrast Welty's "Listening" (p. 47) and Alexie's "Joy of Reading and Writing." Using the Questions for Discussion and Writing following

Welty (p. 51), examine the connections each makes between the acts of reading and writing. Have your experiences with e-mail, Twitter, and other social media influenced this answer? If so, in what ways?

3. Write a paper, either individually or with a partner, on reading as a source of empowerment. Draw on your experiences as a reader, as well as those of Alexie and Welty.

RICHARD WRIGHT

From *Fighting Words*

Richard Wright, son of sharecroppers, was born in Mississippi in 1908. He grew up in a household impoverished in body, soul, and spirit and dominated by a fundamentalist grandmother who forbade reading anything but the Bible. His autobiography, Black Boy (1945), chronicles the discrimination, despair, and anger that impelled Wright to move to Chicago and, ultimately, to Paris, where he lived until his death in 1960. His internationally distinguished reputation puts him in the ranks of the celebrated authors he cites in paragraph 46 of "Fighting Words," an excerpt from Black Boy.

I stood at a counter [in the bank lobby] and picked up the Memphis *Commercial Appeal* and began my free reading of the press. I came finally to the editorial page and saw an article dealing with one H. L. Mencken. I knew by hearsay that he was the editor of the *American Mercury*, but aside from that I knew nothing about him. The article was a furious denunciation of Mencken, concluding with one, hot, short sentence: Mencken is a fool.

I wondered what on earth this Mencken had done to call down upon him the scorn of the South. . . . Undoubtedly he must be advocating ideas that the South did not like. Were there, then, people other than Negroes who criticized the South? . . .

Now, how could I find out about this Mencken? There was a huge library near the riverfront, but I knew that Negroes were not allowed to patronize its shelves any more than they were the parks and playgrounds of the city. I had gone into the library several times to get books for the white men on the job. Which of them would now help me to get books? And how could I read them without causing concern to the white men with whom I worked? . . .

One morning I paused before the [desk of a] Catholic fellow [who was hated by white Southerners].

"I want to ask you a favor," I whispered to him.

"What is it?"

"I want to read. I can't get books from the library. I wonder if you'd let me use your card?"

He looked at me suspiciously.

5

"My card is full most of the time," he said.

"I see," I said and waited, posing my question silently.   10

"You're not trying to get me into trouble, are you, boy?" he asked, staring at me.

"Oh, no, sir."

"What book do you want?"

"A book by H. L. Mencken."

"Which one?"   15

"I don't know. Has he written more than one?"

"He has written several."

"I didn't know that."

"What makes you want to read Mencken?"

"Oh, I just saw his name in the newspaper," I said.   20

"It's good of you to want to read," he said. "But you ought to read the right things."

I said nothing. Would he want to supervise my reading?

"Let me think," he said. "I'll figure out something."

I turned from him and he called me back. He stared at me quizzically.

"Richard, don't mention this to the other white men," he said.   25

"I understand," I said. "I won't say a word."

A few days later he called me to him.

"I've got a card in my wife's name," he said. "Here's mine."

"Thank you, sir."

"Do you think you can manage it?"   30

"I'll manage fine," I said.

"If they suspect you, you'll get in trouble," he said.

"I'll write the same kind of notes to the library that you wrote when you sent me for books," I told him. "I'll sign your name."

He laughed.

"Go ahead. Let me see what you get," he said.   35

That afternoon I addressed myself to forging a note. Now, what were the names of books written by H. L. Mencken? I did not know any of them. I finally wrote what I thought would be a foolproof note: *Dear Madam: Will you please let this nigger boy*—I used the word "nigger" to make the librarian feel that I could not possibly be the author of the note—*have some books by H. L. Mencken?* I forged the white man's name.

I entered the library as I had always done when on errands for whites, but I felt that I would somehow slip up and betray myself. I doffed my hat, stood a respect-ful distance from the desk, looked as unbookish as possible, and waited for the white patrons to be taken care of. When the desk was clear of people, I still waited. The white librarian looked at me.

"What do you want, boy?"

As though I did not possess the power of speech, I stepped forward and sim-ply handed her the forged note, not parting my lips.

"What books by Mencken does he want?" she asked.   40

"I don't know, ma'am," I said, avoiding her eyes. . . .

"You're not using these books, are you?" she asked pointedly.

"Oh, no, ma'am. I can't read." . . .

I said nothing. She stamped the card and handed me the books.

That night in my rented room . . . I opened *A Book of Prefaces* and began to   45
read. I was jarred and shocked by the style, the clear, clean, sweeping sentences. . . .
Yes, this man was fighting, fighting with words. He was using words as a weapon,
using them as one would use a club. Could words be weapons? Well, yes, for here
they were. Then, maybe, perhaps, I could use them as a weapon? No. It frightened
me. I read on and what amazed me was not what he said, but how on earth anybody had the courage to say it.

Occasionally I glanced up to reassure myself that I was alone in the room. Who
were these men about whom Mencken was talking so passionately? Who was Anatole
France? Joseph Conrad? Sinclair Lewis, Sherwood Anderson, Dostoevski, George
Moore, Gustave Flaubert, Maupassant, Tolstoy, Frank Harris, Mark Twain, Thomas
Hardy, Arnold Bennett, Stephen Crane, Zola, Norris, Gorky, Bergson, Ibsen, Balzac,
Bernard Shaw, Dumas, Poe, Thomas Mann, O. Henry, Dreiser, H. G. Wells, Gogol,
T. S. Eliot, Gide, Baudelaire, Edgar Lee Masters, Stendhal, Turgenev, Huneker,
Nietzsche, and scores of others? Were these men real? Did they exist or had they
existed? . . . I concluded the book with the conviction that I had somehow overlooked
something terribly important in life. I had once tried to write, had once reveled in
feeling, had let my crude imagination roam, but the impulse to dream had been
slowly beaten out of me by experience. Now it surged up again and I hungered for
books, new ways of looking and seeing. It was not a matter of believing or disbelieving
what I read, but of feeling something new, of being affected by something that made
the look of the world different.

QUESTIONS FOR DISCUSSION AND WRITING

1. Why did Wright have to lie to take out library books he wanted to read in
   the segregated South? He had to use a white man's library card (paragraphs
   10–40), since none was available to him, and he lied to the librarian who
   asked, "You're not using those books, are you?". . . "On, no, ma'am. I can't
   read" (paragraphs 42 and 43). Why were African Americans denied access to
   books at that time?

2. Judging from the experiences of Welty (p. 47), Alexie (p. 63), and Wright,
   why do you suppose that some people who love to read become writers, while
   many do not?

3. Many autobiographers and other authors write of their excitement at learning
   to read or of discovering particular authors with a wide range of possibilities,
   power, and perspective opening before them. As Wright explains in his concluding paragraph (paragraph 46), his encounters with the universe of major
   authors, ranging from Anatole France and Joseph Conrad to Turgenev and
   Nietzsche, gave him "new ways of looking and seeing . . . of feeling something
   new, of being affected by something that made the look of the world different." Have you ever been excited, electrified by something you read in print or

online? At school or on your own? What was this reading? In what ways has it shaped your current thinking, expanded your understanding of the world? If nothing you've ever read has affected you in this dramatic way, make a list of the characteristics a piece would need to have in order to make an indelible impression on you.

4. Writing as an instrumental medium—producing, for instance, directions, operators' manuals, records of meetings, contracts and other legal documents—forms the foundation of many transactions and professions, including advertising, the law, and many aspects of engineering and computer programming. In contrast, Welty, Alexie, Wright, and other creative writers view writing as a means of exploring oneself, one's gender, and one's culture, and as a form of storytelling that provides insight as well as entertainment. Write a brief paper in two parts, perhaps defining a favorite topic (work, love, ethics) or explaining how to do something you enjoy doing. One part should reflect an instrumental approach to the subject; the other should be a narrative disclosing your passion for the subject and/or the process.

GEORGE SAUNDERS

Thank You, Esther Forbes

George Saunders (b. 1958) has an unusual background for a creative writer: His undergraduate degree is in geophysical engineering from Colorado School of Mines. He turned his skills in observation and technical procedures away from science and toward writing, and today is a professor of creative writing at Syracuse University, where he received his own master of arts degree in creative writing in 1988. He has regularly published in periodicals such as the New Yorker, GQ, *and* Harper's Magazine. *His fiction works are typically collections of short stories and novellas, including* CivilWarLand in Bad Decline *(1996),* Pastoralia *(2000),* The Brief and Frightening Reign of Phil *(2005), and* Tenth of December: Stories *(2013). In an interview with* WAG, *an online magazine, he claimed short works are "the only thing I can do."*

This essay comes from Saunders's collection of nonfiction essays, The Braindead Megaphone *(2007). It is Saunders's first collection of nonfiction essays. In "Thank You, Esther Forbes," Saunders remembers fondly both an influential younger teacher and the book she led him to,* Johnny Tremain. *The young Saunders is drawn not merely to the content of the book, but to the language. Saunders explores how different uses of language—different sentences, different words—can be used to describe the same thing to different effect.*

It began, like so many things in those days, with a nun. Unlike the other nuns at St. Damian School, who, it seemed, had been born nuns, Sister Lynette seemed to have been born an adorable, sun-dappled Kansas girl with an Audrey Hepburn smile, who was then kidnapped by a band of older, plumper, meaner nuns who were trying to break her. I was a little in love with Sister Lynette, with her dry wit and good-heartedness and the wisp of hair that snuck out from under her wimple. I thought of a convent as a place of terrific rigor, where prospective nuns were given access to esoteric knowledge, which they were then to secretly disseminate among select students in Middle America, to save the culture. Hoping to be so identified, I would linger in Sister Lynette's classroom after school (both of us covered in chalk dust, my wool pants smelling like Distressed Sheep) as she told me stories about her Kansas girlhood. I entertained rescue fantasies, in which Sister realized that the best way for her to serve God was to quit the nuns, marry me, and start wearing jeans as we traveled around the country making antiwar speeches. Since I was only in third grade, these fantasies required a pre-fantasy, in which pacifist aliens placed me in a sort of Aging Apparatus.

One afternoon, Sister Lynette handed me a book: *Johnny Tremain,* by Esther Forbes. This is the story of an arrogant apprentice silversmith in Boston during the Revolutionary War, whose prospects are cut short by a tragic accident until he finds a new sense of purpose in the war. The cover was a picture of a young Johnny, looking a bit like Twiggy. On it there was a shiny gold medallion: the Newbery Medal.

It was an award-winner.

Sister Lynette had given me an award-winner.

I was soon carrying it around twenty-four hours a day, the Newbery Medal 5 facing out, as if I, and not Esther Forbes, had written *Johnny Tremain.*

"I think you can handle this," Sister had said as she handed me the book (she'd checked it out of the library), but what I heard was: "Only you, George, in this entire moronic class, can handle this. There is a spark in you, and it is that spark that keeps me from fleeing back to Kansas."

I imagined the scene at the convent—everyone in nun gear, sitting around a TV that was somehow always tuned to *The Flying Nun.* And then Sister Lynette makes her announcement:

"I'm thinking of giving Saunders *Johnny Tremain.*"

A tense silence.

"Isn't that . . . ," asks Sister Humiline, the principal, "an award-winner?"   10

"It is," says Sister Lynette. "But I think he's ready."

"Well, then . . . ," says Sister Humiline. Clearly this is important. Denied this, Sister Lynette might make her break for Kansas. "Let him give it a try, then. But, truly, I wonder if he's got it in him. That book is hard, and he is only a third-grader."

"Even I had trouble with it," pipes up a junior nun.

"I think he can handle it," says Sister Lynette.

And the wonderful thing was: I could. I loved the language, which was dense 15 and seemed not to care that it sounded mathematically efficient ("On rocky islands gulls woke"). The sentences somehow had got more life in them than normal sentences had. They were not merely sentences but compressed moments that burst when you read them. I often left the book open on the kitchen table, so that my mother and her friends could see how at home I was with phrases like "too cripple-handed for chopping open sea chests" or "Isannah drank herself sick and silly on sillabubs."

A sentence, Forbes seemed to believe, not only had to say something, it had to say it uniquely, with verve. A sentence was more than just a fact-conveyor; it also made a certain sound, and could have a thrilling quality of being over-full, saying more than its length should permit it to say. A sequence of such sentences exploding in the brain made the invented world almost unbearably real, each sentence serving as a kind of proof.

The tragic accident that happens early in the book ends Johnny's silversmithing: his right thumb is melded to the palm of his hand by molten silver. During recess, I started holding my hand like his in the pocket of my coat, trying to get through the entire period without uncrippling myself. There was a sweetness in the bitterness I felt as I imagined that I was Johnny and the whole world had turned against me, even my fiancée, Cilia, and her real-life corollary, Susan Pusateri. Had Susan smiled? She would marry me in spite of my deformity. Was she talking energetically to Joey Cannarozzi? She preferred his fully opposable thumb, and I would therefore have to lay siege to the British armory.

After a while, because I liked the idea of being wounded, but didn't much like the idea of actually having that pink flipperlike thing flapping around on my arm, a world-famous surgeon from France would arrive in the Boston in my head and fix my hand, and I would go back to class, face chapped from the wind, holding the book in my now-perfect hand, Newbery Medal facing outward.

"Good book?" Sister Lynette would say from her desk.

"Good book," I would say.   20

Before *Johnny Tremain,* writers and writing gave me the creeps. In our English book, which had one of those 1970s titles that connoted nothing (*Issues and Perspectives,* maybe, or *Amalgam 109*), the sentences ("Larry, aged ten, a tow-headed heavyset boy with a happy smile for all, meandered down to the ballfield, hoping against hope he would at last be invited to join some good-spirited game instigated by the other lads of summer") repulsed me the way a certain kind of moccasin-style house slipper then in vogue among my father's friends repulsed me. I would never, I swore, wear slippers like that. Only old people who had given up on life could wear slippers like that. Likewise the sentences in *Amalgam 109* or *Polyglot Viewpoints* seemed to have given up on life, or to never have taken life sufficiently personally. They weren't lies, exactly, but they weren't true either. They lacked will. They seemed committee-written, seemed to emanate from no-person, to argue against the intimate actual feeling of minute-to-minute life.

Forbes suggested that the sentence was where the battle was fought. With enough attention, a sentence could peel away from its fellows and be, not only from you, but *you.* I later found the same quality in Hemingway, in Isaac Babel, Gertrude Stein, Henry Green: sentences that had been the subject of so much concentration, they had become things in the world instead of attempts to catalog it.

A person can write: "There were, out in the bay, a number of rocks, islands of a sort, and upon these miniature islands, there resided a number of gulls, which, as the sun began to rise, gradually came to life, ready to begin another day of searching for food."

Or she can write: "On rocky islands gulls woke."

The first sentence is perfectly correct. There is, strictly speaking, more infor-   25
mation in it than in the second. But is the increased information justified by the
greater number of words? The second sentence credits our intelligence. Where else
would the islands be, but in a bay? The plural "islands" implies that there are "a
number" of them. If the rocks are "islands of a sort," let's call them "islands." Gulls
search for food every day, no need to point it out.

The second sentence has been loved by its creator. She has given it her full
attention. That missing comma? She meant it. There was, to Forbes, I expect, a
world of difference between, "On rocky islands, gulls woke," and "On rocky islands
gulls woke."

Standing around the school yard, I tried out sentences meant to describe, with
Forbes-like precision, whatever I happened to be seeing: "Sister Lynette was eating lunch in the doorway while watching the third-and fourth-grade kids running around in the parking lot at recess and as she watched them, she thought of
her home in Kansas." That wasn't very Forbes-ish. Sister Lynette wasn't actually
standing in the doorway at all. She was . . . she was "standing on the sidewalk that
ran between the school building itself and the parking lot on which the children
played." Or actually, she was "standing with one foot on that sidewalk and one foot
in the parking lot." Did we need all that? Was her exact position worth the resulting sentence-bulk? Why did we care where she was standing anyway? Did it affect
what came next? Also, she wasn't watching "the third- and fourth-grade kids." She
was watching *some* of them. Actually, on closer inspection, she wasn't. She was
looking across the street, at a run-down house. What did I mean by "run-down"?
What were the specific characteristics of the house that might cause me to think
of it as "run-down"?

I remember those times with great affection: the bitter Chicago cold, the vast
parking lot, the world, suddenly and for the first time, transformed into something
describable, with me, the Potential Describer, at its center.

The world, I started to see, was a different world, depending on what you said
about it, and how you said it. By honing the sentences you used to describe the
world, you changed the inflection of your mind, which changed your perceptions.

The difference between Esther Forbes and the authors of *Polyglot 141* was that   30
Forbes had fully invested herself in her sentences. She had made them her own,
agreed to live or die by them, taken total responsibility for them. How had she
done this? I didn't know. But I do now: she'd revised them. She had abided long
enough with each of them to push past the normal into what we might call the
excessive-meaningful; had held the prose up to sufficient scrutiny to turn it into
something iconic, something that sounded like her and only like her.

What happens when this attention is not paid?

Well, *Polyglot 141* happens.

But worse things can happen than *Polyglot 141*.

A petty bureaucrat writes to his superior: "The lighting must be better protected than now. Lights could be eliminated, since they apparently are never used.
However, it has been observed that when the doors are shut, the load always

presses hard against them as soon as darkness sets in. This is because the load naturally rushes toward the light when darkness sets in, which makes closing the door difficult. Also, because of the alarming nature of darkness, screaming always occurs when the doors are closed. It would therefore be useful to light the lamp before and during the first moments of the operation." The bureaucrat was the ironically named "Mr. Just," his organization the SS, the year 1942.

What Mr. Just did not write—what he would have written, had he been tak- 35 ing full responsibility for his own prose—is: "To more easily kill the Jews, leave the lights on." But writing this would have forced him to admit what he was up to. To avoid writing this, what did he have to do? Disown his prose. Pretend his prose was not him. He may have written a more honest version, and tore it up. He may have intuitively, self-protectively, skipped directly to this dishonest, passive-voice version. Either way, he accepted an inauthentic relation to his own prose, and thereby doomed himself to hell.

Working with language is a means by which we can identify the bullshit within ourselves (and others). If we learn what a truthful sentence looks like, a little flag goes up at a false one. False prose can mark an attempt to evade responsibility ("On structures not unlike rock masses, it was observed that certain animals perhaps prone to flight slept somewhat less aggressively than previously"), or something more diabolical ("The germ-ridden avatars of evil perched on their filthy black rocks in the otherwise pure bay, daring the clear-souled inhabitants of the city to do what was so obviously necessary: kill them before they could infest the city's hopeful, innocent children"); the process of improving our prose disciplines the mind, hones the logic, and, most important of all, tells us what we really think. But this process takes time, and immersion in prior models of beautiful compression.

Forbes was my first model of beautiful compression. She did for me what one writer can do for another: awoke a love for sentences. Behind her prose I sensed the loving hand of an involved human maker. Her thirst for direct, original language seemed like a religion of sorts, a method of orientation, and a comfort, in all countries and weathers, in happiness and sadness, in sickness and in health. Reading *Johnny Tremain*, I felt a premonition that immersion in language would enrich and bring purpose to my life, which has turned out to be true.

So thank you, Esther Forbes. I never knew you, it turned out your Boston never existed, but that nonexistent town, and that boy made out of words, changed things for me forever.

QUESTIONS FOR DISCUSSION AND WRITING

1. Saunders, writing from his perspective as a child, thought the nuns at his school were on a secret mission "to save the culture" (paragraph 1). What does that mean? What is the background for such a statement? Think about what nuns represent in terms of the culture, especially as depicted in Saunders's essay. Think of the other cultural references in the essay—Audrey Hepburn, the television show *The Flying Nun*, even the state of Kansas (as thought of by someone not from Kansas). What do these references suggest about the culture?

2. Saunders makes distinctions between the use of language in textbooks such as *Polyglot Viewpoints* and *Amalgam 109* and Esther Forbes's use of language in *Johnny Tremain*. What is the basis of such distinctions? Use a dictionary to look up the meanings of the words "polyglot" and "amalgam." What is Saunders pointing out by using such words? How is that different from what Forbes does? Ultimately, why does Forbes's use of language have such a stronger impact on Saunders?

3. Discuss what type of writing, and writers, have had the strongest impact on you. What was it about their writing style—use of words, sentences, images— that attracted you? Can you define what good writing is? If you're struggling with this, first define what bad writing is. Find examples of writing that are either good or bad. What elements are in good writing that are not in bad writing, or vice versa?

4. In paragraphs 34–35, Saunders shows how the use of language by a "petty bureaucrat" masks the profoundly evil actions that are taking place in a Nazi death camp in 1942. Why does the bureaucrat write in such a way? Can you think of more recent examples of the use of language, perhaps just words or phrases, that are used by powerful entities such as governments to mask the truth? Be specific. Address the question of why such writing exists, and why it is allowed to exist and even thrive in large organizations and institutions.

5. Ultimately, Saunders's essay is nostalgic. It recalls a time in his childhood when he was profoundly affected by a teacher—and a book—and it recalls both with a degree of pleasure and humor. Can you remember a similar experience of your own, when a person or experience created a lasting impression, perhaps one that guides your choices even today in terms of academic interests or career plans? Be specific. Or is nostalgia simply sentimental and misleading— pulling an adult away from the core realities of the present by wrapping images up the past in a vision that justifies itself? Argue for or against either side.

JOAN DIDION

On Keeping a Notebook

Born in 1934 and reared on a ranch near Sacramento, California, Didion graduated from the University of California, Berkeley (1956). Winning Vogue's Prix de Paris writing contest enabled her to start near the top, working in New York as a Vogue *copywriter and editor for the next eight years. In 1964 she married John Gregory Dunne and moved to Los Angeles, where the couple, both novelists and nonfiction writers, began a long career of collaborating on screenplays until his death in 2003. Among their films are* Panic in Needle Park *(1973) and* A Star Is Born *(1976). Their screenplay for* Up Close and Personal *(1996) took eight years, twenty-seven drafts, and three hundred additional revisions. "We were each the person the other trusted,"*

Didion explains in The Year of Magical Thinking *(2005), a meditation on "marriage and children and memory" prompted by Dunne's death in December 2003 and interwoven with their daughter Quintana's mysterious mortal illness. In 2011 Didion published* Blue Nights, *about her daughter's death.*

Didion's novels, including A Book of Common Prayer *(1977) and* Democracy *(1984), have been praised for their elegant prose and distinctive voice—precise, controlled, and concise. These qualities also characterize her essays, particularly those collected in* Slouching Towards Bethlehem *(1968) and* The White Album *(1979). Many are cynical commentaries on the erosion of traditional American pioneer values expressed in strong family and social structures. In "On Keeping a Notebook" (1966), Didion discusses what a notebook means for someone who writes, or wants to—not to provide "an accurate factual record of what I have been doing or thinking" but a way to demonstrate "how it felt to me." Thus the notebook collects an "indiscriminate and erratic assemblage" of facts, names, events, oddities, all filtered through the writer's consciousness and imagination.*

"'That woman Estelle,'" the note reads, "'is partly the reason why George Sharp and I are separated today.' *Dirty crepe-de-Chine wrapper, hotel bar, Wilmington RR, 9:45 a.m. August Monday morning.*"

Since the note is in my notebook, it presumably has some meaning to me. I study it for a long while. At first I have only the most general notion of what I was doing on an August Monday morning in the bar of the hotel across from the Pennsylvania Railroad station in Wilmington, Delaware (waiting for a train? missing one? 1960? 1961? why Wilmington?), but I do remember being there. The woman in the dirty crepe-de-Chine wrapper had come down from her room for a beer, and the bartender had heard before the reason why George Sharp and she were separated today. "Sure," he said, and went on mopping the floor. "You told me." At the other end of the bar is a girl. She is talking, pointedly, not to the man beside her but to a cat lying in the triangle of sunlight cast through the open door. She is wearing a plaid silk dress from Peck & Peck, and the hem is coming down.

Here is what it is: the girl has been on the Eastern Shore, and now she is going back to the city, leaving the man beside her, and all she can see ahead are the viscous summer sidewalks and the 3 a.m. long-distance calls that will make her lie awake and then sleep drugged through all the steaming mornings left in August (1960? 1961?). Because she must go directly from the train to lunch in New York, she wishes that she had a safety pin for the hem of the plaid silk dress, and she also wishes that she could forget about the hem and the lunch and stay in the cool bar that smells of disinfectant and malt and make friends with the woman in the crepe-de-Chine wrapper. She is afflicted by a little self-pity, and she wants to compare Estelles. That is what that was all about.

Why did I write it down? In order to remember, of course, but exactly what was it I wanted to remember? How much of it actually happened? Did any of it? Why do I keep a notebook at all? It is easy to deceive oneself on all those scores. The impulse to write things down is a peculiarly compulsive one, inexplicable to those who do not share it, useful only accidentally, only secondarily, in the way that any compulsion tries to justify itself. I suppose that it begins or does not begin in the cradle. Although I have felt compelled to write things down since I was five years old, I doubt that my daughter ever will, for she is a singularly blessed and accepting child, delighted with life exactly as life presents itself to her, unafraid to go to sleep and unafraid to wake up. Keepers of private notebooks are a different breed altogether, lonely and resistant rearrangers of things, anxious malcontents, children afflicted apparently at birth with some presentiment of loss.

My first notebook was a Big Five tablet, given to me by my mother with the   5
sensible suggestion that I stop whining and learn to amuse myself by writing down my thoughts. She returned the tablet to me a few years ago; the first entry is an account of a woman who believed herself to be freezing to death in the Arctic night, only to find, when day broke, that she had stumbled onto the Sahara Desert, where she would die of the heat before lunch. I have no idea what turn of a five-year-old's mind could have prompted so insistently "ironic" and exotic a story, but it does reveal a certain predilection for the extreme which has dogged me into adult life; perhaps if I were analytically inclined I would find it a truer story than any I might have told about Donald Johnson's birthday party or the day my cousin Brenda put Kitty Litter in the aquarium.

So the point of my keeping a notebook has never been, nor is it now, to have an accurate factual record of what I have been doing or thinking. That would be a different impulse entirely, an instinct for reality which I sometimes envy but do not possess. At no point have I ever been able successfully to keep a diary; my approach to daily life ranges from the grossly negligent to the merely absent, and on those few occasions when I have tried dutifully to record a day's events, boredom has so overcome me that the results are mysterious at best. What is this business about "shopping, typing piece, dinner with E, depressed"? Shopping for what? Typing what piece? Who is E? Was this "E" depressed, or was I depressed? Who cares?

In fact I have abandoned altogether that kind of pointless entry; instead I tell what some would call lies. "That's simply not true," the members of my family frequently tell me when they come up against my memory of a shared event. "The party was *not* for you, the spider was *not* a black widow, *it wasn't that way at all.*" Very likely they are right, for not only have I always had trouble distinguishing between what happened and what merely might have happened, but I remain unconvinced that the distinction, for my purposes, matters. The cracked crab that I recall having for lunch the day my father came home from Detroit in 1945 must certainly be embroidery, worked into the day's pattern, to lend verisimilitude; I was ten years old and would not now remember the cracked crab. The day's events did not turn on cracked crab. And yet it is precisely that fictitious crab that makes me see the afternoon all over again, a home movie run all too often, the father bearing gifts, the child weeping, an exercise in family love and guilt. Or that is what it was to me. Similarly, perhaps it never did snow that August in Vermont; perhaps there never were flurries in the night wind, and maybe no one else felt the ground hardening and summer already dead even as we pretended to bask in it, but that was how it felt to me, and it might as well have snowed, could have snowed, did snow.

How it felt to me: that is getting closer to the truth about a notebook. I some-times delude myself about why I keep a notebook, imagine that some thrifty virtue derives from preserving everything observed. See enough and write it down, I tell myself, and then some morning when the world seems drained of wonder, some day when I am only going through the motions of doing what I am supposed to do, which is write—on that bankrupt morning I will simply open my notebook and there it will all be, a forgotten account with accumulated interest, paid passage back to the world out there: dialogue overheard in hotels and elevators and at the hat-check counter in Pavillon (one middle-aged man shows his hat check to another and says, "That's my old football number"); impressions of Bettina Aptheker and Benjamin Sonnenberg and Teddy ("Mr. Acapulco") Stauffer; careful *aperçus* about tennis bums and failed fashion models and Greek shipping heir-esses, one of whom taught me a significant lesson (a lesson I could have learned from F. Scott Fitzgerald, but perhaps we all must meet the very rich for ourselves) by asking, when I arrived to interview her in her orchid-filled sitting room on the second day of a paralyzing New York blizzard, whether it was snowing outside.

I imagine, in other words, that the notebook is about other people. But of course it is not. I have no real business with what one stranger said to another at the hat-check counter in Pavillon; in fact I suspect that the line "That's my old foot-ball number" touched not my own imagination at all, but merely some memory of something once read, probably "The Eighty-Yard Run." Nor is my concern with a woman in a dirty crepe-de-Chine wrapper in a Wilmington bar. My stake is always, of course, in the unmentioned girl in the plaid silk dress. *Remember what it was to be me:* that is always the point.

It is a difficult point to admit. We are brought up in the ethic that others, any others, all others, are by definition more interesting than ourselves; taught to be diffident, just this side of self-effacing. ("You're the least important person in the room and don't forget it," Jessica Mitford's governess would hiss in her ear on the advent of any social occasion; I copied that into my notebook because it is only recently that I have been able to enter a room without hearing some such phrase in my inner ear.) Only the very young and the very old may recount their dreams at breakfast, dwell upon self, interrupt with memories of beach picnics and favor-ite Liberty lawn dresses and the rainbow trout in a creek near Colorado Springs. The rest of us are expected, rightly, to affect absorption in other people's favorite dresses, other people's trout.

And so we do. But our notebooks give us away, for however dutifully we record what we see around us, the common denominator of all we see is always, transparently, shamelessly, the implacable "I." We are not talking here about the kind of notebook that is patently for public consumption, a structural conceit for binding together a series of graceful *pensées*; we are talking about something pri-vate, about bits of the mind's string too short to use, an indiscriminate and erratic assemblage with meaning only for its maker.

And sometimes even the maker has difficulty with the meaning. There does not seem to be, for example, any point in my knowing for the rest of my life that, during 1964, 720 tons of soot fell on every square mile of New York City, yet there it is in my notebook, labeled "FACT." Nor do I really need to remember that Ambrose Bierce liked to spell Leland Stanford's name "£eland $tanford" or that "smart women almost always wear black in Cuba," a fashion hint without much potential for practical application. And does not the relevance of these notes seem marginal at best?:

> In the basement museum of the Inyo County Courthouse in Independence, California, sign pinned to a mandarin coat: "This MANDARIN COAT was often worn by Mrs. Minnie S. Brooks when giving lectures on her TEAPOT COLLECTION."
> Redhead getting out of car in front of Beverly Wilshire Hotel, chinchilla stole, Vuitton bags with tags reading:

> MRS LOU FOX
>
> HOTEL SAHARA
>
> VEGAS

Well, perhaps not entirely marginal. As a matter of fact, Mrs. Minnie S. Brooks and her MANDARIN COAT pull me back into my own childhood, for although I never knew Mrs. Brooks and did not visit Inyo County until I was thirty, I grew up in just such a world, in houses cluttered with Indian relics and bits of gold ore and ambergris and the souvenirs my Aunt Mercy Farnsworth brought back from the Orient. It is a long way from that world to Mrs. Lou Fox's world, where we all live now, and is it not just as well to remember that? Might not Mrs. Minnie S. Brooks help me to remember what I am? Might not Mrs. Lou Fox help me to remember what I am not?

But sometimes the point is harder to discern. What exactly did I have in mind when I noted down that it cost the father of someone I know $650 a month to light the place on the Hudson in which he lived before the Crash? What use was I planning to make of this line by Jimmy Hoffa: "I may have my faults, but being wrong ain't one of them"? And although I think it interesting to know where the girls who travel with the Syndicate have their hair done when they find themselves on the West Coast, will I ever make suitable use of it? Might I not be better off just passing it on to John O'Hara? What is a recipe for sauerkraut doing in my notebook? What kind of magpie keeps this notebook? *"He was born the night the Titanic went down."* That seems a nice enough line, and I even recall who said it, but is it not really a better line in life than it could ever be in fiction?

But of course that is exactly it: not that I should ever use the line, but that I   15
should remember the woman who said it and the afternoon I heard it. We were on her terrace by the sea, and we were finishing the wine left from lunch, trying to get what sun there was, a California winter sun. The woman whose husband was born the night the *Titanic* went down wanted to rent her house, wanted to go

back to her children in Paris. I remember wishing that I could afford the house, which cost $1,000 a month. "Someday you will," she said lazily. "Someday it all comes." There in the sun on her terrace it seemed easy to believe in someday, but later I had a low-grade afternoon hangover and ran over a black snake on the way to the supermarket and was flooded with inexplicable fear when I heard the checkout clerk explaining to the man ahead of me why she was finally divorcing her husband. "He left me no choice," she said over and over as she punched the register. "He has a little seven-month-old baby by her, he left me no choice." I would like to believe that my dread then was for the human condition, but of course it was for me, because I wanted a baby and did not then have one and because I wanted to own the house that cost $1,000 a month to rent and because I had a hangover.

It all comes back. Perhaps it is difficult to see the value in having one's self back in that kind of mood, but I do see it; I think we are well advised to keep on nodding terms with the people we used to be whether we find them attractive company or not. Otherwise they turn up unannounced and surprise us, come hammering on the mind's door at 4 a.m. of a bad night and demand to know who deserted them, who betrayed them, who is going to make amends. We forget all too soon the things we thought we could never forget. We forget the loves and the betrayals alike, forget what we whispered and what we screamed, forget who we were. I have already lost touch with a couple of people I used to be; one of them, a seventeen-year-old, presents little threat, although it would be of some interest to me to know again what it feels like to sit on a river levee drinking vodka-and-orange-juice and listening to Les Paul and Mary Ford and their echoes sing "How High the Moon" on the car radio. (You see I still have the scenes, but I no longer perceive myself among those present, no longer could even improvise the dialogue.) The other one, a twenty-three-year-old, bothers me more. She was always a good deal of trouble, and I suspect she will reappear when I least want to see her, skirts too long, shy to the point of aggravation, always the injured party, full of recriminations and little hurts and stories I do not want to hear again, at once saddening me and angering me with her vulnerability and ignorance, an apparition all the more insistent for being so long banished.

It is a good idea, then, to keep in touch, and I suppose that keeping in touch is what notebooks are all about. And we are all on our own when it comes to keeping those lines open to ourselves: your notebook will never help me, nor mine you. *"So what's new in the whiskey business?"* What could that possibly mean to you? To me it means a blonde in a Pucci bathing suit sitting with a couple of fat men by the pool at the Beverly Hills Hotel. Another man approaches, and they all regard one another in silence for a while. "So what's new in the whiskey business?" one of the fat men finally says by way of welcome, and the blonde stands up, arches one foot and dips it in the pool, looking all the while at the cabaña where Baby Pignatari is talking on the telephone. That is all there is to that, except that several years later I saw the blonde coming out of Saks Fifth Avenue in New York with her California complexion and a voluminous mink coat. In the harsh wind that day she looked old and irrevocably tired to me, and even the skins in the mink coat were not worked the way they were doing them that year, not the way she would have wanted them done, and there is the point of the story. For a while after that I did not like to look in the mirror, and my eyes would skim the newspapers and pick out only the deaths, the cancer victims, the premature coronaries, the suicides, and I stopped riding the Lexington Avenue IRT because I noticed for the first time that all the strangers I had seen for years—the man with the seeing-eye dog, the spinster who read the classified pages every day, the fat girl who always got off with me at Grand Central—looked older than they once had.

It all comes back. Even that recipe for sauerkraut: even that brings it back. I was on Fire Island when I first made that sauerkraut, and it was raining, and we drank a lot of bourbon and ate the sauerkraut and went to bed at ten, and I listened to the rain and the Atlantic and felt safe. I made the sauerkraut again last night and it did not make me feel any safer, but that is, as they say, another story.

QUESTIONS FOR DISCUSSION AND WRITING

1. Make a list of all the ways you use writing and another list of all the ways people in your household use writing. Include everything from tweets, twitters, and blogs to love letters to legal documents. Compare your lists with those of others in your class. What is distinctive about your lists? What factors do you think might account for the differences in the composition and style of your and your peers' lists?

2. In a 1999 interview, Didion advises beginning writers to learn "the discipline of sitting down and writing." What methods help you keep writing even when you write "bad stuff"?

3. Observe an ordinary event—people taking seats on a bus, sharing a meal, waiting in an office. Write "just the facts" you see objectively, withholding your attitudes and judgments. Then rewrite the account from your perspective, adding and changing language in order to express your eyewitness experience. What does this exercise suggest about telling the truth and telling lies, one of Didion's major concerns in "On Keeping a Notebook"? How does this revision reflect your personal style?

4. For what purposes do you revise your writing?

PETER ELBOW

Freewriting

Peter Elbow (b. 1935) grew up in New Jersey and was educated at Williams College, Oxford, Harvard, and Brandeis. Known for his innovative methods of teaching writing, Elbow taught and directed writing programs at MIT, Evergreen State College, SUNY–Stony Brook, and the University of Massachusetts at Amherst, from which he retired in 2000. In 2001 Elbow received an award from the National Council of Teachers of English for his "transforming influence and lasting intellectual contribu-tion to the English profession," derived primarily from his numerous articles and two books that have become contemporary classics, Writing with Power *(1986) and* Writing without Teachers *(1973), in which "Freewriting" appears. This manifesto of "power to the people"—in Elbow's view, writing students, most likely those in Fresh-man English—liberates students from teachers and grammar books in urging them to listen to their own voices, "the only source of power," a natural sound, texture, and rhythm "that will make a reader listen." To do this, writers have to listen to their own voices—ssssssh! Try it.*

The most effective way I know to improve your writing is to do freewriting ex-ercises regularly. At least three times a week. They are sometimes called "automatic writing," "babbling," or "jabbering" exercises. The idea is simply to write for ten minutes (later on, perhaps fifteen or twenty). Don't stop for anything. Go quickly without rushing. Never stop to look back, to cross something out, to wonder how to spell something, to wonder what word or thought to use, or to think about what you are doing. If you can't think of a word or a spelling, just use a squiggle or else write, "I can't think of it." Just put down something. The easiest thing is just to put down whatever is in your mind. If you get stuck it's fine to write "I can't think what to say, I can't think what to say" as many times as you want; or to repeat the last word you wrote over and over again; or anything else. The only requirement is that you *never* stop.

What happens to a freewriting exercise is important. It must be a piece of writing which, even if someone reads it, doesn't send any ripples back to you. It is like writing something and putting it in a bottle in the sea. The teacherless class helps your writing by providing maximum feedback. Freewritings help you by providing no feedback at all. When I assign one, I invite the writer to let me read it. But I also tell him to keep it if he prefers. I read it quickly and make no comments at all and I do not speak with him about it. The main thing is that a freewriting must never be evaluated in any way; in fact there must be no discus-sion or comment at all.

Here is an example of a fairly coherent exercise (sometimes they are very incoherent, which is fine):

> I think I'll write what's on my mind, but the only thing on my mind right now is what to write for ten minutes. I've never done this before and I'm not pre-pared in any way—the sky is cloudy today, how's that? now I'm afraid I won't be able to think of what to write when I get to the end of the sentence—well, here I am at the end of the sentence—here I am again, again, again, at least I'm still writing—Now I ask is there some reason to be happy that I'm still writing—ah yes! Here comes the question again—What am I getting out of this? What point is there in it? It's almost obscene to always ask it but I seem to question everything that way and I was gonna say something else pertain-ing to that but I got so busy writing down the first part that I forgot what I was

leading into. This is kind of fun oh don't stop writing—cars and trucks speed-ing by somewhere out the window, pens clittering across peoples' papers. The sky is still cloudy—is it symbolic that I should be mentioning it? Huh? I dunno. Maybe I should try colors, blue, red, dirty words—wait a minute—no can't do that, orange, yellow, arm tired, green pink violet magenta lavender red brown black green—now that I can't think of any more colors—just about done—relief? maybe.

Freewriting may seem crazy but actually it makes simple sense. Think of the difference between speaking and writing. Writing has the advantage of permitting more editing. But that's its downfall too. Almost everybody interposes a massive and complicated series of editings between the time words start to be born into consciousness and when they finally come off the end of the pencil or typewriter onto the page. This is partly because schooling makes us obsessed with the "mis-takes" we make in writing. Many people are constantly thinking about spelling and grammar as they try to write. I am always thinking about the awkwardness, wordiness, and general mushiness of my natural verbal product as I try to write down words.

But it's not just "mistakes" or "bad writing" we edit as we write. We also edit   5 unacceptable thoughts and feelings, as we do in speaking. In writing there is more time to do it so the editing is heavier: when speaking, there's someone right there waiting for a reply and he'll get bored or think we're crazy if we don't come out with *something*. Most of the time in speaking, we settle for the catch-as-catch-can way in which the words tumble out. In writing, however, there's a chance to try to get them right. But the opportunity to get them right is a terrible burden: you can work for two hours trying to get a paragraph "right" and discover it's not right at all. And then give up.

Editing, *in itself*, is not the problem. Editing is usually necessary if we want to end up with something satisfactory. The problem is that editing goes on *at the same time* as producing. The editor is, as it were, constantly looking over the shoul-der of the producer and constantly fiddling with what he's doing while he's in the middle of trying to do it. No wonder the producer gets nervous, jumpy, inhibited, and finally can't be coherent. It's an unnecessary burden to try to think of words and also worry at the same time whether they're the right words.

The main thing about freewriting is that it is *nonediting*. It is an exercise in bringing together the process of producing words and putting them down on the page. Practiced regularly, it undoes the ingrained habit of editing at the same time you are trying to produce. It will make writing less blocked because words will come more easily. You will use up more paper, but chew up fewer pencils.

Next time you write, notice how often you stop yourself from writing down something you were going to write down. Or else cross it out after it's written. "Naturally," you say, "it wasn't any good." But think for a moment about the occa-sions when you spoke well. Seldom was it because you first got the beginning just right. Usually it was a matter of a halting or even garbled beginning, but you kept going and your speech finally became coherent and even powerful. There is a lesson here for writing: trying to get the beginning just right is a formula for failure—and probably a secret tactic to make yourself give up writing. Make some words, whatever they are, and then grab hold of that line and reel in as hard as you can. Afterwards you can throw away lousy beginnings and make new ones. This is the quickest way to get into good writing.

The habit of compulsive, premature editing doesn't just make writing hard. It also makes writing dead. Your voice is damped out by all the interruptions, changes, and hesitations between the consciousness and the page. In your natural way of producing words there is a sound, a texture, a rhythm—a voice—which is the main source of power in your writing. I don't know how it works, but this voice is the force that will make a reader listen to you, the energy that drives the meanings through his thick skull. Maybe you don't *like* your voice; maybe people have made fun of it. But it's the only voice you've got. It's your only source of power. You better get back into it, no matter what you think of it. If you keep writing in it, it may change into something you like better. But if you abandon it, you'll likely never have a voice and never be heard.

Freewritings are vacuums. Gradually you will begin to carry over into your 10 regular writing some of the voice, force, and connectedness that creep into those vacuums.

QUESTIONS FOR DISCUSSION AND WRITING

1. What is freewriting (paragraph 1)? What does Elbow suggest if no ideas come to mind? What differences does he find between the processes of speaking and writing (paragraphs 4 and 5)?

2. Elbow says that "compulsive, premature editing doesn't just make writing hard. It also makes writing dead" (paragraph 9). What does he mean by "editing"? What does he mean by "compulsive, premature editing"? When in the writing process is it appropriate to edit one's work?

3. How, in Elbow's view, does freewriting serve as an antidote to "compulsive, premature editing"? Is he right?

4. In your experience, what other factors might make writing dead? Are these different for your own writing than for "dead" writing you might be required to read? What can you do to bring life to your own writing? To your reading?

5. What does Elbow mean by "voice" (paragraph 9)—a notoriously difficult term to define? Why should it be so hard to define voice when, in good writers as in good speakers, it is as clear and distinctive as a fingerprint?

6. Try freewriting for ten or fifteen minutes a day for a week, following Elbow's suggestions. Experiment by writing in different settings, at different times of the day or night, and, if you wish, in different tones, modes, media. Are any of these writings useful warm-ups for longer pieces—either academic essays or stories— poetry, creative nonfiction? If freewriting works for you, keep it up!

STEPHEN KING

Write or Die

One of the most popular and prolific authors of our time, Stephen King (also writing as Richard Bachman and John Swithen) began writing because he loved reading; the range of authors whom he cites as models includes H. P. Lovecraft, Ernest Hemingway, Elmore Leonard, Joyce Carol Oates, Graham Greene, and T. S. Eliot. Born in 1947, King began submitting stories to magazines and collecting rejection slips when he was twelve. He published his first story at age nineteen. Growing up in rural Maine, he helped his mother support the family with a number of tough jobs, including janitor, mill hand, and laundry laborer. After graduating from the University of Maine (B.A., 1970), King taught high school English while working on his extremely popular first novel, Carrie *(1974). A rush of best-sellers followed:* Salem's Lot *(1975),* The Shining *(1977),* The Stand *(1978),* The Dead Zone *(1979),* Firestarter *(1980), and* Cujo *(1981). After his novella "The Body" (from the collection* Different Seasons, *1982) was turned into the coming-of-age film* Stand by Me, *King's reputation grew beyond his core fans of horror, fantasy, and science fiction. His most recent novels include* Cell *(2006) (cell phone users gone amok),* Under the Dome *(2009) (with overtones of 9/11), and* Joyland *(2013), set in an amusement park.*

King is a compulsive writer, having published, since 1974, over seventy novels in addition to short stories and nonfiction—two books a year, sometimes more, writing through, in, and around major complications in his life, as he explains in On Writing: A Memoir of the Craft *(2000).* On Writing *is part autobiography, part writing manual. "Write or Die," an excerpt from* On Writing, *discusses two key influences on his writing—a guidance counselor at the end of his rope with the young King and a ruthlessly honest newspaper editor.*

Hardly a week after being sprung from detention hall, I was once more invited to step down to the principal's office. I went with a sinking heart, wondering what new shit I'd stepped in.

It wasn't Mr. Higgins who wanted to see me, at least; this time the school guidance counselor had issued the summons. There had been discussions about me, he said, and how to turn my "restless pen" into more constructive channels. He had enquired of John Gould, editor of Lisbon's weekly newspaper, and had discovered Gould had an opening for a sports reporter. While the school couldn't *insist* that I take this job, everyone in the front office felt it would be a good idea. *Do it or die,* the G.C.'s eyes suggested. Maybe that was just paranoia, but even now, almost forty years later, I don't think so.

I groaned inside. I was shut of *Dave's Rag,* almost shut of *The Drum,* and now here was the Lisbon *Weekly Enterprise.* Instead of being haunted by waters, like Norman Maclean in *A River Runs Through It,* I was as a teenager haunted by newspapers. Still, what could I do? I rechecked the look in the guidance counselor's eyes and said I would be delighted to interview for the job.

Gould—not the well-known New England humorist or the novelist who wrote *The Greenleaf Fires* but a relation of both, I think—greeted me warily but with some interest. We would try each other out, he said, if that suited me.

Now that I was away from the administrative offices of Lisbon High, I felt able to muster a little honesty. I told Mr. Gould that I didn't know much about sports. Gould said, "These are games people understand when they're watching them drunk in bars. You'll learn if you try."

He gave me a huge roll of yellow paper on which to type my copy—I think I still have it somewhere—and promised me a wage of half a cent a word. It was the first time someone had promised me wages for writing.

The first two pieces I turned in had to do with a basketball game in which an LHS player broke the school scoring record. One was a straight piece of reporting. The other was a sidebar about Robert Ransom's record-breaking performance. I brought both to Gould the day after the game so he'd have them for Friday, which was when the paper came out. He read the game piece, made two minor corrections, and spiked it. Then he started in on the feature piece with a large black pen.

I took my fair share of English Lit classes in my two remaining years at Lisbon, and my fair share of composition, fiction, and poetry classes in college, but John Gould taught me more than any of them, and in no more than ten minutes. I wish I still had the piece—it deserves to be framed, editorial corrections and all—but I can remember pretty well how it went and how it looked after Gould had combed through it with that black pen of his. Here's an example:

Last night, in the ~~well-loved~~ gymnasium of Lisbon High School, partisans and Jay Hills fans alike were stunned by an athletic performance unequalled in school history. Bob Ransom, ~~known as "Bullet" Bob for both his size and accuracy,~~ scored thirty-seven points. Yes, you heard me right. ~~Plus~~ he did it with grace, speed . . . and with an odd courtesy as well, committing only two personal fouls in his ~~knight-like~~ quest for a record which has eluded Lisbon ~~thinclads~~ ^{players} since ~~the years of Korea~~ ¹⁹⁵³. . .

Gould stopped at "the years of Korea" and looked up at me. "What year was the last record made?" he asked.

Luckily, I had my notes. "1953," I said. Gould grunted and went back to work. When he finished marking my copy in the manner indicated above, he looked up and saw something on my face. I think he must have mistaken it for horror. It wasn't; it was pure revelation. Why, I wondered, didn't English teachers ever do this? It was like the Visible Man Old Raw Diehl had on his desk in the biology room.

"I only took out the bad parts, you know," Gould said. "Most of it's pretty good."

"I know," I said, meaning both things: yes, most of it was good—okay anyway, serviceable—and yes, he had only taken out the bad parts. "I won't do it again."

He laughed. "If that's true, you'll never have to work for a living. You can do this instead. Do I have to explain any of these marks?"

"No," I said.

"When you write a story, you're telling yourself the story," he said. "When you   15 rewrite, your main job is taking out all the things that are *not* the story."

Gould said something else that was interesting on the day I turned in my first two pieces: write with the door closed, rewrite with the door open. Your stuff starts out being just for you, in other words, but then it goes out. Once you know what the story is and get it right—as right as you can, anyway—it belongs to anyone who wants to read it. Or criticize it. If you're very lucky (this is my idea, not John Gould's, but I believe he would have subscribed to the notion), more will want to do the former than the latter. . . .

QUESTIONS FOR DISCUSSION AND WRITING

1. Why do you suppose King initially regarded writing for a newspaper as a punishment rather than an opportunity?

2. How does King's reproduction of Gould's editing illustrate his advice to the young writer? Explain Gould's distinction between writing "with the door closed" and rewriting "with the door open" (paragraph 16). Why are both important?

3. King writes all the time, in and out of disaster, displacement, devastation, and in happier times, as well. Have you become a compulsive writer on social media—Twitter, Facebook, e-mail, and/or a blog? If so, with what consequences? Have these been as productive for you as they have been for King? If not, what can you do to transform the negatives into positives? Write your own essay in response to King's "Write or Die."

CHRISTOPHER HITCHENS

Unspoken Truths

Christopher Hitchens (1949–2011) was a well-known writer who also frequently appeared on talk shows and the lecture circuit. Educated at Balliol College, Oxford, Hitchens was an atheist who wrote the book God Is Not Great: How Religion Poisons Everything *(2007), which was a best-seller. He authored several other books, including* The Trial of Henry Kissinger *(2001),* Letters to a Young Contrarian *(2001), and* Hitch-22: A Memoir *(2010). He published frequently in magazines, including* Vanity Fair, *for which he was a contributing editor from 1992 until his death in 2011. An avowed socialist, Hitchens could not be described as comfortably belonging to a single political camp, but he generally spoke out against authoritarian and totalitarian regimes. Hitchens was angered by what he saw as a weak response to the threats*

*launched against Salmon Rushdie when in 1989 the Ayatollah Khomeini issued a
"fatwa" against Rushdie for his novel* Satanic Verses *(the "fatwa" was an order for
Muslims to kill Rushdie).*

*In this article, written near the end of his life, Hitchens bemoans the literal loss
of his voice and expands on what that means. For a man who was well known for
talking, whether in speeches or debates, televised or in person, the loss of his voice
becomes for Hitchens a cruel precursor to his inevitable death. (Hitchens died of
esophageal cancer; his enthusiastic smoking and drinking likely increased his chance
of getting the disease.) Employing extensive use of figurative language and literary
allusions, Hitchens conveys the distress he feels, yet couches it nevertheless in humor.
He connects writing and talking in ways that those of us who still have a voice may
rarely even consider.*

> I have seen the moment of my greatness flicker,
> And I have seen the eternal Footman hold my coat, and snicker,
> And in short, I was afraid.
> —T. S. Eliot, "The Love Song of J. Alfred Prufrock"

Like so many of life's varieties of experience, the novelty of a diagnosis of malignant
cancer has a tendency to wear off. The thing begins to pall, even to become banal.
One can become quite used to the specter of the eternal Footman, like some lethal
old bore lurking in the hallway at the end of the evening, hoping for the chance to
have a word. And I don't so much object to his holding my coat in that marked manner, as if mutely reminding me that it's time to be on my way. No, it's the snickering
that gets me down.

On a much-too-regular basis, the disease serves me up with a teasing special
of the day, or a flavor of the month. It might be random sores and ulcers, on the
tongue or in the mouth. Or why not a touch of peripheral neuropathy, involving
numb and chilly feet? Daily existence becomes a babyish thing, measured out
not in Prufrock's coffee spoons but in tiny doses of nourishment, accompanied
by heartening noises from onlookers, or solemn discussions of the operations of
the digestive system, conducted with motherly strangers. On the less good days, I
feel like that wooden-legged piglet belonging to a sadistically sentimental family
that could bear to eat him only a chunk at a time. Except that cancer isn't so . . .
considerate.

Most despond-inducing and alarming of all, so far, was the moment when my
voice suddenly rose to a childish (or perhaps piglet-like) piping squeak. It then
began to register all over the place, from a gruff and husky whisper to a papery,
plaintive bleat. And at times it threatened, and now threatens daily, to disappear
altogether. I had just returned from giving a couple of speeches in California,
where with the help of morphine and adrenaline I could still successfully "project"
my utterances, when I made an attempt to hail a taxi outside my home—and nothing happened. I stood, frozen, like a silly cat that had abruptly lost its meow. I used
to be able to stop a New York cab at thirty paces. I could also, without the help of
a microphone, reach the back row and gallery of a crowded debating hall. And it
may be nothing to boast about, but people tell me that if their radio or television

was on, even in the next room, they could always pick out my tones and know that I was "on," too.

Like health itself, the loss of such a thing can't be imagined until it occurs. In common with everybody else, I have played versions of the youthful "Which would you rather?" game, in which most usually it's debated whether blindness or deafness would be the most oppressive. But I don't ever recall speculating much about being struck dumb. (In the American vernacular, to say "I'd really hate to be dumb" might in any case draw another snicker.) Deprivation of the ability to speak is more like an attack of impotence, or the amputation of part of the personality. To a great degree, in public and private, I "was" my voice. All the rituals and etiquette of conversation, from clearing the throat in preparation for the telling of an extremely long and taxing joke to (in younger days) trying to make my proposals more persuasive as I sank the tone by a strategic octave of shame, were innate and essential to me. I have never been able to sing, but I could once recite poetry and quote prose and was sometimes even asked to do so. And timing is everything: the exquisite moment when one can break in and cap a story, or turn a line for a laugh, or ridicule an opponent. I lived for moments like that. Now, if I want to enter a conversation, I have to attract attention in some other way, and live with the awful fact that people are then listening "sympathetically." At least they don't have to pay attention for long: I can't keep it up and anyway can't stand to.

When you fall ill, people send you CDs. Very often, in my experience, these are 5
by Leonard Cohen. So I have recently learned a song, entitled "If It Be Your Will." It's a tiny bit saccharine, but it's beautifully rendered and it opens like this:

> If it be your will,
> That I speak no more:
> And my voice be still,
> As it was before . . .

I find it's best not to listen to this late at night. Leonard Cohen is unimaginable without, and indissoluble from, his voice. (I now doubt that I could be bothered, or bear, to hear that song done by anybody else.) In some ways, I tell myself, I could hobble along by communicating only in writing. But this is really only because of my age. If I had been robbed of my voice earlier, I doubt that I could ever have achieved much on the page. I owe a vast debt to Simon Hoggart of the *Guardian* (son of the author of *The Uses of Literacy*), who about thirty-five years ago informed me that an article of mine was well argued but dull, and advised me briskly to write "more like the way that you talk." At the time, I was near speechless at the charge of being boring and never thanked him properly, but in time I appreciated that my fear of self-indulgence and the personal pronoun was its own form of indulgence.

To my writing classes I used later to open by saying that anybody who could talk could also write. Having cheered them up with this easy-to-grasp ladder, I then replaced it with a huge and loathsome snake: "How many people in this class, would you say, can talk? I mean really talk?" That had its duly woeful effect. I told them to read every composition aloud, preferably to a trusted friend. The rules are much the same: Avoid stock expressions (like the plague, as William Safire used to say) and repetitions. Don't say that as a boy your grandmother used to read to you, unless at that stage of her life she really was a boy, in which case you have probably thrown away a better intro. If something is worth hearing or listening to, it's very probably worth reading. So, this above all: Find your own voice.

The most satisfying compliment a reader can pay is to tell me that he or she feels personally addressed. Think of your own favorite authors and see if that isn't precisely one of the things that engage you, often at first without your noticing it. A good conversation is the only human equivalent: the realizing that decent points are being made and understood, that irony is in play, and elaboration, and that a dull or obvious remark would be almost physically hurtful. This is how philosophy evolved in the symposium, before philosophy was written down. And poetry began with the voice as its only player and the ear as its only recorder. Indeed, I don't know of any really good writer who was deaf, either. How could one ever come, even with the clever signage of the good Abbé de l'Épée, to appreciate the miniscule twinges and ecstasies of nuance that the well-tuned voice imparts? Henry James and Joseph Conrad actually dictated their later novels—which must count as one of the greatest vocal achievements of all time, even though they might have benefited from hearing some passages read back to them—and Saul Bellow dictated much of *Humboldt's Gift*. Without our corresponding feeling for the idiolect, the stamp on the way an individual actually talks, and therefore writes, we would be deprived of a whole continent of human sympathy, and of its minor-key pleasures such as mimicry and parody.

More solemnly: "All I have is a voice," wrote W. H. Auden in "September 1, 1939," his agonized attempt to comprehend, and oppose, the triumph of radical evil. "Who can reach the deaf?" he asked despairingly. "Who can speak for the dumb?" At about the same time, the German–Jewish future Nobelist Nelly Sachs found that the apparition of Hitler had caused her to become literally speechless: robbed of her very voice by the stark negation of all values. Our own everyday idiom preserves the idea, however mildly: When a devoted public servant dies, the obituaries will often say that he was "a voice" for the unheard.

From the human throat terrible banes can also emerge: bawling, droning, 10 whining, yelling, inciting ("the windiest militant trash," as Auden phrased it in the same poem), and even snickering. It's the chance to pitch still, small voices against this torrent of babble and noise, the voices of wit and understatement, for which one yearns. All of the best recollections of wisdom and friendship, from Plato's "Apology" for Socrates to Boswell's *Life of Johnson*, resound with the spoken, unscripted moments of interplay and reason and speculation. It's in engagements like this, in competition and comparison with others, that one can hope to hit upon the elusive, magical *mot juste*. For me, to remember friendship is to recall those conversations that it seemed a sin to break off: the ones that made the sacrifice of the following day a trivial one. That was the way that Callimachus chose to remember his beloved Heraclitus (as adapted into English by William Cory):

They told me, Heraclitus; they told me you were dead.
They brought me bitter news to hear, and bitter tears to shed.
I wept when I remembered how often you and I
Had tired the sun with talking, and sent him down the sky.

Indeed, he rests his claim for his friend's immortality on the sweetness of his tones:

Still are thy pleasant voices, thy nightingales, awake;
For Death, he taketh all away, but them he cannot take

Perhaps a little too much uplift in that closing line . . .

In the medical literature, the vocal "cord" is a mere "fold," a piece of gristle that strives to reach out and touch its twin, thus producing the possibility of sound effects. But I feel that there must be a deep relationship with the word "chord": the resonant vibration that can stir memory, produce music, evoke love, bring tears, move crowds to pity and mobs to passion. We may not be, as we used to boast, the only animals capable of speech. But we are the only ones who can deploy vocal communication for sheer pleasure and recreation, combining it with our two other boasts of reason and humor to produce higher syntheses. To lose this ability is to be deprived of an entire range of faculty: It is assuredly to die more than a little.

My chief consolation in this year of living dyingly has been the presence of friends. I can't eat or drink for pleasure anymore, so when they offer to come it's only for the blessed chance to talk. Some of these comrades can easily fill a hall with paying customers avid to hear them: They are talkers with whom it's a privilege just to keep up. Now at least I can do the listening for free. Can they come and see me? Yes, but only in a way. So now every day I go to a waiting room, and watch the awful news from Japan [about the Fukushima disaster] on cable TV (often closed-captioned, just to torture myself) and wait impatiently for a high dose of protons to be fired into my body at two-thirds the speed of light. What do I hope for? If not a cure, then a remission. And what do I want back? In the most beautiful apposition of two of the simplest words in our language: the freedom of speech.

QUESTIONS FOR DISCUSSION AND WRITING

1. Hitchens begins his article with a quotation from "The Love Song of J. Alfred Prufrock" by T. S. Eliot. What is the essence of the meaning of this passage? How do you respond to Hitchens's statement that it's not so much the idea that Death is urging him to leave, but that "it's the snickering that gets me down" (paragraph 1)? Consider the importance of dignity when dying. In what ways does impending death often "snicker" at a person? Cite specific examples.

2. Hitchens was not simply a writer, but also a well-known debater and talk show guest. He connects his voice with himself, writing ". . . in public and private, I 'was' my voice" (paragraph 4). He compares his inability to speak as being similar to impotence or even amputation. Do these comparisons strike you as

exaggerated or not? Why? Consider how important voice is in your own life, and how the loss of your voice would compare with the loss of other faculties.

3. In paragraph 6, Hitchens relates advice he received early in his career, to write "more like the way you talk." He also observes that he doesn't "know of any really good writer who was deaf" (paragraph 8). In the same paragraph, he also recounts stories of famous writers dictating their novels. Explore the relationship between talking and writing as Hitchens describes it. Do you agree with him or not? Cite specific examples to support your position.

4. This article by Hitchens is loaded with figurative language and allusions. Examine his use of similes and metaphors and consider what effect Hitchens is attempting to achieve by using them. Trace some of his allusions (e.g., who was the Abbé de l'Épée?; who was Boswell's *Life of Johnson* about and what is his connection to talking?). Read W. H. Auden's poem "September 1939" in its entirety. What is the overall effect of Hitchens's use of figurative language and allusions? Do you find it difficult and off-putting? After doing some investigation, do you still feel that way? What are the advantages of writing in such a way? What are some disadvantages?

5. Consider that ultimately Hitchens is writing about his inevitable death—what he wryly calls his "year of living dyingly" (paragraph 13). He refers to the earthquake in Japan, the resulting tsunami, and the nuclear meltdowns that occurred as a consequence. More than 15,000 people are reported to have died in that disaster. He watches this as he waits for his own chemotherapy, a procedure he knows will not cure him. He longs for what he calls his own "freedom of speech" (paragraph 13). In your opinion, is Hitchens's article ultimately hopeful? Morose? Inspired? Depressing? What specific aspects of the essay lead to that ultimate assessment?

ELIE WIESEL

Why I Write: Making No Become Yes

Elie Wiesel devotes his life to serving as the world's conscience of the Holocaust. He was born in 1929 in Sighet, Hungary, "which no longer exists except in the memory of those it expelled." During World War II, he survived harrowing experiences in the concentration camps of Auschwitz and Buchenwald. Members of his family were killed there, among the six million Jews systematically exterminated in Europe. As a teenager, he was liberated from Buchenwald in 1945 and sent to Paris, where he studied philosophy before immigrating to New York in 1956. Wiesel has devoted his life to writing over sixty books of fiction, nonfiction, poetry, and drama on the Holocaust theme, including Night *(1961),* The Accident *(1962),* The Trial of God *(1978),* All Rivers Run to the Sea *(1995),* A Mad Desire to Dance *(2009), and* The Sonderberg Case *(2010). As one critic writes, in Wiesel's writing, "the Holocaust looms as the shadow, the central but unspoken mystery in the life of his protagonists. Even pre-Holocaust events are seen as warnings of impending doom." Wiesel's literary and humanitarian efforts have been acknowledged with a host of awards worldwide, including the Nobel Peace Prize in 1986.*

On receiving the Congressional Gold Medal (1984), Wiesel explained his philosophy of writing: "I have learned that suffering confers no privileges: it depends on what one does with it. That is why survivors have tried to teach their contemporaries how to build on ruins; how to invent hope in a world that offers none; how to proclaim faith to a generation that has seen it shamed and mutilated." He elaborates on this theme in "Why I Write: Making No Become Yes," an essay originally published in the New York Times Book Review *(April 14, 1986).*

Why do I write?

Perhaps in order not to go mad. Or, on the contrary, to touch the bottom of madness. Like Samuel Beckett, the survivor expresses himself "en désespoir de cause"—out of desperation.

Speaking of the solitude of the survivor, the great Yiddish and Hebrew poet and thinker Aaron Zeitlin addresses those—his father, his brother, his friends—who have died and left him: "You have abandoned me," he says to them. "You are together, without me. I am here. Alone. And I make words."

So do I, just like him. I also say words, write words, reluctantly.

There are easier occupations, far more pleasant ones. But for the survivor, 5
writing is not a profession, but an occupation, a duty. Camus calls it "an honor." As he puts it: "I entered literature through worship." Other writers have said they did so through anger, through love. Speaking for myself, I would say—through silence.

It was by seeking, by probing silence that I began to discover the perils and power of the word. I never intended to be a philosopher, or a theologian. The only role I sought was that of witness. I believed that, having survived by chance, I was duty-bound to give meaning to my survival, to justify each moment of my life. I knew the story had to be told. Not to transmit an experience is to betray it. This is what Jewish tradition teaches us. But how to do this? "When Israel is in exile, so is the word," says the Zohar. The word has deserted the meaning it was intended to convey—impossible to make them coincide. The displacement, the shift, is irrevocable.

This was never more true than right after the upheaval. We all knew that we could never, never say what had to be said, that we could never express in words, coherent, intelligible words, our experience of madness on an absolute scale. The walk through flaming night, the silence before and after the selection, the monotonous praying of the condemned, the Kaddish of the dying, the fear and hunger of the sick, the shame and suffering, the haunted eyes, the demented stares. I thought that I would never be able to speak of them. All words seemed inadequate, worn, foolish, lifeless, whereas I wanted them to be searing.

Where was I to discover a fresh vocabulary, a primeval language? The language of night was not human, it was primitive, almost animal—hoarse shouting, screams, muffled moaning, savage howling, the sound of beating. A brute strikes out wildly, a body falls. An officer raises his arm and a whole community walks toward a common grave. A soldier shrugs his shoulders, and a thousand families are torn apart, to be reunited only by death. This was the concentration camp language. It negated all other language and took its place. Rather than a link, it became a wall. Could it be surmounted? Could the reader be brought to the other side? I knew the answer was negative, and yet I knew that "no" had to become "yes." It was the last wish of the dead.

The fear of forgetting remains the main obsession of all those who have passed through the universe of the damned. The enemy counted on people's incredulity and forgetfulness. How could one foil this plot? And if memory grew hollow, empty of substance, what would happen to all we had accumulated along the way? Remember, said the father to his son, and the son to his friend. Gather the names, the faces, the tears. We had all taken an oath: "If, by some miracle, I emerge alive, I will devote my life to testifying on behalf of those whose shadow will fall on mine forever and ever."

That is why I write certain things rather than others—to remain faithful. 10

Of course, there are times of doubt for the survivor, times when one gives in to weakness, or longs for comfort. I hear a voice within me telling me to stop mourning the past. I too want to sing of love and of its magic. I too want to celebrate the sun, and the dawn that heralds the sun. I would like to shout, and shout loudly: "Listen, listen well! I too am capable of victory, do you hear? I too am open to laughter and joy! I want to stride, head high, my face unguarded, without having to point to the ashes over there on the horizon, without having to tamper with facts to hide their tragic ugliness. For a man born blind, God himself is blind, but look, I see, I am not blind." One feels like shouting this, but the shout changes to a murmur. One must make a choice; one must remain faithful. A big word, I know. Nevertheless, I use it, it suits me. Having written the things I have written, I feel I can afford no longer to play with words. If I say that the writer in me wants to remain loyal, it is because it is true. This sentiment moves all survivors; they owe nothing to anyone, but everything to the dead.

I owe them my roots and my memory. I am duty-bound to serve as their emissary, transmitting the history of their disappearance, even if it disturbs, even if it brings pain. Not to do so would be to betray them, and thus myself. And since I am incapable of communicating their cry by shouting, I simply look at them, I see them and write.

While writing, I question them as I question myself. I believe I have said it before, elsewhere. I write to understand as much as to be understood. Will I succeed one day? Wherever one starts, one reaches darkness. God? He remains the God of darkness. Man? The source of darkness. The killers' derision, their victims' tears, the onlookers' indifference, their complicity and complacency—the divine role in all that I do not understand. A million children massacred—I shall never understand.

Jewish children—they haunt my writings. I see them again and again. I shall always see them. Hounded, humiliated, bent like the old men who surround them as though to protect them, unable to do so. They are thirsty, the children, and there is no one to give them water. They are hungry, but there is no one to give them a crust of bread. They are afraid, and there is no one to reassure them.

They walk in the middle of the road, like vagabonds. They are on the way to the   15
station, and they will never return. In sealed cars, without air or food, they travel
toward another world. They guess where they are going, they know it, and they keep
silent. Tense, thoughtful, they listen to the wind, the call of death in the distance.

All these children, these old people, I see them. I never stop seeing them. I
belong to them.

But they, to whom do they belong?

People tend to think that a murderer weakens when facing a child. The child
reawakens the killer's lost humanity. The killer can no longer kill the child before
him, the child inside him.

But with us it happened differently. Our Jewish children had no effect upon
the killers. Nor upon the world. Nor upon God.

I think of them. I think of their childhood. Their childhood is a small Jewish   20
town, and this town is no more. They frighten me; they reflect an image of myself,
one that I pursue and run from at the same time—the image of a Jewish adolescent
who knew no fear, except the fear of God, whose faith was whole, comforting, and
not marked by anxiety.

No, I do not understand. And if I write, it is to warn the reader that he will not
understand either. "You will not understand, you will never understand," were the
words heard everywhere during the reign of night. I can only echo them. You, who
never lived under a sky of blood, will never know what it was like. Even if you read
all the books ever written, even if you listen to all the testimonies ever given, you
will remain on this side of the wall, you will view the agony and death of a people
from afar, through the screen of a memory that is not your own.

An admission of impotence and guilt? I do not know. All I know is that Treb-
linka and Auschwitz cannot be told. And yet I have tried. God knows I have tried.

Have I attempted too much or not enough? Among some twenty-five volumes, only three or four penetrate the phantasmagoric realm of the dead. In my
other books, through my other books, I have tried to follow other roads. For it
is dangerous to linger among the dead, they hold on to you and you run the risk
of speaking only to them. And so I have forced myself to turn away from them
and study other periods, explore other destinies and teach other tales—the Bible
and the Talmud, Hasidism and its fervor, the shtetl and its songs, Jerusalem and
its echoes, the Russian Jews and their anguish, their awakening, their courage.
At times, it has seemed to me that I was speaking of other things with the sole
purpose of keeping the essential—the personal experience—unspoken. At times
I have wondered: And what if I was wrong? Perhaps I should not have heeded my
own advice and stayed in my own world with the dead.

But then, I have not forgotten the dead. They have their rightful place even
in the works about the Hasidic capitals Ruzhany and Korets, and Jerusalem. Even
in my biblical and Midrashic tales, I pursue their presence, mute and motionless. The presence of the dead then beckons in such tangible ways that it affects
even the most removed characters. Thus they appear on Mount Moriah, where
Abraham is about to sacrifice his son, a burnt offering to their common God.
They appear on Mount Nebo, where Moses enters solitude and death. They

appear in Hasidic and Talmudic legends in which victims forever need defending against forces that would crush them. Technically, so to speak, they are of course elsewhere, in time and space, but on a deeper, truer plane, the dead are part of every story, of every scene.

"But what is the connection?" you will ask. Believe me, there is one. After 25 Auschwitz everything brings us back to Auschwitz. When I speak of Abraham, Isaac and Jacob, when I invoke Rabbi Yohanan ben Zakkai and Rabbi Akiba, it is the better to understand them in the light of Auschwitz. As for the Maggid of Mezeritch and his disciples, it is in order to encounter the followers of their followers that I reconstruct their spellbound, spellbinding universe. I like to imagine them alive, exuberant, celebrating life and hope. Their happiness is as necessary to me as it was once to themselves.

And yet—how did they manage to keep their faith intact? How did they manage to sing as they went to meet the Angel of Death? I know Hasidim who never vacillated—I respect their strength. I know others who chose rebellion, protest, rage—I respect their courage. For there comes a time when only those who do not believe in God will not cry out to him in wrath and anguish.

Do not judge either group. Even the heroes perished as martyrs, even the martyrs died as heroes. Who would dare oppose knives to prayers? The faith of some matters as much as the strength of others. It is not ours to judge, it is only ours to tell the tale.

But where is one to begin? Whom is one to include? One meets a Hasid in all my novels. And a child. And an old man. And a beggar. And a madman. They are all part of my inner landscape. The reason why? Pursued and persecuted by the killers, I offer them shelter. The enemy wanted to create a society purged of their presence, and I have brought some of them back. The world denied them, repudiated them, so I let them live at least within the feverish dreams of my characters.

It is for them that I write, and yet the survivor may experience remorse. He has tried to bear witness; it was all in vain.

After the liberation, we had illusions. We were convinced that a new world 30 would be built upon the ruins of Europe. A new civilization would see the light. No more wars, no more hate, no more intolerance, no fanaticism. And all this because the witnesses would speak. And speak they did, to no avail.

They will continue, for they cannot do otherwise. When man, in his grief, falls silent, Goethe says, then God gives him the strength to sing his sorrows. From that moment on, he may no longer choose not to sing, whether his song is heard or not. What matters is to struggle against silence with words, or through another form of silence. What matters is to gather a smile here and there, a tear here and there, a word here and there, and thus justify the faith placed in you, a long time ago, by so many victims.

Why do I write? To wrench those victims from oblivion. To help the dead vanquish death.

Translated from the French by Rosette C Lamont.

QUESTIONS FOR DISCUSSION AND WRITING

1. Wiesel says, "The only role I sought [as a writer] was that of witness" (paragraph 6). What does he mean by "witness"? Could any—or all—of the other writers in this book be considered "witnesses" to their beliefs and values? Explain your answer with references to the writers' works. In what ways does writing as a witness require the reader to "open the door," as King says (paragraph 16)?

2. What does Wiesel mean by "[n]ot to transmit an experience is to betray it" (paragraph 6)? Why is it important to twenty-first-century readers that the experience of the Holocaust, which occurred over seventy years ago, be kept fresh in memory? What does Wiesel expect his readers to do with this knowledge?

3. Pick a cultural, social, or political issue that you feel profoundly invested in, and then write an essay in which you play the role of "witness," explaining why you think this issue should be kept alive and treated seriously. Write it first for yourself—"with the door shut," as Stephen King would say (p. 84). Then, open that door. Think of classmates or other people you know who aren't particularly invested in this issue, and write your essay to them, seeking to change their minds and perhaps move them to action. Discuss the subject with them first, in order to determine the points to emphasize in your argument.

4. In "On Keeping a Notebook" (p. 74) Joan Didion asserts that the "impulse to write things down is a peculiarly compulsive one" (paragraph 4). Although a compulsion could be seen as a type of aberrant behavior, Wiesel (who has written more than sixty books and scores of speeches and articles) uses writing to bear moral witness, over and over, to remind the world to behave in a moral way, with justice and compassion. A quick Internet search will reveal that Stephen King (p. 84) is likewise a compulsive author, providing entertainment, social commentary, and food for thought for millions. Comment on the connections among the compulsivity, creativity, and commitment of Wiesel and King. Are these essentially positive connections?

5. Wiesel writes all the time, in and out of disaster, displacement, devastation, and in happier times, as well. Have you become a compulsive writer on social media—Twitter, Facebook, e-mail, and/or a blog? If so, with what consequences? Have these been as productive for you as they have been for Wiesel? If not, what can you do to transform the negatives into positives? Write your own essay in response to Wiesel's "Why I Write."

CHAPTER 5

Identity and Culture: Who Am I, and Why Does It Matter?

JHUMPA LAHIRI

My Two Lives

Jhumpa Lahiri (b. 1967) explores the challenges and difficulties of life from the perspective of an Indian-American woman. Born in London, Lahiri was brought as a toddler to the United States and raised in Rhode Island. Living between the cultures of the United States and India (or as she states it, living on "either side of the hyphen"), Lahiri has made her immigrant experience the subject of much of her writing. Her debut book was a collection of short stories, Interpreter of Maladies *(1999), which won much acclaim, including the Pulitzer Prize for Fiction. In 2003, Lahiri followed that success with the publication of her first novel,* The Namesake. *It was named a* New York Times *Notable Book and a* Los Angeles Times *Book Prize finalist, among other honors. She followed that with another collection of short stories,* Unaccustomed Earth *(2008). A second novel,* The Lowland: A Novel, *was published in 2013. In addition to having won the Pulitzer Prize, Lahiri has also won the PEN/Hemingway Award (1999) and a Guggenheim Fellowship (2002). She was appointed by President Barack Obama to the President's Committee on the Arts and Humanities.*

In this essay, originally published in Newsweek *in 2006, Lahiri examines her personal past and the difficulties she faced as a girl, and later a young woman, growing up between two cultures. On the one hand, she was living in the United States, speaking English without an accent and absorbing American customs and practices like other young people. On the other hand, there were her parents, speaking Bengali, listening to Nazrul music (created by a popular Bengali singer whose songs espoused rebellion against British rule), and eating Indian foods. Her life reflects in some ways the stories of all immigrant families, of trying to bring together old country and new, so that both sides of the hyphen are present in her life.*

I have lived in the United States for almost 37 years and anticipate growing old in this country. Therefore, with the exception of my first two years in London, "Indian-American" has been a constant way to describe me. Less constant is my relationship to the term. When I was growing up in Rhode Island in the 1970s I felt neither Indian nor American. Like many immigrant offspring I felt intense pressure to be two things, loyal to the old world and fluent in the new, approved of on either side of the hyphen. Looking back, I see that this was generally the case. But my perception as a young girl was that I fell short at both ends, shuttling between two dimensions that had nothing to do with one another.

At home I followed the customs of my parents, speaking Bengali and eating rice and dal with my fingers. These ordinary facts seemed part of a secret, utterly alien way of life, and I took pains to hide them from my American friends. For my parents, home was not our house in Rhode Island but Calcutta, where they were raised. I was aware that the things they lived for—the Nazrul songs they listened to on the reel-to-reel, the family they missed, the clothes my mother wore that were not available in any store in any mall—were at once as precious and as worthless as an outmoded currency.

I also entered a world my parents had little knowledge or control of: school, books, music, television, things that seeped in and became a fundamental aspect of who I am. I spoke English without an accent, comprehending the language in a way my parents still do not. And yet there was evidence that I was not entirely American. In addition to my distinguishing name and looks, I did not attend Sunday school, did not know how to ice-skate, and disappeared to India for months at a time. Many of these friends proudly called themselves Irish-American or Italian-American. But they were several generations removed from the frequently humiliating process of immigration, so that the ethnic roots they claimed had descended underground whereas mine were still tangled and green. According to my parents I was not American, nor would I ever be no matter how hard I tried. I felt doomed by their pronouncement, misunderstood, and gradually defiant. In spite of the first lessons of arithmetic, one plus one did not equal two but zero, my conflicting selves always canceling each other out.

When I first started writing I was not conscious that my subject was the Indian-American experience. What drew me to my craft was the desire to force the two worlds I occupied to mingle on the page as I was not brave enough, or mature enough, to allow in life. My first book was published in 1999, and around then, on the cusp of a new century, the term "Indian-American" has become part of this country's vocabulary. I've heard it so often that these days, if asked about my background, I use the term myself, pleasantly surprised that I do not have to explain further. What a difference from my early life, when there was no such way to describe me, when the most I could do was to clumsily and ineffectually explain.

As I approach middle age, one plus one equals two, both in my work and in   5 my daily existence. The traditions on either side of the hyphen dwelt in me like siblings, still occasionally sparring, one outshining the other depending on the day. But like siblings they are intimately familiar with one another, forgiving and intertwined. When my husband and I were married five years ago in Calcutta we invited friends who had never been to India, and they came full of enthusiasm for a place I avoided talking about in my childhood, fearful of what people might say. Around non-Indian friends, I no longer feel compelled to hide the fact that I speak another language. I speak Bengali to my children, even though I lack the proficiency to teach them to read or write the language. As a child I sought perfection and so denied myself the claim to any identity. As an adult I accept that a bicultural upbringing is a rich but imperfect thing.

While I am American by virtue of the fact that I was raised in this country, I am Indian thanks to the efforts of two individuals. I feel Indian not because of the time I've spent in India or because of my genetic composition but rather because of my parents' steadfast presence in my life. They live three hours from my home; I speak to them daily and see them about once a month. Everything will change once they die. They will take certain things with them—conversations in another tongue, and perceptions about the difficulties of being foreign. Without them, the back-and-forth life my family leads, both literally and figuratively, will at last approach stillness. An anchor will drop, and a line of connection will be severed.

I have always believed that I lack the authority my parents bring to being Indian. But as long as they live they protect me from feeling like an impostor. Their passing will mark not only the loss of the people who created me but the loss of a singular way of life, a singular struggle. The immigrant's journey, no matter how ultimately rewarding, is founded on departure and deprivation, but it secures for the subsequent generation a sense of arrival and advantage. I can see a day coming when my American side, lacking the counterpoint India has until now maintained, begins to gain ascendancy and weight. It is in fiction that I will continue to interpret the term "Indian-American," calculating that shifting equation, whatever answers it may yield.

QUESTIONS FOR DISCUSSION AND WRITING

1. Lahiri describes that as a child, both sides of the hyphen tended to cancel each other out, or as she says, "one plus one did not equal two but zero . . ." (paragraph 3). Why was this so? How does having the status of a child (and the perception of a child) contribute to her particular dilemma? In your opinion, is this likely to be a typical problem for children of immigrants who are disconnected physically by long distances from their parents' homeland? Cite examples.

2. Lahiri states that friends of hers, as children, described themselves as Irish Americans or Italian Americans, but she says they are far removed from the "frequently humiliating process of immigration . . . " (paragraph 3). What is humiliating about the process? Find details from her essay that support this description. If you can, add other possible situations or circumstances that can make immigration a humiliating process. Is this simply a result of culture clashes, or are other factors, such as racial, religious, or classist prejudice, part of the problem? Explain.

3. As a mature adult, Lahiri appears to have settled much of the conflict; in her own words, now "one plus one equals two, both in my work and my daily existence" (paragraph 5). What changed for her over time? How has she resolved the conflicts of her younger days? Does her path to resolution offer a path that other children of immigrants can take as well? Why or why not?

4. Lahiri's parents came to the United States from India by way of Great Britain. Although the United States is not historically connected to India, the British ruled India for more than two hundred years, and many Indians speak English. Consider how the country of origin for an immigrant (or the child of immigrants) plays a factor in establishing a positive relationship between the culture of the new and the culture of the old. Would a child of immigrants from a country with only distant connections to the United States face a more difficult time establishing the sense of harmony that Lahiri achieved? Explain, using specific examples.

ERIC LIU

Notes of a Native Speaker

Eric Liu was born in Poughkeepsie, New York, in 1968. "My own assimilation began long before I was born," writes Liu, whose parents came to the United States from Taiwan in the late 1950s. His father was an IBM executive, and his mother worked as a computer programmer. Liu and his sister grew up with the photos and pilot stories of their grandfather, a general in the Nationalist Chinese air force during World War II. "Shadow-dancing" with his identity as a "Renaissance boy" or an "Asian overachiever," Liu graduated summa cum laude with a bachelor's degree in history from Yale (1990). He interned with Senator Daniel Patrick Moynihan one summer and spent two other summers in Marine Officer Candidate School in Quantico, Virginia. At age twenty-five, Liu became President Bill Clinton's youngest speechwriter. He attended Harvard Law School and then, in 2000, returned to the White House as deputy domestic policy adviser. With Nick Hanauer he wrote The Gardens of Democracy *(2011), a reexamination of democracy. Liu is the curator of Citizen University, a conference on creative citizenship, and the True Patriot Network, dedicated to promoting progressive civic values.*

The title of Liu's memoir, The Accidental Asian: Notes of a Native Speaker *(1998), is a multiracial reference to Anne Tyler's* The Accidental Tourist *(1985), James Baldwin's essay "Notes of a Native Son" (1955), and Richard Wright's* Native Son *(1940). Although Liu grew up speaking a mixture of English and Mandarin, English is his native language. Refusing to look at ten million Americans of Asian descent as an ethnic group, Liu focuses on the diversity of Asian American heritage and downplays race.*

Here are some of the ways you could say I am "white":

I listen to National Public Radio.
I wear khaki Dockers.
I own brown suede bucks.
I eat gourmet greens.
I have few close friends "of color."
I married a white woman.

I am a child of the suburbs.

I furnish my condo à la Crate & Barrel.

I vacation in charming bed-and-breakfasts.

I have never once been the victim of blatant discrimination.

I am a member of several exclusive institutions.

I have been in the inner sanctums of political power.

I have been there as something other than an attendant.

I have the ambition to return.

I am a producer of the culture.

I expect my voice to be heard.

I speak flawless, unaccented English.

I subscribe to *Foreign Affairs*.

I do not mind when editorialists write in the first person plural.

I do not mind how white television casts are.

I am not too ethnic.

I am wary of minority militants.

I consider myself neither in exile nor in opposition.

I am considered "a credit to my race."

I never asked to be white. I am not literally white. That is, I do not have white skin or white ancestors. I have yellow skin and yellow ancestors, hundreds of generations of them. But like so many other Asian Americans of the second generation, I find myself now the bearer of a strange new status: white, by acclamation. Thus it is that I have been described as an "honorary white," by other whites, and as a "banana," by other Asians. Both the honorific and the epithet take as a given this idea: to the extent that I have moved away from the periphery and toward the center of American life, I have become white inside. *Some are born white, others achieve whiteness, still others have whiteness thrust upon them.* This, supposedly, is what it means to assimilate.

There was a time when assimilation did quite strictly mean whitening. In fact, well into the first half of this century, mimicry of the stylized standards of the WASP gentry was the proper, dominant, perhaps even sole method of ensuring that your origins would not be held against you. You "made it" in society not only by putting on airs of anglitude, but also by assiduously bleaching out the marks of a darker, dirtier past. And this bargain, stifling as it was, was open to European immigrants almost exclusively; to blacks, only on the passing occasion; to Asians, hardly at all.

Times have changed, and I suppose you could call it progress that a Chinaman, too, may now aspire to whiteness. But precisely because the times have changed, that aspiration—and the *imputation* of the aspiration—now seems astonishingly outmoded. The meaning of "American" has undergone a revolution in the twenty-nine years I have been alive, a revolution of color, class, and culture. Yet the vocabulary of "assimilation" has remained fixed all this time: fixed in whiteness, which is still our metonym for power; and fixed in shame, which is what the colored are expected to feel for embracing the power.

I have assimilated. I am of the mainstream. In many ways I fit the psychological profile of the so-called banana: imitative, impressionable, rootless, eager to please. As I will admit in this essay, I have at times gone to great lengths to downplay my difference, the better to penetrate the "establishment" of the moment. Yet I'm not sure that what I did was so cut-and-dried as "becoming white." I plead guilty to the charges above: achieving, learning the ways of the upper middle class, distancing myself from radicals of any hue. But having confessed, I still do not know my crime.

To be an accused banana is to stand at the ill-fated intersection of class and race. And because class is the only thing Americans have more trouble talking about than race, a minority's climb up the social ladder is often willfully misnamed and wrongly portrayed. There is usually, in the portrayal, a strong whiff of betrayal: the assimilist is a traitor to his kind, to his class, to his own family. He cannot gain the world without losing his soul. To be sure, something *is* lost in any migration, whether from place to place or from class to class. But something is gained as well. And the result is always more complicated than the monochrome language of "whiteness" and "authenticity" would suggest. . . .

I recently dug up a photograph of myself from freshman year of college that made me smile. I have on the wrong shoes, the wrong socks, the wrong checkered shirt tucked the wrong way into the wrong slacks. I look like what I was: a boy sprung from a middlebrow burg who affected a secondhand preppiness. I look nervous. Compare that image to one from my senior-class dinner: now I am attired in a gray tweed jacket with a green plaid bow tie and a sensible button-down shirt, all purchased at the Yale Co-op. I look confident, and more than a bit contrived.

What happened in between those two photographs is that I experienced, then overcame, what the poet Meena Alexander has called "the shock of arrival." When I was deposited at the wrought-iron gates of my residential college as a freshman, I felt more like an outsider than I'd thought possible. It wasn't just that I was a small Chinese boy standing at a grand WASP temple; nor simply that I was a hayseed neophyte puzzled by the refinements of college style. It was *both*: color and class were all twisted together in a double helix of felt inadequacy.

For a while I coped with the shock by retreating to a group of my own kind— not fellow Asians, but fellow marginal public-school grads who resented the rah-rah Yalies to whom everything came so effortlessly. Aligning myself this way was bearable—I was hiding, but at least I could place myself in a long tradition of underdog exiles at Yale. Aligning myself by race, on the other hand, would have seemed too inhibiting.

I know this doesn't make much sense. I know also that college, in the multicultural era, is supposed to be where the deracinated minority youth discovers the "person of color" inside. To a point, I did. I studied Chinese, took an Asian American history course, a seminar on race politics. But ultimately, college was where the unconscious habits of my adolescent assimilation hardened into self-conscious strategy.

I still remember the moment, in the first week of school, when I came upon a table in Yale Station set up by the Asian American Student Association.

The upperclassman staffing the table was pleasant enough. He certainly did not strike me as a fanatic. Yet, for some reason, I flashed immediately to a scene I'd witnessed days earlier, on the corner outside. Several Lubavitcher Jews, dressed in black, their faces bracketed by dangling side curls, were looking for fellow travelers at this busy crossroads. Their method was crude but memorable. As any vaguely Jewish-looking male walked past, the zealots would quickly approach, extend a pamphlet, and ask, "Excuse me, sir, are you Jewish?" Since most were not, and since those who were weren't about to stop, the result was a frantic, nervous, almost comical buzz all about the corner: Excuse me, are you Jewish? Are you Jewish? Excuse me. Are you Jewish?

I looked now at the clean-cut Korean boy at the AASA table (I think I can distinguish among Asian ethnicities as readily as those Hasidim thought they could tell Gentile from Jew), and though he had merely offered an introductory hello and was now smiling mutely at me, in the back of my mind I heard only this: *Excuse me, are you Asian? Are you Asian? Excuse me. Are you Asian?* I took one of the flyers on the table, even put my name on a mailing list, so as not to appear impolite. But I had already resolved not to be active in any Asians-only group. I thought then: I would never *choose* to be so pigeonholed.

This allergic sensitivity to "pigeonholing" is one of the unhappy hallmarks of the banana mentality. What does the banana fear? That is, what did *I* fear? The possibility of being mistaken for someone more Chinese. The possibility of being known only, or even primarily, for being Asian. The possibility of being written off by whites as a self-segregating ethnic clumper. These were the threats—unseen and, frankly, unsubstantiated—that I felt I should keep at bay.

I didn't avoid making Asian friends in college or working with Asian classmates; I simply never went out of my way to do so. This distinction seemed important—it marked, to my mind, the difference between self-hate and self-respect. That the two should have been so proximate in the first place never struck me as odd, or telling. Nor did it ever occur to me that the reasons I gave myself for dissociating from Asians as a group—that I didn't want to be part of a clique, that I didn't want to get absorbed and lose my individuality—were the very developments that marked my own assimilation. I simply hewed to my ideology of race neutrality and self-reliance. I didn't need that crutch, I told myself nervously, that crutch of racial affinity. What's more, I was vaguely insulted by the presumption that I might.

But again: Who was making the presumption? Who more than I was taking the mere existence of Korean volleyball leagues or Taiwanese social sets or pan-Asian student clubs to mean that *all* people of Asian descent, myself included, needed such quasi-kinship groups? And who more than I interpreted this need as infirmity, as a failure to fit in? I resented the faintly sneering way that some whites regarded Asians as an undifferentiated mass. But whose sneer, really, did I resent more than my own?

I was keenly aware of the unflattering mythologies that attach to Asian 15 Americans: that we are indelibly foreign, exotic, math and science geeks, numbers people rather than people people, followers and not leaders, physically frail but devious and sneaky, unknowable and potentially treacherous. These stereotypes of Asian otherness and inferiority were like immense blocks of ice sitting before me, challenging me to chip away at them. And I did, tirelessly. All the while, though, I was oblivious to rumors of my *own* otherness and inferiority, rumors that rose off those blocks like a fog, wafting into my consciousness and chilling my sense of self.

As I had done in high school, I combated the stereotypes in part by trying to disprove them. If Asians were reputed to be math and science geeks, I would be a student of history and politics. If Asians were supposed to be feeble subalterns, I'd lift weights and go to Marine officer candidate school. If Asians were alien, I'd be ardently patriotic. If Asians were shy and retiring, I'd try to be exuberant and jocular. If they were narrow-minded specialists, I'd be a well-rounded generalist. If they were perpetual outsiders, I'd join every establishment outfit I could and show that I, too, could run with the swift.

I overstate, of course. It wasn't that I chose to do all these things with no other purpose than to cut against a supposed convention. I was neither so Pavlovian nor so calculating that I would simply remake myself into the opposite of what people expected. I actually *liked* history, and wasn't especially good at math. As the grandson of a military officer, I *wanted* to see what officer candidates school would be like, and I enjoyed it, at least once I'd finished. I am *by nature* enthusiastic and allegiant, a joiner, and a bit of a jingo.

At the same time, I was often aware, sometimes even hopeful, that others might think me "exceptional" for my race. I derived satisfaction from being the "atypical" Asian, the only Chinese face at OCS or in this club or that.

The irony is that in working so duteously to defy stereotype, I became a slave to it. For to act self-consciously against Asian "tendencies" is not to break loose from the cage of myth and legend; it is to turn the very key that locks you inside. What spontaneity is there when the value of every act is measured, at least in part, by its power to refute a presumption about why you act? The *typical Asian* I imagined, and the *atypical Asian* I imagined myself to be, were identical in this sense: neither was as much a creature of free will as a human being ought to be.

Let me say it plainly, then: I am not proud to have had this mentality. I believe [20] I have outgrown it. And I expose it now not to justify it but to detoxify it, to prevent its further spread.

Yet it would be misleading, I think, to suggest that my education centered solely on the discomfort caused by race. The fact is, when I first got to college I felt deficient compared with people of *every* color. Part of why I believed it so necessary to achieve was that I lacked the connections, the wealth, the experience, the sophistication that so many of my classmates seemed to have. I didn't get the jokes or the intellectual references. I didn't have the canny attitude. So in addition to all my coursework, I began to puzzle over this, the culture of the influential class.

Over time, I suppose, I learned the culture. My interests and vocabulary became ever more worldly. I made my way onto what Calvin Trillin once described as the "magic escalator" of a Yale education. Extracurriculars opened the door to an alumni internship, which brought me to Capitol Hill, which led to a job and a life in Washington after commencement. Gradually, very gradually,

I found that I was not so much of an outsider anymore. I found that by almost any standard, but particularly by the standards of my younger self, I was actually beginning to "make it."

It has taken me until now, however, to appraise the thoughts and acts of that younger self. I can see now that the straitening path I took was not the only or even the best path. For while it may be possible to transcend race, *it is not always necessary to try.* And while racial identity is sometimes a shackle, it is not *only* a shackle. I could have spared myself a great deal of heartache had I understood this earlier, that the choice of race is not simply "embrace or efface."

I wonder sometimes how I would have turned out had I been, from the start, more comfortable in my own skin. What did I miss by distancing myself from race? What friendships did I forgo, what self-knowledge did I defer? Had certain accidents of privilege been accidents of privation or exclusion, I might well have developed a different view of the world. But I do not know just how my view would have differed.

What I know is that through all those years of shadow-dancing with my iden- 25 tity, something happened, something that had only partially to do with color. By the time I left Yale I was no longer the scared boy of that freshman photo. I had become more sure of myself and of my place—sure enough, indeed, to perceive the folly of my fears. And in the years since, I have assumed a sense of expectation, of access and *belonging,* that my younger self could scarcely have imagined. All this happened incrementally. There was no clear tipping point, no obvious moment of mutation. The shock of arrival, it would seem, is simply that I arrived.

QUESTIONS FOR DISCUSSION AND WRITING

1. In the opening paragraph, how does Liu intend for his list to portray the essence of "whiteness"? Explain why this list is an effective definition of whiteness—or why it fails to define whiteness—for you.

2. Liu says, "college was where the unconscious habits of my . . . assimilation hardened into self-conscious strategy" (paragraph 9). Describe the strategy of assimilation that he developed. What did it consist of? What stages did it go through? What did it accomplish for him?

3. Considering the focus on self-definition in this essay, do you find that it celebrates self-centeredness? Does Liu say too much about himself and not enough about others? What does he gain and what does he lose by focusing on himself? Write an essay in which you either defend or criticize Liu's focus on himself. Include references to yourself, if they fit.

4. Have you ever felt that you had to assimilate yourself into a group? Write about your experience of assimilation, stressing any stages that you went through and explaining the positive or negative aspects of the process. Or, write about someone else's assimilation into a group. Does the desire to assimilate ever justify deception, withholding information, or other forms of manipulating evidence or other people?

SHERMAN ALEXIE

What Sacagawea Means to Me

For Alexie's biographical information, see page 63. "What Sacagawea Means to Me," originally published in Time *(2002), uses the ultra-American image of the theme park as a springboard for creative cultural analysis. Alexie raises questions about ethnicity, gender, and social class in relation to Sacagawea, a Native American woman who, in 1804, was drafted into Lewis and Clark's expedition and lived out a complex relationship to the conquering race.*

In the future, every U.S. citizen will get to be Sacagawea for fifteen minutes. For the low price of admission, every American, regardless of race, religion, gender, and age, will climb through the portal into Sacagawea's Shoshone Indian brain. In the multicultural theme park called Sacagawea Land, you will be kidnapped as a child by the Hidatsa tribe and sold to Toussaint Charbonneau, the French-Canadian trader who will take you as one of his wives and father two of your children. Your first child, Jean-Baptiste, will be only a few months old as you carry him during your long journey with Lewis and Clark. The two captains will lead the adventure, fighting rivers, animals, weather, and diseases for thousands of miles, and you will march right beside them. But you, the aboriginal multitasker, will also breastfeed. And at the end of your Sacagawea journey, you will be shown the exit and given a souvenir T-shirt that reads, IF THE U.S. IS EDEN, THEN SACAGAWEA IS EVE.

Sacagawea is our mother. She is the first gene pair of the American DNA. In the beginning, she was the word, and the word was possibility. I revel in the wondrous possibilities of Sacagawea. It is good to be joyous in the presence of her spirit, because I hope she had moments of joy in what must have been a grueling life. This much is true: Sacagawea died of some mysterious illness when she was only in her twenties. Most illnesses were mysterious in the nineteenth century, but I suspect that Sacagawea's indigenous immune system was defenseless against an immigrant virus. Perhaps Lewis and Clark infected Sacagawea. If that is true, then certain postcolonial historians would argue that she was murdered not by germs but by colonists who carried those germs. I don't know much about the science of disease and immunities, but I know enough poetry to recognize that individual human beings are invaded and colonized by foreign bodies, just as individual civilizations are invaded and colonized by foreign bodies. In that sense, colonization might be a natural process, tragic and violent to be sure, but predictable and ordinary as well, and possibly necessary for the advance, however constructive and destructive, of all civilizations.

After all, Lewis and Clark's story has never been just the triumphant tale of two white men, no matter what the white historians might need to believe. Sacagawea was not the primary hero of this story either, no matter what the Native American historians and I might want to believe. The story of Lewis and Clark is also the story of the approximately forty-five nameless and faceless first- and second-generation European Americans who joined the journey, then left or completed it, often without monetary or historical compensation. Considering the time and place, I imagine those forty-five were illiterate, low-skilled laborers subject to managerial whims and nineteenth-century downsizing. And it is most certainly the story of the black slave York, who also cast votes during this allegedly democratic adventure. It's even the story of Seaman, the domesticated Newfoundland dog who must have been a welcome and friendly presence and who survived the risk of becoming supper during one lean time or another. The Lewis and Clark Expedition was exactly the kind of multicultural, trigenerational, bi-gendered, animal-friendly, government-supported, partly French-Canadian project that should rightly be celebrated by liberals and castigated by conservatives.

In the end, I wonder if colonization might somehow be magical. After all, Miles Davis is the direct descendant of slaves and slave owners. Hank Williams is the direct descendant of poor whites and poorer Indians. In 1876 Emily Dickinson was writing her poems in an Amherst attic while Crazy Horse was killing Custer on the banks of the Little Big Horn. I remain stunned by these contradictions, by the successive generations of social, political, and artistic mutations that can be so beautiful and painful. How did we get from there to here? This country somehow gave life to Maria Tallchief and Ted Bundy, to Geronimo and Joe McCarthy, to Nathan Bedford Forrest and Toni Morrison, to the Declaration of Independence and Executive Order No. 1066, to César Chávez and Richard Nixon, to theme parks and national parks, to smallpox and the vaccine for smallpox.

As a Native American, I want to hate this country and its contradictions. I   5
want to believe that Sacagawea hated this country and its contradictions. But this country exists, in whole and in part, because Sacagawea helped Lewis and Clark. In the land that came to be called Idaho, she acted as diplomat between her long-lost brother and the Lewis and Clark party. Why wouldn't she ask her brother and her tribe to take revenge against the men who had enslaved her? Sacagawea is a contradiction. Here in Seattle, I exist, in whole and in part, because a half-white man named James Cox fell in love with a Spokane Indian woman named Etta Adams who gave birth to my mother. I am a contradiction; I am Sacagawea.

QUESTIONS FOR DISCUSSION AND WRITING

1. The opening paragraph of Alexie's essay places the reader in the frame of the story with sentences such as "You will be kidnapped as a child by the Hidatsa tribe and sold to Toussaint Charbonneau." Why does Alexie change the reader's identity? What ideas is he trying to convey, and what connections is he attempting to create? For example, when he writes "you, the aboriginal multitasker, will also breastfeed," how is he trying to affect you as a male or female Indian or non-Indian reader?

2. Alexie states that "Lewis and Clark's story has never been just the triumphant tale of two white men, no matter what the white historians might need to believe" (paragraph 3). Why would white historians "need to believe" a different account from what Alexie offers? In what ways is Alexie's tale *non-triumphant* or *nonwhite*? Make a list of the ways Alexie attempts to modify,

contradict, or update the story told by traditional historians. You could extend this discussion by bringing to class some traditional accounts of the Lewis and Clark Expedition or writing a research paper on contrasting interpretations of the Lewis and Clark Expedition.

3. Although Alexie is a Native American author deeply concerned with the effects of colonization on his ancestors, he also discusses the "forty-five nameless and faceless first- and second-generation European Americans who joined the journey" (paragraph 3), who are white. Why does he draw attention to this group?

4. In the last two paragraphs of "What Sacagawea Means to Me," Alexie discusses contradictions. Write a paper about one or more of these contradictions in which you explain its meaning or try to resolve it, or both. For example, what should we make of the fact that Emily Dickinson was composing classic American poetry at the same time that Crazy Horse was battling Custer? Are these activities equivalent? Does one cancel out the other? Do they represent a larger contradiction in American society? How can one nation (the "United" States) embody such differences? Or consider the following question: What does America *stand for* if it can produce both Geronimo and Joe McCarthy, both the Declaration of Independence and Executive Order No. 1066 (which provided for the internment of Japanese Americans during World War II)?

5. Compare Alexie's way of discussing the problems experienced by nonwhites in America to that of Leslie Marmon Silko's in "Language and Literature from a Pueblo Indian Perspective" (p. 57) or Alice Walker's "In Search of Our Mothers' Gardens" (p. 307). Which writer's approach to the problem of nonwhite existence and identity is more effective, in your opinion? Why? By yourself or with a partner, write an essay in which you explain which of the two essays is more likely to change readers' perceptions about the experience of being nonwhite in America.

N. SCOTT MOMADAY

The Way to Rainy Mountain

N. Scott Momaday (b. 1934 in Lawton, Oklahoma) grew up on an Indian reservation in the Southwest, where his Cherokee-Caucasian mother and Kiowa father were both teachers. After earning his doctorate at Stanford University (1963), where he was a student of essayist and novelist Wallace Stegner, Momaday taught English at the University of California at Santa Barbara, and at Berkeley, Stanford, and the University of Arizona. For Momaday, identity is "a moral idea, for it accounts for the way in which [a man] reacts to other men and to the world in general." Primarily a poet (Angle of Geese, 1974; The Gourd Dancer, 1976), Momaday has also written two novels—the Pulitzer Prize–winning House Made of Dawn (1968), which *launched a renaissance in Native American writing, and* The Ancient Child *(1989), as well as* The Names: A Memoir *(1976). Like his earlier books, Momaday's more recent collections—*In the Presence of the Sun: Stories and Poems *(1992),* The Man Made of Words: Essays, Stories, Passages *(1997), and* In the Bear's House *(1999)— combine story, poem, prose poem, dialogue, ethnography, history, and personal history. Again the Far Morning: New and Selected Poems *was published in 2011.*

In "The Way to Rainy Mountain," which became the prologue to Momaday's book of the same title, Momaday preserves and validates the Native American oral tradition, retelling Kiowa legends, tracing the history of the Kiowas' migration, lyrically describing the landscape of their journey, and placing himself and his family within that matrix.

A single knoll rises out of the plain in Oklahoma, north and west of the Wichita Range. For my people, the Kiowas, it is an old landmark, and they gave it the name Rainy Mountain. The hardest weather in the world is there. Winter brings blizzards, hot tornadic winds arise in the spring, and in summer the prairie is an anvil's edge. The grass turns brittle and brown, and it cracks beneath your feet. There are green belts along the rivers and creeks, linear groves of hickory and pecan, willow and witch hazel. At a distance in July or August the steaming foliage seems almost to writhe in fire. Great green and yellow grasshoppers are everywhere in the tall grass, popping up like corn to sting the flesh, and tortoises crawl about on the red earth, going nowhere in the plenty of time. Loneliness is an aspect of the land. All things in the plain are isolate; there is no confusion of objects in the eye, but *one* hill or *one* tree or *one* man. To look upon that landscape in the early morning, with the sun at your back, is to lose the sense of proportion. Your imagination comes to life, and this, you think, is where Creation was begun.

I returned to Rainy Mountain in July. My grandmother had died in the spring, and I wanted to be at her grave. She had lived to be very old and at last infirm. Her only living daughter was with her when she died, and I was told that in death her face was that of a child.

I like to think of her as a child. When she was born, the Kiowas were living the last great moment of their history. For more than a hundred years they had controlled the open range from the Smoky Hill River to the Red, from the headwaters of the Canadian to the fork of the Arkansas and Cimarron. In alliance with the Comanches, they had ruled the whole of the southern Plains. War was their sacred business, and they were among the finest horsemen the world has ever known. But warfare for the Kiowas was preeminently a matter of disposition rather than of survival, and they never understood the grim, unrelenting advance of the U.S. Cavalry. When at last, divided and ill-provisioned, they were driven onto the Staked Plains in the cold rains of autumn, they fell into panic. In Palo Duro Canyon they abandoned their crucial stores to pillage and had nothing then but their lives. In order to save themselves, they surrendered to the soldiers at Fort Sill and were imprisoned in the old stone corral that now stands as a military museum. My grandmother was spared the humiliation of those high gray walls by eight or ten years, but she must have known from birth the affliction of defeat, the dark brooding of old warriors.

Her name was Aho, and she belonged to the last culture to evolve in North America. Her forebears came down from the high country in western Montana nearly three centuries ago. They were a mountain people, a mysterious tribe of hunters whose language has never been positively classified in any major group. In the late seventeenth century they began a long migration to the south and east. It was a journey toward the dawn, and it led to a golden age. Along the way the Kiowas were befriended by the Crows, who gave them the culture and religion of the Plains. They acquired horses, and their ancient nomadic spirit was suddenly free of the ground. They acquired Tai-me, the sacred Sun Dance doll, from that moment the object and symbol of their worship, and so shared in the divinity of the sun. Not least, they acquired the sense of destiny, therefore courage and pride. When they entered upon the southern Plains they had been transformed. No longer were they slaves to the simple necessity of survival; they were a lordly and dangerous society of fighters and thieves, hunters and priests of the sun. According to their origin myth, they entered the world through a hollow log. From one point of view, their migration was the fruit of an old prophecy, for indeed they emerged from a sunless world.

Although my grandmother lived out her long life in the shadow of Rainy 5
Mountain, the immense landscape of the continental interior lay like memory in her blood. She could tell of the Crows, whom she had never seen, and of the Black Hills, where she had never been. I wanted to see in reality what she had seen more perfectly in the mind's eye, and traveled fifteen hundred miles to begin my pilgrimage.

Yellowstone, it seemed to me, was the top of the world, a region of deep lakes and dark timber, canyons and waterfalls. But, beautiful as it is, one might have the sense of confinement there. The skyline in all directions is close at hand, the high wall of the woods and deep cleavages of shade. There is a perfect freedom in the mountains, but it belongs to the eagle and the elk, the badger and the bear. The Kiowas reckoned their stature by the distance they could see, and they were bent and blind in the wilderness.

Descending eastward, the highland meadows are a stairway to the plain. In July the inland slope of the Rockies is luxuriant with flax and buckwheat, stonecrop and larkspur. The earth unfolds and the limit of the land recedes. Clusters of trees, and animals grazing far in the distance, cause the vision to reach away and wonder to build upon the mind. The sun follows a longer course in the day, and the sky is immense beyond all comparison. The great billowing clouds that sail upon it are shadows that move upon the grain like water, dividing light. Farther down, in the land of the Crows and Blackfeet, the plain is yellow. Sweet clover takes hold of the hills and bends upon itself to cover and seal the soil. There the Kiowas paused on their way; they had come to the place where they must change their lives. The sun is at home on the plains. Precisely there does it have the certain character of a god. When the Kiowas came to the land of the Crows, they could see the dark lees of the hills at dawn across the Bighorn River, the profusion of light on the grain shelves, the oldest deity ranging after the solstices. Not yet would they veer southward to the caldron of the land that lay below; they must wean their blood from the northern winter and hold the mountains a while longer in their view. They bore Tai-me in procession to the east.

A dark mist lay over the Black Hills, and the land was like iron. At the top of a ridge I caught sight of Devil's Tower upthrust against the gray sky as if in the birth of time the core of the earth had broken through its crust and the motion of the world was begun. There are things in nature that engender an awful quiet in the heart of man; Devil's Tower is one of them. Two centuries ago, because they could not do otherwise, the Kiowas made a legend at the base of the rock. My grandmother said:

> Eight children were there at play, seven sisters and their brother. Suddenly the boy was struck dumb; he trembled and began to run upon his hands and feet. His fingers became claws, and his body was covered with fur. Directly there was a bear where the boy had been. The sisters were terrified; they ran, and the bear after them. They came to the stump of a great tree, and the tree spoke to them. It bade them climb upon it, and as they did so it began to rise into the air. The bear came to kill them, but they were just beyond its reach. It reared against the tree and scored the bark all around with its claws. The seven sisters were borne into the sky, and they became the stars of the Big Dipper.

From that moment, and so long as the legend lives, the Kiowas have kinsmen in the night sky. Whatever they were in the mountains, they could be no more. However tenuous their well-being, however much they had suffered and would suffer again, they had found a way out of the wilderness.

My grandmother had a reverence for the sun, a holy regard that now is all but gone out of mankind. There was a wariness in her, and an ancient awe. She was a Christian in her later years, but she had come a long way about, and she never forgot her birthright. As a child she had been to the Sun Dances; she had taken part in those annual rites, and by then she had learned the restoration of her people in the presence of Tai-me. She was about seven when the last Kiowa Sun Dance was held in 1887 on the Washita River above Rainy Mountain Creek. The buffalo were gone. In order to consummate the ancient sacrifice—to impale the head of a buffalo bull upon the medicine tree—a delegation of old men journeyed into Texas, there to beg and barter for an animal from the Goodnight herd. She was ten when the Kiowas came together for the last time as a living Sun Dance culture. They could find no buffalo; they had to hang an old hide from the sacred tree. Before the dance could begin, a company of soldiers rode out from Fort Sill under orders to disperse the tribe. Forbidden without cause the essential act of their faith, having seen the wild herds slaughtered and left to rot upon the ground, the Kiowas backed away forever from the medicine tree. That was July 20, 1890, at the great bend of the Washita. My grandmother was there. Without bitterness, and for as long as she lived, she bore a vision of deicide.

Now that I can have her only in memory, I see my grandmother in the several postures that were peculiar to her: standing at the wood stove on a winter morning and turning meat in a great iron skillet; sitting at the south window, bent 10 above her beadwork, and afterwards, when her vision failed, looking down for a long time into the fold of her hands; going out upon a cane, very slowly as she did when the weight of age came upon her; praying. I remember her most often at prayer. She made long, rambling prayers out of suffering and hope, having seen many things. I was never sure that I had the right to hear, so exclusive were they of all mere custom and company. The last time I saw her she prayed standing by the side of her bed at night, naked to the waist, the light of a kerosene lamp moving upon her dark skin. Her long, black hair, always drawn and braided in the day, lay upon her shoulders and against her breasts like a shawl. I do not speak Kiowa, and I never understood her prayers, but there was something inherently sad in the sound, some merest hesitation upon the syllables of sorrow. She began in a high and descending pitch, exhausting her breath to silence; then again and again—and always the same intensity of effort, of something that is, and is not, like urgency in the human voice. Transported so in the dancing light among the shadows of her room, she seemed beyond the reach of time. But that was illusion; I think I knew then that I should not see her again.

Houses are like sentinels in the plain, old keepers of the weather watch. There, in a very little while, wood takes on the appearance of great age. All colors wear soon away in the wind and rain, and then the wood is burned gray and the grain appears and the nails turn red with rust. The windowpanes are black and opaque; you imagine there is nothing within, and indeed there are many ghosts, bones given up to the land. They stand here and there against the sky, and you approach them for a longer time than you expect. They belong in the distance; it is their domain.

Once there was a lot of sound in my grandmother's house, a lot of coming and going, feasting and talk. The summers there were full of excitement and reunion. The Kiowas are a summer people; they abide the cold and keep to themselves, but when the season turns and the land becomes warm and vital they cannot hold still; an old love of going returns upon them. The aged visitors who came to my grandmother's house when I was a child were made of lean and leather, and they bore themselves upright. They wore great black hats and bright ample shirts that shook in the wind. They rubbed fat upon their hair and wound their braids with strips of colored cloth. Some of them painted their faces and carried the scars of old and cherished enmities. They were an old council of warlords, come to remind and be reminded of who they were. Their wives and daughters served them well. The women might indulge themselves; gossip was at once the mark and compensation of their servitude. They made loud and elaborate talk among themselves, full of jest and gesture, fright and false alarm. They went abroad in fringed and flowered shawls, bright beadwork and German silver. They were at home in the kitchen, and they prepared meals that were banquets.

There were frequent prayer meetings, and great nocturnal feasts. When I was a child I played with my cousins outside, where the lamplight fell upon the ground and the singing of the old people rose up around us and carried away into the darkness. There were a lot of good things to eat, a lot of laughter and surprise. And afterwards, when the quiet returned, I lay down with my grandmother and could hear the frogs away by the river and feel the motion of the air.

Now there is a funeral silence in the rooms, the endless wake of some final word. The walls have closed in upon my grandmother's house. When I returned to it in mourning, I saw for the first time in my life how small it was. It was late at night, and there was a white moon, nearly full. I sat for a long time on the stone steps by the kitchen door. From there I could see out across the land; I could see the long row of trees by the creek, the low light upon the rolling plains, and the stars of the Big Dipper. Once I looked at the moon and caught sight of a strange thing. A cricket had perched upon the handrail, only a few inches away from me. My line of vision was such that the creature filled the moon like a fossil. It had gone there, I thought, to live and die, for there, of all places, was its small definition made whole and eternal. A warm wind rose up and purled like the longing within me.

The next morning I awoke at dawn and went out on the dirt road to Rainy   15
Mountain. It was already hot, and the grasshoppers began to fill the air. Still, it was early in the morning, and the birds sang out of the shadows. The long yellow grass on the mountain shone in the bright light, and a scissortail hied above the land. There, where it ought to be, at the end of a long and legendary way, was my grand-mother's grave. Here and there on the dark stones were ancestral names. Looking back once, I saw the mountain and came away.

QUESTIONS FOR DISCUSSION AND WRITING

1. If you were to tell a grandchild or another youngster about a place in your childhood that shaped your character, what place would it be? Make a long list of everything you can remember about the place; then sort your list into clusters of things—maybe the atmosphere, the physical qualities, the per-sonal associations that certain physical qualities evoke, whatever works. Think about what made this place special for you and in what ways its special quality became an important part of who you are.

    Write a sketch—complemented by photographs or drawings if you like—that shows your special place to others in your class.

2. In what ways does the special place you wrote about in question 1 fit into the past and the future? How and to what extent does it connect with various dimensions of history? In what ways do Sherman Alexie's (p. 106) and Gloria Anzaldúa's (p. 135) interpretations corroborate or alter Momaday's views of cultural history?

3. Reflect on a story you were told as a child. What, if any, was the moral of the story? How explicit was it? Write about this story, and share your writing with your classmates, reflecting with them on how your story connects with stories they recall. As Momaday does, write about how that childhood story helps shape a story you now tell about yourself as an adult.

4. Reflect on a storytelling performance that has significance for you. Who told the story? How would you describe the scene of the storytelling? Try writing down as much of the story as you can in the language you recall. Consid-ering *The Way to Rainy Mountain*'s "three voices"—mythic, historical, and

immediate—explain which "voice" your story already embodies, and write companion pieces for it that embody the other two voices.

5. To whom might you retell your story from question 4, and what action might that person or persons take in response? What other familiar stories do you want them to keep in mind? Rewrite your story, including references to related stories, as a call to a particular audience to take a particular action. On the basis of your story, what should they do?

6. Sherman Alexie says, "I always want to be on the edge of offending somebody." Thus he has criticized the "Mother Earth Father Sky" clichés that he claims are perpetuated by Indian authors such as Momaday. Compare and contrast Alexie's satiric interpretation of an iconic Indian woman, Sacagawea (p. 106) with Momaday's depiction of his grandmother in "The Way to Rainy Mountain" (p. 108). Is Alexie's criticism of Momaday justified? Has Momaday offered any defense of his depiction of his ancestors and their native land in any of the readings in this chapter?

TONY JUDT

Toni

Born in London, England, in 1948, Tony Judt was educated at Cambridge University and the École Normale Supérieure, Paris. From 1972 to 1978 he was a Fellow of King's College, Cambridge, England; he then taught at the University of California at Berkeley and Oxford University. In 1987 he moved to New York University, where he served as the Erich Maria Remarque Professor in European Studies, Dean for Humanities, and Director of NYU's Erich Maria Remarque Institute. He was a frequent contributor to the New York Review of Books *and other periodicals. In 1996 Judt was elected a Fellow of the American Academy of Arts and Sciences and in 2007 a corresponding Fellow of the British Academy. Judt is the author or editor of twelve books, including* Postwar: A History of Europe Since 1945 *(2005),* Ill Fares the Land *(2010), and two books published posthumously,* The Memory Chalet *(2011) and* Thinking the Twentieth Century *(with Timothy Snyder, 2013). Judt died in 2010 of amyotrophic lateral sclerosis (ALS), commonly known as Lou Gehrig's disease.*

In "Toni," published in NYRblog, an online extension of the New York Review of Books, *Judt examines the complex nature of Jewish identity.*

I never knew Toni Avegael. She was born in Antwerp in February 1926 and lived there most of her life. We were related: She was my father's first cousin. I well remember her older sister Lily: a tall, sad lady whom my parents and I used to visit in a little house somewhere in northwest London. We have long since lost touch, which is a pity.

I am reminded of the Avegael sisters (there was a middle girl, Bella) whenever I ask myself—or am asked—what it means to be Jewish. There is no general-purpose answer to this question: It is always a matter of what it means to be Jewish for me—something quite distinct from what it means for my fellow Jews. To outsiders, such concerns are mysterious. A Protestant who does not believe in the Scriptures, a Catholic who abjures the authority of the Pope in Rome, or a Muslim for whom Muhammad is not the Prophet: These are incoherent categories. But a Jew who rejects the authority of the rabbis is still Jewish (even if only by the rabbis' own matrilineal definition): Who is to tell him otherwise?

I reject the authority of the rabbis—all of them (and for this I have rabbinical authority on my side). I participate in no Jewish community life, nor do I practice Jewish rituals. I don't make a point of socializing with Jews in particular—and for the most part I haven't married them. I am not a "lapsed" Jew, having never con-formed to requirements in the first place. I don't "love Israel" (either in the modern sense or in the original generic meaning of loving the Jewish people), and I don't care if the sentiment is reciprocated. But whenever anyone asks me whether or not I am Jewish, I unhesitatingly respond in the affirmative and would be ashamed to do otherwise.

The ostensible paradox of this condition is clearer to me since coming to New York: The curiosities of Jewish identity are more salient here. Most American Jews of my acquaintance are not particularly well informed about Jewish culture or history; they are blithely ignorant of Yiddish or Hebrew and rarely attend religious ceremonies. When they do, they behave in ways that strike me as curious.

Shortly after arriving in New York, I was invited to a bar mitzvah. On my way 5
to the synagogue, I realized I had forgotten my hat and returned home to recover it—only to observe that almost no one else covered his head during the brief, exig-uous excuse for a religious ceremony. To be sure, this was a "Reform" synagogue and I should have known better: Reform Jews (known in England as "liberals") have been optionally topless in synagogue for over half a century. All the same, the contrast between unctuous performance of ritual and selective departure from established traditions struck me then and strikes me now as a clue to the compen-satory quality of American Jewish identity.

Some years ago I attended a gala benefit dinner in Manhattan for prominent celebrities in the arts and journalism. Halfway through the ceremonies, a middle-aged man leaned across the table and glared at me: "Are you Tony Judt? You really must stop writing these terrible things about Israel!" Primed for such interroga-tions, I asked him what was so terrible about what I had written. "I don't know. You may be right—I've never been to Israel. But we Jews must stick together: We may need Israel one day." The return of eliminationist anti-Semitism was just a matter of time: New York might become unlivable.

I find it odd—and told him so—that American Jews should have taken out a territorial insurance policy in the Middle East lest we find ourselves back in Poland in 1942. But even more curious was the setting for this exchange: The overwhelming majority of the awardees that evening were Jewish. Jews in America are more success-ful, integrated, respected, and influential than at any place or time in the history of the community. Why then is contemporary Jewish identity in the United States so obsessively attached to the recollection—and anticipation—of its own disappearance?

Had Hitler never happened, Judaism might indeed have fallen into deliquescence. With the breakdown of Jewish isolation in the course of the later nineteenth century throughout much of Europe, the religious, communitarian, and ritualistic boundaries of Judaism were eroding: Centuries of ignorance and mutually enforced separation were coming to a close. Assimilation—by migration, marriage, and cultural dilution—was well underway.

In retrospect, the interim consequences can be confusing. In Germany, many Jews thought of themselves as Germans—and were resented for just that reason. In Central Europe, notably in the unrepresentative urban triangle of Prague-Budapest-Vienna, a secularized Jewish intelligentsia—influential in the liberal professions—established a distinctive basis for postcommunitarian Jewish life. But the world of Kafka, Kraus, and Zweig was brittle: Dependent upon the unique circumstances of a disintegrating liberal empire, it was helpless in the face of the tempests of ethnonationalism. For those in search of cultural roots, it offers little beyond regret and nostalgia. The dominant trajectory for Jews in those years was assimilation.

I can see this in my own family. My grandparents came out of the shtetl and   10 into unfriendly alien environments—an experience that temporarily reinforced a defensive Jewish self-awareness. But for their children, those same environments represented normal life. My parents' generation of European Jews neglected their Yiddish, frustrated the expectations of their immigrant families, and spurned communitarian rituals and restrictions. As late as the 1930s, it was reasonable to suppose that their own children—my generation—would be left with little more than a handful of memories of "the old country": something like the pasta-and-St.-Patrick's-Day nostalgia of Italian-Americans or Irish-Americans, and with about as much meaning.

But things turned out differently. A generation of emancipated young Jews, many of whom had fondly imagined themselves fully integrated into a post-communitarian world, was forcibly re-introduced to Judaism as civic identity: one that they were no longer free to decline. Religion—once the foundation of Jewish experience—was pushed ever further to the margin. In Hitler's wake, Zionism (hitherto a sectarian minority preference) became a realistic option. Jewishness became a secular attribute, externally attributed.

Ever since, Jewish identity in contemporary America has had a curious dybbuk-like quality: It lives on by virtue of a double, near-death experience. The result is a sensitivity to past suffering that can appear disproportionate even to fellow Jews. Shortly after publishing an essay on Israel's future, I was invited to London for an interview with the *Jewish Chronicle*—the local Jewish paper of record. I went with trepidation, anticipating further aspersions upon my imperfect identification with the Chosen People. To my surprise, the editor turned off the microphone: "Before we start," she began, "I'd like to ask you something. How can you stand to live among those awful American Jews?"

And yet, maybe those "awful American Jews" are onto something despite themselves. For what can it mean—following the decline of faith, the abatement of persecution, and the fragmentation of community—to insist upon one's Jewish-ness? A "Jewish" state where one has no intention of living and whose intolerant clerisy excludes ever more Jews from official recognition? An "ethnic" member-ship criterion that one would be embarrassed to invoke for any other purpose?

There was a time when being Jewish was a lived condition. In the United States today, religion no longer defines us: Just 46 percent of Jews belong to a synagogue, only 27 percent attend at least once a month, and no more than 21 percent of the synagogue members (10 percent of the whole) are Orthodox. In short, the "old believers" are but a minority. Modern-day Jews live on preserved memory. Being Jewish largely consists of remembering what it once meant to be Jewish. Indeed, of all the rabbinical injunctions, the most enduring and distinctive is *Zakhor!*— Remember! But most Jews have internalized this injunction without any very secure sense of what it requires of them. We are the people who remember . . . something.

What, then, should we remember? Great-grandma's latkes back in Pilvistock? 15 I doubt it: Shorn of setting and symbols, they are nothing but apple cakes. Child-hood tales of Cossack terrors (I recall them well)? What possible resonance could these have to a generation who has never known a Cossack? Memory is a poor foundation for any collective enterprise. The authority of historical injunction, lacking contemporary iteration, grows obscure.

In this sense, American Jews are instinctively correct to indulge their Holo-caust obsession: It provides reference, liturgy, example, and moral instruction—as well as historical proximity. And yet they are making a terrible mistake: They have confused a means of remembering with a reason to do so. Are we really Jews for no better reason than that Hitler sought to exterminate our grandparents? If we fail to rise above this consideration, our grandchildren will have little cause to identify with us.

In Israel today, the Holocaust is officially invoked as a reminder of how hateful non-Jews can be. Its commemoration in the diaspora is doubly exploited: to justify uncompromising Israelophilia and to service lachrymose self-regard. This seems to me a vicious abuse of memory. But what if the Holocaust served instead to bring us closer, so far as possible, to a truer understanding of the tradition we evoke?

Here, remembering becomes part of a broader social obligation by no means confined to Jews. We acknowledge readily enough our duties to our contempo-raries; but what of our obligations to those who came before us? We talk glibly of what we owe the future—but what of our debt to the past? Except in crassly practi-cal ways—preserving institutions or edifices—we can only service that debt to the full by remembering and conveying beyond ourselves the duty to remember.

Unlike my table companion, I don't expect Hitler to return. And I refuse to remember his crimes as an occasion to close off conversation: to repackage Jewishness as a defensive indifference to doubt or self-criticism and a retreat into self-pity. I choose to invoke a Jewish past that is impervious to orthodoxy: that opens conversations rather than closes them. Judaism for me is a sensibil-ity of collective self-questioning and uncomfortable truth-telling: the *dafka*-like quality of awkwardness and dissent for which we were once known. It is not enough to stand at a tangent to other peoples' conventions; we should also be the most unforgiving critics of our own. I feel a debt of responsibility to this past. It is why I am Jewish.

Toni Avegael was transported to Auschwitz in 1942 and gassed to death there as a Jew. I am named after her.   20

QUESTIONS FOR DISCUSSION AND WRITING

1. What is Judt's thesis, his main claim, in this essay? Where is the thesis located? Why do you suppose Judt chose to place it there?

2. Do you find Judt's thesis convincing? Why or why not?

3. What is the "ostensible paradox" Judt discusses in paragraph 4? What does he mean by "Judaism as civic identity" (paragraph 11)?

4. According to Judt, what constitutes the elements of his Jewish identity? To what extent does your religion or lack of one help make up who you are? Extend Judt's consideration of identity by adding elements beyond religious identification. What other categories would you include? Support your answer with examples from your own life.

5. According to Judt, what effects has the Holocaust had on Jewish identity for those Jews who survived it and their descendents? Support your answer with specific examples from the text.

6. Judt uses words such as shtetl (paragraph 10), dybbuk (paragraph 12), and *dafka* (paragraph 19). If you are not familiar with these terms, look them up in a dictionary. Why do you suppose Judt uses these terms?

7. Judt opens his essay with a mention of Toni Avegael and returns to her in the final paragraph. What is the effect of that final paragraph? How would the essay have been different if the information about Toni Avegael's fate were included at the beginning, when Judt first mentions her? In what ways does the information in the final paragraph support what Judt says throughout the essay?

8. How might Elie Wiesel (p. 91) respond to Judt's article? Are there points of agreement between what the two say? Be specific.

JAMES BALDWIN

Stranger in the Village

Through his fiction, James Baldwin (1924–1987) undertook to arouse the conscience of America during a time of social strife and racial polarization. Born in Harlem, he supplemented his education with intensive and obsessive reading. Baldwin's work would draw extensively on his Harlem youth—especially his struggle with a stepfather who called him ugly and refused to recognize his talent. Editing school newspapers, writing stories, and publishing articles, Baldwin entered literary circles but, disgusted by racial encounters and an unsatisfactory personal life, moved to Paris in 1948. During a sojourn in Switzerland he completed his first novel, Go Tell It on the Mountain *(1953). The novels that followed center on family relations, homosexual love, and race; the best known are* Giovanni's Room *(1956) and* Another Country *(1962). Two of his plays,* The Amen Corner *(1955) and* Blues for Mister Charlie *(1964), have been produced on Broadway. Baldwin's two best-selling essay collections,* Notes of a Native Son *(1955) and* The Fire Next Time *(1963), give voice to the urgent emotional and spiritual dangers of racism. Essayist Phillip Lopate calls Baldwin "the greatest American essayist in the second half of the twentieth century." Baldwin retained his U.S. citizenship but lived primarily in France until his death, returning to the United States several times to lend his support to civil rights marches with Martin Luther King Jr., Stokely Carmichael, and Malcolm X.*

In "Stranger in the Village," from Notes of a Native Son *(1955), Baldwin's account of his experience as the only black person living in a Swiss village leads into a meditation on blackness, whiteness, and the unique challenge of an American identity.*

From all available evidence no black man had ever set foot in this tiny Swiss village before I came. I was told before arriving that I would probably be a "sight" for the village; I took this to mean that people of my complexion were rarely seen in Switzerland, and also that city people are always something of a "sight" outside of the city. It did not occur to me—possibly because I am an American—that there could be people anywhere who had never seen a Negro.

It is a fact that cannot be explained on the basis of the inaccessibility of the village. The village is very high, but it is only four hours from Milan and three hours from Lausanne. It is true that it is virtually unknown. Few people making plans for a holiday would elect to come here. On the other hand, the villagers are able, presumably, to come and go as they please—which they do: to another town at the foot of the mountain, with a population of approximately five thousand, the nearest place to see a movie or go to the bank. In the village there is no movie house, no bank, no library, no theater; very few radios, one jeep, one station wagon; and at the moment, one typewriter, mine, an invention which the woman next door to me here had never seen. There are about six hundred people living here, all Catholic—I conclude this from the fact that the Catholic church is open all year round, whereas the Protestant chapel, set off on a hill a little removed from the village, is open only in the summertime when the tourists arrive. There are four or five hotels, all closed now, and four or five *bistros*, of which, however, only two do any business during the winter. These two do not do a great deal, for life in the village seems to end around nine or ten o'clock. There are a few stores, butcher, baker, *épicerie*, a hardware store, and a money-changer—who cannot change travelers' checks, but must send them down to the bank, an operation which takes two or three days. There is something called the *Ballet Haus*, closed in the winter and used for God knows what, certainly not ballet, during the summer. There seems to be only one schoolhouse in the village, and this for the quite young children; I suppose this to mean that their older brothers and sisters at some point descend from these mountains in order to complete their education—possibly, again, to the town just below. The landscape is absolutely forbidding, mountains towering on all four sides, ice and snow as far as the eye can reach. In this white wilderness, men and women and children move all day, carrying washing, wood, buckets of milk or water, sometimes skiing on Sunday afternoons. All week long boys and young men are to be seen shoveling snow off the rooftops, or dragging wood down from the forest in sleds.

The village's only real attraction, which explains the tourist season, is the hot spring water. A disquietingly high proportion of these tourists are cripples, or semi-cripples, who come year after year—from other parts of Switzerland, usually—to take the waters. This lends the village, at the height of the season, a rather terrifying air of sanctity, as though it were a lesser Lourdes. There is often something beautiful, there is always something awful, in the spectacle of a person who has lost one of his faculties, a faculty he never questioned until it was gone, and who struggles to recover it. Yet people remain people, on crutches or indeed on deathbeds; and wherever I passed, the first summer I was here, among the native villagers or among the lame, a wind passed with me—of astonishment, curiosity, amusement, and outrage. That first summer I stayed two weeks and never intended to return. But I did return in the winter, to work; the village offers, obviously, no distractions whatever and has the further advantage of being extremely cheap. Now it is winter again, a year later, and I am here again. Everyone in the village knows my name, though they scarcely ever use it, knows that I come from America—though, this, apparently, they will never really believe: black men come from Africa—and everyone knows that I am the friend of the son of a woman who was born here, and that I am staying in their chalet. But I remain as much a stranger today as I was the first day I arrived, and the children shout *Neger! Neger!* as I walk along the streets.

It must be admitted that in the beginning I was far too shocked to have any real reaction. In so far as I reacted at all, I reacted by trying to be pleasant—it being a great part of the American Negro's education (long before he goes to school) that he must make people "like" him. This smile-and-the-world-smiles-with-you routine worked about as well in this situation as it had in the situation for which it was designed, which is to say that it did not work at all. No one, after all, can be liked whose human weight and complexity cannot be, or has not been, admitted. My smile was simply another unheard-of phenomenon which allowed them to see my teeth—they did not, really, see my smile and I began to think that, should I take to snarling, no one would notice any difference. All of the physical characteristics of the Negro which had caused me, in America, a very different and almost forgotten pain were nothing less than miraculous—or infernal—in the eyes of the village people. Some thought my hair was the color of tar, that it had the texture of wire, or the texture of cotton. It was jocularly suggested that I might let it all grow long and make myself a winter coat. If I sat in the sun for more than five minutes some daring creature was certain to come along and gingerly put his fingers on my hair, as though he were afraid of an electric shock, or put his hand on my hand, astonished that the color did not rub off. In all of this, in which it must be conceded there was the charm of genuine wonder and in which there was certainly no element of intentional unkindness, there was yet no suggestion that I was human: I was simply a living wonder.

I knew that they did not mean to be unkind, and I know it now; it is necessary, 5 nevertheless, for me to repeat this to myself each time that I walk out of the chalet. The children who shout *Neger!* have no way of knowing the echoes this sound raises in me. They are brimming with good humor and the more daring swell with pride when I stop to speak with them. Just the same, there are days when I cannot pause and smile, when I have no heart to play with them; when, indeed, I mutter sourly to myself, exactly as I muttered on the streets of a city these children have never seen, when I was no bigger than these children are now: *Your* mother *was a nigger.* Joyce is right about history being a nightmare—but it may be the nightmare from which no one *can* awaken. People are trapped in history and history is trapped in them.

There is a custom in the village—I am told it is repeated in many villages—of "buying" African natives for the purpose of converting them to Christianity. There stands in the church all year round a small box with a slot for money, decorated with a black figurine, and into this box the villagers drop their francs. During the *carnaval* which precedes Lent, two village children have their faces blackened—out of which bloodless darkness their blue eyes shine like ice—and fantastic horsehair wigs are placed on their blond heads; thus disguised, they solicit among the villagers for money for the missionaries in Africa. Between the box in the church and the blackened children, the village "bought" last year six or eight African natives. This was reported to me with pride by the wife of one of the *bistro* owners and I was careful to express astonishment and pleasure at the solicitude shown by the village for the souls of black folks. The *bistro* owner's wife beamed with a pleasure far more genuine than my own and seemed to feel that I might now breathe more easily concerning the souls of at least six of my kinsmen.

I tried not to think of these so lately baptized kinsmen, of the price paid for them, or the peculiar price they themselves would pay, and said nothing about my father, who having taken his own conversion too literally never, at bottom, forgave the white world (which he described as heathen) for having saddled him with a Christ in whom, to judge at least from their treatment of him, they themselves no longer believed. I thought of white men arriving for the first time in an African village, strangers there, as I am a stranger here, and tried to imagine the astounded populace touching their hair and marveling at the color of their skin. But there is a great difference between being the first white man to be seen by Africans and being the first black man to be seen by whites. The white man takes the astonishment as tribute, for he arrives to conquer and to convert the natives, whose inferiority in relation to himself is not even to be questioned; whereas I, without a thought of conquest, find myself among a people whose culture controls me, has even, in a sense, created me, people who have cost me more in anguish and rage than they will ever know, who yet do not even know of my existence. The astonishment with which I might have greeted them, should they have stumbled into my African village a few hundred years ago, might have rejoiced their hearts. But the astonishment with which they greet me today can only poison mine.

And this is so despite everything I may do to feel differently, despite my friendly conversations with the *bistro* owner's wife, despite their three-year-old son who has at last become my friend, despite the *saluts* and *bonsoirs*[1] which I exchange with people as I walk, despite the fact that I know that no individual can be taken to task for what history is doing, or has done. I say that the culture of these people controls me—but they can scarcely be held responsible for European culture. America comes out of Europe, but these people have never seen America, nor have most of them seen more of Europe than the hamlet at the foot of their mountain. Yet they move with an authority which I shall never have; and they regard me, quite rightly, not only as a stranger in their village but as a suspect latecomer, bearing no credentials, to everything they have—however unconsciously—inherited.

For this village, even were it incomparably more remote and incredibly more primitive, is the West, the West onto which I have been so strangely grafted. These people cannot be, from the point of view of power, strangers anywhere in the world; they have made the modern world, in effect, even if they do not know it. The most illiterate among them is related, in a way that I am not, to Dante, Shakespeare, Michelangelo, Aeschylus, Da Vinci, Rembrandt, and Racine; the cathedral at Chartres says something to them which it cannot say to me, as indeed would New York's Empire State Building, should anyone here ever see it. Out of their hymns and dances come Beethoven and Bach. Go back a few centuries and they are in their full glory—but I am in Africa, watching the conquerors arrive.

The rage of the disesteemed is personally fruitless, but it is also absolutely   10
inevitable; this rage, so generally discounted, so little understood even among the people whose daily bread it is, is one of the things that makes history. Rage can only with difficulty, and never entirely, be brought under the domination of the intelligence and is therefore not susceptible to any arguments whatever. This is a fact which ordinary representatives of the *Herrenvolk*,[2] having never felt this rage and being unable to imagine, quite fail to understand. Also, rage cannot be hidden, it can only be dissembled. This dissembling deludes the thoughtless, and strengthens rage and adds, to rage, contempt. There are, no doubt, as many ways of coping with the resulting complex of tensions as there are black men in the world, but no black man can hope ever to be entirely liberated from this internal warfare—rage, dissembling, and contempt having inevitably accompanied his first realization of the power of white men. What is crucial here is that, since white men represent in the black man's world so heavy a weight, white men have for black men a reality which is far from being reciprocal; and hence all black men have toward all white men an attitude which is designed, really, either to rob the white man of the jewel of his naïveté, or else to make it cost him dear.

The black man insists, by whatever means he finds at his disposal, that the white man cease to regard him as an exotic rarity and recognize him as a human being. This is a very charged and difficult moment, for there is a great deal of will power involved in the white man's naïveté. Most people are not naturally reflective

---

[1] "Hellos" and "good evenings."
[2] Master race.

any more than they are naturally malicious, and the white man prefers to keep the black man at a certain human remove because it is easier for him thus to preserve his simplicity and avoid being called to account for crimes committed by his forefathers, or his neighbors. He is inescapably aware, nevertheless, that he is in a better position in the world than black men are, nor can he quite put to death the suspicion that he is hated by black men therefore. He does not wish to be hated, neither does he wish to change places, and at this point in his uneasiness he can scarcely avoid having recourse to those legends which white men have created about black men, the most usual effect of which is that the white man finds himself enmeshed, so to speak, in his own language which describes hell, as well as the attributes which lead one to hell, as being as black as night.

Every legend, moreover, contains its residuum of truth, and the root function of language is to control the universe by describing it. It is of quite considerable significance that black men remain, in the imagination, and in overwhelming numbers in fact, beyond the disciplines of salvation; and this despite the fact that the West has been "buying" African natives for centuries. There is, I should hazard, an instantaneous necessity to be divorced from this so visibly unsaved stranger, in whose heart, moreover, one cannot guess what dreams of vengeance are being nourished; and, at the same time, there are few things on earth more attractive than the idea of the unspeakable liberty which is allowed the unredeemed. When, beneath the black mask, a human being begins to make himself felt one cannot escape a certain awful wonder as to what kind of human being it is. What one's imagination makes of other people is dictated, of course, by the laws of one's own personality and it is one of the ironies of black-white relations that, by means of what the white man imagines the black man to be, the black man is enabled to know who the white man is.

I have said, for example, that I am as much a stranger in this village today as I was the first summer I arrived, but this is not quite true. The villagers wonder less about the texture of my hair than they did then, and wonder rather more about me. And the fact that their wonder now exists on another level is reflected in their attitudes and in their eyes. There are the children who make those delightful, hilarious, sometimes astonishingly grave overtures of friendship in the unpredictable fashion of children; other children, having been taught that the devil is a black man, scream in genuine anguish as I approach. Some of the older women never pass without a friendly greeting, never pass, indeed, if it seems that they will be able to engage me in conversation; other women look down or look away or rather contemptuously smirk. Some of the men drink with me and suggest that I learn how to ski—partly, I gather, because they cannot imagine what I would look like on skis—and want to know if I am married, and ask questions about my *métier*. But some of the men have accused *le sale nègre*[3]—behind my back—of stealing wood and there is already in the eyes of some of them that peculiar, intent, paranoiac malevolence which one sometimes surprises in the eyes of American white men when, out walking with their Sunday girl, they see a Negro male approach.

---

[3]The dirty Negro.

There is a dreadful abyss between the streets of this village and the streets of the city in which I was born, between the children who shout *Neger!* today and those who shouted *Nigger!* yesterday—the abyss is experience, the American experience. The syllable hurled behind me today expresses, above all, wonder: I am a stranger here. But I am not a stranger in America and the same syllable riding on the American air expresses the war my presence has occasioned in the American soul.

For this village brings home to me this fact: that there was a day, and not really a very distant day, when Americans were scarcely Americans at all but discontented Europeans, facing a great unconquered continent and strolling, say, into a marketplace and seeing black men for the first time. The shock this spectacle afforded is suggested, surely, by the promptness with which they decided that these black men were not really men but cattle. It is true that the necessity on the part of the settlers of the New World of reconciling their moral assumptions with the fact—and the necessity—of slavery enhanced immensely the charm of this idea, and it is also true that this idea expresses, with a truly American bluntness, the attitude which to varying extents all masters have had toward all slaves.

But between all former slaves and slave-owners and the drama which begins for Americans over three hundred years ago at Jamestown, there are at least two differences to be observed. The American Negro slave could not suppose, for one thing, as slaves in past epochs had supposed and often done, that he would ever be able to wrest the power from his master's hands. This was a supposition which the modern era, which was to bring about such vast changes in the aims and dimensions of power, put to death; it only begins, in unprecedented fashion, and with dreadful implications, to be resurrected today. But even had this supposition persisted with undiminished force, the American Negro slave could not have used it to lend his condition dignity, for the reason that this supposition rests on another: that the slave in exile yet remains related to his past, has some means—if only in memory—of revering and sustaining the forms of his former life, is able, in short, to maintain his identity.

This was not the case with the American Negro slave. He is unique among the black men of the world in that his past was taken from him, almost literally, at one blow. One wonders what on earth the first slave found to say to the first dark child he bore. I am told that there are Haitians able to trace their ancestry back to African kings, but any American Negro wishing to go back so far will find his journey through time abruptly arrested by the signature on the bill of sale which served as the entrance paper for his ancestor. At the time—to say nothing of the circumstances—of the enslavement of the captive black man who was to become the American Negro, there was not the remotest possibility that he would ever take power from his master's hands. There was no reason to suppose that his situation would ever change, nor was there, shortly, anything to indicate that his situation had ever been different. It was his necessity, in the words of E. Franklin Frazier, to find a "motive for living under American culture or die." The identity of the American Negro comes out of this extreme situation, and the evolution of this identity was a source of the most intolerable anxiety in the minds and the lives of his masters.

For the history of the American Negro is unique also in this: that the question of his humanity, and of his rights therefore as a human being, became a burning one for several generations of Americans, so burning a question that it ultimately became one of those used to divide the nation. It is out of this argument that the venom of the epithet *Nigger!* is derived. It is an argument which Europe has never had, and hence Europe quite sincerely fails to understand how or why the argument arose in the first place, why its effects are frequently disastrous and always so unpredictable, why it refuses until today to be entirely settled. Europe's black possessions remained—and do remain—in Europe's colonies, at which remove they represented no threat whatever to European identity. If they posed any problem at all for the European conscience it was a problem which remained comfortingly abstract: in effect, the black man, as a *man* did not exist for Europe. But in America, even as a slave, he was an inescapable part of the general social fabric and no American could escape having an attitude toward him. Americans attempt until today to make an abstraction of the Negro, but the very nature of these abstractions reveals the tremendous effects the presence of the Negro has had on the American character.

When one considers the history of the Negro in America it is of the greatest importance to recognize that the moral beliefs of a person, or a people, are never really as tenuous as life—which is not moral—very often causes them to appear; these create for them a frame of reference and a necessary hope, the hope being that when life has done its worst they will be enabled to rise above themselves and to triumph over life. Life would scarcely be bearable if this hope did not exist. Again, even when the worst has been said, to betray a belief is not by any means to have put oneself beyond its power; the betrayal of a belief is not the same thing as ceasing to believe. If this were not so there would be no moral standards in the world at all. Yet one must also recognize that morality is based on ideas and that all ideas are dangerous—dangerous because ideas can only lead to action and where the action leads no man can say. And dangerous in this respect: that confronted with the impossibility of remaining faithful to one's beliefs, and the equal impossibility of becoming free of them, one can be driven to the most inhuman excesses. The ideas on which American beliefs are based are not, though Americans often seem to think so, ideas which originated in America. They came out of Europe. And the establishment of democracy on the American continent was scarcely as radical a break with the past as was the necessity, which Americans faced, of broadening this concept to include black men.

This was, literally, a hard necessity. It was impossible, for one thing, for 20 Americans to abandon their beliefs, not only because these beliefs alone seemed able to justify the sacrifices they had endured and the blood that they had spilled, but also because these beliefs afforded them their only bulwark against a moral chaos as absolute as the physical chaos of the continent it was their destiny to conquer. But in the situation in which Americans found themselves, these beliefs threatened an idea which, whether or not one likes to think so, is the very warp and woof of the heritage of the West, the idea of white supremacy.

Americans have made themselves notorious by the shrillness and the brutality with which they have insisted on this idea, but they did not invent it; and it has escaped the world's notice that those very excesses of which Americans have been guilty imply a certain, unprecedented uneasiness over the idea's life and power, if not, indeed, the idea's validity. The idea of white supremacy rests simply on the fact that white men are the creators of civilization (the present civilization, which is the only one that matters; all previous civilizations are simply "contributions" to our own) and are therefore civilization's guardians and defenders. Thus it was impossible for Americans to accept the black man as one of themselves, for to do so was to jeopardize their status as white men. But not so to accept him was to deny his human reality, his human weight and complexity, and the strain of denying the overwhelmingly undeniable forced Americans into rationalizations so fantastic that they approached the pathological.

At the root of the American Negro problem is the necessity of the American white man to find a way of living with the Negro in order to be able to live with himself. And the history of this problem can be reduced to the means used by Americans—lynch law and law, segregation and legal acceptance, terrorization and concession—either to come to terms with this necessity, or to find a way around it, or (most usually) to find a way of doing both these things at once. The resulting spectacle, at once foolish and dreadful, led someone to make the quite accurate observation that "the Negro-in-America is a form of insanity which overtakes white men."

In this long battle, a battle by no means finished, the unforeseeable effects of which will be felt by many future generations, the white man's motive was the protection of his identity; the black man was motivated by the need to establish an identity. And despite the terrorization which the Negro in America endured and endures sporadically until today, despite the cruel and totally inescapable ambivalence of his status in his country, the battle for his identity has long ago been won. He is not a visitor to the West, but a citizen there, an American; as American as the Americans who despise him, the Americans who fear him, the Americans who love him—the Americans who became less than themselves, or rose to be greater than themselves by virtue of the fact that the challenge he represented was inescapable. He is perhaps the only black man in the world whose relationship to white men is more terrible, more subtle, and more meaningful than the relationship of bitter possessed to uncertain possessors. His survival depended, and his development depends, on his ability to turn his peculiar status in the Western world to his own advantage and, it may be, to the very great advantage of that world. It remains for him to fashion out of his experience that which will give him sustenance, and a voice.

The cathedral at Chartres, I have said, says something to the people of this village which it cannot say to me; but it is important to understand that this cathedral says something to me which it cannot say to them. Perhaps they are struck by the power of the spires, the glory of the windows; but they have known God, after all, longer than I have known him, and in a different way, and I am terrified by the slippery bottomless well to be found in the crypt, down which heretics were hurled to death, and by the obscene, inescapable gargoyles jutting out of the stone and seeming to say that God and the devil can never be divorced. I doubt that the villagers think of the devil when they face a cathedral because they have never been identified with the devil. But I must accept the status which myth, if nothing else, gives me in the West before I can hope to change the myth.

Yet, if the American Negro has arrived at his identity by virtue of the abso- 25 luteness of his estrangement from his past, American white men still nourish the illusion that there is some means of recovering the European innocence, of returning to a state in which black men do not exist. This is one of the greatest errors Americans can make. The identity they fought so hard to protect has, by virtue of that battle, undergone a change: Americans are as unlike any other white people in the world as it is possible to be. I do not think, for example, that it is too much to suggest that the American vision of the world—which allows so little reality, generally speaking, for any of the darker forces in human life, which tends until today to paint moral issues in glaring black and white—owes a great deal to the battle waged by Americans to maintain between themselves and black men a human separation which could not be bridged. It is only now beginning to be borne in on us—very faintly, it must be admitted, very slowly, and very much against our will—that this vision of the world is dangerously inaccurate, and perfectly useless. For it protects our moral high-mindedness at the terrible expense of weakening our grasp of reality. People who shut their eyes to reality simply invite their own destruction, and anyone who insists on remaining in a state of innocence long after that innocence is dead turns himself into a monster.

The time has come to realize that the interracial drama acted out on the American continent has not only created a new black man, it has created a new white man, too. No road whatever will lead Americans back to the simplicity of this European village where white men still have the luxury of looking on me as a stranger. I am not, really, a stranger any longer for any American alive. One of the things that distinguishes Americans from other people is that no other people has ever been so deeply involved in the lives of black men, and vice versa. This fact faced, with all its implications, it can be seen that the history of the American Negro problem is not merely shameful, it is also something of an achievement. For even when the worst has been said, it must also be added that the perpetual challenge posed by this problem was always, somehow, perpetually met. It is precisely this black-white experience which may prove of indispensable value to us in the world we face today. This world is white no longer, and it will never be white again.

QUESTIONS FOR DISCUSSION AND WRITING

1. The "physical characteristics of the Negro" cause James Baldwin problems in Europe as well as in the United States (paragraph 4). What are these problems? What are the differences between the problems he experiences on either side of the Atlantic? What are some of the similarities? How does Baldwin respond to them?

2. What is Baldwin's attitude toward the villagers' practice of "'buying' African natives for the purpose of converting them to Christianity" (paragraph 6)? What

is the villagers' attitude toward it? Does Baldwin understand the villagers' "reason" to feel that way? Do they understand his reason not to? Why or why not?

3. Baldwin analyzes the "root of the American Negro problem" (paragraph 22). What does Baldwin consider the basis of "the problem"? In what ways has American society changed in the half century since Baldwin wrote that could cause a different judgment today? Is the election of Barack Obama as U.S. president in itself a sufficient indicator of major social changes? Explain your answer with particular reference to education, economics, and politics.

4. Have you ever felt like a "stranger in a strange land," displaced or alien in an unfamiliar culture—of a school, town, state or region, country? What was the nature of this experience? Did you like being an "outsider"? Why or why not? Whether or not you liked it, did you learn or grow from this, and if so, in what ways? Does this estrangement still continue? If so, with what effects? Or have you gotten beyond this, and if so, with what consequences, for better or for worse? Do you know of others in comparable situations, anywhere in the world? Write an analysis, even if it's inconclusive.

TAMARA WINFREY HARRIS

No Disrespect: Black Women and the Burden of Respectability

Tamara Winfrey Harris (b. 1969) is a freelance writer operating in the Indianapolis area. Harris graduated from Iowa State University in 1991, and since then has written extensively. She is a regular contributor to publications such as Ms., Newsweek, Huffington Post, *and* Bitch *magazine, where this article initially appeared online in the Summer 2012 issue. Harris describes herself as interested in race and gender and particularly how they come together with pop culture and politics. She is an editor for the Web site* Love Isn't Enough, *dedicated to parenting in "a colorstruck world." She also contributes to the Web site* Racialicious *and is writing a book on what she terms "the exploration of black women and marriage, and the racist and sexist underpinnings of the 'black marriage crisis' narrative."*

In this article, Harris explores the question of "respectability politics"—the idea that minorities, but especially black women, must present themselves as respectable, as defined by the dominant culture. The majority culture—white, heterosexual, middle class—essentially rewards those who conform to and assimilate its own values. Harris points out that blacks themselves have largely bought into respectability politics as well, which appears, for example, in criticism directed at Viola Davis and Octavia Spencer for playing maids in the 2011 film The Help. *The point of the criticism is that such acclaimed actresses should hold out for roles that do not involve stereotypical characters or situations. However, Harris argues that respectability politics itself serves to limit and disregard large portions of the population, privileging certain kinds of experiences over others.*

In February 2012, PBS host Tavis Smiley interviewed Viola Davis and Octavia Spencer about their Oscar nominations for their roles as Aibileen and Minny, Jim Crow–era domestic workers in *The Help*. "I'm pulling for both of you to win on Academy Award night," Smiley ventured. "But there's something that sticks in my craw about celebrating Hattie McDaniel so many years ago for playing a maid"— a reference to the actor who won for her role as Mammy in 1939's *Gone with the Wind*. "I want you to win," Smiley concluded, "but I'm ambivalent about what you're winning for."

Davis countered that it is hard for black actresses to find multifaceted roles in Hollywood, and that pressure from the black community to eschew portrayals that are not heroic makes it even harder: "That very mind-set that you have, and that a lot of African-Americans have, is absolutely destroying the black artist. . . . If your criticism is that you just don't want to see the maid . . . then I have an issue with that. Do I always have to be noble?"

For black women, particularly those in the public eye, the answer to this question is often a resounding "Yes." They are required to be noble examples of black excellence. To be better. To be respectable. And the bounds of respectability are narrowly defined by professional and personal choices reflecting the social mores of the majority culture—patriarchal, Judeo-Christian, heteronormative, and middle class.

Spencer ended up taking home an Oscar later that month for Best Supporting Actress (Davis lost to Meryl Streep for Best Actress), but Smiley had articulated a discomfort many in the black community felt about their big-screen roles. For all its popularity and acclaim, *The Help* illustrates that Hollywood still filters (and distorts) the lives and histories of minorities through the eyes of the majority; celebrates white saviors; and, 72 years post-Mammy, is still more comfortable casting black women as maids than as prime ministers, action heroes, or romantic leads.

Where Smiley trod lightly, some people have been more explicit in their criti- 5 cism of Davis and Spencer. In an open letter to Davis on the film-industry site Indiewire, black filmmaker Tanya Steele wrote, "Currently, the vanguard of black culture is still healing wounds from their past. Wounds that racism has created, wounds that drive you to gain acceptance in the larger culture. The acknowledgment comes in the form of a paycheck, exposure, star status, acceptance. An acceptance that is more important than our legacy. Isn't it that simple? How else could a black woman . . . take the role?"

Much-needed criticisms of *The Help* and the characters of Aibileen and Minny have come from sources like the Association of Black Women Historians, which, in its own open letter, challenged various aspects of the book and film, including misrepresentations of elements of black life and the lack of attention given to sexual harassment and civil rights activism. But there is something else floating in the ether: the idea that the role of a maid is simply too ignoble for a twenty-first-century black actress. That idea is merely respectability politics at work.

Respectability politics work to counter negative views of blackness by aggressively adopting the manners and morality that the dominant culture deems "respectable." The approach emerged in reaction to white racism that labeled blackness as "other"—degenerate and substandard—with roots in an assimilationist narrative that prevailed in the late-nineteenth-century United States. Black activists and allies believed that acceptance and respect for African-Americans would come by showing the majority culture "we are just like you."

Black women in particular had their own set of stereotypes to battle, as they had long been labeled by white society as lascivious Jezebels, animalistic beasts of burden, and disreputable antiwomen. According to Dr. Sarah Jackson, a race and media studies scholar at Boston's Northeastern University, to counter these stereotypes newly freed African-American women were forced to adhere to the sexist strictures of the Cult of True Womanhood, which positioned white women as inherently chaste, pious, childlike, submissive, and (as Sojourner Truth famously said in her "Ain't I a Woman" speech) in need of being "helped over mud puddles." In other words: respectable.

And here emerges one fallacy of respectability politics: An oppressed community can implicitly endorse deeply flawed values, including many that form the foundation of their own oppression. The idea that domestic work is shameful is a product of class bias that disdains the working class, and of gender bias that devalues "women's work." And while Truth spoke longingly about the delicate way white women were treated, that treatment was deeply sexist.

On the other hand, respectability has been important for marginalized peo- 10 ple throughout history. Black women's clubs that formed in the early twentieth century, spearheaded by women like Ida B. Wells, uplifted the black community and "proved" the respectability of African-American women by replicating similar organizations led by white women. Black civil rights activists showed up at marches and protests in their Sunday best—despite discomfort, and sometimes only to be spat on or sprayed by fire hoses. Those jackets and ties, heels and hats, sent a message: Your stereotypes are untrue; we deserve equality; we, too, are respectable. Jackson notes, "Assimilation was an effective way to join the national conversation at a time when there was a great disparity in not just the visibility of black Americans, but in the opportunity and legal protections afforded them."

Negative views of blackness have surely not disappeared in the twenty-first century. And the black community still uses respectability politics as a form of resistance. But perhaps now more than ever—when there are so many different ways to be black and to be a woman—respectability politics have the potential to harm as much as uplift. As often happens, black women carry a double burden, as they are asked to uphold a respectability built on both racist and sexist foundations. And the burden isn't just about professional decisions—say, which roles an actress should choose—but personal ones as well.

When neo-soul singer Erykah Badu announced her third pregnancy in 2008, some fans attacked her for having children outside of marriage with more than one father. One online commenter labeled the singer, known for rocking a mega 'fro, "trash with great hair." A Zimbio.com article that referred to Badu's "growing list of baby daddies" featured a "Knocked Up Again" headline. A blog article wondered baldly if the singer was "a ho." She was derided as a poor example of black woman-hood. The storm got so heavy that Badu bit back in a lengthy and poetically unapolo-getic online post about her family that ended with an entreaty to "Kiss my placenta."

Three years later, when Beyoncé announced she was expecting, she was pub-licly applauded for doing pregnancy "the right way," and celebrated for being a model of black womanhood. Even Diddy's 18-year-old son, Justin Combs, weighed in on Bey's proper use of her uterus. Combs tweeted: "Beyoncé dated, married, THEN got pregnant . . . young ladies take notes." (No word on whether Combs's dad, who has never married but has five children, is also taking notes.)

Jackson calls the differing reactions to Badu's and Beyoncé's pregnancies "a sexist, puritanical, moral panic. The idea that a woman who doesn't have her chil-dren in wedlock is discrediting an entire race of people is ridiculous. It only serves to further demonize single women, who are working hard at motherhood, and are sexually independent. And it reinforces the historical idea of sexual deviance and unfit motherhood that has been used to marginalize black women."

Badu's personal choices raised the specter of the Jezebel. And rather than   15
reject that problematic stereotype, critics pilloried Badu as a poor example to the black and broader communities—as not respectable. But the hand-wringing over the singer's familial status is less about the welfare of her children and more about a black woman publicly violating sexist morality by having children (read: sex) outside of marriage.

"The traditionalist [respectability] narrative has come dangerously close to being exclusionary to the very community we are trying to uplift," says Jackson. In rightfully pushing back at negative and untrue caricatures of modern black moth-erhood centered around "welfare queens," we can unwittingly demonize any black mother whose family falls outside of traditional, heterosexual, and patriarchal paradigms—no matter how thoughtful her decisions, how involved her partners, or how well cared for her children. If we buy that the only "right" way for a woman to build a family is through a state-sanctioned marriage to a man, then we have made a large percentage of black women "wrong."

Respectability politics serve to curtail the individual liberties of people who have spent centuries fighting to be free. For black female actors and other artists, this may mean making choices based not on what's best for their careers and per-sonal lives, but instead, on what serves to convince the majority culture that people like them deserve respect.

Take Halle Berry's Academy Award–winning performance in the 2001 film *Monster's Ball*, which was as controversial as it was critically acclaimed. Berry drew particular criticism for a daring sex scene with costar Billy Bob Thornton. A black woman on screen, bouncing and writhing naked with a white man, was viewed as base and degrading by many in the black community. Angela Bassett, who had turned down Berry's role, was critical.

"I wasn't going to be a prostitute on film," Bassett told *Newsweek*. (In fact, Berry's character was not a prostitute, but a woman who begins a relationship with her husband's executioner.) "I couldn't do that because it's such a stereotype about black women and sexuality. Film is forever. It's about putting something out there you can be proud of 10 years later. I mean, Meryl Streep won Oscars without all that."

By choosing a highly sexualized role, Bassett implied, Berry was reinforcing 20 stereotypes about black women. Put another way, Berry was reinforcing the way white society views black women.

For women, to be sexual, to be sexual with different partners, or to be sexual outside of marriage is not deemed respectable. This is especially true for black women. Respectability politics allow both the white and black communities to lay claim to black women's bodies.

"For black women, our quest to have ownership over our bodies and ourselves has always been at least 50 percent public. It's never been just a private quest for dignity and respect," says American and Africana studies scholar Kimberly C. Ellis. Ellis, also known as Dr. Goddess, performs one-woman shows that leverage spoken word, comedy, and music to mine issues of race, class, and gender.

Though Ellis says she does not adhere to the standards advanced by the politics of respectability, she is still conscientious about the characters she creates. "The question is, do we have the responsibility to define ourselves within what Dr. Cornel West calls 'the white normative gaze' or the responsibility to demonstrate our full humanity?"

But Ellis says she "can't act as though there is not an active agenda to attack and destroy any image of black dignity and leadership and power in order to affect public policy and political will."

The image of black female dignity is routinely attacked by a 24/7 media-industrial complex that serves up a steady stream of caricature. Scripts featuring fully formed black female roles may be difficult to find, but the exploding popularity of unscripted television has placed an increasing number of stereotypical black female characters in the public eye—characters presumed to represent "real" black womanhood. In her book *Reality Bites Back,* Jennifer Pozner points out that producers in the reality TV genre specifically seek out "characters" that represent gender and racial stereotypes—namely angry black women.

Bravo's popular *Real Housewives* franchise—a reality juggernaut that keeps 25 spawning new shows—follows the antics of groups of bourgeois women from various U.S. cities. Nearly all participants are presented as bullying, narcissistic, backstabbing, money-grubbing, cliquey, disloyal, arrogant, self-involved, willfully ignorant, poorly spoken, wasteful, and tackily nouveau riche. It makes for good television. But the mostly African-American Atlanta cast's dysfunction is accepted as uniquely black, a confirmation of a host of stereotypes about poor, ignorant, urban people; loud, angry black women; and shiftless black men. The cast is discussed in the blogosphere using racialized terms, including, frequently, "ghetto." By contrast, the Beverly Hills, Orange County, New York, and New Jersey wives are not seen as representative of white culture or white womanhood. They are not discussed using racialized terms. And few white people are spending time being embarrassed by their hijinks.

The question is: Who is most to blame for the images of black women we see? In the case of the *Real Housewives* franchise, it is series creator and Bravo executive Andy

Cohen, who selects the casts and guides storylines through editing and behind-the-scenes maneuvering. But modern purveyors of respectability politics have concerned themselves with black women like *Real Housewives of Atlanta* star NeNe Leakes. Loud, aggressive, and crass, Leakes is often charged with setting black women back through her behavior. For instance, earlier this year, in an interview with HelloBeautiful.com, actor Brian White *(Stomp the Yard)* derided Leakes while calling her presence on television an accurate depiction of reality, and urged the black community to do better by saying, "You can't call it a stereotype if it's the majority."

Engaging with respectability politics is not just arbitrary policing. In the case of black women, it is rooted in the realities of racism and the specific way it intersects with sexism and class. When members of the community react to a black actress in a highly sexualized role, they can be pushing back at the destructive notion of black woman as rump-shaker, as belly warmer, as unrapeable object of pleasure. They may be anticipating the fallout from one more salacious black female character—another brick in a wall of sexual stereotype that has dogged American women of African descent for centuries. When we rage at the prevalence of NeNe Leakes–type portrayals, we do so knowing black women carry that neck-rolling stereotype on their backs into every interview for a potential new job and every interaction with authority.

Representation matters. It changes minds and cements biases. Individual black women are more likely to be viewed as representatives of their race by the majority culture. Black women and girls do suffer from seeing limited and/or relentlessly negative reflections of themselves in the media. Those limited images do reinforce stereotypes about black women and often prevent people from recognizing their humanity. And those stereotypes do burden black women in their real, everyday lives.

What can we do about that?

Policing the behavior of black women is not the answer. If it is wrong for a 30 contemporary black actress to portray a maid, what message are we sending to black women who do domestic work? If it is wrong to be shown having sex with white men, what does that say about black women in interracial relationships with white men? If Erykah Badu is a whore for having children out of wedlock, what does that say about all black single mothers? Indeed, since more than half of births to all women under 30 occur outside of marriage (regardless of race), what does it say about women as a whole?

The goal of respectability politics may be noble, but the execution is flawed, damaging, and ineffective. By indulging in respectability politics, we acquiesce to the racially biased idea that the actions of individual black people are representative of the whole. We add to the pre-existing burdens of racism and sexism. And we fail to solve our problem, because we move the responsibility for eradicating race and gender biases from the powerful institutions and systems that perpetrate them to those oppressed by them. It is easier to try to control the oppressed than challenge the oppressor, but it is rarely a humane or useful approach.

Jackson adds, "I worry about putting all our eggs in the basket of media representation. We're relying on institutions that historically have been run by nonblack and nonfemale entities—institutions that are invested in regurgitating old stereotypes and tired perspectives."

Rather than critiquing the individual choices of black actresses, Jackson proposes an alternative. "There are countless firsthand narratives by black women. We need to be critiquing Hollywood for not adapting more work about black women by black women. If Hollywood and the black community were willing to get behind films like *Pariah*"—a 2011 independent film, written and directed by Dee Rees, about a Brooklyn teen dealing with friendship, family, and sexual identity—"we wouldn't be having this conversation. [Hollywood] may still make *The Help*, but it wouldn't be such a big problem."

Marginalized people might also lead the way in rejecting the essentialist notion of respectability that has provided a foundation for our own misery. Black women have been on the front lines of many a revolution. A battle that opens the door for all people—domestic workers and duchesses, the chaste and the promiscuous, the conventional and the daring—to be seen as valuable, to be seen as respectable, is a fight well worth having.

QUESTIONS FOR DISCUSSION AND WRITING

1. Harris's article begins by recounting an interview with actresses Viola Davis and Octavia Spencer in which the host claims he'd like for them to win the Oscars for their performances "but I'm ambivalent about what you're winning for" (paragraph 1). By this, he is referring to their portrayals of maids in the movie *The Help*, which is set in the South before segregation laws were struck down. In your opinion, should actors from minority groups accept only roles that display respectable characters? If you've seen the movie (or read the novel), do you agree with the characterization that the maids are not respectable characters? Why or why not?

2. Harris states that respectability politics "work to counter negative views of blackness by aggressively adopting the manners and morality that the dominant culture deems 'respectable'" (paragraph 7). What is the attraction of respectability politics, especially for those who have been discriminated against for generations? What are the inherent problems in respectability politics? Cite specific examples from life that you have seen or experienced yourself. Do you agree with Harris that, ultimately, respectability politics is actually destructive? Why or why not?

3. Harris notes that during the era of civil rights protests, activists wore "their Sunday best" (paragraph 10). If wearing nice clothing was part of an attempt to convince those in the dominant culture that their stereotypes about blacks were wrong, should the argument then be made that this was a mistake? Why or why not? What about other forms of assimilation? What advantages are there to adopting the styles, values, habits, and ethics of the dominant culture? What are the disadvantages?

4. In terms of current pop culture figures, Harris points to NeNe Leakes, a woman who appears on *The Real Housewives of Atlanta*. Physically large and

intimidating, Leakes is also described as "loud, aggressive, and crass" (paragraph 26). In other words, she fulfills some negative stereotypes the dominant culture has about black women. Harris points out that the prominence of a person like Leakes can follow other black women, as she says, "into every interview for a potential new job and every interaction with authority" (paragraph 27). Misbehavior by white women on shows like *The Real Housewives of Beverly Hills* is not viewed as reflecting upon the entire race. In your experience and opinion, how susceptible are people to embracing negative portrayals of minority women as seen in popular culture? Are there ways to combat that?

5. Ultimately, Harris appears to move toward a position of accepting virtually all behavior. As she states, "open the door to all people" (paragraph 34) so that all are seen as respectable. However, does this lead to an empty relativism, in which all things are good—and thus nothing is wrong? If everything (and everyone) is respectable, what is the value of respectability? Does such an approach lead to a world in which people must refrain from making judgments about quality and value? Is that good or bad? Why or why not?

GLORIA ANZALDÚA

From *Beyond Traditional Notions of Identity*

Gloria Anzaldúa, among the first openly lesbian Chicana authors, was born in 1942 in southwest Texas, a borderland between the United States and Mexico that she considers "una herida abierta," an open wound, where "the Third World grates against the First and bleeds." The daughter of a sharecropper and a field worker, she labored in the fields weekends and summers throughout high school and college, before graduating with a bachelor's degree from Pan American University in 1969. She earned a master's degree in English and education from the University of Texas in Austin (1972) and a doctorate from the University of California at Santa Cruz. Her work, such as This Bridge Called My Back: Writings by Radical Women of Color *(co-edited with Cherríe Moraga, 1981) and* Borderlands/La Frontera, The New Mestiza *(1987), powerfully addresses—in two English and six Spanish dialects—issues of poverty, racism, and gender. Anzaldúa died in 2004. "Beyond Traditional Notions of Identity," revisiting* This Bridge Called My Back *after two decades, was published in the* Chronicle of Higher Education *October 11, 2002.*

More than two decades ago, Cherríe Moraga and I edited a multigenre collection giving voice to radical women of color, *This Bridge Called My Back: Writings by Radical Women of Color*. Every generation that reads *This Bridge Called My Back* rewrites it. Like the trestle bridge, and other things that have reached their zenith, it will decline unless we attach it to new growth or append new growth to it. In a new collection of writings and art, *this bridge we call home: radical visions for transformation*, AnaLouise Keating and I, together with our contributors, attempt to continue the dialogue of the past 21 years, rethink the old ideas, and germinate new theories. We move from focusing on what has been done to us (victimhood) to a more extensive level of agency, one that questions what we're doing to each other, to those in distant countries, and to the earth's environment.

Twenty-one years ago we struggled with the recognition of difference within the context of commonality. Today we grapple with the recognition of commonality within the context of difference. While *This Bridge Called My Back* displaced whiteness, *this bridge we call home* carries that displacement further. It questions the terms *white* and *women of color* by showing that whiteness may not be applied to all whites, because some possess women-of-color consciousness, just as some women of color bear white consciousness. We intend to change notions of identity, viewing it as part of a more complex system covering a larger terrain, and demonstrating that the politics of exclusion based on traditional categories diminishes our humanness.

Today categories of race and gender are more permeable and flexible than they were for those of us growing up before the 1980s. Today we need to move beyond separate and easy identifications, creating bridges that cross race and other classifications among different groups via intergenerational dialogue. Rather than legislating and restricting racial identities, we hope to make them more pliant.

We must learn to incorporate additional underrepresented voices; we must attempt to break the impasse between women of color and other groups. By including women and men of different "races," nationalities, classes, sexualities, genders, and ages in our discussions, we complicate the debates within feminist theory both inside and outside the academy and inside and outside the United States.

Our goal is not to use differences to separate us from others, but neither is it   5
to gloss over those differences. Many of us identify with groups and social positions not limited to our ethnic, racial, religious, class, gender, and national classifications. Though most people self-define by what they exclude, we define who we are by what we include—what I call the new tribalism. I fear that many *mujeres de color* will not want whites or men to join the dialogue. We risk the displeasure of those women. There are no safe spaces. "Home" can be unsafe and dangerous because it bears the likelihood of intimacy and thus thinner boundaries.

QUESTIONS FOR DISCUSSION AND WRITING

1. Anzaldúa explains that two decades earlier her work had "struggled with the recognition of difference within the context of commonality" but that now "we grapple with the recognition of commonality within the context of difference" (paragraph 2). Explain how this perspective applies to Eric Liu's "Notes of a Native Speaker" (p. 100), Sherman Alexie's "What Sacagawea Means to Me" (p. 106), and Richard Rodriguez's "Aria" (p. 211).

2. What does Anzaldúa mean by "Today categories of race and gender are more permeable and flexible than they were for those of us growing up before the 1980s" (paragraph 3)?

3. "Today," says Anzaldúa, "we need to . . . [create] bridges that cross race and other classifications among different groups via intergenerational dialogue" (paragraph 3). With a partner, preferably one of a racial or ethnic group different from yours and possibly of another generation, write an essay expanding on this idea.

BOBBIE ANN MASON

Being Country

Born (1940) in Mayfield, Kentucky, Bobbie Ann Mason grew up on a dairy farm, and in Clear Springs: A Memoir *(1999), she describes her family's "independence, stability, authenticity" along with their "crippling social isolation." She earned a bachelor's degree at the University of Kentucky (1962), a master's at the State University of New York at Binghamton (1966), and a doctorate at the University of Connecticut (1972). She contributes regularly to* Mother Jones, *the* Atlantic Monthly, *and the* New Yorker. *Her novel* In Country *(1984) was made into a film in 1989. Other works include* Shiloh and Other Stories *(1983) and* Feather Crowns *(1994). Her most recent novel is* The Girl in the Blue Beret *(2011). Her themes are often the encroachment of modern life—television, fast food, shopping malls, the Vietnam War—into traditional rural life; her characters, farmers and working-class people, try to cope with change and balance their individual needs with those of their families.*

Mason's writing style, unsentimental and spare, echoes the language of rural western Kentuckians. She uses names—places, roads, brand names, popular musicians, and TV characters—to portend changes to rural life, changes that have already become commonplace elsewhere. In "Being Country" from Clear Springs, *Mason uses physical images from her youth, the routines and rhythms of farm life, and a constant concern for food—home-grown, home-cooked food—to illustrate rural experience.*

One day Mama and Granny were shelling beans and talking about the proper method of drying apples. I was nearly eleven and still entirely absorbed with the March girls in *Little Women*. Drying apples was not in my dreams. Beth's death was weighing darkly on me at that moment, and I threw a little tantrum—what Mama called a hissy fit.

"Can't y'all talk about anything but food?" I screamed.

There was a shocked silence. "Well, what else is there?" Granny asked.

Granny didn't question a woman's duties, but I did. I didn't want to be hulling beans in a hot kitchen when I was fifty years old. I wanted to *be* somebody, maybe an airline stewardess. Also, I had been listening to the radio. I had notions.

Our lives were haunted by the fear of crop failure. We ate as if we didn't know   5 where our next meal might come from. All my life I have had a recurrent food dream: I face a buffet or cafeteria line, laden with beautiful foods. I spend the entire dream choosing the foods I want. My anticipation is deliciously agonizing. I always wake up just as I've made my selections but before I get to eat.

Working with food was fraught with anxiety and desperation. In truth, no one in memory had missed a meal—except Peyton Washam on the banks of Panther Creek wistfully regarding his seed corn. But the rumble of poor Peyton's belly must have survived to trouble our dreams. We were at the mercy of nature, and it wasn't to be trusted. My mother watched the skies at evening for a portent of the morrow. A cloud that went over and then turned around and came back was an especially bad sign. Our livelihood—even our lives—depended on forces outside our control.

I think this dependence on nature was at the core of my rebellion. I hated the constant sense of helplessness before vast forces, the continuous threat of failure. Farmers didn't take initiative, I began to see; they reacted to whatever presented itself. I especially hated women's part in the dependence.

My mother allowed me to get spoiled. She never even tried to teach me to cook. "You didn't want to learn," she says now. "You were a lady of leisure, and you didn't want to help. You had your nose in a book."

I believed progress meant freedom from the field and the range. That meant moving to town, I thought.

Because we lived on the edge of Mayfield, I was acutely conscious of being   10 country. I felt inferior to people in town because we grew our food and made our clothes, while they bought whatever they needed. Although we were self-sufficient and resourceful and held clear title to our land, we lived in a state of psychological poverty. As I grew older, this acute sense of separation from town affected me more deeply. I began to sense that the fine life in town—celebrated in magazines, on radio, in movies—was denied us. Of course we weren't poor at all. Poor people had too many kids, and they weren't landowners; they rented decrepit little houses with plank floors and trash in the yard. "Poor people are wormy and eat wild onions," Mama said. We weren't poor, but we were country.

We had three wardrobes—everyday clothes, school clothes, and Sunday clothes. We didn't wear our school clothes at home, but we could wear them to town. When we got home from church, we had to change back into everyday clothes before we ate Mama's big Sunday dinner.

"Don't eat in your good clothes!" Mama always cried. "You'll spill something on them."

Mama always preferred outdoor life, but she was a natural cook. At harvest time, after she'd come in from the garden and put out a wash, she would whip out a noontime dinner for the men in the field—my father and grandfather and maybe some neighbors and a couple of hired hands: fried chicken with milk gravy, ham, mashed potatoes, lima beans, field peas, corn, slaw, sliced tomatoes, fried apples, biscuits, and peach pie. This was not considered a banquet, only plain hearty food, fuel for work. All the ingredients except the flour, sugar, and salt came from our farm—the chickens, the hogs, the milk and butter, the Irish potatoes, the beans, peas, corn, cabbage, apples, peaches. Nothing was processed, except by Mama. She was always butchering and plucking and planting and hoeing and shredding and slicing and creaming (scraping cobs for the creamed corn) and pressure-cooking and canning and freezing and thawing and mixing and shaping and baking and frying.

We would eat our pie right on the same plate as our turnip greens so as not to mess up another dish. The peach cobbler oozed all over the turnip-green juice and the pork grease. "It all goes to the same place," Mama said. It was boarding-house reach, no "Pass the peas, please." Conversation detracted from the sensuous pleasure of filling yourself. A meal required meat and vegetables and dessert. The beverages were milk and iced tea ("ice-tea"). We never used napkins or ate tossed salad. Our salads were Jell-O and slaw. We ate "poke salet" and wilted lettuce. Mama picked tender, young pokeweed in the woods in the spring, before it turned poison, and cooked it a good long time to get the bitterness out. We liked it with vinegar and minced boiled eggs. Wilted lettuce was tender new lettuce, shredded, with sliced radishes and green onions, and blasted with hot bacon grease to blanch the rawness. "Too many fresh vegetables in summer gives people the scours," Daddy said.

Food was better in town, we thought. It wasn't plain and everyday. The centers 15 of pleasure were there—the hamburger and barbecue places, the movie shows, all the places to buy things. Woolworth's, with the pneumatic tubes overhead rushing money along a metallic mole tunnel up to a balcony; Lochridge & Ridgway, with an engraved sign on the third-story cornice: STOVES, APPLIANCES, PLOWS. On the mezzanine at that store, I bought my first phonograph records, brittle 78s of big-band music—Woody Herman and Glenn Miller, and Glen Gray and his Casa Loma Orchestra playing "No Name Jive." A circuit of the courthouse square took you past the grand furniture stores, the two dime stores, the shoe stores, the men's stores, the ladies' stores, the banks, the drugstores. You'd walk past the poolroom and an exhaust fan would blow the intoxicating smell of hamburgers in your face. Before she bought a freezer, Mama stored meat in a rented food locker in town, near the ice company. She stored the butchered calf there, and she fetched hunks of him each week to fry. But hamburgers in town were better. They were greasier, and they came in waxed-paper packages.

At the corner drugstore, on the square, Mama and Janice and I sat at filigreed wrought-iron tables on a black-and-white mosaic tile floor, eating peppermint ice cream. It was very cold in there, under the ceiling fans. The ice cream was served elegantly, in paper cones sunk into black plastic holders. We were uptown.

The A&P grocery, a block away, reeked of the rich aroma of ground coffee. Daddy couldn't stand the smell of coffee, but Mama loved it. Daddy retched and scoffed in his exaggerated fashion. "I can't stand that smell!" Granny perked coffee, and Granddaddy told me it would turn a child black. I hated coffee. I wouldn't touch it till I was thirty. We savored store-bought food—coconuts, pineapples, and Vienna sausages and potted meat in little cans that opened with keys. We rarely went to the uptown A&P. We usually traded at a small mom-and-pop grocery, where the proprietors slapped the hands of black children who touched the candy case. I wondered if they were black from coffee.

QUESTIONS FOR DISCUSSION AND WRITING

1. Mason says she "wanted to be somebody" (paragraph 4), particularly someone who is not preoccupied with food. Judging by the essay, to what extent does she succeed? What passages support your view?

2. Although town food is touted as more sophisticated and desirable than farm food, is Mason working a subtle irony in the juxtaposition? Homemade "gravy, ham, mashed potatoes" were ordinary, but town hamburgers "were better. They were greasier, and they came in waxed-paper packages" (paragraph 15). If there is an irony here, what is it, and how might Mason have intended for it to work?

3. Mason uses lists to describe Mama's work with food. How do these lists affect you as a reader? What difference would it make if Mason had chosen to break them up into shorter sentences?

4. Compare and contrast Mason's lists with the list that opens Eric Liu's "Notes of a Native Speaker" (p. 100). Write an essay that includes a description of some activity with which you are very familiar, using lists to convey the movements and sensations—sight, sound, smell, touch, taste—that accompany the activity. See if you can make your reader experience the same things you experience.

5. In your upbringing, did you ever yearn, as Mason did, for fundamentally different surroundings? For example, did you ever wish you could live a different sort of life? Explain why you were attracted to a different place or different people—or even different foods. If you eventually got to experience these things, describe what the experience was like and discuss whether it met your expectations.

CHAPTER 6

Relationships and Life Choices: How Should We Be with Ourselves, Others, and the World?

BRIAN DOYLE

Joyas Voladoras

Brian Doyle, editor of Portland Magazine *(University of Portland, in Oregon) has published nine collections of essays, including* Two Voices: A Father and Son Discuss Family and Faith, *coauthored with his father, Jim Doyle (1996);* Credo *(1999);* Saints Passionate & Peculiar *(2002); and* Leaping: Revelations and Epiphanies *(2003). Doyle's essays have appeared in the* American Scholar, *the* Atlantic Monthly, *and* Harper's. *His award-winning work has been included in the* Best American Essays *anthologies of 1998, 1999, 2003, and 2009. His first novel,* Mink River, *was published in 2010, and his second,* Cat's Foot, *in 2012. "Joyas Voladoras," originally published in the* American Scholar *(2004), represents Doyle at his characteristic best: short (six paragraphs), ranging from earth to heaven and back again through precise, evocative details that get at the heart of the matter—in this case, the human heart and its endurance through the experiences, common yet profound, that connect all creatures small and great.*

Consider the hummingbird for a long moment. A hummingbird's heart beats ten times a second. A hummingbird's heart is the size of a pencil eraser. A hummingbird's heart is a lot of the hummingbird. *Joyas voladoras*, flying jewels, the first white explorers in the Americas called them, and the white men had never seen such creatures, for hummingbirds came into the world only in the Americas, nowhere else in the universe, more than three hundred species of them whirring and zooming and nectaring in hummer time zones nine times removed from ours, their hearts hammering faster than we could clearly hear if we pressed our elephantine ears to their infinitesimal chests.

Each one visits a thousand flowers a day. They can dive at sixty miles an hour. They can fly backwards. They can fly more than five hundred miles without pausing to rest. But when they rest they come close to death: on frigid nights, or when they are starving, they retreat into torpor, their metabolic rate slowing to a fifteenth of their normal sleep rate, their hearts sludging nearly to a halt, barely beating, and if they are not soon warmed, if they do not soon find that which is sweet, their hearts grow cold, and they cease to be. Consider for a moment those hummingbirds who did not open their eyes again today, this very day, in the Americas: bearded hel-metcrests and booted racket-tails, violet-tailed sylphs and violet-capped wood-nymphs, crimson topazes and purple-crowned fairies, red-tailed comets and amethyst woodstars, rainbow-bearded thornbills and glittering-bellied emeralds, velvet-purple coronets and golden-bellied star-frontlets, fiery-tailed awlbills and Andean hillstars, spatuletails and pufflegs, each the most amazing thing you have never seen, each thunderous wild heart the size of an infant's fingernail, each mad heart silent, a brilliant music stilled.

Hummingbirds, like all flying birds but more so, have incredible enormous immense ferocious metabolisms. To drive those metabolisms they have racecar hearts that eat oxygen at an eye-popping rate. Their hearts are built of thinner, leaner fibers than ours. Their arteries are stiffer and more taut. They have more mitochondria in their heart muscles—anything to gulp more oxygen. Their hearts are stripped to the skin for the war against gravity and inertia, the mad search for food, the insane idea of flight. The price of their ambition is a life closer to death; they suffer more heart attacks and aneurysms and ruptures than any other living creature. It's expensive to fly. You burn out. You fry the machine. You melt the engine. Every creature on earth has approximately two billion heartbeats to spend in a lifetime. You can spend them slowly, like a tortoise, and live to be two hundred years old, or you can spend them fast, like a hummingbird, and live to be two years old.

The biggest heart in the world is inside the blue whale. It weighs more than seven tons. It's as big as a room. It *is* a room, with four chambers. A child could walk around in it, head high, bending only to step through the valves. The valves are as big as the swinging doors in a saloon. This house of a heart drives a creature a hundred feet long. When this creature is born it is twenty feet long and weighs four tons. It is way bigger than your car. It drinks a hundred gallons of milk from its mama every day and gains two hundred pounds a day, and when it is seven or eight years old it endures an unimaginable puberty and then it essentially disappears from human ken, for next to nothing is known of the mating habits, travel patterns, diet, social life, language, social structure, diseases, spirituality, wars, stories, despairs, and arts of the blue whale. There are perhaps ten thousand blue whales in the world, living in every ocean on earth, and of the largest mammal who ever lived we know nearly nothing. But we know this: the animals with the largest hearts in the world generally travel in pairs, and their penetrating moaning cries, their piercing yearning tongue, can be heard underwater for miles and miles.

Mammals and birds have hearts with four chambers. Reptiles and turtles   5 have hearts with three chambers. Fish have hearts with two chambers. Insects and mollusks have hearts with one chamber. Worms have hearts with one chamber, although they may have as many as eleven single-chambered hearts. Unicellular bacteria have no hearts at all; but even they have fluid eternally in motion, washing from one side of the cell to the other, swirling and whirling. No living being is without interior liquid motion. We all churn inside.

So much held in a heart in a lifetime. So much held in a heart in a day, an hour, a moment. We are utterly open with no one, in the end—not mother and father, not wife or husband, not lover, not child, not friend. We open windows to each but we live alone in the house of the heart. Perhaps we must. Perhaps we could not bear to be so naked, for fear of a constantly harrowed heart. When young we think there will come one person who will savor and sustain us always; when we are older we know this is the dream of a child, that all hearts finally are bruised and scarred, scored and torn, repaired by time and will, patched by force of character, yet fragile and rickety forevermore, no matter how ferocious the defense and how many bricks you bring to the wall. You can brick up your heart as stout and tight and hard and cold and impregnable as you possibly can and down it comes in an instant, felled by a woman's second glance, a child's apple breath, the shatter of glass in the road, the words "I have something to tell you," a cat with a broken spine dragging itself into the forest to die, the brush of your mother's papery ancient hand in a thicket of your hair, the memory of your father's voice early in the morning echoing from the kitchen where he is making pancakes for his children.

QUESTIONS FOR DISCUSSION AND WRITING

1. The essay's title, "Joyas Voladoras," means "flying jewels," the name the first explorers of the Americas gave to hummingbirds, says Doyle (paragraph 1). What characteristics of hummingbirds does each of the first three paragraphs focus on?

2. Doyle connects the two halves of his essay with "Every creature on earth has approximately two billion heartbeats to spend in a lifetime" (paragraph 3). What themes are common to both halves of the essay? What features unify hummingbirds, whales, humans?

3. Explain the significance of the last two sentences in paragraph 5, "No living being is without interior liquid motion. We all churn inside," in relation to the final paragraph. What sorts of "churning" does paragraph 6 identify?

4. Doyle writes that "all hearts finally are bruised and scarred, scored and torn, repaired by time and will, patched by force of character, yet fragile and rickety forevermore" (paragraph 6). Based on your own understanding of family relationships and life choices, is Doyle right? Explain.

5. After discussion with a classmate, good friend, or relative, write an essay in which you address Doyle's comment: "We are utterly open with no one, in the end—not mother and father, not wife or husband, not lover, not child, not friend. We open windows to each other but we live alone in the house of the heart" (p. 142).

JONATHAN FRANZEN

Liking Is for Cowards. Go for What Hurts.

Having appeared on the cover of Time *magazine with the headline "Great American Novelist," Jonathan Franzen (b. 1957) is no hidden literary treasure. His novel* The Corrections *was picked by Oprah Winfrey for her book club, which quickly became controversial when Franzen expressed reservations about the pick. He was worried that men would be put off by the Oprah seal of approval; he wanted to reach a male readership that he felt was in steady decline. Ironically, after Oprah rescinded the pick, news of the controversy actually helped the book's sales. In 2010, Franzen's fourth novel,* Freedom, *was again picked by Oprah for her book club. This time Franzen did appear on the Oprah Winfrey show, without incident, to talk both about* Freedom *and about the controversy surrounding* The Corrections. *Over the course of his career, Franzen has accumulated many honors. Among them his selection as a Fulbright Scholar when he was still a college student at Swarthmore, a Guggenheim Fellowship in 1996, the National Book Award in 2001 for* The Corrections, *and his election to the American Academy of Arts and Letters in 2010.*

In this essay, Franzen goes after one of his favorite targets: technology. Franzen is interested in how technology actually works against our own humanity. Beginning with an analogy comparing his love for his BlackBerry (a once-popular smartphone) with romantic love, Franzen examines the promises of technology, and how they echo the language used for our erotic relationships. Franzen encourages the reader to examine the questions of what is truly important and what is not, and explores the threat that technology— especially what he terms "techno-consumerism"—poses to our own humanity.

A couple of weeks ago, I replaced my three-year-old BlackBerry Pearl with a much more powerful BlackBerry Bold. Needless to say, I was impressed with how far the technology had advanced in three years. Even when I didn't have anybody to call or text or e-mail, I wanted to keep fondling my new Bold and experiencing the marvelous clarity of its screen, the silky action of its track pad, the shocking speed of its responses, the beguiling elegance of its graphics.

I was, in short, infatuated with my new device. I'd been similarly infatuated with my old device, of course; but over the years the bloom had faded from our relationship. I'd developed trust issues with my Pearl, accountability issues, compatibility issues, and even, toward the end, some doubts about my Pearl's very sanity, until I'd finally had to admit to myself that I'd outgrown the relationship.

Do I need to point out that—absent some wild, anthropomorphizing projection in which my old BlackBerry felt sad about the waning of my love for it—our relationship was entirely one-sided? Let me point it out anyway.

Let me further point out how ubiquitously the word "sexy" is used to describe late-model gadgets; and how the extremely cool things that we can do now with these gadgets—like impelling them to action with voice commands, or doing that spreading-the-fingers iPhone thing that makes images get bigger—would have looked, to people a hundred years ago, like a magician's incantations, a magician's hand gestures; and how, when we want to describe an erotic relationship that's working perfectly, we speak, indeed, of magic.

Let me toss out the idea that, as our markets discover and respond to what 5 consumers most want, our technology has become extremely adept at creating products that correspond to our fantasy ideal of an erotic relationship, in which the beloved object asks for nothing and gives everything, instantly, and makes us feel all powerful, and doesn't throw terrible scenes when it's replaced by an even sexier object and is consigned to a drawer.

To speak more generally, the ultimate goal of technology, the telos of techne, is to replace a natural world that's indifferent to our wishes—a world of hurricanes and hardships and breakable hearts, a world of resistance—with a world so responsive to our wishes as to be, effectively, a mere extension of the self.

Let me suggest, finally, that the world of techno-consumerism is therefore troubled by real love, and that it has no choice but to trouble love in turn.

Its first line of defense is to commodify its enemy. You can all supply your own favorite, most nauseating examples of the commodification of love. Mine include the wedding industry, TV ads that feature cute young children or the giving of automobiles as Christmas presents, and the particularly grotesque equation of diamond jewelry with everlasting devotion. The message, in each case, is that if you love somebody you should buy stuff.

A related phenomenon is the transformation, courtesy of Facebook, of the verb "to like" from a state of mind to an action that you perform with your computer mouse, from a feeling to an assertion of consumer choice. And liking, in general, is commercial culture's substitute for loving. The striking thing about all consumer products—and none more so than electronic devices and applications—is that they're designed to be immensely likable. This is, in fact, the definition of a consumer product, in contrast to the product that is simply itself and whose makers aren't fixated on your liking it. (I'm thinking here of jet engines, laboratory equipment, serious art and literature.)

But if you consider this in human terms, and you imagine a person defined 10 by a desperation to be liked, what do you see? You see a person without integrity, without a center. In more pathological cases, you see a narcissist—a person who can't tolerate the tarnishing of his or her self-image that not being liked represents, and who therefore either withdraws from human contact or goes to extreme, integrity-sacrificing lengths to be likable.

If you dedicate your existence to being likable, however, and if you adopt whatever cool persona is necessary to make it happen, it suggests that you've despaired of being loved for who you really are. And if you succeed in manipulating other people into liking you, it will be hard not to feel, at some level, contempt for those people, because they've fallen for your shtick. You may find yourself becoming depressed, or alcoholic, or, if you're Donald Trump, running for president (and then quitting).

Consumer technology products would never do anything this unattractive, because they aren't people. They are, however, great allies and enablers of narcissism. Alongside their built-in eagerness to be liked is a built-in eagerness to reflect well on us. Our lives look a lot more interesting when they're filtered through the sexy Facebook interface. We star in our own movies, we photograph ourselves incessantly, we click the mouse and a machine confirms our sense of mastery.

And, since our technology is really just an extension of ourselves, we don't have to have contempt for its manipulability in the way we might with actual people. It's all one big endless loop. We like the mirror and the mirror likes us. To friend a person is merely to include the person in our private hall of flattering mirrors.

I may be overstating the case, a little bit. Very probably, you're sick to death of hearing social media disrespected by cranky fifty-one-year-olds. My aim here is mainly to set up a contrast between the narcissistic tendencies of technology and the problem of actual love. My friend Alice Sebold likes to talk about "getting down in the pit and loving somebody." She has in mind the dirt that love inevitably splatters on the mirror of our self-regard.

The simple fact of the matter is that trying to be perfectly likable is incompat-   15
ible with loving relationships. Sooner or later, for example, you're going to find yourself in a hideous, screaming fight, and you'll hear coming out of your mouth things that you yourself don't like at all, things that shatter your self-image as a fair, kind, cool, attractive, in-control, funny, likable person. Something realer than lik-ability has come out in you, and suddenly you're having an actual life.

Suddenly there's a real choice to be made, not a fake consumer choice between a BlackBerry and an iPhone, but a question: Do I love this person? And, for the other person, does this person love me?

There is no such thing as a person whose real self you like every particle of. This is why a world of liking is ultimately a lie. But there is such a thing as a person whose real self you love every particle of. And this is why love is such an existential threat to the techno-consumerist order: It exposes the lie.

This is not to say that love is only about fighting. Love is about bottomless empathy, born out of the heart's revelation that another person is every bit as real as you are. And this is why love, as I understand it, is always specific. Trying to love all of humanity may be a worthy endeavor, but, in a funny way, it keeps the focus on the self, on the self's own moral or spiritual well-being. Whereas, to love a specific person, and to identify with his or her struggles and joys as if they were your own, you have to surrender some of your self.

The big risk here, of course, is rejection. We can all handle being disliked now and then, because there's such an infinitely big pool of potential likers. But to expose your whole self, not just the likable surface, and to have it rejected, can be catastrophically painful. The prospect of pain generally, the pain of loss, of breakup, of death, is what makes it so tempting to avoid love and stay safely in the world of liking.

And yet pain hurts but it doesn't kill. When you consider the alternative—an   20
anesthetized dream of self-sufficiency, abetted by technology—pain emerges as the natural product and natural indicator of being alive in a resistant world. To go through a life painlessly is to have not lived. Even just to say to yourself, "Oh, I'll get to that love and pain stuff later, maybe in my thirties" is to consign yourself to ten years of merely taking up space on the planet and burning up its resources. Of being (and I mean this in the most damning sense of the word) a consumer.

When I was in college, and for many years after, I liked the natural world. Didn't love it, but definitely liked it. It can be very pretty, nature. And since I was looking for things to find wrong with the world, I naturally gravitated to environmentalism, because there were certainly plenty of things wrong with the environment. And the more I looked at what was wrong—an exploding world population, exploding levels of resource consumption, rising global tempera-tures, the trashing of the oceans, the logging of our last old-growth forests—the angrier I became.

Finally, in the mid-1990s, I made a conscious decision to stop worrying about the environment. There was nothing meaningful that I personally could do to save the planet, and I wanted to get on with devoting myself to the things I loved. I still tried to keep my carbon footprint small, but that was as far as I could go without falling back into rage and despair.

BUT then a funny thing happened to me. It's a long story, but basically I fell in love with birds. I did this not without significant resistance, because it's very uncool to be a birdwatcher, because anything that betrays real passion is by definition uncool. But little by little, in spite of myself, I developed this passion, and although one-half of a passion is obsession, the other half is love.

And so, yes, I kept a meticulous list of the birds I'd seen, and, yes, I went to inordinate lengths to see new species. But, no less important, whenever I looked at a bird, any bird, even a pigeon or a robin, I could feel my heart overflow with love. And love, as I've been trying to say today, is where our troubles begin.

Because now, not merely liking nature but loving a specific and vital part of it, 25 I had no choice but to start worrying about the environment again. The news on that front was no better than when I'd decided to quit worrying about it—was considerably worse, in fact—but now those threatened forests and wetlands and oceans weren't just pretty scenes for me to enjoy. They were the home of animals I loved.

And here's where a curious paradox emerged. My anger and pain and despair about the planet were only increased by my concern for wild birds, and yet, as I began to get involved in bird conservation and learned more about the many threats that birds face, it became easier, not harder, to live with my anger and despair and pain.

How does this happen? I think, for one thing, that my love of birds became a portal to an important, less self-centered part of myself that I'd never even known existed. Instead of continuing to drift forward through my life as a global citizen, liking and disliking and withholding my commitment for some later date, I was forced to confront a self that I had to either straight-up accept or flat-out reject.

Which is what love will do to a person. Because the fundamental fact about all of us is that we're alive for a while but will die before long. This fact is the real root cause of all our anger and pain and despair. And you can either run from this fact or, by way of love, you can embrace it.

When you stay in your room and rage or sneer or shrug your shoulders, as I did for many years, the world and its problems are impossibly daunting. But when you go out and put yourself in real relation to real people, or even just real animals, there's a very real danger that you might love some of them.

And who knows what might happen to you then?   30

QUESTIONS FOR DISCUSSION AND WRITING

1. Franzen begins the essay speaking about his Blackberry in the same language and tone one might use in regard to a romantic lover (paragraphs 1–4). Why? What is the point of anthropomorphizing a device, a mere gadget? Examine further his use of language and his invocation of the word "magic"

(paragraph 4)—a word used to describe the amazing abilities of today's technological devices and a word often used to describe a special and strong romantic attachment. Are we substituting one for the other? Or, in your opinion, is Franzen overdoing the comparison? Explain.

2. Franzen states in paragraph 6 that "the ultimate goal of technology, the telos of techne, is to replace a natural world that's indifferent to our wishes." What does he mean by this? Look up the words "telos" and "techne" in a dictionary if you're not already familiar with them. Also, what does Franzen mean when he describes the "natural world"?

3. Because technology like smartphones, laptops, and other consumer-oriented devices have no will of their own, Franzen argues that they essentially become much more likable than real humans, who do have a will. The threat is to the creation and sustenance of human relationships. Franzen points out that to love someone means to put one's own feelings at risk as well. Do you agree that today's technology is creating incentives to avoid meaningful human relationships? Why or why not?

4. Franzen in particular singles out Facebook as an example of how technology enables narcissism. After all, people can build their own profiles, post pictures and videos (perhaps only the flattering ones), and basically make themselves seem more in control of their own lives. As he says, "We like the mirror and the mirror likes us" (paragraph 13). Is Franzen exaggerating the problem, or does he have a valid point? Defend your answer with specific examples.

5. Franzen, perhaps surprisingly, takes the essay in a different direction toward its conclusion: He discusses his experiences with environmentalism. He argues that his first foray into environmentalism only wound up making him angry. He states in paragraph 22, "There was nothing meaningful that I personally could do to save the planet. . . ." So he turned away from environmentalism, only to return later when he developed a passion for birds. His point is that he needed something real—in this case, birds—to connect with the problems of the environment. How convincing do you find his point: that we need something real (animal or human) to move us to care and to love? How does that connect to his root fear, that technology is removing us from our humanity? Explain.

TERRY TEMPEST WILLIAMS

The Clan of One-Breasted Women

When the U.S. government decided to test atomic weapons in a "virtually uninhabited" section of Utah in the 1950s, environmentalist Terry Tempest Williams's family was among the "virtual uninhabitants," as she puts it. In one of the most troubling episodes in U.S. history, Williams (b. 1955) and other Utah residents were being exposed to fallout while the federal government assured them that they were safe; thousands died of radiation-related diseases. As she watched the women in her family die of cancer, and as the government refused to acknowledge the claims of the test victims, she came to realize that "tolerating blind obedience in the name of patriotism or religion ultimately takes our lives." Williams earned degrees in English (B.S., 1979) and environmental education (M.S., 1984) at the University of Utah. All of her books—including The Secret Language of Snow *(1984), a children's book;* Pieces of White Shell: A Journey to Navajo Land *(1984);* Leap *(2000); and* When Women Were Birds *(2012)—reflect her belief in the vital link among human beings, animals, and the earth. These themes prevail in her best-known work,* Refuge: An Unnatural History of Family and Place *(1992). In "The Clan of One-Breasted Women" (1991), the epilogue to* Refuge, *Williams tells the story of her family's history with cancer. Her analysis becomes an emotional and ethical protest against the federal government's routine denial that anyone was harmed by the radioactive fallout.*

I belong to a Clan of One-Breasted Women. My mother, my grandmothers, and six aunts have all had mastectomies. Seven are dead. The two who survive have just completed rounds of chemotherapy and radiation.

I've had my own problems: two biopsies for breast cancer and a small tumor between my ribs diagnosed as a "borderline malignancy."

This is my family history.

Most statistics tell us breast cancer is genetic, hereditary, with rising percentages attached to fatty diets, childlessness, or becoming pregnant after thirty. What they don't say is living in Utah may be the greatest hazard of all.

We are a Mormon family with roots in Utah since 1847. The "word of wisdom" 5
in my family aligned us with good foods—no coffee, no tea, tobacco, or alcohol. For the most part, our women were finished having their babies by the time they were thirty. And only one faced breast cancer prior to 1960. Traditionally, as a group of people, Mormons have a low rate of cancer.

Is our family a cultural anomaly? The truth is, we didn't think about it. Those who did, usually the men, simply said, "bad genes." The women's attitude was stoic. Cancer was part of life. On February 16, 1971, the eve of my mother's surgery, I accidentally picked up the telephone and overheard her ask my grandmother what she could expect.

"Diane, it is one of the most spiritual experiences you will ever encounter."

I quietly put down the receiver.

Two days later, my father took my brothers and me to the hospital to visit her. She met us in the lobby in a wheelchair. No bandages were visible. I'll never forget her radiance, the way she held herself in a purple velvet robe, and how she gathered us around her.

"Children, I am fine. I want you to know I felt the arms of God around me." 10

We believed her. My father cried. Our mother, his wife, was thirty-eight years old.

A little over a year after Mother's death, Dad and I were having dinner together. He had just returned from St. George, where the Tempest Company was completing the gas lines that would service southern Utah. He spoke of his love for the country, the sandstone landscape, bare-boned and beautiful. He had just finished hiking the Kolob trail in Zion National Park. We got caught up in reminiscing, recalling with fondness our walk up Angel's Landing on his fiftieth birthday and the years our family had vacationed there.

Over dessert, I shared a recurring dream of mine. I told my father that for years, as long as I could remember, I saw this flash of light in the night in the desert—that this image had so permeated my being that I could not venture south without seeing it again, on the horizon, illuminating buttes and mesas.

"You did see it," he said.

"Saw what?"   15

"The bomb. The cloud. We were driving home from Riverside, California. You were sitting on Diane's lap. She was pregnant. In fact, I remember the day, September 7, 1957. We had just gotten out of the Service. We were driving north, past Las Vegas. It was an hour or so before dawn, when this explosion went off. We not only heard it, but felt it. I thought the oil tanker in front of us had blown up. We pulled over and suddenly, rising from the desert floor, we saw it, clearly, this golden-stemmed cloud, the mushroom. The sky seemed to vibrate with an eerie pink glow. Within a few minutes, a light ash was raining on the car."

I stared at my father.

"I thought you knew that," he said. "It was a common occurrence in the fifties."

It was at this moment that I realized the deceit I had been living under. Children growing up in the American Southwest, drinking contaminated milk from contaminated cows, even from the contaminated breasts of their mothers, my mother—members, years later, of the Clan of One-Breasted Women.

It is a well-known story in the Desert West, "The Day We Bombed Utah," 20 or more accurately, the years we bombed Utah: aboveground atomic testing in Nevada took place from January 27, 1951, through July 11, 1962. Not only were the winds blowing north covering "low-use segments of the population" with fallout and leaving sheep dead in their tracks, but the climate was right. The United States of the 1950s was red, white, and blue. The Korean War was raging. McCarthyism was rampant. Ike was it, and the cold war was hot. If you were against nuclear testing, you were for a communist regime.

Much has been written about this "American nuclear tragedy." Public health was secondary to national security. The Atomic Energy Commissioner, Thomas Murray, said, "Gentlemen, we must not let anything interfere with this series of tests, nothing."

Again and again, the American public was told by its government, in spite of burns, blisters, and nausea, "It has been found that the tests may be conducted with adequate assurance of safety under conditions prevailing at the bombing reservations." Assuaging public fears was simply a matter of public relations. "Your best action," an Atomic Energy Commission booklet read, "is not to be worried about fallout." A news release typical of the times stated, "We find no basis for concluding that harm to any individual has resulted from radioactive fallout."

On August 30, 1979, during Jimmy Carter's presidency, a suit was filed, *Irene Allen* v. *The United States of America*. Mrs. Allen's case was the first on an alphabetical list of twenty-four test cases, representative of nearly twelve hundred plaintiffs seeking compensation from the United States government for cancers caused by nuclear testing in Nevada.

Irene Allen lived in Hurricane, Utah. She was the mother of five children and had been widowed twice. Her first husband, with their two oldest boys, had watched the tests from the roof of the local high school. He died of leukemia in 1956. Her second husband died of pancreatic cancer in 1978.

In a town meeting conducted by Utah Senator Orrin Hatch, shortly before the 25 suit was filed, Mrs. Allen said, "I am not blaming the government, I want you to know that, Senator Hatch. But I thought if my testimony could help in any way so this wouldn't happen again to any of the generations coming up after us . . . I am happy to be here this day to bear testimony of this."

God-fearing people. This is just one story in an anthology of thousands.

On May 10, 1984, Judge Bruce S. Jenkins handed down his opinion. Ten of the plaintiffs were awarded damages. It was the first time a federal court had determined that nuclear tests had been the cause of cancers. For the remaining fourteen test cases, the proof of causation was not sufficient. In spite of the split decision, it was considered a landmark ruling. It was not to remain so for long.

In April 1987, the Tenth Circuit Court of Appeals overturned Judge Jenkins's ruling on the ground that the United States was protected from suit by the legal doctrine of sovereign immunity, a centuries-old idea from England in the days of absolute monarchs.

In January 1988, the Supreme Court refused to review the Appeals Court decision. To our court system it does not matter whether the United States government was irresponsible, whether it lied to its citizens, or even that citizens died from the fallout of nuclear testing. What matters is that our government is immune: "The King can do no wrong."

In Mormon culture, authority is respected, obedience is revered, and inde- 30 pendent thinking is not. I was taught as a young girl not to "make waves" or "rock the boat."

"Just let it go," Mother would say. "You know how you feel, that's what counts."

For many years, I have done just that—listened, observed, and quietly formed my own opinions, in a culture that rarely asks questions because it has all the answers. But one by one, I have watched the women in my family die common, heroic deaths. We sat in waiting rooms hoping for good news, but always receiving the bad. I cared for them, bathed their scarred bodies, and kept their secrets. I watched beautiful women become bald as Cytoxan, cisplatin, and Adriamycin were injected into their veins. I held their foreheads as they vomited green-black bile, and I shot them with morphine when the pain became inhuman. In the end, I witnessed their last peaceful breaths, becoming a midwife to the rebirth of their souls.

The price of obedience has become too high.

The fear and inability to question authority that ultimately killed rural communities in Utah during atmospheric testing of atomic weapons is the same fear I saw in my mother's body. Sheep. Dead sheep. The evidence is buried.

I cannot prove that my mother, Diane Dixon Tempest, or my grandmothers, 35
Lettie Romney Dixon and Kathryn Blackett Tempest, along with my aunts developed cancer from nuclear fallout in Utah. But I can't prove they didn't.

My father's memory was correct. The September blast we drove through in
1957 was part of Operation Plumbbob, one of the most intensive series of bomb
tests to be initiated. The flash of light in the night in the desert, which I had always
thought was a dream, developed into a family nightmare. It took fourteen years,
from 1957 to 1971, for cancer to manifest in my mother—the same time, Howard
L. Andrews, an authority in radioactive fallout at the National Institutes of Health,
says radiation cancer requires to become evident. The more I learn about what it
means to be a "downwinder," the more questions I drown in.

What I do know, however, is that as a Mormon woman of the fifth generation
of Latter-day Saints, I must question everything, even if it means losing my faith,
even if it means becoming a member of a border tribe among my own people.
Tolerating blind obedience in the name of patriotism or religion ultimately takes
our lives.

When the Atomic Energy Commission described the country north of the
Nevada Test Site as "virtually uninhabited desert terrain," my family and the birds
at Great Salt Lake were some of the "virtual uninhabitants."

One night, I dreamed women from all over the world circled a blazing fire in the
desert. They spoke of change, how they hold the moon in their bellies and wax
and wane with its phases. They mocked the presumption of even-tempered beings
and made promises that they would never fear the witch inside themselves. The
women danced wildly as sparks broke away from the flames and entered the night
sky as stars.

And they sang a song given to them by Shoshone grandmothers: 40

Ah ne nah, nah	Consider the rabbits
nin nah nah—	How gently they walk on the earth—
ah ne nah, nah	Consider the rabbits
nin nah nah—	How gently they walk on the earth—
Nyaga mutzi	We remember them
oh ne nay—	We can walk gently also—
Nyaga mutzi	We remember them
oh ne nay—	We can walk gently also—

The women danced and drummed and sang for weeks, preparing themselves for
what was to come. They would reclaim the desert for the sake of their children, for
the sake of the land.

A few miles downwind from the fire circle, bombs were being tested. Rabbits
felt the tremors. Their soft leather pads on paws and feet recognized the shaking sands, while the roots of mesquite and sage were smoldering. Rocks were hot
from the inside out and dust devils hummed unnaturally. And each time there was
another nuclear test, ravens watched the desert heave. Stretch marks appeared. The
land was losing its muscle.

The women couldn't bear it any longer. They were mothers. They had suffered labor pains but always under the promise of birth. The red hot pains beneath the desert promised death only, as each bomb became a stillborn. A contract had been made and broken between human beings and the land. A new contract was being drawn by the women, who understood the fate of the earth as their own.

Under the cover of darkness, ten women slipped under a barbed-wire fence and entered the contaminated country. They were trespassing. They walked toward the town of Mercury, in moonlight, taking their cues from coyote, kit fox, antelope squirrel, and quail. They moved quietly and deliberately through the maze of Joshua trees. When a hint of daylight appeared they rested, drinking tea and sharing their rations of food. The women closed their eyes. The time had come to protest with the heart, that to deny one's genealogy with the earth was to commit treason against one's soul.

At dawn, the women draped themselves in mylar, wrapping long streamers of silver plastic around their arms to blow in the breeze. They wore clear masks that became the faces of humanity. And when they arrived at the edge of Mercury, they carried all the butterflies of a summer day in their wombs. They paused to allow their courage to settle.

The town that forbids pregnant women and children to enter because of radia- 45 tion risks was asleep. The women moved through the streets as winged messengers, twirling around each other in slow motion, peeking inside homes and watching the easy sleep of men and women. They were astonished by such stillness and periodically would utter a shrill note or low cry just to verify life.

The residents finally awoke to these strange apparitions. Some simply stared. Others called authorities, and in time, the women were apprehended by wary soldiers dressed in desert fatigues. They were taken to a white, square building on the other edge of Mercury. When asked who they were and why they were there, the women replied, "We are mothers and we have come to reclaim the desert for our children."

The soldiers arrested them. As the ten women were blindfolded and handcuffed, they began singing:

You can't forbid us everything
You can't forbid us to think—
You can't forbid our tears to flow
And you can't stop the songs that we sing.

The women continued to sing louder and louder, until they heard the voices of their sisters moving across the mesa:

Ah ne nah, nah
nin nah nah—
Ah ne nah, nah
nin nah nah—
Nyaga mutzi
oh ne nay—

Nyaga mutzi
oh ne nay—

"Call for reinforcements," one soldier said.

"We have," interrupted one woman, "we have—and you have no idea of our numbers."

I crossed the line at the Nevada Test Site and was arrested with nine other Utahns for trespassing on military lands. They are still conducting nuclear tests in the desert. Ours was an act of civil disobedience. But as I walked toward the town of Mercury, it was more than a gesture of peace. It was a gesture on behalf of the Clan of One-Breasted Women.

As one officer cinched the handcuffs around my wrists, another frisked my 50 body. She found a pen and a pad of paper tucked inside my left boot.

"And these?" she asked sternly.

"Weapons," I replied.

Our eyes met. I smiled. She pulled the leg of my trousers back over my boot.

"Step forward, please," she said as she took my arm.

We were booked under an afternoon sun and bused to Tonopah, Nevada. It was 55 a two-hour ride. This was familiar country. The Joshua trees standing their ground had been named by my ancestors, who believed they looked like prophets pointing west to the Promised Land. These were the same trees that bloomed each spring, flowers appearing like white flames in the Mojave. And I recalled a full moon in May, when Mother and I had walked among them, flushing out mourning doves and owls.

The bus stopped short of town. We were released.

The officials thought it was a cruel joke to leave us stranded in the desert with no way to get home. What they didn't realize was that we were home, soul-centered and strong, women who recognized the sweet smell of sage as fuel for our spirits.

QUESTIONS FOR DISCUSSION AND WRITING

1. Terry Tempest Williams's family is prominent in Utah; her father was a member of the Stake High Council of the regional Mormon Church. Why does Williams define her "family history" (paragraph 3) in terms of women with breast cancer rather than men of power?

2. "The Clan of One-Breasted Women" is the ten-page epilogue to Williams's book *Refuge*. How many sections is the epilogue divided into? Why is it important to notice the demarcation of these sections? What is the significance—structurally and thematically—of the two "dreams" she describes (paragraphs 13 and 39)?

3. As a little girl, Williams was taught by her Mormon culture "not to 'make waves.'" As an adult woman, especially as a conscientious writer, she changed her behavior pattern: "[A]s a Mormon woman of the fifth generation of Latter-day Saints, I must question everything . . ." (paragraph 37). What is the significance of this change to her intellectual and spiritual growth?

4. According to Williams, the Atomic Energy Commission, which is made up of mostly male members, declared the "desert terrain" to be "virtually uninhabited" (paragraph 38). What factors (socioeconomic, geographic, political, psychological, cultural) might prompt continued disregard for the inhabitants? How does the existence of new, heavily populated desert communities in Arizona and Nevada (not to mention Middle Eastern countries) affect your answer?

5. What are the differences, for Terry Tempest Williams, between writing as a form of advocacy and the act of civil disobedience she describes in "The Clan of One-Breasted Women"? Consider in your response Martin Luther King Jr.'s advocacy of a "direct-action campaign" in support of civil rights and the role his "Letter from Birmingham Jail" (p. 406) played in influencing protesters' behavior.

6. Using Terry Tempest Williams and Henry David Thoreau (p. 161) as examples, write an essay in which you argue for or against the precept that where we live determines what we live for. Or argue the converse, that what we live for determines where and how we live, to whom we belong, and indeed, who we are.

E. B. WHITE

Once More to the Lake

*E. B. (Elwyn Brooks) White (1899–1985) is beloved for his children's books—*Stuart Little *(1945),* Charlotte's Web *(1952), and* The Trumpet of the Swan *(1970)—and famous for his distinguished essays. He grew up in Mount Vernon, New York, a place of ponds and spacious yards and amateur musicales; and his family spent August at Belgrade Lake, Maine. In later years, White humorously reflected that his childhood lacked the deprivation and loneliness often thought to be essential to becoming a writer. After graduating from Cornell, where he edited the* Daily Sun, *in 1926 White joined the staff of the country's most sophisticated and politically astute magazine, the* New Yorker. *White wrote the "Talk of the Town" and "Notes and Comment" columns for thirty years. Between 1938 and 1943, he also wrote the "One Man's Meat" column for* Harper's. *The essays from these three columns were collected in* One Man's Meat *(1942) and* The Points of My Compass *(1962). In 1937 White helped his former English professor at Cornell, William Strunk Jr., to revise* The Elements of Style *(originally published in 1918). Now known as "Strunk and White," this classic handbook for writers advocates clarity, precision, and simple elegance.*

*"Once More to the Lake" (*Harper's, *August 1941) became a staple of the essay canon because of the elegant simplicity of White's style. With sophistication, light irony, and gentle common sense, White examines the humorous and serious sides of ordinary life—and human relationships, here just on the brink of World War II.*

One summer, along about 1904, my father rented a camp on a lake in Maine and took us all there for the month of August. We all got ringworm from some kittens and had to rub Pond's Extract on our arms and legs night and morning, and my father rolled over in a canoe with all his clothes on; but outside of that the vacation was a success and from then on none of us ever thought there was any place in the world like that lake in Maine. We returned summer after summer—always on August 1 for one month. I have since become a saltwater man, but sometimes in summer there are days when the restlessness of the tides and the fearful cold of the sea water and the incessant wind that blows across the afternoon and into the evening make me wish for the placidity of a lake in the woods. A few weeks ago this feeling got so strong I bought myself a couple of bass hooks and a spinner and returned to the lake where we used to go, for a week's fishing and to revisit old haunts.

I took along my son, who had never had any fresh water up his nose and who had seen lily pads only from train windows. On the journey over to the lake I began to wonder what it would be like. I wondered how time would have marred this unique, this holy spot—the coves and streams, the hills that the sun set behind, the camps and the paths behind the camps. I was sure that the tarred road would have found it out, and I wondered in what other ways it would be desolated. It is strange how much you can remember about places like that once you allow your mind to return into the grooves that lead back. You remember one thing, and that suddenly reminds you of another thing. I guess I remembered clearest of all the early mornings, when the lake was cool and motionless, remembered how the bedroom smelled of the lumber it was made of and of the wet woods whose scent entered through the screen. The partitions in the camp were thin and did not extend clear to the top of the rooms, and as I was always the first up I would dress softly so as not to wake the others, and sneak out into the sweet outdoors and start out in the canoe, keeping close along the shore in the long shadows of the pines. I remembered being very careful never to rub my paddle against the gunwale for fear of disturbing the stillness of the cathedral.

The lake had never been what you would call a wild lake. There were cottages sprinkled around the shores, and it was in farming country although the shores of the lake were quite heavily wooded. Some of the cottages were owned by nearby farmers, and you would live at the shore and eat your meals at the farmhouse. That's what our family did. But although it wasn't wild, it was a fairly large and undisturbed lake and there were places in it that, to a child at least, seemed infinitely remote and primeval.

I was right about the tar: it led to within half a mile of the shore. But when I got back there, with my boy, and we settled into a camp near a farmhouse and into the kind of summertime I had known, I could tell that it was going to be pretty much the same as it had been before—I knew it, lying in bed the first morning smelling the bedroom and hearing the boy sneak quietly out and go off along the shore in a boat. I began to sustain the illusion that he was I, and therefore, by simple transposition, that I was my father. This sensation persisted, kept cropping up all the time we were there. It was not an entirely new feeling, but in this setting it grew much stronger. I seemed to be living a dual existence. I would be in the middle of some simple act, I would be picking up a bait box or laying down a table fork, or I would be saying something and suddenly it would be not I but my father who was saying the words or making the gesture. It gave me a creepy sensation.

We went fishing the first morning. I felt the same damp moss covering the worms in the bait can, and saw the dragonfly alight on the tip of my rod as it hovered a few inches from the surface of the water. It was the arrival of this fly that convinced me beyond any doubt that everything was as it always had been, that the years were a mirage and that there had been no years. The small waves were the same, chucking the rowboat under the chin as we fished at anchor, and the boat was the same boat, the same color green and the ribs broken in the same places, and under the floorboards the same fresh water leavings and débris—the dead hellgrammite, the wisps of moss, the rusty discarded fishhook, the dried blood from yesterday's catch. We stared silently at the tips of our rods, at the drag-onflies that came and went. I lowered the tip of mine into the water, tentatively, pensively dislodging the fly, which darted two feet away, poised, darted two feet back, and came to rest again a little farther up the rod. There had been no years between the ducking of this dragonfly and the other one—the one that was part of memory. I looked at the boy, who was silently watching his fly, and it was my hands that held his rod, my eyes watching. I felt dizzy and didn't know which rod I was at the end of.

We caught two bass, hauling them in briskly as though they were mackerel, pulling them over the side of the boat in a businesslike manner without any land-ing net, and stunning them with a blow on the back of the head. When we got back for a swim before lunch, the lake was exactly where we had left it, the same number of inches from the dock, and there was only the merest suggestion of a breeze. This seemed an utterly enchanted sea, this lake you could leave to its own devices for a few hours and come back to, and find that it had not stirred, this constant and trustworthy body of water. In the shallows, the dark, water-soaked sticks and twigs, smooth and old, were undulating in clusters on the bottom against the clean ribbed sand, and the track of the mussel was plain. A school of minnows swam by, each minnow with its small individual shadow, doubling the attendance, so clear and sharp in the sunlight. Some of the other campers were in swimming, along the shore, one of them with a cake of soap, and the water felt thin and clear and unsubstantial. Over the years there had been this person with the cake of soap, this cultist, and here he was. There had been no years.

Up to the farmhouse to dinner through the teeming dusty field, the road under our sneakers was only a two-track road. The middle track was missing, the one with the marks of the hooves and the splotches of dried, flaky manure. There had always been three tracks to choose from in choosing which track to walk in; now the choice was narrowed down to two. For a moment I missed terribly the middle alternative. But the way led past the tennis court, and something about the way it lay there in the sun reassured me; the tape had loosened along the backline, the alleys were green with plantains and other weeds, and the net (installed in June and removed in September) sagged in the dry noon, and the whole place steamed with midday heat and hunger and emptiness. There was a choice of pie for dessert, and one was blueberry and one was apple, and the waitresses were the same country girls, there having been no passage of time, only the illusion of it as in a dropped curtain—the waitresses were still fifteen; their hair had been washed, that was the only difference—they had been to the movies and seen the pretty girls with the clean hair.

Summertime, oh, summertime, pattern of life indelible with fade-proof lake, the wood unshatterable, the pasture with the sweetfern and the juniper forever and ever, summer without end; this was the background, and the life along the shore was the design, the cottages with their innocent and tranquil design, their tiny docks with the flagpole and the American flag floating against the white clouds in the blue sky, the little paths over the roots of the trees leading from camp to camp and the paths leading back to the outhouses and the can of lime for sprinkling, and at the souvenir counters at the store the miniature birch-bark canoes and the postcards that showed things looking a little better than they looked. This was the American family at play, escaping the city heat, wondering whether the new-comers in the camp at the head of the cove were "common" or "nice," wondering whether it was true that the people who drove up for Sunday dinner at the farm-house were turned away because there wasn't enough chicken.

It seemed to me, as I kept remembering all this, that those times and those summers had been infinitely precious and worth saving. There had been jollity and peace and goodness. The arriving (at the beginning of August) had been so big a business in itself, at the railway station the farm wagon drawn up, the first smell of the pine-laden air, the first glimpse of the smiling farmer, and the great importance of the trunks and your father's enormous authority in such matters, and the feel of the wagon under you for the long ten-mile haul, and at the top of the last long hill catching the first view of the lake after eleven months of not seeing this cherished body of water. The shouts and cries of the other campers when they saw you, and the trunks to be unpacked, to give up their rich burden. (Arriving was less exciting nowadays, when you sneaked up in your car and parked it under a tree near the camp and took out the bags and in five minutes it was all over, no fuss, no loud wonderful fuss about trunks.)

Peace and goodness and jollity. The only thing that was wrong now, really, 10 was the sound of the place, an unfamiliar nervous sound of the outboard motors. This was the note that jarred, the one thing that would sometimes break the illusion and set the years moving. In those other summertimes all motors were inboard; and when they were at a little distance, the noise they made was a seda-tive, an ingredient of summer sleep. They were one-cylinder and two-cylinder engines, and some were make-and-break and some were jump-spark, but they all made a sleepy sound across the lake. The one-lungers throbbed and fluttered, and the twin-cylinder ones purred and purred, and that was a quiet sound, too. But now the campers all had outboards. In the daytime, in the hot mornings, these motors made a petulant, irritable sound; at night in the still evening when the afterglow lit the water, they whined about one's ears like mosquitoes. My boy loved our rented outboard, and his great desire was to achieve single-handed mastery over it, and authority, and he soon learned the trick of choking it a little (but not too much), and the adjustment of the needle valve. Watching him I would remember the things you could do with the old one-cylinder engine with the heavy flywheel, how you could have it eating out of your hand if you got really close to it spiritually. Motorboats in those days didn't have clutches, and you would make a landing by shutting off the motor at the proper time and coasting in with a dead rudder. But there was a way of reversing them, if you learned the trick, by cutting the switch and putting it on again exactly on the final dying revolution of the flywheel, so that it would kick back against compression and begin reversing. Approaching a dock in a strong following breeze, it was difficult to slow up sufficiently by the ordinary coasting method, and if a boy felt he had complete mastery over his motor, he was tempted to keep it running beyond its time and then reverse it a few feet from the dock. It took a cool nerve, because if you threw the switch a twentieth of a second too soon you would catch the flywheel when it still had speed enough to go up past center, and the boat would leap ahead, charging bull-fashion at the dock.

We had a good week at the camp. The bass were biting well and the sun shone endlessly, day after day. We would be tired at night and lie down in the accumulated heat of the little bedrooms after the long hot day and the breeze would stir almost imperceptibly outside and the smell of the swamp drift in through the rusty screens. Sleep would come easily and in the morning the red squirrel would be on the roof, tapping out his gay routine. I kept remembering everything, lying in bed in the mornings—the small steamboat that had a long rounded stern like the lip of a Ubangi, and how quietly she ran on the moonlight sails, when the older boys played their mandolins and the girls sang and we ate doughnuts dipped in sugar, and how sweet the music was on the water in the shining night, and what it had felt like to think about girls then. After breakfast we would go up to the store and the things were in the same place—the minnows in a bottle, the plugs and spinners disarranged and pawed over by the youngsters from the boys' camp, the Fig Newtons and the Beeman's gum. Outside, the road was tarred and cars stood in front of the store. Inside, all was just as it had always been, except there was more Coca-Cola and not so much Moxie and root beer and birch beer and sarsaparilla. We would walk out with the bottle of pop apiece and sometimes the pop would backfire up our noses and hurt. We explored the streams, quietly, where the turtles slid off the sunny logs and dug their way into the soft bottom; and we lay on the town wharf and fed worms to the tame bass. Everywhere we went I had trouble making out which was I, the one walking at my side, the one walking in my pants.

One afternoon while we were at that lake a thunderstorm came up. It was like the revival of an old melodrama that I had seen long ago with childish awe. The second-act climax of the drama of the electrical disturbance over a lake in America had not changed in any important respect. This was the big scene, still the big scene. The whole thing was so familiar, the first feeling of oppression and heat and a general air around camp of not wanting to go very far away. In mid-afternoon (it was all the same) a curious darkening of the sky, and a lull in everything that had made life tick; and then the way the boats suddenly swung the other way at their moorings with the coming of a breeze out of the new quarter, and the premonitory rumble. Then the kettle drum, then the snare, then the bass drum and cymbals, then crackling light against the dark, and the gods grinning and licking their chops in the hills. Afterward the calm, the rain steadily rustling in the calm lake, the return of light and hope and spirits, and the campers running out in joy and relief to go swimming in the rain, their bright cries perpetuating the deathless joke about how they were getting simply drenched, and the children screaming with delight at the new sensation of bathing in the rain, and the joke about getting drenched linking the generations in a strong indestructible chain. And the comedian who waded in carrying an umbrella.

When the others went swimming my son said he was going in, too. He pulled his dripping trunks from the line where they had hung all through the shower and wrung them out. Languidly, and with no thought of going in, I watched him, his hard little body, skinny and bare, saw him wince slightly as he pulled up around his vitals the small, soggy, icy garment. As he buckled the swollen belt, suddenly my groin felt the chill of death.

QUESTIONS FOR DISCUSSION AND WRITING

1. Explain Brian Doyle's observation of the human condition (p. 141) in relation to "Once More to the Lake." In your own experience, is his observation accurate? Would you accept all of what he says? If not, explain how you would modify this statement: "When young we think there will come one person who will savor and sustain us always; when we are older we know this is the dream of a child, that all hearts finally are bruised and scarred, scored and torn, repaired by time and will, patched by force of character, yet fragile and rickety forevermore, no matter how ferocious the defense and how many bricks you bring to the wall" (p. 143).

2. Although Tolstoy has famously said, "All happy families are alike," White and Alice Walker (p. 307) offer snapshots of happy families, and each is different. What characteristics have they in common? In what ways do they differ? Write a definition of a happy family, based on these readings and your own family (happy or not) and those of others. How does the ideal compare with the reality? Is it consistent over time or often changing?

3. Is there any hint of problems to come in E. B. White's commentary on idyllic three-generation family relationships in "Once More to the Lake"? In what ways does White remind readers of both the presence and passing of time?

4. Children learn from the adults around them, for better and for worse. Identify some of the values, as well as skills, that White's son learned from his father, just as White had learned from his own father. Under what circumstances do children learn the truth of Doyle's observations quoted in question 1?

HENRY DAVID THOREAU
Where I Lived, and What I Lived For

"The mass of men lead lives of quiet desperation," wrote Henry David Thoreau (1817–1862) in Walden, *a book that taught the civilized world how to live closer to nature and eternal truth, or "reality," as he termed it. A poet, diarist, and essayist, his works are essential statements of American romantic idealism. After graduating from Harvard (1837), he worked intermittently as a teacher, gardener, and surveyor while doing his real work as an original thinker. As a transcendentalist, Thoreau believed that intuitive understanding transcends the limits of human experience and that ideas and the natural world are powerful—and more important than material goods. These views pervade his two major works,* A Week on the Concord and Merrimack Rivers *(1849) and* Walden, or Life in the Woods *(1854), the latter being Thoreau's interpretation of his two years at Concord's Walden Pond. There he lived frugally in the small cabin he built himself, feasting on the wonders of his natural surroundings, scarcely a mile from his Massachusetts birthplace.*

"Where I Lived, and What I Lived For," from the second chapter of Walden, *gained worldwide renown as a philosophical manifesto and meditation on nature. Here Thoreau, in the guise of a rustic philosopher, spans the universe from earth to heaven, exploring what is essential to a good life well lived, and what is not. His mind having been shaped by classical learning and wide reading, he experienced modern life as frenetic, chaotic, and banal. He identifies the various enemies of self-knowledge—a preoccupation with speed (the railroad) and trivia (the latest news). "Our life is frittered away by detail," he boldly claims—then points the way back to genuine experience.*

I went to the woods because I wished to live deliberately, to front only the essential facts of life, and see if I could not learn what it had to teach, and not, when I came to die, discover that I had not lived. I did not wish to live what was not life, living is so dear; nor did I wish to practice resignation, unless it was quite necessary. I wanted to live deep and suck out all the marrow of life, to live so sturdily and Spartan-like as to put to rout all that was not life, to cut a broad swath and shave close, to drive life into a corner, and reduce it to its lowest terms, and, if it proved to be mean, why then to get the whole and genuine meanness of it, and publish its meanness to the world; or if it were sublime, to know it by experience, and be able to give a true account of it in my next excursion. For most men, it appears to me, are in a strange uncertainty about it, whether it is of the devil or of God, and have *somewhat hastily* concluded that it is the chief end of man here to "glorify God and enjoy him forever."

Still we live meanly, like ants; though the fable tells us that we were long ago changed into men; like pygmies we fight with cranes; it is error upon error, and clout upon clout, and our best virtue has for its occasion a superfluous and evitable wretchedness. Our life is frittered away by detail. An honest man has hardly need to count more than his ten fingers, or in extreme cases he may add his ten toes, and lump the rest. Simplicity, simplicity, simplicity! I say, let your affairs be as two or three, and not a hundred or a thousand; instead of a million count half a dozen, and keep your accounts on your thumb-nail. In the midst of this chopping sea of civilized life, such are the clouds and storms and quicksands and thousand-and-one items to be allowed for, that a man has to live, if he would not founder and go to the bottom and not make his port at all, by dead reckoning, and he must be a great calculator indeed who succeeds. Simplify, simplify. Instead of three meals a day, if it be necessary eat but one; instead of a hundred dishes, five; and reduce other things in proportion. Our life is like a German Confederacy, made up of petty states, with its boundary forever fluctuating, so that even a German cannot tell you how it is bounded at any moment. The nation itself, with all its so-called internal improvements, which, by the way are all external and superficial, is just such an unwieldy and overgrown establishment, cluttered with furniture and tripped up by its own traps, ruined by luxury and heedless expense, by want of calculation and a worthy aim, as the million households in the lands; and the only cure for it, as for them, is in a rigid economy, a stern and more than Spartan simplicity of life and elevation of purpose. It lives too fast. Men think that it is essential that the *Nation* have commerce, and export ice, and talk through a telegraph, and ride thirty miles an hour, without a doubt, whether *they* do or not; but whether we should live like baboons or like men, is a little uncertain. If we do not get out sleepers, and forge rails, and devote days and nights to the work, but go to tinkering upon our *lives* to improve *them*, who will build railroads? And if railroads are not built, how shall we get to heaven in season? But if we stay at home and mind our business, who will want railroads? We do not ride on the railroad; it rides upon us. Did you ever think what those sleepers are that underlie the railroad? Each one is a man, an Irishman, or a Yankee man. The rails are laid on them, and they are covered with sand, and the cars run smoothly over them. They are sound sleepers, I assure you. And every few years a new lot is laid down and run over; so that, if some have the pleasure of riding on a rail, others have the misfortune to be ridden upon. And when they run over a man that is walking in his sleep, a supernumerary sleeper in the wrong position, and wake him up, they suddenly stop the cars, and make a hue and cry about it, as if this were an exception. I am glad to know that it takes a gang of men for every five miles to keep the sleepers down and level in their beds as it is, for this is a sign that they may sometimes get up again.

Why should we live with such hurry and waste of life? We are determined to be starved before we are hungry. Men say that a stitch in time saves nine, and so they take a thousand stitches today to save nine to-morrow. As for *work*, we haven't any of any consequence. We have the Saint Vitus' dance, and cannot possibly keep our heads still. If I should only give a few pulls at the parish bell-rope, as for a fire, that is, without setting the bell, there is hardly a man on his farm in the outskirts of Concord, notwithstanding that press of engagements which was his excuse so many times this morning, nor a boy, nor a woman, I might almost say, but would foresake all and follow that sound, not mainly to save property from the flames, but, if we will confess the truth, much more to see it burn, since burn it must, and we, be it known, did not set it on fire,—or to see it put out, and have a hand in it, if that is done as handsomely; yes, even if it were the parish church itself. Hardly a man takes a half-hour's nap after dinner, but when he wakes he holds up his head and asks, "What's the news?" as if the rest of mankind had stood his sentinels. Some give directions to be waked every half-hour, doubtless for no other purpose; and then, to pay for it, they tell what they have dreamed. After a night's sleep the news is as indispensable as the breakfast. "Pray tell me anything new that has happened to a man anywhere on this globe,"—and he reads it over his coffee and rolls, that a man has had his eyes gouged out this morning on the Wachito River; never dreaming the while that he lives in the dark unfathomed mammoth cave of this world, and has but the rudiment of an eye himself.

For my part, I could easily do without the post-office. I think that there are very few important communications made through it. To speak critically, I never received more than one or two letters in my life—I wrote this some years ago—that were worth the postage. The penny-post is, commonly, an institution through which you seriously offer a man that penny for his thoughts which is so often safely offered in jest. And I am sure that I never read any memorable news in a newspaper. If we read of one man robbed, or murdered, or killed by accident, or one house burned, or one vessel wrecked, or one steamboat blown up, or one cow run over on the Western Railroad, or one mad dog killed, or one lot of grasshoppers in the winter,—we never need read of another. One is enough. If you are acquainted with the principle, what do you care for a myriad instances and applications? To a philosopher all *news*, as it is called, is gossip, and they who edit and read it are old women over their tea. Yet not a few are greedy after this gossip. There was such a rush, as I hear, the other day at one of the offices to learn the foreign news by the last arrival, that several large squares of plate glass belonging to the establishment were broken by the pressure,—news which I seriously think a ready wit might write a twelvemonth, or twelve years, beforehand with sufficient accuracy. As for Spain, for instance, if you know how to throw in Don Carlos and the Infanta, and Don Pedro and Seville and Granada, from time to time in the right proportions,—they may have changed the names a little since I saw the papers,—and serve up a bull-fight when other entertainments fail, it will be true to the letter, and give us as good an idea of the exact state or ruin of things in Spain as the most succinct and lucid reports under this head in the newspapers: and as for England, almost the last significant scrap of news from that quarter was the revolution of 1649; and if you have learned the history of her crops for an average year, you never need attend to that thing again, unless your speculations are of a merely pecuniary character. If one may judge who rarely looks into the newspapers, nothing new does ever happen in foreign parts, a French revolution not excepted.

What news! how much more important to know what that is which was never 5 old! "Kieou-he-yu (great dignitary of the state of Wei) sent a man to Khoung-tseu to know his news. Khoung-tseu caused the messenger to be seated near him, and questioned him in these terms: What is your master doing? The messenger answered with respect: My master desires to diminish the number of his faults, but he cannot come to the end of them. The messenger being gone, the philosopher remarked: What a worthy messenger! What a worthy messenger!" The preacher, instead of vexing the ears of drowsy farmers on their day of rest at the end of the week,—for Sunday is the fit conclusion of an ill-spent week, and not the fresh and brave beginning of a new one,—with this one other draggle-tail of a sermon, should shout with thundering voice, "Pause! Avast! Why so seeming fast, but deadly slow?"

Shams and delusions are esteemed for soundless truths, while reality is fabulous. If men would steadily observe realities only, and not allow themselves to be deluded, life, to compare it with such things as we know, would be like a fairy tale and the Arabian Nights Entertainments. If we respected only what is inevitable and has a right to be, music and poetry would resound along the streets. When we are unhurried and wise, we perceive that only great and worthy things have any permanent and absolute existence, that petty fears and petty pleasures are but the shadow of the reality. This is always exhilarating and sublime. By closing the eyes and slumbering, and consenting to be deceived by shows, men establish and confirm their daily life of routine and habit everywhere, which still is built on purely illusory foundations. Children, who play life, discern its true law and relations more clearly than men, who fail to live it worthily, but who think that they are wiser by experience, that is, by failure. I have read in a Hindoo book, that "there was a king's son, who, being expelled in infancy from his native city, was brought up by a forester, and, growing up to maturity in that state, imagined himself to belong to the barbarous race with which he lived. One of his father's ministers having discovered him, revealed to him what he was, and the misconception of his character was removed, and he knew himself to be a prince. "So soul," continues the Hindoo philosopher, "from the circumstances in which it is placed, mistakes its own character, until the truth is revealed to it by some holy teacher, and then it knows itself to be *Brahme*." I perceive that we inhabitants of New England live this mean life that we do because our vision does not penetrate the surface of things. We think that that is which *appears* to be. If a man should walk through this town and see only the reality, where, think you, would the "Mill-dam" go to? If he should give us an account of the realities he beheld there, we should not recognize the place in his description. Look at the meeting-house, or a court-house, or a jail, or a shop, or a dwelling-house, and say what that thing really is before a true gaze, and they would all go to pieces in your account of them. Men esteem truth remote, in the outskirts of the system, behind the farthest star, before Adam and after the last man. In eternity there is indeed something true and sublime. But all these times and places and occasions are now and here. God himself culminates in the present moment, and will never be more divine in the lapse of all the ages. And we are enabled to apprehend at all what is sublime and noble only by the perpetual instilling and drenching of the reality that surrounds us. The universe constantly and obediently answers to our conceptions; whether we travel fast or slow, the track is laid for us. Let us spend our lives in conceiving then. The poet or the artist never yet had so fair and noble a design but some of his posterity at least could accomplish it.

Let us spend one day as deliberately as Nature, and not be thrown off the track by every nutshell and mosquito's wing that falls on the rails. Let us rise early and fast, or breakfast, gently and without perturbation; let company come and let company go, let the bells ring and the children cry,—determined to make a day of it. Why should we knock under and go with the stream? Let us not be upset and overwhelmed in that terrible rapid and whirlpool called a dinner, situated in the meridian shallows. Weather this danger and you are safe, for the rest of the way is down hill. With unrelaxed nerves, with morning vigor, sail by it, looking another way, tied to the mast like Ulysses. If the engine whistles, let it whistle till it is hoarse for its pains. If the bell rings, why should we run? We will consider what kind of music they are like. Let us settle ourselves, and work and wedge our feet downward through the mud and slush of opinion, and prejudice, and tradition, and delusion, and appearance, that alluvion which covers the globe, through Paris and London, through New York and Boston and Concord, through Church and State, through poetry and philosophy and religion, till we come to a hard bottom and rocks in place, which we can call *reality*, and say, This is, and no mistake; and then begin, having a *point d'appui*, below freshet and frost and fire, a place where you might found a wall or a state, or set a lamppost safely, or perhaps a gauge, not a Nilometer, but a Realometer, that future ages might know how deep a freshet of shams and appearances had gathered from time to time. If you stand right fronting and face to face to a fact, you will see the sun glimmer on both its surfaces, as if it were a cimeter, and feel its sweet edge dividing you through the heart and marrow, and so you will happily conclude your mortal career. Be it life or death, we crave only reality. If we are really dying, let us hear the rattle in our throats and feel cold in the extremities; if we are alive, let us go about our business.

Time is but the stream I go a-fishing in. I drink at it; but while I drink I see the sandy bottom and detect how shallow it is. Its thin current slides away, but eternity remains. I would drink deeper; fish in the sky, whose bottom is pebbly with stars. I cannot count one. I know not the first letter of the alphabet. I have always been regretting that I was not as wise as the day I was born. The intellect is a cleaver; it discerns and rifts its way into the secret of things. I do not wish to be any more busy with my hands than is necessary. My head is hands and feet. I feel all my best faculties concentrated in it. My instinct tells me that my head is an organ for burrowing, as some creatures use their snout and fore paws, and with it I would mine and burrow my way through these hills. I think that the richest vein is somewhere hereabouts; so by the divining-rod and thin rising vapors I judge; and here I will begin to mine.

QUESTIONS FOR DISCUSSION AND WRITING

1. In "Where I Lived, and What I Lived For," Thoreau argues that "we are enabled to apprehend at all what is sublime and noble only by the perpetual instilling and drenching of the reality that surrounds us" (paragraph 6). In observing this reality, "we perceive that only great and worthy things have any permanent and absolute existence, that petty fears and petty pleasures are but the shadow of the reality." In a culture dominated by social networking and high technology, to what extent is it possible to live life focused on the sublime without being distracted by "petty fears and petty pleasure"? Explain.

2. Thoreau begins his essay "Civil Disobedience" with the Jeffersonian sentiment, "That government is best which governs least" and follows it with the
claim that the best government "governs not at all." How does this apparent
support of political anarchy coexist with his claim in "Where I Lived, and
What I Lived For" that nature can teach "the essential facts of life"?

3. After reading "Where I Lived, and What I Lived For," describe how Thoreau
envisions the development of individual conscience. Consider Thoreau's challenge to "spend one day as deliberately as Nature, and not be thrown off the track
by every nutshell and mosquito's wing that falls on the rails" (paragraph 7). Try
doing so, and write a paper explaining and analyzing your experience. Would
you ever repeat the experiment?

4. Thoreau was part of a literary, political, and philosophical movement called
Transcendentalism, which sought a better relationship with the world and,
particularly in Thoreau's case, with nature. Do some research on Transcendentalism and then listen to the T. M. Luhrmann and Kurt Anderson interview,
"When God Talks Back: Understanding the American Evangelical Relationship
with God" (in the e-Pages at bedfordstmartins.com/arlington). What might
Thoreau say to the subjects discussed in the Luhrmann interview?

T. M. LUHRMANN AND KURT ANDERSON

When God Talks Back: Understanding the American Evangelical Relationship with God
[AUDIO INTERVIEW]

*"I really wanted to know what people meant when they said that God spoke to them,
that God told them something."*

 In the e-Pages at bedfordstmartins.com/arlington

MALCOLM GLADWELL

Drinking Games

A staff writer at the New Yorker *since 1996, Malcolm Gladwell (b. 1963) has also had
great success as a writer of nonfiction books, including* The Tipping Point *(2000),*
Blink *(2005), and* Outliers *(2008). His books examine the sometimes unexpected in
the world of social sciences. For example,* The Tipping Point *is described as a book
about change—in particular, the causes of social changes that often happen quickly*

and without adequate reason. Blink *is about what Gladwell calls "rapid cognition"—suddenly jumping to a conclusion or understanding about something or someone.* Outliers *examines unusual phenomena—happenings far outside the norm. Gladwell has also published a collection of journalism,* What the Dog Saw *(2009). All four of his books became* New York Times *best-sellers. He won a National Magazine Award in 1999 and in 2005 was named one of* Time *magazine's 100 Most Influential People. A Canadian, Gladwell was named to the Order of Canada in 2011, the second highest honor of merit in Canada.*

In this article, which initially appeared in the New Yorker *in the February 15, 2010, issue, Gladwell examines the topic of alcohol consumption and how culture plays a role in it. Gladwell, looking at research done decades ago in Bolivia by Dwight and Anna Heath, notes how a small, fairly isolated group of people, the Camba, drank 180-proof alcohol in a ritualistic manner. Despite the extremely high potency of the drink, the Camba experienced none of the typical problems associated with alcohol abuse, such as fighting or sexual harassment. Looking closer to home—in this case, New Haven, Connecticut, home of Yale University, researcher Dwight Heath also examined drinking practices among Irish Americans and Italian Americans, and found that although both groups tended to drink frequently, the Irish Americans tended to experience more problems as a result of heavy drinking, while the Italian Americans drank frequently, but not heavily. The result was to examine how alcohol's impact is not based simply on the genetics or physical attributes of a drinker, but on the culture in which the drinker lives.*

How much people drink may matter less than how they drink it.

1.

In 1956, Dwight Heath, a graduate student in anthropology at Yale University, was preparing to do field work for his dissertation. He was interested in land reform and social change, and his first choice as a study site was Tibet. But six months before he was to go there he got a letter from the Chinese government rejecting his request for a visa. "I had to find a place where you can master the literature in four months, and that was accessible," Heath says now. "It was a hustle." Bolivia was the next best choice. He and his wife, Anna Cooper Heath, flew to Lima with their baby boy, and then waited for five hours while mechanics put boosters on the plane's engines. "These were planes that the U.S. had dumped after World War II," Heath recalls. "They weren't supposed to go above ten thousand feet. But La Paz, where we were headed, was at twelve thousand feet." As they flew into the Andes, Cooper Heath says, they looked down and saw the remnants of "all the planes where the boosters didn't work."

From La Paz, they traveled five hundred miles into the interior of eastern Bolivia, to a small frontier town called Montero. It was the part of Bolivia where the Amazon Basin meets the Chaco—vast stretches of jungle and lush prairie. The area was inhabited by the Camba, a mestizo people descended from the indigenous Indian populations and Spanish settlers. The Camba spoke a language that was a mixture of the local Indian languages and seventeenth-century Andalusian Spanish. "It was an empty spot on the map," Heath says. "There was a railroad coming. There was a highway coming. There was a national government . . . coming."

They lived in a tiny house just outside of town. "There was no pavement, no sidewalks," Cooper Heath recalls. "If there was meat in town, they'd throw out the hide in front, so you'd know where it was, and you would bring banana leaves in your hand, so it was your dish. There were adobe houses with stucco and tile roofs, and the town plaza, with three palm trees. You heard the rumble of oxcarts. The padres had a jeep. Some of the women would serve a big pot of rice and some sauce. That was the restaurant. The guy who did the coffee was German. The year we came to Bolivia, a total of eighty-five foreigners came into the country. It wasn't exactly a hot spot."

In Montero, the Heaths engaged in old-fashioned ethnography—"vacuuming ₅ up everything," Dwight says, "learning everything." They convinced the Camba that they weren't missionaries by openly smoking cigarettes. They took thousands of photographs. They walked around the town and talked to whomever they could, and then Dwight went home and spent the night typing up his notes. They had a Coleman lantern, which became a prized social commodity. Heath taught some of the locals how to build a split-rail fence. They sometimes shared a beer in the evenings with a Bolivian Air Force officer who had been exiled to Montero from La Paz. "He kept on saying, 'Watch me, I will be somebody,'" Dwight says. (His name was René Barrientos; eight years later he became the president of Bolivia, and the Heaths were invited to his inauguration.) After a year and a half, the Heaths packed up their photographs and notes and returned to New Haven. There Dwight Heath sat down to write his dissertation—only to discover that he had nearly missed what was perhaps the most fascinating fact about the community he had been studying.

Today, the Heaths are in their late seventies. Dwight has neatly combed gray hair and thick tortoiseshell glasses, a reserved New Englander through and through. Anna is more outgoing. They live not far from the Brown University campus, in Providence, in a house filled with hundreds of African statues and sculptures, with books and papers piled high on tables, and they sat, in facing armchairs, and told the story of what happened half a century ago, finishing each other's sentences.

"It was August or September of 1957," Heath said. "We had just gotten back. She's tanned. I'm tanned. I mean, really tanned, which you didn't see a lot of in New Haven in those days."

"I'm an architecture nut," Anna said. "And I said I wanted to see the inside of this building near the campus. It was always closed. But Dwight says, 'You never know,' so he walked over and pulls on the door and it opens." Anna looked over at her husband.

"So we go in," Dwight went on, "and there was a couple of little white-haired guys there. And they said, 'You're tanned. Where have you been?' And I said Bolivia. And one of them said, 'Well, can you tell me how they drink?'" The building was Yale's Center of Alcohol Studies. One of the white-haired men was

E. M. Jellinek, perhaps the world's leading expert on alcoholism at the time; the other was Mark Keller, the editor of the well-regarded *Quarterly Journal of Studies on Alcohol*. Keller stood up and grabbed Heath by the lapels: "I don't know anyone who has ever been to Bolivia. Tell me about it!" He invited Heath to write up his alcohol-related observations for his journal.

After the Heaths went home that day, Anna said to Dwight, "Do you realize   10 that every weekend we were in Bolivia we went out drinking?" The code he used for alcohol in his notebooks was 30A, and when he went over his notes he found 30A references everywhere. Still, nothing about the alcohol question struck him as particularly noteworthy. People drank every weekend in New Haven, too. His focus was on land reform. But who was he to say no to the *Quarterly Journal of Studies on Alcohol*? So he sat down and wrote up what he knew. Only after his article, "Drinking Patterns of the Bolivian Camba," was published, in September of 1958, and the queries and reprint requests began flooding in from around the world, did he realize what he had found. "This is so often true in anthropology," Anna said. "It is not anthropologists who recognize the value of what they've done. It's everyone else. The anthropologist is just reporting."

2.

The abuse of alcohol has, historically, been thought of as a moral failing. Muslims and Mormons and many kinds of fundamentalist Christians do not drink, because they consider alcohol an invitation to weakness and sin. Around the middle of the last century, alcoholism began to be widely considered a disease: It was recognized that some proportion of the population was genetically susceptible to the effects of drinking. Policymakers, meanwhile, have become increasingly interested in using economic and legal tools to control alcohol-related behavior: That's why the drinking age has been raised from eighteen to twenty-one, why drunk-driving laws have been toughened, and why alcohol is taxed heavily. Today, our approach to the social burden of alcohol is best described as a mixture of all three: we moralize, medicalize, and legalize.

In the 1950s, however, the researchers at the Yale Center of Alcohol Studies found something lacking in this emerging approach, and the reason had to do with what they observed right in their own town. New Haven was a city of immigrants—Jewish, Irish, and, most of all, Italian. Recent Italian immigrants made up about a third of the population, and whenever the Yale researchers went into the Italian neighborhoods they found an astonishing thirst for alcohol. The overwhelming majority of Italian-American men in New Haven drank. A group led by the director of the Yale alcohol-treatment clinic, Giorgio Lolli, once interviewed a sixty-one-year-old father of four who consumed more than three thousand calories a day of food and beverages—of which a third was wine, "He usually has an 8-oz. glass of wine immediately following his breakfast every morning," Lolli and his colleagues wrote. "He always takes wine with his noonday lunch—as much as 24 oz." But he didn't display the pathologies that typically accompany that kind of alcohol consumption. The man was successfully employed, and had been drunk only twice in his life. He was, Lolli concluded, "a healthy, happy individual who has made a satisfactory adjustment to life."

By the late fifties, Lolli's clinic had admitted twelve hundred alcoholics. Plenty of them were Irish. But just forty were Italians (all of whom were second- or third-generation immigrants). New Haven was a natural experiment. Here were two groups who practiced the same religion, who were subject to the same laws and constraints, and who, it seemed reasonable to suppose, should have the same assortment within their community of those genetically predisposed to alcoholism. Yet the heavy-drinking Italians had nothing like the problems that afflicted their Irish counterparts.

"That drinking must precede alcoholism is obvious," Mark Keller once wrote. "Equally obvious, but not always sufficiently considered, is the fact that drinking is not necessarily followed by alcoholism." This was the puzzle of New Haven, and why Keller demanded of Dwight Heath, that day on the Yale campus, Tell me how the Camba drink. The crucial ingredient, in Keller's eyes, had to be cultural.

The Heaths had been invited to a party soon after arriving in Montero, and every weekend and holiday thereafter. It was their Coleman lantern. "Whatever the occasion, it didn't matter," Anna recalled. "As long as the party was at night, we were first on the list."

The parties would have been more aptly described as drinking parties. The host would buy the first bottle and issue the invitations. A dozen or so people would show up on Saturday night, and the party would proceed—often until everyone went back to work on Monday morning. The composition of the group was informal: Sometimes people passing by would be invited. But the structure of the party was heavily ritualized. The group would sit in a circle. Someone might play the drums or a guitar. A bottle of rum, from one of the sugar refineries in the area, and a small drinking glass were placed on a table. The host stood, filled the glass with rum, and then walked toward someone in the circle. He stood before the "toastee," nodded, and raised the glass. The toastee smiled and nodded in return. The host then drank half the glass and handed it to the toastee, who would finish it. The toastee eventually stood, refilled the glass, and repeated the ritual with someone else in the circle. When people got too tired or too drunk, they curled up on the ground and passed out, rejoining the party when they awoke. The Camba did not drink alone. They did not drink on work nights. And they drank only within the structure of this elaborate ritual.

"The alcohol they drank was awful," Anna recalled. "Literally, your eyes poured tears. The first time I had it, I thought, I wonder what will happen if I just vomit in the middle of the floor. Not even the Camba said they liked it. They say it tastes bad. It burns. The next day they are sweating this stuff. You can smell it." But the Heaths gamely persevered. "The anthropology graduate student in the 1950s felt that he had to adapt," Dwight Heath said. "You don't want to offend anyone, you don't want to decline anything. I gritted my teeth and accepted those drinks."

"We didn't get drunk that much," Anna went on, "because we didn't get toasted as much as the other folks around. We were strangers. But one night there was this really big party—sixty to eighty people. They'd drink. Then pass out. Then wake up and party for a while. And I found, in their drinking patterns, that I could turn my drink over to Dwight. The husband is obliged to drink for his wife. And Dwight is holding the Coleman lantern with his arm wrapped around it, and I said, 'Dwight, you are burning your arm.' "She mimed her husband peeling his forearm off the hot surface of the lantern. "And he said—very deliberately—'So I am.'"

When the Heaths came back to New Haven, they had a bottle of the Camba's rum analyzed and learned that it was a hundred and eighty proof. It was laboratory alcohol—the concentration that scientists use to fix tissue. No one had ever heard of anyone drinking it. This was the first of the astonishing findings of the Heaths' research—and, predictably, no one believed it at first.

"One of the world's leading physiologists of alcohol was at the Yale center," [20] Heath recalled. "His name was Leon Greenberg. He said to me, 'Hey, you spin a good yarn. But you couldn't really have drunk that stuff.' And he needled me just enough that he knew he would get a response. So I said, 'You want me to drink it? I have a bottle.' So one Saturday I drank some under controlled conditions. He was taking blood samples every twenty minutes and, sure enough, I did drink it, the way I said I'd drunk it."

Greenberg had an ambulance ready to take Heath home. But Heath decided to walk. Anna was waiting up for him in the third-floor walkup they rented, in an old fraternity house. "I was hanging out the window waiting for him, and there's the ambulance driving along the street, very slowly, and next to it is Dwight. He waves, and he looks fine. Then he walks up the three flights of stairs and says, 'Ahh, I'm drunk,' and falls flat on his face. He was out for three hours."

The bigger surprise was what happened when the Camba drank. The Camba had weekly benders with laboratory-proof alcohol, and, Dwight Heath said, "There was no social pathology—none. No arguments, no disputes, no sexual aggression, no verbal aggression. There was pleasant conversation or silence." On the Brown University campus, a few blocks away, beer—which is to Camba rum approximately what a peashooter is to a bazooka—was known to reduce the student population to a raging hormonal frenzy on Friday nights. "The drinking didn't interfere with work," Heath went on. "It didn't bring in the police. And there was no alcoholism, either."

3.

What Heath found among the Camba is hard to believe. We regard alcohol's behavioral effects as inevitable. Alcohol disinhibits, we assume, as reliably as caffeine enlivens. It gradually unlocks the set of psychological constraints that keep our behavior in check, and makes us do things that we would not ordinarily do. It's a drug, after all.

But, after Heath's work on the Camba, anthropologists began to take note of all the puzzling ways in which alcohol wasn't reliable in its effects. In the classic 1969 work *Drunken Comportment*, for example, the anthropologists Craig MacAndrew and Robert B. Edgerton describe an encounter that Edgerton had while studying a tribe in central Kenya. One of the tribesmen, he was told, was "very dangerous" and "totally beyond control" after he had been drinking, and one day Edgerton ran across the man:

> I heard a commotion, and saw people running past me. One young man stopped and urged me to flee because this dangerous drunk was coming down the path attacking all whom he met. As I was about to take this advice and leave, the drunk burst wildly into the clearing where I was sitting. I stood up, ready to run, but much to my surprise, the man calmed down, and as he walked slowly past me, he greeted me in polite, even deferential terms, before he turned and dashed away. I later learned that in the course of his "drunken rage" that day he had beaten two men, pushed down a small boy, and eviscerated a goat with a large knife.

The authors include a similar case from Ralph Beals's work among the Mixe Indians of Oaxaca, Mexico: [25]

> The Mixe indulge in frequent fist fights, especially while drunk. Although I probably saw several hundred, I saw no weapons used, although nearly all men carried machetes and many carried rifles. Most fights start with a drunken quarrel. When the pitch of voices reaches a certain point, everyone expects a fight. The men hold out their weapons to the onlookers, and then begin to fight with their fists, swinging wildly until one falls down [at which point] the victor helps his opponent to his feet and usually they embrace each other.

The angry Kenyan tribesman was disinhibited toward his own people but inhibited toward Edgerton. Alcohol turned the Mixe into aggressive street fighters, but they retained the presence of mind to "hold out their weapons to the onlookers." Something that truly disinhibits ought to be indiscriminate in its effects. That's not the picture of alcohol that these anthropologists have given us. (MacAndrew and Edgerton, in one of their book's many wry asides, point out that we are all acquainted with people who can hold their liquor. "In the absence of anything observably untoward in such a one's drunken comportment," they ask, "are we seriously to presume that he is devoid of inhibitions?")

Psychologists have encountered the same kinds of perplexities when they have set out to investigate the effects of drunkenness. One common "belief is that alcohol causes self-inflation." It makes us see ourselves through rose-tinted glasses. Oddly, though, it doesn't make us view everything about ourselves through rose-tinted glasses. When the psychologists Claude Steele and Mahzarin Banaji gave a group of people a personality questionnaire while they were sober and then again when they were drunk, they found that the only personality aspects that were inflated by drinking were those where there was a gap between real and ideal states. If you are good-looking and the world agrees that you are good-looking, drinking doesn't make you think you're even better-looking. Drinking only makes you feel you're better-looking if you think you're good-looking and the world doesn't agree.

Alcohol is also commonly believed to reduce anxiety. That's what a disinhibiting agent should do: relax us and make the world go away. Yet this effect also turns out to be selective. Put a stressed-out drinker in front of an exciting football game and he'll forget his troubles. But put him in a quiet bar somewhere, all by himself, and he'll grow more anxious.

Steele and his colleague Robert Josephs's explanation is that we've misread the effects of alcohol on the brain. Its principal effect is to narrow our emotional and mental field of vision. It causes, they write, "a state of shortsightedness in which superficially understood, immediate aspects of experience have a disproportionate influence on behavior and emotion."

Alcohol makes the thing in the foreground even more salient and the thing 30 in the background disappear. That's why drinking makes you think you are attractive when the world thinks otherwise: The alcohol removes the little constraining voice from the outside world that normally keeps our self-assessments in check. Drinking relaxes the man watching football because the game is front and center, and alcohol makes every secondary consideration fade away. But in a quiet bar his problems are front and center—and every potentially comforting or mitigating thought recedes. Drunkenness is not disinhibition. Drunkenness is myopia.

Myopia theory changes how we understand drunkenness. Disinhibition suggests that the drinker is increasingly insensitive to his environment—that he is in the grip of an autonomous physiological process. Myopia theory, on the contrary, says that the drinker is, in some respects, increasingly sensitive to his environment: He is at the mercy of whatever is in front of him.

A group of Canadian psychologists led by Tara MacDonald recently went into a series of bars and made the patrons read a short vignette. They had to imagine that they had met an attractive person at a bar, walked him or her home, and ended up in bed—only to discover that neither of them had a condom. The subjects were then asked to respond on a scale of one (very unlikely) to nine (very likely) to the proposition: "If I were in this situation, I would have sex." You'd think that the subjects who had been drinking heavily would be more likely to say that they would have sex—and that's exactly what happened. The drunk people came in at 5.36, on average, on the nine-point scale. The sober people came in at 3.91. The drinkers couldn't sort through the long-term consequences of unprotected sex. But then MacDonald went back to the bars and stamped the hands of some of the patrons with the phrase "AIDS kills." Drinkers with the hand stamp were slightly less likely than the sober people to want to have sex in that situation: They couldn't sort through the kinds of rationalizations necessary to set aside the risk of AIDS. Where norms and standards are clear and consistent, the drinker can become more rule-bound than his sober counterpart.

In other words, the frat boys drinking in a bar on a Friday night don't have to be loud and rowdy. They are responding to the signals sent by their immediate environment—by the pulsing music, by the crush of people, by the dimmed light, by the countless movies and television shows and general cultural expectations that say that young men in a bar with pulsing music on a Friday night have permission to be loud and rowdy. "Persons learn about drunkenness what their societies import to them, and comporting themselves in consonance with these understandings, they become living confirmations of their society's teachings," MacAndrew and Edgerton conclude. "Since societies, like individuals, get the sorts of drunken comportment that they allow, they deserve what they get."

4.

This is what connects the examples of Montero and New Haven. On the face of it, the towns are at opposite ends of the spectrum. The Camba got drunk every weekend on laboratory-grade alcohol. The Italians drank wine, in civil amounts, every day. The Italian example is healthy and laudable. The Camba's fiestas were excessive and surely took a long-term physical toll. But both communities understood the importance of rules and structure. Camba society, Dwight Heath says, was marked by a singular lack of "communal expression." They were itinerant farmworkers. Kinship ties were weak. Their daily labor tended to be solitary and the hours long. There were few neighborhood or civic groups. Those weekly drinking parties were not chaotic revels; they were the heart of Camba community life. They had a function, and the elaborate rituals—one bottle at a time, the toasting, the sitting in a circle—served to give the Camba's drinking a clear structure.

In the late 1940s, Phyllis Williams and Robert Straus, two sociologists at Yale, [35] selected ten first- and second-generation Italian-Americans from New Haven to keep diaries detailing their drinking behavior, and their entries show how well that community understood this lesson as well. Here is one of their subjects, Philomena Sappio, a forty-year-old hairdresser from an island in the Bay of Naples, describing what she drank one week in October of 1948:

Fri.—Today for dinner 4 oz. of wine [noon]. In the evening, I had fish with 8 oz. of wine [6 P.M.].

Sat.—Today I did not feel like drinking at all. Neither beer nor any other alcohol. I drank coffee and water.

Sun.—For dinner I made lasagna at noon, and had 8 oz. of wine. In the evening, I had company and took one glass of liqueur [1 oz. Strega] with my company. For supper—did not have supper because I wasn't hungry.

Mon.—At dinner I drank coffee, at supper 6 oz. of wine [5 P.M.].

Tues.—At dinner, 4 oz. wine [noon]. One of my friends and her husband took me and my daughter out this evening in a restaurant for supper. We had a splendid supper. I drank 1 oz. of vermouth [5:30 P.M.] and 12 oz. of wine [6 P.M.].

Wed.—For dinner, 4 oz. of wine [noon] and for supper 6 oz. of wine [6 P.M.].

Thurs.—At noon, coffee and at supper, 6 oz. of wine [6 P.M.].

Fri.—Today at noon I drank orange juice; at supper in the evening [6 P.M.] 8 oz. of wine.

Sappio drinks almost every day, unless she isn't feeling well. She almost always drinks wine. She drinks only at mealtimes. She rarely has more than a glass—except on a special occasion, as when she and her daughter are out with friends at a restaurant.

Here is another of Williams and Straus's subjects—Carmine Trotta, aged sixty, born in a village outside Salerno, married to a girl from his village, father of three, proprietor of a small grocery store, resident of an exclusively Italian neighborhood:

> Fri.—I do not generally eat anything for breakfast if I have a heavy supper the night before. I leave out eggnog and only take coffee with whisky because I like to have a little in the morning with coffee or with eggnog or a few crackers.
>
> Mon.—When I drink whisky before going to bed I always put it in a glass of water.
>
> Wed.—Today is my day off from business, so I [drank] some beer because it was very hot. I never drink beer when I am working because I don't like the smell of beer on my breath for my customers.
>
> Thurs.—Every time that I buy a bottle of whisky I always divide same. One half at home and one half in my shop.

Sappio and Trotta do not drink for the same purpose as the Camba: Alcohol has no larger social or emotional reward. It's food, consumed according to the same quotidian rhythms as pasta or cheese. But the content of the rules matters less than the fact of the rule, the existence of a drinking regimen that both encourages and constrains alcohol's use. "I went to visit one of my friends this evening," Sappio writes. "We saw television and she offered me 6 oz. of wine to drink, and it was good [9 P.M.]." She did not say that her friend put the bottle on the table or offered her a second glass. Evidently, she brought out one glass of wine for each of them, and they drank together, because one glass is what you had, in the Italian neighborhoods of New Haven, at 9 P.M. while watching television.

5.

Why can't we all drink like the Italians of New Haven? The flood of immigrants who came to the United States in the nineteenth century brought with them a wealth of cultural models, some of which were clearly superior to the patterns of their new host—and, in a perfect world, the rest of us would have adopted the best ways of the newcomers. It hasn't worked out that way, though. Americans did not learn to drink like Italians. On the contrary, when researchers followed up on Italian-Americans, they found that by the third and fourth generations they were, increasingly, drinking like everyone else.

There is something about the cultural dimension of social problems that 40 eludes us. When confronted with the rowdy youth in the bar, we are happy to raise his drinking age, to tax his beer, to punish him if he drives under the influence, and to push him into treatment if his habit becomes an addiction. But we are reluctant to provide him with a positive and constructive example of how to drink. The consequences of that failure are considerable, because, in the end, culture is a more powerful tool in dealing with drinking than medicine, economics, or the law. For all we know, Philomena Sappio could have had within her genome a grave susceptibility to alcohol. Because she lived in the protective world of New Haven's immigrant Italian community, however, it would never have become a problem. Today, she would be at the mercy of her own inherent weaknesses. Nowhere in the multitude of messages and signals sent by popular culture and social institutions about drinking is there any consensus about what drinking is supposed to mean.

"Mind if I vent for a while?" a woman asks her husband, in one popular—and depressingly typical—beer ad. He is sitting on the couch. She has just come home from work. He replies, "Mind? I'd prefer it!" And he jumps up, goes to the refrigerator, and retrieves two cans of Coors Light—a brand that comes with a special vent intended to make pouring the beer easier. "Let's vent!" he cries out. She looks at him oddly: "What are you talking about?" "I'm talking about venting!" he replies, as she turns away in disgust. "What are you talking about?" The voice-over intones, "The vented wide-mouthed can from Coors Light. It lets in air for a smooth, refreshing pour." Even the Camba, for all their excesses, would never have been so foolish as to pretend that you could have a conversation about drinking and talk only about the can.

QUESTIONS FOR DISCUSSION AND WRITING

1. Gladwell reports a statement made by Anna Heath, who, with her husband Dwight, went to Bolivia in the 1950s and wound up opening up a new range of research: "It is not anthropologists who recognize the value of what they've done. It's everyone else. The anthropologist is just reporting" (p. 169). How does this relate to the examination of alcohol use and abuse? What did the Heaths almost unknowingly discover in their visit to the Camba in Bolivia? What might be some consequences of their research that go beyond the realms of anthropology?

2. A detailed study was also done of the drinking habits of two groups living in New Haven, Connecticut: the Irish Americans and the Italian Americans. Although both groups drank frequently, the Italian Americans did not encounter the same problems with alcohol that the Irish Americans did. Why? However, as the generations progressed, later generations of Italian Americans were more likely to develop problems with their alcohol use. Why is this? Can there be other explanations—such as genetic proclivity—that could adequately explain such an occurrence or not? Develop your answer with specific details. To get more facts, do additional research on your own about causes of alcoholism.

3. Dwight Heath describes the skepticism a fellow Yale researcher had about his story of drinking 180-proof rum, so Heath drank some under controlled circumstances. Why did Heath's colleague not believe him until this test? What

does this say about the difference between reliance on anecdotal evidence versus evidence gathered in controlled situations? Under what circumstances then can conclusions be drawn from noncontrolled circumstances or observations? Explain.

4. In paragraph 24, Gladwell states, "anthropologists began to take note of all the puzzling ways alcohol wasn't reliable in its effects." What does Gladwell mean by unreliable effects? Look at the examples that Gladwell cites. What do they have in common? Can you cite examples of your own, either that you have witnessed yourself or that you have heard or read about? What can explain such unreliability?

5. Later in the essay, Gladwell points out that alcohol's "principal effect is to narrow our emotional and mental field of vision" (paragraph 29). What does this mean? What are the consequences of this effect?

6. If, ultimately, culture has a much greater influence on the use and abuse of alcohol, what does this mean for those fighting a personal battle with alcoholism? Does Gladwell's essay offer practical lessons or advice to help improve people's approach to alcohol consumption? Be specific.

MICHAEL POLLAN

The Food Movement, Rising

Michael Pollan (b. 1955) had already written one New York Times *best-seller—*The Botany of Desire: A Plant's Eye View of the World *in 2001—when he firmly entered into the public's consciousness with his book* The Omnivore's Dilemma: A Natural History of Four Meals *(2006). Not only was it a best-seller, but it was also named one of the ten best books of the year by the* New York Times *and the* Washington Post. *It won the California Book Award, the Northern California Book Award, and the James Beard Award.* The Omnivore's Dilemma *discussed the contemporary way in which food comes to our plates, compared to the ways of the past. It argued that the modern industrial-style agricultural practices have removed us from nature, much to our detriment. Pollan's book, unlike many other works that focus on how fast food and processed foods have done damage to the human body, examined the large-scale environmental impacts of agribusiness. Since then, Pollan has published* In Defense of Food: An Eater's Manifesto *(2008) and* Food Rules: An Eater's Manual *(2010). Both books were also best sellers. In 2010, Pollan was named to* Time *magazine's 100 Most Influential People list, which is just one of many honors and awards he has received for his writings. He currently is a professor of journalism at the University of California, Berkeley.*

In "The Food Movement, Rising," which initially appeared in the New York Times Review of Books *on May 20, 2010, Pollan argues that food—and food problems—have been largely absent from public discussion, until recently. For most of the long stretch of human history, acquiring enough food to eat was a fundamental concern, but in recent times, especially in developed nations, there has been little worry about food availability. However, a new concern has arisen: The food we eat— and how we grow that food—may be creating serious damage to the environment. This has spawned a variety of reactions. Some argue for more locally grown food and food grown organically; others respond that such approaches are inherently elitist because they drive up the costs of food, which the rich can afford but the poor cannot. In the background, but relevant, are discussions about food and eating: Is it merely fuel for the body? Is it a way for families and communities to bond? How is eating a political statement? What is our future in terms of food and eating? No matter what the answers, it's clear to Pollan that discussions about the nature of food and eating are going to be vital to our future.*

1. FOOD MADE VISIBLE

It might sound odd to say this about something people deal with at least three times a day, but food in America has been more or less invisible, politically speaking, until very recently. At least until the early 1970s, when a bout of food price inflation and the appearance of books critical of industrial agriculture (by Wendell Berry, Francis Moore Lappé, and Barry Commoner, among others) threatened to propel the subject to the top of the national agenda, Americans have not had to think very hard about where their food comes from, or what it is doing to the planet, their bodies, and their society.

Most people count this a blessing, Americans spend a smaller percentage of their income on food than any people in history—slightly less than 10 percent— and a smaller amount of their time preparing it: a mere thirty-one minutes a day on average, including clean-up. The supermarkets brim with produce summoned from every corner of the globe, a steady stream of novel food products (17,000 new ones each year) crowds the middle aisles, and in the freezer case you can find "home meal replacements" in every conceivable ethnic stripe, demanding nothing more of the eater than opening the package and waiting for the microwave to chirp. Considered in the long sweep of human history, in which getting food dominated not just daily life but economic and political life as well, having to worry about food as little as we do, or did, seems almost a kind of dream.

The dream that the age-old "food problem" had been largely solved for most Americans was sustained by the tremendous postwar increases in the productivity of American farmers, made possible by cheap fossil fuel (the key ingredient in both chemical fertilizers and pesticides) and changes in agricultural policies. Asked by President Nixon to try to drive down the cost of food after it had spiked in the early 1970s, Agriculture Secretary Earl Butz shifted the historical focus of federal farm policy from supporting prices for farmers to boosting yields of a small handful of commodity crops (corn and soy especially) at any cost.

The administration's cheap food policy worked almost too well: Crop prices fell, forcing farmers to produce still more simply to break even. This led to a deep depression in the farm belt in the 1980s followed by a brutal wave of consolidation. Most importantly, the price of food came down, or at least the price of the kinds of foods that could be made from corn and soy: processed foods and sweetened beverages and feedlot meat. (Prices for fresh produce have increased since the 1980s.) Washington had succeeded in eliminating food as a political issue—an objective dear to most governments at least since the time of the French Revolution.

But although cheap food is good politics, it turns out there are significant 5 costs—to the environment, to public health, to the public purse, even to the culture—and as these became impossible to ignore in recent years, food has come back into view. Beginning in the late 1980s, a series of food safety scandals opened people's eyes to the way their food was being produced, each one drawing the curtain back a little further on a food system that had changed beyond recognition. When BSE, or mad cow disease, surfaced in England in 1986, Americans learned that cattle, which are herbivores, were routinely being fed the flesh of other cattle; the practice helped keep meat cheap but at the risk of a hideous brain-wasting disease.

The 1993 deaths of four children in Washington State who had eaten hamburgers from Jack in the Box were traced to meat contaminated with *E. Coli* 0157:H7, a mutant strain of the common intestinal bacteria first identified in feedlot cattle in 1982. Since then, repeated outbreaks of food-borne illness linked to new antibiotic-resistant strains of bacteria (campylobacter, salmonella, MRSA) have turned a bright light on the shortsighted practice of routinely administering antibiotics to food animals, not to treat disease but simply to speed their growth and allow them to withstand the filthy and stressful conditions in which they live.

In the wake of these food safety scandals, the conversation about food politics that briefly flourished in the 1970s was picked up again in a series of books, articles, and movies about the consequences of industrial food production. Beginning in 2001 with the publication of Eric Schlosser's *Fast Food Nation*, a surprise best-seller, and, the following year, Marion Nestle's *Food Politics*, the food journalism of the last decade has succeeded in making clear and telling connections between the methods of industrial food production, agricultural policy, food-borne illness, childhood obesity, the decline of the family meal as an institution, and, notably, the decline of family income beginning in the 1970s.

Besides drawing women into the work force, falling wages made fast food both cheap to produce and a welcome, if not indispensable, option for pinched and harried families. The picture of the food economy Schlosser painted resembles an upside-down version of the social compact sometimes referred to as "Fordism": Instead of paying workers well enough to allow them to buy things like cars, as Henry Ford proposed to do, companies like Wal-Mart and McDonald's pay their workers so poorly that they can afford only the cheap, low-quality food these companies sell, creating a kind of nonvirtuous circle driving down both wages and the quality of food. The advent of fast food (and cheap food in general) has, in effect, subsidized the decline of family incomes in America.

2. FOOD POLITICS

Cheap food has become an indispensable pillar of the modern economy. But it is no longer an invisible or uncontested one. One of the most interesting social movements to emerge in the last few years is the "food movement," or perhaps I should say "movements," since it is unified as yet by little more than the recognition that industrial food production is in need of reform because its social/environmental/public health/animal welfare/gastronomic costs are too high.

As that list suggests, the critics are coming at the issue from a great many   10
different directions. Where many social movements tend to splinter as time goes on, breaking into various factions representing divergent concerns or tactics, the food movement starts out splintered. Among the many threads of advocacy that can be lumped together under that rubric we can include school lunch reform; the campaign for animal rights and welfare; the campaign against genetically modified crops; the rise of organic and locally produced food; efforts to combat obesity and type 2 diabetes; "food sovereignty" (the principle that nations should be allowed to decide their agricultural policies rather than submit to free trade regimes); farm bill reform; food safety regulation; farmland preservation; student organizing around food issues on campus; efforts to promote urban agriculture and ensure that communities have access to healthy food; initiatives to create gardens and cooking classes in schools; farm worker rights; nutrition labeling; feedlot pollution; and the various efforts to regulate food ingredients and marketing, especially to kids.

It's a big, lumpy tent, and sometimes the various factions beneath it work at cross-purposes. For example, activists working to strengthen federal food safety regulations have recently run afoul of local food advocates, who fear that the burden of new regulation will cripple the current revival of small-farm agriculture. Joel Salatin, the Virginia meat producer and writer who has become a hero to the food movement, fulminates against food safety regulation on libertarian grounds in his *Everything I Want to Do Is Illegal: War Stories from the Local Food Front*. Hunger activists like Joel Berg, in *All You Can Eat: How Hungry Is America?*, criticize supporters of "sustainable" agriculture—i.e., producing food in ways that do not harm the environment—for advocating reforms that threaten to raise the cost of food to the poor. Animal rights advocates occasionally pick fights with sustainable meat producers (such as Joel Salatin), as Jonathan Safran Foer does in his recent vegetarian polemic, *Eating Animals*.

But there are indications that these various voices may be coming together in something that looks more and more like a coherent movement. Many in the animal welfare movement, from PETA to Peter Singer, have come to see that a smaller-scale, more humane animal agriculture is a goal worth fighting for, and surely more attainable than the abolition of meat eating. Stung by charges of elitism, activists for sustainable farming are starting to take seriously the problem of hunger and poverty. They're promoting schemes and policies to make fresh local food more accessible to the poor, through programs that give vouchers redeemable at farmers' markets to participants in the Special Supplemental Nutrition Program for Women, Infants, and Children (WIC) and food stamp recipients. Yet a few underlying tensions remain: The "hunger lobby" has traditionally supported farm subsidies in exchange for the farm lobby's support of nutrition programs, a marriage of, convenience dating to the 1960s that vastly complicates reform of the farm bill—a top priority for the food movement.

The sociologist Troy Duster reminds us of an all-important axiom about social movements: "No movement is as coherent and integrated as it seems from afar," he says, "and no movement is as incoherent and fractured as it seems from up close." Viewed from a middle distance, then, the food movement coalesces around the recognition that today's food and farming economy is "unsustainable"—that it can't go on in its current form much longer without courting a breakdown of some kind, whether environmental, economic, or both.

For some in the movement, the more urgent problem is environmental: The food system consumes more fossil fuel energy than we can count on in the future (about a fifth of the total American use of such energy) and emits more greenhouse gas than we can afford to emit, particularly since agriculture is the one human system that should be able to substantially rely on photosynthesis: solar energy. It will be difficult if not impossible to address the issue of climate change without reforming the food system. This is a conclusion that has only recently been embraced by the environmental movement, which historically has disdained all agriculture as a lapse from wilderness and a source of pollution.[1] But in the last few years, several of the major environmental groups have come to appreciate that a diversified, sustainable agriculture—which can sequester large amounts of carbon in the soil—holds the potential not just to mitigate but actually to help solve environmental problems, including climate change. Today, environmental organizations like the Natural Resources Defense Council and the Environmental Working Group are taking up the cause of food system reform, lending their expertise and clout to the movement.

But perhaps the food movement's strongest claim on public attention today is   15 the fact that the American diet of highly processed food laced with added fats and sugars is responsible for the epidemic of chronic diseases that threatens to bankrupt the health care system. The Centers for Disease Control estimates that fully three quarters of U.S. health care spending goes to treat chronic diseases, most of which are preventable and linked to diet: heart disease, stroke, type 2 diabetes, and at least a third of all cancers. The health care crisis probably cannot be addressed without addressing the catastrophe of the American diet, and that diet is the direct (even if unintended) result of the way that our agriculture and food industries have been organized.

Michelle Obama's recent foray into food politics, beginning with the organic garden she planted on the White House lawn last spring, suggests that the administration has made these connections. Her new "Let's Move" campaign to combat childhood obesity might at first blush seem fairly anodyne, but in announcing the

---

[1] Al Gore's *An Inconvenient Truth* made scant mention of food or agriculture, but in his recent follow-up book, *Our Choice: A Plan to Solve the Climate Crisis* (2009), he devotes a long chapter to the subject of our food choices and their bearing on climate.

initiative in February, and in a surprisingly tough speech to the Grocery Manufacturers Association in March,[2] the first lady has effectively shifted the conversation about diet from the industry's preferred ground of "personal responsibility" and exercise to a frank discussion of the way food is produced and marketed. "We need you not just to tweak around the edges," she told the assembled food makers, "but to entirely rethink the products that you're offering, the information that you provide about these products, and how you market those products to our children."

Mrs. Obama explicitly rejected the conventional argument that the food industry is merely giving people the sugary, fatty, and salty foods they want, contending that the industry "doesn't just respond to people's natural inclinations—it also actually helps to shape them," through the ways it creates products and markets them.

So far at least, Michelle Obama is the food movement's most important ally in the administration, but there are signs of interest elsewhere. Under Commissioner Margaret Hamburg, the FDA has cracked down on deceptive food marketing and is said to be weighing a ban on the nontherapeutic use of antibiotics in factory farming. Attorney General Eric Holder recently avowed the Justice Department's intention to pursue antitrust enforcement in agribusiness, one of the most highly concentrated sectors in the economy.[3] At his side was Agriculture Secretary Tom Vilsack, the former governor of Iowa, who has planted his own organic vegetable garden at the department and launched a new "Know Your Farmer, Know Your Food" initiative aimed at promoting local food systems as a way to both rebuild rural economies and improve access to healthy food.

Though Vilsack has so far left mostly undisturbed his department's traditional deference to industrial agriculture, the new tone in Washington and the appointment of a handful of respected reformers (such as Tufts professor Kathleen Merrigan as deputy secretary of agriculture) has elicited a somewhat defensive, if not panicky, reaction from agribusiness. The Farm Bureau recently urged its members to go on the offensive against "food activists," and a trade association representing pesticide makers called CropLife America wrote to Michelle Obama suggesting that her organic garden had unfairly maligned chemical agriculture and encouraging her to use "crop protection technologies"—i.e., pesticides.

The first lady's response is not known; however, the president subsequently 20 rewarded CropLife by appointing one of its executives to a high-level trade post. This and other industry-friendly appointments suggest that while the administration may be sympathetic to elements of the food movement's agenda, it isn't about to take on agribusiness, at least not directly, at least until it senses at its back a much larger constituency for reform.

---

[2] Ms. Obama's speech can be read at www.whitehouse.gov/the-press-office/remarks-first-lady-a-grocery-manufacturers-association-conference.

[3] Speaking in March at an Iowa "listening session" about agribusiness concentration, Holder said, "long periods of reckless deregulation have restricted competition" in agriculture. Indeed: four companies (JBS/Swift, Tyson, Cargill, and National Beef Packers) slaughter 85 percent of U.S. beef cattle; two companies (Monsanto and DuPont) sell more than 50 percent of U.S. corn seed; one company (Dean Foods) controls 40 percent of the U.S. milk supply.

One way to interpret Michelle Obama's deepening involvement in food issues is as an effort to build such a constituency, and in this she may well succeed. It's a mistake to underestimate what a determined first lady can accomplish. Lady Bird Johnson's "highway beautification" campaign also seemed benign, but in the end it helped raise public consciousness about "the environment" (as it would soon come to be known) and put an end to the public's tolerance for littering. And while Michelle Obama has explicitly limited her efforts to exhortation ("we can't solve this problem by passing a bunch of laws in Washington," she told the Grocery Manufacturers, no doubt much to their relief), her work is already creating a climate in which just such a "bunch of laws" might flourish: A handful of state legislatures, including California's, are seriously considering levying new taxes on sugar in soft drinks, proposals considered hopelessly extreme less than a year ago.

The political ground is shifting, and the passage of health care reform may accelerate that movement. The bill itself contains a few provisions long promoted by the food movement (like calorie labeling on fast food menus), but more important could be the new political tendencies it sets in motion. If health insurers can no longer keep people with chronic diseases out of their patient pools, it stands to reason that the companies will develop a keener interest in preventing those diseases. They will then discover that they have a large stake in things like soda taxes and in precisely which kinds of calories the farm bill is subsidizing. As the insurance industry and the government take on more responsibility for the cost of treating expensive and largely preventable problems like obesity and type 2 diabetes, pressure for reform of the food system, and the American diet, can be expected to increase.

3. BEYOND THE BARCODE

It would be a mistake to conclude that the food movement's agenda can be reduced to a set of laws, policies, and regulations, important as these may be. What is attracting so many people to the movement today (and young people in particular) is a much less conventional kind of politics, one that is about something more than food. The food movement is also about community, identity, pleasure, and, most notably, about carving out a new social and economic space removed from the influence of big corporations on the one side and government on the other. As the Diggers used to say during their San Francisco be-ins during the 1960s, food can serve as "an edible dynamic"—a means to a political end that is only nominally about food itself.

One can get a taste of this social space simply by hanging around a farmers' market, an activity that a great many people enjoy today regardless of whether they're in the market for a bunch of carrots or a head of lettuce. Farmers' markets are thriving, more than five thousand strong, and there is a lot more going on in them than the exchange of money for food. Someone is collecting signatures on a petition. Someone else is playing music. Children are everywhere, sampling fresh produce, talking to farmers. Friends and acquaintances stop to chat. One sociologist calculated that people have ten times as many conversations at the farmers' market than they do in the supermarket. Socially as well as sensually, the farmers' market offers a remarkably rich and appealing environment. Someone buying food here may be acting not just as a consumer but also as a neighbor, a citizen, a parent, a cook. In many cities and towns, farmers' markets have taken on (and not for the first time) the function of a lively new public square.

Though seldom articulated as such, the attempt to redefine, or escape, the traditional role of consumer has become an important aspiration of the food movement. In various ways it seeks to put the relationship between consumers and producers on a new, more neighborly footing, enriching the kinds of information exchanged in the transaction, and encouraging us to regard our food dollars as "votes" for a different kind of agriculture and, by implication, economy. The modern marketplace would have us decide what to buy strictly on the basis of price and self-interest; the food movement implicitly proposes that we enlarge our understanding of both those terms, suggesting that not just "good value" but ethical and political values should inform our buying decisions, and that we'll get more satisfaction from our eating when they do.

That satisfaction helps to explain why many in the movement don't greet the spectacle of large corporations adopting its goals, as some of them have begun to do, with unalloyed enthusiasm. Already Wal-Mart sells organic and local food, but this doesn't greatly warm the hearts of food movement activists. One important impetus for the movement, or at least its locavore wing—those who are committed to eating as much locally produced food as possible—is the desire to get "beyond the barcode"—to create new economic and social structures outside of the mainstream consumer economy. Though not always articulated in these terms, the local food movement wants to decentralize the global economy, if not secede from it altogether, which is why in some communities, such as Great Barrington, Massachusetts, local currencies (the "BerkShare") have popped up.

In fact it's hard to say which comes first: the desire to promote local agriculture or the desire to promote local economies more generally by cutting ties, to whatever degree possible, to the national economic grid.[4] This is at bottom a communitarian impulse, and it is one that is drawing support from the right as well as the left. Though the food movement has deep roots in the counterculture of the 1960s, its critique of corporate food and federal farm subsidies, as well as its emphasis on building community around food, has won it friends on the right. In his 2006 book *Crunchy Cons*, Rod Dreher identifies a strain of libertarian conservatism, often evangelical, that regards fast food as anathema to family values, and has seized on local food as a kind of culinary counterpart to home schooling.

It makes sense that food and farming should become a locus of attention for Americans disenchanted with consumer capitalism. Food is the place in daily life where corporatization can be most vividly felt: Think about the homogenization of taste and experience represented by fast food. By the same token, food offers

25

---

[4]For an interesting case study about a depressed Vermont mining town that turned to local food and agriculture to revitalize itself, see Ben Hewitt, *The Town That Food Saved: How One Community Found Vitality in Local Food* (Rodale, 2009).

us one of the shortest, most appealing paths out of the corporate labyrinth, and into the sheer diversity of local flavors, varieties, and characters on offer at the farmers' market.

Put another way, the food movement has set out to foster new forms of civil society. But instead of proposing that space as a counterweight to an overbearing state, as is usually the case, the food movement poses it against the dominance of corporations and their tendency to insinuate themselves into any aspect of our lives from which they can profit. As Wendell Berry writes, the corporations

> will grow, deliver, and cook your food for you and (just like your mother) beg you to eat it. That they do not yet offer to insert it, prechewed, into your mouth is only because they have found no profitable way to do so.

The corporatization of something as basic and intimate as eating is, for many 30 of us today, a good place to draw the line.

The Italian-born organization Slow Food, founded in 1986 as a protest against the arrival of McDonald's in Rome, represents perhaps the purest expression of these politics. The organization, which now has 100,000 members in 132 countries, began by dedicating itself to "a firm defense of quiet material pleasure" but has lately waded into deeper political and economic waters. Slow Food's founder and president, Carlo Petrini, a former leftist journalist, has much to say about how people's daily food choices can rehabilitate the act of consumption, making it something more creative and progressive. In his new book *Terra Madre: Forging a New Global Network of Sustainable Food Communities*, Petrini urges eaters and food producers to join together in "food communities" outside of the usual distribution channels, which typically communicate little information beyond price and often exploit food producers. A farmers' market is one manifestation of such a community, but Petrini is no mere locavore. Rather, he would have us practice on a global scale something like "local" economics, with its stress on neighborliness, as when, to cite one of his examples, eaters in the affluent West support nomad fisher folk in Mauritania by creating a market for their bottarga, or dried mullet roe. In helping to keep alive such a food tradition and way of life, the eater becomes something more than a consumer; she becomes what Petrini likes to call a "coproducer."

Ever the Italian, Petrini puts pleasure at the center of his politics, which might explain why Slow Food is not always taken as seriously as it deserves to be. For why shouldn't pleasure figure in the politics of the food movement? Good food is potentially one of the most democratic pleasures a society can offer, and is one of those subjects, like sports, that people can talk about across lines of class, ethnicity, and race.

The fact that the most humane and most environmentally sustainable choices frequently turn out to be the most delicious choices (as chefs such as Alice Waters and Dan Barber have pointed out) is fortuitous to say the least; it is also a welcome challenge to the more dismal choices typically posed by environmentalism, which most of the time is asking us to give up things we like. As Alice Waters has often said, it was not politics or ecology that brought her to organic agriculture, but rather the desire to recover a certain taste—one she had experienced as an exchange student in France. Of course democratizing such tastes, which under current policies tend to be more expensive, is the hard part, and must eventually lead the movement back to more conventional politics lest it be tagged as elitist.

But the movement's interest in such seemingly mundane matters as taste and the other textures of everyday life is also one of its great strengths. Part of the movement's critique of industrial food is that, with the rise of fast food and the collapse of everyday cooking, it has damaged family life and community by under-mining the institution of the shared meal. Sad as it may be to bowl alone, eating alone can be sadder still, not least because it is eroding the civility on which our political culture depends.

That is the argument made by Janet Flammang, a political scientist, in a   35 provocative new book called *The Taste for Civilization: Food, Politics, and Civil Society.* "Significant social and political costs have resulted from fast food and convenience foods," she writes, "grazing and snacking instead of sitting down for leisurely meals, watching television during mealtimes instead of conversing"— 40 percent of Americans watch television during meals—"viewing food as fuel rather than sustenance, discarding family recipes and foodways, and denying that eating has social and political dimensions." The cultural contradictions of capital-ism—its tendency to undermine the stabilizing social forms it depends on—are on vivid display at the modern American dinner table.

In a challenge to second-wave feminists who urged women to get out of the kitchen, Flammang suggests that by denigrating "foodwork"—everything involved in putting meals on the family table—we have unthinkingly wrecked one of the nurseries of democracy: the family meal. It is at "the temporary democracy of the table" that children learn the art of conversation and acquire the habits of civility—sharing, listening, taking turns, navigating differences, arguing without offending—and it is these habits that are lost when we eat alone and on the run. "Civility is not needed when one is by oneself."[5]

These arguments resonated during the Senate debate over health care reform, when the *New York Times* reported that the private Senate dining room, where senators of both parties used to break bread together, stood empty. Flammang attributes some of the loss of civility in Washington to the aftermath of the 1994 Republican Revolution, when Newt Gingrich, the new Speaker of the House, urged his freshman legislators not to move their families to Washington. Mem-bers now returned to their districts every weekend, sacrificing opportunities for socializing across party lines and, in the process, the "reservoirs of good will

[5]See David M. Herszenhorn, "In Senate Health Care Vote, New Partisan Vitriol," the *New York Times,* December 23, 2009: "Senator Max Baucus, Democrat of Montana and chairman of the Finance Com-mittee, said the political—and often personal—divisions that now characterize the Senate were epito-mized by the empty tables in the senators' private dining room, a place where members of both parties used to break bread. 'Nobody goes there anymore,' Mr. Baucus said. 'When I was here 10, 15, 30 years ago, that is the place you would go to talk to senators, let your hair down, just kind of compare notes, no spouses allowed, no staff, nobody. It is now empty.'"

replenished at dinner parties." It is much harder to vilify someone with whom you have shared a meal.

Flammang makes a convincing case for the centrality of food work and shared meals, much along the lines laid down by Carlo Petrini and Alice Waters, but with more historical perspective and theoretical rigor. A scholar of the women's movement, she suggests that "American women are having second thoughts" about having left the kitchen.[6] However, the answer is not for them simply to return to it, at least not alone, but rather "for everyone—men, women, and children—to go back to the kitchen, as in preindustrial days, and for the workplace to lessen its time demands on people." Flammang points out that the historical priority of the American labor movement has been to fight for money, while the European labor movement has fought for time, which she suggests may have been the wiser choice.

At the very least this is a debate worth having, and it begins by taking food issues much more seriously than we have taken them. Flammang suggests that the invisibility of these issues until recently owes to the identification of food work with women and the (related) fact that eating, by its very nature, falls on the wrong side of the mind–body dualism. "Food is apprehended through the senses of touch, smell, and taste," she points out,

> which rank lower on the hierarchy of senses than sight and hearing, which are typically thought to give rise to knowledge. In most of philosophy, religion, and literature, food is associated with body, animal, female, and appetite— things civilized men have sought to overcome with reason and knowledge.

Much to our loss. But food is invisible no longer and, in light of the mounting   40 costs we've incurred by ignoring it, it is likely to demand much more of our attention in the future, as eaters, parents, and citizens. It is only a matter of time before politicians seize on the power of the food issue, which besides being increasingly urgent is also almost primal, indeed is in some deep sense proto-political. For where do all politics begin if not in the high chair?—at that fateful moment when mother, or father, raises a spoonful of food to the lips of the baby who clamps shut her mouth, shakes her head no, and for the very first time in life awakens to and asserts her sovereign power.

QUESTIONS FOR DISCUSSION AND WRITING

1. Considering that throughout almost all of the United States, food is readily available, what is the nature of today's food problem, as Pollan sees it? Examine Pollan's short history of food production in the United States, which he picks up in the 1970s and carries to the present. Is there an underlying theme to his criticism of contemporary food production practices? In your opinion, is this criticism valid? Why or why not?

---

[6]The stirrings of a new "radical homemakers" movement lends some support to the assertion. See Shannon Hayes's *Radical Homemakers: Reclaiming Domesticity from a Consumer Culture* (Left to Write Press, 2010).

2. Henry Ford is said to have given his workers pay raises so they could buy the cars they were making, which is what Pollan refers to as "Fordism" in paragraph 8. Pollan argues that modern food companies like McDonald's and Walmart are engaged in the reverse: paying their employees so little they are forced to buy the cheap food offered by these companies. Cheap food is typically unhealthy food, high in fat, salt, and/or sugar, and containing little nutritional value. One response to critics of cheap food, however, is that the stance is elitist: Arguments against cheap food work for the well-to-do but are irrelevant to people who cannot afford higher quality food and do not have the time to regularly prepare fresh meals at home. What is your response to that argument? Can the eating habits of poorer Americans be improved without turning to elitist solutions? How? If not, what will be the long-term ramifications for America?

3. As Pollan notes, the food movement is not a single, unified group, but includes locavores, vegans, advocates for small farms, advocates for the poor, environmentalists, animal rights activists, and others who may have, at times, conflicting goals. According to Pollan, how can these groups be united? What role can high-profile people, such as First Lady Michelle Obama, play in the food movement? Do the generally left-wing politics of many in the food movement create a barrier for broader acceptance of its ideas? Why or why not?

4. Pollan reserves most of his optimism for farmers' markets, which, he says, are "thriving, more than five thousand strong" (paragraph 24). Have you ever been to a farmers' market? If so, describe the experience. Pollan looks at the farmers' market as a way to "put the relationship between consumers and producers on a new, more neighborly footing" (paragraph 25). Why is such a relationship necessary or beneficial, in your opinion?

5. How are food and family connected? Is the contemporary family—often eating alone at separate times, or together with the television on, and eating processed foods or take-out meals—also part of the problem with food? Or, are people simply making the family (and particularly the working mother) a scapegoat for problems not within the family's (or mother's) power to control? Explain.

LISA MILLER

Divided We Eat

What's for dinner? Lisa Miller (b. 1963) explores the implications of the different answers people may give to that question, especially as it reflects differences in economics and social class in the United States. A senior editor for Newsweek *magazine, Miller wrote the weekly "Belief Watch" column and was in charge of the magazine's coverage of religion. She won the Wilbur Award for Outstanding Magazine Column in 2010. Before working at* Newsweek, *Miller worked at the* Wall Street Journal, *the* Harvard Business Review, *the* New Yorker, *and* Self *magazine. She is the author of the nonfiction book* Heaven: Our Enduring Fascination with the Afterlife. *Miller is a 1984 graduate of Oberlin College. Currently, she is a contributing editor for* New York *magazine and the religion columnist for the* Washington Post.

In this article, which was the cover story for Newsweek's *November 29, 2010, issue, Miller tackles the food divide: Well-to-do Americans are becoming pickier about the foods they eat, choosing local, organic foods that can be costly; at the same time, the number of Americans experiencing "food insecurity"—the real possibility of running out of food and the money to buy more—is increasing. The food one eats is becoming a sign of social status, like cars and clothes in past generations. The final irony is this: America's poorest are typically the most obese as well, subsisting on processed foods and fast foods that are high in fat, salt, and calories, but low in nutrition.*

For breakfast, I usually have a cappuccino—espresso made in an Alessi pot and mixed with organic milk, which has been gently heated and hand-fluffed by my husband. I eat two slices of imported cheese—Dutch Parrano, the label says, "the hippest cheese in New York" (no joke)—on homemade bread with butter. I am what you might call a food snob. My nutritionist neighbor drinks a protein shake while her 5-year-old son eats quinoa porridge sweetened with applesauce and laced with kale flakes. She is what you might call a health nut. On a recent morning, my neighbor's friend Alexandra Ferguson sipped politically correct Nicaraguan coffee in her comfy kitchen while her two young boys chose from among an assortment of organic cereals. As we sat, the six chickens Ferguson and her husband, Dave, keep for eggs in a backyard coop peered indoors from the stoop. The Fergusons are known as locavores.

Alexandra says she spends hours each day thinking about, shopping for, and preparing food. She is a disciple of Michael Pollan, whose 2006 book *The Omnivore's Dilemma* made the locavore movement a national phenomenon, and believes that eating organically and locally contributes not only to the health of her family but to the existential happiness of farm animals and farmers—and, indeed, to the survival of the planet. "Michael Pollan is my new hero, next to Jimmy Carter," she told me. In some neighborhoods, a lawyer who raises chickens in her backyard might be considered eccentric, but we live in Park Slope, Brooklyn, a community that accommodates and celebrates every kind of foodie. Whether you believe in eating for pleasure, for health, for justice, or for some idealized vision of family life, you will find neighbors who reflect your food values. In Park Slope, the contents of a child's lunchbox can be fodder for a 20-minute conversation.

Over coffee, I cautiously raise a subject that has concerned me of late: less than five miles away, some children don't have enough to eat; others exist almost exclusively on junk food. Alexandra concedes that her approach is probably out of reach for those people. Though they are not wealthy by Park Slope standards— Alexandra works part time and Dave is employed by the city—the Fergusons spend approximately 20 percent of their income, or $1,000 a month, on food. The average American spends 13 percent, including restaurants and takeout.

And so the conversation turns to the difficulty of sharing their interpretation of the Pollan doctrine with the uninitiated. When they visit Dave's family in Tennessee, tensions erupt over food choices. One time, Alexandra remembers, she irked her mother-in-law by purchasing a bag of organic apples, even though her mother-in-law had already bought the nonorganic kind at the grocery store. The old apples were perfectly good, her mother-in-law said. Why waste money—and apples?

The Fergusons recall Dave's mother saying something along these lines "When 5 we come to your place, we don't complain about your food. Why do you complain about ours? It's not like our food is poison."

"I can't convince my brother to spend another dime on food," adds Dave.

"This is our charity. This is my giving to the world," says Alexandra, finally, as she packs lunchboxes—organic peanut butter and jelly on grainy bread, a yogurt, and a clementine—for her two boys. "We contribute a lot."

According to data released last week by the U.S. Department of Agriculture, 17 percent of Americans—more than 50 million people—live in households that are "food insecure," a term that means a family sometimes runs out of money to buy food, or it sometimes runs out of food before it can get more money. Food insecurity is especially high in households headed by a single mother. It is most severe in the South, and in big cities. In New York City, 1.4 million people are food insecure, and 257,000 of them live near me, in Brooklyn. Food insecurity is linked, of course, to other economic measures like housing and employment, so it surprised no one that the biggest surge in food insecurity since the agency established the measure in 1995 occurred between 2007 and 2008, at the start of the economic downturn. (The 2009 numbers, released last week, showed little change.) The proportion of households that qualify as "hungry"—with what the USDA calls "very low food security"—is small, about 6 percent. Reflected against the obsessive concerns of the foodies in my circle, and the glare of attention given to the plight of the poor and hungry abroad, even a fraction of starving children in America seems too high.

Mine seems on some level like a naive complaint. There have always been rich people and poor people in America and, in a capitalist economy, the well-to-do have always had the freedom to indulge themselves as they please. In hard times, food has always marked a bright border between the haves and the have-nots. In the earliest days of the Depression, as the poor waited on bread lines, the middle and upper classes in America became devoted to fad diets. Followers of the Hollywood 18-Day Diet, writes Harvey Levenstein in his 1993 book *Paradox of Plenty*, "could live on fewer than six hundred calories a day by limiting each meal to half a grapefruit, melba toast, coffee without cream or sugar, and, at lunch and dinner, some raw vegetables."

But modern America is a place of extremes, and what you eat for dinner has 10 become the definitive marker of social status; as the distance between rich and poor continues to grow, the freshest, most nutritious foods have become luxury goods that only some can afford. Among the lowest quintile of American families, mean household income has held relatively steady between $10,000 and $13,000 for the past two decades (in inflation-adjusted dollars); among the highest, income has jumped 20 percent to $170,800 over the same period, according to census data. What this means, in practical terms, is that the richest Americans can afford to buy berries out of season at Whole Foods—the upscale grocery chain that recently reported a 58 percent increase in its quarterly profits—while the food insecure often eat what they can: highly caloric, mass-produced foods like pizza and packaged cakes that fill them up quickly. The number of Americans on food stamps has surged by 58.5 percent over the last three years.

Corpulence used to signify the prosperity of a few but has now become a marker of poverty. Obesity has risen as the income gap has widened: more than a third of U.S. adults and 17 percent of children are obese, and the problem is acute among the poor. While obesity is a complex problem—genetics, environment, and activity level all play a role—a 2008 study by the USDA found that children and women on food stamps were likelier to be overweight than those who were not. According to studies led by British epidemiologist Kate Pickett, obesity rates are highest in developed countries with the greatest income disparities. America is among the most obese of nations; Japan, with its relatively low income inequality, is the thinnest.

Adam Drewnowski, an epidemiologist at the University of Washington, has spent his career showing that Americans' food choices correlate to social class. He argues that the most nutritious diet—lots of fruits and vegetables, lean meats, fish, and grains—is beyond the reach of the poorest Americans, and it is economic elitism for nutritionists to uphold it as an ideal without broadly addressing issues of affordability. Lower-income families don't subsist on junk food and fast food because they lack nutritional education, as some have argued. And though many poor neighborhoods are, indeed, food deserts—meaning that the people who live there don't have access to a well-stocked supermarket—many are not. Lower-income families choose sugary fat, and processed foods because they're cheaper—and because they taste good. In a paper published last spring, Drewnowski showed how the prices of specific foods changed between 2004 and 2008 based on data from Seattle-area supermarkets. While food prices overall rose about 25 percent, the most nutritious foods (red peppers, raw oysters, spinach, mustard greens, romaine lettuce) rose 29 percent, while the least nutritious foods (white sugar, hard candy, jelly beans, and cola) rose just 16 percent.

"In America," Drewnowski wrote in an e-mail "food has become the premier marker of social distinctions, that is to say—social class. It used to be clothing and fashion, but no longer, now that 'luxury' has become affordable and available to all." He points to an article in the *New York Times*, written by Pollan, which describes a meal element by element, including "a basket of morels and porcini gathered near Mount Shasta." "Pollan," writes Drewnowski, "is drawing a picture of class privilege that is as acute as anything written by Edith Wharton or Henry James."

I finish writing the previous paragraph and go downstairs. There, in the mail, I find the Christmas catalog from the luxury retail store Barneys. HAVE A FOODIE HOLIDAY, its cover reads. Inside, models are covered—literally—with food. A woman in a red $2,000 Lanvin trench has an enormous cabbage on her head.

Another, holding a green Proenza Schouler clutch, wears a boiled crab in her bouffant. Most disconcerting is the Munnu diamond pendant ($80,500) worn by a model, who seems to have traded her hair for an octopus. Its tentacles dangle past her shoulders, and the girl herself wears the expression of someone who's stayed too long at the party. Food is no longer trendy or fashionable. It is fashion.

Tiffiney Davis, a single mom, lives about four miles away from me, in subsidized 15 housing, in a gentrifying neighborhood called Red Hook. Steps from her apartment, you can find ample evidence of foodie culture: Fairway, the supermarket where I buy my Dutch cheese, is right there, as is a chic bakery, and a newfangled lobster pound. Davis says she has sometimes worried about having enough food. She works in Manhattan, earning $13 an hour for a corporate catering company (which once had a contract with *Newsweek*), and she receives food stamps. She spends $100 a week on food for herself and her two kids. Sometimes she stretches her budget by bringing food home from work.

Davis is sheepish about what her family eats for breakfast. Everybody rises at 6, and there's a mad rush to get the door, so often they eat bodega food. Her daughter, Malaezia, 10, will have egg and cheese on a roll; her son, 13-year-old Tashawn, a muffin and soda. She herself used to pop into at Dunkin' Donuts for two doughnuts and a latte, but when New York chain restaurants started posting calories on their menus, she stopped. "I try my best to lessen the chemicals and the fattening stuff," she says, "but it's hard."

Time is just part of the problem, Davis explains, as she prepares Sunday dinner in her cheerful kitchen. Tonight she's making fried chicken wings with bottled barbecue sauce; yellow rice from a box; black beans from a can; broccoli; and carrots, cooked in olive oil and honey. A home-cooked dinner doesn't happen every night. On weeknights, everyone gets home, exhausted—and then there's homework. Several nights a week, they get takeout: Chinese, or Domino's, or McDonald's. Davis doesn't buy fruits and vegetables mostly because they're too expensive, and in the markets where she usually shops, they're not fresh. "I buy bananas and bring them home and 10 minutes later they're no good . . . Whole Foods sells fresh, beautiful tomatoes," she says. "Here, they're packaged and full of chemicals anyway. So I mostly buy canned foods."

In recent weeks the news in New York City has been full with a controversial proposal to ban food-stamp recipients from using their government money to buy soda. Local public-health officials insist they need to be more proactive about slowing obesity; a recent study found that 40 percent of the children in New York City's kindergarten through eighth-grade classrooms were either overweight or obese. (Nationwide, 36 percent of 6- to 11-year-olds are overweight or obese.) Opponents of the proposal call it a "nanny state" measure, another instance of government interference, and worse—of the government telling poor people what to do, as if they can't make good decisions on their own. "I think it's really difficult," says Pickett, the British epidemiologist. "Everybody needs to be able to feel that they have control over what they spend. And everybody should be able to treat themselves now and again. Why shouldn't a poor child have a birthday party with cake and soda?"

But Davis enthusiastically supports the proposal. A 9-year-old boy in her building recently died of an asthma attack, right in front of his mother. He was obese, she says, but his mom kept feeding him junk. "If these people don't care at all about calorie counts, then the government should. People would live a lot longer," she says.

Claude Fischler, a French sociologist, believes that Americans can fight both [20] obesity and food insecurity by being more, well, like the French. Americans take an approach to food and eating that is unlike any other people in history. For one thing, we regard food primarily as (good or bad) nutrition. When asked "What is eating well?" Americans generally answer in the language of daily allowances: They talk about calories and carbs, fats, and sugars. They don't see eating as a social activity, and they don't see food—as it has been seen for millennia—as a shared resource, like a loaf of bread passed around the table. When asked "What is eating well?" the French inevitably answer in terms of "conviviality": togetherness, intimacy, and good tastes unfolding in a predictable way.

Even more idiosyncratic than our obsession with nutrition, says Fischler, is that Americans see food choice as a matter of personal freedom, an inalienable right. Americans want to eat what they want: morels or Big Macs. They want to eat where they want, in the car or alfresco. And they want to eat when they want. With the exception of Thanksgiving, when most of us dine off the same turkey menu, we are food libertarians. In surveys, Fischler has found no single time of day (or night) when Americans predictably sit together and eat. By contrast, 54 percent of the French dine at 12:30 each day. Only 9.5 percent of the French are obese.

When I was a child I was commanded to "eat your eggs. There are starving children in Africa." And when I was old enough to think for myself, I could easily see that my own eaten or uneaten eggs would not do a single thing to help the children of Africa. This is the Brooklyn conundrum, playing out all over the country. Locally produced food is more delicious than the stuff you get in the supermarket; it's better for the small farmers and the farm animals; and, as a movement, it's better for the environment. It's easy—and probably healthy, if you can afford it—to make that choice as an individual or a family, says the New York University nutritionist Marion Nestle. Bridging the divide is much harder. "Choosing local or organic is something you can actually do. It's very difficult for people to get involved in policy."

Locavore activists in New York and other cities are doing what they can to help the poor with access to fresh food. Incentive programs give food-stamp recipients extra credit if they buy groceries at farmers' markets. Food co-ops and community-garden associations are doing better urban outreach. Municipalities are establishing bus routes between poor neighborhoods and those where well-stocked supermarkets exist.

Joel Berg, executive director of the New York City Coalition Against Hunger, says these programs are good, but they need to go much, much further. He believes, like Fischler, that the answer lies in seeing food more as a shared resource, like water, than as a consumer product, like shoes. "It's a nuanced conversation, but I think 'local' or 'organic' as the shorthand for all things good is way too simplistic," says Berg. "I think we need a broader conversation about scale, working conditions, and environmental impact. It's a little too much of people buying easy virtue."

Even the locavore hero Pollan agrees. "Essentially," he says, "we have a sys- 25
tem where wealthy farmers feed the poor crap and poor farmers feed the wealthy
high-quality food." He points to Walmart's recent announcement of a program
that will put more locally grown food on its shelves as an indication that big retail-
ers are looking to sell fresh produce in a scalable way. These fruits and vegetables
might not be organic, but the goal, says Pollan, is not to be absolutist in one's food
ideology. "I argue for being conscious," he says, "but perfectionism is an enemy
of progress." Pollan sees a future where, in an effort to fight diabetes and obesity,
health-insurance companies are advocates for small and medium-size farmers.
He dreams of a broad food-policy conversation in Washington. "The food movement," he reminds me, "is still very young."

Berg believes that part of the answer lies in working with Big Food. The food
industry hasn't been entirely bad: It developed the technology to bring apples to
Wisconsin in the middle of winter, after all. It could surely make sustainably produced fruits and vegetables affordable and available. "We need to bring social justice to bigger agriculture as well," Berg says.

My last stop was at Jabir Suluki's house in Clinton Hill, about two miles from my
home. Suluki has toast for breakfast, with a little cheese on top, melted in the toaster
oven. He is not French—he was born and raised in Brooklyn—but he might as well
be. Every day, between 5 and 7, he prepares dinner for his mother and himself—and
any of his nieces and nephews who happen to drop by. He prepares food with the
confidence of a person descended from a long line of home cooks—which he is.

Both Suluki and his mother are diabetic. For them, healthy, regular meals are
a necessity—and so he does what he can on $75 a week. "To get good food, you
really got to sacrifice a lot. It's expensive. But I take that sacrifice, because it's worth
it." Suluki uses his food stamps at the farmers' market. He sorts through the rotten
fruit at the local supermarket. He travels to Queens, when he can get a ride, and
buys cheap meat in bulk. He is adamant that it is the responsibility of parents to
feed their children good food in moderate portions, and that it's possible to do so
on a fixed income.

For dinner he and his mother ate Salisbury steak made from ground turkey, with a little ground beef thrown in and melted cheese on top "because turkey doesn't have any taste"; roasted potatoes and green peppers; and frozen green
beans, "heated quickly so they still have a crunch." For dessert, his mother ate two
pieces of supermarket coffeecake.

Suluki thinks a lot about food, and the role it plays in the life of his neighbors. 30
He doesn't have soda in his refrigerator, but he opposes the New York City soda
proposal because, in light of the government's food and farm subsidies—and in
light of all the other kinds of unhealthy cheap foods for sale in his supermarket—
he sees it as hypocrisy. "You can't force junk on people and then criticize it at the
same time." Suluki is a community organizer, and sees the web of problems before
us—hunger, obesity, health—as something for the community to solve. "We can't
just attack this problem as individuals," he tells me. "A healthy community produces healthy people." That's why, on the weekends, he makes a big pot of rice and
beans, and brings it down to the food pantry near his house.

QUESTIONS FOR DISCUSSION AND WRITING

1. Miller begins her article with a discussion of her food choices for breakfast that include high-end or exotic foods, including "the hippest cheese in New York" (paragraph 1). What do these food choices, both hers and those of her neighbors, say about them in terms of socioeconomic class, education, and politics? Examine, for example, the statement that her friends, the Fergusons, are "locavores" (paragraph 1). If you are not familiar with that term, look it up. What are the implications of being a locavore? What conditions (such as economic or environmental) are necessary in order for someone to function as a locavore? What does this tell you about the Fergusons?

2. Miller states that up to 17 percent of Americans are "food insecure"—a situation in which a family may run out of money or food before the next paycheck (paragraph 8). Does this number surprise you? Why or why not? Later, the article points out that the poorest Americans also are typically more obese than the average American. How does this happen? Argue whether or not attempts to combat this by having the government control access to fast foods (such as sugary sodas) are a good idea or not. For example, is it acceptable for the government to prevent food stamps from being spent on junk food, candy, and soda? Why or why not? Be specific in your response.

3. Miller points out that the United States has large income inequality; a country like Japan with low income inequality has less trouble with obesity. Is drawing this connection between income inequality reasonable or not? Do other cultural factors not connected to income inequality play an important role in obesity issues? Cite specific examples to support your answer.

4. Another international comparison that Miller makes addresses differences in attitudes toward food and eating habits. She compares the United States to France, pointing out that the French approach meals on more social terms, whereas in the United States meals are seen in terms of nutrition. A related factor is that the French eat together more often, and at regular times, and one result is that the French have a much lower level of obesity than is seen in the United States. What are your attitudes toward eating? Think about the habits of eating you learned while growing up and now practice as an adult. How have these habits affected how you eat, what you eat, when you eat, with whom you eat, and so forth?

5. Ultimately, food may well reflect other, large cultural divides that exist within a community (such as Miller's Brooklyn) and the nation as a whole. Does an attempt to help people eat healthier represent a privileging of one culture over another (for example, the upper-middle-class perspective over the working-class perspective)? Can that be justified in terms of public health, or is it a patronizing attempt to modify the behavior of others to conform to social expectations? Support your answer with concrete details and examples.

CHAPTER 7

Education and the American Character: What Do We Teach? What Do We Learn? And Why Does This Matter?

DAVID SEDARIS

What I Learned and What I Said at Princeton

David Sedaris was born in Raleigh, North Carolina, in 1957. He dropped out of Kent State University in 1977 and ten years later graduated from the Art Institute of Chicago. His career as a humorist began unexpectedly, with his first reading from "SantaLand Diaries" on National Public Radio in 1992, a self-satirizing account of his career as a Santa's elf during Christmas season that focused on the backstage seed-iness of playing Crumpet the Elf. In recent years his biting satirical tone has softened somewhat in stories about living in Paris with his life's companion, Hugh, as in Me Talk Pretty One Day *(2000), or about his dysfunctional family, in* Dress Your Family in Corduroy and Denim *(2004). Nevertheless,* When You Are Engulfed in Flames *(2008) does include essays on chimpanzees at a typing school and hostility toward a paraplegic. His most recent book is* Let's Explore Diabetes with Owls *(2013).*

Despite the claims of his baccalaureate address delivered at Princeton in June 2006 (New Yorker, June 26, 2006), Sedaris did not attend the university of which he speaks so fondly: "This chapel, for instance—I remember when it was just a clearing, cordoned off with sharp sticks. Prayer was compulsory back then, and you couldn't just fake it by moving your lips. . . . I'm dating myself, but this was before Jesus Christ."

It's been interesting to walk around campus this afternoon, as when *I* went to Princeton things were completely different. This chapel, for instance—I remember when it was just a clearing, cordoned off with sharp sticks. Prayer was compulsory back then, and you couldn't just fake it by moving your lips; you had to know the words, and really mean them. I'm dating myself, but this was before Jesus Christ. We worshipped a God named Sashatiba, who had five eyes, including one right here, on the Adam's apple. None of us ever met him, but word had it that he might appear at any moment, so we were always at the ready. *Whatever you do, don't look at his neck,* I used to tell myself.

It's funny now, but I thought about it a lot. Some people thought about it a little too much, and it really affected their academic performance. Again, I date myself, but back then we were on a pass-fail system. If you passed, you got to live, and if you failed you were burned alive on a pyre that's now the Transgender Studies Building. Following the first grading period, the air was so thick with smoke you could barely find your way across campus. There were those who said that it smelled like meat, no different from a barbecue, but I could tell the difference. I mean, really. Since when do you grill hair? Or those ugly, chunky shoes we all used to wear?

It kept you on your toes, though, I'll say that much. If I'd been burned alive because of bad grades, my parents would have killed me, especially my father, who meant well but was just a little too gung ho for my taste. He had the whole outfit: Princeton breastplate, Princeton nightcap; he even got the velvet cape with the tiger head hanging like a rucksack from between the shoulder blades. In those days, the mascot was a sabretooth, so you can imagine how silly it looked, and how painful it was to sit down. Then, there was his wagon, completely covered with decals and bumper stickers: "I hold my horses for Ivy League schools," "My son was accepted at the best university in the United States and all I got was a bill for a hundred and sixty-eight thousand dollars." On and on, which was just so . . . *wrong.*

One of the things they did back then was start you off with a modesty seminar, an eight-hour session that all the freshmen had to sit through. It might be different today, but in my time it took the form of a role-playing exercise, my classmates and I pretending to be graduates, and the teacher assuming the part of an average citizen: the soldier, the bloodletter, the whore with a heart of gold.

"Tell me, young man. Did you attend a university of higher learning?" 5

To anyone holding a tool or a weapon, we were trained to respond, "What? Me go to college?" If, on the other hand, the character held a degree, you were allowed to say, "Sort of," or, sometimes, "I think so."

"So where do you sort of think you went?"

And it was the next bit that you had to get just right. Inflection was everything, and it took the foreign students forever to master it.

"Where do you sort of think you went?"

And we'd say, "Umm, Princeton?"—as if it were an oral exam, and we weren't 10 quite sure that this was the correct answer.

"Princeton, my goodness," the teacher would say. "That must have been quite something!"

You had to let him get it out, but once he started in on how brilliant and committed you must be it was time to hold up your hands, saying, "Oh, it isn't that hard to get into."

Then he'd say, "Really? But I heard—"

"Wrong," you'd tell him. "You heard wrong. It's not that great of a school."

This was the way it had to be done—you had to play it down, which wasn't 15 easy when your dad was out there, reading your acceptance letter into a bullhorn.

I needed to temper my dad's enthusiasm a bit, and so I announced that I would be majoring in patricide. The Princeton program was very strong back then, the best in the country, but it wasn't the sort of thing your father could get too worked up about. Or, at least, most fathers wouldn't. Mine was over the moon. "Killed by a Princeton graduate!" he said. "And my own son, no less."

My mom was actually jealous. "So what's wrong with matricide?" she asked. "What, I'm not good enough to murder?"

They started bickering, so in order to make peace I promised to consider a double major.

"And how much more is that going to cost us?" they said.

Those last few months at home were pretty tough, but then I started my fresh-   20
man year, and got caught up in the life of the mind. My idol-worship class was the best, but my dad didn't get it. "What the hell does that have to do with patricide?" he asked.

And I said, "Umm. *Everything*?"

He didn't understand that it's all connected, that one subject leads to another and forms a kind of chain that raises its head and nods like a cobra when you're sucking on a bong after three days of no sleep. On acid it's even wilder, and appears to eat things. But, not having gone to college, my dad had no concept of a well-rounded liberal-arts education. He thought that all my classes should be murder-related, with no lunch breaks or anything. Fortunately, it doesn't work that way.

In truth, I had no idea what I wanted to study, so for the first few years I took everything that came my way. I enjoyed pillaging and astrology, but the thing that ultimately stuck was comparative literature. There wasn't much of it to compare back then, no more than a handful of epic poems and one novel about a lady detective, but that's part of what I liked about it. The field was new, and full of possibilities, but try telling that to my parents.

"You mean you *won't* be killing us?" my mother said. "But I told everyone you were going for that double major."

Dad followed his "I'm so disappointed" speech with a lecture on career   25
opportunities. "You're going to study literature and get a job doing *what*?" he said. "*Literaturizing*?"

We spent my entire vacation arguing; then, just before I went back to school, my father approached me in my bedroom. "Promise me you'll keep an open mind," he said. And, as he left, he slipped an engraved dagger into my book bag.

I had many fine teachers during my years at Princeton, but the one I think of most often was my fortune-telling professor—a complete hag with wild gray hair, warts the size of new potatoes, the whole nine yards. She taught us to forecast the weather up to two weeks in advance, but ask her for anything weightier and you were likely to be disappointed.

The alchemy majors wanted to know how much money they'd be making after graduation. "Just give us an approximate figure," they'd say, and the professor would shake her head and cover her crystal ball with a little cozy given to her by one of her previous classes. When it came to our futures, she drew the line, no matter how hard we begged—and, I mean, we really tried. I was as let down as the next guy, but, in retrospect, I can see that she acted in our best interests. Look at yourself on the day that you graduated from college, then look at yourself today. I did that recently, and it was, like, "What the hell happened?"

The answer, of course, is life. What the hag chose not to foretell—and what we, in our certainty, could not have fathomed—is that stuff comes up. Weird doors open. People fall into things. Maybe the engineering whiz will wind up brewing cider, not because he has to but because he finds it challenging. Who knows? Maybe the athlete will bring peace to all nations, or the class moron will go on to become the President of the United States—though that's more likely to happen at Harvard or Yale, schools that will pretty much let in anybody.

There were those who left Princeton and soared like arrows into the bosoms   30
of power and finance, but I was not one of them. My path was a winding one, with plenty of obstacles along the way. When school was finished, I went back home, an Ivy League graduate with four years' worth of dirty laundry and his whole life ahead of him. "What are you going to do now?" my parents asked.

And I said, "Well, I was thinking of washing some of these underpants."

That took six months. Then I moved on to the shirts.

"Now what?" my parents asked.

And, when I told them I didn't know, they lost what little patience they had left. "What kind of a community-college answer is that?" my mother said. "You went to the best school there is—how can you not know something?"

And I said, "I don't know."   35

In time, my father stopped wearing his Princeton gear. My mother stopped talking about my "potential," and she and my dad got themselves a brown-and-white puppy. In terms of intelligence, it was just average, but they couldn't see that at all. "Aren't you just the smartest dog in the world?" they'd ask, and the puppy would shake their hands just like I used to do.

My first alumni weekend cheered me up a bit. It was nice to know that I wasn't the only unemployed graduate in the world, but the warm feeling evaporated when I got back home and saw that my parents had given the dog my bedroom. In place of the Princeton pennant they'd bought for my first birthday was a banner reading, "Westminster or bust."

I could see which way the wind was blowing, and so I left, and moved to the city, where a former classmate, a philosophy major, got me a job on his rag-picking crew. When the industry moved overseas—this the doing of *another* former classmate—I stayed put, and eventually found work skinning hides for a ratcatcher, a thin, serious man with the longest beard I had ever seen.

At night, I read and reread the handful of books I'd taken with me when I left home, and eventually, out of boredom as much as anything else, I started to write myself. It wasn't much, at first: character sketches, accounts of my day, parodies of articles in the alumni newsletter. Then, in time, I became more ambitious, and began crafting little stories about my family. I read one of them out loud to the ratcatcher, who'd never laughed at anything but roared at the description of my mother and her puppy. "My mom was just the same," he said. "I graduated from

Brown, and two weeks later she was raising falcons on my top bunk!" The story about my dad defecating in his neighbor's well pleased my boss so much that he asked for a copy, and sent it to his own father.

This gave me the confidence to continue, and in time I completed an entire 40 book, which was subsequently published. I presented a first edition to my parents, who started with the story about our neighbor's well, and then got up to close the drapes. Fifty pages later, they were boarding up the door and looking for ways to disguise themselves. Other people had loved my writing, but these two didn't get it at all. "What's wrong?" I asked.

My father adjusted his makeshift turban, and sketched a mustache on my mother's upper lip. "What's wrong?" he said. "I'll tell you what's wrong: you're killing us."

"But I thought that's what you wanted?"

"We did," my mother wept, "but not this way."

It hadn't occurred to me until that moment, but I seemed to have come full circle. What started as a dodge had inadvertently become my life's work, an irony I never could have appreciated had my extraordinary parents not put me through Princeton.

QUESTIONS FOR DISCUSSION AND WRITING

1. Sedaris actually delivered this commencement address at Princeton (June 2006). Despite his opening claim, "when *I* went to Princeton things were completely different" (paragraph 1), he never attended Princeton. At what point does he expect his audience to know this? Why is it important to recognize that Sedaris is writing a satire? Identify at least ten aspects of college that he is satirizing. Write your own satire on the topic that most appeals to you.

2. Why have you enrolled in the college you're attending? How did you choose it? In either a satire or a straightforward paper, discuss your criteria, and highlight the major issues influencing your decision. Which issues pertained to the actual education you expected to receive and to your understanding of its quality? If you've been there long enough to assess the accuracy of your predictions, include these assessments.

3. Can all students' parents be expected to be as proud of their child's acceptance as Sedaris's dad allegedly was, "reading [his] acceptance letter into a bullhorn" (paragraph 15)? Or is this pride reserved essentially for parents and students in elitist schools? Where does Sedaris critique this? How would he expect his audience of newly minted Princeton graduates to react?

4. Sedaris satirizes parents' relations with their college student children, both while the children are in college and after they have graduated and moved back home (paragraph 30 and following). Do you think most college graduates' expectations are fulfilled by their undergraduate experiences? What do you expect to occur as a consequence of earning a college degree? What

evidence have you that your expectations will be fulfilled? Or not? Write a paper analyzing this.

5. Or, discuss the ideas raised in question 4 with your parents (or others who have a stake in your education) and write a dialogue that captures the essence of this conversation. What are the major points of agreement? Disagreement? What can you do to ensure that your expectations will be fulfilled?

6. Sedaris's piece was originally given as a talk. After reading it, listen to Michael Oatman's take on higher education, "Admittance to a Better Life," in the e-Pages at bedfordstmartins.com/arlington. To what extent does the oral delivery of Oatman's essay affect how you receive it? Are there parts of Sedaris's speech that likely would have worked better if you were listening to him speak? Compare the aural and textual nature of both essays. Be specific.

MICHAEL OATMAN

Admittance to a Better Life [AUDIO ESSAY]

"I still wonder what happened to that happy-go-lucky semi-thug who used to hang out with drug dealers on dimly lit street corners. Well, I'm in the library parsing a Jane Austen novel looking for dramatic irony, while many of my old friends are dead or in jail."

 In the e-Pages at bedfordstmartins.com/arlington.

TIM KREIDER

In Praise of Not Knowing

Tim Kreider (b. 1967) is an American cartoonist who also dabbles in writing political and social commentary. His comic The Pain—When Will It End? *was originally self-published, then published in alternative newspapers. Since 2000, it has been published as a webcomic. Politically, Kreider typically takes on conservatives such as gun owners and the religious right, but he is also known for his strong, and ultimately futile, defense of categorizing Pluto as a planet. This article was originally published in the* New York Times, *to which Kreider is a frequent contributor.*

In this article, Kreider examines the Internet on the basis of what so many people feel is its chief asset: easy, quick access to "zettabtyes of information." Kreider points out, however, that the easy access to information has an unexpected and perhaps unwanted effect: the removal of wonder from our lives. Focusing on youth culture, he points out that generations of young people, including himself, often bonded by being "in the know." However, with the Internet, everyone can be "in the

*know," so there is nothing left—all can be explained. This leaves us not only with an
excess of data, but with an absence of imagination and mystery, as well.*

When I was 17, I took a record of John Cage's piano pieces out of the library. The
pieces were interesting, but what really arrested my attention was the B-side of
the album—a work called "The Dreamer That Remains," by a composer I'd never
heard of named Harry Partch. This was music from another planet: unearthly
yowling strings, metallic twangs, rippling liquid percussion. I couldn't even identify the instruments.

I loaned the record to a friend of mine, the only other person in the world
I then knew who liked classical music. The piece's refrain, in which a chorus of
corpses in a funeral home sing, "Let us loiter together/And know one another,"
became a two-man in-joke between us. For years, as far as we could tell, we were
the only people who knew about Harry Partch. He was, in a sense, ours.

This was in the '80s, a time when there was simply no way of learning much
more about Harry Partch, at least not that I knew of. If I were a 17-year-old discovering Harry Partch today, I could Google him, and I'd immediately find the Harry
Partch Information Center and Corporeal Meadows, where I'd learn all about his
system of intonation with a 43-note octave and his instruments made of bamboo,
jet-engine nose cones, artillery-shell casings, and whiskey bottles, with names like
the Gourd Tree, Boo II, Zymo-Xyl, and Marimba Eroica. I'd even find listings for
the rare public performances of Partch's work. Maybe most important, I'd be able
to connect with hundreds of other people who were interested in Harry Partch,
avant-garde music, and other weird stuff, and not have to feel so eccentric and
freakish and alone.

All of which is good, of course. That's what the Internet is for, yes? Information—zettabytes of information—at our instantaneous disposal.

Except if I'm recalling correctly, adolescents secretly like feeling eccentric and   5
freakish and alone, hoarding pop arcana, and cultivating ever-dweebier erudition.
They recite lines from cult movies like *The Rocky Horror Picture Show, Repo Man,*
and *Napoleon Dynamite* as though they were passwords to a speakeasy; wear buttons bearing the names of obscure music groups as if they were campaign ribbons;
and list favorite films and books and bands on their Facebook pages as if they were
as essential as name and age and gender.

That proprietary sense that my friend and I had about Harry Partch, our sense
of belonging to an exclusive club of cognoscenti, is why teenagers get so disgusted
when everybody else in the world finds out about their favorite band. It's fun being
In the Know, but once everyone's in it, there's nothing to know anymore.

There was, back then, a genre of literature whose purpose was simply to let you
know about cool stuff you might not have heard about. The beloved *Famous Monsters
of Filmland* magazine consisted of stills from half-forgotten horror films like *It! The
Terror from Beyond Space* and *Taste the Blood of Dracula.* The copy seemed to have
been written not only for but by 10-year-old boys who'd stayed up all night: crazed,
breathless, and completely exhaustive scene-by-scene descriptions of the entire plots
of those movies.

When I was older, I pored over a book called *Cult Films* that described the plots of movies like *King of Hearts, Harold and Maude,* and *Behind the Green Door.* This was not only before the Internet, but also before home video. The only way you were ever going to see any of these films was if they happened to be on TV late at night or came to a repertory theater near you, which, if you lived in suburban Maryland, good luck.

There are some celebrated films that have long been hard to find on DVD or the Internet: Stanley Kubrick's first feature, *Fear and Desire,* the British absurdist black comedy *The Bed-Sitting Room,* Joseph Losey's *Secret Ceremony.* When I found out the former two, at least, had become available, I was almost disappointed. It was fun not being able to see them, not having every last thing a click away. Because what we cannot find inflames the imagination.

Kurt Cobain once said in an interview that long before he'd heard any actual   10 punk rock music, he studied magazine photos of punk musicians and imagined what the music sounded like. It must have sounded to him—who knows?—something like what would later be called grunge.

Instant accessibility leaves us oddly disappointed, bored, endlessly craving more. I've often had the experience of reading a science article that purported to explain some question I'd always wondered about, only to find myself getting distracted as soon as I started reading the explanation. Not long ago the Hubble telescope observed that Pluto's surface is changing rapidly, and noticeably reddening. It's not a bland white ball of ice, but the color of rust and soot. We're not likely to learn anything more until the *New Horizons* spacecraft gets there in 2015. In the meantime, we just get to wonder.

I find this mysterious and tantalizing. As soon as I began reading possible explanations—ultraviolet light interacting with chemicals, blah blah blah—I started to lose interest. Just knowing that there is an answer is somehow deflating. If some cryptozoologist actually bagged a Yeti and gave it a Latin name, it would just be another animal. An intriguing animal, no doubt, but would it really be any more bizarre or improbable than a giraffe or a giant squid?

I hope kids are still finding some way, despite Google and Wikipedia, of not knowing things. Learning how to transform mere ignorance into mystery, simple not knowing into wonder, is a useful skill. Because it turns out that the most important things in this life—why the universe is here instead of not, what happens to us when we die, how the people we love really feel about us—are things we're never going to know.

QUESTIONS FOR DISCUSSION AND WRITING

1. Kreider begins the article with an anecdote about discovering the avant-garde composer Harry Partch, virtually by accident. He bemoans the idea that today a quick search with Google will reveal all sorts of information about Partch, information that before the Internet would have been difficult and time-consuming to find. He says, "All of which is good, of course" (paragraph 4). Do you believe that Kreider means that? Why or why not? What can be bad about instant access to so much information?

2. In your experience, how frequently does the Internet create the opportunity for chance encounters with new information (such as when Kreider found Partch on the B-side of a John Cage album)? Or does the Internet generally require that you already know what you want to find in order for you to find it? Can you cite examples of spontaneous or chance discoveries that you made while searching for information on the Internet? If not, why do you suppose that is?

3. Kreider cites the idea that youth sometimes "secretly like feeling eccentric and freakish and alone" (paragraph 5). Do you agree with that statement or not? Can you think of cultural touchstones that you share with other friends, such as citing lines from movies or listening to obscure bands? Does this constitute what Kreider means by "being In the Know" (paragraph 6)? Do you agree or disagree with Kreider that the Internet makes such bonding less possible because it gives exposure to virtually everything and everyone? Defend your answer.

4. Kreider speaks of "cool stuff" (paragraph 7) as typically obscure, half-forgotten works, whether they be books, films, music, or other forms of artistic expression. Think about the implications: That which is unpopular is cool, and that which is popular is uncool. Consider that many youth believe that being cool will result in being popular (and vice versa). Think of pop culture icons ("pop" being short for "popular"), including rap artists, actors, and other entertainers, who are embraced for being cool. In light of this, does Kreider's idea seem like a paradox? Can that paradox be resolved?

5. In paragraph 13, Kreider states that he hopes young people are still finding "how to transform mere ignorance into mystery, simple not knowing into wonder." Why is this important to Kreider? Do you agree or disagree? Cite specific examples to defend your answer.

JONATHAN KOZOL

The Human Cost of an Illiterate Society

Jonathan Kozol (b. 1936) grew up in Newton, Massachusetts, graduated from Harvard (B.A., 1958), and received a Rhodes scholarship but abandoned it to spend four years in Paris writing a novel, The Fume of Poppies *(1958). Moved by the murders of civil rights activists in the South, he returned to the United States to become deeply involved in the civil rights movement and issues of social justice, to which he has devoted the rest of his life as an author, educator, and activist. Kozol's first nonfiction book,* Death at an Early Age: The Destruction of the Hearts and Minds of Negro Children in the Boston Public Schools *(1967), won a National Book Award. Other award-winning books include* Rachel and Her Children: Homeless Families in America *(1988),* Savage Inequalities: Children in America's Schools *(1991), and*

Amazing Grace: The Lives of Children and the Conscience of a Nation *(1995). His most recent book is* Fire in the Ashes *(2012).*

"The Human Cost of an Illiterate Society," a chapter from Illiterate America *(1985), shows how illiteracy degrades people's quality of life, makes them vulnerable to others' interpretations of the written word, and prevents their full participation in democratic society.*

> *PRECAUTIONS. READ BEFORE USING.*
> *Poison: Contains sodium hydroxide (caustic soda-lye).*
> *Corrosive: Causes severe eye and skin damage, may cause blindness.*
> *Harmful or fatal if swallowed.*
> *If swallowed, give large quantities of milk or water.*
> *Do not induce vomiting.*
> *Important: Keep water out of can at all times to prevent contents from violently erupting. . . .*
>
> —Warning on a Can of Drāno

We are speaking here no longer of the dangers faced by passengers on Eastern Airlines or the dollar costs incurred by U.S. corporations and taxpayers. We are speaking now of human suffering and of the ethical dilemmas that are faced by a society that looks upon such suffering with qualified concern but does not take those actions which its wealth and ingenuity would seemingly demand.

Questions of literacy, in Socrates' belief, must at length be judged as matters of morality. Socrates could not have had in mind the moral compromise peculiar to a nation like our own. Some of our Founding Fathers did, however, have this question in their minds. One of the wisest of those Founding Fathers (one who may not have been most compassionate but surely was more prescient than some of his peers) recognized the special dangers that illiteracy would pose to basic equity in the political construction that he helped to shape.

"A people who mean to be their own governors," James Madison wrote, "must arm themselves with the power knowledge gives. A popular government without popular information or the means of acquiring it, is but a prologue to a farce or a tragedy, or perhaps both."

Tragedy looms larger than farce in the United States today. Illiterate citizens seldom vote. Those who do are forced to cast a vote of questionable worth. They cannot make informed decisions based on serious print information. Sometimes they can be alerted to their interests by aggressive voter education. More frequently, they vote for a face, a smile, or a style, not for a mind or character or body of beliefs.

The number of illiterate adults exceeds by 16 million the entire vote cast for 5 the winner in the 1980 presidential contest. If even one third of all illiterates could vote, and read enough and do sufficient math to vote in their self-interest, Ronald Reagan would not likely have been chosen president. There is, of course, no way to know for sure. We do know this: Democracy is a mendacious term when used by those who are prepared to countenance the forced exclusion of one third of our electorate. So long as 60 million people are denied significant participation, the government is neither of, nor for, nor by, the people. It is a government, at best, of those two thirds whose wealth, skin color, or parental privilege allows them opportunity to profit from the provocation and instruction of the written word.

The undermining of democracy in the United States is one "expense" that sensitive Americans can easily deplore because it represents a contradiction that endangers citizens of all political positions. The human price is not so obvious at first.

Since I first immersed myself within this work I have often had the following dream: I find that I am in a railroad station or a large department store within a city that is utterly unknown to me and where I cannot understand the printed words. None of the signs or symbols is familiar. Everything looks strange: like mirror writing of some kind. Gradually I understand that I am in the Soviet Union. All the letters on the walls around me are Cyrillic. I look for my pocket dictionary but I find that it has been mislaid. Where have I left it? Then I recall that I forgot to bring it with me when I packed my bags in Boston. I struggle to remember the name of my hotel. I try to ask somebody for directions. One person stops and looks at me in a peculiar way. I lose the nerve to ask. At last I reach into my wallet for an ID card. The card is missing. Have I lost it? Then I remember that my card was confiscated for some reason, many years before. Around this point, I wake up in a panic.

This panic is not so different from the misery that millions of adult illiterates experience each day within the course of their routine existence in the U.S.A.

Illiterates cannot read the menu in a restaurant.

They cannot read the cost of items on the menu in the *window* of the restaurant   10 before they enter.

Illiterates cannot read the letters that their children bring home from their teachers. They cannot study school department circulars that tell them of the courses that their children must be taking if they hope to pass the SAT exams. They cannot help with homework. They cannot write a letter to the teacher. They are afraid to visit in the classroom. They do not want to humiliate their child or themselves.

Illiterates cannot read instructions on a bottle of prescription medicine. They cannot find out when a medicine is past the year of safe consumption; nor can they read of allergenic risks, warnings to diabetics, or the potential sedative effect of certain kinds of nonprescription pills. They cannot observe preventive health care admonitions. They cannot read about "the seven warning signs of cancer" or the indications of blood-sugar fluctuations or the risks of eating certain foods that aggravate the likelihood of cardiac arrest.

Illiterates live, in more than literal ways, an uninsured existence. They cannot understand the written details on a health insurance form. They cannot read the waivers that they sign preceding surgical procedures. Several women I have known in Boston have entered a slum hospital with the intention of obtaining a tubal ligation and have emerged a few days later after having been subjected to a hysterectomy. Unaware of their rights, incognizant of jargon, intimidated by the unfamiliar air of fear and atmosphere of ether that so many of us find oppressive in the confines even of the most attractive and expensive medical facilities, they have signed their names to documents they could not read and which nobody, in the hectic situation that prevails so often in those overcrowded hospitals that serve the urban poor, had even bothered to explain.

Childbirth might seem to be the last inalienable right of any female citizen within a civilized society. Illiterate mothers, as we shall see, already have been cheated of the power to protect their progeny against the likelihood of demolition in deficient public schools and, as a result, against the verbal servitude within which they themselves exist. Surgical denial of the right to bear that child in the first place represents an ultimate denial, an unspeakable metaphor, a final darkness that denies even the twilight gleamings of our own humanity. What greater violation of our biological, our biblical, our spiritual humanity could possibly exist than that which takes place nightly, perhaps hourly these days, within such overburdened and benighted institutions as the Boston City Hospital? Illiteracy has many costs; few are so irreversible as this.

Even the roof above one's head, the gas or other fuel for heating that protects the residents of northern city slums against the threat of illness in the winter months become uncertain guarantees. Illiterates cannot read the lease that they must sign to live in an apartment which, too often, they cannot afford. They cannot manage check accounts and therefore seldom pay for anything by mail. Hours and entire days of difficult travel (and the cost of bus or other public transit) must be added to the real cost of whatever they consume. Loss of interest on the check accounts they do not have, and could not manage if they did, must be regarded as another of the excess costs paid by the citizen who is excluded from the common instruments of commerce in a numerate society. 15

"I couldn't understand the bills," a woman in Washington, D.C., reports, "and then I couldn't write the checks to pay them. We signed things we didn't know what they were."

Illiterates cannot read the notices that they receive from welfare offices or from the IRS. They must depend on word-of-mouth instruction from the welfare worker—or from other persons whom they have good reason to mistrust. They do not know what rights they have, what deadlines and requirements they face, what options they might choose to exercise. They are half-citizens. Their rights exist in print but not in fact.

Illiterates cannot look up numbers in a telephone directory. Even if they can find the names of friends, few possess the sorting skills to make use of the yellow pages; categories are bewildering and trade names are beyond decoding capabilities for millions of nonreaders. Even the emergency numbers listed on the first page of the phone book—"Ambulance," "Police," and "Fire"—are too frequently beyond the recognition of nonreaders.

Many illiterates cannot read the admonition on a pack of cigarettes. Neither the Surgeon General's warning nor its reproduction on the package can alert them to the risks. Although most people learn by word of mouth that smoking is related to a number of grave physical disorders, they do not get the chance to read the detailed stories which can document this danger with the vividness that turns concern into determination to resist. They can see the handsome cowboy or the slim

Virginia lady lighting up a filter cigarette; they cannot heed the words that tell them that this product is (not "may be") dangerous to their health. Sixty million men and women are condemned to be the unalerted, high-risk candidates for cancer.

Illiterates do not buy "no-name" products in the supermarkets. They must   20 depend on photographs or the familiar logos that are printed on the packages of brand-name groceries. The poorest people, therefore, are denied the benefits of the least costly products.

Illiterates depend almost entirely upon label recognition. Many labels, however, are not easy to distinguish. Dozens of different kinds of Campbell's soup appear identical to the nonreader. The purchaser who cannot read and does not dare to ask for help, out of the fear of being stigmatized (a fear which is unfortunately realistic), frequently comes home with something which she never wanted and her family never tasted.

Illiterates cannot read instructions on a pack of frozen food. Packages sometimes provide an illustration to explain the cooking preparations; but illustrations are of little help to someone who must "boil water, drop the food—*within* its plastic wrapper—in the boiling water, wait for it to simmer, instantly remove."

Even when labels are seemingly clear, they may be easily mistaken. A woman in Detroit brought home a gallon of Crisco for her children's dinner. She thought that she had bought the chicken that was pictured on the label. She had enough Crisco now to last a year—but no more money to go back and buy the food for dinner.

Recipes provided on the packages of certain staples sometimes tempt a semiliterate person to prepare a meal her children have not tasted. The longing to vary the uniform and often starchy content of low-budget meals provided to the family that relies on food stamps commonly leads to ruinous results. Scarce funds have been wasted and the food must be thrown out. The same applies to distribution of food-surplus produce in emergency conditions. Government inducements to poor people to "explore the ways" by which to make a tasty meal from tasteless noodles, surplus cheese, and powdered milk are useless to nonreaders. Intended as benevolent advice, such recommendations mock reality and foster deeper feelings of resentment and of inability to cope. (Those, on the other hand, who cautiously refrain from "innovative" recipes in preparation of their children's meals must suffer the opprobrium of "laziness," "lack of imagination. . . .")

Illiterates cannot travel freely. When they attempt to do so, they encounter   25 risks that few of us can dream of. They cannot read traffic signs and, while they often learn to recognize and to decipher symbols, they cannot manage street names which they haven't seen before. The same is true for bus and subway stops. While ingenuity can sometimes help a man or woman to discern directions from familiar landmarks, buildings, cemeteries, churches, and the like, most illiterates are virtually immobilized. They seldom wander past the streets and neighborhoods they know. Geographical paralysis becomes a bitter metaphor for their entire existence. They are immobilized in almost every sense we can imagine. They can't move up. They can't move out. They cannot see beyond. Illiterates may take an oral test for drivers' permits in most sections of America. It is a questionable concession.

Where will they go? How will they get there? How will they get home? Could it be that some of us might like it better if they stayed where they belong?

Travel is only one of many instances of circumscribed existence. Choice, in almost all of its facets, is diminished in the life of an illiterate adult. Even the printed TV schedule, which provides most people with the luxury of preselection, does not belong within the arsenal of options in illiterate existence. One consequence is that the viewer watches only what appears at moments when he happens to have time to turn the switch. Another consequence, a lot more common, is that the TV set remains in operation night and day. Whatever the program offered at the hour when he walks into the room will be the nutriment that he accepts and swallows. Thus, to passivity, is added frequency—indeed, almost uninterrupted continuity. Freedom to select is no more possible here than in the choice of home or surgery or food.

"You don't choose," said one illiterate woman. "You take your wishes from somebody else." Whether in perusal of a menu, selection of highways, purchase of groceries, or determination of affordable enjoyment, illiterate Americans must trust somebody else: a friend, a relative, a stranger on the street, a grocery clerk, a TV copywriter.

"All of our mail we get, it's hard for her to read. Settin' down and writing a letter, she can't do it. Like if we get a bill . . . we take it over to my sister-in-law . . . My sister-in-law reads it."

Billing agencies harass poor people for the payment of the bills for purchases that might have taken place six months before. Utility companies offer an agreement for a staggered payment schedule on a bill past due. "You have to trust them," one man said. Precisely for this reason, you end up by trusting no one and suspecting everyone of possible deceit. A submerged sense of distrust becomes the corollary to a constant need to trust. "They are cheating me . . . I have been tricked . . . I do not know . . ."

Not knowing: This is a familiar theme. Not knowing the right word for the ₃₀ right thing at the right time is one form of subjugation. Not knowing the world that lies concealed behind those words is a more terrifying feeling. The longitude and latitude of one's existence are beyond all easy apprehension. Even the hard, cold stars within the firmament above one's head begin to mock the possibilities for self-location. Where am I? Where did I come from? Where will I go?

"I've lost a lot of jobs," one man explains. "Today, even if you're a janitor, there's still reading and writing . . . They leave a note saying, 'Go to room so-and-so . . .' You can't do it. You can't read it. You don't know."

"The hardest thing about it is that I've been places where I didn't know where I was. You don't know where you are . . . You're lost."

"Like I said: I have two kids. What do I do if one of my kids starts choking? I go running to the phone . . . I can't look up the hospital phone number. That's if we're at home. Out on the street, I can't read the sign. I get to a pay phone. 'Okay, tell us where you are. We'll send an ambulance.' I look at the street sign. Right there, I can't tell you what it says. I'd have to spell it out, letter for letter. By that time, one of my kids would be dead . . . These are the kinds of fears you go with, every single day . . ."

"Reading directions, I suffer with. I work with chemicals . . . That's scary to begin with . . ."

"You sit down. They throw the menu in front of you. Where do you go from there? Nine times out of ten you say, 'Go ahead. Pick out something for the both of us.' I've eaten some weird things, let me tell you!"

Menus. Chemicals. A child choking while his mother searches for a word she does not know to find assistance that will come too late. Another mother speaks about the inability to help her kids to read: "I can't read to them. Of course that's leaving them out of something they should have. Oh, it matters. You *believe* it matters! I ordered all these books. The kids belong to a book club. Donny wanted me to read a book to him. I told Donny: 'I can't read.' He said: 'Mommy, you sit down. I'll read it to you.' I tried it one day, reading from the pictures. Donny looked at me. He said, 'Mommy, that's not right.' He's only five. He knew I couldn't read . . ."

A landlord tells a woman that her lease allows him to evict her if her baby cries and causes inconvenience to her neighbors. The consequence of challenging his words conveys a danger which appears, unlikely as it seems, even more alarming than the danger of eviction. Once she admits that she can't read, in the desire to maneuver for the time in which to call a friend, she will have defined herself in terms of an explicit impotence that she cannot endure. Capitulation in this case is preferable to self-humiliation. Resisting the definition of oneself in terms of what one cannot do, what others take for granted, represents a need so great that other imperatives (even one so urgent as the need to keep one's home in winter's cold) evaporate and fall away in face of fear. Even the loss of home and shelter, in this case, is not so terrifying as the loss of self.

"I come out of school. I was sixteen. They had their meetings. The directors meet. They said that I was wasting their school paper. I was wasting pencils . . ."

Another illiterate, looking back, believes she was not worthy of her teacher's time. She believes that it was wrong of her to take up space within her school. She believes that it was right to leave in order that somebody more deserving could receive her place.

Children choke. Their mother chokes another way: on more than chicken bones.

People eat what others order, know what others tell them, struggle not to see themselves as they believe the world perceives them. A man in California speaks about his own loss of identity, of self-location, definition:

"I stood at the bottom of the ramp. My car had broke down on the freeway. There was a phone. I asked for the police. They was nice. They said to tell them where I was. I looked up at the signs. There was one that I had seen before. I read it to them: one way street. They thought it was a joke. I told them I couldn't read. There was other signs above the ramp. They told me to try. I looked around for somebody to help. All the cars was going by real fast. I couldn't make them understand that I was lost. The cop was nice. He told me: 'Try once more.' I did my best. I couldn't read. I only knew the sign above my head. The cop was trying to be nice. He knew that I was trapped. 'I can't send out a car to you if you can't tell me where you are.' I felt afraid. I nearly cried. I'm forty-eight years old. I only said: 'I'm on a one-way street . . .'"

Perhaps we might slow down a moment here and look at the realities described above. This is the nation that we live in. This is a society that most of us did not create but which our President and other leaders have been willing to sustain by virtue of malign neglect. Do we possess the character and courage to address a problem which so many nations, poorer than our own, have found it natural to correct?

The answers to these questions represent a reasonable test of our belief in the democracy to which we have been asked in public school to swear allegiance.

QUESTIONS FOR DISCUSSION AND WRITING

1. Quoting Socrates, Kozol argues that questions of literacy are ultimately "matters of morality" (paragraph 2) and that illiteracy is a threat to democracy. How does he support this argument?

2. Kozol opens his chapter on the cost of illiteracy with the warning on a can of Drāno. Why does he include the warning without further explanation about its significance to the chapter? Writing about the human cost of illiteracy, Kozol faces a dilemma that is innate to his subject and medium: One must first be literate to read his book, so those he wants to help have no access to his written message. To what extent does his medium limit the effectiveness of his message?

3. Kozol repeats the same phrase ("Illiterates cannot") to introduce his topic sentences. What is the effect of this repetition? What could be some of the advantages and risks for Kozol in using this rhetorical design? Why does he choose the negative pattern for the repeated opening phrase?

4. Kozol's argument is true for people who have to live in a civilization based on the power of the written word. Yet it is possible to challenge Kozol and perhaps ourselves from a different perspective. Drawing on Henry David Thoreau (p. 161), Leslie Marmon Silko (p. 57), and Richard Rodriguez (p. 211), imagine that you are a member of an ancient yet highly advanced oral civilization, and write an essay with a title such as "The Human Cost of a Literate Society."

RICHARD RODRIGUEZ

Aria: A Memoir of a Bilingual Childhood

Richard Rodriguez, born in San Francisco in 1944, is the author of Days of Obligation: An Argument with My Mexican Father *(1993) and* Brown: An Erotic History of the Americas *(2002). His memoir,* Hunger of Memory: The Education of Richard Rodriguez *(1982), is a moving and provocative account of growing up bilingual and bicultural as the son of Mexican immigrants in a largely white neighborhood in Sacramento. The book became a focal point in the 1980s' national debate about bilingual education, a debate that continues into the twenty-first century with various "English-only" initiatives.*

In his memoir's opening chapter, "Aria," Rodriguez reflects on the difficult transition from his private, Spanish-speaking world to the public, English-speaking one. Although the English-only classroom brought estrangement from his family and heritage, Rodriguez nevertheless argues in Hunger of Memory *against both bilingual education and affirmative action—programs he acknowledges having benefited from as a scholarship student at both Stanford (B.A., 1967) and Columbia (M.A., 1969) and as a doctoral student in English at the University of California at Berkeley.*

I remember, to start with, that day in Sacramento, in a California now nearly thirty years past, when I first entered a classroom—able to understand about fifty stray English words. The third of four children, I had been preceded by my older brother and sister to a neighborhood Roman Catholic school. But neither of them had revealed very much about their classroom experiences. They left each morning and returned each afternoon, always together, speaking Spanish as they climbed the five steps to the porch. And their mysterious books, wrapped in brown shopping-bag paper, remained on the table next to the door, closed firmly behind them.

An accident of geography sent me to a school where all my classmates were white and many were the children of doctors and lawyers and business executives. On that first day of school, my classmates must certainly have been uneasy to find themselves apart from their families, in the first institution of their lives. But I was astonished. I was fated to be the "problem student" in class.

The nun said, in a friendly but oddly impersonal voice: "Boys and girls, this is Richard Rodriguez." (I heard her sound it out: *Rich-heard Road-ree-guess.*) It was the first time I had heard anyone say my name in English. "Richard," the nun repeated more slowly, writing my name down in her book. Quickly I turned to see my mother's face dissolve in a watery blur behind the pebbled-glass door.

Now, many years later, I hear of something called "bilingual education"—a scheme proposed in the late 1960s by Hispanic-American social activists, later endorsed by a congressional vote. It is a program that seeks to permit non-English-speaking children (many from lower-class homes) to use their "family language" as the language of school. Such, at least, is the aim its supporters announce. I hear them, and am forced to say no: It is not possible for a child, any child, ever to use his family's language in school. Not to understand this is to misunderstand the public uses of schooling and to trivialize the nature of intimate life.

Memory teaches me what I know of these matters. The boy reminds the adult. 5 I was a bilingual child, but of a certain kind: "socially disadvantaged," the son of working-class parents, both Mexican immigrants.

In the early years of my boyhood, my parents coped very well in America. My father had steady work. My mother managed at home. They were nobody's victims. When we moved to a house many blocks from the Mexican-American section of town, they were not intimidated by those two or three neighbors who initially tried to make us unwelcome. ("Keep your brats away from my sidewalk!") But despite all they achieved, or perhaps because they had so much to achieve, they lacked any deep feeling of ease, of belonging in public. They regarded the people at work or in crowds as being very distant from us. Those were the others, *los gringos*. That term was interchangeable in their speech with another, even more telling: *los americanos*.

I grew up in a house where the only regular guests were my relations. On a certain day, enormous families of relatives would visit us, and there would be so many people that the noise and the bodies would spill out to the backyard and onto the front porch. Then for weeks no one would come. (If the doorbell rang, it was usually a salesman.) Our house stood apart—gaudy yellow in a row of white bungalows. We were the people with the noisy dog, the people who raised chickens. We were the foreigners on the block. A few neighbors would smile and wave at us. We waved back. But until I was seven years old, I did not know the name of the old couple living next door or the names of the kids living across the street.

In public, my father and mother spoke a hesitant, accented, and not always grammatical English. And then they would have to strain, their bodies tense, to catch the sense of what was rapidly said by *los gringos*. At home, they returned to Spanish. The language of their Mexican past sounded in counterpoint to the English spoken in public. The words would come quickly, with ease. Conveyed through those sounds was the pleasing, soothing, consoling reminder that one was at home.

During those years when I was first learning to speak, my mother and father addressed me only in Spanish; in Spanish I learned to reply. By contrast, Englis[h] (*inglés*) was the language I came to associate with gringos, rarely he[ard in the] house. I learned my first words of English overhearing my p[arents speak to] strangers. At six years of age, I knew just enough word[s ... to be sent] on errands to stores one block away—but no more.

I was then a listening child, careful to hear [the differe]nt sounds of 10
Spanish and English. Wide-eyed with hearing, I'd [li]sten to sounds more than to words. First, there were English (*gringo*) sounds. So many words still were unknown to me that when the butcher or the lady at the drugstore said something, exotic polysyllabic sounds would bloom in the midst of their sentences. Often the speech of people in public seemed to me very loud, booming with confidence. The man behind the counter would literally ask, "What can I do for you?" But by being so firm and clear, the sound of his voice said that he was a gringo; he belonged in public society. There were also the high, nasal notes of middle-class American speech—which I rarely am conscious of hearing today because I hear them so often, but could not stop hearing when I was a boy. Crowds at Safeway or at bus stops were noisy with the birdlike sounds of *los gringos*. I'd move away from them all—all the chirping chatter above me.

My own sounds I was unable to hear, but I knew that I spoke English poorly. My words could not extend to form complete thoughts. And the words I did speak I didn't know well enough to make distinct sounds. (Listeners would usually lower their heads to hear better what I was trying to say.) But it was one thing for *me* to speak English with difficulty; it was more troubling to hear my parents speaking in public: their high-whining vowels and guttural consonants; their sentences that got stuck with "eh" and "ah" sounds; the confused syntax; the hesitant rhythm of sounds so different from the way gringos spoke. I'd notice, moreover, that my parents' voices were softer than those of gringos we would meet.

I am tempted to say now that none of this mattered. (In adulthood I am embarrassed by childhood fears.) And, in a way, it didn't matter very much that my parents could not speak English with ease. Their linguistic difficulties had no serious consequences. My mother and father made themselves understood at the county hospital clinic and at government offices. And yet, in another way, it mattered very much. It was unsettling to hear my parents struggle with English. Hearing them, I'd grow nervous, and my clutching trust in their protection and power would be weakened.

There were many times like the night at a brightly lit gasoline station (a blaring white memory) when I stood uneasily hearing my father talk to a teenage attendant. I do not recall what they were saying, but I cannot forget the sounds my father made as he spoke. At one point his words slid together to form one long word—sounds as confused as the threads of blue and green oil in the puddle next to my shoes. His voice rushed through what he had left to say. Toward the end, he reached falsetto notes, appealing to his listener's understanding. I looked away at the lights of passing automobiles. I tried not to hear any more. But I heard only too well the attendant's reply, his calm, easy tones. Shortly afterward, headed for home, I shivered when my father put his hand on my shoulder. The very first chance that I got, I evaded his grasp and ran on ahead into the dark, skipping with feigned boyish exuberance.

But then there was Spanish: *español*, the language rarely heard away from the house; *español*, the language which seemed to me therefore a private language, my family's language. To hear its sounds was to feel myself specially recognized as one of the family, apart from *los otros*. A simple remark, an inconsequential comment could convey that assurance. My parents would say something to me and I would feel embraced by the sounds of their words. Those sounds said: *I am speaking with ease in Spanish. I am addressing you in words I never use with los gringos. I recognize you as someone special, close, like no one outside. You belong with us. In the family. Ricardo.*

At the age of six, well past the time when most middle-class children no longer notice the difference between sounds uttered at home and words spoken in public, I had a different experience. I lived in a world compounded of sounds. I was a child longer than most. I lived in a magical world, surrounded by sounds both pleasing and fearful. I shared with my family a language enchantingly private—different from that used in the city around us. 15

Just opening or closing the screen door behind me was an important experience. I'd rarely leave home all alone or without feeling reluctance. Walking down the sidewalk, under the canopy of tall trees, I'd warily notice the (suddenly) silent neighborhood kids who stood warily watching me. Nervously, I'd arrive at the grocery store to hear there the sounds of the gringo, reminding me that in this so-big world I was a foreigner. But if leaving home was never routine, neither was coming back. Walking toward our house, climbing the steps from the sidewalk, in summer when the front door was open, I'd hear voices beyond the screen door talking in Spanish. For a second or two I'd stay, linger there listening. Smiling, I'd hear my mother call out, saying in Spanish, "Is that you, Richard?" Those were her words, but all the while her sounds would assure me: *You are home now. Come closer inside. With us.* "*Sí*," I'd reply.

Once more inside the house, I would resume my place in the family. The sounds would grow harder to hear. Once more at home, I would grow less conscious of them. It required, however, no more than the blurt of the doorbell to alert me all over again to listen to sounds. The house would turn instantly quiet while my mother went to the door. I'd hear her hard English sounds. I'd wait to hear her voice turn to soft-sounding Spanish, which assured me, as surely as did the clicking tongue of the lock on the door, that the stranger was gone.

Plainly it is not healthy to hear such sounds so often. It is not healthy to distinguish public from private sounds so easily. I remained cloistered by sounds, timid and shy in public, too dependent on the voices at home. And yet I was a very happy child when I was at home. I remember many nights when my father would come back from work, and I'd hear him call out to my mother in Spanish, sounding relieved. In Spanish, his voice would sound the light and free notes that he never could manage in English. Some nights I'd jump up just hearing his voice. My brother and I would come running into the room where he was with our mother. Our laughing (so deep was the pleasure!) became screaming. Like others who feel the pain of public alienation, we transformed the knowledge of our public separateness into a consoling reminder of our intimacy. Excited, our voices joined in a celebration of sounds. *We are speaking now the way we never speak out in public— we are together*, the sounds told me. Some nights no one seemed willing to loosen the hold that sounds had on us. At dinner we invented new words that sounded Spanish, but made sense only to us. We pieced together new words by taking, say, an English verb and giving it Spanish endings. My mother's instructions at bedtime would be lacquered with mock-urgent tones. Or a word like *sí*, sounded in several notes, would convey added measures of feeling. Tongues lingered around the edges of words, especially fat vowels, and we happily sounded that military drum roll, the twirling roar of the Spanish *r*. Family language, my family's sounds: the voices of my parents and sisters and brother. Their voices insisting: *You belong here. We are family members. Related. Special to one another. Listen!* Voices singing and sighing, rising and straining, then surging, teeming with pleasure which burst syllables into fragments of laughter. At times it seemed there was steady quiet only when, from another room, the rustling whispers of my parents faded and I edged closer to sleep.

Supporters of bilingual education imply today that students like me miss a great deal by not being taught in their family's language. What they seem not to recognize is that, as a socially disadvantaged child, I regarded Spanish as a private language. It was a ghetto language that deepened and strengthened my feeling of public separateness. What I needed to learn in school was that I had the right, and the obligation, to speak the public language. The odd truth is that my first-grade classmates could have become bilingual, in the conventional sense of the word, more easily than I. Had they been taught early (as upper-middle-class children often are taught) a "second language" like Spanish or French, they could have regarded it simply as another public language. In my case, such bilingualism could not have been so quickly achieved. What I did not believe was that I could speak a single public language.

Without question, it would have pleased me to have heard my teachers address   20 me in Spanish when I entered the classroom. I would have felt much less afraid. I would have imagined that my instructors were somehow "related" to me; I would indeed have heard their Spanish as my family's language. I would have trusted them and responded with ease. But I would have delayed—postponed for how long?—having to learn the language of public society. I would have evaded—and for how long?—learning the great lesson of school: that I had a public identity.

Fortunately, my teachers were unsentimental about their responsibility. What they understood was that I needed to speak public English. So their voices would search me out, asking me questions. Each time I heard them I'd look up in surprise to see a nun's face frowning at me. I'd mumble, not really meaning to answer. The nun would persist. "Richard, stand up. Don't look at the floor. Speak up. Speak to the entire class, not just to me!" But I couldn't believe English could be my language to use. (In part, I did not want to believe it.) I continued to mumble. I resisted the teacher's demands. (Did I somehow suspect that once I learned this public language my family life would be changed?) Silent, waiting for the bell to sound, I remained dazed, diffident, afraid.

Because I wrongly imagined that English was intrinsically a public language and Spanish was intrinsically private, I easily noted the difference between classroom language and the language at home. At school, words were directed to a general audience of listeners. ("Boys and girls . . .") Words were meaningfully ordered. And the point was not self-expression alone, but to make oneself understood by many others. The teacher quizzed: "Boys and girls, why do we use that word in this sentence? Could we think of a better word to use there? Would the sentence change its meaning if the words were differently arranged? Isn't there a better way of saying much the same thing?" (I couldn't say. I wouldn't try to say.)

Three months passed. Five. A half year. Unsmiling, ever watchful, my teachers noted my silence. They began to connect my behavior with the slow progress my brother and sisters were making. Until, one Saturday morning, three nuns arrived at the house to talk to our parents. Stiffly they sat on the blue living-room sofa. From the doorway of another room, spying on the visitors, I noted the incongruity, the clash of two worlds, the faces and voices of school intruding upon the familiar setting of home. I overheard one voice gently wondering, "Do your children speak only Spanish at home, Mrs. Rodriguez?" While another voice added, "That Richard especially seems so timid and shy."

That Rich-heard!

With great tact, the visitors continued, "Is it possible for you and your hus-   25 band to encourage your children to practice their English when they are home?" Of course my parents complied. What would they not do for their children's well-being? And how could they question the Church's authority which those women represented? In an instant they agreed to give up the language (the sounds) which had revealed and accentuated our family's closeness. The moment after the visitors left, the change was observed. "*Ahora*, speak to us only *en inglés*," my father and mother told us.

At first, it seemed a kind of game. After dinner each night, the family gathered together to practice "our" English. It was still then *inglés*, a language foreign to us, so we felt drawn to it as strangers. Laughing, we would try to define words we could not pronounce. We played with strange English sounds, often overanglicizing our pronunciations. And we filled the smiling gaps of our sentences with familiar Spanish sounds. But that was cheating, somebody shouted, and everyone laughed.

In school, meanwhile, like my brother and sisters, I was required to attend a daily tutoring session. I needed a full year of this special work. I also needed my teachers to keep my attention from straying in class by calling out, "*Rich-heard*"—their English voices slowly loosening the ties to my other name, with its three notes, *Ri-car-do*. Most of all, I needed to hear my mother and father speak to me in a moment of seriousness in "broken"—suddenly heartbreaking—English. This scene was inevitable. One Saturday morning I entered the kitchen where my parents were talking, but I did not realize that they were talking in Spanish until, the moment they saw me, their voices changed and they began speaking English. The gringo sounds they uttered startled me. Pushed me away. In that moment of trivial misunderstanding and profound insight, I felt my throat twisted by unsounded grief. I simply turned and left the room. But I had no place to escape to where I could grieve in Spanish. My brother and sisters were speaking English in another part of the house.

Again and again in the days following, as I grew increasingly angry, I was obliged to hear my mother and father encouraging me: "Speak to us *en inglés*." Only then did I determine to learn classroom English. Thus, sometime afterward it happened: One day in school, I raised my hand to volunteer an answer to a question. I spoke out in a loud voice and I did not think it remarkable when the entire class understood. That day I moved very far from being the disadvantaged child I had been only days earlier. Taken hold at last was the belief, the calming assurance, that I *belonged* in public.

Shortly after, I stopped hearing the high, troubling sounds of *los gringos*. A more and more confident speaker of English, I didn't listen to how strangers sounded when they talked to me. With so many English-speaking people around me, I no longer heard American accents. Conversations quickened. Listening to persons whose voices sounded eccentrically pitched, I might note their sounds for a few seconds, but then I'd concentrate on what they were saying. Now when I heard someone's tone of voice—angry or questioning or sarcastic or happy or sad—I didn't distinguish it from the words it expressed. Sound and word were thus tightly wedded. At the end of each day I was often bemused, and always relieved, to realize how "soundless," though crowded with words, my day in public had been. An eight-year-old boy, I finally came to accept what had been technically true since my birth: I was an American citizen.

But diminished by then was the special feeling of closeness at home. Gone was   30
the desperate, urgent, intense feeling of being at home among those with whom
I felt intimate. Our family remained a loving family, but one greatly changed. We
were no longer so close, no longer bound tightly together by the knowledge of
our separateness from *los gringos*. Neither my older brother nor my sisters rushed
home after school any more. Nor did I. When I arrived home, often there would be
neighborhood kids in the house. Or the house would be empty of sounds.

Following the dramatic Americanization of their children, even my parents
grew more publicly confident—especially my mother. First she learned the names
of all the people on the block. Then she decided we needed to have a telephone in
our house. My father, for his part, continued to use the word *gringo,* but it was no
longer charged with bitterness or distrust. Stripped of any emotional content, the
word simply became a name for those Americans not of Hispanic descent. Hearing him, sometimes, I wasn't sure if he was pronouncing the Spanish word *gringo*,
or saying gringo in English.

There was a new silence at home. As we children learned more and more
English, we shared fewer and fewer words with our parents. Sentences needed to
be spoken slowly when one of us addressed our mother or father. Often the parent
wouldn't understand. The child would need to repeat himself. Still the parent misunderstood. The young voice, frustrated, would end up saying, "Never mind"—the
subject was closed. Dinners would be noisy with the clinking of knives and forks
against dishes. My mother would smile softly between her remarks; my father, at
the other end of the table, would chew and chew his food while he stared over the
heads of his children.

My mother! My father! After English became my primary language, I no longer knew what words to use in addressing my parents. The old Spanish words
(those tender accents of sound) I had earlier used—*mamá* and *papá*—I couldn't
use any more. They would have been all-too-painful reminders of how much had
changed in my life. On the other hand, the words I heard neighborhood kids call
their parents seemed equally unsatisfactory. "Mother" and "father," "ma," "papa,"
"pa," "dad," "pop" (how I hated the all-American sound of that last word)—all
these I felt were unsuitable terms of address for *my* parents. As a result, I never
used them at home. Whenever I'd speak to my parents, I would try to get their
attention by looking at them. In public conversations, I'd refer to them as my "parents" or my "mother" and "father."

My mother and father, for their part, responded differently, as their children
spoke to them less. My mother grew restless, seemed troubled and anxious at the
scarceness of words exchanged in the house. She would question me about my
day when I came home from school. She smiled at my small talk. She pried at the
edges of my sentences to get me to say something more. ("What . . . ?") She'd join
conversations she overheard, but her intrusions often stopped her children's talking. By contrast, my father seemed to grow reconciled to the new quiet. Though
his English somewhat improved, he tended more and more to retire into silence.
At dinner he spoke very little. One night his children and even his wife helplessly
giggled at his garbled English pronunciation of the Catholic "Grace Before Meals."

Thereafter he made his wife recite the prayer at the start of each meal, even on formal occasions when there were guests in the house.

Hers became the public voice of the family. On official business it was she, not 35 my father, who would usually talk to strangers on the phone or in stores. We children grew so accustomed to his silence that years later we would routinely refer to his "shyness." (My mother often tried to explain: Both of his parents died when he was eight. He was raised by an uncle who treated him as little more than a menial servant. He was never encouraged to speak. He grew up alone—a man of few words.) But I realized my father was not shy whenever I'd watch him speaking Spanish with relatives. Using Spanish, he was quickly effusive. Especially when talking with other men, his voice would spark, flicker, flare alive with varied sounds. In Spanish he expressed ideas and feelings he rarely revealed when speaking English. With firm Spanish sounds he conveyed a confidence and authority that English would never allow him.

The silence at home, however, was not simply the result of fewer words passing between parents and children. More profound for me was the silence created by my inattention to sounds. At about the time I no longer bothered to listen with care to the sounds of English in public, I grew careless about listening to the sounds made by the family when they spoke. Most of the time I would hear someone speaking at home and didn't distinguish his sounds from the words people uttered in public. I didn't even pay much attention to my parents' accented and ungrammatical speech—at least not at home. Only when I was with them in public would I become alert to their accents. But even then their sounds caused me less and less concern. For I was growing increasingly confident of my own public identity.

I would have been happier about my public success had I not recalled, sometimes, what it had been like earlier, when my family conveyed its intimacy through a set of conveniently private sounds. Sometimes in public, hearing a stranger, I'd hark back to my lost past. A Mexican farm worker approached me one day downtown. He wanted directions to some place. "*Hijito, . . .*" he said. And his voice stirred old longings. Another time I was standing beside my mother in the visiting room of a Carmelite convent, before the dense screen which rendered the nuns shadowy figures. I heard several of them speaking Spanish in their busy, singsong, overlapping voices, assuring my mother that, yes, yes, we were remembered, all our family was remembered, in their prayers. Those voices echoed faraway family sounds. Another day a dark-faced old woman touched my shoulder lightly to steady herself as she boarded a bus. She murmured something to me I couldn't quite comprehend. Her Spanish voice came near, like the face of a never-before-seen relative in the instant before I was kissed. That voice, like so many of the Spanish voices I'd hear in public, recalled the golden age of my childhood.

Bilingual educators say today that children lose a degree of "individuality" by becoming assimilated into public society. (Bilingual schooling is a program popularized in the seventies, that decade when middle-class "ethnics" began to resist the process of assimilation—the "American melting pot.") But the bilingualists oversimplify when they scorn the value and necessity of assimilation. They do not seem to realize that a person is individualized in two ways. So they do not realize that, while one suffers a diminished sense of *private* individuality by being assimilated into public society, such assimilation makes possible the achievement of *public* individuality.

Simplistically again, the bilingualists insist that a student should be reminded of his difference from others in mass society, of his "heritage." But they equate mere separateness with individuality. The fact is that only in private—with intimates—is separateness from the crowd a prerequisite for individuality; an intimate "tells" me that I am unique, unlike all others, apart from the crowd. In public, by contrast, full individuality is achieved, paradoxically, by those who are able to consider themselves members of the crowd. Thus it happened for me. Only when I was able to think of myself as an American, no longer an alien in gringo society, could I seek the rights and opportunities necessary for full public individuality. The social and political advantages I enjoy as a man began on the day I came to believe that my name is indeed *Rich-heard Road-ree-guess*. It is true that my public society today is often impersonal; in fact, my public society is usually mass society. But despite the anonymity of the crowd, and despite the fact that the individuality I achieve in public is often tenuous—because it depends on my being one in a crowd—I celebrate the day I acquired my new name. Those middle-class ethnics who scorn assimilation seem to me filled with decadent self-pity, obsessed by the burden of public life. Dangerously, they romanticize public separateness and trivialize the dilemma of those who are truly socially disadvantaged.

If I rehearse here the changes in my private life after my Americanization, it is 40 finally to emphasize a public gain. The loss implies the gain. The house I returned to each afternoon was quiet. Intimate sounds no longer greeted me at the door. Inside there were other noises. The telephone rang. Neighborhood kids ran past the door of the bedroom where I was reading my schoolbooks—covered with brown shopping-bag paper. Once I learned the public language, it would never again be easy for me to hear intimate family voices. More and more of my day was spent hearing words, not sounds. But that may only be a way of saying that on the day I raised my hand in class and spoke loudly to an entire roomful of faces, my childhood started to end.

QUESTIONS FOR DISCUSSION AND WRITING

1. What distinctions does Rodriguez draw between public and private language? Support your response with quotations from the text.

2. Do you find Rodriguez's argument convincing? Why or why not?

3. Looking closely at the passages in "Aria" where Rodriguez represents differing languages, describe the effects of each representation on you as a reader. What do you think is gained and lost through representations of language variation?

4. In the library or on the Internet, locate some contemporary debates about bilingual and ESL (English as a Second Language) curricula. What differences between these two curricula can you identify? Which passages from "Aria" could be used to support bilingual, ESL, or "English-only" agendas today?

MAYA SCHENWAR

Radical "Unschooling" Moms Are Changing the Stay-at-Home Landscape

Maya Schenwar is the executive director of Truthout, a Web site that states its purpose is "to spark action by revealing systemic injustice and providing a platform for transformative ideas. . . ." Its purpose is nothing less than to save humanity and the planet. Schenwar is a 2005 graduate of Swarthmore College. Before becoming executive director, she was a contributing editor at Punk Planet *magazine, and she contributed to many online publications, including* Bitch *magazine, from which this article is taken.*

In this article, Schenwar ventures into the topic of homeschooling. Typically the domain of "hippie earth mothers" and "creationist Christians" trying to keep their children away from the ideas that run counter to their personal beliefs, homeschoolers have been joined by a new faction: feminists who also worry about the corrupting influence of public schools. Much like their hippie and creationist colleagues, these new homeschoolers decry the morality of public education, which they see as steeped in sexism, racism, classism, heterosexism, and elitism. Unlike their counterparts, however, they may prefer a type of homeschooling called "unschooling," in which parents act not simply as teachers themselves, but as facilitators who guide their children toward their own explorations. However, the role comes with a contradiction: The feminist becomes a stay-at-home mother, who needs financial support from another, often the children's father.

Not long ago, homeschooling was thought of as the domain of hippie earth mothers letting their kids "do their own thing" or creationist Christians shielding their kids from monkey science and premarital sex. As recently as 1980, homeschooling was illegal in 30 states. Despite the fact that such figures as Abraham Lincoln, Margaret Atwood, Sandra Day O'Connor, and, um, Jennifer Love Hewitt were products of a home education, the practice is still often seen as strange and even detrimental.

These days, homeschooling is legal across the country, and parents are homeschooling for secular reasons as well as faith-based ones: quality of education, freedom to travel, their kids' special needs, or simply a frustration with the educational system. Most significantly, many progressive parents are taking their kids' education into their own hands to instill open-mindedness and social consciousness along with reading, science, and math.

For these parents, "unschooling" is an attractive option. In this approach to homeschooling, kids choose what they'll study and investigate their questions outside the confines of a classroom. In traditional homeschooling, parents play the role of teachers, determining the curriculum, handing out assignments, and administering tests. Unschooling parents, on the other hand, act as facilitators, guiding their kids' explorations. Even though the diy approach may appeal to progressives who identify with the anti-establishment ethos of the punk movement, homeschooling still raises tricky questions for progressive mothers.

Namely, this one: Can women trade their careers for their families without sacrificing a few of their feminist values—the very values that inspired many of them to homeschool in the first place? It's no wonder that punk feminist moms like Kim Campbell, who has homeschooled her kids for seven years, occasionally feel like walking oxymorons.

Despite her indie values, Campbell worries that her economic dependence on 5 her husband could set a bad example for her daughter. "The first half year that we homeschooled, I had a complete identity crisis over the matter," she says. "At the time I knew that I was making a great decision, but I couldn't figure out how to square it with what I'd always considered my feminist sensibilities." For Campbell and a growing contingent of other feminist unschoolers across the country, educating their kids has also been a process of figuring out how homeschooling jibes with their feminism.

Nina Packebush, a Washington state mom of three and self-described "radical parent," started teaching her son at home because he was dyslexic and had ADHD, and his school wasn't providing the personal attention he needed. As Packebush sought out teaching resources, she discovered a gaping hole in standard history textbooks.

"I noticed that women and people of color were virtually nonexistent," Packebush says. "Don't even try to find any mention of lgbt people in history. One thing led to another, and soon I was homeschooling because I was a feminist." When her youngest child reached school age, Packebush chose to keep her out of the classroom solely because of its gender-biased curriculum.

Instead of using the standard Houghton Mifflin textbooks, Packebush provides a variety of mass-market books, like *Freedom's Children,* for her kids. Beyond that, she follows where her kids' interests lead; unschooling emphasizes that learning opportunities can pop up at any time. When Packebush's older daughter became interested in zine-making, it became their curriculum. Packebush even started up her own zine, The Edgy-Catin' Mama.

Sarah Schira, who maintains TheDenimJumper.com, a Web site for "sassy secular homeschoolers," says that simply hanging out is one of the best routes to consciousness building. "One of the strengths of homeschooling is the incredible amount of time we spend together," she says. "We listen to the news on the radio all the time, and they hear our reactions, the political discussions it raises. We talk a lot about societal institutions and the role that larger, almost invisible factors play in shaping events and free choice."

Spending an "incredible amount of time" with your kids is great when they're 8 10 and 10, like Schira's. But what about when they're 12 . . . or 17? Can homeschoolers encourage the development of their kids' social consciousness without dictating it? It seems that the answer comes back to unschooling and the notion of parents as facilitators, not commanders-in-chief. Granted, kids will always be influenced by their parents' views, but if parents stress self-realization as a family value, kids may be more motivated to apply their lessons and grapple with important issues on their own terms.

That doesn't mean that freedom can't be a hard pill to swallow, even for a radical parent. At 18, Packebush's son Jason announced that he planned to become a porn star and asked what she'd do to stop him. "Well, I won't see your movies," she replied, biting back cries of rage. Eventually, Jason lost interest in the porn-star dream, and Packebush chalked up a couple of coolness points. "It's important to trust your kids," she says, "even if they choose something that hits you right in the guts."

As challenging and rewarding as homeschooling may be, some don't see it as real work. A slew of recent books, including Leslie Bennetts's bestseller *The Feminine Mistake,* argue that while stay-at-home moms, like homeschoolers, may believe they are choosing to leave the workforce, their decisions are actually influenced by insidious patriarchal forces. Many homeschooling moms counter that removing themselves from the marketplace means freeing themselves from its many sexist influences. If they have the financial means—or the ingenuity—to opt out, they'd rather live outside the workforce. Schira says that by rejecting the idea that success is all about money, she's reconceptualizing what happiness means. "I have come to recognize that I don't want the kind of life being offered by our culture," she says. "I don't want things. I don't want status. I want interdependence, harmony, new solutions to old problems."

Of course, resorting to one income brings out the five-ton mammoth in the room: Most homeschoolers are women and most of their income providers are men. Packebush, who was married when she began homeschooling, says that even in her "hip, alternative, feminist marriage," she was the one doing most of the childcare and teaching. "The vast majority of the people doing homeschooling are women," she says.

Often, that's because moms want to be their family's primary teachers. But raising radical, revolutionary children isn't feminist if the mom's individuality is getting lost in the lives of her kids. It's tough for homeschooling mothers to maintain their free time. Forums for homeschoolers abound with tips for dealing with burnout. The workload can be overwhelming, and even with a "fuck money" attitude, it's natural to feel undercompensated at times. Homeschooling mothers must negotiate a fine line between protesting capitalism and becoming unpaid labor.

Considering progressive parents' efforts to break with capitalism—spending 15 less, living alternatively, working cooperatively—it makes sense that many homeschoolers don't want their kids going anywhere near the mainstream school system. For Coleen Murphy, a New Orleans mom who was homeschooled herself, the negative social aspects of public education are a major reason she homeschools her two young boys.

"I see the school system as largely reinforcing the very worst aspects of societal norms, such as classism, racism, sexism, and good old mean-spiritedness, while limiting or removing access and opportunities to experience the best of what happens when human beings come together—acting with compassion; helping others because your help is needed, rather than to win some gold stars or other false rewards; asking questions because we want to know the answers rather than in order to display which of us knows the most how to please authority figures."

Along with the question of self-expression comes gender expression and unschooled kids are prone to ignoring (or at least toning down) the gender distinctions that rule most schools. Take Diana, a homeschooled seventeen-year-old from New Haven, Connecticut, who swears by Kate Bornstein's book *Gender Outlaw* and is very grateful to have missed out on the school social scene. "Not going to high school or middle school, I've never had that onslaught of pressure to do all sorts of pointless competitive things, like lose my virginity before I wanted to, or be sexy so men will like me, or be queer for the enjoyment of an audience," she says.

Avoiding homophobia is central to many parents' decision to homeschool. Packebush thinks queer, feminist homeschooling is on the rise because parents see it as an escape from the rampant sexism, homophobia, and transphobia of public schools. "Gender construction is one of the biggest reasons I keep my kids out of school."

Unschoolers' conceptions of gender are shaped not only by their open-minded parents, but also by their immediate environment. Having fewer kids around may mean less of a tendency to stereotype by gender or other handy labels. On the other hand, most schools also bring together individuals from different backgrounds, and although the routine clashes based on race, class, gender, and sexual orientation can make a mainstream school a shitty place to be, that diversity can also be instructive. It's easy to be color-blind when you're not exposed to racism; it's easy to "ignore" gender when you're not confronted with sexism. Getting to know a varied group of people at a young age—and seeing how discrimination impacts everyone—could build awareness of the conflicts inherent in our society.

For this reason, many feminist homeschoolers make a concerted effort to 20 expose their kids to a diverse crowd. Though many homeschoolers roll their eyes at the most prominent pop-culture depiction of a homeschooled kid—Lindsay Lohan's character in *Mean Girls*—Jesse Cordes Selbin, a nineteen-year-old who was homeschooled for seven years, says she identifies with her. Selbin spent a considerable portion of her teens in Sweden and says interacting with a wider world helped her put the often-brutal social scene of many schools in perspective. "My parents homeschooled me so that I could get more experience in the world, not so that I could shelter myself from it."

As the feminist homeschooling movement gains momentum, mothers will increasingly be faced with tough, identity-defining questions: Does being a feminist mean you have to have a paid job? What does it mean to raise a feminist kid? Is there a feminist definition of success, and should there be? It's important to keep in mind that a homeschooling mom is many things besides a homeschooling mom—even if she can't stop talking about her kid's latest papier-mâché dinosaur. Forging these more complex identities entails recognizing all the hats they wear besides "homeschooler." Packebush is a zinester, Schira is a webmaster and writer, and so on. They're Marxists, or anarchists, or punks, or please-don't-define-me-the-reason-I-homeschool-is-to-get-away-from-this-label-slapping-bullshit human beings.

As for Kim Campbell, she's still unschooling and still fighting critics of her decision with a vengeance. When others question whether her decision to "stop working" is feminist, she responds, "Honey, you don't know from work!"

QUESTIONS FOR DISCUSSION AND WRITING

1. Schenwar begins by pointing out how attitudes toward homeschooling have changed over time; in the past, homeschooling was the norm, then it became not only rare but illegal in thirty states, and now, it has become more popular again. What is your own attitude toward homeschooling? What do you think about the portrayal of homeschooling as the realm of fringe aspects?

2. In paragraph 4, Schenwar talks about "punk feminist moms"—what does she mean by that? How can the feminist values of independence and self-assertion be reconciled with the economic dependence that comes with being at home full-time?

3. Another aspect of the article is the idea of "unschooling" (paragraph 3). Rather than having parents act as teachers—teaching a curriculum, giving tests, and so on—the parent instead acts as a facilitator, a guide. Schenwar calls this a "diy approach" (paragraph 3), meaning a "do it yourself approach." What is your attitude about unschooling? What problems can you see with unschooling? What sort of parents would make good unschooling teachers? What sort of parents would not?

4. Another unexpected development is that the promotion of freedom for children can have undesired results, as when one homeschooler's son announces that he wants to become a porn star (paragraph 11). Can you imagine other unintended consequences that could develop from such an approach? What role do discipline and respect play in the expression of values these homeschoolers are trying to promote?

5. A problem feminist homeschoolers have to face, just like other homeschoolers, is that they are attempting to raise their children to have values that differ from those of mainstream culture, yet eventually these children will have to interact with and within that same culture. In your opinion, should parents keep their children away from the larger society when the values of that society are counter to their own? Cite specific examples.

JOHN TAYLOR GATTO

Against School: How Public Education Cripples Our Kids, and Why

John Taylor Gatto (b. 1935) is a career teacher who was named New York City Teacher of the Year three times. He quit in 1991, while still the New York State Teacher of the Year, writing in an op-ed piece in the Wall Street Journal *that he no longer wished to hurt children. In 1992, he published his first book,* Dumbing Us Down: The Hidden Curriculum of Compulsory Schooling. *In 1997, he won the Alexis de*

Tocqueville Award for Excellence in Advancement of Educational Freedom. His most recent book, published in 2008, is Weapons of Mass Instruction: A Schoolteacher's Journey through the Dark World of Compulsory Schooling. *Gatto is a relentless critic of compulsory schooling, promoting instead homeschooling and especially "unschooling"—allowing children to explore on their own what they want to learn.*

In this article, which originally appeared in the Harper's *magazine forum "School on a Hill," Gatto argues against compulsory schooling by giving a history of how mass education came about. Instead of benign motivations, such as improving people to become better citizens and develop their own talents, Gatto argues that the motivations behind the push for mass education are far darker and more sinister. Citing original texts from the early twentieth century, Gatto puts forward the argument that the actual purpose of the modern school system is to basically denigrate and control people, essentially to take away their own humanity. This served the purposes of mass production by large corporations.*

I taught for thirty years in some of the worst schools in Manhattan, and in some of the best, and during that time I became an expert in boredom. Boredom was everywhere in my world, and if you asked the kids, as I often did, *why* they felt so bored, they always gave the same answers: They said the work was stupid, that it made no sense, that they already knew it. They said they wanted to be doing something real, not just sitting around. They said teachers didn't seem to know much about their subjects and clearly weren't interested in learning more. And the kids were right: Their teachers were every bit as bored as they were.

Boredom is the common condition of schoolteachers, and anyone who has spent time in a teachers' lounge can vouch for the low energy, the whining, the dispirited attitudes, to be found there. When asked why *they* feel bored, the teachers tend to blame the kids, as you might expect. Who wouldn't get bored teaching students who are rude and interested only in grades? If even that. Of course, teachers are themselves products of the same twelve-year compulsory school programs that so thoroughly bore their students, and as school personnel they are trapped inside structures even more rigid than those imposed upon the children. Who, then, is to blame?

We all are. My grandfather taught me that. One afternoon when I was seven I complained to him of boredom, and he batted me hard on the head. He told me that I was never to use that term in his presence again, that if I was bored it was my fault and no one else's. The obligation to amuse and instruct myself was entirely my own, and people who didn't know that were childish people, to be avoided if possible. Certainly not to be trusted. That episode cured me of boredom forever, and here and there over the years I was able to pass on the lesson to some remarkable student. For the most part, however, I found it futile to challenge the official notion that boredom and childishness were the natural state of affairs in the classroom. Often I had to defy custom, and even bend the law, to help kids break out of this trap.

The empire struck back, of course; childish adults regularly conflate opposition with disloyalty. I once returned from a medical leave to discover that all evidence of my having been granted the leave had been purposely destroyed, that my job had been terminated, and that I no longer possessed even a teaching license. After nine months of tormented effort I was able to retrieve the license when a school secretary testified to witnessing the plot unfold. In the meantime my family suffered more than I care to remember. By the time I finally retired in 1991, I had more than enough reason to think of our schools—with their long-term, cell-block-style, forced confinement of both students and teachers—as virtual factories of childishness. Yet I honestly could not see why they had to be that way. My own experience had revealed to me what many other teachers must learn along the way, too, yet keep to themselves for fear of reprisal: If we wanted to we could easily and inexpensively jettison the old, stupid structures and help kids take an education rather than merely receive a schooling. We could encourage the best qualities of youthfulness—curiosity, adventure, resilience, the capacity for surprising insight—simply by being more flexible about time, texts, and tests, by introducing kids to truly competent adults, and by giving each student what autonomy he or she needs in order to take a risk every now and then.

But we don't do that. And the more I asked why not, and persisted in think- 5 ing about the "problem" of schooling as an engineer might, the more I missed the point: What if there is no "problem" with our schools? What if they are the way they are, so expensively flying in the face of common sense and long experience in how children learn things, not because they are doing something wrong but because they are doing something right? Is it possible that George W. Bush accidentally spoke the truth when he said we would "leave no child behind"? Could it be that our schools are designed to make sure not one of them ever really grows up?

Do we really need school? I don't mean education, just forced schooling: six classes a day, five days a week, nine months a year, for twelve years. Is this deadly routine really necessary? And if so, for what? Don't hide behind reading, writing, and arithmetic as a rationale, because 2 million happy homeschoolers have surely put that banal justification to rest. Even if they hadn't, a considerable number of well-known Americans never went through the twelve-year wringer our kids currently go through, and they turned out all right. George Washington, Benjamin Franklin, Thomas Jefferson, Abraham Lincoln? Someone taught them, to be sure, but they were not products of a school system, and not one of them was ever "graduated" from a secondary school. Throughout most of American history, kids generally didn't go to high school, yet the unschooled rose to be admirals, like Farragut; inventors, like Edison; captains of industry, like Carnegie and Rockefeller; writers, like Melville and Twain and Conrad; and even scholars, like Margaret Mead. In fact, until pretty recently people who reached the age of thirteen weren't looked upon as children at all. Ariel Durant, who co-wrote an enormous, and very good, multivolume history of the world with her husband, Will, was happily married at fifteen, and who could reasonably claim that Ariel Durant was an uneducated person? Unschooled, perhaps, but not uneducated.

We have been taught (that is, schooled) in this country to think of "success" as synonymous with, or at least dependent upon, "schooling," but historically that isn't true in either an intellectual or a financial sense. And plenty of people throughout the world today find a way to educate themselves without resorting to a system of compulsory secondary schools that all too often resemble prisons. Why, then, do Americans confuse education with just such a system? What exactly is the purpose of our public schools?

Mass schooling of a compulsory nature really got its teeth into the United States between 1905 and 1915, though it was conceived of much earlier and pushed for throughout most of the nineteenth century. The reason given for this enormous upheaval of family life and cultural traditions was, roughly speaking, threefold:

1. To make good people.

2. To make good citizens.

3. To make each person his or her personal best.

These goals are still trotted out today on a regular basis, and most of us accept them in one form or another as a decent definition of public education's mission, however short schools actually fall in achieving them. But we are dead wrong. Compounding our error is the fact that the national literature holds numerous and surprisingly consistent statements of compulsory schooling's true purpose. We have, for example, the great H. L. Mencken, who wrote in the *American Mercury* for April 1924 that the aim of public education is not

> to fill the young of the species with knowledge and awaken their intelligence. . . . Nothing could be further from the truth. The aim . . . is simply to reduce as many individuals as possible to the same safe level, to breed and train a standardized citizenry, to put down dissent and originality. That is its aim in the United States . . . and that is its aim everywhere else.

Because of Mencken's reputation as a satirist, we might be tempted to dismiss 10 this passage as a bit of hyperbolic sarcasm. His article, however, goes on to trace the template for our own educational system back to the now vanished, though never to be forgotten, military state of Prussia. And although he was certainly aware of the irony that we had recently been at war with Germany, the heir to Prussian thought and culture, Mencken was being perfectly serious here. Our educational system really is Prussian in origin, and that really is cause for concern.

The odd fact of a Prussian provenance for our schools pops up again and again once you know to look for it. William James alluded to it many times at the turn of the century. Orestes Brownson, the hero of Christopher Lasch's 1991 book, *The True and Only Heaven*, was publicly denouncing the Prussianization of American schools back in the 1840s. Horace Mann's "Seventh Annual Report" to the Massachusetts State Board of Education in 1843 is essentially a paean to the land of Frederick the Great and a call for its schooling to be brought here. That Prussian culture loomed large in America is hardly surprising, given our early association with that utopian state. A Prussian served as Washington's aide during the Revolutionary War, and so many German-speaking people had settled here by 1795 that Congress considered publishing a German-language edition of the federal laws. But what shocks is that we should so eagerly have adopted one of the very worst aspects of Prussian culture: an educational system deliberately designed to produce mediocre intellects, to hamstring the inner life, to deny students appreciable leadership skills, and to ensure docile and incomplete citizens—all in order to render the populace "manageable."

It was from James Bryant Conant—president of Harvard for twenty years, WWI poison-gas specialist, WWII executive on the atomic-bomb project, high commissioner of the American zone in Germany after WWII, and truly one of the most influential figures of the twentieth century—that I first got wind of the real purposes of American schooling. Without Conant, we would probably not have the same style and degree of standardized testing that we enjoy today, nor would we be blessed with gargantuan high schools that warehouse 2,000 to 4,000 students at a time, like the famous Columbine High in Littleton, Colorado. Shortly after I retired from teaching I picked up Conant's 1959 book-length essay, *The Child the Parent and the State*, and was more than a little intrigued to see him mention in passing that the modern schools we attend were the result of a "revolution" engineered between 1905 and 1930. A revolution? He declines to elaborate, but he does direct the curious and the uninformed to Alexander Inglis's 1918 book, *Principles of Secondary Education*, in which "one saw this revolution through the eyes of a revolutionary."

Inglis, for whom a lecture in education at Harvard is named, makes it perfectly clear that compulsory schooling on this continent was intended to be just what it had been for Prussia in the 1820s: a fifth column into the burgeoning democratic movement that threatened to give the peasants and the proletarians a voice at the bargaining table. Modern, industrialized, compulsory schooling was to make a sort of surgical incision into the prospective unity of these underclasses. Divide children by subject, by age-grading, by constant rankings on tests, and by many other more subtle means, and it was unlikely that the ignorant mass of mankind, separated in childhood, would ever reintegrate into a dangerous whole.

Inglis breaks down the purpose—the actual purpose—of modem schooling into six basic functions, any one of which is enough to curl the hair of those innocent enough to believe the three traditional goals listed earlier:

1. The *adjustive* or *adaptive* function. Schools are to establish fixed habits of reaction to authority. This, of course, precludes critical judgment completely. It also pretty much destroys the idea that useful or interesting material should be taught, because you can't test for reflexive obedience until you know whether you can make kids learn, and do, foolish and boring things.

2. The *integrating* function. This might well be called "the conformity function," because its intention is to make children as alike as possible. People who conform are predictable, and this is of great use to those who wish to harness and manipulate a large labor force.

3. The *diagnostic and directive* function. School is meant to determine each student's proper social role. This is done by logging evidence mathematically and anecdotally on cumulative records. As in "your permanent record." Yes, you do have one.

4. The *differentiating* function. Once their social role has been "diagnosed," children are to be sorted by role and trained only so far as their destination in the social machine merits—and not one step further. So much for making kids their personal best.

5. The *selective* function. This refers not to human choice at all but to Darwin's theory of natural selection as applied to what he called "the favored races." In short, the idea is to help things along by consciously attempting to improve the breeding stock. Schools are meant to tag the unfit—with poor grades, remedial placement, and other punishments—clearly enough that their peers will accept them as inferior and effectively bar them from the reproductive sweepstakes. That's what all those little humiliations from first grade onward were intended to do: wash the dirt down the drain.

6. The *propaedeutic* function. The societal system implied by these rules will require an elite group of caretakers. To that end, a small fraction of the kids will quietly be taught how to manage this continuing project, how to watch over and control a population deliberately dumbed down and declawed in order that government might proceed unchallenged and corporations might never want for obedient labor.

That, unfortunately, is the purpose of mandatory public education in this   15
country. And lest you take Inglis for an isolated crank with a rather too cynical take on the educational enterprise, you should know that he was hardly alone in championing these ideas. Conant himself, building on the ideas of Horace Mann and others, campaigned tirelessly for an American school system designed along the same lines. Men like George Peabody, who funded the cause of mandatory schooling throughout the South, surely understood that the Prussian system was useful in creating not only a harmless electorate and a servile labor force but also a virtual herd of mindless consumers. In time a great number of industrial titans came to recognize the enormous profits to be had by cultivating and tending just such a herd via public education, among them Andrew Carnegie and John D. Rockefeller.

There you have it. Now you know. We don't need Karl Marx's conception of a grand warfare between the classes to see that it is in the interest of complex management, economic or political, to dumb people down, to demoralize them, to divide them from one another, and to discard them if they don't conform. Class may frame the proposition, as when Woodrow Wilson, then president of Princeton University, said the following to the New York City School Teachers Association in 1909: "We want one class of persons to have a liberal education, and we want another class of persons, a very much larger class, of necessity, in every society, to forgo the privileges of a liberal education and fit themselves to perform specific difficult manual tasks." But the motives behind the disgusting decisions that bring about these ends need not be class-based at all. They can stem purely from fear, or from the by now familiar belief that "efficiency" is the paramount virtue, rather than love, liberty, laughter, or hope. Above all, they can stem from simple greed.

There were vast fortunes to be made, after all, in an economy based on mass production and organized to favor the large corporation rather than the small business or the family farm. But mass production required mass consumption, and at the turn of the twentieth century most Americans considered it both unnatural and unwise to buy things they didn't actually need. Mandatory schooling was a godsend on that count. School didn't have to train kids in any direct sense to think they should consume nonstop, because it did something even better: it encouraged them not to think at all. And that left them sitting ducks for another great invention of the modern era—marketing.

Now, you needn't have studied marketing to know that there are two groups of people who can always be convinced to consume more than they need to: addicts and children. School has done a pretty good job of turning our children into addicts, but it has done a spectacular job of turning our children into children. Again, this is no accident. Theorists from Plato to Rousseau to our own Dr. Inglis knew that if children could be cloistered with other children, stripped of responsibility and independence, encouraged to develop only the trivializing emotions of greed, envy, jealousy, and fear, they would grow older but never truly grow up. In the 1934 edition of his once well-known book *Public Education in the United States*, Ellwood P. Cubberley detailed and praised the way the strategy of successive school enlargements had extended childhood by two to six years, and forced schooling was at that point still quite new. This same Cubberley—who was dean of Stanford's School of Education, a textbook editor at Houghton Mifflin, and Conant's friend and correspondent at Harvard—had written the following in the 1922 edition of his book *Public School Administration*: "Our schools are . . . factories in which the raw products (children) are to be shaped and fashioned. . . . And it is the business of the school to build its pupils according to the specifications laid down."

It's perfectly obvious from our society today what those specifications were. Maturity has by now been banished from nearly every aspect of our lives. Easy divorce laws have removed the need to work at relationships; easy credit has removed the need for fiscal self-control; easy entertainment has removed the need to learn to entertain oneself; easy answers have removed the need to ask questions. We have become a nation of children, happy to surrender our judgments and our wills to political exhortations and commercial blandishments that would insult actual adults. We buy televisions, and then we buy the things we see on the television. We buy computers, and then we buy the things we see on the computer. We buy $150 sneakers whether we need them or not, and when they fall apart too soon we buy another pair. We drive SUVs and believe the lie that they constitute a kind of life insurance, even when we're upside-down in them. And, worst of all, we don't bat an eye when Ari Fleischer tells us to "be careful what you say," even if we remember having been told somewhere back in school that America is the land of the free. We simply buy that one too. Our schooling, as intended, has seen to it.

Now for the good news. Once you understand the logic behind modern schooling, 20 its tricks and traps are fairly easy to avoid. School trains children to be employees and consumers; teach your own to be leaders and adventurers. School trains children to obey reflexively; teach your own to think critically and independently. Well-schooled kids have a low threshold for boredom; help your own to develop an inner life so that they'll never be bored. Urge them to take on the serious material, the *grown-up* material, in history, literature, philosophy, music, art, economics, theology—all the stuff schoolteachers know well enough to avoid. Challenge your kids with plenty of solitude so that they can learn to enjoy their own company, to conduct inner dialogues. Well-schooled people are conditioned to dread being alone, and they seek constant companionship through the TV, the computer, the cell phone, and through shallow friendships quickly acquired and quickly abandoned. Your children should have a more meaningful life, and they can.

First, though, we must wake up to what our schools really are: laboratories of experimentation on young minds, drill centers for the habits and attitudes that corporate society demands. Mandatory education serves children only incidentally; its real purpose is to turn them into servants. Don't let your own have their childhoods extended, not even for a day. If David Farragut could take command of a captured British warship as a preteen, if Thomas Edison could publish a broadsheet at the age of twelve, if Ben Franklin could apprentice himself to a printer at the same age (then put himself through a course of study that would choke a Yale senior today), there's no telling what your own kids could do. After a long life, and thirty years in the public school trenches, I've concluded that genius is as common as dirt. We suppress our genius only because we haven't yet figured out how to manage a population of educated men and women. The solution, I think, is simple and glorious. Let them manage themselves.

QUESTIONS FOR DISCUSSION AND WRITING

1. "Boredom" is a word Gatto uses frequently at the beginning of his article, both the boredom that students feel (paragraph 1) and the boredom that teachers feel (paragraph 2). He then references an incident with his grandfather, the point of which is that people are responsible to themselves not to become bored—it is no one else's fault or responsibility. How well do you relate to this passage? How frequently are you bored in the classroom? What is (or are) the source(s) of that boredom? Is boredom an inevitable by-product of the educational system? Why or why not?

2. In paragraph 4, Gatto states, "We could encourage the best qualities of youthfulness—curiosity, adventure, resilience, the capacity for surprising insight—simply by being more flexible about time, texts, and tests, by introducing kids to truly competent adults, and by giving each student what autonomy he or she needs in order to take a risk every now and then." Based on your own experiences in schooling, what prevents these things from happening? Given that in any one year millions of students are in school, is it possible to create a public education system in which such things could happen? What would such a system look like?

3. Gatto argues that the school system in the United States was intentionally modeled on the Prussian system. Gatto states that education in Prussia was

deliberately designed "to produce mediocre intellects, to hamstring the inner life, to deny students appreciable leadership skills, and to ensure docile and incompetent citizens" (paragraph 11). Do you agree that this statement also characterizes today's educational system in the United States? Why or why not? Cite specific examples to defend your answer.

4. Another idea underpinning much of what Gatto argues is his idea about childhood and adulthood. Simply put, he argues that "we have become a nation of children" (paragraph 19), in which we are encouraged to indulge in immature behavior, the type of behavior a hundred years ago would hardly be tolerated. He speaks of easy divorce and easy credit, overspending and overconsumption, the constant need for entertainment, and the acceptance of simple answers to difficult questions. Can you cite specific examples of this that you have seen or experienced in your own life? More importantly, can you determine how schooling is complicit in encouraging these sorts of behavior?

5. In paragraph 21, Gatto argues that we extend our children's childhood too long, citing historical examples of people such as Thomas Edison and Benjamin Franklin, who were already working hard and accomplishing great things at an age when most people are still in school. His argument seems in many ways to go against the common cultural mandate not to let children grow up too fast—the implication that childhood is superior to adulthood. What would this shortening of childhood entail? What problems might be encountered in pushing more adult responsibilities and expectations on younger people?

6. Gatto concludes his argument by stating that "genius is as common as dirt" and that the solution is obvious: "Let them [students] manage themselves" (paragraph 21). What problems might be presented by "unschooling" children, that is, allowing children the freedom to explore the world for themselves, not bound by teachers, classrooms, and schools? In your opinion, does unschooling—instead of mass, compulsory education—hold the promise to actually better educate children? Defend your answer.

PLATO

The Allegory of the Cave

Born in Athens (c. 428–347 B.C.E.), Plato was the most famous pupil of Socrates. Together with Aristotle, these three thinkers are the philosophical forebears of Western thought. The dialogues of Plato display the Socratic method of philosophical exploration, in which Socrates poses step-by-step questions about concepts of "good," "justice," and "piety." Each question has a simple answer, but cumulatively they reveal contradictions, ambiguities, and other barriers to understanding. For this reason, Plato's The Republic *argues that a just government should be guided by statesmen whose learning—attained through dialogue rather than through the senses—makes them both persuasive and wise.*

"The Allegory of the Cave," from The Republic, *tells of prisoners who understand life only through shadows flickering on the wall of their cave. Like all allegories, this story conveys abstract ideas through more concrete representation, in this case, Plato's belief that "ideas," or pure forms, exist only in the spiritual realm. Before birth, we see ideas perfectly, but on earth our memories fade and our senses perceive only unreliable shadows of those ideas. Plato's allegory thus suggests that, like the prisoners, people on earth understand life only through sense perceptions similar to shadows; as a result, they know reality only incompletely.*

Next, said I, here is a parable to illustrate the degrees in which our nature may be enlightened or unenlightened. Imagine the condition of men living in a sort of cavernous chamber underground, with an entrance open to the light and a long passage all down the cave. Here they have been from childhood, chained by the leg and also by the neck, so that they cannot move and can see only what is in front of them, because the chains will not let them turn their heads. At some distance higher up is the light of a fire burning behind them; and between the prisoners and the fire is a track with a parapet built along it, like the screen at a puppet-show, which hides the performers while they show their puppets over the top.

I see, said he.

Now behind this parapet imagine persons carrying along various artificial objects, including figures of men and animals in wood or stone or other materials, which project above the parapet. Naturally, some of these persons will be talking, others silent.

It is a strange picture, he said, and a strange sort of prisoners.

Like ourselves, I replied; for in the first place prisoners so confined would 5 have seen nothing of themselves or of one another, except the shadows thrown by the fire-light on the wall of the Cave facing them, would they?

Not if all their lives they had been prevented from moving their heads.

And they would have seen as little of the objects carried past.

Of course.

Now, if they could talk to one another, would they not suppose that their words referred only to those passing shadows which they saw?

Necessarily.   10

And suppose their prison had an echo from the wall facing them? When one of the people crossing behind them spoke, they could only suppose that the sound came from the shadow passing before their eyes.

No doubt.

In every way, then, such prisoners would recognize as reality nothing but the shadows of those artificial objects.

Inevitably.

Now consider what would happen if their release from the chains and the 15 healing of their unwisdom should come about in this way. Suppose one of them were set free and forced suddenly to stand up, turn his head, and walk with eyes lifted to the light; all these movements would be painful, and he would be too dazzled to make out the objects whose shadows he had been used to see. What do you think he would say, if someone told him that what he had formerly seen was meaningless illusion, but now, being somewhat nearer to reality and turned towards more real objects, he was getting a truer view? Suppose further that he were shown the various objects being carried by and were made to say, in reply to questions, what each of them was. Would he not be perplexed and believe the objects now shown him to be not so real as what he formerly saw?

Yes, not nearly so real.

And if he were forced to look at the fire-light itself, would not his eyes ache, so that he would try to escape and turn back to the things which he could see distinctly, convinced that they really were clearer than these other objects now being shown to him?

Yes.

And suppose someone were to drag him away forcibly up the steep and rugged ascent and not let him go until he had hauled him out into the sunlight, would he not suffer pain and vexation at such treatment, and, when he had come out into the light, find his eyes so full of its radiance that he could not see a single one of the things that he was now told were real?

Certainly he would not see them all at once.   20

He would need, then, to grow accustomed before he could see things in that upper world. At first it would be easiest to make out shadows, and then the images of men and things reflected in water, and later on the things themselves. After that, it would be easier to watch the heavenly bodies and the sky itself by night, looking at the light of the moon and stars rather than the Sun and the Sun's light in the day-time.

Yes, surely.

Last of all, he would be able to look at the Sun and contemplate its nature, not as it appears when reflected in water or any alien medium, but as it is in itself in its own domain.

No doubt.

And now he would begin to draw the conclusion that it is the Sun that produces 25 the seasons and the course of the year and controls everything in the visible world, and moreover is in a way the cause of all that he and his companions used to see.

Clearly he would come at last to that conclusion.

Then if he called to mind his fellow prisoners and what passed for wisdom in his former dwelling-place, he would surely think himself happy in the change and be sorry for them. They may have had a practice of honoring and commending one another, with prizes for the man who had the keenest eye for the passing shadows and the best memory for the order in which they followed or accompanied one another, so that he could make a good guess as to which was going to come next. Would our released prisoner be likely to covet those prizes or to envy the men exalted to honor and power in the Cave? Would he not feel like Homer's Achilles, that he would far sooner 'be on earth as a hired servant in the house of a landless man' or endure anything rather than go back to his old beliefs and live in the old way?

Yes, he would prefer any fate to such a life.

Now imagine what would happen if he went down again to take his former seat in the Cave. Coming suddenly out of the sunlight, his eyes would be filled with darkness. He might be required once more to deliver his opinion on those shadows, in competition with the prisoners who had never been released, while his eyesight was still dim and unsteady; and it might take some time to become used to the darkness. They would laugh at him and say that he had gone up only to come back with his sight ruined; it was worth no one's while even to attempt the ascent. If they could lay hands on the man who was trying to set them free and lead them up, they would kill him.

Yes, they would.   30

Every feature in this parable, my dear Glaucon, is meant to fit our earlier analysis. The prison dwelling corresponds to the region revealed to us through the sense of sight, and the fire-light within it to the power of the Sun. The ascent to see the things in the upper world you may take as standing for the upward journey of the soul into the region of the intelligible; then you will be in possession of what I surmise, since that is what you wish to be told. Heaven knows whether it is true; but this, at any rate, is how it appears to me. In the world of knowledge, the last thing to be perceived and only with great difficulty is the essential Form of Goodness. Once it is perceived, the conclusion must follow that, for all things, this is the cause of whatever is right and good; in the visible world it gives birth to light and to the lord of light, while it is itself sovereign in the intelligible world and the parent of intelligence and truth. Without having had a vision of this Form no one can act with wisdom, either in his own life or in matters of state.

QUESTIONS FOR DISCUSSION AND WRITING

1. Visualize Plato's parable by means of an outline or a drawing. How many stages are there in the process through which "our nature may be enlightened or unenlightened" (paragraph 1)? In what sequence are these stages arranged? Why does Plato choose this order?

2. Does Plato challenge the ways you think about thinking? About understanding the world? After discussion, write an essay in which you define what you mean by thinking, and illustrate this with examples. In your estimation, does "thinking" equal "intelligence"? What can thinking in itself accomplish? Then, examine some of the different types of intelligence Howard Gardner (p. 237) discusses to question your original definition.

3. Imagine you're a teacher (in a specific field that you know a lot about), a coach, a chef, a musician—someone giving instruction to a person who doesn't know much about the subject at hand but is eager to learn. How could you best teach this novice the fundamentals? How could you decide whether or not that person had sufficient "intelligence" in that area to make it worth proceeding for more advanced instruction? Work out a plan of action and, if time permits, try it out on an actual pupil. After you've tested this out, what refinements in the initial plan would you make?

4. Why does Plato use the prisoners in a cave (almost a dungeon) as a metaphor of people in search of knowledge? What can we learn from this metaphor about Plato's evaluation of knowledge and the human capacity for acquiring knowledge? Can human beings acquire complete and certain knowledge? Why or why not?

5. Describe the characteristics of the Socratic dialogue based on specific details from "The Allegory of the Cave." Who talks most often? Who responds with brief phrases? What problems does the unequal use of language reveal about the form of the Socratic dialogue? What possible truths does this format discourage us from discovering?

HOWARD GARDNER

Who Owns Intelligence?

Howard Gardner was born in Scranton, Pennsylvania, in 1943. As a boy, he was a gifted pianist. He attended Harvard University (B.A., 1965; Ph.D., 1971) and, as a Harvard professor, has researched normal and gifted children's creativity. Brain Damage: Gateway to the Mind *(1975) reports on his research with aphasic adults—those unable to process language. Recipient of a 1981 MacArthur "genius" fellowship, Gardner soon turned his attention to the theory of intelligence used in the social sciences and standardized testing. His conclusion—that people possess more than one type of intelligence—inspired his enduring book* Frames of Mind: The Theory of Multiple Intelligences *(1983), first published in 1983; 25th anniversary edition, 2008. Here he categorizes intelligence as "object-related" (math and logic), "object-free" (music and language), and "personal" (our perceptions of ourselves and of others). Other books build on his earlier research:* Multiple Intelligences: The Theory in Practice *(1993), and* Intelligence Reframed: Multiple Intelligences for the Twenty-first Century *(1999);* Changing Minds: The Art and Science of Changing Our Own and Other People's Minds *(2004);* Five Minds for the Future *(2007);* Truth, Beauty, and Goodness Reframed: Educating for the Virtues in the Age of Truthiness and Twitter *(2011); and* The App Generation: How Today's Youth Navigate Identity, Intimacy, and Imagination in a Digital World *(with Katie Davis; 2013).* The Disciplined Mind: Beyond Facts and Standardized Tests *(2000) counters E. D. Hirsch Jr.'s emphasis on acquisition of factual knowledge in* Cultural Literacy *(1987) and instead argues for deep understanding of a few traditional disciplines.*

Gardner summarizes current theory and his own beliefs in "Who Owns Intelligence?" (Atlantic, 1999). After first reviewing the history of the IQ test, the first measure of intellectual potential to be developed by modern psychology, he surveys current theories of intelligence, arguing that several schools of "experts are competing for the 'ownership' of intelligence in the next century."

Almost a century ago Alfred Binet, a gifted psychologist, was asked by the French Ministry of Education to help determine who would experience difficulty in school. Given the influx of provincials to the capital, along with immigrants of uncertain stock, Parisian officials believed they needed to know who might not advance smoothly through the system. Proceeding in an empirical manner, Binet posed many questions to youngsters of different ages. He ascertained which questions when answered correctly predicted success in school, and which questions when answered incorrectly foretold school difficulties. The items that discriminated most clearly between the two groups became, in effect, the first test of intelligence.

Binet is a hero to many psychologists. He was a keen observer, a careful scholar, an inventive technologist. Perhaps even more important for his followers, he devised the instrument that is often considered psychology's greatest success story. Millions of people who have never heard Binet's name have had aspects of their fate influenced by instrumentation that the French psychologist inspired. And thousands of psychometricians—specialists in the measurement of psychological variables—earn their living courtesy of Binet's invention.

Although it has prevailed over the long run, the psychologists' version of intelligence is now facing its biggest threat. Many scholars and observers—and even some iconoclastic psychologists—feel that intelligence is too important to be left to the psychometricians. Experts are extending the breadth of the concept—proposing many intelligences, including emotional intelligence and moral intelligence. They are experimenting with new methods of ascertaining intelligence, including some that avoid tests altogether in favor of direct measures of brain activity. They are forcing citizens everywhere to confront a number of questions: What is intelligence? How ought it to be assessed? And how do our notions of intelligence fit with what we value about human beings? In short, experts are competing for the "ownership" of intelligence in the next century.

The outline of the psychometricians' success story is well known. Binet's colleagues in England and Germany contributed to the conceptualization and instrumentation of intelligence testing—which soon became known as IQ tests. (An IQ, or intelligence quotient, designates the ratio between mental age and chronological age. Clearly we'd prefer that a child in our care have an IQ of 120, being smarter than average for his or her years, than an IQ of 80, being older than average for his or her intelligence.) Like other Parisian fashions of the period, the intelligence test migrated easily to the United States. First used to determine who was "feeble-minded," it was soon used to assess "normal" children, to identify the "gifted," and to determine who was fit to serve in the Army. By the 1920s the intelligence test had become a fixture in educational practice in the United States and much of Western Europe.

Early intelligence tests were not without their critics. Many enduring concerns were first raised by the influential journalist Walter Lippmann, in a series of published debates with Lewis Terman, of Stanford University, the father of IQ testing in America. Lippmann pointed out the superficiality of the questions, their possible cultural biases, and the risks of trying to determine a person's intellectual potential with a brief oral or paper-and-pencil measure. 5

Perhaps surprisingly, the conceptualization of intelligence did not advance much in the decades following Binet's and Terman's pioneering contributions. Intelligence tests came to be seen, rightly or wrongly, as primarily a tool for selecting people to fill academic or vocational niches. In one of the most famous—if irritating—remarks about intelligence testing, the influential Harvard psychologist E. G. Boring declared, "Intelligence is what the tests test." So long as these tests did what they were supposed to do (that is, give some indication of school success), it did not seem necessary or prudent to probe too deeply into their meaning or to explore alternative views of the human intellect.

Psychologists who study intelligence have argued chiefly about three questions. The first: Is intelligence singular, or does it consist of various more or less independent intellectual faculties? The purists—ranging from the turn-of-the-century English psychologist Charles Spearman to his latter-day disciples Richard J. Herrnstein and Charles Murray (of *The Bell Curve* fame)—defend the notion of a single overarching "g," or general intelligence. The pluralists—ranging from L. L. Thurstone, of the University of Chicago, who posited seven vectors of the mind, to J. P. Guilford, of the University of Southern California, who discerned 150 factors of the intellect—construe intelligence as composed of some or even many dissociable components. In his much cited *The Mismeasure of Man* (1981) the paleontologist Stephen Jay Gould argued that the conflicting conclusions reached on this issue reflect alternative assumptions about statistical procedures rather than the way the mind is. Still, psychologists continue the debate, with a majority sympathetic to the general-intelligence perspective.

The public is more interested in the second question: Is intelligence (or are intelligences) largely inherited? This is by and large a Western question. In the Confucian societies of East Asia individual differences in endowment are assumed to be modest, and differences in achievement are thought to be due largely to effort. In the West, however, many students of the subject sympathize with the view—defended within psychology by Lewis Terman, among others—that intelligence is inborn and one can do little to alter one's intellectual birthright.

Studies of identical twins reared apart provide surprisingly strong support for the "heritability" of psychometric intelligence. That is, if one wants to predict someone's score on an intelligence test, the scores of the biological parents (even if the child has not had appreciable contact with them) are more likely to prove relevant than the scores of the adoptive parents. By the same token, the IQs of identical twins are more similar than the IQs of fraternal twins. And, contrary to common sense (and political correctness), the IQs of biologically related people grow closer in the later years of life. Still, because of the intricacies of behavioral genetics and the difficulties of conducting valid experiments with human child-rearing, a few defend the proposition that intelligence is largely environmental rather than heritable, and some believe that we cannot answer the question at all.

Most scholars agree that even if psychometric intelligence is largely inher- 10
ited, it is not possible to pinpoint the sources of differences in average IQ between groups, such as the fifteen-point difference typically observed between

African-American and white populations. That is because in our society the contemporary—let alone the historical—experiences of these two groups cannot be equated. One could ferret out the differences (if any) between black and white populations only in a society that was truly color-blind.

One other question has intrigued laypeople and psychologists: Are intelligence tests biased? Cultural assumptions are evident in early intelligence tests. Some class biases are obvious—who except the wealthy could readily answer a question about polo? Others are more subtle. Suppose the question is what one should do with money found on the street. Although ordinarily one might turn it over to the police, what if one had a hungry child? Or what if the police force were known to be hostile to members of one's ethnic group? Only the canonical response to such a question would be scored as correct.

Psychometricians have striven to remove the obviously biased items from such measures. But biases that are built into the test situation itself are far more difficult to deal with. For example, a person's background affects his or her reaction to being placed in an unfamiliar locale, being instructed by someone dressed in a certain way, and having a printed test booklet thrust into his or her hands. And as the psychologist Claude M. Steele has argued . . . , the biases prove even more acute when people know that their academic potential is being measured and that their racial or ethnic group is widely considered to be less intelligent than the dominant social group.

The idea of bias touches on the common assumption that tests in general, and intelligence tests in particular, are inherently conservative instruments—tools of the establishment. It is therefore worth noting that many testing pioneers thought of themselves as progressives in the social sphere. They were devising instruments that could reveal people of talent even if those people came from "remote and apparently inferior backgrounds," to quote from a college catalogue of the 1950s. And occasionally the tests did discover intellectual diamonds in the rough. More often, however, they picked out the privileged. The still unresolved question of the causal relationship between IQ and social privilege has stimulated many a dissertation across the social sciences.

Paradoxically, one of the clearest signs of the success of intelligence tests is that they are no longer widely administered. In the wake of legal cases about the propriety of making consequential decisions about education on the basis of IQ scores, many public school officials have become test-shy. By and large, the testing of IQ in the schools is restricted to cases involving a recognized problem (such as a learning disability) or a selection procedure (determining eligibility for a program that serves gifted children).

Despite this apparent setback, intelligence testing and the line of thinking 15 that underlies it have actually triumphed. Many widely used scholastic measures, chief among them the SAT (renamed the Scholastic Assessment Test a few years ago), are thinly disguised intelligence tests that correlate highly with scores on standard psychometric instruments. Virtually no one raised in the developed world today has gone untouched by Binet's seemingly simple invention of a century ago.

MULTIPLE INTELLIGENCES

The concept of intelligence has in recent years undergone its most robust challenge since the days of Walter Lippmann. Some who are informed by psychology but not bound by the assumptions of the psychometricians have invaded this formerly sacrosanct territory. They have put forth their own ideas of what intelligence is, how (and whether) it should be measured, and which values should be invoked in considerations of the human intellect. For the first time in many years the intelligence establishment is clearly on the defensive—and the new century seems likely to usher in quite different ways of thinking about intelligence.

One evident factor in the rethinking of intelligence is the perspective introduced by scholars who are not psychologists. Anthropologists have commented on the parochialism of the Western view of intelligence. Some cultures do not even have a concept called intelligence, and others define intelligence in terms of traits that we in the West might consider odd—obedience, good listening skills, or moral fiber, for example. Neuroscientists are skeptical that the highly differentiated and modular structure of the brain is consistent with a unitary form of intelligence. Computer scientists have devised programs deemed intelligent; these programs often go about problem-solving in ways quite different from those embraced by human beings or other animals.

Even within the field of psychology the natives have been getting restless. Probably the most restless is the Yale psychologist Robert J. Sternberg. A prodigious scholar, Sternberg, who is forty-nine, has written dozens of books and hundreds of articles, the majority of them focusing in one or another way on intelligence. Sternberg began with the strategic goal of understanding the actual mental processes mobilized by standard test items, such as the solving of analogies. But he soon went beyond standard intelligence testing by insisting on two hitherto neglected forms of intelligence: the "practical" ability to adapt to varying contexts (as we all must in these days of divorcing and downsizing), and the capacity to automate familiar activities so that we can deal effectively with novelty and display "creative" intelligence.

Sternberg has gone to greater pains than many other critics of standard intelligence testing to measure these forms of intelligence with the paper-and-pencil laboratory methods favored by the profession. And he has found that a person's ability to adapt to diverse contexts or to deal with novel information can be differentiated from success at standard IQ-test problems. His efforts to create a new intelligence test have not been crowned with easy victory. Most psychometricians are conservative—they like the tests that have been in use for decades, and if new ones are to be marketed, these must correlate well with existing instruments. So much for openness to novelty within psychometrics.

Others in the field seem less bound by its strictures. The psychologist and jour- 20
nalist Daniel Goleman has achieved worldwide success with his book *Emotional Intelligence* (1995). Contending that this new concept (sometimes nicknamed EQ) may matter as much as or more than IQ, Goleman draws attention to such pivotal human abilities as controlling one's emotional reactions and "reading" the signals

of others. In the view of the noted psychiatrist Robert Coles, author of *The Moral Intelligence of Children* (1997), among many other books, we should prize character over intellect. He decries the amorality of our families, hence our children; he shows how we might cultivate human beings with a strong sense of right and wrong, who are willing to act on that sense even when it runs counter to self-interest. Other, frankly popular accounts deal with leadership intelligence (LQ), executive intelligence (EQ or ExQ), and even financial intelligence.

Like Coles's and Goleman's efforts, my work on "multiple intelligences" eschews the psychologists' credo of operationalization and test-making. I began by asking two questions: How did the human mind and brain evolve over millions of years? and How can we account for the diversity of skills and capacities that are or have been valued in different communities around the world?

Armed with these questions and a set of eight criteria, I have concluded that all human beings possess at least eight intelligences: linguistic and logical-mathematical (the two most prized in school and the ones central to success on standard intelligence tests), musical, spatial, bodily-kinesthetic, naturalist, interpersonal, and intrapersonal.

I make two complementary claims about intelligence. The first is universal. We all possess these eight intelligences—and possibly more. Indeed, rather than seeing us as "rational animals," I offer a new definition of what it means to be a human being, cognitively speaking: *Homo sapiens sapiens* is the animal that possesses these eight forms of mental representation.

My second claim concerns individual differences. Owing to the accidents of heredity, environment, and their interactions, no two of us exhibit the same intelligences in precisely the same proportions. Our "profiles of intelligence" differ from one another. This fact poses intriguing challenges and opportunities for our education system. We can ignore these differences and pretend that we are all the same; historically, that is what most education systems have done. Or we can fashion an education system that tries to exploit these differences, individualizing instruction and assessment as much as possible.

INTELLIGENCE AND MORALITY

As the century of Binet and his successors draws to a close, we'd be wise to take stock of, and to anticipate, the course of thinking about intelligence. Although my crystal ball is no clearer than anyone else's (the species may lack "future intelligence"), it seems safe to predict that interest in intelligence will not go away.

To begin with, the psychometric community has scarcely laid down its arms. New versions of the standard tests continue to be created, and occasionally new tests surface as well. Researchers in the psychometric tradition churn out fresh evidence of the predictive power of their instruments and the correlations between measured intelligence and one's life chances. And some in the psychometric tradition are searching for the biological basis of intelligence: the gene or complex of genes that may affect intelligence, the neural structures that are crucial for intelligence, or telltale brain-wave patterns that distinguish the bright from the less bright.

Beyond various psychometric twists, interest in intelligence is likely to grow in other ways. It will be fed by the creation of machines that display intelligence and by the specific intelligence or intelligences. Moreover, observers as diverse as Richard Herrnstein and Robert B. Reich, President Clinton's first Secretary of Labor, have agreed that in coming years a large proportion of society's rewards will go to those people who are skilled symbol analysts—who can sit at a computer screen (or its technological successor), manipulate numbers and other kinds of symbols, and use the results of their operations to contrive plans, tactics, and strategies for enterprises ranging from business to science to war games. These people may well color how intelligence is conceived in decades to come—just as the need to provide good middle-level bureaucrats to run an empire served as a primary molder of intelligence tests in the early years of the century.

Surveying the landscape of intelligence, I discern three struggles between opposing forces. The extent to which, and the manner in which, these various struggles are resolved will influence the lives of millions of people. I believe that the three struggles are interrelated; that the first struggle provides the key to the other two; and that the ensemble of struggles can be resolved in an optimal way.

The first struggle concerns the breadth of our definition of intelligence. One camp consists of the purists, who believe in a single form of intelligence—one that basically predicts success in school and in school-like activities. Arrayed against the purists are the progressive pluralists, who believe that many forms of intelligence exist. Some of these pluralists would like to broaden the definition of intelligence considerably, to include the abilities to create, to lead, and to stand out in terms of emotional sensitivity or moral excellence.

The second struggle concerns the assessment of intelligence. Again, one readily encounters a traditional position. Once chiefly concerned with paper-and-pencil tests, the traditionally oriented practitioner is now likely to use computers to provide the same information more quickly and more accurately. But other positions abound. Purists disdain psychological tasks of any complexity, preferring to look instead at reaction time, brain waves, and other physiological measures of intellect. In contrast, simulators favor measures closely resembling the actual abilities that are prized. And skeptics warn against the continued expansion of testing. They emphasize the damage often done to individual life chances and self-esteem by a regimen of psychological testing, and call for less technocratic, more humane methods—ranging from self-assessment to the examination of portfolios of student work to selection in the service of social equity.

The final struggle concerns the relationship between intelligence and the qualities we value in human beings. Although no one would baldly equate intellect and human worth, nuanced positions have emerged on this issue. Some (in the *Bell Curve* mold) see intelligence as closely related to a person's ethics and values; they believe that brighter people are more likely to appreciate moral complexity and to behave judiciously. Some call for a sharp distinction between the realm of intellect on the one hand, and character, morality, or ethics on the other. Society's ambivalence on this issue can be discerned in the figures that become the culture's heroes. For every Albert Einstein or Bobby Fischer who is celebrated for his intellect, there is a Forrest Gump or a Chauncey Gardiner[1] who is celebrated for human—and humane—traits that would never be captured on any kind of intelligence test.

Thanks to the work of the past decade or two, the stranglehold of the psychometricians has at last been broken. This is a beneficent development. Yet now that the psychometricians have been overcome, we risk deciding that anything goes—that emotions, morality, creativity, must all be absorbed into the "new (or even the New Age) intelligence." The challenge is to chart a concept of intelligence that reflects new insights and discoveries and yet can withstand rigorous scrutiny.

An analogy may help. One can think of the scope of intelligence as represented by an elastic band. For many years the definition of intelligence went unchallenged, and the band seemed to have lost its elasticity. Some of the new definitions expand the band, so that it has become taut and resilient; and yet earlier work on intelligence is still germane. Other definitions so expand the band that it is likely finally to snap—and the earlier work on intelligence will no longer be of use.

Until now the term "intelligence" has been limited largely to certain kinds of problem-solving involving language and logic—the skills at a premium in the bureaucrat or the law professor. However, human beings are able to deal with numerous kinds of content besides words, numbers, and logical relations—for example, space, music, the psyches of other human beings. Like the elastic band, definitions of intelligence need to be expanded to include human skill in dealing with these diverse contents. And we must not restrict attention to solving problems that have been posed by others; we must consider equally the capacity of individuals to fashion products—scientific experiments, effective organizations— that draw on one or more human intelligences. The elastic band can accommodate such broadening as well.

So long as intelligences are restricted to the processing of contents in the 35 world, we avoid epistemological problems—as we should. "Intelligence" should not be expanded to include personality, motivation, will, attention, character, creativity, and other important and significant human capacities. Such stretching is likely to snap the band.

Let's see what happens when one crosses one of these lines—for example, when one attempts to conflate intelligence and creativity. Beginning with a definition, we extend the descriptor "creative" to those people (or works or institutions) who meet two criteria: they are innovative, and their innovations are eventually accepted by a relevant community.

No one denies that creativity is important—and, indeed, it may prove even more important in the future, when nearly all standard (algorithmic) procedures will be carried out by computers. Yet creativity should not be equated with intelligence. An expert may be intelligent in one or more domains but not necessarily

---

[1]Chauncey Gardiner is the hero of Jerzy Kosinski's novel *Being There* (1971), who begins as Chauncey, an actual gardener, and becomes a U.S. president; understanding nothing, he talks about the only thing he knows—gardening—but is hailed as a genius who uses the garden to describe the world situation. [Editors' note.]

inclined toward, or successful in, innovation. Similarly, although it is clear that the ability to innovate requires a certain degree of intelligence, we don't find a significant correlation between measures of intellect and of creativity. Indeed, creativity seems more dependent on a certain kind of temperament and personality—risk-taking, tough-skinned, persevering, above all having a lust to alter the status quo and leave a mark on society—than on efficiency in processing various kinds of information. By collapsing these categories together we risk missing dimensions that are important but separate; and we may think that we are training (or selecting) one when we are actually training (or selecting) the other.

Next consider what happens when one stretches the idea of intelligence to include attitudes and behaviors—and thus confronts human values within a culture. A few values can be expressed generically enough that they command universal respect: the Golden Rule is one promising candidate. Most values, however, turn out to be specific to certain cultures or subcultures—even such seeming unproblematic ones as the unacceptability of killing or lying. Once one conflates morality and intelligence, one needs to deal with widely divergent views of what is good or bad and why. Moreover, one must confront the fact that people who score high on tests of moral reasoning may act immorally outside the test situation—even as courageous and self-sacrificing people may turn out to be unremarkable on formal tests of moral reasoning or intelligence. It is far preferable to construe intelligence itself as morally neutral and then decide whether a given use of intelligence qualifies as moral, immoral, or amoral in context.

As I see it, no intelligence is moral or immoral in itself. One can be gifted in language and use that gift to write great verse, as did Johann Wolfgang von Goethe, or to foment hatred, as did Joseph Goebbels. Mother Teresa and Lyndon Johnson, Mohandas Gandhi and Niccolò Machiavelli, may have had equivalent degrees of interpersonal intelligence, but they put their skills to widely divergent uses.

Perhaps there is a form of intelligence that determines whether or not a situation harbors moral consideration or consequences. But the term "moral intelligence" carries little force. After all, Adolf Hitler and Joseph Stalin may well have had an exquisite sense of which situations contained moral considerations. However, either they did not care or they embraced their own peculiar morality according to which eliminating Jews was the moral thing to do in quest of a pure Aryan society, or wiping out a generation was necessary in the quest to establish a communist state. 40

THE BORDERS OF INTELLIGENCE

Writing as a scholar rather than as a layperson, I see two problems with the notion of emotional intelligence. First, unlike language or space, the emotions are not contents to be processed; rather, cognition has evolved so that we can make sense of human beings (self and others) that possess and experience emotions. Emotions are part and parcel of all cognition, though they may well prove more salient at certain times or under certain circumstances: they accompany our interactions with others, our listening to great music, our feelings when we solve—or fail to solve—a difficult mathematical problem. If one calls some intelligences emotional, one suggests that other intelligences are not—and that implication flies in the face of experience and empirical data.

The second problem is the conflation of emotional intelligence and a certain preferred pattern of behavior. This is the trap that Daniel Goleman sometimes falls into in his otherwise admirable *Emotional Intelligence*. Goleman singles out as emotionally intelligent those people who use their understanding of emotions to make others feel better, to solve conflicts, or to cooperate in home or work situations. No one would dispute that such people are wanted. However, people who understand emotion may not necessarily use their skills for the benefit of society.

For this reason I prefer the term "emotional sensitivity"—a term (encompassing my interpersonal and intrapersonal intelligences) that could apply to people who are sensitive to emotions in themselves and in others. Presumably, clinicians and salespeople excel in sensitivity to others, poets and mystics in sensitivity to themselves. And some autistic or psychopathological people seem completely insensitive to the emotional realm. I would insist, however, on a strict distinction between emotional sensitivity and being a "good" or "moral" person. A person may be sensitive to the emotions of others but use that sensitivity to manipulate or to deceive them, or to create hatred.

I call, then, for a delineation of intelligence that includes the full range of contents to which human beings are sensitive, but at the same time designates as off limits such valued but separate human traits as creativity, morality, and emotional appropriateness. I believe that such a delineation makes scientific and epistemological sense. It reinvigorates the elastic band without stretching it to the breaking point. It helps to resolve the two remaining struggles: how to assess, and what kinds of human beings to admire.

Once we decide to restrict intelligence to human information-processing 45 and product-making capacities, we can make use of the established technology of assessment. That is, we can continue to use paper-and-pencil or computer-adapted testing techniques while looking at a broader range of capacities, such as musical sensitivity and empathy with others. And we can avoid ticklish and possibly unresolvable questions about the assessment of values and morality that may well be restricted to a particular culture and that may well change over time.

Still, even with a limited perspective on intelligence, important questions remain about which assessment path to follow—that of the purist, the simulator, or the skeptic. Here I have strong views. I question the wisdom of searching for a "pure" intelligence—be it general intelligence, musical intelligence, or interpersonal intelligence. I do not believe that such alchemical intellectual essences actually exist; they are a product of our penchant for creating terminology rather than determinable and measurable entities. Moreover, the correlations that have thus far been found between supposedly pure measures and the skills that we actually value in the world are too modest to be useful.

What does exist is the use of intelligences, individually and in concert, to carry out tasks that are valued by a society. Accordingly, we should be assessing the extent to which human beings succeed in carrying out tasks of consequence that presumably involve certain intelligences. To be concrete, we should not test musical intelligence by looking at the ability to discriminate between two tones or timbres; rather, we should be teaching people to sing songs or play instruments or transform melodies and seeing how readily they master such feats. At the same time, we should abjure a search for pure emotional sensitivity—for example, a test that matches facial expressions to galvanic skin response. Rather, we should place (or observe) people in situations that call for them to be sensitive to the aspirations and motives of others. For example, we could see how they handle a situation in which they and colleagues have to break up a fight between two teenagers, or persuade a boss to change a policy of which they do not approve.

Here powerful new simulations can be invoked. We are now in a position to draw on technologies that can deliver realistic situations or problems and also record the success of subjects in dealing with them. A student can be presented with an unfamiliar tune on a computer and asked to learn that tune, transpose it, orchestrate it, and the like. Such exercises would reveal much about the student's intelligence in musical matters.

Turning to the social (or human, if you prefer) realm, subjects can be presented with simulated interactions and asked to judge the shifting motivations of each actor. Or they can be asked to work in an interactive hypermedia production with unfamiliar people who are trying to accomplish some sort of goal, and to respond to their various moves and countermoves. The program can alter responses in light of the moves of the subject. Like a high-stakes poker game, such a measure should reveal much about the interpersonal or emotional sensitivity of a subject.

A significant increase in the breadth—the elasticity—of our concept of intel- 50 ligence, then, should open the possibility for innovative forms of assessment far more realistic than the classic short-answer examinations. Why settle for an IQ or an SAT test, in which the items are at best remote proxies for the ability to design experiments, write essays, critique musical performances, and so forth? Why not instead ask people actually (or virtually) to carry out such tasks? And yet by not opening up the Pandora's box of values and subjectivity, one can continue to make judicious use of the insights and technologies achieved by those who have devoted decades to perfecting mental measurement.

To be sure, one can create a psychometric instrument for any conceivable human virtue, including morality, creativity, and emotional intelligence in its several senses. Indeed, since the publication of Daniel Goleman's book dozens of efforts have been made to create tests for emotional intelligence. The resulting instruments are not, however, necessarily useful. Such instruments are far more likely to satisfy the test maker's desire for reliability (a subject gets roughly the same score on two separate administrations of the test) than the need for validity (the test measures the trait that it purports to measure).

Such instruments-on-demand prove dubious for two reasons. First, beyond some platitudes, few can agree on what it means to be moral, ethical, a good person: consider the differing values of Jesse Helms and Jesse Jackson, Margaret Thatcher and Margaret Mead. Second, scores on such tests are much more likely to reveal test-taking savvy (skills in language and logic) than fundamental character.

In speaking about character, I turn to a final concern: the relationship between intelligence and what I will call virtue—those qualities that we admire and wish to hold up as examples for our children. No doubt the desire to expand intelligence to encompass ethics and character represents a direct response to the general feeling that our society is lacking in these dimensions; the expansionist view of intelligence reflects the hope that if we transmit the technology of intelligence to these virtues, we might in the end secure a more virtuous population.

I have already indicated my strong reservations about trying to make the word "intelligence" all things to all people—the psychometric equivalent of the true, the beautiful, and the good. Yet the problem remains: how, in a post-Aristotelian, post-Confucian era in which psychometrics looms large, do we think about the virtuous human being?

My analysis suggests one promising approach. We should recognize that intelligences, creativity, and morality—to mention just three desiderata—are separate. Each may require its own form of measurement or assessment, and some will prove far easier to assess objectively than others. Indeed, with respect to creativity and morality, we are more likely to rely on overall judgments by experts than on any putative test battery. At the same time, testing prevents us from looking for people who combine several of these attributes—who have musical and interpersonal intelligence, who are psychometrically intelligent and creative in the arts, who combine emotional sensitivity and a high standard of moral conduct.

Let me introduce another analogy at this point. In college admissions much attention is paid to scholastic performance, as measured by College Board examinations and grades. However, other features are also weighed, and sometimes a person with lower test scores is admitted if he or she proves exemplary in terms of citizenship or athletics or motivation. Admissions officers do not confound these virtues (indeed, they may use different scales and issue different grades), but they recognize the attractiveness of candidates who exemplify two or more desirable traits.

We have left the Eden of classical times, in which various intellectual and ethical values necessarily commingled, and we are unlikely ever to re-create it. We should recognize that these virtues can be separate and will often prove to be remote from one another. When we attempt to aggregate them, through phrases like "emotional intelligence," "creative intelligence," and "moral intelligence," we should realize that we are expressing a wish rather than denoting a necessary or even a likely coupling.

We have an aid in converting this wish to reality: the existence of powerful examples—people who succeed in exemplifying two or more cardinal human virtues. To name names is risky—particularly when one generation's heroes can become the subject of the next generation's pathographies. Even so, I can without apology mention Niels Bohr, George C. Marshall, Rachel Carson, Arthur Ashe, Louis Armstrong, Pablo Casals, Ella Fitzgerald.

In studying the lives of such people, we discover human possibilities. Young human beings learn primarily from the examples of powerful adults around them—those who are admirable and also those who are simply glamorous.

Sustained attention to admirable examples may well increase the future incidence of people who actually do yoke capacities that are scientifically and epistemologically separate.

In one of the most evocative phrases of the century the British novelist E. M. Forster counseled us, "Only connect." I believe that some expansionists in the territory of intelligence, though well motivated, have prematurely asserted connections that do not exist. But I also believe that as human beings, we can help to forge connections that may be important for our physical and psychic survival. 60

Just how the precise borders of intelligence are drawn is a question we can leave to scholars. But the imperative to broaden our definition of intelligence in a responsible way goes well beyond the academy. Who "owns" intelligence promises to be an issue even more critical in the next century than it has been in this era of the IQ test.

QUESTIONS FOR DISCUSSION AND WRITING

1. Identify and examine Gardner's "eight intelligences": "linguistic and logical-mathematical . . . musical, spatial, bodily-kinesthetic, naturalist, interpersonal, and intrapersonal" (paragraph 22). Does Plato's "The Allegory of the Cave" (p. 233) address any of these? If so, which sorts of intelligence?

2. For Gardner, which kinds of intelligence are primary? Why? If Gardner considers each kind of intelligence equivalent to every other kind, does he make a different case for the importance of each? On what grounds? Do you agree with him? If so, explain why. If not, make a case for a hierarchical arrangement of the different kinds of intelligence Gardner identifies. Does your hierarchy depend on, for example, a person's choice of profession or passionate involvement? For instance, a person with high musical intelligence might or might not have equally high bodily-kinesthetic intelligence, and this could lead to a differential expenditure of time, energy, and talent in one area or the other. Yet good musicians need excellent muscular coordination and good timing, among other things, just as good athletes do. So don't oversimplify your discussion. Draw on your own experience and that of people you know.

3. What is "alchemy"? What does Gardner mean by speaking of "pure intelligence" as "alchemical" (paragraph 46)?

4. What are Gardner's reasons for differentiating intelligence from creativity and from morality? Illustrate your answer with examples you have seen in action.

5. Does Gardner challenge the ways you think about thinking? About understanding the world? After discussion, write an essay in which you define what you mean by thinking, and illustrate this with examples. In your estimation, does "thinking" equal "intelligence"? What can thinking in itself accomplish? Then, examine some of the different types of intelligence Gardner discusses to question your original definition.

LINDA SIMON

The Naked Source

Linda Simon (b. 1946) earned a doctorate in English and American literature from Brandeis University in 1983, and is currently professor of English at Skidmore College. She has written several biographical studies, including The Biography of Alice B. Toklas *(1977),* Of Virtue Rare: Margaret Beaufort, Matriarch of the House of Tudor *(1982),* Genuine Reality: A Life of William James *(1998), and* Dark Light: Electricity and Anxiety from the Telegraph to the X-Ray *(2004), making her an authority on the interpretation of primary data that underpins biographical and historical writing.*

"The Naked Source," originally published in the Michigan Quarterly Review *(1998), is a manifesto for revamping historical education. Primary sources—naked data—wait for us to interpret them and render them into coherent narratives by using our curiosity, imagination, intuition, and perseverance. History is more than stuff to learn for a test—it's a way of making sense of the world.*

It is true that my students do not know history. That annals of the American past, as students tell it, are compressed into a compact chronicle: John Kennedy and Martin Luther King flourish just a breath away from FDR and Woodrow Wilson, who themselves come right on the heels of Jefferson and Lincoln. The far and distant past is more obscure still.

Some, because they are bright and inquisitive, have learned names, dates, and the titles of major events. But even these masters of Trivial Pursuit often betray their ignorance of a real sense of the past. Teachers all have favorite oneliners that point to an abyss in historical knowledge. Mine is: Sputnik *who*?

There is no debate here. Students do not know history. Students should learn history. There is less agreement about what they should know, why they should know it, and far less agreement about how they should pursue this study of the past.

When I ask my students why they need to know history, they reply earnestly: We need to learn history because those who do not know history are doomed to repeat the mistakes of the past. They have heard this somewhere, although no one can attribute the remark. And if they are told that George Santayana said it, they know not who Santayana was, although if you care to inform them they will dutifully record his name, dates (1863–1952), and the title of the work (*The Life of Reason*) in which the remark was made.

Is that so? I ask. What will not be repeated?   5

Inevitably they respond emotionally with the example of the Holocaust. Some have watched an episode of a PBS series. Some have seen the film *The Diary of Anne Frank*. Such genocide, they reply, will not be repeated because we know about it. Undaunted by examples of contemporary genocide, they remain firm in their conviction. Genocide, they maintain. And the Great Depression.

The Great Depression has made a big impact on the adolescent imagination. Given any work of literature written at any time during the 1930s, some students will explain it as a direct response to the Great Depression. Wasn't everyone depressed, after all? And aren't most serious works of literature grim, glum, dark, and deep. There you have it.

But now we know about the Great Depression. And so it will not, cannot, happen again.

I am not persuaded that requiring students to read Tacitus or Thucydides, Carl Becker or Francis Parkman, Samuel Eliot Morison or Arnold Toynbee will remedy this situation, although I believe that students, and we, might well benefit from these writers' illumination. What students lack, after all, is a sense of historical-mindedness, a sense that lives were lived in a context, a sense that events (the Battle of Barnet, for example) had consequences (if men were slain on the battlefield, they could not return to the farm), a sense that answers must generate questions, more questions, and still more subtle questions.

As it is, students learning history, especially in the early grades, are asked 10 prescribed questions and are given little opportunity to pursue their own inquiry or satisfy their own curiosity. The following questions are from current high school texts:

> Has the role of the present United Nations proved that the hopes and dreams of Woodrow Wilson were achievable? If so, how? If not, why?

> What were the advantages of an isolationist policy for the United States in the nineteenth century? Were there disadvantages?

Questions such as these perpetuate the idea that history is a body of knowledge on which students will be tested. The first question, in other words, asks students: Did you read the section in the text on the role of the United Nations? Did you read the section on Wilson's aims in proposing the League of Nations? Can you put these two sections together?

The second question asks students: Did you understand the term *isolationist*? Did you read the section on U.S. foreign relations in the nineteenth century? Can you summarize the debate that the authors of the textbook recount?

Questions such as these perpetuate the idea that history can uncover "facts" and "truth," that history is objective, and that students, if only they are diligent, can recover "right answers" about the past. Questions such as these ignore the role of historians. Even those bright students who can recall dates and events rarely can recall the name of a historian, much less any feeling about who this particular man or woman was. For many students, historical facts are things out there, like sea shells or autumn leaves, and it hardly matters who fetches them. The sea shell will look the same whether it is gathered in Charles Beard's pocket or Henri Pirenne's.

What students really need to learn, more than "history," is a sense of the historical method of inquiry. They need to know what it is that historians do and how they do it. They need to understand the role of imagination and intuition in the telling of histories, they need to practice, themselves, confronting sources, making judgments, and defending conclusions.

When I ask my freshmen what they think historians do, they usually offer 15 me some lofty phrases about "influencing the course of future events." But what

I mean is: what do historians do after breakfast? That is a question few of my students can answer. And they are surprised when I read them the following passage by British historian A. L. Rowse from his book *The Use of History*.

> You might think that in order to learn history you need a library of books to begin with. Not at all: that only comes at the end. What you need at the beginning is a pair of stout walking shoes, a pencil and a notebook; perhaps I should add a good county guide covering the area you mean to explore . . . and a map of the country . . . that gives you field footpaths and a wealth of things of interest, marks churches and historic buildings and ruins, wayside crosses and holy wells, prehistoric camps and dykes, the sites of battles. When you can't go for a walk, it is quite a good thing to study the map and plan where you would like to go. I am all in favor of the open-air approach to history; the most delightful and enjoyable, the most imaginative and informative, and—what not everybody understands—the best training.

It is the best training because it gives the would-be historian an encounter with the things that all historians look at and puzzle over: primary sources about the past. Historians look at battlefields and old buildings, read letters and diaries and documents, interview eyewitnesses or participants in events. And they ask questions of these sources. Gradually, after asking increasingly sophisticated questions, they make some sense, for themselves, of what once happened.

What professional historians do, however, is not what most students do when they set out to learn history within the confines of a course. Instead of putting students face to face with primary sources, instructors are more likely to send them to read what other people say about the past. Students begin with a library of books of secondary sources, or they may begin with a text. But that, cautions Rowse, should come "at the end." Instead of allowing students to gain experience in weighing evidence and making inferences, the structures of many courses encourage them to amass information. "I found it!" exclaim enthusiastic students. They need to ask, "But what does it mean?"

They need to ask that question of the kinds of sources that historians actually use. Instead of reading Morison's rendering of Columbus's voyages, for example, students might read Columbus himself: his journal, his letters to the Spanish monarchs. Then they can begin to decide for themselves what sort of man this was and what sort of experience he had. Morison—as excellent a historian as he is—comes later. With some sense of the sources that Morison used, students can begin to evaluate his contribution to history, to understand how he drew conclusions from the material available to him, to see how "facts" are augmented by historical intuition. They can begin to understand, too, that the reconstruction of the past is slow and painstaking work.

Courses that cover several decades or even millennia may give students a false impression of historical inquiry. Historians, like archaeologists or epidemiologists, move slowly through bumpy and perilous terrain. They are used to travelling for miles only to find themselves stranded at a dead end. Once, in the archives of Westminster Abbey, I eagerly awaited reading a fragment of a letter from King

Henry VI (after all, that is how it was described in the card catalog), only to lift out of an envelope the corner of a page, about an inch across, with the faintest ink-mark the only evidence that it had, five hundred years before, been a letter at all.

Slowly the historian assembles pieces of the past. A household expense record 20 might be the only artifact proving that a certain medieval woman existed. How much can be known about her? How much can be known by examining someone's checkbook today? Yet historians must make do with just such odd legacies: wills and land deeds, maps and drawings, family portraits or photographs. Can you imagine the excitement over the discovery of a diary or a cache of letters? At last, a text. But the diary may prove a disappointment, a frustration. William James recorded the title of a book he may have been reading or the name of a visitor. Didn't he understand that a historian or biographer would need the deep, reflective ruminations of which we know he was more than capable?

Students have not had these experiences. When they are asked to write, they write *about* history. The research paper or the term paper seems to many of them another form of test—this time a take-home drawn out over weeks. Even if they have learned that "voice" and "audience" are important for a writer, they see history papers as different. They must be objective; they must learn proper footnoting and documentation. They must compile an impressive bibliography. Most important, they must find something out. The research paper produces nothing so much as anxiety, and the student often feels overwhelmed by the project.

They might, instead, be asked to write history as historians do it. They might be introduced to archives—in their college, in their community, in their state capital. They might be encouraged to interview people, and to interview them again and again until they begin to get the kind of information that will enlighten them about a particular time or event. They might be encouraged to read newspapers on microfilm or the bound volumes of old magazines that are yellowing in the basement of their local library. And then they might be asked to write in that most challenging form: the historical narrative.

"I can recall experiencing upon the completing of my first work of history," George Kennan wrote once, ". . . a moment of panic when the question suddenly presented itself to me: What is it that I have done here? Perhaps what I have written is not really history but rather some sort of novel, the product of my own imagination,—an imagination stimulated, inspired and informed, let us hope, by the documents I have been reading, but imagination nevertheless." Most historians share Kennan's reaction.

Students, of course, can never discover the boundary between "fact" and imaginative construction unless they have contact with primary sources. They cannot know where the historian has intervened to analyze the information he or she has discovered. "Most of the facts that you excavate," Morison wrote in "History as a Literary Art," "are dumb things; it is for you to make them speak by proper selection, arrangement, and emphasis." Morison suggested that beginning historians look to such writers as Sherwood Anderson and Henry James for examples of the kind of palpable description and intense characterization that can make literature—historical or fictional—come alive.

Students need to be persuaded that they are writing literature, not taking a   25
test, when they set out to be historians. Their writing needs to be read and evaluated not only for the facts that they have managed to compile, but for the sense of the past that they have conveyed. They need to discover that the past was not only battles and elections, Major Forces and Charismatic Leaders, but ordinary people, growing up, courting, dancing to a different beat, camping by a river that has long since dried up, lighting out for a territory that no longer exists. Except in the imagination of historians, as they confront the naked source, unaided.

QUESTIONS FOR DISCUSSION AND WRITING

1. Do you agree with Simon that "[t]here is no debate here. Students do not know history" (paragraph 3)? Consider your experience with history classes. Have you studied the past in the way that Simon recommends, or have you merely amassed dates and names to repeat back on tests?

2. Simon asserts that well-written history is a type of literature—not merely a compilation of facts. The historian actually interprets the primary data and makes up a plausible story. How does this image of the historian at work match your experience as a reader of history?

3. Write a historical narrative based on primary sources like those discussed by Simon. Investigate a person or an event from your local history—your family or hometown, for example. Use diaries, old news reports, town records, archives, or photographs. You might also interview people who know about the subject of your study.

4. Explore an aspect of history that intrigues you by writing a two-part essay sequence. First, write a short essay in which you describe a period, an event, or a person that you would like to learn more about; also explain why this subject interests you. Include a list of questions about your subject that you would like to answer. Next, find several sources of information—history books, encyclopedias, videos, Web sites—and write a second, longer essay about your subject. Explain what you learned, what surprises you encountered, and how closely the historical record matches what you expected to find. Were you able to answer all of your questions? Why or why not? Where could you turn to find the answers?

PEG TYRE

The Writing Revolution

According to her Web site, Peg Tyre (b. 1960) is "a nationally renowned writer and thinker about education." Tyre has published several books; her most recent is The Good School: How Smart Parents Get Their Kids the Education They Deserve

(2011). That book discusses how parents who care about getting the best education for their children can make sense of the blizzard of information, and misinformation, about schools and teachers. She also wrote The Trouble with Boys: A Surprising Report Card on Our Sons, Their Problems at School and What Parents & Educators Must Do *(2008), which was a New York Times bestseller and won the 2009 award for Books for a Better Life. Tyre has taught at Columbia Graduate School of Journalism and has lectured at Harvard, Yale, Columbia, Emory, and the Googleplex in Mountain View, California.*

In this article, initially published in the Atlantic, *Tyre focuses on New Dorp, a public high school on Staten Island that was woefully underperforming. After having tried other reforms that didn't work—such as firing bad teachers, breaking the school into smaller units, and engaging private business—the school returned to improving student writing as the key. They found that many students were unable to formulate anything coherent beyond a simple sentence. So, New Dorp put in place a rigorous writing program that went back to the basics of grammar—basics that were never taught to these students. The results were astonishing and significant: higher passing rates, higher graduation rates, and more students moving from high school into college.*

In 2009, when Monica DiBella entered New Dorp, a notorious public high school on Staten Island, her academic future was cloudy. Monica had struggled to read in early childhood, and had repeated first grade. During her elementary-school years, she got more than one hundred hours of tutoring, but by fourth grade, she'd fallen behind her classmates again. In the years that followed, Monica became comfortable with math and learned to read passably well, but never seemed able to express her thoughts in writing. During her freshman year at New Dorp, a '70s-style brick behemoth near a grimy beach, her history teacher asked her to write an essay on Alexander the Great. At a loss, she jotted down her opinion of the Macedonian ruler: "I think Alexander the Great was one of the best military leaders." An essay? "Basically, that wasn't going to happen," she says, sweeping her blunt-cut brown hair from her brown eyes. "It was like, well, I got a sentence down. What now?" Monica's mother, Santa, looked over her daughter's answer—six simple sentences, one of which didn't make sense—with a mixture of fear and frustration. Even a coherent, well-turned paragraph seemed beyond her daughter's ability. An essay? "It just didn't seem like something Monica could ever do."

For decades, no one at New Dorp seemed to know how to help low-performing students like Monica, and unfortunately, this troubled population made up most of the school, which caters primarily to students from poor and working-class families. In 2006, 82 percent of freshmen entered the school reading below grade level. Students routinely scored poorly on the English and history Regents exams, a New York State graduation requirement: the essay questions were just too difficult. Many would simply write a sentence or two and shut the test booklet. In the spring of 2007, when administrators calculated graduation rates, they found that four out of ten students who had started New Dorp as freshmen had dropped out, making it one of the 2,000 or so lowest-performing high schools in the nation. City officials, who had been closing comprehensive high schools all over New York and opening smaller, specialized ones in their stead, signaled that New Dorp was in the crosshairs.

And so the school's principal, Deirdre DeAngelis, began a detailed investigation into why, ultimately, New Dorp's students were failing. By 2008, she and her faculty had come to a singular answer: bad writing. Students' inability to translate thoughts into coherent, well-argued sentences, paragraphs, and essays was severely impeding intellectual growth in many subjects. Consistently, one of the largest differences between failing and successful students was that only the latter could express their thoughts on the page. If nothing else, DeAngelis and her teachers decided, beginning in the fall of 2009, New Dorp students would learn to write well. "When they told me about the writing program," Monica says, "well, I was skeptical." With disarming candor, sharp-edged humor, and a shy smile, Monica occupies the middle ground between child and adult—she can be both naive and knowing. "On the other hand, it wasn't like I had a choice. I go to high school. I figured I'd give it a try."

New Dorp's Writing Revolution, which placed an intense focus, across nearly every academic subject, on teaching the skills that underlie good analytical writing, was a dramatic departure from what most American students—especially low performers—are taught in high school. The program challenged long-held assumptions about the students and bitterly divided the staff. It also yielded extraordinary results. By the time they were sophomores, the students who had begun receiving the writing instruction as freshmen were already scoring higher on exams than any previous New Dorp class. Pass rates for the English Regents, for example, bounced from 67 percent in June 2009 to 89 percent in 2011; for the global-history exam, pass rates rose from 64 to 75 percent. The school reduced its Regents-repeater classes—cram courses designed to help struggling students collect a graduation requirement—from five classes of thirty-five students to two classes of twenty students.

The number of kids enrolling in a program that allows them to take college- 5 level classes shot up from 148 students in 2006 to 412 students last year. Most important, although the makeup of the school has remained about the same— roughly 40 percent of students are poor, a third are Hispanic, and 12 percent are black—a greater proportion of students who enter as freshmen leave wearing a cap and gown. This spring, the graduation rate is expected to hit 80 percent, a staggering improvement over the 63 percent figure that prevailed before the Writing Revolution began. New Dorp, once the black sheep of the borough, is being held up as a model of successful school turnaround. "To be able to think critically and express that thinking, it's where we are going," says Dennis Walcott, New York City's schools chancellor. "We are thrilled with what has happened there."

In the coming months, the conversation about the importance of formal writing instruction and its place in a public-school curriculum—the conversation that was central to changing the culture at New Dorp—will spread throughout the nation. Over the next two school years, forty-six states will align themselves with the Common Core State Standards. For the first time, elementary-school students— who today mostly learn writing by constructing personal narratives, memoirs, and small works of fiction—will be required to write informative and persuasive essays.

By high school, students will be expected to produce mature and thoughtful essays, not just in English class but in history and science classes as well.

Common Core's architect, David Coleman, says the new writing standards are meant to reverse a pedagogical pendulum that has swung too far, favoring self-expression and emotion over lucid communication. "As you grow up in this world, you realize people really don't give a shit about what you feel or what you think," he famously told a group of educators last year in New York. Early accounts suggest that the new writing standards will deliver a high-voltage shock to the American public. Last spring, Florida school officials administered a writing test that, for the first time, required tenth-graders to produce an expository essay aligned with Common Core goals. The pass rate on the exam plummeted from 80 percent in 2011 to 38 percent this year.

According to the Nation's Report Card, in 2007, the latest year for which this data is available, only 1 percent of all twelfth-graders nationwide could write a sophisticated, well-organized essay. Other research has shown that 70 to 75 percent of students in grades four through twelve write poorly. Over the past thirty years, as knowledge-based work has come to dominate the economy, American high schools have raised achievement rates in mathematics by providing more-extensive and higher-level instruction. But high schools are still graduating large numbers of students whose writing skills better equip them to work on farms or in factories than in offices; for decades, achievement rates in writing have remained low.

Although New Dorp teachers had observed students failing for years, they never connected that failure to specific flaws in their own teaching. They watched passively as Deirdre DeAngelis got rid of the bad apples on the staff; won foundation money to break the school into smaller, more personalized learning communities; and wooed corporate partners to support after-school programs. Nothing seemed to move the dial.

Her decision in 2008 to focus on how teachers supported writing inside each 10 classroom was not popular. "Most teachers," said Nell Scharff, an instructional expert DeAngelis hired, "entered into the process with a strongly negative attitude." They were doing their job, they told her hotly. New Dorp students were simply not smart enough to write at the high-school level. You just had to listen to the way the students talked, one teacher pointed out—they rarely communicated in full sentences, much less expressed complex thoughts. "It was my view that these kids didn't want to engage their brains," Fran Simmons, who teaches freshman English, told me. "They were lazy."

Scharff, a lecturer at Baruch College, a part of the City University of New York, kept pushing, asking: "What skills that lead to good writing did struggling students lack?" She urged the teachers to focus on the largest group: well-behaved kids like Monica who simply couldn't seem to cobble together a paragraph. "Those kids were showing up" every day, Scharff said. "They seem to want to do well." Gradually, the bellyaching grew fainter. "Every quiz, every unit test, every homework assignment became a new data point," Scharff recalled. "We combed through their writing. Again and again, we asked: 'How did the kids in our target group go wrong? What skills were missing?'"

Maybe the struggling students just couldn't read, suggested one teacher. A few teachers administered informal diagnostic tests the following week and reported back. The students who couldn't write well seemed capable, at the very least, of decoding simple sentences. A history teacher got more granular. He pointed out that the students' sentences were short and disjointed. What words, Scharff asked, did kids who wrote solid paragraphs use that the poor writers didn't? Good essay writers, the history teacher noted, used coordinating conjunctions to link and expand on simple ideas—words like *for, and, nor, but, or, yet,* and *so.* Another teacher devised a quick quiz that required students to use those conjunctions. To the astonishment of the staff, she reported that a sizable group of students could not use those simple words effectively. The harder they looked, the teachers began to realize, the harder it was to determine whether the students were smart or not—the tools they had to express their thoughts were so limited that such a judgment was nearly impossible.

The exploration continued. One teacher noted that the best-written paragraphs contained complex sentences that relied on dependent clauses like *although* and *despite,* which signal a shifting idea within the same sentence. Curious, Fran Simmons devised a little test of her own. She asked her freshman English students to read *Of Mice and Men* and, using information from the novel, answer the following prompt in a single sentence:

"Although George . . ."

She was looking for a sentence like: *Although George worked very hard, he could not attain the American Dream.*

Some of Simmons's students wrote a solid sentence, but many were stumped. 15 More than a few wrote the following: "Although George and Lenny were friends."

A lightbulb, says Simmons, went on in her head. These fourteen- and fifteen-year-olds didn't know how to use some basic parts of speech. With such grammatical gaps, it was a wonder they learned as much as they did. "Yes, they could read simple sentences," but works like the Gettysburg Address were beyond them—not because they were too lazy to look up words they didn't know, but because "they were missing a crucial understanding of how language works. They didn't understand that the key information in a sentence doesn't always come at the beginning of that sentence."

Some teachers wanted to know how this could happen. "We spent a lot of time wondering how our students had been taught," said English teacher Stevie D'Arbanville. "How could they get passed along and end up in high school without understanding how to use the word *although?*"

But the truth is, the problems affecting New Dorp students are common to a large subset of students nationally. Fifty years ago, elementary-school teachers taught the general rules of spelling and the structure of sentences. Later instruction focused on building solid paragraphs into full-blown essays. Some kids mastered it, but many did not. About twenty-five years ago, in an effort to enliven instruction and get more kids writing, schools of education began promoting a different approach. The popular thinking was that writing should be *"caught,* not *taught,"* explains Steven Graham, a professor of education instruction at Arizona State University. Roughly, it was supposed to work like this: Give students interesting creative-writing assignments; put that writing in a fun, social context in which kids share their work. Kids, the theory goes, will "catch" what they need in order to be successful writers. Formal lessons in grammar, sentence structure, and essay-writing took a back seat to creative expression.

The catch method works for some kids, to a point. "Research tells us some students catch quite a bit, but not everything," Graham says. And some kids don't catch much at all. Kids who come from poverty, who had weak early instruction, or who have learning difficulties, he explains, "can't catch anywhere near what they need" to write an essay. For most of the 1990s, elementary- and middle-school children kept journals in which they wrote personal narratives, poetry, and memoirs and engaged in "peer editing," without much attention to formal composition. Middle- and high-school teachers were supposed to provide the expository- and persuasive-writing instruction.

Then, in 2001, came No Child Left Behind. The program's federally mandated 20 tests assess two subjects—math and reading—and the familiar adage "What gets tested gets taught" has turned out to be true. *Literacy,* which once consisted of the ability to read for knowledge, write coherently, and express complex thoughts about the written word, has become synonymous with *reading.* Formal writing instruction has become even more of an afterthought.

Teacher surveys conducted by Arthur Applebee, the director of the Center on English Learning and Achievement at the University at Albany (part of the State University of New York system), found that even when writing instruction is offered, the teacher mostly does the composing and students fill in the blanks. "Writing as a way to study, to learn, or to construct new knowledge or generate new networks of understanding," says Applebee, "has become increasingly rare."

Back on Staten Island, more New Dorp teachers were growing uncomfortably aware of their students' profound deficiencies—and their own. "At teachers college, you read a lot of theory, like Paulo Freire's *Pedagogy of the Oppressed,* but don't learn how to teach writing," said Fran Simmons. How could the staff backfill the absent foundational skills their students needed in order to learn to write?

Seeking out ideas, DeAngelis took a handful of teachers to visit the Windward School, a small private school for first-through-ninth-graders located in a leafy section of White Plains, a suburb of New York City. To be accepted there, children have to possess at least average intelligence, have a language-based learning disability, and have parents who can afford the $45,000 yearly tuition. Students attend Windward for two or three years before reentering mainstream schools, and because so many affluent children move in and out of Windward, the writing program there, which was developed by the former Windward head Judith Hochman, has become something of a legend among private-school administrators. "Occasionally, we'd have a student attend Windward. And they'd come back and we'd find that that student had writing *down,"* says Scott Nelson, the headmaster at Rye Country Day, an exclusive independent school in Westchester County. Nelson figured that Rye Country Day kids could benefit en masse from the Windward expository-writing program. Three years ago, Nelson sent his entire middle-school English and social-studies staff to be trained by Hochman.

The Hochman Program, as it is sometimes called, would not be unfamiliar to nuns who taught in Catholic schools circa 1950. Children do not have to "catch" a single thing. They are explicitly taught how to turn ideas into simple sentences, and how to construct complex sentences from simple ones by supplying the answer to three prompts—*but, because,* and *so.* They are instructed on how to use appositive clauses to vary the way their sentences begin. Later on, they are taught how to recognize sentence fragments, how to pull the main idea from a paragraph, and how to form a main idea on their own. It is, at least initially, a rigid, unswerving formula. "I prefer *recipe*," Hochman says, "but *formula*? Yes! Okay!"

Hochman, seventy-five, has chin-length blond hair and big features. Her 25 voice, usually gentle, rises almost to a shout when she talks about poor writing instruction. "The thing is, kids need a formula, at least at first, because what we are asking them to do is very difficult. So God, let's stop acting like they should just know how to do it. Give them a formula! Later, when they understand the rules of good writing, they can figure out how to break them." Because the tenets of good writing are difficult to teach in the abstract, the writing program at Windward involves a large variety of assignments, by teachers of nearly every subject. After DeAngelis visited the school, she says, "I had one question and one question only: How can we steal this and bring it back to New Dorp?"

For her part, Hochman was intrigued by the challenge New Dorp presented. Research has shown that thinking, speaking, and reading comprehension are interconnected and reinforced through good writing instruction. If the research was correct, Hochman told DeAngelis, a good writing program at New Dorp should lead to significant student improvement all around.

Within months, Hochman became a frequent visitor to Staten Island. Under her supervision, the teachers at New Dorp began revamping their curriculum. By fall 2009, nearly every instructional hour except for math class was dedicated to teaching essay writing along with a particular subject. So in chemistry class in the winter of 2010, Monica DiBella's lesson on the properties of hydrogen and oxygen was followed by a worksheet that required her to describe the elements with subordinating clauses—for instance, she had to begin one sentence with the word *although.*

> *Although*... "hydrogen is explosive and oxygen supports combustion," Monica wrote, "a compound of them puts out fires."
>
> *Unless* . . . "hydrogen and oxygen form a compound, they are explosive and dangerous."
>
> *If*... This was a hard one. Finally, she figured out a way to finish the sentence. *If* . . . "hydrogen and oxygen form a compound, they lose their original properties of being explosive and supporting combustion."

As her understanding of the parts of speech grew, Monica's reading comprehension improved dramatically. "Before, I could read, sure. But it was like a sea of words," she says. "The more writing instruction I got, the more I understood which words were important."

Classroom discussion became an opportunity to push Monica and her classmates to listen to each other, think more carefully, and speak more precisely, in ways they could then echo in persuasive writing. When speaking, they were required to use specific prompts outlined on a poster at the front of each class.

"I agree/disagree with_____ because . . ."

"I have a different opinion . . ."

"I have something to add . . ."

"Can you explain your answer?"

The structured speaking was a success during Monica's fifth-period-English discussion of the opening scene of Arthur Miller's *Death of a Salesman*. "What is Willie Loman's state of mind? Is he tired? If he is tired, why would he be so tired?" asked the teacher, Angelo Caterina. "Willie Loman seems tired because he is getting old," ventured a curly-haired girl who usually sat in the front. "Can you explain your answer?" Monica called out. The curly-haired girl bit her lip while her eyes searched the book in front of her. "The stage direction says he's sixty-three. That's old!" Other hands shot up. Reading from the prompt poster made the students sound as if they'd spent the previous period in the House of Lords instead of the school cafeteria. "I agree that his age is listed in the stage direction," said John Feliciano. "But I disagree with your conclusion. I think he is tired because his job is very hard and he has to travel a lot."

Robert Fawcett, a loose-limbed boy in a white T-shirt, got his turn. Robert had been making money working alongside the school's janitors. "I disagree with those conclusions," he said, glancing at the prompts. "The way Willie Loman describes his job suggests that the kind of work he does is making him tired. It is repetitive. It can feel pointless. It can make you feel exhausted." The class was respectfully silent for a moment, acknowledging that Robert had analyzed the scene and derived a fresh idea from his own experience.

By sophomore year, Monica's class was learning how to map out an introductory paragraph, then how to form body paragraphs. "There are phrases—*specifically, for instance, for example*—that help you add detail to a paragraph," Monica explains. She reflects for a moment. "Who could have known that, unless someone taught them?" Homework got a lot harder. Teachers stopped giving fluffy assignments such as "Write a postcard to a friend describing life in the trenches of World War I" and instead demanded that students fashion an expository essay describing three major causes of the conflict.

Some writing experts caution that championing expository and analytic writing at the expense of creative expression is shortsighted. "The secret weapon of our economy is that we foster creativity," says Kelly Gallagher, a high-school writing teacher who has written several books on adolescent literacy. And formulaic instruction will cause some students to tune out, cautions Lucy Calkins, a professor at Columbia University's Teachers College. While she welcomes a bigger dose of expository writing in schools, she says lockstep instruction won't accelerate learning. "Kids need to see their work reach other readers . . . They need to have choices in the questions they write about, and a way to find their voice."

To be sure, the writing program hasn't solved all of New Dorp's problems. The high rate of poverty makes the students vulnerable to drug abuse and violence. And in some subjects, scores on the Regents exams this year showed less growth than the teachers had hoped for. Still, word of the dramatic turnaround has spread: Principals and administrators from other failing high schools as far away as Chicago have been touring New Dorp. As other schools around New York City and the nation scramble to change their curriculum to suit the Common Core standards, New Dorp teachers say they're ready.

In a profoundly hopeful irony, New Dorp's reemergence as a viable institu-   35 tion has hinged not on a radical new innovation but on an old idea done better. The school's success suggests that perhaps certain instructional fundamentals— fundamentals that schools have devalued or forgotten—need to be rediscovered, updated, and reintroduced. And if that can be done correctly, traditional instruction delivered by the teachers already in classrooms may turn out to be the most powerful lever we have for improving school performance after all.

As for Monica DiBella, her prospects have also improved. She expresses more complex and detailed ideas when she raises her hand. Whereas she once read far below grade level, this year she earned a 77 on her English Regents exam (a 75 or above signals that a student is on track to engage in college-level coursework) and a 91 in American history ("Yep, you heard that right," Monica tells me). Although many of her classmates can now bang out an essay with ease, she admits she still struggles with writing. She hurried through the essay on her global-history exam, and the results fell far short of a masterpiece. The first paragraph reads:

> Throughout history, societies have developed significant technological innovations. The technological innovations have had both positive and negative effect on the society of humankind. Two major technological advances were factory systems and chemical pesticides.

But Dina Zoleo, who taught Monica as a junior, points out that the six-paragraph essay shows Monica's newfound ability to write solid, logically ordered paragraphs about what she's learned, citing examples and using transitions between ideas. Together with her answers in the multiple-choice section of the test, it was enough to earn Monica an 84. She's now begun the process of applying to college. "I always wanted to go to college, but I never had the confidence that I could say and write the things I know." She smiles and sweeps the bangs from her eyes. "Then someone showed me how."

QUESTIONS FOR DISCUSSION AND WRITING

1. Think about your own history with writing and writing instruction. How well were you taught grammar? When did you begin to write essays? How much of the writing you were encouraged to do was personal narrative or creative

writing, and how much of it involved expository or argumentative essays? As you think back on your own school experiences with writing, how well do you think that instruction prepared you for college-level writing?

2. Part of the backdrop to this article is a decades-long discussion over how to improve education, particularly education in public schools that primarily serve poor and working-class families. Other potential reforms listed (which were not successful at New Dorp) included firing incompetent teachers, breaking large schools into smaller learning communities, and involving private industry (paragraph 9). Does the fact that the reforms didn't work at New Dorp mean that the reforms themselves are not effective or needed? Investigate in-depth one of these reforms and analyze why that reform may not have worked at New Dorp. In what kind of school or situation might those reforms be more effective?

3. In paragraph 18, Tyre gives a brief history of how writing instruction moved away from the teaching of principles of spelling and sentence construction toward self-expression. Underpinning that was the notion that students would "catch" the lessons in grammar and sentence construction. Why has this not worked? Which students are less likely to "catch" the lessons? Why?

4. The Common Core State Standards, first mentioned in paragraph 6, move students away from writing personal narratives and creative writing toward writing essays that are informative or persuasive. What dangers might you see in this movement? Is such an approach inherently elitist—meaning that it serves the purpose of preparing working-class students to write at the college level, when many of them might not want to go to college at all, but pursue working-class careers? Is there still benefit for such students in the Common Core? Be specific.

5. Hochman speaks of a recipe or formula (paragraphs 24 and 25) for student writers, which allows them to write essays. She argues that students need to learn a formula first; once they understand the principles, then they can break the rules. Do you agree or disagree? Cite specific examples in your response.

6. Based on your own experiences and observations, why do you think so many writing assignments at the elementary, middle, and high school levels are more personal or creative rather than informative or persuasive? Defend your answer with specific examples.

CHAPTER 8

Gender: What Makes Us Men and Women?

ANDREA CORNWALL

Boys and Men Must Be Included in the Conversation on Equality

A social anthropologist at the University of Sussex in the School of Global Studies, Andrea Cornwall (b. 1963) specializes in researching democracy, citizen participation, participatory research, and gender and sexuality. She has published frequently in her field, as both an editor and a writer. Her credits include being editor for The Participation Reader *(2011) and a co-editor for* Men and Development: Politicizing Masculinity *(2011). She is a fellow at the Institute of Development Studies at the University of Sussex, which states on its Web site that "Our vision is a world in which poverty does not exist, social justice prevails and economic growth is focused on improving human wellbeing." She has also written what she terms a "truer-than-fiction" look at the bureaucracy behind aid, called* The Beast of Bureaucracy: Tales from Valhalla *(2007).*

In this article, which initially appeared in the Guardian, *a newspaper based in London, Cornwall addresses an important issue: If true equality is to be reached, boys and men must also be involved. Lately, the male side of the human race has been either ignored or vilified in the quest for gender equality. Moreover, boys and men have their own matters to deal with, including problems associated with male privilege and the difficulties many boys and men face because of gender role expectations. Cornwall urges the reader to approach the pursuit of equality not as a zero-sum game (in which one side wins and the other side loses), but as a more meaningful "transformation" of the structure of gender relations.*

Girls are cool. Girls can save the world. Girls can—according to the colorful stickers produced by the Nike Foundation—pull off miracles: "lifting" economies, ending the spread of HIV, leading the revolution. Investing in girls, the U.K.'s Department for International Development tells us, is a surefire way to "stop poverty before it starts."

Few of today's international development agencies would give boys the time of day. They're not seen as part of the solution to development's ills. When boys make an appearance in today's development narratives, they're cast as hazardous menace or hopeless loser. Not for them the lifting, ending, and leading that's become the script for girls. Boys are, after all, men-in-the-making, assumed to have access to—and be able to utilize—all the patriarchal privilege that's going.

Don't get me wrong. There's a lot of really inspiring work going on with girls, and there's good reason to focus on their empowerment. But I'm disturbed about the promotion of Girl Power as the development panacea. There's something dangerously retributive about an approach that simply flips an inequity around and approaches power as a zero-sum game.

Yes, girls can be extracted from their everyday lives and "empowered" as individuals. But the reality is that these lives are lived as part of families, communities, and societies. Cutting boys and men out of the picture isn't going to make them go away. And the current narrative misses not only the fact that transforming the ways boys become men can be a key strategy in achieving gender justice, but also the contribution boys and men can make to that struggle.

It's not as if boys are having a particularly easy time. Male privilege can 5 become a burden when boys and men are unable to live up to the expectations associated with it. The stubbornness of dominant ideals of masculinity offers them little let-up in what they're supposed to do and be. Shifting labor markets leave boys and men shut out of employment opportunities. Boys are failing at school. They're falling through the cracks. And boys and men whose gender expression or sexual orientation departs from dominant sexual or social norms are all too often subjected to violent abuse and exclusion.

Educating girls is hugely important for development—but so is schooling for boys that can create and sustain new, more egalitarian, norms. Frank Karioris observes: "If it is true that men who are more educated are more likely to challenge norms and participate in domestic roles and caregiving, but men's overall achievement rate in education is declining; then it would seem logical to assume that there will be a decrease in men's involvement in challenging norms, and increased resistance to men sharing in the domestic or caregiving roles. This . . . is a movement away from gender equality."

So what can be done? One thing is clear: Women and girls can't be expected to take responsibility for this as well. Women's rights activists are tired of being told to "engage," "involve," or "bring men in," as if it's their job to persuade men to care about issues that ought to be their concern. As Alan Greig has so eloquently put it, it's not about bringing men in by talking to them nicely and making sure they're not put off: It's about naming male privilege, and getting men engaged in holding other men to account.

Around the world, we're seeing work that's inspired by an agenda for change that doesn't leave boys and men out of the equation—mobilizing men to stop violence against women, and challenging and changing men's attitudes to intimate relationships and fatherhood. By tackling deadly ideals of masculinity and opening up alternative ways of being a man, these initiatives are transforming boys' and men's intimate and interpersonal relationships and creating the basis for greater equality.

The new book *Men and Development: Politicizing Masculinities* draws together lessons from this work and argues that progress depends on going beyond the personal—getting political about matters long regarded as "women's issues," such as unequal pay, unequal domestic labor burdens, and unequal representation in politics. These are issues on which we hear little talk and see little action by men, yet they remain the basis on which any meaningful structural transformation of gender injustice depends.

One inspiring lesson from the Occupy movement is that people can be moti- 10 vated to engage politically when they connect their own personal frustrations with a bigger picture of structural inequity. Rather than put "girls and women" in one corner—as deserving subjects who can be put to work for development— and leave "boys and men" to be picked up only when they turn bad, we need a fresh approach. Specifically, we need new ways of connecting the trouble that the inequitable distribution of power and privilege creates for us as individuals with a broader struggle for social justice.

Girls themselves are making these connections. In a couple of weeks' time, the women's fund Mama Cash is sponsoring an exchange between high school girl students from Chile and Nicaragua. What's on their agenda? Not Girl Power, but tackling gender stereotypes in the curriculum and advocating for better sexuality education for young people. Mama Cash program officer Alejandra Sarda reflected: "They don't have this separation between genders. You just don't see it. They have problems that need to be addressed. But they also see that boys have to be part of the conversation. We can learn a lot from how they're organizing."

QUESTIONS FOR DISCUSSION AND WRITING

1. Cornwall begins her essay with the statement, "Girls are cool" (paragraph 1). What does she mean by this? Cite examples in the media and pop culture that reinforce such a statement. For example, look at television commercials, particularly ones directed toward a female audience. How are girls and women typically portrayed? How are men portrayed? What do such cultural messages tell the audience about the abilities and tendencies of women? Of men?

2. Cornwall's discussion about gender is also occurring in the context of "international development" (paragraph 2). Where do agencies of international development operate? How is gender a factor in aid development? How are gender relations in developing nations different from those in developed nations? Be specific in your response. You may need to do some research on your own.

3. Cornwall also talks about "male privilege" (paragraph 5) and how that, too, can be a burden. In what ways might male privilege be a burden? Be specific. Compare male privilege in the developed world to male privilege in the developing world. What are the differences? Be specific.

4. In paragraph 6, Cornwall calls for an education to "sustain new, more egalitarian, norms. . . ." What does she mean by this? Note that she follows this call with a quote from Frank Karioris stating that male educational achievement is falling, which is expected to lead to less male involvement in promoting equality. Why? Do you agree with that assessment? Why or why not? Again, be specific.

5. Cornwall cites the Occupy movement as helping people to see that their individual life circumstances are indeed connected to "bigger picture" (paragraph 10) issues of inequity. Cite specific examples of this that you have seen in your own life or in the lives of those around you. Discuss how those individual circumstances relate to specific larger issues.

EDUARDO PORTER

The New Mating Market

A columnist for the New York Times, *Eduardo Porter writes about business and economics. He started his career in Mexico, writing about finance for* Notimex, *a Mexican news agency. He also worked in Brazil before coming to the United States and writing for the* Wall Street Journal. *He has been with the* New York Times *since 2004 and used to sit on the* Times *Editorial Board. Perhaps unusual for a writer of finance and economics, Porter has a bachelor's degree in physics, and a master of science (M.Sc.) degree in quantum fields and fundamental forces. His book,* The Price of Everything *(2011), shows how price affects many of our everyday behaviors, such as how we to choose to buy a cup of coffee or have a baby.*

In this excerpt from The Price of Everything, *Porter examines how and why Americans are still choosing to have so many children. He begins by examining traditional explanations, such as the call of religion and having children as insurance for one's old age. However, a greater motivation can be found, he argues, in that the United States makes it easier for women to both work and have children at the same time. Social changes have loosened the prohibition against women having children out of wedlock, but also, changing gender models—in which men are more willing to help out with household tasks and childrearing—have played a huge role. The result is that the American birth rate continues to outstrip birth rates in countries that are more economically advanced but socially traditional, which force women to make a choice between career and children. In America, women can have both.*

One of the world's demographic mysteries is why, considering the current changes in the structure of the family, Americans still have so many kids.

Religion is one possibility. It is more popular in the United States than in pretty much every other wealthy nation. I heard a story on the radio about a small evangelical movement called the Quiverfull, a name based on Psalm 127 in the Bible, which says, "Like arrows in the hands of a warrior are sons born in one's youth. Blessed is the man whose quiver is full of them." The group frowns on contraception. Apparently, its members believe that if they have enough children, they will be able to take over the Congress in a few generations. "The womb is such a powerful weapon," suggested one of their leaders. "It's a weapon against the enemy."

The reason for America's prolificacy could also be that pensions in the United States are particularly stingy, making kids more useful as old-age insurance. A typical worker in the United States receives as little as 40 percent of his or her last wages from Social Security. European pensions are more generous. In Italy, fertility started rising slowly in 1996 after plummeting for ages. Perhaps not coincidentally, that was the year in which pension reform kicked in, reducing the payments promised to younger workers from 80 percent of their last wage to only 65 percent. Indeed, economists found that the odds of having a kid rose 10 percent for those workers who had their pensions cut, relative to those who hadn't.

But the most convincing explanation seems to be that the United States has been better at accommodating work and childbearing than other nations. In the United States and some other countries, such as Sweden and Denmark, men have taken over some household tasks, lowering the cost of childbearing for women, allowing them to juggle kids and work outside the home. Some analysts also suggest that the weakening of the marriage bond has had a comparatively mild impact on American fertility because American women chose to have kids on their own. Countries like Italy or Spain, where traditional sexual roles are more entrenched, have had a tougher time overcoming beliefs that tie childbearing to marriage and a more traditional division of labor. Where mothers are expected to rear the young single-handedly, women face a starker choice: either employment or reproduction. As job opportunities have appeared, many have opted to work, dropping out of the mothering business altogether.

The fact that the archetypal marital transaction has been rendered obsolete 5 does not mean modern marriage has nothing to offer. Marriage can yield substantial savings on everything from rent to magazine subscriptions. One study comparing the expenditures of single and married men and women in Canada found that singles living by themselves can spend substantially more than half of what a couple spends to achieve the same standard of living.

Marriage is also a form of insurance. Families with two sources of income are more financially secure than one and are thus more willing to take financial risks. A study of Italian women found that single women invest less in risky assets than married women, suggesting they feel more financially vulnerable. Other researchers found that the legalization of divorce in Ireland in 1996 led to higher savings rates among couples, as they hedged against the higher probability of breaking up and bolstered their finances. Married couples became 10 to 13 percent less likely to be in debt. And savings grew fastest among those who weren't religious and thus were more likely to divorce.

Marriage in the United States is a more symmetrical institution than it has ever been: Both parents work; both care for the children. Today, in 57 percent of married couples, both spouses earn money. In a quarter of these the wife makes more than the husband, up from 16 percent two decades ago. Partners are more similar, in age, education, and earnings prospects. Rather than a kid factory, it is now more like a club, where husbands and wives pool the resources they earn from work to buy leisure and other goods—like child care—from the market.

The classic Hollywood formula where the rich executive married his secretary after discovering she was a pretty young woman once she took off her glasses no longer has any purchase on reality. Today, Americans are about four times as likely to marry someone with the same level of education as they are to marry someone who is more or less educated. And if one spouse in a marriage has more education than the other, it is likely to be the wife. As husbands and wives have become less dependent on each other to produce what the family unit needs, marriage, once meant to last until death, has become a more diverse arrangement than it ever was.

The changes have taken a toll. Marriage has become unstable among poorer, less educated Americans. They marry and have children at a younger age, but divorce relatively soon, cohabit, and remarry. Among the least educated—people with no high school degree—marriage has become a rarity, and single mothers abound.

College graduates, by contrast, are marrying more. In the 1960 census 29 per- 10 cent of women in their sixties with a college degree said they had never been married. By the 2000 census the share of never-married women in their sixties with a college degree was 8 percent. The better educated are marrying later, in their thirties and forties rather than their twenties, but they are much more likely to stay married. Twenty-three percent of white women with a college education who married in 1970 divorced within ten years. By 1990 the share had fallen to 16 percent.

These different experiences of marriage have a clear economic rationale. For the poor and less educated, marriage retained the old rationale of the shared production unit—where women and men trade complementary skills in the workplace and at home. Husbands make money in the workforce and trade it with their wives for child care and domestic labor. Marriage couldn't adapt to the fact that women now often had more stable jobs than men.

For the more educated, the transformation was easier to take in stride. They could allow marriage to be transformed into a partnership built not around production but around consumption. For those who could more easily buy goods, services, and leisure, marriage became more about sharing the fun. Yet the experiences of women like Cathy Watson-Short, the former Silicon Valley executive, suggest that even highly educated American families are still learning to cope with some of the changes. The tension between the workplace and the home seems to be prompting some to reconsider working. The share of prime-aged women in the workforce peaked almost ten years ago, at 77 percent, and has declined modestly since then. The participation rate of married mothers with kids of preschool age in the job market dropped some 4 percentage points from its peak in 1998 to 60 percent in 2005. A 1997 survey by the Pew Research Center found that a third of working mothers said they would ideally work full time. By 2007 the share had declined to about a fifth.

Until the financial crisis of 2008, which put many families under increasing financial strain, fertility rates had been edging up for the first time in many years. Many of the young women who had delayed marriage and childbirth fifteen years earlier to start a professional career had become older professionals considering children for the first time. In the late 1970s only about 10 percent of forty-year-old women reported having a young child at home. By the early years of this century, the share had jumped to 30 percent. Some economists suggested this burst of late childbearing could put a lid on the labor supply of women.

It seems unlikely, however, that this pause means that women have rejected their new identity forged in the workplace. After nearly a century of women marching into work, I don't see any signs suggesting a wholesale retreat back into the home.

QUESTIONS FOR DISCUSSION AND WRITING

1. Porter begins this excerpt with a note of surprise that Americans are having as many children as they do. What is behind his surprise? He mentions the "changes in the structure of the family" (paragraph 1). What changes is he referring to, and why would conventional wisdom lead to the conclusion that there would be fewer children?

2. In discussing religion as a motivation for having children, Porter cites a small movement called "the Quiverfull" (paragraph 2). Think about various larger religious groups in the United States. What are their attitudes toward children? How do large religious groups view issues such as marriage, sex, contraception, abortion, and so on? How prominent are such attitudes across the general population, and how do they affect how many children are born?

3. Social changes have made what Porter calls the "archetypal marital transaction" obsolete (paragraph 5). What does Porter mean by a marital transaction? What are some of the economic benefits of marriage? How does the possibility of divorce affect the economics of marriage? Cite specific examples that you see in your own life or the lives of people you know.

4. At the core of Porter's argument is the idea that the United States makes it easier for women to both work and bear children. He compares that to patterns in more traditional, yet developed nations, such as Spain and Italy, where the rate of childbearing has declined. What specific policies or actions exist in the United States to help working women have children? What social mores or expectations exist that do the same?

5. Porter draws another connection—with income: The higher the income, the more stable the marriage. Instead of struggling to make ends meet, married couples can share "the fun" (paragraph 12). He even notes that in the prosperous time before the Great Recession hit in 2008, fertility rates were increasing. Explain this connection between money and children. How does this also connect to the fact that more women are waiting until they are older to start having children?

BARBARA EHRENREICH

Bonfire of the Disney Princesses

The daughter of a miner from Butte, Montana, Barbara Ehrenreich (b. 1941) has enjoyed considerable success as a writer, particularly one interested in social activism. She describes her own writing career as having three tracks: her essays and opinion pieces; her books; and her activism for the causes of health care, peace, women's rights, and economic justice. Many know Ehrenreich for her book Nickel and Dimed *(2001), in which she purposely went undercover, seeking work as a low-skilled worker (hiding her doctoral education and work background). She worked variously as a waitress, housekeeper, and hotel maid, as well as in other low-wage occupations. What she uncovered is how difficult the work life is for America's working class in today's economy, and how difficult and exhausting such work is. The book became a bestseller and started many conversations about the value of work and human dignity. Among her other books is* Bait and Switch *(2005), in which she examines the lives of unemployed white collar workers and how they, even those individuals who have done "everything right," are vulnerable to downward, not upward, mobility.*

In this article, originally posted on the Huffpost Healthy Living Web site, Ehrenreich takes on that most archetypal of feminine images: the Disney Princess. Snow White, Cinderella, Ariel, and others have lived in the imaginations of children, in some cases for generations. But Ehrenreich asks the question, What messages are these heroines sending to young girls? She explores the sexualization of the character and, by extension, of young girls. And, Ehrenreich goes beyond the message that the Princess is all about finding the Prince: She connects the sexualization of girls to the far more serious issue of sexual abuse of children by adults. Ehrenreich argues that sexual discovery is an important part of growing up, but that it should be done by the children themselves, not molded by adult interference. She concludes with a call to action that is only partly tongue-in-cheek: Rise up and reject the Disney sexualization of young girls.

Contrary to the rumors I have been trying to spread for some time, Disney Princess products are not contaminated with lead. More careful analysis shows that the entire product line—books, DVDs, ball gowns, necklaces, toy cell phones, toothbrush holders, T-shirts, lunch boxes, backpacks, wallpaper, sheets, stickers, etc.— is saturated with a particularly potent time-release form of the date rape drug.

We cannot blame China this time, because the drug is in the concept, which was spawned in the Disney studios. Before 2000, the Princesses were just the separate, disunited, heroines of Disney animated films—Snow White, Cinderella, Ariel, Aurora, Pocahontas, Jasmine, Belle, and Mulan. Then Disney's Andy Mooney got the idea of bringing the gals together in a team. With a wave of the wand ($10.99 at Target, tiara included) they were all elevated to royal status and set loose on the world as an imperial cabal, and have since have busied themselves achieving global domination. Today, there is no little girl in the wired, industrial world who does not seek to display her allegiance to the pink-and-purple clad Disney dynasty.

Disney likes to think of the Princesses as role models, but what a sorry bunch of wusses they are. Typically, they spend much of their time in captivity or a coma, waking up only when a Prince comes along and kisses them. The most striking exception is Mulan, who dresses as a boy to fight in the army, but—like the other Princess of color, Pocahontas—she lacks full Princess status and does not warrant a line of tiaras and gowns. Otherwise the Princesses have no ambitions and no marketable skills, although both Snow White and Cinderella are good at housecleaning.

And what could they aspire to, beyond landing a Prince? In Princessland, the only career ladder leads from baby-faced adolescence to a position as an evil enchantress, stepmother, or witch. Snow White's wicked stepmother is consumed with envy for her stepdaughter's beauty; the sea witch Ursula covets Ariel's lovely voice; Cinderella's stepmother exploits the girl's cheap, uncomplaining, labor. No need for complicated witch-hunting techniques—pin-prickings and dunkings—in Princessland. All you have to look for is wrinkles.

Feminist parents gnash their teeth. For this their little girls gave up Dora, who 5 bounds through the jungle saving baby jaguars, whose mother is an archaeologist, and whose adventures don't involve smoochy rescues by Diego? There was drama in Dora's life too, and the occasional bad actor like Swiper the fox. Even Barbie looks like a suffragette compared to Disney's Belle. So what's the appeal of the pink tulle Princess cult?

Seen from the witchy end of the female life cycle, the Princesses exert their pull through a dark and undeniable eroticism. They're sexy little wenches, for one thing. Snow White has gotten slimmer and bustier over the years; Ariel wears nothing but a bikini top (though, admittedly, she is half fish.) In faithful imitation, the three-year-old in my life flounces around with her tiara askew and her Princess gown sliding off her shoulder, looking for all the world like a London socialite after a hard night of cocaine and booze. Then she demands a poison apple and falls to the floor in a beautiful swoon. Pass the Rohypnol-laced margarita, please.

It may be old-fashioned to say so, but sex—and especially some middle-aged man's twisted version thereof—doesn't belong in the pre-K playroom. Children are going to discover it soon enough, but they've got to do so on their own.

There's a reason, after all, why we're generally more disgusted by sexual abusers than adults who inflict mere violence on children: We sense that sexual abuse more deeply messes with a child's mind. One's sexual inclinations—straightforward or kinky, active or passive, heterosexual or homosexual—should be free to develop without adult intervention or manipulation. Hence our harshness toward the kind of sexual predators who leer at kids and offer candy. But Disney, which also owns ABC, Lifetime, ESPN, A&E, and Miramax, is rewarded with $4 billion a year for marketing the masochistic Princess cult and its endlessly proliferating paraphernalia.

Let's face it, no parent can stand up against this alone. Try to ban the Princesses from your home, and you might as well turn yourself in to Child Protective Services before the little girls get on their Princess cell phones. No, the only way to topple royalty is through a mass uprising of the long-suffering serfs. Assemble with your neighbors and make a holiday bonfire out of all that plastic and tulle! March on Disney World with pitchforks held high!

QUESTIONS FOR DISCUSSION AND WRITING

1. Ehrenreich begins her essay by humorously comparing Disney Princess products to lead poisoning. However, she moves from that metaphor to a more shocking and powerful one: comparing the products to a "time-release form

of the date rape drug" (paragraph 1). Why does she make this comparison? How is it connected to the issues she addresses later in the essay? Is her comparison overly dramatic? Why or why not?

2. Ehrenreich says that Disney would have young girls consider the princesses as role models, but she herself calls them "a sorry bunch of wusses" (paragraph 3). Why? What characteristics of the typical Disney heroine seem to offend Ehrenreich? What do the princesses typically lack?

3. What role do men play in the lives of the typical Disney heroine? What does that say about the nature of men, particularly in relation to women? In your opinion, is this sending helpful or destructive messages to young girls (and boys) about mature relationships? Defend your answer.

4. Another aspect of the Disney heroine is conflict with older women (Cinderella's evil stepmother, Snow White's evil stepmother, Ariel's nemesis Ursula, and so on). Implied is the idea that the only difference between the heroine and her enemy is age—meaning that once the wrinkles begin to set in, the heroine becomes the enemy. Why? What does this say about the competition women are in—for beauty, for the Prince, for love and acceptance? Is Disney supporting ageism, the idea that younger is better and older people (especially older women) are of little value? To defend your answer, cite other examples not in Ehrenreich's essay.

5. Ehrenreich argues that the public is "more disgusted by sexual abusers than adults who inflict mere violence on children" (paragraph 8). How is sexual abuse connected to her discussion of the Disney heroine? What aspects of the Disney characters—appearances and behaviors—sexualize characters meant for consumption by young children? The implied comparison suggests that Disney is like a sexual predator, only one that is rewarded, not imprisoned, for its actions. Do you agree or disagree? Is Disney a culprit in the sexualization of young children? Defend your answer with specific details.

HANNA ROSIN

A Boy's Life

Hanna Rosin (b. 1970) has written for a wide variety of publications, including the online magazine Slate, *for which she is a cofounder and editor of* DoubleX, *the women's section, as well as traditional magazines and newspapers like the* Atlantic, *the* New Yorker, GQ, *and the* Washington Post. *She wrote* The End of Men: And the Rise of Women *(2012), in which she argues that the dominance of men over women is coming to an end as women have pulled ahead of men in many, if not all, measurements of achievement. Rosin was born in Israel, raised in Queens, and educated at Stanford University. This article, "A Boy's Life," earned her a nomination for the National Magazine Award in 2009.*

In this article, Rosin examines the lives of transgender children and their parents. Transgender children are convinced that their real gender is not their physical gender; as one boy said, "God made a mistake" by not making him a girl. Rosin examines the real-life problems parents of such children face, and the dilemma over what to do about their child's gender identification issues. Some argue to simply accept the fact that a boy wants to be a girl, or vice versa. Others, however, caution against such acceptance, arguing that these children are too young to make lifelong decisions about their gender identification. Spurring the controversy forward is the development of blockers—hormone injections, that, if given before puberty, prevent boys from developing more masculine features or girls from developing their feminine features. However, because puberty sets in at such a young age, this important decision may have to be made too early.

The local newspaper recorded that Brandon Simms was the first millennium baby born in his tiny southern town, at 12:50 a.m. He weighed eight pounds, two ounces and, as his mother, Tina, later wrote to him in his baby book, "had a darlin' little face that told me right away you were innocent." Tina saved the white knit hat with the powder-blue ribbon that hospitals routinely give to new baby boys. But after that, the milestones took an unusual turn. As a toddler, Brandon would scour the house for something to drape over his head—a towel, a doily, a moons-and-stars bandanna he'd snatch from his mother's drawer. "I figure he wanted something that felt like hair," his mother later guessed. He spoke his first full sentence at a local Italian restaurant: "I like your high heels," he told a woman in a fancy red dress. At home, he would rip off his clothes as soon as Tina put them on him, and instead try on something from her closet—a purple undershirt, lingerie, shoes. "He ruined all my heels in the sandbox," she recalls.

At the toy store, Brandon would head straight for the aisles with the Barbies or the pink and purple dollhouses. Tina wouldn't buy them, instead steering him to neutral toys: puzzles or building blocks or cool neon markers. One weekend, when Brandon was 2½, she took him to visit her ten-year-old cousin. When Brandon took to one of the many dolls in her huge collection—a blonde Barbie in a pink sparkly dress—Tina let him bring it home. He carried it everywhere, "even slept with it, like a teddy bear."

For his third Christmas, Tina bought Brandon a first-rate Army set—complete with a Kevlar hat, walkie-talkies, and a hand grenade. Both Tina and Brandon's father had served in the Army, and she thought their son might identify with the toys. A photo from that day shows him wearing a towel around his head, a bandanna around his waist, and a glum expression. The Army set sits unopened at his feet. Tina recalls his joy, by contrast, on a day later that year. One afternoon, while Tina was on the phone, Brandon climbed out of the bathtub. When she found him, he was dancing in front of the mirror with his penis tucked between his legs. "Look, Mom, I'm a girl," he told her. "Happy as can be," she recalls.

"Brandon, God made you a boy for a special reason," she told him before they said prayers one night when he was five, the first part of a speech she'd prepared. But he cut her off: "God made a mistake," he said.

Tina had no easy explanation for where Brandon's behavior came from. Gen- 5
der roles are not very fluid in their no-stoplight town, where Confederate flags line
the main street. Boys ride dirt bikes through the woods starting at age five; local
county fairs feature muscle cars for boys and beauty pageants for girls of all ages.
In the Army, Tina operated heavy machinery, but she is no tomboy. When she was
younger, she wore long flowing dresses to match her long, wavy blond hair; now
she wears it in a cute, Renée Zellweger–style bob. Her husband, Bill (Brandon's
stepfather), lays wood floors and builds houses for a living. At a recent meeting
with Brandon's school principal about how to handle the boy, Bill aptly summed up
the town philosophy: "The way I was brought up, a boy's a boy and a girl's a girl."

School had always complicated Brandon's life. When teachers divided the
class into boys' and girls' teams, Brandon would stand with the girls. In all of his
kindergarten and first-grade self-portraits—"I have a pet," "I love my cat," "I love
to play outside"—the "I" was a girl, often with big red lips, high heels, and a princess dress. Just as often, he drew himself as a mermaid with a sparkly purple tail, or
a tail cut out from black velvet. Late in second grade, his older stepbrother, Travis,
told his fourth-grade friends about Brandon's "secret"—that he dressed up at home
and wanted to be a girl. After school, the boys cornered and bullied him. Brandon
went home crying and begged Tina to let him skip the last week.

Since he was four, Tina had been taking Brandon to a succession of therapists.
The first told her he was just going through a phase; but the phase never passed.
Another suggested that Brandon's chaotic early childhood might have contributed to his behavior. Tina had never married Brandon's father, whom she'd met
when they were both stationed in Germany. Twice, she had briefly stayed with
him, when Brandon was five months old and then when he was three. Both times,
she'd suspected his father of being too rough with the boy and had broken off the
relationship. The therapist suggested that perhaps Brandon overidentified with his
mother as the protector in the family, and for a while, this theory seemed plausible
to Tina. In play therapy, the therapist tried to get Brandon to discuss his feelings
about his father. She advised Tina to try a reward system at home. Brandon could
earn up to $21 a week for doing three things: looking in the mirror and saying
"I'm a boy"; not dressing up; and not wearing anything on his head. It worked for
a couple of weeks, but then Brandon lost interest.

Tina recounted much of this history to me in June at her kitchen table,
where Brandon, now eight, had just laid out some lemon pound cake he'd baked
from a mix. She, Bill, Brandon, his half sister, Madison, and Travis live in a
comfortable double-wide trailer that Bill set up himself on their half acre of
woods. I'd met Tina a month earlier, and she'd agreed to let me follow Brandon's
development over what turned out to be a critical few months of his life, on
the condition that I change their names and disguise where they live. While we
were at the table talking, Brandon was conducting a kind of nervous fashion
show; over the course of several hours, he came in and out of his room wearing eight or nine different outfits, constructed from his costume collection, his
mom's shoes and scarves, and his little sister's bodysuits and tights. Brandon is
a gymnast and likes to show off splits and back bends. On the whole, he is quiet

and a little somber, but every once in a while—after a great split, say—he shares a shy, crooked smile.

About a year and a half ago, Tina's mom showed her a Barbara Walters *20/20* special she'd taped. The show featured a six-year-old boy named "Jazz" who, since he was a toddler, had liked to dress as a girl. Everything about Jazz was familiar to Tina: the obsession with girls' clothes, the Barbies, wishing his penis away, even the fixation on mermaids. At the age of three, Jazz had been diagnosed with "gender-identity disorder" and was considered "transgender," Walters explained. The show mentioned a "hormone imbalance," but his parents had concluded that there was basically nothing wrong with him. He "didn't ask to be born this way," his mother explained. By kindergarten, his parents were letting him go to school with shoulder-length hair and a pink skirt on.

Tina had never heard the word *transgender*; she'd figured no other little boy   10
on Earth was like Brandon. The show prompted her to buy a computer and Google "transgender children." Eventually, she made her way to a subculture of parents who live all across the country; they write in to listservs with grammar ranging from sixth-grade-level to professorial, but all have family stories much like hers. In May, she and Bill finally met some of them at the Trans-Health Conference in Philadelphia, the larger of two annual gatherings in the United States that many parents attend. Four years ago, only a handful of kids had come to the conference. This year, about fifty showed up, along with their siblings—enough to require a staff dedicated to full-time children's entertainment, including Jack the Balloon Man, Sue's Sand Art, a pool-and-pizza party, and a treasure hunt.

Diagnoses of gender-identity disorder among adults have tripled in Western countries since the 1960s; for men, the estimates now range from 1 in 7,400 to 1 in 42,000 (for women, the frequency of diagnosis is lower). Since 1952, when Army veteran George Jorgensen's sex-change operation hit the front page of the New York *Daily News*, national resistance has softened a bit, too. Former NASCAR driver J. T. Hayes recently talked to *Newsweek* about having had a sex-change operation. Women's colleges have had to adjust to the presence of "trans-men," and the president-elect of the Gay and Lesbian Medical Association is a trans-woman and a successful cardiologist. But nothing can do more to normalize the face of transgender America than the sight of a seven-year-old (boy or girl?) with pink cheeks and a red balloon puppy in hand saying to Brandon, as one did at the conference:

"Are you transgender?"

"What's that?" Brandon asked.

"A boy who wants to be a girl."

"Yeah. Can I see your balloon?"

Around the world, clinics that specialize in gender-identity disorder in children report an explosion in referrals over the past few years. Dr. Kenneth Zucker, who runs the most comprehensive gender-identity clinic for youth in Toronto, has seen his waiting list quadruple in the past four years, to about eighty kids—an increase he attributes to media coverage and the proliferation of new sites on the

Internet. Dr. Peggy Cohen-Kettenis, who runs the main clinic in the Netherlands, has seen the average age of her patients plummet since 2002. "We used to get calls mostly from parents who were concerned about their children being gay," says Catherine Tuerk, who since 1998 has run a support network for parents of children with gender-variant behavior, out of Children's National Medical Center in Washington, D.C. "Now about 90 percent of our calls are from parents with some concern that their child may be transgender."

In breakout sessions at the conference, transgender men and women in their fifties and sixties described lives of heartache and rejection: years of hiding makeup under the mattress, estranged parents, suicide attempts. Those in their twenties and thirties conveyed a dedicated militancy: They wore nose rings and Mohawks, ate strictly vegan, and conducted heated debates about the definitions of *queer* and *he-she* and *drag queen*. But the kids treated the conference like a family trip to Disneyland. They ran around with parents chasing after them, fussing over twisted bathing-suit straps or wiping crumbs from their lips. They looked effortlessly androgynous, and years away from sex, politics, or any form of rebellion. For Tina, the sight of them suggested a future she'd never considered for Brandon: a normal life as a girl. "She could end up being a *mommy* if she wants, just like me," one adoring mother leaned over and whispered about her 5-year-old (natal) son.

It took the gay rights movement thirty years to shift from the Stonewall riots to gay marriage; now its transgender wing, long considered the most subversive, is striving for suburban normalcy too. The change is fueled mostly by a community of parents who, like many parents of this generation, are open to letting even preschool children define their own needs. Faced with skeptical neighbors and school officials, parents at the conference discussed how to use the kind of quasi-therapeutic language that, these days, inspires deference: Tell the school the child has a "medical condition" or a "hormonal imbalance" that can be treated later, suggested a conference speaker, Kim Pearson; using terms like *gender-identity disorder* or *birth defect* would be going too far, she advised. The point was to take the situation out of the realm of deep pathology or mental illness, while at the same time separating it from voluntary behavior, and to put it into the idiom of garden-variety "challenge." As one father told me, "Between all the kids with language problems and learning disabilities and peanut allergies, the school doesn't know who to worry about first."

A recent medical innovation holds out the promise that this might be the first 15 generation of transsexuals who can live inconspicuously. About three years ago, physicians in the United States started treating transgender children with puberty blockers, drugs originally intended to halt precocious puberty. The blockers put teens in a state of suspended development. They prevent boys from growing facial and body hair and an Adam's apple, or developing a deep voice or any of the other physical characteristics that a male-to-female transsexual would later spend tens of thousands of dollars to reverse. They allow girls to grow taller, and prevent them from getting breasts or a period.

At the conference, blockers were the hot topic. One mother who'd found out about them too late cried, "The guilt I feel is overwhelming." The preteens sized each other up for signs of the magic drug, the way other teens might look for hip, expensive jeans: a 16-year-old (natal) girl, shirtless, with no sign of breasts; a 17-year-old (natal) boy with a face as smooth as Brandon's. "Is there anybody out there," asked Dr. Nick Gorton, a physician and trans-man from California, addressing a room full of older transsexuals, "who would not have taken the shot if it had been offered?" No one raised a hand.

After a day of sessions, Tina's mind was moving fast. "These kids look happier," she told me. "This is nothing we can fix. In his brain, in his *mind*, Brandon's a girl." With Bill, she started to test out the new language. "What's it they say? It's nothing wrong. It's just a medical condition, like diabetes or something. Just a variation on human behavior." She made an unlikely friend, a lesbian mom from Seattle named Jill who took Tina under her wing. Jill had a five-year-old girl living as a boy and a future already mapped out. "He'll just basically be living life," Jill explained about her (natal) daughter. "I already legally changed his name and called all the parents at the school. Then, when he's in eighth grade, we'll take him to the [endocrinologist] and get the blockers, and no one will ever know. He'll just sail right through."

"I live in a small town," Tina pleaded with Jill. "This is all just really *new*. I never even heard the word *transgender* until recently, and the shrinks just kept telling me this is fixable."

In my few months of meeting transgender children, I talked to parents from many different backgrounds, who had made very different decisions about how to handle their children. Many accepted the "new normalcy" line, and some did not. But they all had one thing in common: In such a loaded situation, with their children's future at stake, doubt about their choices did not serve them well. In Brandon's case, for example, doubt would force Tina to consider that if she began letting him dress as a girl, she would be defying the conventions of her small town, and the majority of psychiatric experts, who advise strongly against the practice. It would force her to consider that she would have to begin making serious medical decisions for Brandon in only a couple of years, and that even with the blockers, he would face a lifetime of hormone injections and possibly major surgery. At the conference, Tina struggled with these doubts. But her new friends had already moved past them.

"Yeah, it is fixable," piped up another mom, who'd been on the *20/20* special. 20 "We call it the disorder we cured with a skirt."

In 1967, Dr. John Money launched an experiment that he thought might confirm some of the more radical ideas emerging in feminist thought. Throughout the '60s, writers such as Betty Friedan were challenging the notion that women should be limited to their prescribed roles as wives, housekeepers, and mothers. But other feminists pushed further, arguing that the whole notion of gender was a social construction, and easy to manipulate. In a 1955 paper, Money had written: "Sexual behavior and orientation as male or female does not have an innate, instinctive basis." We learn whether we are male or female "in the course of the various experiences of growing up." By the sixties, he was well known for having established the first American clinic to perform voluntary sex-change operations, at the Johns Hopkins Hospital, in Baltimore. One day, he got a letter from the parents of infant twin boys, one of whom had suffered a botched circumcision that had burned off most of his penis.

Money saw the case as a perfect test for his theory. He encouraged the parents to have the boy, David Reimer, fully castrated and then to raise him as a girl. When the child reached puberty, Money told them, doctors could construct a vagina and give him feminizing hormones. Above all, he told them, they must not waver in their decision and must not tell the boy about the accident.

In paper after paper, Money reported on Reimer's fabulous progress, writing that "she" showed an avid interest in dolls and dollhouses, that she preferred dresses, hair ribbons, and frilly blouses. Money's description of the child in his book *Sexual Signatures* prompted one reviewer to describe her as "sailing contentedly through childhood as a genuine girl." *Time* magazine concluded that the Reimer case cast doubt on the belief that sex differences are "immutably set by the genes at conception."

The reality was quite different, as *Rolling Stone* reporter John Colapinto brilliantly documented in the 2000 best-seller *As Nature Made Him*. Reimer had never adjusted to being a girl at all. He wanted only to build forts and play with his brother's dump trucks, and insisted that he should pee standing up. He was a social disaster at school, beating up other kids and misbehaving in class. At fourteen, Reimer became so alienated and depressed that his parents finally told him the truth about his birth, at which point he felt mostly relief, he reported. He eventually underwent phalloplasty, and he married a woman. Then four years ago, at age thirty-eight, Reimer shot himself dead in a grocery-store parking lot.

Today, the notion that gender is purely a social construction seems nearly as 25 outmoded as bra-burning or free love. Feminist theory is pivoting with the rest of the culture, and is locating the key to identity in genetics and the workings of the brain. In the new conventional wisdom, we are all pre-wired for many things previously thought to be in the realm of upbringing, choice, or subjective experience: happiness, religious awakening, cheating, a love of chocolate. Behaviors are fundamental unless we are chemically altered. Louann Brizendine, in her 2006 best-selling book, *The Female Brain*, claims that everything from empathy to chattiness to poor spatial reasoning is "hardwired into the brains of women." Dr. Milton Diamond, an expert on human sexuality at the University of Hawaii and long the intellectual nemesis of Money, encapsulated this view in an interview on the BBC in 1980, when it was becoming clear that Money's experiment was failing: "Maybe we really have to think . . . that we don't come to this world neutral; that we come to this world with some degree of maleness and femaleness which will transcend whatever the society wants to put into [us]."

Diamond now spends his time collecting case studies of transsexuals who have a twin, to see how often both twins have transitioned to the opposite sex. To him, these cases are a "confirmation" that "the biggest sex organ is not between the legs but between the ears." For many gender biologists like Diamond, transgender children now serve the same allegorical purpose that David Reimer once did, but they support the opposite conclusion: they are seen as living proof that "gender identity is influenced by some innate or immutable factors," writes Melissa Hines, the author of *Brain Gender*.

This is the strange place in which transsexuals have found themselves. For years, they've been at the extreme edges of transgressive sexual politics. But now children like Brandon are being used to paint a more conventional picture: Before they have much time to be shaped by experience, before they know their sexual orientation, even in defiance of their bodies, children can know their gender, from the firings of neurons deep within their brains. What better rebuke to the *Our Bodies, Ourselves* era of feminism than the notion that even the body is dispensable, that the hard nugget of difference lies even deeper?

In most major institutes for gender-identity disorder in children worldwide, a psychologist is the central figure. In the United States, the person intending to found "the first major academic research center," as he calls it, is Dr. Norman Spack, an endocrinologist who teaches at Harvard Medical School and is committed to a hormonal fix. Spack works out of a cramped office at Children's Hospital in Boston, where the walls are covered with diplomas and notes of gratitude scrawled in crayons or bright markers ("Thanks, Dr. Spack!!!"). Spack is bald, with a trim beard, and often wears his Harvard tie under his lab coat. He is not confrontational by nature, but he can hold his own with his critics: "To those who say I am interrupting God's work, I point to Leviticus, which says, 'Thou shalt not stand idly by the blood of your neighbor'"—an injunction, as he sees it, to prevent needless suffering.

Spack has treated young-adult transsexuals since the 1980s, and until recently he could never get past one problem: "They are never going to fail to draw attention to themselves." Over the years, he'd seen patients rejected by families, friends, and employers after a sex-change operation. Four years ago, he heard about the innovative use of hormone blockers on transgender youths in the Netherlands; to him, the drugs seemed like the missing piece of the puzzle.

The problem with blockers is that parents have to begin making medical 30 decisions for their children when the children are quite young. From the earliest signs of puberty, doctors have about eighteen months to start the blockers for ideal results. For girls, that's usually between ages ten and twelve; for boys, between twelve and fourteen. If the patients follow through with cross-sex hormones and sex-change surgery, they will be permanently sterile, something Spack always discusses with them. "When you're talking to a twelve-year-old, that's a heavy-duty conversation," he said in a recent interview. "Does a kid that age really think about fertility? But if you don't start treatment, they will always have trouble fitting in."

When Beth was eleven, she told her mother, Susanna, that she'd "rather be dead" than go to school anymore as a girl. (The names of all the children and parents used as case studies in this story are pseudonyms.) For a long time, she had refused to shower except in a bathing suit, and had skipped out of health class every Thursday, when the standard puberty videos were shown. In March 2006, when Beth, now Matt, was 12, they went to see Spack. He told Matt that if he went down this road, he would never biologically have children.

"I'll adopt!" Matt said.

"What is most important to him is that he's comfortable in who he is," says Susanna. They left with a prescription—a "godsend," she calls it.

Now, at fifteen and on testosterone, Matt is tall, with a broad chest and hairy legs. Susanna figures he's the first trans-man in America to go shirtless without having had any chest surgery. His mother describes him as "happy" and "totally at home in his masculine body." Matt has a girlfriend; he met her at the amusement park where Susanna works. Susanna is pretty sure he's said something to the girl about his situation, but knows he hasn't talked to her parents.

Susanna imagines few limitations in Matt's future. Only a minority of trans- 35 men get what they call "bottom" surgery, because phalloplasty is still more cosmetic than functional, and the procedure is risky. But otherwise? Married? "Oh, yeah. And his career prospects will be good because he gets very good grades. We envision a kind of family life, maybe in the suburbs, with a good job." They have "no fears" about the future, and "zero doubts" about the path they've chosen.

Blockers are entirely reversible; should a child change his or her mind about becoming the other gender, a doctor can stop the drugs and normal puberty will begin. The Dutch clinic has given them to about seventy children since it started the treatment, in 2000; clinics in the United States and Canada have given them to dozens more. According to Dr. Peggy Cohen-Kettenis, the psychologist who heads the Dutch clinic, no case of a child stopping the blockers and changing course has yet been reported.

This suggests one of two things: Either the screening is excellent, or once a child begins, he or she is set firmly on the path to medical intervention. "Adolescents may consider this step a guarantee of sex reassignment," wrote Cohen-Kettenis, "and it could make them therefore less rather than more inclined to engage in introspection." In the Netherlands, clinicians try to guard against this with an extensive diagnostic protocol, including testing and many sessions "to confirm that the desire for treatment is very persistent," before starting the blockers.

Spack's clinic isn't so comprehensive. A part-time psychologist, Dr. Laura Edwards-Leeper, conducts four-hour family screenings by appointment. (When I visited during the summer, she was doing only one or two a month.) But often she has to field emergency cases directly with Spack, which sometimes means skipping the screening altogether. "We get these calls from parents who are just frantic," she says. "They need to get in immediately, because their child is about to hit puberty and is having serious mental-health issues, and we really want to accommodate that. It's like they've been waiting their whole lives for this and they are just desperate, and when they finally get in to see us . . . it's like a rebirth."

Spack's own conception of the psychology involved is uncomplicated: "If a girl starts to experience breast budding and feels like cutting herself, then she's probably transgendered. If she feels immediate relief on the [puberty-blocking] drugs, that confirms the diagnosis," he told the Boston Globe. He thinks of the blockers not as an addendum to years of therapy but as "preventative" because they forestall the trauma that comes from social rejection. Clinically, men who become women are usually described as "male-to-female," but Spack, using the parlance of activist parents, refers to them as "affirmed females"—"because how can you be a male-to-female if really you were always a female in your brain?"

For the transgender community, *born in the wrong body* is the catchphrase 40 that best captures this moment. It implies that the anatomy deceives where the brain tells the truth; that gender destiny is set before a baby takes its first breath. But the empirical evidence does not fit this argument so neatly. Milton Diamond says his study of identical transgender twins shows the same genetic predisposition that has been found for homosexuality: If one twin has switched to the opposite sex, there is a 50 percent chance that the other will as well. But his survey has not yet been published, and no one else has found nearly that degree of correlation. Eric Vilain, a geneticist at UCLA who specializes in sexual development and sex differences in the brain, says the studies on twins are mixed and that, on the whole, "there is no evidence of a biological influence on transsexualism yet."

In 1995, a study published in *Nature* looked at the brains of six adult male-to-female transsexuals and showed that certain regions of their brains were closer in size to those of women than of men. This study seemed to echo a famous 1991 study about gay men, published in *Science* by the neuroscientist Simon LeVay. LeVay had studied a portion of the hypothalamus that governs sexual behavior, and he discovered that in gay men, its size was much closer to women's than to straight men's; his findings helped legitimize the notion that homosexuality is hardwired. But in the transsexual study, the sample size was small, and the subjects had already received significant feminizing hormone treatments, which can affect brain structure.

Transsexualism is far less common than homosexuality, and the research is in its infancy. Scattered studies have looked at brain activity, finger size, familial recurrence, and birth order. One hypothesis involves hormonal imbalances during pregnancy. In 1988, researchers injected hormones into pregnant rhesus monkeys; the hormones seemed to masculinize the brains but not the bodies of their female babies. "Are we expecting to find some biological component [to gender identity]?" asks Vilain. "Certainly I am. But my hunch is, it's going to be mild. My hunch is that sexual orientation is probably much more hardwired than gender identity. I'm not saying [gender identity is] entirely determined by the social environment. I'm just saying that it's much more malleable."

Vilain has spent his career working with intersex patients, who are born with the anatomy of both sexes. He says his hardest job is to persuade the parents to leave the genitals ambiguous and wait until the child has grown up, and can choose his or her own course. This experience has influenced his views on parents with young transgender kids. "I'm torn here. I'm very ambivalent. I know [the parents] are saying the children are born this way. But I'm still on the fence. I consider the child my patient, not the parents, and I don't want to alleviate the anxiety of the parents by surgically fixing the child. We don't know the long-term effects of making these decisions for the child. We're playing God here, a little bit."

Even some supporters of hormone blockers worry that the availability of the drugs will encourage parents to make definitive decisions about younger and younger kids. This is one reason why doctors at the clinic in the Netherlands ask parents not to let young children live as the other gender until they are about to go on blockers. "We discourage it because the chances are very high that your child will not be a transsexual," says Cohen-Kettenis. The Dutch studies of their own patients show that among young children who have gender-identity disorder, only 20 to 25 percent still want to switch gender at adolescence; other studies show similar or even lower rates of persistence.

The most extensive study on transgender boys was published in 1987 as The "Sissy Boy Syndrome" and the Development of Homosexuality. For fifteen years, Dr. Richard Green followed forty-four boys who exhibited extreme feminine behaviors, and a control group of boys who did not. The boys in the feminine group all played with dolls, preferred the company of girls to boys, and avoided "rough-and-tumble play." Reports from their parents sound very much like the testimonies one reads on the listservs today. "He started . . . cross-dressing when he was about three," reported one mother. "[He stood] in front of the mirror and he took his penis and he folded it under, and he said, 'Look, Mommy, I'm a girl,'" said another.

Green expected most of the boys in the study to end up as transsexuals, but nothing like that happened. Three-fourths of the forty-four boys turned out to be gay or bisexual (Green says a few more have since contacted him and told him they too were gay). Only one became a transsexual. "We can't tell a pre-gay from a pre-transsexual at eight," says Green, who recently retired from running the adult gender-identity clinic in England. "Are you helping or hurting a kid by allowing them to live as the other gender? If everyone is caught up in facilitating the thing, then there may be a hell of a lot of pressure to remain that way, regardless of how strongly the kid still feels gender-dysphoric. Who knows? That's a study that hasn't found its investigator yet."

Out on the sidewalk in Philadelphia, Tina was going through Marlboro after Marlboro, stubbing them out half-smoked against city buildings. The conference's first day had just ended, with Tina asking another mom, "So how do you know if one of these kids stays that way or if he changes?" and the mom suggesting she could wait awhile and see.

"Wait? Wait for what?" Tina suddenly said to Bill. "He's already waited six years, and now I don't care about any of that no more." Bill looked worried, but she threw an Army phrase at him: "Suck it up and drive on, soldier."

The organizers had planned a pool party for that night, and Tina had come to a decision: Brandon would wear exactly the kind of bathing suit he'd always wanted. She had spotted a Macy's a couple of blocks away. I walked with her and Bill and Brandon into the hush and glow, the headless mannequins sporting golf shorts with $80 price tags. They quietly took the escalator one floor up, to the girls' bathing-suit department. Brandon leaped off at the top and ran to the first suit that caught his eye: a teal Hannah Montana bikini studded with jewels and glitter. "Oh, I love this one," he said.

"So that's the one you want?" asked Tina.

Brandon hesitated. He was used to doing his cross-dressing somewhat furtively. Normally he would just grab the shiniest thing he saw, for fear his chance would evaporate. But as he came to understand that both Tina and Bill were on board, he slowed down a bit. He carefully looked through all the racks. Bill, calm now, was helping him. "You want a one-piece or two-piece?" Bill asked. Tina, meanwhile, was having a harder time. "I'll get used to it," she said. She had tried twice to call Brandon "she," Tina suddenly confessed, but "it just don't sound right," she said, her eyes tearing.

Brandon decided to try on an orange one-piece with polka dots, a sky-blue-and-pink two-piece, and a Hawaiian-print tankini with a brown background and pink hibiscus flowers. He went into a dressing room and stayed there a long, long time. Finally, he called in the adults. Brandon had settled on the least showy of the three: the Hawaiian print with the brown background. He had it on and was shyly looking in the mirror. He wasn't doing backflips or grinning from ear to ear; he was still and at peace, gently fingering the price tag. He mentioned that he didn't want to wear the suit again until he'd had a chance to wash his feet.

At the pool party, Brandon immediately ran into a friend he'd made earlier, the transgender boy who'd shared his balloon puppy. The pool was in a small room in the corner of a hotel basement, with low ceilings and no windows. The echoes of seventy giddy children filled the space. Siblings were there, too, so it was impossible to know who had been born a boy and who a girl. They were all just smooth limbs and wet hair and an occasional slip that sent one crying to his or her mother.

Bill sat next to me on a bench and spilled his concerns. He was worried about Tina's stepfather, who would never accept this. He was worried that Brandon's father might find out and demand custody. He was worried about Brandon's best friend, whose parents were strict evangelical Christians. He was worried about their own pastor, who had sternly advised them to take away all of Brandon's girl-toys and girl-clothes. "Maybe if we just pray hard enough," Bill had told Tina.

Brandon raced by, arm in arm with his new friend, giggling. Tina and Bill didn't know this yet, but Brandon had already started telling the other kids that his name was Bridget, after the pet mouse he'd recently buried ("My beloved Bridget. Rest with the Lord," the memorial in his room read). The comment of an older transsexual from Brooklyn who'd sat behind Tina in a session earlier that day echoed in my head. He'd had his sex-change operation when he was in his fifties, and in his wild, wispy wig, he looked like a biblical prophet, with breasts. "You think you have troubles now," he'd yelled out to Tina. "Wait until next week. Once you let the genie out of the bottle, she's not going back in!"

Dr. Kenneth Zucker has been seeing children with gender-identity disorder in Toronto since the mid-seventies, and has published more on the subject than any other researcher. But lately he has become a pariah to the most-vocal activists in the American transgender community. In 2012, the *Diagnostic and Statistical Manual of Mental Disorders*—the bible for psychiatric professionals—will be updated. Many in the transgender community see this as their opportunity to remove gender-identity disorder from the book, much the same way homosexuality was delisted in 1973. Zucker is in charge of the committee that will make the recommendation. He seems unlikely to bless the condition as psychologically healthy, especially in young children.

I met Zucker in his office at the Centre for Addiction and Mental Health, where piles of books alternate with the Barbies and superheroes that he uses for play therapy. Zucker has a white mustache and beard, and his manner is somewhat Talmudic. He responds to every question with a methodical three-part answer, often ending by climbing a chair to pull down a research paper he's written. On one of his file cabinets, he's tacked up a flyer from a British parents' advocacy group that reads: "Gender dysphoria is increasingly understood . . . as having biological origins," and describes "small parts of the brain" as "progressing along different pathways." During the interview, he took it down to make a point: "In terms of empirical data, this is not true. It's just dogma, and I've never liked dogma. Biology is not destiny."

In his case studies and descriptions of patients, Zucker usually explains gender dysphoria in terms of what he calls "family noise": neglectful parents who caused a boy to overidentify with his domineering older sisters; a mother who expected a daughter and delayed naming her newborn son for eight weeks. Zucker's belief is that with enough therapy, such children can be made to feel comfortable in their birth sex. Zucker has compared young children who believe they are meant to live as the other sex to people who want to amputate healthy limbs, or who believe they are cats, or those with something called ethnic-identity disorder. "If a five-year-old black kid came into the clinic and said he wanted to be white, would we endorse that?" he told me. "I don't think so. What we would want to do is say, 'What's going on with this kid that's making him feel that it would be better to be white?'"

Young children, he explains, have very concrete reasoning; they may believe that if they want to wear dresses, they are girls. But he sees it as his job—and the parents'—to help them think in more-flexible ways. "If a kid has massive separation anxiety and does not want to go to school, one solution would be to let them stay home. That would solve the problem at one level, but not at another. So it is with gender identity." Allowing a child to switch genders, in other words, would probably not get to the root of the psychological problem, but only offer a superficial fix.

Zucker calls his approach "developmental," which means that the most impor- 60
tant factor is the age of the child. Younger children are more malleable, he believes, and can learn to "be comfortable in their own skin." Zucker says that in twenty-five years, not one of the patients who started seeing him by age six has switched gender. Adolescents are more fixed in their identity. If a parent brings in, say, a thirteen-year-old who has never been treated and who has severe gender dysphoria, Zucker will generally recommend hormonal treatment. But he considers that a fraught choice. "One has to think about the long-term developmental path. This kid will go through lifelong hormonal treatment to approximate the phenotype of a male and may require some kind of surgery and then will have to deal with the fact that he doesn't have a phallus; it's a tough road, with a lot of pain involved."

Zucker put me in touch with two of his success stories, a boy and a girl, now both living in the suburbs of Toronto. Meeting them was like moving into a parallel world where every story began the same way as those of the American families I'd met, but then ran in the opposite direction.

When he was four, the boy, John, had tested at the top of the gender-dysphoria scale. Zucker recalls him as "one of the most anxious kids I ever saw." He had bins full of Barbies and Disney princess movies, and he dressed in homemade costumes. Once, at a hardware store, he stared up at the glittery chandeliers and wept, "I don't want to be a daddy! I want to be a mommy!"

His parents, well-educated urbanites, let John grow his hair long and play with whatever toys he preferred. But then a close friend led them to Zucker, and soon they began to see themselves as "in denial," recalls his mother, Caroline. "Once we came to see his behavior for what it was, it became painfully sad." Zucker believed John's behavior resulted from early-childhood medical trauma—he was born with tumors on his kidneys and had had invasive treatments every three months—and from his dependence during that time on his mother, who has a dominant personality.

When they reversed course, they dedicated themselves to the project with a thoroughness most parents would find exhausting and off-putting. They boxed up all of John's girl-toys and videos and replaced them with neutral ones. Whenever John cried for his girl-toys, they would ask him, "Do you think playing with those would make you feel better about being a boy?" and then would distract him with an offer to ride bikes or take a walk. They turned their house into a 1950s kitchen-sink drama, intended to inculcate respect for patriarchy, in the crudest and simplest terms: "Boys don't wear pink, they wear blue," they would tell him, or "Daddy is smarter than Mommy—ask him." If John called for Mommy in the middle of the night, Daddy went, every time.

When I visited the family, John was lazing around with his older brother, idly [65] watching TV and playing video games, dressed in a polo shirt and Abercrombie & Fitch shorts. He said he was glad he'd been through the therapy, "because it made me feel happy," but that's about all he would say; for the most part, his mother spoke for him. Recently, John was in the basement watching the Grammys. When Caroline walked downstairs to say good night, she found him draped in a blanket, vamping. He looked up at her, mortified. She held his face and said, "You never have to be embarrassed of the things you say or do around me." Her position now is that the treatment is "not a cure; this will always be with him"—but also that he has nothing to be ashamed of. About a year ago, John carefully broke the news to his parents that he is gay. "You'd have to carefully break the news to me that you were straight," his dad told him. "He'll be a man who loves men," says his mother. "But I want him to be a happy man who loves men."

The girl's case was even more extreme in some ways. She insisted on peeing standing up and playing only with boys. When her mother bought her Barbies, she'd pop their heads off. Once, when she was six, her father, Mike, said out of the blue: "Chris, you're a girl." In response, he recalls, she "started screaming and freaking out," closing her hand into a fist and punching herself between the legs, over and over. After that, her parents took her to see Zucker. He connected Chris's behavior to the early years of her parents' marriage; her mother had gotten pregnant and Mike had been resentful of having to marry her, and verbally abusive. Chris, Zucker told them, saw her mother as weak and couldn't identify with her. For four years, they saw no progress. When Chris turned eleven and other girls in school started getting their periods, her mother found her on the bed one night, weeping. She "said she wanted to kill herself," her mother told me. "She said, 'In my head, I've always been a boy.'"

But about a month after that, everything began to change. Chris had joined a softball team and made some female friends; her mother figured she had cottoned to the idea that girls could be tough and competitive. Then one day, Chris went to her mother and said, "Mom, I need to talk to you. We need to go shopping." She bought clothes that were tighter and had her ears pierced. She let her hair grow out. Eventually she gave her boys' clothes away.

Now Chris wears her hair in a ponytail, walks like a girl, and spends hours on the phone, talking to girlfriends about boys. Her mother recently watched her through a bedroom window as she was jumping on their trampoline, looking slyly at her own reflection and tossing her hair around. At her parents' insistence, Chris has never been to a support group or a conference, never talked to another girl who wanted to be a boy. For all she knew, she was the only person in the world who felt as she once had felt.

The week before I arrived in Toronto, the Barbara Walters special about Jazz had been re-aired, and both sets of parents had seen it. "I was aghast," said John's mother. "It really affected us to see this poor little peanut, and her parents just going to the teacher and saying 'He is a "she" now.' Why would you assume a four-year-old would understand the ramifications of that?"

"We were shocked," Chris's father said. "They gave up on their kid too early. 70 Regardless of our beliefs and our values, you look at Chris, and you look at these kids, and they have to go through a sex-change operation and they'll never look right and they'll never have a normal life. Look at Chris's chance for a happy, decent life, and look at theirs. Seeing those kids, it just broke our hearts."

Catherine Tuerk, who runs the support group for parents in Washington, D.C., started out as an advocate for gay rights after her son came out, in his twenties. She has a theory about why some parents have become so comfortable with the trans-gender label: "Parents have told me it's almost easier to tell others, 'My kid was born in the wrong body,' rather than explaining that he might be gay, which is in the back of everyone's mind. When people think about being gay, they think about sex—and thinking about sex and kids is taboo."

Tuerk believes lingering homophobia is partly responsible for this, and in some cases, she may be right. When Bill saw two men kissing at the conference, he said, "That just don't sit right with me." In one of Zucker's case studies, a seventeen-year-old girl requesting cross-sex hormones tells him, "Doc, to be honest, lesbians make me sick . . . I want to be normal." In Iran, homosexuality is punishable by death, but sex-change operations are legal—a way of normalizing aberrant attractions.

Overall, though, Tuerk's explanation touches on something deeper than latent homophobia: a subconscious strain in American conceptions of childhood. You see it in the hyper-vigilance about "good touch" and "bad touch." Or in the banishing of Freud to the realm of the perverse. The culture seems invested in an almost Victorian notion of childhood innocence, leaving no room for sexual volition, even in the far future.

When Tuerk was raising her son, in the '70s, she and her husband, a psychiatrist, both fell prey to the idea that their son's gayness was somehow their fault, and that they could change it. These were the years when the child psychologist Bruno Bettelheim blamed cold, distant "refrigerator mothers" for everything from autism to schizophrenia in their children. Children, to Bettelheim, were messy, unhappy creatures, warped by the sins of their parents. Today's children are nothing like that, at least not in their parents' eyes. They are pure vessels, channeling biological impulses beyond their control—or their parents'. Their requests are innocent, unsullied by baggage or desire. Which makes it much easier to say yes to them.

Tuerk was thrilled when the pendulum swung from nurture toward nature; "I can tell you the exact spot where I was, in Chevy Chase Circle, when someone said the words to me: 'There's a guy in Baltimore, and he thinks people are born gay.'" But she now thinks the pendulum may have swung too far. For the minority who are truly transgender, "the sooner they get into the right clothes, the less they're going to suffer. But for the rest? I'm not sure if we're helping or hurting them by pushing them in this direction." 75

It's not impossible to imagine Brandon's life going in another direction. His early life fits neatly into a Zucker case study about family noise. Tina describes Brandon as "never leaving my side" during his early years. The diagnosis writes itself: father, distant and threatening; mother, protector; child overidentifies with strong maternal figure. If Tina had lived in Toronto, if she'd had the patience for six years of Dr. Zucker's therapy, if the therapy had been free, then who knows?

Yet Zucker's approach has its own disturbing elements. It's easy to imagine that his methods—steering parents toward removing pink crayons from the box, extolling a patriarchy no one believes in—could instill in some children a sense of shame and a double life. A 2008 study of twenty-five girls who had been seen in Zucker's clinic showed positive results; twenty-two were no longer gender-dysphoric, meaning they were comfortable living as girls. But that doesn't mean they were happy. I spoke to the mother of one Zucker patient in her late twenties, who said her daughter was repulsed by the thought of a sex change but was still suffering—she'd become an alcoholic, and was cutting herself. "I'd be surprised if she outlived me," her mother said.

When I was reporting this story, I was visibly pregnant with my third child. My pregnancy brought up a certain nostalgia for the parents I met, because it reminded them of a time when life was simpler, when a stranger could ask them whether their baby was a boy or a girl and they could answer straightforwardly. Many parents shared journals with me that were filled with anguish. If they had decided to let their child live as the other gender, that meant cutting off ties with family and friends who weren't supportive, putting away baby pictures, mourning the loss of the child they thought they had. It meant sending their child out alone into a possibly hostile world. If they chose the other route, it meant denying their child the things he or she most wanted, day after day, in the uncertain hope that one day, it would all pay off. In either case, it meant choosing a course on the basis of hazy evidence, and resolving to believe in it.

About two months after the conference, I visited Brandon again. On Father's Day, Tina had made up her mind to just let it happen. She'd started calling him "Bridget" and, except for a few slipups, "she." She'd packed up all the boy-clothes and given them to a neighbor, and had taken Bridget to JC Penney for a new wardrobe. When I saw her, her ears were pierced and her hair was just beginning to tickle her earlobes. "If it doesn't move any faster, I'll have to get extensions!" Tina said.

That morning, Tina was meeting with Bridget's principal, and the principal of a nearby school, to see if she could transfer. "I want her to be known as Bridget, not Bridget-who-used-to-be-Brandon." Tina had memorized lots of lines she'd heard at the conference, and she delivered them well, if a little too fast. She told the principals that she had "pictures and medical documentation." She showed them a book called *The Transgender Child*. "I thought we could fix it," she said, "but gender's in your brain." Brandon's old principal looked a little shell-shocked. But the one from the nearby school, a young woman with a sweet face and cropped curly hair, seemed more open. "This is all new to me," she said. "It's a lot to learn."

The week before, Tina had gone to her mother's house, taking Bridget along. Bridget often helps care for her grandmother, who has lupus; the two are close. After lunch, Bridget went outside in a pair of high heels she'd found in the closet. Tina's stepfather saw the child and lost it: "Get them damned shoes off!" he yelled.

"Make me," Bridget answered.

Then the stepfather turned to Tina and said, "You're ruining his fucking life," loud enough for Bridget to hear.

Tina's talk with Karen, the mother of Bridget's best friend, Abby, hadn't gone too smoothly, either. Karen is an evangelical Christian, with an anti–gay-marriage bumper sticker on her white van. For two years, she'd picked up Brandon nearly every day after school, and brought him over to play with Abby. But that wasn't going to happen anymore. Karen told Tina she didn't want her children "exposed to that kind of thing." "God doesn't make mistakes," she added.

Bridget, meanwhile, was trying to figure it all out—what she could and couldn't do, where the limits were. She'd always been a compliant child, but now she was misbehaving. Her cross-dressing had amped up; she was trying on makeup, and demanding higher heels and sexier clothes. When I was over, she came out of the house dressed in a cellophane getup, four-inch heels, and lip gloss. "It's like I have to teach her what's appropriate for a girl her age," says Tina.

Thursdays, the family spends the afternoon at a local community center, where both Bridget and her little sister, Madison, take gymnastics. She'd normally see Abby there; the two of them are in the same class and usually do their warm-up together, giggling and going over their day. On the car ride over, Bridget was trying to navigate that new relationship, too.

"Abby's not my best friend anymore. She hits me. But she's really good at drawing."

"Well, don't you go hitting nobody," Tina said. "Remember, sticks and stones."

When they arrived at the center and opened the door, Abby was standing right there. She looked at Bridget/Brandon. And froze. She turned and ran away. Madison, oblivious, followed her, yelling, "Wait for us!"

Bridget sat down on a bench next to Tina. Although they were miles from 90 home, she'd just seen a fourth-grade friend of her stepbrother's at the pool table, and she was nervous.

"Hey, we need to work on this," said Tina. "If anybody says anything, you say, 'I'm not Brandon. I'm Bridget, his cousin from California. You want to try it?'"

"No. I don't want to."

"Well, if someone keeps it up, you just say, 'You're crazy.'"

Tina had told me over the phone that Brandon was easily passing as a girl, but that wasn't really true, not yet. With his hair still short, he looked like a boy wearing tight pink pants and earrings. This meant that for the moment, everywhere in this small town was a potential land mine. At the McDonald's, the cashier eyed him suspiciously: "Is that Happy Meal for a boy or a girl?" At the playground, a group of teenage boys with tattoos and their pants pulled low down did a double take. By the evening, Tina was a nervous wreck. "Gosh darn it! I left the keys in the car," she said. But she hadn't. She was holding them in her hand.

After gymnastics, the kids wanted to stop at the Dairy Queen, but Tina couldn't take being stared at in one more place. "Drive-thru!" she yelled. "And I don't want to hear any more whining from you."

On the quiet, wooded road leading home, she could finally relax. It was cool 95 enough to roll down the windows and get some mountain air. After high school, Tina had studied to be a travel agent; she had always wanted to just "work on a cruise ship or something, just go, go, go." Now she wanted things to be easy for Brandon, for him to disappear and pop back as Bridget, a new kid from California, new to this town, knowing nobody. But in a small town, it's hard to erase yourself and come back as your opposite.

Maybe one day they would move, she said. But thinking about that made her head hurt. Instead of the future, she drifted to the past, when things were easier.

"Remember that camping trip we took once, Brandon?" she asked, and he did. And together, they started singing one of the old camp songs she'd taught him.

Smokey the Bear, Smokey the Bear,

Howlin' and a-prowlin' and a-sniffin' the air.

He can find a fire before it starts to flame.

That's why they call him Smokey,

That's how he got his name.

"You remember that, Brandon?" she asked again. And for the first time all day, they seemed happy.

QUESTIONS FOR DISCUSSION AND WRITING

1. When you read the story of Brandon, the young boy who wants to be a girl, what was your reaction? Was the story shocking, sad, appalling, or even funny to you? Why do you suppose you reacted the way that you did? Consider how acceptance of homosexuality has greatly increased in this society in the past

generation. Is changing one's gender undergoing a similar acceptance? If so, why? If not, why not? Be specific.

2. In paragraph 12, Rosin argues that transgendered people are seeking "suburban normalcy." What does she mean by that? Why is it desired? She puts that goal into the same context as homosexuals seeking the right to gay marriage. Are there any problems with that comparison? Why or why not?

3. A fundamental question is whether the desires of a very young child should be taken seriously. In most everyday situations, a lot may not be at stake, but in the case of using hormone injections as blockers—stopping the child from undergoing puberty—a tremendous amount is at stake. Consider that older transsexuals at a conference all claim they would have gotten that treatment if it had been available for them (paragraph 14). How can parents be sure they are making the right decision for their child? What issues or roadblocks would parents have to overcome when deciding on this course of action?

4. Dr. Kenneth Zucker, who has been treating children with gender-identity disorder for close to forty years, argues that the children can, and should, be treated. He compares such a child to one who might reject his or her own ethnicity: "If a five-year-old black kid came into the clinic and said he wanted to be white, would we endorse that?" says Dr. Zucker (paragraph 56). Zucker claims no empirical data support transsexuality being based in biology; rather, he argues, it is based on psychology and therefore is treatable. In your opinion, are there problems with the comparing gender identity with ethnic identity? Why or why not? Be specific.

5. Zucker puts the author in contact with two of his "success stories" (paragraph 59): a boy who eventually stopped wanting to be a girl, and a girl who stopped wanting to be a boy. Do their stories convince you that Zucker is right? If so, why? If not, why not? Be specific.

DEIRDRE N. McCLOSKEY

Yes, Ma'am

Deirdre N. McCloskey was born Donald McCloskey in 1942, in Ann Arbor, Michigan. As Donald, McCloskey earned undergraduate and graduate degrees in economics at Harvard University and became a professor at the University of Chicago and the University of Iowa as well as a scholar noted for taking a sometimes controversial cross-disciplinary approach that combined economic theory and practice with history, philosophy, and rhetoric. In the mid-1990s, after years of internal struggle, McCloskey—who had been married for three decades and had two children—began the process of a gender change, resulting in complete gender reassignment surgery in 1996 and a new identity as Deirdre N. McCloskey.

Since 2000 Deirdre McCloskey has been Distinguished Professor of Economics, History, English, and Communication at the University of Illinois at Chicago and was Visiting Tinbergen Professor (2002–2006) of Philosophy, Economics, and Art and Cultural Studies at Erasmus University of Rotterdam. Her most recent (of sixteen) books include How to Be Human—Though an Economist *(2001),* The Bourgeois Virtues: Ethics for an Age of Capitalism *(2006),* The Cult of Statistical Significance: How the Standard Error Costs Us Jobs, Justice, and Lives *(with Stephen Ziliak, 2008), and* Bourgeois Dignity: Why Economics Can't Explain the Modern World *(2010). Describing herself as a "postmodern free-market quantitative Episcopalian feminist Aristotelian," McCloskey has also published nearly 400 articles on economic theory, economic history, philosophy, rhetoric, feminism, ethics, and law. Her highly personal* Crossing: A Memoir *appeared in 1999 to much critical acclaim.*

Those contemplating a sex change are generally required by their physicians to live life as a member of the opposite sex for a year or more before gender reassignment surgery, and even after surgery they must continue to adapt physically to their new identity. In the following chapter from Crossing, *McCloskey describes her early attempts to assume a physical identity that strangers would accept as that of a woman. She also considers the gestural differences between women and men and the hostility directed at those perceived to be cross-gendered.*

It's hard to pass. You just try it, Dee would say. I mean really try to pass as the opposite gender, not just put on a joke dress and a lampshade hat for the Lions picnic. You'll be surprised at how many gender clues there are and how easy it is to get them wrong. Scores of them, natural and unnatural, genetic and socially constructed.

No, hundreds. Women stand and sit at angles. Men offer their hands to shake. Women put their hands to their chests when speaking of themselves. Men barge through. Women look frequently at nonspeaking participants in a conversation. Men don't look at each other when talking. Women carry papers and books clutched to their midriffs, men balance things on their hips. Women smile at other women when entering their space. Men never smile at male strangers. Women put their hands on their hips with fingers pointing backward. Men use wide gestures. Women frequently fold their hands together in their laps. Men walk from their shoulders, women from their hips. And on and on.

Dee watched other women in her culture for characteristic gestures and practiced them on the spot. **The way the hands gesture together, as though in a little dance. The way the fingers lie up the arm when the arms are crossed. Standing with feet in a ballet pose. Pulling your hair from under a coat just put on.** (It was some time before her hair was long enough to make that feminine gesture useful.) Years into her transition she could amuse herself in a dull moment in a mall or airport by breaking down other women's gestures and trying them out. Like square dancing: hundreds of calls.

Rest one elbow on the back of the other hand, laid horizontally across your middle, the free hand stretching vertically to frame your face from the bottom, palm out. In touching your face, which you should do frequently, hold the hand in a graceful pose. For situations such as display at the dinner table, learn the hand pose used in ballet—fingers arched and separated, middle finger almost touching the thumb. Pinky up, but not too much, since it's an obvious parody of the lady-like. Overacting evokes the theatrical tradition of drag. Try to create a somewhat splayed effect with the fingers, angled up, instead of masculine cupping. When shaking hands—don't be the first to offer—use no strong grip, and place your hand sideward into the other person's. Check your hair frequently. Play idly with your jewelry. Check your clothing (a set of gestures that women's clothes require more often than men's, or else you stride out of the ladies' room with the back of your skirt up around your behind). Always stand more on one foot than the other. Stand with your legs crossed (a youngish gesture, this). Never stand manlike with feet parallel and legs spread wide. Angle your feet when you stop at the corner before crossing. Rest with hands together, not sprawled all over like a man's. When sitting cross your legs, either knee over knee angled to one side (never lower leg crossed horizontally over the knee, like the Greek boy in the statue removing a splinter) or to one side beneath the chair ankle over ankle. Never slouch when you sit. Stick your rear end solidly into the back of the chair, and never stretch your legs out, crossed at the ankles. Keep your knees together when you sit—"close the gates of hell" used to be the misogynist joke about it—which is easier if your knees are naturally angled inward, as girls' and especially women's are. If your feet are not crossed when sit-ting, keep your legs together from feet to knees. "Take up less space" is one formula; another is "keep your wrists loose," and still another "keep your elbows close to your body," this one imitating the effect of a female angle in the elbow, a piece of biology. But the formulas are hard to apply, like formal grammatical rules. Imitate, imitate, the way girls learn it. Deirdre was congratulated three years into full time: "Last year your motions were a little abrupt; now they are convincingly feminine." The gesture language is probably imitated with the same ease and at the same age as the spoken language, and like the spoken language it is hard to learn as an adult. Little girls act different from little boys, independent of the slight structural differ-ences in their bodies. By age ten many girls even know the secret smile.

Much of behavior is gendered. A lot of it is culturally specific and variable 5 from person to person. European men cross their legs in a way that in America is coded as feminine. American soldiers in Vietnam would sneer at what they read as femininity in their Vietnamese allies and enemies: "They're all queer, you know." Mediterranean and Middle Eastern women make broader gestures, not the little dance of hands that upper-middle-class women in America use. The gender clues figure in any culture in an abundance that only a gender crosser or Dustin Hoff-man preparing for *Tootsie* can grasp.

Of course if you are *aiming* to be funny then you want to be read, even if you are skillful at giving appropriate gender clues. Passing is not at issue. The Aus-tralian comedian who has developed the character "Dame Edna" is good at it. Without a leer or a nudge, he simply is the absurd Dame and sometimes spends hours in character, yet of course his audience knows. Miss Piggy of the Muppets is similar. She is gloriously who she is, yet everyone knows it's cross-speaking—her voice is always that of a man using falsetto. Getting read is part of the joke.

If you are not trying to be funny, you do not want to get read. Really, you don't. A sincere but detected attempt to jump the gender border from male to female— and no joking about it—creates anxiety in men, to be released by laughter if they can handle it or by a length of steel pipe if they can't. A 1997 survey claimed that 60 percent of cross-gendered people had been assaulted. Deirdre knew a gender crosser who had been beaten by four young men outside a bar even in peaceful Iowa City. The director of Gender PAC noted that "RuPaul is funny so long as she stays in a television studio. But try walking to the subway and she'll be a grease spot on the sidewalk before she makes it home." (If a female-to-male crosser was read by men maybe he would be regarded as cute, or rational: after all, it's rational to prefer to be a man, isn't it? Like the daily prayer by Orthodox Jewish men thanking God for not making them women. On the other hand, Brandon Teena, a pre-op female-to-male thief outed by the Falls City, Nebraska, police department was raped, complained about it to the police, who did nothing, and the next week in 1993 was murdered. Not by women.)

The anxiety is weirdly strong. A standard routine in the movies is that two men are forced to sleep with each other by circumstances (oh, sure), and then one of them dreams that he's sleeping with a woman. The other man, horrified by the amorous advances, rejects them violently, and the awakened dreamer is ashamed. The routine enacts over and over again the male anxiety about being homosexual, much less being a woman, and the violent reaction the anxiety arouses. With this threat of violence in mind, Donald's sister had given him her own pepper spray. The pepper spray, though, wouldn't be much good against a steel pipe.

Women who read a cross-dresser are not violent, but frightened and indignant. Who is this guy? What's he up to? Deirdre knew from being a woman on trains late at night in Holland or walking by Dutch cafés in the summertime or living later in the less demonstrative but more dangerous environment of America that women have daily experiences of men in fact being up to something, often something sexual, often enough something dangerous. At first it was flattering, the knocking on windows of the *eetcafé* as she went by, the propositions to come into the jazz club and have a drink. Then it was tedious or frightening. Women experience dangerous men all day long and are on the alert. The alertness is not male bashing, merely prudence in the company of people with greater upper-body strength and the inclination to use it, intoxicated by lethal fantasies about What She Really Wants. Women who read a gender crosser are putting her in this category of dangerous men. To be read by women is utterly demoralizing. After all, the gender crosser is trying to join the women, to pass as one, and instead they are treating her like a man, maybe nuts, probably dangerous, definitely another one of those bloody *men*.

On all counts it is better for a gender crosser to pass rapidly to the other side, and making the crossing rapid ought to be the purpose of medical intervention, such as facial surgery, and social intervention, such as counseling on gender clues. Women acquainted with a gender crosser sometimes think of her interest in facial surgery as vanity. Natural-born women have no problem passing as women. "You're silly to want operations," says a woman out of a face with pointed chin, no browridges, high cheekbones. Deirdre's mother declared that getting electrolysis,

10

which she regarded as merely temporary, was "vain." But a nose job or a facelift or electrolysis that will make a gender crosser passable will also make her less likely to be scorned or raped or killed—at any rate at no more than the shocking rates for genetic women. Deirdre knew a not very passable gender crosser in tolerant Holland who had been raped three times. It is merely prudent to pass.

Some radical feminists object to gender crossing. They complain of the gender crosser that she (when they have the ruth to call her "she") is adopting oppressive stereotypes about women and therefore contributing to society's discrimination. The gender crosser, they claim, is pulling women back to the 1950s, white gloves and pillbox hats, lovely garden parties, and a *Leave It to Beaver* vision of a woman's life.

There is little truth in the stereotype argument. The crossphobe who uses it ordinarily doesn't know any gender crossers. A gender crosser with a job or career outside the home tries to keep it and does not in practice dissolve into a 1950s heaven of full-time cookie baking and teatime gossip. Far from becoming passive and stereotypically feminine, the gender crossers Deirdre knew often retained much of their masculine sides. The crossphobes mix up gender crossers with drag queens or female impersonators, whose shtick is indeed a parody of women—sometimes demeaning and stereotypical, though often enough loving and amusing. In 1958 the sociologist Harold Garfinkel described a gender crosser named Agnes. Latter-day crossphobes attack Agnes as "displaying rigidly traditional ideas of what a woman is" or having "stereotypical views of femininity" or "constructing an extremely narrow and constricted view of womanhood." Agnes was nineteen, a typist, at the height of the feminine mystique. But no allowances: "I don't support you in your effort to have an operation, because you have stereotypical views of what it means to be a woman." Unlike all the other nineteen-year-old typists in 1958. (Agnes had the operation, and was fine, because Garfinkel and a psychiatrist named Stoller did support her.)

A gender crosser trying to be a woman must reproduce enough of the characteristic gestures to escape being read, and often—especially in voice—this is difficult. It becomes second nature, and a comfort to oneself even when alone. But if you fail you are classed with people stereotyping women. Or murdered. The crossphobe radical feminists are allies in hatred with the gay-bashing murderers of Matthew Shephard.

The complaint about stereotyping will be delivered by a genetic woman whose every gesture and syllable is stereotypically feminine. At seminars in which Deirdre was attacked for stereotyping she would reply with the same stereotypically feminine gestures or turns of phrase just used by the crossphobe—who had been practicing them since she was a little girl. This was Garfinkel's point, that gender is something "done," a performance, not an essence springing from genitals or chromosomes. Deirdre would say, "Of course I [putting her hand to her chest in the feminine way of referring to oneself, just used by the crossphobe] would never [doing a deprecating double flap with her hands in the style of American middle-class women] want to damage women by *stereotyping* [raising her voice in the falsetto of emphasis stereotypical of women, for instance the crossphobe attacking the genuineness of gender crossers]."

The passing worked better, slowly, each month, if she dressed carefully and worked   15
at it. Each little acceptance delighted her. The signal was being called "mevrouw"
in Holland, "ma'am" in America, "madame" in France, "madam" in England. *Yes:
call me madam*.

She is getting up to leave a Dutch tram at Oostzeedijk, intent on how to make
the transfer to the subway. *Let's see: across there and down. Remember to watch
for the bicycles*. The tram has almost stopped and she is pressing the exit button
when she hears finally through her English thoughts and the haze of a foreign
tongue, *"Mevrouw! Mevrouw!" It's me they're calling*, she thinks. *Oh. I've left a
package*. She smiles in thanks and snatches up the package, slipping out the door
as it closes, still smiling. They see her as "ma'am."

At the grocery store she is accosted by a woman giving out samples of a Dutch
delicacy. It doesn't look very good. The woman babbles at Dee in Dutch, and Dee
catches only the blessed "mevrouw." She smiles and shakes her head no thank you
and pushes the cart toward the canned goods.

In May in Paris with an economist friend, Nancy, who is visiting there for a
year, she walks out of a hat store, wearing the lovely lace floppy number just purchased. An elegant Frenchman goes by and says with a smile, "Un beau chapeau,
madame!" Deirdre's French is poor, and she is still wondering if he could have
said what she thought he had said when he politely repeats it in English over his
shoulder as he walks on, "A beautiful hat, madame!" She would say when telling
the story, "I could have kissed him. If he had proposed, I would have married him
on the spot. Even though he was shorter."

A month later she wears the hat (which can be worn only in Paris or at special
events) to a daylong concert of classical music in the park in Rotterdam. Sitting at
luncheon on the grass with some members of her women's group, she feels particularly lovely. A Dutchman passes by and makes in Dutch the same remark the
Frenchman had made, "A beautiful hat, mevrouw!"

The women's group meets at a restaurant in Rotterdam. It is a year since she   20
abandoned the male role. The waiter asks the *"dames"* (DAH-mez) what they
want, including Deirdre without notice or comment. *One of the dames. Yes*.

QUESTIONS FOR DISCUSSION AND WRITING

1. In her opening paragraphs, McCloskey observes a number of "gender clues,"
   distinctions between the physical behavior and gestures of women and men.
   Are these distinctions borne out by your own observations?

2. At the end of paragraph 4, McCloskey claims that children early on learn
   gendered behavior through imitation. In paragraph 5, she makes the further
   point that gender-identified behavior differs from culture to culture. What do
   these ideas suggest about her views on gender?

3. McCloskey writes that both men and women respond negatively when they
   detect in someone a "sincere . . . attempt to jump the gender border from male
   to female," but in different ways (paragraphs 7–9). How does she account for
   these different negative reactions?

4. McCloskey refers to herself throughout this essay in the third person—as "she," "Dee," "Deirdre," and even "Donald" (her pre-crossing name). Why might she have chosen to do this? What is its effect on you as a reader?

5. "Some radical feminists object to gender crossing," McCloskey writes at the beginning of paragraph 11. Starting with McCloskey's elaboration of this point, write an essay in which you explore your views about gendered behavior, as described in paragraphs 4–5, and gender stereotypes, such as the female homemakers and garden clubbers and the male breadwinners and sports enthusiasts depicted in popular films and television. Expand your perspective with references to other essays in this chapter.

6. Compare McCloskey's discussion of how gender is presented with that of Colleen Kinder, who, in "Blot Out," in the e-Pages at bedfordstmartins.com/arlington, writes of her experience of going literally undercover in Cairo, Egypt, in traditional women's dress. In what ways do McCloskey and Kinder see gender as a performance? What does each see as dangers in trying to "pass"? What elements of gender is each trying to reshape?

COLLEEN KINDER

Blot Out   [TEXT ESSAY]

"After walking alone as a blonde, nonvirginal, youngish woman in the streets of Africa's most densely populated city, where almost everyone is a boy or a man, and looking, visibility is the last thing I desire."

 In the e-Pages at bedfordstmartins.com/arlington.

NATALIE ANGIER

Men, Women, Sex and Darwin

"It's bad luck to be born either sex" is Natalie Angier's favorite quotation (from anthropologist Sarah Hrdy). Angier (b. 1958) grew up in the Bronx, New York, and earned a bachelor's degree in physics and English from Barnard College (1978). In 1991 she received the Pulitzer Prize for her science writing in the New York Times, where she has worked since 1990. Her books include Natural Obsessions (1988), on the world of cancer research; The Beauty of the Beastly (1995), on invertebrates; and The Canon: A Whirligig Tour of the Beautiful Basics of Science (2007). In Woman: An Intimate Geography (1999), Angier analyzes female genetics, anatomy, physiology, and endocrinology from the fetus to menopause, arguing that males and females are more androgynous than is often supposed. In the ongoing debate over whether

genetics or culture more strongly influence the behavior of men and women, Angier favors "nurture" over "nature." In "Men, Women, Sex and Darwin," first published in the New York Times Magazine *(February 1999), she provides evidence to contradict the psychologists who claim that sexual stereotypes have evolved over millions of years and are programmed into human genes.*

Life is short but jingles are forever. None more so, it seems, than the familiar ditty, variously attributed to William James, Ogden Nash and Dorothy Parker: "Hoggamus, higgamus, / Men are polygamous, / Higgamus, hoggamus, / Women monogamous."

Lately the pith of that jingle has found new fodder and new fans, through the explosive growth of a field known as evolutionary psychology. Evolutionary psychology professes to have discovered the fundamental modules of human nature, most notably the essential nature of man and of woman. It makes sense to be curious about the evolutionary roots of human behavior. It's reasonable to try to understand our impulses and actions by applying Darwinian logic to the problem. We're animals. We're not above the rude little prods and jests of natural and sexual selection. But evolutionary psychology as it has been disseminated across mainstream consciousness is a cranky and despotic Cyclops, its single eye glaring through an overwhelmingly masculinist lens. I say "masculinist" rather than "male" because the view of male behavior promulgated by hard-core evolutionary psychologists is as narrow and inflexible as their view of womanhood is.

I'm not interested in explaining to men what they really want or how they should behave. If a fellow chooses to tell himself that his yen for the fetching young assistant in his office and his concomitant disgruntlement with his aging wife make perfect Darwinian sense, who am I to argue with him? I'm only proposing here that the hard-core evolutionary psychologists have got a lot about women wrong—about some of us, anyway—and that women want more and deserve better than the cartoon *Olive Oyl* handed down for popular consumption.

The cardinal premises of evolutionary psychology of interest to this discussion are as follows: 1. Men are more promiscuous and less sexually reserved than women are. 2. Women are inherently more interested in a stable relationship than men are. 3. Women are naturally attracted to high-status men with resources. 4. Men are naturally attracted to youth and beauty. 5. Humankind's core preferences and desires were hammered out long, long ago, a hundred thousand years or more, in the legendary Environment of Evolutionary Adaptation, or E.E.A., also known as the ancestral environment, also known as the Stone Age, and they have not changed appreciably since then, nor are they likely to change in the future.

In sum: Higgamus, hoggamus, Pygmalionus, *Playboy* magazine, *eternitas*. Amen. 5

Hard-core evolutionary psychology types go to extremes to argue in favor of the yawning chasm that separates the innate desires of women and men. They declare ringing confirmation for their theories even in the face of feeble and amusingly contradictory data. For example: Among the cardinal principles of the evo-psycho set is that men are by nature more polygamous than women are, and much more accepting of casual, even anonymous, sex. Men can't help themselves, they say: they are always hungry for sex, bodies, novelty and nubility. Granted, men needn't act on such desires, but the drive to sow seed is there nonetheless, satyric and relentless, and women cannot fully understand its force. David Buss, a professor of psychology at the University of Texas at Austin and one of the most outspoken of the evolutionary psychologists, says that asking a man not to lust after a pretty young woman is like telling a carnivore not to like meat.

At the same time, they recognize that the overwhelming majority of men and women get married, and so their theories must extend to different innate mate preferences among men and women. Men look for the hallmarks of youth, like smooth skin, full lips and perky breasts; they want a mate who has a long child-bearing career ahead of her. Men also want women who are virginal and who seem as though they'll be faithful and not make cuckolds of them. The sexy, vampy types are fine for a Saturday romp, but when it comes to choosing a marital partner, men want modesty and fidelity.

Women want a provider, the theory goes. They want a man who seems rich, stable and ambitious. They want to know that they and their children will be cared for. They want a man who can take charge, maybe dominate them just a little, enough to reassure them that the man is genotypically, phenotypically, eternally, a king. Women's innate preference for a well-to-do man continues to this day, the evolutionary psychologists insist, even among financially independent and professionally successful women who don't need a man as a provider. It was adaptive in the past to look for the most resourceful man, they say, and adaptations can't be willed away in a generation or two of putative cultural change.

And what is the evidence for these male-female verities? For the difference in promiscuity quotas, the hard-cores love to raise the example of the differences between gay men and lesbians. Homosexuals are seen as a revealing population because they supposedly can behave according to the innermost impulses of their sex, untempered by the need to adjust to the demands and wishes of the opposite sex, as heterosexuals theoretically are. What do we see in this ideal study group? Just look at how gay men carry on! They are perfectly happy to have hundreds, thousands, of sexual partners, to have sex in bathhouses, in bathrooms, in Central Park. By contrast, lesbians are sexually sedate. They don't cruise sex clubs. They couple up and stay coupled, and they like cuddling and hugging more than they do serious, genitally based sex.

In the hard-core rendering of inherent male-female discrepancies in promis- 10 cuity, gay men are offered up as true men, real men, men set free to be men, while lesbians are real women, ultra-women, acting out every woman's fantasy of love and commitment. Interestingly, though, in many neurobiology studies gay men are said to have somewhat feminized brains, with hypothalamic nuclei that are closer in size to a woman's than to a straight man's, and spatial-reasoning skills that are modest and ladylike rather than manfully robust. For their part, lesbians are posited to have somewhat masculinized brains and skills—to be sportier, more mechanically inclined, less likely to have played with dolls or tea sets when young—all as an ostensible result of exposure to prenatal androgens. And so gay men are sissy boys in some contexts and Stone Age manly men in others, while lesbians are battering rams one day and flower into the softest and most sexually divested girlish girls the next.

On the question of mate preferences, evo-psychos rely on surveys, most of them compiled by David Buss. His surveys are celebrated by some, derided by others, but in any event they are ambitious—performed in 37 countries, he says, on six continents. His surveys, and others emulating them, consistently find that men rate youth and beauty as important traits in a mate, while women give comparatively greater weight to ambition and financial success. Surveys show that surveys never lie. Lest you think that women's mate preferences change with their own mounting economic clout, surveys assure us that they do not. Surveys of female medical students, according to John Marshall Townsend, of Syracuse University, indicate that they hope to marry men with an earning power and social status at least equal to and preferably greater than their own.

Perhaps all this means is that men can earn a living wage better, even now, than women can. Men make up about half the world's population, but they still own the vast majority of the world's wealth—the currency, the minerals, the timber, the gold, the stocks, the amber fields of grain. In her superb book *Why So Slow?* Virginia Valian, a professor of psychology at Hunter College, lays out the extent of lingering economic discrepancies between men and women in the United States. In 1978 there were two women heading Fortune 1000 companies; in 1994, there were still two; in 1996, the number had jumped all the way to four. In 1985, 2 percent of the Fortune 1000's senior-level executives were women; by 1992, that number had hardly budged, to 3 percent. A 1990 salary and compensation survey of 799 major companies showed that of the highest-paid officers and directors, less than one-half of 1 percent were women. Ask, and he shall receive. In the United States the possession of a bachelor's degree adds $28,000 to a man's salary but only $9,000 to a woman's. A degree from a high-prestige school contributes $11,500 to a man's income but *subtracts* $2,400 from a woman's. If women continue to worry that they need a man's money, because the playing field remains about as level as the surface of Mars, then we can't conclude anything about innate preferences. If women continue to suffer from bag-lady syndrome even as they become prosperous, if they still see their wealth as provisional and capsizable, and if they still hope to find a man with a dependable income to supplement their own, then we can credit women with intelligence and acumen, for inequities abound.

There's another reason that smart, professional women might respond on surveys that they'd like a mate of their socioeconomic status or better. Smart, professional women are smart enough to know that men can be tender of ego—is it genetic?—and that it hurts a man to earn less money than his wife, and that resentment is a noxious chemical in a marriage and best avoided at any price. "A woman who is more successful than her mate threatens his position in the male hierarchy," Elizabeth Cashdan, of the University of Utah, has written. If women could be persuaded that men didn't mind their being high achievers, were in fact pleased and proud to be affiliated with them, we might predict that the women would stop caring about the particulars of their mates' income. The anthropologist

Sarah Blaffer Hrdy writes that "when female status and access to resources do not depend on her mate's status, women will likely use a range of criteria, not primarily or even necessarily prestige and wealth, for mate selection." She cites a 1996 *New York Times* story about women from a wide range of professions—bankers, judges, teachers, journalists—who marry male convicts. The allure of such men is not their income, for you can't earn much when you make license plates for a living. Instead, it is the men's gratitude that proves irresistible. The women also like the fact that their husbands' fidelity is guaranteed. "Peculiar as it is," Hrdy writes, "this vignette of sex-reversed claustration makes a serious point about just how little we know about female choice in breeding systems where male interests are not paramount and patrilines are not making the rules."

Do women love older men? Do women find gray hair and wrinkles attractive on men—as attractive, that is, as a fine, full head of pigmented hair and a vigorous, firm complexion? The evolutionary psychologists suggest yes. They believe that women look for the signs of maturity in men because a mature man is likely to be a comparatively wealthy and resourceful man. That should logically include baldness, which generally comes with age and the higher status that it often confers. Yet, as Desmond Morris points out, a thinning hairline is not considered a particularly attractive state.

Assuming that women find older men attractive, is it the men's alpha status? Or   15 could it be something less complimentary to the male, something like the following—that an older man is appealing not because he is powerful but because in his maturity he has lost some of his power, has become less marketable and desirable and potentially more grateful and gracious, more likely to make a younger woman feel that there is a balance of power in the relationship? The rude little calculation is simple: He is male, I am female—advantage, man. He is older, I am younger—advantage, woman. By the same token, a woman may place little value on a man's appearance because she values something else far more: room to breathe. Who can breathe in the presence of a handsome young man, whose ego, if expressed as a vapor, would fill Biosphere II? Not even, I'm afraid, a beautiful young woman.

In the end, what is important to question, and to hold to the fire of alternative interpretation, is the immutability and adaptive logic of the discrepancy, its basis in our genome rather than in the ecological circumstances in which a genome manages to express itself. Evolutionary psychologists insist on the essential discordance between the strength of the sex drive in males and females. They admit that many nonhuman female primates gallivant about rather more than we might have predicted before primatologists began observing their behavior in the field—more, far more, than is necessary for the sake of reproduction. Nonetheless, the credo of the coy female persists. It is garlanded with qualifications and is admitted to be an imperfect portrayal of female mating strategies, but then, that little matter of etiquette attended to, the credo is stated once again.

"Amid the great variety of social structure in these species, the basic theme . . . stands out, at least in minimal form: males seem very eager for sex and work hard to find it; females work less hard," Robert Wright says in *The Moral Animal*. "This isn't to say the females don't like sex. They love it, and may initiate it. And, intriguingly, the females of the species most closely related to humans—chimpanzees and bonobos—seem particularly amenable to a wild sex life, including a variety of partners. Still, female apes don't do what male apes do: search high and low, risking life and limb, to find sex, and to find as much of it, with as many different partners, as possible; it has a way of finding them." In fact female chimpanzees do search high and low and take great risks to find sex with partners other than the partners who have a way of finding them. DNA studies of chimpanzees in West Africa show that half the offspring in a group of closely scrutinized chimpanzees turned out not to be the offspring of the resident males. The females of the group didn't rely on sex "finding" its way to them; they proactively left the local environs, under such conditions of secrecy that not even their vigilant human observers knew they had gone, and became impregnated by outside males. They did so even at the risk of life and limb—their own and those of their offspring. Male chimpanzees try to control the movements of fertile females. They'll scream at them and hit them if they think the females aren't listening. They may even kill an infant they think is not their own. We don't know why the females take such risks to philander, but they do, and to say that female chimpanzees "work less hard" than males do at finding sex does not appear to be supported by the data.

Evo-psychos pull us back and forth until we might want to sue for whiplash. On the one hand we are told that women have a lower sex drive than men do. On the other hand we are told that the madonna-whore dichotomy is a universal stereotype. In every culture, there is a tendency among both men and women to adjudge women as either chaste or trampy. The chaste ones are accorded esteem. The trampy ones are consigned to the basement, a notch or two below goats in social status. A woman can't sleep around without risking terrible retribution, to her reputation, to her prospects, to her life. "Can anyone find a single culture in which women with unrestrained sexual appetites *aren't* viewed as more aberrant than comparably libidinous men?" Wright asks rhetorically.

Women are said to have lower sex drives than men, yet they are universally punished if they display evidence to the contrary—if they disobey their "natural" inclination toward a stifled libido. Women supposedly have a lower sex drive than men do, yet it is not low enough. There is still just enough of a lingering female infidelity impulse that cultures everywhere have had to gird against it by articulating a rigid dichotomy with menacing implications for those who fall on the wrong side of it. There is still enough lingering female infidelity to justify infibulation, purdah, claustration. Men have the naturally higher sex drive, yet all the laws, customs, punishments, shame, strictures, mystiques and antimystiques are aimed with full hominid fury at that tepid, sleepy, hypoactive creature, the female libido.

"It seems premature . . . to attribute the relative lack of female interest in sexual [20] variety to women's biological nature alone in the face of overwhelming evidence that women are consistently beaten for promiscuity and adultery," the primatologist Barbara Smuts has written. "If female sexuality is muted compared to that of men, then why must men the world over go to extreme lengths to control and contain it?"

Why indeed? Consider a brief evolutionary apologia for President Clinton's adulteries written by Steven Pinker, of the Massachusetts Institute of Technology.

"Most human drives have ancient Darwinian rationales," he wrote. "A prehistoric man who slept with fifty women could have sired fifty children, and would have been more likely to have descendants who inherited his tastes. A woman who slept with fifty men would have no more descendants than a woman who slept with one. Thus, men should seek quantity in sexual partners; women, quality." And isn't it so, he says, everywhere and always so? "In our society," he continues, "most young men tell researchers that they would like eight sexual partners in the next two years; most women say that they would like one." Yet would a man find the prospect of a string of partners so appealing if the following rules were applied: that no matter how much he may like a particular woman and be pleased by her performance and want to sleep with her again, he will have no say in the matter and will be dependent on her mood and good graces for all future contact; that each act of casual sex will cheapen his status and make him increasingly less attractive to other women; and that society will not wink at his randiness but rather sneer at him and think him pathetic, sullied, smaller than life? Until men are subjected to the same severe standards and threat of censure as women are, and until they are given the lower hand in a so-called casual encounter from the start, it is hard to insist with such self-satisfaction that, hey, it's natural, men like a lot of sex with a lot of people and women don't.

Reflect for a moment on Pinker's philandering caveman who slept with 50 women. Just how good a reproductive strategy is this chronic, random shooting of the gun? A woman is fertile only five or six days a month. Her ovulation is concealed. The man doesn't know when she's fertile. She might be in the early stages of pregnancy when he gets to her; she might still be lactating and thus not ovulating. Moreover, even if our hypothetical Don Juan hits a day on which a woman is ovulating, the chances are around 65 percent that his sperm will fail to fertilize her egg; human reproduction is complicated, and most eggs and sperm are not up to the demands of proper fusion. Even if conception occurs, the resulting embryo has about a 30 percent chance of miscarrying at some point in gestation. In sum, each episode of fleeting sex has a remarkably small probability of yielding a baby—no more than 1 or 2 percent at best.

And because the man is trysting and running, he isn't able to prevent any of his casual contacts from turning around and mating with other men. The poor fellow. He has to mate with many scores of women for his wham-bam strategy to pay off. And where are all these women to be found, anyway? Population densities during that purportedly all-powerful psyche shaper the "ancestral environment" were quite low, and long-distance travel was dangerous and difficult.

There are alternatives to wantonness, as a number of theorists have emphasized. If, for example, a man were to spend more time with one woman rather than dashing breathlessly from sheet to sheet, if he were to feel compelled to engage in what animal behaviorists call mate guarding, he might be better off, reproductively speaking, than the wild Lothario, both because the odds of impregnating the woman would increase and because he'd be monopolizing her energy and keeping her from the advances of other sperm bearers. It takes the average couple three to four months of regular sexual intercourse to become pregnant. That number of days is approximately equal to the number of partners our hypothetical libertine needs to sleep with to have one encounter result in a "fertility unit," that is, a baby. The two strategies, then, shake out about the same. A man can sleep with a lot of women—the quantitative approach—or he can sleep with one woman for months at a time, and be madly in love with her—the qualitative tactic.

It's possible that these two reproductive strategies are distributed in discrete 25 packets among the male population, with a result that some men are born philanderers and can never attach, while others are born romantics and perpetually in love with love; but it's also possible that men teeter back and forth from one impulse to the other, suffering an internal struggle between the desire to bond and the desire to retreat, with the circuits of attachment ever there to be toyed with, and their needs and desires difficult to understand, paradoxical, fickle, treacherous and glorious. It is possible, then, and for perfectly good Darwinian reason, that casual sex for men is rarely as casual as it is billed.

It needn't be argued that men and women are exactly the same, or that humans are meta-evolutionary beings, removed from nature and slaves to culture, to reject the perpetually regurgitated model of the coy female and the ardent male. Conflicts of interest are always among us, and the outcomes of those conflicts are interesting, more interesting by far than what the ultra-evolutionary psychology line has handed us. Patricia Gowaty, of the University of Georgia, sees conflict between males and females as inevitable and pervasive. She calls it sexual dialectics. Her thesis is that females and males vie for control over the means of reproduction. Those means are the female body, for there is as yet no such beast as the parthenogenetic man.

Women are under selective pressure to maintain control over their reproduction, to choose with whom they will mate and with whom they will not—to exercise female choice. Men are under selective pressure to make sure they're chosen or, barring that, to subvert female choice and coerce the female to mate against her will. "But once you have this basic dialectic set in motion, it's going to be a constant push-me, pull-you," Gowaty says. "That dynamism cannot possibly result in a unitary response, the caricatured coy woman and ardent man. Instead there are going to be some coy, reluctantly mating males and some ardent females, and any number of variations in between.

"A female will choose to mate with a male whom she believes, consciously or otherwise, will confer some advantage on her and her offspring. If that's the case, then her decision is contingent on what she brings to the equation." For example, she says, "the 'good genes' model leads to oversimplified notions that there is a 'best male' out there, a top-of-the-line hunk whom all females would prefer to mate with if they had the wherewithal. But in the viability model, a female brings her own genetic complement to the equation, with the result that what looks good genetically to one woman might be a clash of colors for another."

Maybe the man's immune system doesn't complement her own, for example, Gowaty proposes. There's evidence that the search for immune variation is one of the subtle factors driving mate selection, which may be why we care about how our lovers smell; immune molecules may be volatilized and released in sweat, hair, the oil on our skin. We are each of us a chemistry set, and each of us has a distinctive mix of reagents. "What pleases me might not please somebody else," Gowaty says.

"There is no one-brand great male out there. We're not all programmed to look for the alpha male and only willing to mate with the little guy or the less aggressive guy because we can't do any better. But the propaganda gives us a picture of the right man and the ideal woman, and the effect of the propaganda is insidious. It becomes self-reinforcing. People who don't fit the model think, I'm weird, I'll have to change my behavior." It is this danger, that the ostensible "discoveries" of evolutionary psychology will be used as propaganda, that makes the enterprise so disturbing.

Variation and flexibility are the key themes that get set aside in the breath- 30
less dissemination of evolutionary psychology. "The variation is tremendous, and is rooted in biology," Barbara Smuts said to me. "Flexibility itself is the adaptation." Smuts has studied olive baboons, and she has seen males pursuing all sorts of mating strategies. "There are some whose primary strategy is dominating other males, and being able to gain access to more females because of their fighting ability," she says. "Then there is the type of male who avoids competition and cultivates long-term relationships with females and their infants. These are the nice, affiliative guys. There's a third type, who focuses on sexual relationships. He's the consorter. . . . And as far as we can tell, no one reproductive strategy has advantages over the others."

Women are said to need an investing male. We think we know the reason. Human babies are difficult and time consuming to raise. Stone Age mothers needed husbands to bring home the bison. Yet the age-old assumption that male parental investment lies at the heart of human evolution is now open to serious question. Men in traditional foraging cultures do not necessarily invest resources in their offspring. Among the Hadza of Africa, for example, the men hunt, but they share the bounty of that hunting widely, politically, strategically. They don't deliver it straight to the mouths of their progeny. Women rely on their senior female kin to help feed their children. The women and their children in a gathering-hunting society clearly benefit from the meat that hunters bring back to the group. But they benefit as a group, not as a collection of nuclear family units, each beholden to the father's personal pound of wildeburger.

This is a startling revelation, which upends many of our presumptions about the origins of marriage and what women want from men and men from women. If the environment of evolutionary adaptation is not defined primarily by male parental investment, the bedrock of so much of evolutionary psychology's theories, then we can throw the door wide open and ask new questions, rather than endlessly repeating ditties and calling the female coy long after she has run her petticoats through the Presidential paper shredder.

For example: Nicholas Blurton Jones, of the University of California at Los Angeles, and others have proposed that marriage developed as an extension of men's efforts at mate guarding. If the cost of philandering becomes ludicrously high, the man might be better off trying to claim rights to one woman at a time. Regular sex with a fertile woman is at least likely to yield offspring at comparatively little risk to his life, particularly if sexual access to the woman is formalized through a public ceremony—a wedding. Looked at from this perspective, one must wonder why an ancestral woman bothered to get married, particularly if she and her female relatives did most of the work of keeping the family fed from year to year. Perhaps, Blurton Jones suggests, to limit the degree to which she was harassed. The cost of chronic male harassment may be too high to bear. Better to agree to a ritualized bond with a male and to benefit from whatever hands-off policy that marriage may bring, than to spend all of her time locked in one sexual dialectic or another.

Thus marriage may have arisen as a multifaceted social pact: between man and woman, between male and male and between the couple and the tribe. It is a reasonable solution to a series of cultural challenges that arose in concert with the expansion of the human neocortex. But its roots may not be what we think they are, nor may our contemporary mating behaviors stem from the pressures of an ancestral environment as it is commonly portrayed, in which a woman needed a mate to help feed and clothe her young. Instead, our "deep" feelings about marriage may be more pragmatic, more contextual and, dare I say it, more egalitarian than we give them credit for being.

If marriage is a social compact, a mutual bid between man and woman to   35 contrive a reasonably stable and agreeable microhabitat in a community of shrewd and well-armed members, then we can understand why, despite rhetoric to the contrary, men are as eager to marry as women are. A raft of epidemiological studies have shown that marriage adds more years to the life of a man than it does to that of a woman. Why should that be, if men are so "naturally" ill suited to matrimony?

What do women want? None of us can speak for all women, or for more than one woman, really, but we can hazard a mad guess that a desire for emotional parity is widespread and profound. It doesn't go away, although it often hibernates under duress, and it may be perverted by the restrictions of habitat or culture into something that looks like its opposite. The impulse for liberty is congenital. It is the ultimate manifestation of selfishness, which is why we can count on its endurance.

QUESTIONS FOR DISCUSSION AND WRITING

1. Throughout much of her article, Angier uses humorous words ("wildeburger") and phrases ("trysting and running") as well as informal words ("guy") and expressions ("hey"). With your classmates, gather other examples of such features. What kind of reader does Angier seem to be addressing? How do these expressions affect you as a reader? In what passages does she *avoid* using such expressions? Speculate on why she varies her style.

2. Angier writes that the "impulse for liberty is congenital" (paragraph 36). How do evolutionary psychologists explain the manifestations of this impulse? How does Angier explain them?

3. Which of the various stereotypical behaviors of men and women that Angier mentions have you seen or heard discussed in the press, in the media, or in conversation? What causes these behaviors, in your opinion—nature or culture?

4. What do primate studies reveal about the relative sexual activity of males and females? What implications for human beings are drawn by evolutionary psychologists and by Angier? Write an essay explaining why you find Angier's approach more or less persuasive than that of the evolutionary psychologists.

5. Write an essay comparing and contrasting the ways in which evolutionary psychologists and Angier view the notion that females choose males who can best care for them and their infants.

ALICE WALKER

In Search of Our Mothers' Gardens

Author of the Pulitzer Prize–winning novel The Color Purple *(1982), Alice Walker is a poet, novelist, essayist, and civil rights activist. She was born (1944) and raised in segregated Eatonton, Georgia, where her parents, Willie Lee and Minnie Walker, were sharecroppers. Walker graduated from Sarah Lawrence (B.A., 1965). During the civil rights movement, she was a voter registration worker in Georgia and a Head Start worker in Mississippi, before teaching at various colleges, including Tougaloo, Wellesley, and her alma mater. Walker addresses the human implications of social issues in her essay collections, including* Living by the Word *(1988) and* Anything We Love Can Be Saved: A Writer's Activism *(1997); short-story collections, such as* In Love and Trouble *(1973) and* You Can't Keep a Good Woman Down *(1981); and novels, including* Meridian *(1976) and* Possessing the Secret of Joy *(1992). Walker's poetry includes* Revolutionary Petunias, and Other Poems *(1973) and* Her Blue Body Everything We Know: Earthling Poems, 1965–1990 *(1991). Her four children's books include* Why War Is Never a Good Idea *(2007). Her most recent book is a memoir,* The Chicken Chronicles *(2011).*

Walker wrote "In Search of Our Mothers' Gardens" for a 1973 Radcliffe symposium on "The Black Woman: Myths and Realities." In 1974 she revised the speech, which was published in Ms. *and later collected in* In Search of Our Mothers' Gardens: Womanist Prose *(1983), coining* womanist *to denote her philosophical and political commitment to "the survival and wholeness of entire people, male and female." The essay combines historical analysis, literary criticism, and autobiography to explore the "creative spirit" of generations of African American women. Walker urges readers to recognize that many such women expressed their "creative spirit" through quilting, gardening, blues singing, storytelling, and poetry.*

I

I described her own nature and temperament. Told how they needed a larger life for their expression. . . . I pointed out that in lieu of proper channels, her emotions had overflowed into paths and dissipated them. I talked beautifully I thought, about an art that would be born, an art that would open the way for women the likes of her. I asked her to hope, and build up an inner life against the coming of that day. . . . I sang, with a strange quiver in my voice, a promise song.

–"Avey," Jean Toomer, Cane

The poet speaking to a prostitute who falls asleep while he's talking—

When the poet Jean Toomer walked through the South in the early twenties, he discovered a curious thing: Black women whose spirituality was so intense, so deep, so *unconscious*, they were themselves unaware of the richness they held. They stumbled blindly through their lives: creatures so abused and mutilated in body, so dimmed and confused by pain, that they considered themselves unworthy even of hope. In the selfless abstractions their bodies became to the men who used them, they became more than "sexual objects," more even than mere women: they became Saints. Instead of being perceived as whole persons, their bodies became shrines; what was thought to be their minds became temples suitable for worship. These crazy "Saints" stared out at the world, wildly, like lunatics—or quietly, like suicides; and the "God" that was in their gate was as mute as a great stone.

Who were these "Saints"? These crazy, loony, pitiful women?

Some of them without a doubt, were our mothers and grandmothers.

In the still heat of the post-Reconstruction South, this is how they seemed 5 to Jean Toomer: exquisite butterflies trapped in an evil honey, toiling away their lives in an era, a century, that did not acknowledge them, except as "the *mule* of the world." They dreamed dreams that no one knew—not even themselves, in any coherent fashion—and saw visions no one could understand. They wandered or sat about the countryside crooning lullabies to ghosts, and drawing the mother of Christ in charcoal on courthouse walls.

They forced their minds to desert their bodies and their striving spirits sought to rise, the frail whirlwinds from the hard red clay. And when those frail whirlwinds fell, in scattered particles, upon the ground, no one mourned. Instead, men lit candles to celebrate the emptiness that remained, as people do who enter a beautiful but vacant space to resurrect a God.

Our mothers and grandmothers, some of them: moving to music not yet written. And they waited.

They waited for a day when the unknown thing that was in them would be made known; but guessed, somehow in their darkness, that on the day of their revelation they would be long dead. Therefore to Toomer they walked, and even ran, in slow motion. For they were going nowhere immediate, and the future was not yet within their grasp. And men took our mothers and grandmothers, "but got no pleasure from it." So complex was their passion and their calm.

To Toomer, they lay vacant and fallow as autumn fields, with harvest time never in sight: and he saw them enter loveless marriages, without joy; and become prostitutes, without resistance; and become mothers of children without fulfillment.

For these grandmothers and mothers of ours were not "Saints," but Artists; 10 driven to a numb and bleeding madness by the springs of creativity in them for which there was no release. They were Creators, who lived lives of spiritual waste, because they were so rich in spirituality—which is the basis of Art—that the strain of enduring their unused and unwanted talent drove them insane. Throwing away this spirituality was their pathetic attempt to lighten the soul to a weight their work-worn, sexually abused bodies could bear.

What did it mean for a Black woman to be an artist in our grandmothers' time? In our great-grandmothers' day? It is a question with an answer cruel enough to stop the blood.

Did you have a genius of a great-great-grandmother who died under some ignorant and depraved white overseer's lash? Or was she required to bake biscuits for a lazy backwater tramp, when she cried out in her soul to paint watercolors of sunsets, or the rain falling on the green and peaceful pasturelands? Or was her body broken and forced to bear children (who were more often than not sold away from her)—eight, ten, fifteen, twenty children—when her one joy was the thought of modeling heroic figures of Rebellion, in stone or clay?

How was the creativity of the Black woman kept alive, year after year and century after century, when for most of the years Black people have been in America, it was a punishable crime for a Black person to read or write? And the freedom to paint, to sculpt, to expand the mind with action, did not exist. Consider, if you can bear to imagine it, what might have been the result if singing, too, had been forbidden by law. Listen to the voices of Bessie Smith, Billie Holiday, Nina Simone, Roberta Flack, and Aretha Franklin, among others, and imagine those voices muzzled for life. Then you may begin to comprehend the lives of our "crazy," "Sainted" mothers and grandmothers. The agony of the lives of women who might have been Poets, Novelists, Essayists, and Short Story Writers (over a period of centuries), who died with their real gifts stifled within them.

And, if this were the end of the story, we would have cause to cry out in my paraphrase of Okot p'Bitek's great poem:

O, my clanswomen
Let us all cry together!
Come,
Let us mourn the death of our mother,
The death of a Queen
The ash that was produced
By a great fire!
O this homestead is utterly dead
Close the gates
With *lacari* thorns,
For our mother
The creator of the Stool is lost!
And all the young women
Have perished in the wilderness.[1]

But this is not the end of the story, for all the young women—our mothers and grandmothers, *ourselves*—have not perished in the wilderness. And if we ask ourselves why, and search for and find the answer, we will know beyond all efforts to erase it from our minds, just exactly who, and of what, we Black American women are.

---

[1]Okot p'Bitek, *Song of Lawino: An Africa Lament* (Nairobi: East African Publishing House, 1966). [Editors' note.]

One example, perhaps the most pathetic, most misunderstood one, can provide a backdrop for our mothers' work: Phillis Wheatley, a slave in the 1700s.

Virginia Woolf, in her book, *A Room of One's Own*, wrote that in order for a woman to write fiction she must have two things, certainly: a room of her own (with a key and lock) and enough money to support herself.

What then are we to make of Phillis Wheatley, a slave, who owned not even herself? This sickly, frail, Black girl who required a servant of her own at times—her health was so precarious—and who, had she been white, would have been easily considered the intellectual superior of all the women and most of the men in the society of her day.

Virginia Woolf wrote further, speaking of course not of our Phillis, that "any woman born with a great gift in the sixteenth century [insert *eighteenth century*, insert *Black woman*, insert *born or made a slave*] would certainly have gone crazed, shot herself, or ended her days in some lonely cottage outside the village, half witch, half wizard [insert *Saint*], feared and mocked at. For it needs little skill and psychology to be sure that a highly gifted girl who had tried to use her gift for poetry would have been so thwarted and hindered by contrary instincts [add *chains, guns, the lash, the ownership of one's body by someone else, submission to an alien religion*] that she must have lost her health and sanity to a certainty."

The key words, as they relate to Phillis, are "contrary instincts." For when we 20 read the poetry of Phillis Wheatley—as when we read the novels of Nella Larsen or the oddly false-sounding autobiography of that freest of all Black women writers, Zora Hurston—evidence of "contrary instincts" is everywhere. Her loyalties were completely divided, as was, without question, her mind.

But how could this be otherwise? Captured at seven, a slave of wealthy, doting whites who instilled in her the "savagery" of the Africa they "rescued" her from . . . one wonders if she was even able to remember her homeland as she had known it, or as it really was.

Yet, because she did try to use her gift for poetry in a world that made her a slave, she was "so thwarted and hindered by . . . contrary instincts that she . . . lost her health. . . ." In the last years of her brief life, burdened not only with the need to express her gift but also with a penniless, friendless "freedom" and several small children for whom she was forced to do strenuous work to feed, she lost her health, certainly. Suffering from malnutrition and neglect and who knows what mental agonies, Phillis Wheatley died.

So torn by "contrary instincts" was Black, kidnapped, enslaved Phillis that her description of "the Goddess"—as she poetically called the Liberty she did not have—is ironically, cruelly humorous. And, in fact, has held Phillis up to ridicule for more than a century. It is usually read prior to hanging Phillis's memory as that of a fool. She wrote:

The Goddess comes, she moves divinely fair,
Olive and laurel binds her *golden* hair:
Wherever shines this native of the skies,
Unnumber'd charms and recent graces rise.

[Emphasis Mine]

It is obvious that Phillis, the slave, combed the "Goddess's" hair every morning; prior, perhaps, to bringing in the milk, or fixing her mistress's lunch. She took her imagery from the one thing she saw elevated above all others.

With the benefit of hindsight we ask, "How could she?"   25

But at last, Phillis, we understand. No more snickering when your stiff, struggling, ambivalent lines are forced on us. We know now that you were not an idiot nor a traitor; only a sickly little Black girl, snatched from your home and country and made a slave; a woman who still struggled to sing the song that was your gift, although in a land of barbarians who praised you for your bewildered tongue. It is not so much what you sang, as that you kept alive, in so many of our ancestors, the notion of song.

II

Black women are called, in the folklore that so aptly identifies one's status in society, "the *mule* of the world," because we have been handed the burdens that everyone else—*everyone* else—refused to carry. We have been called "Matriarchs," "Superwomen," and "Mean and Evil Bitches." Not to mention "Castrators" and "Sapphire's Mama." When we have pleaded for understanding, our character has been distorted; when we have asked for simple caring, we have been handed empty inspirational appellations, then stuck in the farthest corner. When we have asked for love, we have been given children. In short, even our plainer gifts, our labors of fidelity and love, have been knocked down our throats. To be an Artist and a Black woman, even today, lowers our status in many respects, rather than raises it: and yet, Artists we will be.

Therefore we must fearlessly pull out of ourselves and look at and identify with our lives the living creativity some of our great-grandmothers were not allowed to know. I stress *some* of them because it is well known that the majority of our great-grandmothers knew, even without "knowing" it, the reality of their spirituality, even if they didn't recognize it beyond what happened in the singing at church—and they never had any intention of giving it up.

How they did it: those millions of Black women who were not Phillis Wheatley, or Lucy Terry or Frances Harper or Zora Hurston or Nella Larsen or Bessie Smith— nor Elizabeth Catlett, nor Katherine Dunham, either—brings me to the title of this essay, "In Search of Our Mothers' Gardens," which is a personal account that is yet shared, in its theme and its meaning, by all of us. I found, while thinking about the far-reaching world of the creative Black woman, that often the truest answer to a question that really matters can be found very close.

In the late 1920s my mother ran away from home to marry my father. Mar- 30 riage, if not running away, was expected of seventeen-year-old girls. By the time she was twenty, she had two children and was pregnant with a third. Five children later, I was born. And this is how I came to know my mother: she seemed a large, soft, loving-eyed woman who was rarely impatient in our home. Her quick, violent temper was on view only a few times a year, when she battled with the white landlord who had the misfortune to suggest to her that her children did not need to go to school.

She made all the clothes we wore, even my brothers' overalls. She made all the towels and sheets we used. She spent the summers canning vegetables and fruits. She spent the winter evenings making quilts enough to cover all our beds.

During the "working" day, she labored beside—not behind—my father in the fields. Her day began before sunup, and did not end until late at night. There was never a moment for her to sit down, undisturbed, to unravel her own private thoughts; never a time free from interruption—by work or the noisy inquiries of her many children. And yet, it is to my mother—and all our mothers who were not famous—that I went in search of the secret of what has fed that muzzled and often mutilated, but vibrant, creative spirit that the Black woman has inherited, and that pops out in wild and unlikely places to this day.

But when, you will ask, did my overworked mother have time to know or care about feeding the creative spirit?

The answer is so simple that many of us have spent years discovering it. We have constantly looked high, when we should have looked high—and low.

For example: in the Smithsonian Institution in Washington, D.C., there hangs a quilt unlike any other in the world. In fanciful, inspired, and yet simple and identifiable figures, it portrays the story of the Crucifixion. It is considered rare, beyond price. Though it follows no known pattern of quiltmaking, and though it is made of bits and pieces of worthless rags, it is obviously the work of a person of powerful imagination and deep spiritual feelings. Below this quilt I saw a note that says it was made by "an anonymous Black woman in Alabama, a hundred years ago." 35

If we could locate this "anonymous" Black woman from Alabama, she would turn out to be one of our grandmothers—an artist who left her mark in the only materials she could afford, and in the only medium her position in society allowed her to use.

As Virginia Woolf wrote further, in *A Room of One's Own*:

"Yet genius of a sort must have existed among women as it must have existed among the working class. [Change this to *slaves* and *the wives and daughters of sharecroppers*.] Now and again an Emily Brontë or a Robert Burns [change this to *a Zora Hurston or a Richard Wright*] blazes out and proves its presence. But certainly it never got itself on to paper. When, however, one reads of a witch being ducked, of a woman possessed by devils [or *Sainthood*], of a wise woman selling herbs [our rootworkers], or even a very remarkable man who had a mother, then I think we are on the track of a suppressed poet, of some mute and inglorious Jane Austen. . . . Indeed, I would venture to guess that Anon, who wrote so many poems without singing them, was often a woman. . . ."

And so our mothers and grandmothers have, more often than not anonymously, handed on the creative spark, the seed of the flower they themselves never hoped to see: or like a sealed letter they could not plainly read.

And so it is, certainly, with my own mother. Unlike Ma Rainey's songs, which retained their creator's name even while blasting forth from Bessie Smith's mouth, no song or poem will bear my mother's name. Yet so many of the stories that I 40 write, that we all write, are my mother's stories. Only recently did I fully realize this: that through years of listening to my mother's stories of her life, I have absorbed not only the stories themselves, but something of the manner in which she spoke, something of the urgency that involves the knowledge that her stories—like her life—must be recorded. It is probably for this reason that so much of what I have written is about characters whose counterparts in real life are so much older than I am.

But the telling of these stories, which came from my mother's lips as naturally as breathing, was not the only way my mother showed herself as an artist. For stories, too, were subject to being distracted, to dying without conclusion. Dinners must be started, and cotton must be gathered before the big rains. The artist that was and is my mother showed itself to me only after many years. This is what I finally noticed:

Like Mem, a character in *The Third Life of Grange Copeland*, my mother adorned with flowers whatever shabby house we were forced to live in. And not just your typical straggly country stand of zinnias, either. She planted ambitious gardens—and still does—with over fifty different varieties of plants that bloom profusely from early March until late November. Before she left home for the fields, she watered her flowers, chopped up the grass, and laid out new beds. When she returned from the fields she might divide clumps of bulbs, dig a cold pit, uproot and replant roses, or prune branches from her taller bushes or trees—until night came and it was too dark to see.

Whatever she planted grew as if by magic, and her fame as a grower of flowers spread over three counties. Because of her creativity with her flowers, even my memories of poverty are seen through a screen of blooms—sunflowers, petunias, roses, dahlias, forsythia, spirea, delphiniums, verbena . . . and on and on.

And I remember people coming to my mother's yard to be given cuttings from her flowers; I hear again the praise showered on her because whatever rocky soil she landed on, she turned into a garden. A garden so brilliant with colors, so original in its design, so magnificent with life and creativity, that to this day people drive by our house in Georgia—perfect strangers and imperfect strangers—and ask to stand or walk among my mother's art.

I notice that it is only when my mother is working in her flowers that she is 45 radiant, almost to the point of being invisible—except as Creator: hand and eye. She is involved in work her soul must have. Ordering the universe in the image of her personal conception of Beauty.

Her face, as she prepares the Art that is her gift, is a legacy of respect she leaves to me, for all that illuminates and cherishes life. She had handed down respect for the possibilities—and the will to grasp them.

For her, so hindered and intruded upon in so many ways, being an artist has still been a daily part of her life. This ability to hold on, even in very simple ways, is work Black women have done for a very long time.

This poem is not enough, but it is something, for the woman who literally covered the holes in our walls with sunflowers:

They were women then
My mama's generation
Husky of voice—Stout of
Step
With fists as well as
Hands
How they battered down
Doors
And ironed
Starched white
Shirts
How they led
Armies
Headragged Generals
Across mined
Fields
Booby-trapped
Ditches
To discover books
Desks
A place for us
How they knew what we
Must know
Without knowing a page
Of it
Themselves.

Guided by my heritage of love and beauty and a respect for strength—in search of my mother's garden, I found my own.

And perhaps in Africa over two hundred years ago, there was just such a 50 mother; perhaps she painted vivid and daring decorations in oranges and yellows and greens on the walls of her hut; perhaps she sang—in a voice like Roberta Flack's—*sweetly* over the compounds of her village; perhaps she wove the most stunning mats or told the most ingenious stories of all the village story-tellers. Perhaps she was herself a poet—though only her daughter's name is signed to the poems that we know.

Perhaps Phillis Wheatley's mother was also an artist.

Perhaps in more than Phillis Wheatley's biological life is her mother's signature made clear.

QUESTIONS FOR DISCUSSION AND WRITING

1. How do *you* recognize a work of art? What counts as art? What role do institutions such as the Smithsonian play in defining what counts—for others and for you—as a work of art? How can one distinguish "art" from "Art"? What passages from Walker's essay support your analysis?

2. Who represents "white culture" in Walker's essay, and what is the role of white culture in Walker's development?

3. What role does gender play in Walker's definition of what counts as art? How does Walker redefine art by considering women's production of it?

4. What definition of *creativity* does Walker provide in "In Search of Our Mothers' Gardens," and how do her examples help you understand its meaning? What is the value of Walker's parenthetical revision of the short passage by Virginia Woolf (paragraph 38)? How does Woolf comment on the nature of imagination?

VIRGINIA WOOLF

Professions for Women

Virginia Woolf (1882–1941) was a significant figure in London literary society in the 1920s–30s. As a prolific writer of novels, essays, short stories, letters, and diaries, she— along with James Joyce—changed the face of modern literature, in part by exploring human consciousness from the inside out, as "stream of consciousness," rather than the outside in. Although the plots of her novels may seem uneventful and the subjects commonplace, Woolf's experimental techniques and inventive style transform the ordinary into world-class beauty and brilliance. Thus, a day in the life of Mrs. Dalloway *(1925), who is giving a party, encapsulates Mrs. Dalloway's life history and that of modern England, as well, in characteristically precise, diamond-edged language. In* To the Lighthouse *(1927), depicting a day of the Ramsay family's seaside summer vacation, Woolf's imaginative perspective invites readers into the mind of Mrs. Ramsay, an unerring interpreter of her cantankerous husband, her brood of rambunctious and romantic children, and a flock of guests—all of whom receive her tender, loving care and a critical eye. The central character in* Orlando *(1928) is transformed from a Renaissance man (self-confident, assertive) into a late nineteenth-century woman (demure and flirtatious, in accord with the values of the time).*

Woolf's book-length essay A Room of One's Own *(1929), concludes that "a woman must have money and a room of her own if she is to write fiction," a feminist point of view reflected, as well, in "Professions for Women." This was originally delivered as a speech to the Women's Service League in 1931 and then published in* The Death of the Moth and Other Essays *(1942). Here Woolf continues to explore the multiple barriers that women must overcome to attain autonomy and professional success in male-dominated society. To do this women have to kill off "The Angel in the House," the embodiment of the nurturing, self-effacing feminine ideal.*

When your secretary invited me to come here, she told me that your Society is concerned with the employment of women and she suggested that I might tell you something about my own professional experiences. It is true I am a woman; it is true I am employed; but what professional experiences have I had? It is difficult to say. My profession is literature; and in that profession there are fewer experiences for women than in any other, with the exception of the stage—fewer, I mean, that are peculiar to women. For the road was cut many years ago—by Fanny Burney, by Aphra Behn, by Harriet Martineau, by Jane Austen, by George Eliot—many famous women, and many more unknown and forgotten, have been before me, making the path smooth, and regulating my steps. Thus, when I came to write, there were very few material obstacles in my way. Writing was a reputable and harmless occupation. The family peace was not broken by the scratching of a pen. No demand was made upon the family purse. For ten and sixpence one can buy paper enough to write all the plays of Shakespeare—if one has a mind that way. Pianos and models, Paris, Vienna and Berlin, masters and mistresses, are not needed by a writer. The cheapness of writing paper is, of course, the reason why women have succeeded as writers before they have succeeded in the other professions.

But to tell you my story—it is a simple one. You have only got to figure to yourselves a girl in a bedroom with a pen in her hand. She had only to move that pen from left to right—from ten o'clock to one. Then it occurred to her to do what is simple and cheap enough after all—to slip a few of those pages into an envelope, fix a penny stamp in the corner, and drop the envelope into the red box at the corner. It was thus that I became a journalist; and my effort was rewarded on the first day of the following month—a very glorious day it was for me—by a letter from an editor containing a cheque for one pound ten shillings and sixpence. But to show you how little I deserve to be called a professional woman, how little I know of the struggles and difficulties of such lives, I have to admit that instead of spending that sum upon bread and butter, rent, shoes and stockings, or butcher's bills, I went out and bought a cat—a beautiful cat, a Persian cat, which very soon involved me in bitter disputes with my neighbors.

What could be easier than to write articles and to buy Persian cats with the profits? But wait a moment. Articles have to be about something. Mine, I seem to remember, was about a novel by a famous man. And while I was writing this review, I discovered that if I were going to review books I should need to do battle with a certain phantom. And the phantom was a woman, and when I came to know her better I called her after the heroine of a famous poem, The Angel in the House. It was she who used to come between me and my paper when I was writing reviews. It was she who bothered me and wasted my time and so tormented me that at last I killed her. You who come of a younger and happier generation may not have heard of her—you may not know what I mean by the Angel in the House. I will describe her as shortly as I can. She was intensely sympathetic. She was immensely charming. She was utterly unselfish. She excelled in the difficult arts of family life. She sacrificed herself daily. If there was a chicken, she took the leg; if there was a draught she sat in it—in short she was so constituted that she never had a mind or a wish of her own, but preferred to sympathize always with the minds and wishes of others. Above all—I need not say it—she was pure. Her purity was supposed to be her chief beauty—her blushes, her great grace. In those days—the last of Queen Victoria—every house had its Angel. And when I came to write I encountered her with the very first words. The shadow of her wings fell on my page; I heard the rustling of her skirts in the room. Directly, that is to say, I took my pen in hand to review that novel by a famous man, she slipped behind me and whispered: "My dear, you are a young woman. You are writing about a book that has been written by a man. Be sympathetic; be tender; flatter; deceive; use all the arts and wiles of our sex. Never let anybody guess that you have a mind of your own. Above all, be pure." And she made as if to guide my pen. I now record the one act for which I take some credit to myself, though the credit rightly belongs to some excellent ancestors of mine who left me a certain sum of money—shall we say five hundred pounds a year?—so that it was not necessary for me to depend solely on charm for my living. I turned upon her and caught her by the throat. I did my best to kill her. My excuse, if I were to be had up in a court of law, would be that I acted in self-defense. Had I not killed her she would have killed me. She would have plucked the heart out of my writing. For, as I found, directly I put pen to paper, you cannot review even a novel without having a mind of your own, without expressing what you think to be the truth about human relations, morality, sex. And all these questions, according to the Angel in the House, cannot be dealt with freely and openly by women; they must charm, they must conciliate, they must—to put it bluntly—tell lies if they are to succeed. Thus, whenever I felt the shadow of her wing or the radiance of her halo upon my page, I took up the inkpot and flung it at her. She died hard. Her fictitious nature was of great assistance to her. It is far harder to kill a phantom than a reality. She was always creeping back when I thought I had dispatched her. Though I flatter myself that I killed her in the end, the struggle was severe; it took much time that had better have been spent upon learning Greek grammar; or in roaming the world in search of adventures. But it was a real experience; it was an experience that was bound to befall all women writers at that time. Killing the Angel in the House was part of the occupation of a woman writer.

But to continue my story. The Angel was dead; what then remained? You may say that what remained was a simple and common object—a young woman in a bedroom with an inkpot. In other words, now that she had rid herself of falsehood, that young woman had only to be herself. Ah, but what is "herself"? I mean, what is a woman? I assure you, I do not know. I do not believe that you know. I do not believe that anybody can know until she has expressed herself in all the arts and professions open to human skill. That indeed is one of the reasons why I have come here—out of respect for you, who are in process of showing us by your experiments what a woman is, who are in process of providing us, by your failures and successes, with that extremely important piece of information.

But to continue the story of my professional experiences. I made one pound 5 ten and six by my first review; and I bought a Persian cat with the proceeds. Then I grew ambitious. A Persian cat is all very well, I said; but a Persian cat is not enough. I must have a motor car. And it was thus that I became a novelist—for it is a very strange thing that people will give you a motor car if you will tell them a story. It is a still stranger thing that there is nothing so delightful in the world as telling stories. It is far pleasanter than writing reviews of famous novels. And yet, if I am to obey your secretary and tell you my professional experiences as a novelist, I must tell you about a very strange experience that befell me as a novelist. And to understand it you must try first to imagine a novelist's state of mind. I hope I am not giving away professional secrets if I say that a novelist's chief desire is to be as unconscious as possible. He has to induce in himself a state of perpetual lethargy. He wants life to proceed with the utmost quiet and regularity. He wants to see the same faces, to read the same books, to do the same things day after day, month after month, while he is writing, so that nothing may break the illusion in which he is living—so that nothing may disturb or disquiet the mysterious nosings about, feelings round, darts, dashes and sudden discoveries of that very shy and illusive spirit, the imagination. I suspect that this state is the same both for men and women. Be that as it may, I want you to imagine me writing a novel in a state of trance. I want you to figure to yourselves a girl sitting with a pen in her hand, which for minutes, and indeed for hours, she never dips into the inkpot. The image that comes to my mind when I think of this girl is the image of a fisherman lying sunk in dreams on the verge of a deep lake with a rod held out over the water. She was letting her imagination sweep unchecked round every rock and cranny of the world that lies submerged in the depths of our unconscious being. Now came the experience, the experience that I believe to be far commoner with women writers than with men. The line raced through the girl's fingers. Her imagination had rushed away. It had sought the pools, the depths, the dark places where the largest fish slumber. And then there was a smash. There was an explosion. There was foam and confusion. The imagination had dashed itself against something hard. The girl was roused from her dream. She was indeed in a state of the most acute and difficult distress. To speak without figure she had thought of something, something about the body, about the passions which it was unfitting for her as a woman to say. Men, her reason told her, would be shocked. The consciousness of what men will say of a woman who speaks the truth about her passions had roused her from her artist's state of unconsciousness. She could write no more. The trance was over. Her imagination could work no longer. This I believe to be a very common experience with women writers—they are impeded by the extreme conventionality of the other sex. For though men sensibly allow themselves great freedom in these respects, I doubt that they realize or can control the extreme severity with which they condemn such freedom in women.

These then were two very genuine experiences of my own. These were two of the adventures of my professional life. The first—killing the Angel in the House—I think I solved. She died. But the second, telling the truth about my own experiences as a body, I do not think I solved. I doubt that any woman has solved it yet. The obstacles against her are still immensely powerful—and yet they are very difficult to define. Outwardly, what is simpler than to write books? Outwardly, what obstacles are there for a woman rather than for a man? Inwardly, I think, the case is very different; she has still many ghosts to fight, many prejudices to overcome. Indeed it will be a long time still, I think, before a woman can sit down to write a book without finding a phantom to be slain, a rock to be dashed against. And if this is so in literature, the freest of all professions for women, how is it in the new professions which you are now for the first time entering?

Those are the questions that I should like, had I time, to ask you. And indeed, if I have laid stress upon these professional experiences of mine, it is because I believe that they are, though in different forms, yours also. Even when the path is nominally open—when there is nothing to prevent a woman from being a doctor, a lawyer, a civil servant—there are many phantoms and obstacles, as I believe, looming in her way. To discuss and define them is I think of great value and importance; for thus only can the labour be shared, the difficulties be solved. But besides this, it is necessary also to discuss the ends and the aims for which we are fighting, for which we are doing battle with these formidable obstacles. Those aims cannot be taken for granted; they must be perpetually questioned and examined. The whole position, as I see it—here in this hall surrounded by women practising for the first time in history I know not how many different professions—is one of extraordinary interest and importance. You have won rooms of your own in the house hitherto exclusively owned by men. You are able, though not without great labour and effort, to pay the rent. You are earning your five hundred pounds a year. But this freedom is only a beginning; the room is your own, but it is still bare. It has to be furnished; it has to be decorated; it has to be shared. How are you going to furnish it, how are you going to decorate it? With whom are you going to share it, and upon what terms? These, I think, are questions of the utmost importance and interest. For the first time in history you are able to ask for them; for the first time you are able to decide for yourselves what the answers should be. Willingly would I stay and discuss those questions and answers—but not tonight. My time is up; and I must cease.

QUESTIONS FOR DISCUSSION AND WRITING

1. What does Woolf mean by "The Angel in the House" (paragraph 3)?

2. "I did my best to kill [The Angel in the House]. . . . Had I not killed her she would have killed me. She would have plucked the heart out of my writing" (paragraph 3). Explain this conflict and the struggle it took for Woolf to succeed as a professional writer. What other claims did society and family make on a woman's time and efforts?

3. Woolf originally delivered "Professions for Women" as a talk in 1931. Have conditions for women's education and professional expectations changed so much as to make Woolf's analysis irrelevant today? Why or why not?

4. Write an essay in which you examine what would be the ideal conditions for anyone—man or woman—to lead a fulfilling life that combined multiple roles, as spouse, parent, worker? What sorts of jobs and support systems would best promote this ideal?

CHAPTER 9

Technology: What Are the Consequences of Life in a Connected World?

MARIA KONNIKOVA

Do You Think Like Sherlock Holmes? What the Detective Can Teach Us about Observation, Attention, and Happiness

Maria Konnikova (b. 1984) is a magna cum laude graduate of Harvard University and is currently a doctoral candidate in psychology at Columbia University. Konnikova is originally from Moscow but came to the United States at the age of four. Her works have appeared in publications such as the Atlantic, *the* New York Times, *the* Boston Globe, *and the* Wall Street Journal, *as well as the online magazine* Slate. *She is also a frequent contributor to* Scientific American. *Her book* Mastermind: How to Think Like Sherlock Holmes *(2013) is a* New York Times *best-seller.*

In this article, which was originally posted on the Slate *Web site, Konnikova argues that we should learn to think more like Sherlock Holmes, not for the purpose of solving crimes, of course, but to better observe the world around us. In particular, she argues that today's fascination with electronic media, from cell phones, to e-mail, to Twitter, to Facebook, makes us less able to see—and observe—our world. The implications may be greater than we realize. Konnikova notes that we do not really multitask in the way we think; rather, we typically can focus on only one thing at a time. Furthermore, doing one thing and thinking about another—letting the mind wander—is actually more likely to make us unhappy than happy.*

I do not think like Sherlock Holmes. Not in the least. That was the rather disheartening conclusion I reached while researching a book on the detective's mental prowess. I'd hoped to discover that I had the secret to Sherlockian thought. What I found instead was that it would be hard work indeed to even begin to approximate the essence of the detective's approach to the world: his ever-mindful mindset and his relentless mental energy. Holmes was a man eternally on, who relished that on-ness and floundered in its absence. It would be exhausting to think like Sherlock. And would it really be worth it in the end?

It all began with those pesky steps, the stairs leading up to the legendary residence that Sherlock Holmes shares with Dr. Watson, 221B Baker Street. Why couldn't Watson recall the number of steps? "I believe my eyes are as good as yours," Watson tells his new flatmate—as, in fact, they are. But the competence of the eyes isn't the issue. Instead, the distinction lies in how those eyes are deployed. "You see, but you do not observe," Holmes tells his companion. And Holmes? "Now, I know there are seventeen steps," he continues, "because I have both seen and observed."

To both see and observe: Therein lies the secret. When I first heard the words as a child, I sat up with recognition. Like Watson, I didn't have a clue. Some twenty years later, I read the passage a second time in an attempt to decipher the psychology behind its impact. I realized I was no better at observing than I had been at the tender age of seven. Worse, even. With my constant companion Sir Smartphone and my newfound love of Lady Twitter, my devotion to Count Facebook, and that itch my fingers got whenever I hadn't checked my e-mail for, what, ten minutes already? OK, five—but it seemed a lifetime. Those Baker Street steps would always be a mystery.

The confluence of seeing and observing is central to the concept of mindfulness, a mental alertness that takes in the present moment to the fullest, that is able to concentrate on its immediate landscape and free itself of any distractions.

Mindfulness allows Holmes to observe those details that most of us don't even realize we don't see. It's not just the steps. It's the facial expressions, the sartorial details, the seemingly irrelevant minutiae of the people he encounters. It's the sizing up of the occupants of a house by looking at a single room. It's the ability to distinguish the crucial from the merely incidental in any person, any scene, any situation. And, as it turns out, all of these abilities aren't just the handy fictional work of Arthur Conan Doyle. They have some real science behind them. After all, Holmes was born of Dr. Joseph Bell, Conan Doyle's mentor at the University of Edinburgh, not some, well, more fictional inspiration. Bell was a scientist and physician with a sharp mind, a keen eye, and a notable prowess at pinpointing both his patients' disease and their personal details. Conan Doyle once wrote to him, "Round the centre of deduction and inference and observation which I have heard you inculcate, I have tried to build up a man who pushed the thing as far as it would go."

Over the past several decades, researchers have discovered that mindfulness can lead to improvements in physiological well-being and emotional regulation. It can also strengthen connectivity in the brain, specifically in a network of the posterior cingulate cortex, the adjacent precuneus, and the medial prefrontal cortex that maintains activity when the brain is resting. Mindfulness can even enhance our levels of wisdom, both in terms of dialectism (being cognizant of change and contradictions in the world) and intellectual humility (knowing your own limitations). What's more, mindfulness can lead to improved problem solving, enhanced imagination, and better decision making. It can even be a weapon against one of the most disturbing limitations that our attention is up against: inattentional blindness.

When inattentional blindness (sometimes referred to as attentional blindness) strikes, our focus on one particular element in a scene or situation or problem causes the other elements to literally disappear. Images that hit our retina are not then processed by our brain but instead dissolve into the who-knows-where, so that we have no conscious experience of having ever been exposed to them to begin with. The phenomenon was made famous by Daniel Simons and Christopher Chabris: In their provocative study, students repeatedly failed to see a person in a gorilla suit who walked onto a basketball court midgame, pounded his chest, and walked off. But the phenomenon actually dates to research conducted by Ulric Neisser, the father of cognitive psychology, in the 1960s and 1970s.

One evening, Neisser noticed that when he looked out the window at twilight, he had the ability to see either the twilight or the reflection of the room on the glass. Focusing on the one made the other vanish. No matter what he did, he couldn't pay active attention to both. He termed this phenomenon "selective looking" and went on to study its effects in study after study of competing attentional demands. Show a person two superimposed videos, and he fails to notice when card players suddenly stop their game, stand up, and start shaking hands—or fails to realize that someone spoke to him in one ear while he's been listening to a conversation with the other. In a real-world illustration of the innate inability to split attention in any meaningful way, a road construction crew once paved over a dead deer in the road. They simply did not see it, so busy were they ensuring that their assignment was properly carried out.

Inattentional blindness, more than anything else, illustrates the limitations of our attentional abilities. Try as we might, we can never see both twilight and reflection. We can't ever multitask the way we think we can. Each time we try, either the room or the world outside it will disappear from conscious processing. That's why Holmes is so careful about where and when he deploys that famed keenness of observation. Were he to spread himself too thin—imagine modern-day Holmes, be it Benedict Cumberbatch or Jonny Lee Miller, pulling out his cell to check his e-mail as he walks down the street and has a conversation at the same time, something you'll never see either of these current incarnations actually doing—he'd be unable to deploy his observation as he otherwise would. Enter the e-mail, exit the Baker Street steps—and then some.

It's not an easy task, that constant cognitive vigilance, the eternal awareness [10] of our own limitations and the resulting strategic allocation of attention. Even Holmes, I'm willing to bet, couldn't reach that level of mindfulness and deliberate thought all at once. It came with years of motivation and practice. To think like Holmes, we have to both want to think like him and practice doing so over and over and over, even when the effort becomes exhausting and seems a pointless waste of energy. Mindfulness takes discipline.

Even after I discovered my propensity for sneaking over to e-mail or Twitter when I wasn't quite sure what to write next, the discovery alone wasn't enough to curb my less-than-ideal work habits. I thought it would be. And I tried, I really did. But somehow, up that browser window popped, seemingly of its own volition. What, me? Attempt to multitask while writing my book? Never.

And so, I took the Odyssean approach: I tied myself to the mast to resist the sirens' call of the Internet. I downloaded Freedom, a program that blocked my access completely for a specified amount of time, and got to writing. The results shocked me. I was woefully bad at maintaining my concentration for large chunks

of time. Over and over, my fingers made their way to that habitual key-press combination that would switch the window from my manuscript to my online world—
only to discover that that world was off-limits for another . . . how long is left? Has
it really been only 20 minutes?

Over time, the impulse became less frequent. And what's more, I found that
my writing—and my thinking, it bears note—was improving with every day of
Internet-less interludes. I could think more fluidly. My brain worked more consci-
entiously. In those breaks when, before, there would be a quick check of e-mail or
a surreptitious run to my Twitter feed, there would be a self-reflecting concentration that quickly rummaged through my brain attic. (You can't write about Holmes
without mentioning his analogy for the human mind at least once.) I came up with
multiple ways of moving forward where before I would find myself stuck. Pieces
that had taken hours to write suddenly were completed in a fraction of the time.

Until that concrete evidence of effectiveness, I had never quite believed that
focused attention would make such a big difference. As much research as I'd read,
as much science as I'd examined, it never quite hit home. It had taken Freedom,
but I was finally taking Sherlock Holmes at his word. I was learning the benefits of
both seeing and observing—and I was no longer trading in the one for the other
without quite realizing what I was doing.

Self-binding software, of course, is not always an option to keep our brains   15
mindfully on track. Who is to stop us from checking our phone mid-dinner or
having the TV on as background noise? But here's what I learned. Those little
nudges to limit your own behavior have a more lasting effect, even in areas where
you've never used them. They make you realize just how limited your attention
is in reality—and how often we wave our own limitations off with a disdainful
motion. Not only did that nagging software make me realize how desperately I was
chained to my online self, but I began to notice how often my hand reached for my
phone when I was walking down the street or sitting in the subway, how utterly
unable I had become to just do what I was doing, be it walking or sitting or even
reading a book, without trying to get in just a little bit more.

I did my best to resist. Now, something that was once thoughtless habit
became a guilt-inducing twinge. I would force myself to replace the phone without
checking it, to take off my headphones and look around, to resist the urge to place
a call just because I was walking to an appointment and had a few minutes of spare
time. It was hard. But it was worth it, if only for my enhanced perceptiveness, for
the quickly growing pile of material that I wouldn't have even noticed before, for
the tangible improvements in thought and clarity that came with every deferred
impulse. It's not for nothing that study after study has shown the benefits of nature
on our thinking: Being surrounded by the natural world makes us more reflective,
more creative, sharper in our cognition. But if we're too busy talking on the phone
or sending a text, we won't even notice that we've walked by a tree.

If we follow Holmes' lead, if we take his admonition to not only see but also
observe, and do so as a matter of course, we may not only find ourselves better
able to rattle off the number of those proverbial steps in a second, but we may
be surprised to discover that the benefits extend much further: We may even be

happier as a result. Even brief exercises in mindfulness, for as little as five minutes a day, have been shown to shift brain activity in the frontal lobes toward a pattern associated with positive and approach-oriented emotional states. And the mind-wandering, multitasking alternative? It may do more than make us less attentive. It may also make us less happy.

As Daniel Gilbert discovered after tracking thousands of participants in real time, a mind that is wandering away from the present moment is a mind that isn't happy. He developed an iPhone app that would prompt subjects to answer questions on what they were currently doing and what they were thinking about at various points in the day. In 46.9 percent of samples Gilbert and his colleagues collected, people were not thinking about whatever it was they were doing—even if what they were doing was actually quite pleasant, like listening to music or playing a game. And their happiness? The more their minds wandered, the less happy they were—regardless of the activity. As Gilbert put it in a paper in *Science*, "The ability to think about what is not happening is a cognitive achievement that comes at an emotional cost."

Thinking like Sherlock Holmes isn't just a way to enhance your cognitive powers. It is also a way to derive greater happiness and satisfaction from life.

QUESTIONS FOR DISCUSSION AND WRITING

1. Konnikova admits right from the start that she does not think like Sherlock Holmes. What does she mean by this? How does she define the way Holmes thinks? Why does she question whether thinking like Holmes would really be worth the effort after all?

2. Konnikova states, "The confluence of seeing and observing is central to the concept of mindfulness . . ." (paragraph 4). How does she define mindfulness? What is important about mindfulness and its relation to the thought processes of Holmes? Do you consider yourself mindful, using Konnikova's definition of the term? Why or why not?

3. A key aspect of Konnikova's argument is that in today's world, mental distractions are all around, including popular social media such as Twitter and Facebook, as well as cell phones and e-mail. What is so damaging about these distractions? How do they contribute to what Konnikova calls "inattentional blindness" (paragraph 7)?

4. The concept of inattentional blindness—in which we can focus our attention on only one thing at a time, to the exclusion of all others—has far-reaching implications. How does this apply to today's obsession with multitasking, the idea that a person needs to be doing more than one thing at a time? Consider how this might affect students studying with music on, or alternating between writing an essay and checking Facebook. How might Konnikova respond to students who argue that such distractions help them relax? How might people other than students be affected by inattentional blindness in their occupation or activities? Cite specific examples.

5. Konnikova points out how difficult it was even for herself to resist habits that distract her from the tasks at hand. She even purposely prevents herself from accessing the Internet for a time by using a program that is (somewhat) ironically called Freedom. How distracted are you when doing tasks? What do you do, if anything, to avoid distractions (e.g., shut off your phone, turn off the stereo and television, restrict your access to the Internet)? Do you even think that you need to?

6. In her conclusion, Konnikova argues that more than efficiency is at stake. She cites studies showing that people are generally happier when they are able to concentrate and focus on the task at hand and that mind wandering is actually a sign of unhappiness. Thus, she concludes, learning to think like Holmes (with the power of concentration and mindfulness) is a way to "derive greater happiness and satisfaction from life" (paragraph 19). On the basis of your own experience and observation, do you agree or disagree? Defend your answer with specific details.

SHERRY TURKLE

How Computers Change the Way We Think

Sherry Turkle, a clinical psychologist, sociologist, and media commentator on the effects of technology, is Abby Rockefeller Mauzé Professor of the Social Studies of Science and Technology at the Massachusetts Institute of Technology and director of the MIT Initiative on Technology and Self, a center of research and reflection on the evolving connections between people and artifacts. She was born in 1948, and earned from Harvard a B.A. (1970), and a Ph.D. in sociology and personality psychology (1976). Her research and writing often focus on the cultural and psychological implications of computer technology, for she regards "computers as carriers of culture, as objects that give rise to new metaphors, to new relationships between people and machines, between different people, and most significantly between people and their ways of thinking about themselves." Turkle is the author of The Second Self: Computers and the Human Spirit *(1984; revised 2005); and* Life on the Screen: Identity in the Age of the Internet *(1997). She has edited three collections on the relationships between things and thinking, including* Evocative Objects: Things We Think With *(2007). Her most recent book is* Alone Together: Why We Expect More from Technology and Less from Each Other *(2011). "How Computers Change the Way We Think" was first published in the* Chronicle of Higher Education *(2004).*

The tools we use to think change the ways in which we think. The invention of written language brought about a radical shift in how we process, organize, store, and transmit representations of the world. Although writing remains our primary information technology, today when we think about the impact of technology on our habits of mind, we think primarily of the computer.

My first encounters with how computers change the way we think came soon after I joined the faculty at the Massachusetts Institute of Technology in the late 1970s, at the end of the era of the slide rule and the beginning of the era of the personal computer. At a lunch for new faculty members, several senior professors in engineering complained that the transition from slide rules to calculators had affected their students' ability to deal with issues of scale. When students used slide rules, they had to insert decimal points themselves. The professors insisted that that required students to maintain a mental sense of scale, whereas those who relied on calculators made frequent errors in orders of magnitude. Additionally, the students with calculators had lost their ability to do "back of the envelope" calculations, and with that, an intuitive feel for the material.

That same semester, I taught a course in the history of psychology. There, I experienced the impact of computational objects on students' ideas about their emotional lives. My class had read Freud's essay on slips of the tongue, with its famous first example: The chairman of a parliamentary session opens a meeting by declaring it closed. The students discussed how Freud interpreted such errors as revealing a person's mixed emotions. A computer-science major disagreed with Freud's approach. The mind, she argued, is a computer. And in a computational dictionary—like we have in the human mind—"closed" and "open" are designated by the same symbol, separated by a sign for opposition. "Closed" equals "minus open." To substitute "closed" for "open" does not require the notion of ambivalence or conflict.

"When the chairman made that substitution," she declared, "a bit was dropped; a minus sign was lost. There was a power surge. No problem."

The young woman turned a Freudian slip into an information-processing error. An explanation in terms of meaning had become an explanation in terms of mechanism. 5

Such encounters turned me to the study of both the instrumental and the subjective sides of the nascent computer culture. As an ethnographer and psychologist, I began to study not only what the computer was doing *for* us, but what it was doing *to* us, including how it was changing the way we see ourselves, our sense of human identity.

In the 1980s, I surveyed the psychological effects of computational objects in everyday life—largely the unintended side effects of people's tendency to project thoughts and feelings onto their machines. In the 20 years since, computational objects have become more explicitly designed to have emotional and cognitive effects. And those "effects by design" will become even stronger in the decade to come. Machines are being designed to serve explicitly as companions, pets, and tutors. And they are introduced in school settings for the youngest children.

Today, starting in elementary school, students use e-mail, word processing, computer simulations, virtual communities, and PowerPoint software. In the process, they are absorbing more than the content of what appears on their screens. They are learning new ways to think about what it means to know and understand.

What follows is a short and certainly not comprehensive list of areas where I see information technology encouraging changes in thinking. There can be no simple way of cataloging whether any particular change is good or bad. That is contested terrain. At every step we have to ask, as educators and citizens, whether current technology is leading us in directions that serve our human purposes. Such questions are not technical; they are social, moral, and political. For me, addressing that subjective side of computation is one of the more significant challenges for the next decade of information technology in higher education. Technology does not determine change, but it encourages us to take certain directions. If we make those directions clear, we can more easily exert human choice.

THINKING ABOUT PRIVACY

Today's college students are habituated to a world of online blogging, instant messaging, and Web browsing that leaves electronic traces. Yet they have had little experience with the right to privacy. Unlike past generations of Americans, who grew up with the notion that the privacy of their mail was sacrosanct, our children are accustomed to electronic surveillance as part of their daily lives.   10

I have colleagues who feel that the increased incursions on privacy have put the topic more in the news, and that this is a positive change. But middle-school and high-school students tend to be willing to provide personal information online with no safeguards, and college students seem uninterested in violations of privacy and in increased governmental and commercial surveillance. Professors find that students do not understand that in a democracy, privacy is a right, not merely a privilege. In 10 years, ideas about the relationship of privacy and government will require even more active pedagogy. (One might also hope that increased education about the kinds of silent surveillance that technology makes possible may inspire more active political engagement with the issue.)

AVATARS OR A SELF?

Chat rooms, role-playing games, and other technological venues offer us many different contexts for presenting ourselves online. Those possibilities are particularly important for adolescents because they offer what Erik Erikson described as a moratorium, a time out or safe space for the personal experimentation that is so crucial for adolescent development. Our dangerous world—with crime, terrorism, drugs, and AIDS—offers little in the way of safe spaces. Online worlds can provide valuable spaces for identity play.

But some people who gain fluency in expressing multiple aspects for self may find it harder to develop authentic selves. Some children who write narratives for their screen avatars may grow up with too little experience of how to share their real feelings with other people. For those who are lonely yet afraid of intimacy, information technology has made it possible to have the illusion of companionship without the demands of friendship.

FROM POWERFUL IDEAS TO POWERPOINT

In the 1970s and early 1980s, some educators wanted to make programming part of the regular curriculum for K–12 education. They argued that because information technology carries ideas, it might as well carry the most powerful ideas that computer science has to offer. It is ironic that in most elementary schools today, the ideas being carried by information technology are not ideas from computer science like procedural thinking, but more likely to be those embedded in productivity tools like PowerPoint presentation software.

PowerPoint does more than provide a way of transmitting content. It carries   15
its own way of thinking, its own aesthetic—which not surprisingly shows up in the aesthetic of college freshmen. In that aesthetic, presentation becomes its own powerful idea.

To be sure, the software cannot be blamed for lower intellectual standards. Misuse of the former is as much a symptom as a cause of the latter. Indeed, the culture in which our children are raised is increasingly a culture of presentation, a corporate culture in which appearance is often more important than reality. In contemporary political discourse, the bar has also been lowered. Use of rhetorical devices at the expense of cogent argument regularly goes without notice. But it is precisely because standards of intellectual rigor outside the educational sphere have fallen that educators must attend to how we use, and when we introduce, software that has been designed to simplify the organization and processing of information.

In "The Cognitive Style of PowerPoint" (Graphics Press, 2003), Edward R. Tufte suggests that PowerPoint equates bulleting with clear thinking. It does not teach students to begin a discussion or construct a narrative. It encourages presentation, not conversation. Of course, in the hands of a master teacher, a PowerPoint presentation with few words and powerful images can serve as the jumping-off point for a brilliant lecture. But in the hands of elementary-school students, often introduced to PowerPoint in the third grade, and often infatuated with its swooshing sounds, animated icons, and flashing text, a slide show is more likely to close down debate than open it up.

Developed to serve the needs of the corporate boardroom, the software is designed to convey absolute authority. Teachers used to tell students that clear exposition depended on clear outlining, but presentation software has fetishized the outline at the expense of the content.

Narrative, the exposition of content, takes time. PowerPoint, like so much in the computer culture, speeds up the pace.

WORD PROCESSING VS. THINKING

The catalog for the Vermont Country Store advertises a manual typewriter,   20
which the advertising copy says "moves at a pace that allows time to compose your thoughts." As many of us know, it is possible to manipulate text on a computer screen and see how it looks faster than we can think about what the words mean.

Word processing has its own complex psychology. From a pedagogical point of view, it can make dedicated students into better writers because it allows them to revise text, rearrange paragraphs, and experiment with the tone and shape of an essay. Few professional writers would part with their computers; some claim that they simply cannot think without their hands on the keyboard. Yet the ability to quickly fill the page, to see it before you can think it, can make bad writers even worse.

A seventh grader once told me that the typewriter she found in her mother's attic is "cool because you have to type each letter by itself. You have to know what you are doing in advance or it comes out a mess." The idea of thinking ahead has become exotic.

TAKING THINGS AT INTERFACE VALUE

We expect software to be easy to use, and we assume that we don't have to know how a computer works. In the early 1980s, most computer users who spoke of transparency meant that, as with any other machine, you could "open the hood" and poke around. But only a few years later, Macintosh users began to use the term when they talked about seeing their documents and programs represented by attractive and easy-to-interpret icons. They were referring to an ability to make things work without needing to go below the screen surface. Paradoxically, it was the screen's opacity that permitted that kind of transparency. Today, when people say that something is transparent, they mean that they can see how to make it work, not that they know how it works. In other words, transparency means epistemic opacity.

The people who built or bought the first generation of personal computers understood them down to the bits and bytes. The next generation of operation systems were more complex, but they still invited that old-time reductive understanding. Contemporary information technology encourages different habits of mind. Today's college students are already used to taking things at (inter) face value; their successors in 2014 will be even less accustomed to probing below the surface.

SIMULATION AND ITS DISCONTENTS

Some thinkers argue that the new opacity is empowering, enabling anyone to use the most sophisticated technological tools and to experiment with simulation in complex and creative ways. But it is also true that our tools carry the message that they are beyond our understanding. It is possible that in daily life, epistemic opacity can lead to passivity.

I first became aware of that possibility in the early 1990s, when the first generation of complex simulation games were introduced and immediately became popular for home as well as school use. SimLife teaches the principles of evolution by getting children involved in the development of complex ecosystems; in that sense it is an extraordinary learning tool. During one session in which I played SimLife with Tim, a 13-year-old, the screen before us flashed a message: "Your orgot is being eaten up." "What's an orgot?" I asked. Tim didn't know. "I just ignore that," he said confidently. "You don't need to know that kind of stuff to play."

For me, that story serves as a cautionary tale. Computer simulations enable their users to think about complex phenomena as dynamic, evolving systems. But they also accustom us to manipulating systems whose core assumptions we may not understand and that may not be true.

We live in a culture of simulation. Our games, our economic and political systems, and the ways architects design buildings, chemists envisage molecules, and surgeons perform operations all use simulation technology. In 10 years the degree to which simulations are embedded in every area of life will have increased exponentially. We need to develop a new form of media literacy: readership skills for the culture of simulation.

We come to written text with habits of readership based on centuries of civilization. At the very least, we have learned to begin with the journalist's traditional questions: who, what, when, where, why, and how. Who wrote these words, what is their message, why were they written, and how are they situated in time and place, politically and socially? A central project for higher education during the next 10 years should be creating programs in information-technology literacy, with the goal of teaching students to interrogate simulations in much the same spirit, challenging their built-in assumptions.

Despite the ever-increasing complexity of software, most computer environ-   30 ments put users in worlds based on constrained choices. In other words, immersion in programmed worlds puts us in reassuring environments where the rules are clear. For example, when you play a video game, you often go through a series of frightening situations that you escape by mastering the rules—you experience life as a reassuring dichotomy of scary and safe. Children grow up in a culture of video games, action films, fantasy epics, and computer programs that all rely on that familiar scenario of almost losing but then regaining total mastery: There is danger. It is mastered. A still-more-powerful monster appears. It is subdued. Scary. Safe.

Yet in the real world, we have never had a greater need to work our way out of binary assumptions. In the decade ahead, we need to rebuild the culture around information technology. In that new socio-technical culture, assumptions about the nature of mastery would be less absolute. The new culture would make it easier, not more difficult, to consider life in shades of gray, to see moral dilemmas in terms other than a battle between Good and Evil. For never has our world been more complex, hybridized, and global. Never have we so needed to have many contradictory thoughts and feelings at the same time. Our tools must help us accomplish that, not fight against us.

Information technology is identity technology. Embedding it in a culture that supports democracy, freedom of expression, tolerance, diversity, and complexity of opinion is one of the next decade's greatest challenges. We cannot afford to fail.

When I first began studying the computer culture, a small breed of highly trained technologists thought of themselves as "computer people." That is no longer the case. If we take the computer as a carrier of a way of knowing, a way of seeing the world and our place in it, we are all computer people now.

QUESTIONS FOR DISCUSSION AND WRITING

1. Turkle begins her list of areas where information technology encourages "changes in thinking" with the observation, "There can be no simple way of cataloging whether any particular change is good or bad. That is contested terrain. At every step we have to ask . . . whether current technology is leading us in directions that serve our human purposes" (paragraph 9). Make a list of some of the major technological tools and technologies that you use regularly and identify their positives and negatives. What are their best and worst features? Could you do without any (word processor, Internet and its many ramifications, including social networking sites, and more—and others, such as a cell phone, that Turkle doesn't discuss), on either a permanent or temporary basis? Why or why not?

2. Are the new technologies Turkle discusses here changing the ways people think, and write and read—as Nicholas Carr argues in "Is Google Making Us Stupid?" (p. 331)? What are some of the ethical as well as intellectual issues underlying this conversation?

3. At the end of "How Computers Change the Way We Think" Turkle concludes that current computing habits and software may undermine "democracy, freedom of expression, tolerance, diversity, and complexity of opinion" (paragraph 32). Can you supplement the evidence Turkle offers with information derived from your own experiences? Is she right? Are there positive features, also embedded in technology, that can counteract the negatives? Identify some and show how these might work.

4. Turkle raises privacy issues (paragraphs 10 and 11). Which are the most significant? Are you coming of age in a time when privacy is no longer a concern? Or do you expect privacy issues and violations to influence—even haunt—you for the rest of your life? Illustrate your answers and explain. Are you worried? Should you be? Which of the aspects of privacy might "inspire more active political engagement," as Turkle hopes (paragraph 11)?

NICHOLAS CARR

Is Google Making Us Stupid?

Technology author Nicholas Carr (b. 1959) earned a B.A. from Dartmouth and an M.A. from Harvard. Carr has been a columnist for the Guardian *and the* Industry Standard; *his writing on technology has appeared in the* New York Times Magazine, Wired, *the* Financial Times, *and* Die Zeit. *Carr's blog (since 2005), Rough Type, focuses on the impact of information technologies on people, society, business, the world. This orientation is reflected in* Does IT Matter? *(2004) and* The Shallows: What the Internet Is Doing to Our Brains *(2010). Likewise, in* The Big Switch: Rewiring the World from Edison to Google *(2008), he demonstrates how and why* "[T]he interplay of technological and economic forces rarely produces the results we at first expect. . . . [T]he economic forces that the World Wide Computer is unleashing . . . the replacement of skilled as well as unskilled workers with software, the global trade in knowledge work, and the ability of companies to aggregate volunteer labor and harvest its economic value—we're left with a prospect that is far from Utopian. The erosion of the middle class may well accelerate, as the divide widens between a relatively small group of extraordinarily wealthy people—the digital elite—and a very large set of people who face eroding fortunes and a persistent struggle to make ends meet. In the YouTube economy, everyone is free to play, but only a few reap the rewards."

"Is Google Making Us Stupid?" (Atlantic, *2008) was a precursor to Carr's* The Shallows. *The essay was included in* The Best American Science and Nature Writing, The Best Technology Writing, *and* The Best Spiritual Writing. *In this triple-winner, Carr argues that "media are not just passive channels of information. They supply the stuff of thought, but they also shape the process of thought. And what the Net seems to be doing is chipping away my capacity for concentration and contemplation. My mind now expects to take in information the way the Net distributes it: in a swiftly moving stream of particles." Carr's essay thoughtfully explores the high price of "zipping among lots of bits of information"—the "loss of depth in our thinking."*

"Dave, stop. Stop, will you? Stop, Dave. Will you stop, Dave?" So the supercomputer HAL pleads with the implacable astronaut Dave Bowman in a famous and weirdly poignant scene toward the end of Stanley Kubrick's *2001: A Space Odyssey.* Bowman, having nearly been sent to a deep-space death by the malfunctioning machine, is calmly coldly disconnecting the memory circuits that control its artificial brain. "Dave, my mind is going," HAL says, forlornly. "I can feel it. I can feel it."

I can feel it, too. Over the past few years I've had an uncomfortable sense that someone, or something, has been tinkering with my brain, remapping the neural circuitry, reprogramming the memory. My mind isn't going—so far as I can tell—but it's changing. I'm not thinking the way I used to think. I can feel it most strongly when I'm reading. Immersing myself in a book or a lengthy article used to be easy. My mind would get caught up in the narrative or the turns of the argument, and I'd spend hours strolling through long stretches of prose. That's rarely the case anymore. Now my concentration often starts to drift after two or three pages. I get fidgety, lose the thread, begin looking for something else to do. I feel as if I'm always dragging my wayward brain back to the text. The deep reading that used to come naturally has become a struggle.

I think I know what's going on. For more than a decade now, I've been spending a lot of time online, searching and surfing and sometimes adding to the great databases of the Internet. The Web has been a godsend to me as a writer. Research that once required days in the stacks or periodical rooms of libraries can now be done in minutes. A few Google searches, some quick clicks on hyperlinks, and I've got the telltale fact or pithy quote I was after. Even when I'm not working, I'm as likely as not to be foraging in the Web's info-thickets—reading and writing e-mails, scanning headlines and blog posts, watching videos and listening to podcasts, or just tripping from link to link to link. (Unlike footnotes, to which they're sometimes likened, hyperlinks don't merely point to related works; they propel you toward them.)

For me, as for others, the Net is becoming a universal medium, the conduit for most of the information that flows through my eyes and ears and into my mind. The advantages of having immediate access to such an incredibly rich store of information are many, and they've been widely described and duly applauded. "The perfect recall of silicon memory," Wired's Clive Thompson has written, "can be an enormous boon to thinking." But that boon comes at a price. As the media theorist Marshall McLuhan pointed out in the 1960s, media are not just passive channels of information. They supply the stuff of thought, but they also shape the process of thought. And what the Net seems to be doing is chipping away my capacity for concentration and contemplation. My mind now expects to take in information the way the Net distributes it: in a swiftly moving stream of particles. Once I was a scuba diver in the sea of words. Now I zip along the surface like a guy on a Jet Ski.

I'm not the only one. When I mention my troubles with reading to friends   5 and acquaintances—literary types, most of them—many say they're having similar experiences. The more they use the Web, the more they have to fight to stay focused on long pieces of writing. Some of the bloggers I follow have also begun mentioning the phenomenon. Scott Karp, who writes a blog about online media, recently confessed that he has stopped reading books altogether. "I was a lit major in college, and used to be [a] voracious book reader," he wrote. "What happened?" He speculates on the answer: "What if I do all my reading on the web not so much because the way I read has changed, i.e. I'm just seeking convenience, but because the way I THINK has changed?"

Bruce Friedman, who blogs regularly about the use of computers in medicine, also has described how the Internet has altered his mental habits. "I now have almost totally lost the ability to read and absorb a longish article on the web or in print," he wrote earlier this year. A pathologist who has long been on the faculty of the University of Michigan Medical School, Friedman elaborated on his comment in a telephone conversation with me. His thinking, he said, has taken on a "staccato" quality, reflecting the way he quickly scans short passages of text from many sources online. "I can't read War and Peace anymore," he admitted. "I've lost the ability to do that. Even a blog post of more than three or four paragraphs is too much to absorb. I skim it."

Anecdotes alone don't prove much. And we still await the long-term neurological and psychological experiments that will provide a definitive picture of how Internet use affects cognition. But a recently published study of online research habits, conducted by scholars from University College London, suggests that we may well be in the midst of a sea change in the way we read and think.

As part of the five-year research program, the scholars examined computer logs documenting the behavior of visitors to two popular research sites, one operated by the British Library and one by a U.K. educational consortium, that provide access to journal articles, e-books, and other sources of written information. They found that people using the sites exhibited "a form of skimming activity," hopping from one source to another and rarely returning to any source they'd already visited. They typically read no more than one or two pages of an article or book before they would "bounce" out to another site. Sometimes they'd save a long article, but there's no evidence that they ever went back and actually read it. The authors of the study report:

> It is clear that users are not reading online in the traditional sense; indeed there are signs that new forms of "reading" are emerging as users "power browse" horizontally through titles, contents pages and abstracts going for quick wins. It almost seems that they go online to avoid reading in the traditional sense.

Thanks to the ubiquity of text on the Internet, not to mention the popularity of text-messaging on cell phones, we may well be reading more today than we did in the 1970s or 1980s, when television was our medium of choice. But it's a different kind of reading, and behind it lies a different kind of thinking—perhaps even a new sense of the self. "We are not only *what* we read," says Maryanne Wolf, a developmental psychologist at Tufts University and the author of *Proust and the Squid: The Story and Science of the Reading Brain.* "We are *how* we read." Wolf worries that the style of reading promoted by the Net, a style that puts "efficiency" and "immediacy" above all else, may be weakening our capacity for the kind of deep reading that emerged when an earlier technology, the printing press, made long and complex works of prose commonplace. When we read online, she says, we tend to become "mere decoders of information." Our ability to interpret text, to make the rich mental connections that form when we read deeply and without distraction, remains largely disengaged.

Reading, explains Wolf, is not an instinctive skill for human beings. It's not etched into our genes the way speech is. We have to teach our minds how to translate the symbolic characters we see into the language we understand. And the media or other technologies we use in learning and practicing the craft of reading play an important part in shaping the neural circuits inside our brains. Experiments demonstrate that readers of ideograms, such as the Chinese, develop a mental circuitry for reading that is very different from the circuitry found in those of us whose written language employs an alphabet. The variations extend across many regions of the brain, including those that govern such essential cognitive functions as memory and the interpretation of visual and auditory stimuli. We can expect as well that the circuits woven by our use of the Net will be different from those woven by our reading of books and other printed works.

Sometime in 1882, Friedrich Nietzsche bought a typewriter—a Malling-Hansen   10
Writing Ball, to be precise. His vision was failing, and keeping his eyes focused on

a page had become exhausting and painful, often bringing on crushing headaches. He had been forced to curtail his writing, and he feared that he would soon have to give it up. The typewriter rescued him, at least for a time. Once he had mastered touch-typing, he was able to write with his eyes closed, using only the tips of his fingers. Words could once again flow from his mind to the page.

But the machine had a subtler effect on his work. One of Nietzsche's friends, a composer, noticed a change in the style of his writing. His already terse prose had become even tighter, more telegraphic. "Perhaps you will through this instrument even take to a new idiom," the friend wrote in a letter, noting that, in his own work, his "'thoughts' in music and language often depend on the quality of pen and paper."

"You are right," Nietzsche replied, "our writing equipment takes part in the forming of our thoughts." Under the sway of the machine, writes the German media scholar Friedrich A. Kittler, Nietzsche's prose "changed from arguments to aphorisms, from thoughts to puns, from rhetoric to telegram style."

The human brain is almost infinitely malleable. People used to think that our mental meshwork, the dense connections formed among the 100 billion or so neurons inside our skulls, was largely fixed by the time we reached adulthood. But brain researchers have discovered that that's not the case. James Olds, a professor of neuroscience who directs the Krasnow Institute for Advanced Study at George Mason University, says that even the adult mind "is very plastic." Nerve cells routinely break old connections and form new ones. "The brain," according to Olds, "has the ability to reprogram itself on the fly, altering the way it functions."

As we use what the sociologist Daniel Bell has called our "intellectual technologies"—the tools that extend our mental rather than our physical capacities—we inevitably begin to take on the qualities of those technologies. The mechanical clock, which came into common use in the 14th century, provides a compelling example. In *Technics and Civilization,* the historian and cultural critic Lewis Mumford described how the clock "disassociated time from human events and helped create the belief in an independent world of mathematically measurable sequences." The "abstract framework of divided time" became "the point of reference for both action and thought."

The clock's methodical ticking helped bring into being the scientific mind 15 and the scientific man. But it also took something away. As the late MIT computer scientist Joseph Weizenbaum observed in his 1976 book, *Computer Power and Human Reason: From Judgment to Calculation,* the conception of the world that emerged from the widespread use of timekeeping instruments "remains an impoverished version of the older one, for it rests on a rejection of those direct experiences that formed the basis for, and indeed constituted, the old reality." In deciding when to eat, to work, to sleep, to rise, we stopped listening to our senses and started obeying the clock.

The process of adapting to new intellectual technologies is reflected in the changing metaphors we use to explain ourselves to ourselves. When the mechanical clock arrived, people began thinking of their brains as operating "like clockwork." Today, in the age of software, we have come to think of them as operating "like computers." But the changes, neuroscience tells us, go much deeper than metaphor. Thanks to our brain's plasticity, the adaptation occurs also at a biological level.

The Internet promises to have particularly far-reaching effects on cognition. In a paper published in 1936, the British mathematician Alan Turing proved that a digital computer, which at the time existed only as a theoretical machine, could be programmed to perform the function of any other information-processing device. And that's what we're seeing today. The Internet, an immeasurably powerful computing system, is subsuming most of our other intellectual technologies. It's becoming our map and our clock, our printing press and our typewriter, our calculator and our telephone, and our radio and TV.

When the Net absorbs a medium, that medium is re-created in the Net's image. It injects the medium's content with hyperlinks, blinking ads, and other digital gewgaws, and it surrounds the content with the content of all the other media it has absorbed. A new e-mail message, for instance, may announce its arrival as we're glancing over the latest headlines at a newspaper's site. The result is to scatter our attention and diffuse our concentration.

The Net's influence doesn't end at the edges of a computer screen, either. As people's minds become attuned to the crazy quilt of Internet media, traditional media have to adapt to the audience's new expectations. Television programs add text crawls and pop-up ads, and magazines and newspapers shorten their articles, introduce capsule summaries, and crowd their pages with easy-to-browse info-snippets. When, in March of this year, *The New York Times* decided to devote the second and third pages of every edition to article abstracts, its design director, Tom Bodkin, explained that the "shortcuts" would give harried readers a quick "taste" of the day's news, sparing them the "less efficient" method of actually turning the pages and reading the articles. Old media have little choice but to play by the new-media rules.

Never has a communications system played so many roles in our lives—or   20
exerted such broad influence over our thoughts—as the Internet does today. Yet, for all that's been written about the Net, there's been little consideration of how, exactly, it's reprogramming us. The Net's intellectual ethic remains obscure.

About the same time that Nietzsche started using his typewriter, an earnest young man named Frederick Winslow Taylor carried a stopwatch into the Midvale Steel plant in Philadelphia and began a historic series of experiments aimed at improving the efficiency of the plant's machinists. With the approval of Midvale's owners, he recruited a group of factory hands, set them to work on various metal-working machines, and recorded and timed their every movement as well as the operations of the machines. By breaking down every job into a sequence of small, discrete steps and then testing different ways of performing each one, Taylor created a set of precise instructions—an "algorithm," we might say today—for how each worker should work. Midvale's employees grumbled about the strict new regime, claiming that it turned them into little more than automatons, but the factory's productivity soared.

More than a hundred years after the invention of the steam engine, the Industrial Revolution had at last found its philosophy and its philosopher.

Taylor's tight industrial choreography—his "system," as he liked to call it—was embraced by manufacturers throughout the country and, in time, around the world. Seeking maximum speed, maximum efficiency, and maximum output, factory owners used time-and-motion studies to organize their work and configure the jobs of their workers. The goal, as Taylor defined it in his celebrated 1911 treatise, *The Principles of Scientific Management,* was to identify and adopt, for every job, the "one best method" of work and thereby to effect "the gradual substitution of science for rule of thumb throughout the mechanic arts." Once his system was applied to all acts of manual labor, Taylor assured his followers, it would bring about a restructuring not only of industry but of society, creating a utopia of perfect efficiency. "In the past the man has been first," he declared; "in the future the system must be first."

Taylor's system is still very much with us; it remains the ethic of industrial manufacturing. And now, thanks to the growing power that computer engineers and software coders wield over our intellectual lives, Taylor's ethic is beginning to govern the realm of the mind as well. The Internet is a machine designed for the efficient and automated collection, transmission, and manipulation of information, and its legions of programmers are intent on finding the "one best method"—the perfect algorithm—to carry out every mental movement of what we've come to describe as "knowledge work."

Google's headquarters, in Mountain View, California—the Googleplex—is the Internet's high church, and the religion practiced inside its walls is Taylorism. Google, says its chief executive, Eric Schmidt, is "a company that's founded around the science of measurement," and it is striving to "systematize everything" it does. Drawing on the terabytes of behavioral data it collects through its search engine and other sites, it carries out thousands of experiments a day, according to the *Harvard Business Review,* and it uses the results to refine the algorithms that increasingly control how people find information and extract meaning from it. What Taylor did for the work of the hand, Google is doing for the work of the mind.

The company has declared that its mission is "to organize the world's information and make it universally accessible and useful." It seeks to develop "the perfect search engine," which it defines as something that "understands exactly what you mean and gives you back exactly what you want." In Google's view, information is a kind of commodity, a utilitarian resource that can be mined and processed with industrial efficiency. The more pieces of information we can "access" and the faster we can extract their gist, the more productive we become as thinkers. 25

Where does it end? Sergey Brin and Larry Page, the gifted young men who founded Google while pursuing doctoral degrees in computer science at Stanford, speak frequently of their desire to turn their search engine into an artificial intelligence, a HAL-like machine that might be connected directly to our brains. "The ultimate search engine is something as smart as people—or smarter," Page said in a speech a few years back. "For us, working on search is a way to work on artificial intelligence." In a 2004 interview with *Newsweek,* Brin said, "Certainly if you had all the world's information directly attached to your brain, or an artificial brain that was smarter than your brain, you'd be better off." Last year, Page told a convention of scientists that Google is "really trying to build artificial intelligence and to do it on a large scale."

Such an ambition is a natural one, even an admirable one, for a pair of math whizzes with vast quantities of cash at their disposal and a small army of computer scientists in their employ. A fundamentally scientific enterprise, Google is motivated by a desire to use technology, in Eric Schmidt's words, "to solve problems that have never been solved before," and artificial intelligence is the hardest problem out there. Why wouldn't Brin and Page want to be the ones to crack it?

Still, their easy assumption that we'd all "be better off" if our brains were supplemented, or even replaced, by an artificial intelligence is unsettling. It suggests a belief that intelligence is the output of a mechanical process, a series of discrete steps that can be isolated, measured, and optimized. In Google's world, the world we enter when we go online, there's little place for the fuzziness of contemplation. Ambiguity is not an opening for insight but a bug to be fixed. The human brain is just an outdated computer that needs a faster processor and a bigger hard drive.

The idea that our minds should operate as high-speed data-processing machines is not only built into the workings of the Internet, it is the network's reigning business model as well. The faster we surf across the Web—the more links we click and pages we view—the more opportunities Google and other companies gain to collect information about us and to feed us advertisements. Most of the proprietors of the commercial Internet have a financial stake in collecting the crumbs of data we leave behind as we flit from link to link—the more crumbs, the better. The last thing these companies want is to encourage leisurely reading or slow, concentrated thought. It's in their economic interest to drive us to distraction.

Maybe I'm just a worrywart. Just as there's a tendency to glorify technological progress, there's a countertendency to expect the worst of every new tool or machine. In Plato's *Phaedrus,* Socrates bemoaned the development of writing. He feared that, as people came to rely on the written word as a substitute for the knowledge they used to carry inside their heads, they would, in the words of one of the dialogue's characters, "cease to exercise their memory and become forgetful." And because they would be able to "receive a quantity of information without proper instruction," they would "be thought very knowledgeable when they are for the most part quite ignorant." They would be "filled with the conceit of wisdom instead of real wisdom." Socrates wasn't wrong—the new technology did often have the effects he feared—but he was shortsighted. He couldn't foresee the many ways that writing and reading would serve to spread information, spur fresh ideas, and expand human knowledge (if not wisdom).

The arrival of Gutenberg's printing press, in the 15th century, set off another round of teeth gnashing. The Italian humanist Hieronimo Squarciafico worried that the easy availability of books would lead to intellectual laziness, making men "less studious" and weakening their minds. Others argued that cheaply printed books and broadsheets would undermine religious authority, demean the work of scholars and scribes, and spread sedition and debauchery. As New York University professor Clay Shirky notes, "Most of the arguments made against the printing press were correct, even prescient." But, again, the doomsayers were unable to imagine the myriad blessings that the printed word would deliver.

So, yes, you should be skeptical of my skepticism. Perhaps those who dismiss critics of the Internet as Luddites or nostalgists will be proved correct, and from our hyperactive, data-stoked minds will spring a golden age of intellectual discovery and universal wisdom. Then again, the Net isn't the alphabet, and although it may replace the printing press, it produces something altogether different. The kind of deep reading that a sequence of printed pages promotes is valuable not just for the knowledge we acquire from the author's words but for the intellectual vibrations those words set off within our own minds. In the quiet spaces opened up by the sustained, undistracted reading of a book, or by any other act of contemplation, for that matter, we make our own associations, draw our own inferences and analogies, foster our own ideas. Deep reading, as Maryanne Wolf argues, is indistinguishable from deep thinking.

If we lose those quiet spaces, or fill them up with "content," we will sacrifice something important not only in our selves but in our culture. In a recent essay, the playwright Richard Foreman eloquently described what's at stake:

> I come from a tradition of Western culture, in which the ideal (my ideal) was the complex, dense and "cathedral-like" structure of the highly educated and articulate personality—a man or woman who carried inside themselves a personally constructed and unique version of the entire heritage of the West. [But now] I see within us all (myself included) the replacement of complex inner density with a new kind of self—evolving under the pressure of information overload and the technology of the "instantly available."

As we are drained of our "inner repertory of dense cultural inheritance," Foreman concluded, we risk turning into "'pancake people'—spread wide and thin as we connect with that vast network of information accessed by the mere touch of a button."

I'm haunted by that scene in *2001*. What makes it so poignant, and so weird, is the computer's emotional response to the disassembly of its mind: its despair as one circuit after another goes dark, its childlike pleading with the astronaut— "I can feel it. I can feel it. I'm afraid"—and its final reversion to what can only be called a state of innocence. HAL's outpouring of feeling contrasts with the emotionlessness that characterizes the human figures in the film, who go about their business with an almost robotic efficiency. Their thoughts and actions feel scripted, as if they're following the steps of an algorithm. In the world of *2001*, people have become so machinelike that the most human character turns out to be a machine. That's the essence of Kubrick's dark prophecy: as we come to rely on computers to mediate our understanding of the world, it is our own intelligence that flattens into artificial intelligence.

QUESTIONS FOR DISCUSSION AND WRITING

1. In paragraphs 2 and 3 Carr explains how the fact that he reads so many materials on the Internet is "remapping the neural circuitry, reprogramming the memory.... I'm not thinking the way I used to think." What is his explanation for how continuous exposure to the Internet shapes "the process of thought" and is "chipping away my capacity for concentration and contemplation" (paragraph 4)? Is his explanation convincing? Why or why not?

2. Do the positive features of reading online (such as ease of locating and accessing millions of documents, worldwide) outweigh the losses Carr identifies, such as becoming "'mere decoders of information'" and disengagement from the process of making "the rich mental connections that form when we read deeply and without distraction" (paragraph 8)?

3. Carr says that the "Internet, an immeasurably powerful computing system, is subsuming most of our other intellectual technologies. It's becoming our map and our clock, our printing press and our typewriter, our calculator and our telephone, and our radio and TV" (paragraph 17). Does your use of the Internet verify Carr's assertion of its functions? (If so, today do you access these technologies via computer or cell phone?) He continues the analysis, explaining how the presence of "hyperlinks, blinking ads, and other digital gewgaws ... scatter our attention and diffuse our concentration" (paragraph 18). Pick an article of interest to you, perhaps on the Internet version of the *New York Times,* and as you read it keep track of all the electronic distractions that occur during your reading. What effects do these distractions have on your ability to understand, remember, process, and store the information in the article? Has this experience been typical?

4. Is Carr accurate in claiming that Google really wants our minds to "operate as high-speed data processing machines" for the financial benefit of the advertisers whose "economic interest [is] to drive us to distraction" (paragraph 29)? Carr quotes Richard Foreman, who says that "we risk turning into 'pancake people'—spread wide and thin as we connect with that vast network of information accessed by the mere touch of a button" (paragraph 33). Is this pessimistic conclusion justified? Why or why not?

5. If you and your peers are considerably younger than Carr, who was born in 1959, do you, on occasion, dive deep into the text as Carr used to, "a scuba diver in the sea of words" (paragraph 4)? Or have you always read in the way that he now reads, zipping "along the surface like a guy on a Jet Ski" (paragraph 4)? If so, in what ways have your experiences of reading—in print or online—differed from Carr's? Are these differences significant? Discuss alternative styles of reading—in print and on the Internet—with classmates and make a chart of the similarities and differences. Analyze your observations.

ADAM GOPNIK

The Information: How the Internet Gets Inside Us

The son of two professors, Adam Gopnik (b. 1956) graduated from McGill University in Montreal, Canada, and went on to study at the New York University Institute of Fine Arts. Gopnik is a staff writer for the New Yorker. *His book* Paris to the Moon *(2000) is a collection of essays that he wrote while he and his family spent five years living in Paris. A more recent book is* The Table Comes First: Family, France and the Meaning of Food *(2011), in which Gopnik examines our relationship, indeed, our preoccupation, with food. He has also written books for children, including* The King in the Window *(2005) and* Steps across the Water *(2010). He has won the National Magazine Award for Essays and Criticism three times as well as the George Polk Award for Magazine Reporting.*

When the first Harry Potter book appeared, in 1997, it was just a year before the universal search engine Google was launched. And so Hermione Granger, that charming grind, still goes to the Hogwarts library and spends hours and hours working her way through the stacks, finding out what a basilisk is or how to make a love potion. The idea that a wizard in training might have, instead, a magic pad where she could inscribe a name and in half a second have an avalanche of news stories, scholarly articles, books, and images (including images she shouldn't be looking at) was a Quidditch broom too far. Now, having been stuck with the library shtick, she has to go on working the stacks in the Harry Potter movies, while the kids who have since come of age nudge their parents. "Why is she doing that?" they whisper. "Why doesn't she just Google it?"

That the reality of machines can outpace the imagination of magic, and in so short a time, does tend to lend weight to the claim that the technological shifts in communication we're living with are unprecedented. It isn't just that we've lived one technological revolution among many; it's that our technological revolution is the big social revolution that we live with. The past twenty years have seen a revolution less in morals, which have remained mostly static, than in means: You could already say "fuck" on HBO back in the eighties; the change has been our ability to tweet or IM or text it. The set subject of our novelists is information; the set obsession of our dons is what it does to our intelligence.

The scale of the transformation is such that an ever-expanding literature has emerged to censure or celebrate it. A series of books explaining why books no longer matter is a paradox that Chesterton would have found implausible, yet there they are, and they come in the typical flavors: the eulogistic, the alarmed, the sober, and the gleeful. When the electric toaster was invented, there were, no doubt, books that said that the toaster would open up horizons for breakfast undreamed of in the days of burning bread over an open flame; books that told you that the toaster would bring an end to the days of creative breakfast, since our children, growing up with uniformly sliced bread, made to fit a single opening, would never know what a loaf of their own was like; and books that told you that sometimes the toaster would make breakfast better and sometimes it would make breakfast worse, and that the cost for finding this out would be the price of the book you'd just bought.

All three kinds appear among the new books about the Internet: call them the Never-Betters, the Better-Nevers, and the Ever-Wasers. The Never-Betters believe that we're on the brink of a new utopia, where information will be free and democratic, news will be made from the bottom up, love will reign, and cookies will bake themselves. The Better-Nevers think that we would have been better off if the whole thing had never happened, that the world that is coming to an end is superior to the one that is taking its place, and that, at a minimum, books and magazines create private space for minds in ways that twenty-second bursts of information don't. The Ever-Wasers insist that at any moment in modernity something like this is going on, and that a new way of organizing data and connecting users is always thrilling to some and chilling to others—that something like this is going on is exactly what makes it a modern moment. One's hopes rest with the Never-Betters; one's head with the Ever-Wasers; and one's heart? Well, twenty or so books in, one's heart tends to move toward the Better-Nevers, and then bounce back toward someplace that looks more like home.

Among the Never-Betters, the N.Y.U. professor Clay Shirky—the author of 5 *Cognitive Surplus* and many articles and blog posts proclaiming the coming of the digital millennium—is the breeziest and seemingly most self-confident. "Seemingly," because there is an element of overdone provocation in his stuff (So people aren't reading Tolstoy? Well, Tolstoy sucks) that suggests something a little nervous going on underneath. Shirky believes that we are on the crest of an ever-surging wave of democratized information: The Gutenberg printing press produced the Reformation, which produced the Scientific Revolution, which produced the Enlightenment, which produced the Internet, each move more liberating than the one before. Though it may take a little time, the new connective technology, by joining people together in new communities and in new ways, is bound to make for more freedom. It's the *Wired* version of Whig history: ever better, onward and upward, progress unstopped. In John Brockman's anthology *Is the Internet Changing the Way You Think?*, the evolutionary psychologist John Tooby shares the excitement—"We see all around us transformations in the making that will rival or exceed the printing revolution"—and makes the same extended parallel to Gutenberg: "Printing ignited the previously wasted intellectual potential of huge segments of the population. . . . Freedom of thought and speech—where they exist—were unforeseen offspring of the printing press."

Shirky's and Tooby's version of Never-Betterism has its excitements, but the history it uses seems to have been taken from the back of a cereal box. The idea, for instance, that the printing press rapidly gave birth to a new order of information, democratic and bottom-up, is a cruel cartoon of the truth. If the printing press did propel the Reformation, one of the biggest ideas it propelled was Luther's newly invented absolutist anti-Semitism. And what followed the Reformation wasn't the Enlightenment, a new era of openness and freely disseminated knowledge. What followed the Reformation was, actually, the Counter-Reformation, which used the same means—i.e., printed books—to spread ideas about what jerks the reformers were, and unleashed a hundred years of religious warfare. In the 1750s, more than two centuries later, Voltaire was still writing in a book about the horrors of those other books that urged burning men alive in auto-da-fé. Buried in Tooby's little parenthetical—"where they exist"—are millions of human bodies. If ideas of democracy and freedom emerged at the end of the printing-press era, it wasn't by some technological logic but because of parallel inventions, like the ideas of limited government and religious tolerance, very hard won from history.

Of course, if you stretch out the time scale enough, and are sufficiently casual about causes, you can give the printing press credit for anything you like. But all the media of modern consciousness—from the printing press to radio and the movies—were used just as readily by authoritarian reactionaries, and then by modern totalitarians, to reduce liberty and enforce conformity as they ever were by libertarians to expand it. As Andrew Pettegree shows in his fine new study, *The Book in the Renaissance*, the mainstay of the printing revolution in seventeenth-century Europe was not dissident pamphlets but royal edicts, printed by the thousand: Almost all the new media of that day were working, in essence, for kinglouis.gov.

Even later, full-fledged totalitarian societies didn't burn books. They burned some books, while keeping the printing presses running off such quantities that by the mid-fifties Stalin was said to have more books in print than Agatha Christie. (Recall that in *1984* Winston's girlfriend works for the Big Brother publishing house.) If you're going to give the printed book, or any other machine-made thing, credit for all the good things that have happened, you have to hold it accountable for the bad stuff, too. The Internet may make for more freedom a hundred years from now, but there's no historical law that says it has to.

Many of the more knowing Never-Betters turn for cheer not to messy history and mixed-up politics but to psychology—to the actual expansion of our minds. The argument, advanced in Andy Clark's *Supersizing the Mind* and in Robert K. Logan's *The Sixth Language*, begins with the claim that cognition is not a little processing program that takes place inside your head, Robby the Robot style. It is a constant flow of information, memory, plans, and physical movements, in which as much thinking goes on out there as in here. If television produced the global village, the Internet produces the global psyche: everyone keyed in like a neuron, so that to the eyes of a watching Martian we are really part of a single planetary brain. Contraptions don't change consciousness; contraptions are part of consciousness. We may not act better than we used to, but we sure think differently than we did.

Cognitive entanglement, after all, is the rule of life. My memories and my wife's intermingle. When I can't recall a name or a date, I don't look it up; I just ask her. Our machines, in this way, become our substitute spouses and plug-in companions. Jerry Seinfeld said that the public library was everyone's pathetic friend, giving up its books at a casual request and asking you only to please return them in a month or so. Google is really the world's Thurber wife: smiling patiently and smugly as she explains what the difference is between eulogy and elegy and what the best route is to that little diner outside Hackensack. The new age is one in which we have a know-it-all spouse at our fingertips.

But, if cognitive entanglement exists, so does cognitive exasperation. Husbands and wives deny each other's memories as much as they depend on them. That's fine until it really counts (say, in divorce court). In a practical, immediate way, one sees the limits of the so-called "extended mind" clearly in the mob-made Wikipedia, the perfect product of that new vast, supersized cognition: When there's easy agreement, it's fine, and when there's widespread disagreement on values or facts, as with, say, the origins of capitalism, it's fine, too; you get both sides. The trouble comes when one side is right and the other side is wrong and doesn't know it. The Shakespeare authorship page and the Shroud of Turin page are scenes of constant conflict and are packed with unreliable information. Creationists crowd cyberspace every bit as effectively as evolutionists, and extend their minds just as fully. Our trouble is not the overall absence of smartness but the intractable power of pure stupidity, and no machine, or mind, seems extended enough to cure that.

The books by the Better-Nevers are more moving than those by the Never-Betters for the same reason that Thomas Gray was at his best in that graveyard: Loss is always the great poetic subject, Nicholas Carr, in *The Shallows*, William Powers, in *Hamlet's BlackBerry*, and Sherry Turkle, in *Alone Together*, all bear intimate witness to a sense that the newfound land, the ever-present BlackBerry-and-instant-message world, is one whose price, paid in frayed nerves and lost reading hours and broken attention, is hardly worth the gains it gives us. "The medium does matter," Carr has written. "As a technology, a book focuses our attention, isolates us from the myriad distractions that fill our everyday lives. A networked computer does precisely the opposite. It is designed to scatter our attention. . . . Knowing that the depth of our thought is tied directly to the intensity of our attentiveness, it's hard not to conclude that as we adapt to the intellectual environment of the Net our thinking becomes shallower."

These three Better-Nevers have slightly different stories to tell. Carr is most concerned about the way the Internet breaks down our capacity for reflective thought. His testimony about how this happened in his own life is plangent and familiar, but he addles it a bit by insisting that the real damage is being done at the neurological level, that our children are having their brains altered by too much instant messaging and the like. This sounds impressive but turns out to be redundant. Of course the changes are in their brains; where else would they be? It's the equivalent of saying that playing football doesn't just affect a kid's fitness; it changes the muscle tone that creates his ability to throw and catch footballs.

Powers's reflections are more family-centered and practical. He recounts, very touchingly, stories of family life broken up by the eternal consultation of smartphones and computer monitors:

> Somebody excuses themselves for a bathroom visit or a glass of water and doesn't return. Five minutes later, another of us exits on a similarly mundane excuse along the lines of "I have to check something." . . . Where have all the humans gone? To their screens of course. Where they always go these

days. The digital crowd has a way of elbowing its way into everything, to the point where a family can't sit in a room together for half an hour without somebody, or everybody, peeling off. . . . As I watched the Vanishing Family Trick unfold, and played my own part in it, I sometimes felt as if love itself, or the acts of heart and mind that constitute love, were being leached out of the house by our screens.

He then surveys seven Wise Men—Plato, Thoreau, Seneca, the usual gang— 15 who have something to tell us about solitude and the virtues of inner space, all of it sound enough, though he tends to overlook the significant point that these worthies were not entirely in favor of the kinds of liberties that we now take for granted and that made the new dispensation possible. (He knows that Seneca instructed the Emperor Nero, but sticks in a footnote to insist that the bad, fiddling-while-Rome-burned Nero asserted himself only after he fired the philosopher and started to act like an Internet addict.)

Similarly, Nicholas Carr cites Martin Heidegger for having seen, in the mid-fifties, that new technologies would break the meditational space on which Western wisdoms depend. Since Heidegger had not long before walked straight out of his own meditational space into the arms of the Nazis, it's hard to have much nostalgia for this version of the past. One feels the same doubts when Sherry Turkle, in *Alone Together*, her touching plaint about the destruction of the old intimacy-reading culture by the new remote-connection-Internet culture, cites studies that show a dramatic decline in empathy among college students, who apparently are "far less likely to say that it is valuable to put oneself in the place of others or to try and understand their feelings." What is to be done? Other Better-Nevers point to research that's supposed to show that people who read novels develop exceptional empathy. But if reading a lot of novels gave you exceptional empathy, university English departments should be filled with the most compassionate and generous-minded of souls, and, so far, they are not.

One of the things that John Brockman's collection on the Internet and the mind illustrates is that when people struggle to describe the state that the Internet puts them in, they arrive at a remarkably familiar picture of disassociation and fragmentation. Life was once whole, continuous, stable; now it is fragmented, multipart, shimmering around us, unstable and impossible to fix. The world becomes Keats's "waking dream," as the writer Kevin Kelly puts it.

The odd thing is that this complaint, though deeply felt by our contemporary Better-Nevers, is identical to Baudelaire's perception about modern Paris in 1855, or Walter Benjamin's about Berlin in 1930, or Marshall McLuhan's in the face of three-channel television (and Canadian television, at that) in 1965. When department stores had Christmas windows with clockwork puppets, the world was going to pieces; when the city streets were filled with horse-drawn carriages running by bright-colored posters, you could no longer tell the real from the simulated; when people were listening to shellac 78s and looking at color newspaper supplements, the world had become a kaleidoscope of disassociated imagery; and when the broadcast air was filled with droning black-and-white images of men in suits reading news, all of life had become indistinguishable from your fantasies of it. It was Marx, not Steve Jobs, who said that the character of modern life is that everything falls apart.

We must, at some level, need this to be true, since we think it's true about so many different kinds of things. We experience this sense of fracture so deeply that we ascribe it to machines that, viewed with retrospective detachment, don't seem remotely capable of producing it. If all you have is a hammer, the saying goes, everything looks like a nail; and, if you think the world is broken, every machine looks like the hammer that broke it.

It is an intuition of this kind that moves the final school, the Ever-Wasers, 20 when they consider the new digital age. A sense of vertiginous overload is the central experience of modernity, they say; at every moment, machines make new circuits for connection and circulation, as obvious-seeming as the postage stamps that let nineteenth-century scientists collaborate by mail, or as newfangled as the Wi-Fi connection that lets a sixteen-year-old in New York consult a tutor in Bangalore. Our new confusion is just the same old confusion.

Among Ever-Wasers, the Harvard historian Ann Blair may be the most ambitious. In her book *Too Much to Know: Managing Scholarly Information before the Modern Age*, she makes the case that what we're going through is like what others went through a very long while ago. Against the cartoon history of Shirky or Tooby, Blair argues that the sense of "information overload" was not the consequence of Gutenberg but already in place before printing began. She wants us to resist "trying to reduce the complex causal nexus behind the transition from Renaissance to Enlightenment to the impact of a technology or any particular set of ideas." Anyway, the crucial revolution was not of print but of paper: "During the later Middle Ages a staggering growth in the production of manuscripts, facilitated by the use of paper, accompanied a great expansion of readers outside the monastic and scholastic contexts." For that matter, our minds were altered less by books than by index slips. Activities that seem quite twenty-first century, she shows, began when people cut and pasted from one manuscript to another; made aggregated news in compendiums; passed around précis. "Early modern finding devices" were forced into existence: lists of authorities, lists of headings.

Everyone complained about what the new information technologies were doing to our minds. Everyone said that the flood of books produced a restless, fractured attention. Everyone complained that pamphlets and poems were breaking kids' ability to concentrate, that big good handmade books were ignored, swept aside by printed works that, as Erasmus said, "are foolish, ignorant, malignant, libelous, mad." The reader consulting a card catalogue in a library was living a revolution as momentous, and as disorienting, as our own. The book index was the search engine of its era, and needed to be explained at length to puzzled researchers—as, for that matter, did the Hermione-like idea of "looking things up." That uniquely evil and necessary thing, the comprehensive review of many different books on a related subject, with the necessary oversimplification of their ideas that it demanded, was already around in 1500, and already being accused of missing all the points. In the period when many of the big, classic books that we no longer have time to read were being written, the general complaint was that there wasn't enough time to read big, classic books.

Blair's and Pettegree's work on the relation between minds and machines, and the combination of delight and despair we find in their collisions, leads you to a broader thought: At any given moment, our most complicated machine will be taken as a model of human intelligence, and whatever media kids favor will be identified as the cause of our stupidity. When there were automatic looms, the mind was like an automatic loom; and, since young people in the loom period liked novels, it was the cheap novel that was degrading our minds. When there were telephone exchanges, the mind was like a telephone exchange, and, in the same period, since the nickelodeon reigned, moving pictures were making us dumb. When mainframe computers arrived and television was what kids liked, the mind was like a mainframe and television was the engine of our idiocy. Some machine is always showing us Mind; some entertainment derived from the machine is always showing us Non-Mind.

Armed with such parallels, the Ever-Wasers smile condescendingly at the Better-Nevers and say, "Of course, some new machine is always ruining every-thing. We've all been here before." But the Better-Nevers can say, in return, "What if the Internet is actually doing it?" The hypochondriac frets about this bump or that suspicious freckle and we laugh—but sooner or later one small bump, one jagged-edge freckle, will be the thing for certain. Worlds really do decline, "Oh, they always say that about the barbarians, but every generation has its barbarians, and every generation assimilates them," one Roman reassured another when the Vandals were at the gates, and next thing you knew there wasn't a hot bath or a good book for another thousand years.

And, if it was ever thus, how did it ever get to be thus in the first place? The digital world is new, and the real gains and losses of the Internet era are to be found not in altered neurons or empathy tests but in the small changes in mood, life, manners, feelings it creates—in the texture of the age. There is, for instance, a simple, spooky sense in which the Internet is just a loud and unlimited library in which we now live—as if one went to sleep every night in the college stacks, surrounded by pamphlets and polemics and possibilities. There is the sociology section, the science section, old sheet music and menus, and you can go to the periodicals room anytime and read old issues of the *New Statesman*. (And you can whisper loudly to a friend in the next carrel to get the hockey scores.) To see that that is so is at least to drain some of the melodrama from the subject. It is odd and new to be living in the library; but there isn't anything odd and new about the library.

Yet surely having something wrapped right around your mind is different from having your mind wrapped tightly around something. What we live in is not the age of the extended mind but the age of the inverted self. The things that have usually lived in the darker recesses or mad corners of our mind—sexual obses-sions and conspiracy theories, paranoid fixations and fetishes—are now out there: You click once and you can read about the Kennedy autopsy or the Nazi salute or hog-tied Swedish flight attendants. But things that were once external and subject to the social rules of caution and embarrassment—above all, our interactions with other people—are now easily internalized, made to feel like mere workings of the id left on its own. (I've felt this myself, writing anonymously on hockey forums: It is easy to say vile things about Gary Bettman, the commissioner of the NHL, with a feeling of glee rather than with a sober sense that what you're saying should be tempered by a little truth and reflection.) Thus the limitless malice of Internet commenting: It's not newly unleashed anger but what we all think in the first order, and have always in the past socially restrained if only thanks to the look on the listener's face—the monstrous music that runs through our minds is now played out loud.

A social network is crucially different from a social circle, since the function of a social circle is to curb our appetites and of a network to extend them. Everything once inside is outside, a click away; much that used to be outside is inside, experienced in solitude. And so the peacefulness, the serenity that we feel away from the Internet, and which all the Better-Nevers rightly testify to, has less to do with being no longer harried by others than with being less oppressed by the force of your own inner life. Shut off your computer, and your self stops raging quite as much or quite as loud.

It is the wraparound presence, not the specific evils, of the machine that oppresses us. Simply reducing the machine's presence will go a long way toward alleviating the disorder. Which points, in turn, to a dog-not-barking-in-the-nighttime detail that may be significant. In the Better-Never books, television isn't scanted or ignored; it's celebrated. When William Powers, in *Hamlet's BlackBerry*, describes the deal his family makes to have an Unplugged Sunday, he tells us that the No Screens agreement doesn't include television: "For us, television had always been a mostly communal experience, a way of coming together rather than pulling apart." ("Can you please turn off your damn computer and come watch television with the rest of the family," the dad now cries to the teenager.)

Yet everything that is said about the Internet's destruction of "interiority" was said for decades about television, and just as loudly. Jerry Mander's *Four Arguments for the Elimination of Television*, in the 1970s, turned on television's addictive nature and its destruction of viewers' inner lives; a little later, George Trow proposed that television produced the absence of context, the disintegration of the frame—the very things, in short, that the Internet is doing now. And Bill McKibben ended his book on television by comparing watching TV to watching ducks on a pond (advantage: ducks), in the same spirit in which Nicholas Carr leaves his computer screen to read *Walden*.

Now television is the harmless little fireplace over in the corner, where the 30 family gathers to watch *Entourage*. TV isn't just docile; it's positively benevolent. This makes you think that what made television so evil back when it was evil was not its essence but its omnipresence. Once it is not everything, it can be merely something. The real demon in the machine is the tirelessness of the user. A meatless Monday has advantages over enforced vegetarianism, because it helps release the pressure on the food system without making undue demands on the eaters.

In the same way, an unplugged Sunday is a better idea than turning off the Internet completely, since it demonstrates that we can get along just fine without the screens, if only for a day.

Hermione, stuck in the nineties, never did get her iPad, and will have to manage in the stacks. But perhaps the instrument of the new connected age was already in place in fantasy. For the Internet screen has always been like the palantír in Tolkien's *Lord of the Rings*—the "seeing stone" that lets the wizards see the entire world. Its gift is great; the wizard can see it all. Its risk is real: Evil things will register more vividly than the great mass of dull good. The peril isn't that users lose their knowledge of the world. It's that they can lose all sense of proportion. You can come to think that the armies of Mordor are not just vast and scary, which they are, but limitless and undefeatable, which they aren't.

Thoughts are bigger than the things that deliver them. Our contraptions may shape our consciousness, but it is our consciousness that makes our credos, and we mostly live by those. Toast, as every breakfaster knows, isn't really about the quality of the bread or how it's sliced or even the toaster. For man cannot live by toast alone. It's all about the butter.

QUESTIONS FOR DISCUSSION AND WRITING

1. Gopnik begins with a reference to Hermione Granger from the Harry Potter books. What is the connection between magic and technology? How does the Internet reflect this connection?

2. Indeed, Gopnik's writing style relies heavily on the use of allusions and references to other writers and thinkers. Did you find the article difficult to comprehend because of that? Did you, like the younger viewer of a Harry Potter movie, "just Google it" (paragraph 1) to understand Gopnik? Did that strike you as ironic? Purposeful? Explain.

3. In paragraph 4, Gopnik divides reactions to technological changes into three categories: the Never-Betters (who are technophiles), the Better-Nevers (who are technophobes), and the Ever-Wasers (who think change is no big deal one way or the other). To which category do you belong? Why? What problems do you see with the other two approaches toward technology?

4. Gopnik writes, "the real gains and losses of the Internet era are to be found not in altered neurons or empathy tests but in the small changes in mood, life, manners, feelings it creates—in the texture of the age" (paragraph 25). If you are too young to remember life before the Internet, what does this statement mean to you? Is it meaningless? Can you describe today's digital world? If you are old enough to remember life before the Internet, how has the "texture of the age" changed? Be specific.

5. In paragraph 29, Gopnik makes a comparison between the Internet and television. He points out that for decades, television was deemed the prime culprit for much that was perceived to be wrong about society; now, in the eyes

of critics, that role has been taken by the Internet. What does Gopnik argue about that comparison? Do you agree or disagree? Defend your answer.

6. Gopnik ends on an optimistic note: "Thoughts are bigger than the things that deliver them" (paragraph 32). This seems to be a response to Marshall McLuhan's famous statement: "The medium is the message" (McLuhan is mentioned by Gopnik in paragraph 18). In your opinion, which one is right, and why?

JAMES GLEICK

How Google Dominates Us

James Gleick (b. 1954) is a Harvard-educated author who writes frequently on science-related topics. His credits include The Information: A History, a Theory, a Flood *(2011) and* Chaos: Making a New Science *(1987), which won a National Book Award and was a finalist for the Pulitzer Prize. After graduating from Harvard with a degree in English and linguistics, Gleick began his writing career in Minneapolis, where he helped found the newspaper* Metropolis. *After that, he worked for the* New York Times *for ten years. Besides winning the National Book Award for* Chaos, *Gleick has been a McGraw Distinguished Lecturer at Princeton University. In addition to the* New York Review of Books, *in which this article was published, Gleick has also written for the* Atlantic, *the* New Yorker, Slate, *and the* Washington Post. *He is on the board for both the Authors Guild and the Key West Literary Seminar.*

In this article, which is broadly a review of four books written about the ubiquitous search engine Google, Gleick shows how Google went from being a new start-up in the dorms at Stanford University to a powerhouse business with more ad revenue than all newspapers and magazines combined. At the center of the argument is a key notion: The product isn't the information we're looking up; we, the users, are the product for Google. Google gathers information, lots of information, about the searches conducted by Google users, and sells specifically directed advertising based on those searches. The precision and sophistication with which Google does this is astonishing, and this ability has more consequences than just presenting advertising. Although the company's motto is, "Don't be evil," some might argue that Google in many ways has been just that.

Tweets Alain de Botton, philosopher, author, and now online aphorist:

> The logical conclusion of our relationship to computers: expectantly to type "what is the meaning of my life" into Google.

You can do this, of course. Type "what is th" and faster than you can find the *e* Google is sending choices back at you: what is the cloud? what is the mean? what is the american dream? what is the illuminati? Google is trying to read your mind. Only it's not your mind. It's the World Brain. And whatever that is, we know that a twelve-year-old company based in Mountain View, California, is wired into it like no one else.

Google is where we go for answers. People used to go elsewhere or, more likely, stagger along not knowing. Nowadays you can't have a long dinner-table argument about who won the Oscar for that Neil Simon movie where she plays an actress who doesn't win an Oscar; at any moment someone will pull out a pocket device and Google it. If you need the art-history meaning of "picturesque," you could find it in *The Book of Answers*, compiled two decades ago by the New York Public Library's reference desk, but you won't. Part of Google's mission is to make the books of answers redundant (and the reference librarians, too). "A hamadryad is a wood-nymph, also a poisonous snake in India, and an Abyssinian baboon," says the narrator of John Banville's 2009 novel, *The Infinities*. "It takes a god to know a thing like that." Not anymore.

The business of finding facts has been an important gear in the workings of human knowledge, and the technology has just been upgraded from rubber band to nuclear reactor, No wonder there's some confusion about Google's exact role in that—along with increasing fear about its power and its intentions.

Most of the time Google does not actually have the answers. When people 5 say, "I looked it up on Google," they are committing a solecism. When they try to erase their embarrassing personal histories "on Google," they are barking up the wrong tree. It is seldom right to say that anything is true "according to Google." Google is the oracle of redirection. Go there for "hamadryad," and it points you to Wikipedia. Or the Free Online Dictionary. Or the Official Hamadryad Web Site (it's a rock band, too, wouldn't you know). Google defines its mission as "to organize the world's information," not to possess it or accumulate it. Then again, a substantial portion of the world's printed books have now been copied onto the company's servers, where they share space with millions of hours of video and detailed multilevel imagery of the entire globe, from satellites and from its squadrons of roving street-level cameras. Not to mention the great and growing trove of information Google possesses regarding the interests and behavior of, approximately, everyone.

When I say Google "possesses" all this information, that's not the same as owning it. What it means to own information is very much in flux.

In barely a decade Google has made itself a global brand bigger than Coca-Cola or GE; it has created more wealth faster than any company in history; it dominates the information economy. How did that happen? It happened more or less in plain sight. Google has many secrets but the main ingredients of its success have not been secret at all, and the business story has already provided grist for dozens of books. Steven Levy's new account, *In the Plex,* is the most authoritative to date and in many ways the most entertaining. Levy has covered personal computing for almost thirty years, for *Newsweek* and *Wired* and in six previous books, and has visited Google's headquarters periodically since 1999, talking with its founders, Larry Page and Sergey Brin, and, as much as has been possible for a journalist, observing the company from the inside. He has been able to record some provocative, if slightly self-conscious, conversations like this one in 2004 about their hopes for Google:

"It will be included in people's brains," said Page. "When you think about something and don't really know much about it, you will automatically get information."

"That's true," said Brin. "Ultimately I view Google as a way to augment your brain with the knowledge of the world. Right now you go into your computer and type a phrase, but you can imagine that it could be easier in the future, that you can have just devices you talk into, or you can have computers that pay attention to what's going on around them."

Page said, "Eventually you'll have the implant, where if you think about a fact, it will just tell you the answer."

In 2004, Google was still a private company, five years old, already worth $25 billion, and handling about 85 percent of Internet searches. Its single greatest innovation was the algorithm called PageRank, developed by Page and Brin when they were Stanford graduate students running their research project from a computer in a dorm room. The problem was that most Internet searches produced useless lists of low-quality results. The solution was a simple idea: to harvest the implicit knowledge already embodied in the architecture of the World Wide Web, organically evolving.

The essence of the Web is the linking of individual "pages" on Web sites, one to another. Every link represents a recommendation—a vote of interest, if not quality. So the algorithm assigns every page a rank, depending on how many other pages link to it. Furthermore, all links are not valued equally. A recommendation is worth more when it comes from a page that has a high rank itself. The math isn't trivial—PageRank is a probability distribution, and the calculation is recursive, each page's rank depending on the ranks of pages that depend . . . and so on. Page and Brin patented PageRank and published the details even before starting the company they called Google.

Most people have already forgotten how dark and unsignposted the Internet 10 once was. A user in 1996, when the Web comprised hundreds of thousands of "sites" with millions of "pages," did not expect to be able to search for "Olympics" and automatically find the official site of the Atlanta games. That was too hard a problem. And what was a search supposed to produce for a word like "university"? AltaVista, then the leading search engine, offered up a seemingly unordered list of academic institutions, topped by the Oregon Center for Optics.

Levy recounts a conversation between Page and an AltaVista engineer, who explained that the scoring system would rank a page higher if "university" appeared multiple times in the headline. AltaVista seemed untroubled that the Oregon center did not qualify as a major university. A conventional way to rank universities would be to consult experts and assess measures of quality: graduate rates, retention rates, test scores. The Google approach was to trust the Web and its numerous links, for better and for worse.

PageRank is one of those ideas that seem obvious after the fact. But the business of Internet search, young as it was, had fallen into some rigid orthodoxies. The main task of a search engine seemed to be the compiling of an index. People naturally thought of existing technologies for organizing the world's information, and these were found in encyclopedias and dictionaries. They could see that alphabetical order was about to become less important, but they were slow to appreciate how dynamic and ungraspable their target, the Internet, really was. Even after Page and Brin flipped on the light switch, most companies continued to wear blindfolds.

The Internet had entered its first explosive phase, boom and then bust for many ambitious start-ups, and one thing everyone knew was that the way to make money was to attract and retain users. The buzzword was "portal"—the user's point of entry, like Excite, Go.com, and Yahoo—and portals could not make money by rushing customers into the rest of the Internet. "Stickiness," as Levy says, "was the most desired metric in Web sites at the time." Portals did not want their search functions to be too good. That sounds stupid, but then again how did Google intend to make money when it charged users nothing? Its user interface at first was plain, minimalist, and emphatically free of advertising—nothing but a box for the user to type a query, followed by two buttons, one to produce a list of results and one with the famously brash tag "I'm feeling lucky."

The Google founders, Larry and Sergey, did everything their own way. Even in the unbuttoned culture of Silicon Valley they stood out from the start as originals, "Montessori kids" (per Levy), unconcerned with standards and proprieties, favoring big red gym balls over office chairs, deprecating organization charts and formal titles, showing up for business meetings in roller-blade gear. It is clear from all these books that they believed their own hype; they believed with moral fervor in the primacy and power of information. (Sergey and Larry did not invent the company's famous motto—"Don't be evil"—but they embraced it, and now they may as well own it.)

As they saw it from the first, their mission encompassed not just the Internet but all the world's books and images, too. When Google created a free e-mail service—Gmail—its competitors were Microsoft, which offered users two megabytes of storage of their past and current e-mail, and Yahoo, which offered four megabytes. Google could have trumped that with six or eight; instead it provided 1,000—a gigabyte. It doubled that a year later and promised "to keep giving people more space forever."

They have been relentless in driving computer science forward. Google Translate has achieved more in machine translation than the rest of the world's artificial intelligence experts combined. Google's new mind-reading type-ahead feature, Google Instant, has "to date" (boasts the 2010 annual report) "saved our users over 100 billion keystrokes and counting." (If you are seeking information about the Gobi Desert, for example, you receive results well before you type the word "desert.")

Somewhere along the line they gave people the impression that they didn't care for advertising—that they scarcely had a business plan at all. In fact it's clear that advertising was fundamental to their plan all along. They did scorn conventional marketing, however; their attitude seemed to be that Google would market itself. As, indeed, it did. Google was a verb and a meme. "The media seized on Google as a marker of a new form of behavior," writes Levy.

Endless articles rhapsodized about how people would Google their blind dates to get an advance dossier or how they would type in ingredients on hand to Google a recipe or use a telephone number to Google a reverse lookup. Columnists shared their self-deprecating tales of Googling themselves. . . . A contestant on the TV show *Who Wants to Be a Millionaire?* arranged with his brother to tap Google during the Phone-a-Friend lifeline. . . . And a fifty-two-year-old man suffering chest pains Googled "heart attack symptoms" and confirmed that he was suffering a coronary thrombosis.

Google's first marketing hire lasted a matter of months in 1999; his experience included Miller Beer and Tropicana and his proposal involved focus groups and television commercials. When Doug Edwards interviewed for a job as marketing manager later that year, he understood that the key word was "viral." Edwards lasted quite a bit longer, and now he's the first Google insider to have published his memoir of the experience. He was, as he says proudly in his subtitle to *I'm Feeling Lucky*, Google employee number 59. He provides two other indicators of how early that was: so early that he nabbed the e-mail address doug@google.com; and so early that Google's entire server hardware lived in a rented "cage."

> Less than six hundred square feet, it felt like a shotgun shack blighting a neighborhood of gated mansions. Every square inch was crammed with racks bristling with stripped-down CPUs [central processing units]. There were twenty-one racks and more than fifteen hundred machines, each sprouting cables like Play-Doh pushed through a spaghetti press. Where other cages were right-angled and inorganic, Google's swarmed with life, a giant termite mound dense with frenetic activity and intersecting curves.

Levy got a glimpse of Google's data storage a bit later and remarked, "If you 20 could imagine a male college freshman made of gigabytes, this would be his dorm."

Not anymore. Google owns and operates a constellation of giant server farms spread around the globe—huge windowless structures, resembling aircraft hangars or power plants, some with cooling towers. The server farms stockpile the exabytes of information and operate an array of staggeringly clever technology. This is Google's share of the cloud (that notional place where our data live) and it is the lion's share.

How thoroughly and how radically Google has already transformed the information economy has not been well understood. The merchandise of the information economy is not information; it is attention. These commodities have an inverse relationship. When information is cheap, attention becomes expensive. Attention is what we, the users, give to Google, and our attention is what Google sells—concentrated, focused, and crystallized.

Google's business is not search but advertising. More than 96 percent of its $29 billion in revenue last year came directly from advertising, and most of the rest came from advertising-related services. Google makes more from advertising than all the nation's newspapers combined. It's worth understanding precisely how this works. Levy chronicles the development of the advertising engine: a "fantastic achievement in building a money machine from the virtual smoke and mirrors of the Internet." In *The Googlization of Everything (and Why We Should Worry),* a book that can be read as a sober and admonitory companion, Siva Vaidhyanathan, a media scholar at the University of Virginia, puts it this way: "We are not Google's customers: we are its product. We—our fancies, fetishes, predilections, and preferences—are what Google sells to advertisers."

The evolution of this unparalleled money machine piled one brilliant innovation atop another, in fast sequence:

1. Early in 2000, Google sold "premium sponsored links": simple text ads assigned to particular search terms. A purveyor of golf balls could have its ad shown to everyone who searched for "golf" or, even better, "golf balls." Other search engines were already doing this. Following tradition, they charged according to how many people saw each ad. Salespeople sold the ads to big accounts, one by one.

2. Late that year, engineers devised an automated self-service system, dubbed AdWords. The opening pitch went, "Have a credit card and 5 minutes? Get your ad on Google today," and suddenly thousands of small businesses were buying their first Internet ads.

3. From a short-lived start-up called GoTo (by 2003 Google owned it) came two new ideas. One was to charge per click rather than per view. People who click on an ad for golf balls are more likely to buy them than those who simply see an ad on Google's Web site. The other idea was to let advertisers bid for keywords—such as "golf ball"—against one another in fast online auctions. Pay-per-click auctions opened a cash spigot. A click meant a successful ad, and some advertisers were willing to pay more for that than a human salesperson could have known. Plaintiffs' lawyers seeking clients would bid as much as fifty dollars for a single click on the keyword "mesothelioma"—the rare form of cancer caused by asbestos.

4. Google—monitoring its users' behavior so systematically—had instant knowledge of which ads were succeeding and which were not. It could view "click-through rates" as a measure of ad quality. And in determining the winners of auctions, it began to consider not just the money offered but the appeal of the ad: An effective ad, getting lots of clicks, would get better placement.

Now Google had a system of profitable cycles in place, positive feedback 25 pushing advertisers to make more effective ads and giving them data to help them do it and giving users more satisfaction in clicking on ads, while punishing noise and spam. "The system enforced Google's insistence that advertising shouldn't be a transaction between publisher and advertiser but a three-way relationship that also included the user," writes Levy. Hardly an equal relationship, however. Vaidhyanathan sees it as exploitative: "The Googlization of everything entails the harvesting, copying, aggregating, and ranking of information about and contributions made by each of us."

By 2003, AdWords Select was serving hundreds of thousands of advertisers and making so much money that Google was deliberating hiding its success from the press and from competitors. But it was only a launching pad for the next brilliancy.

5. So far, ads were appearing on Google's search pages, discreet in size, clearly marked, at the top or down the right side. Now the company expanded its platform outward. The aim was to develop a form of artificial intelligence that could analyze chunks of text—Web sites, blogs, e-mail, books—and match them with keywords. With two billion Web pages already in its index and with its close tracking of user behavior, Google had exactly the information needed to tackle this problem. Given a Web site (or a blog or an e-mail), it could predict which advertisements would be effective.

This was, in the jargon, "content-targeted advertising." Google called its program AdSense. For anyone hoping to—in the jargon—"monetize" their content, it was the Holy Grail. The biggest digital publishers, such as the *New York Times,* quickly signed up for AdSense, letting Google handle growing portions of their advertising business. And so did the smallest publishers, by the millions—so grew the "long tail" of possible advertisers, down to individual bloggers. They signed up because the ads were so powerfully, measurably productive. "Google conquered the advertising world with nothing more than applied mathematics," wrote Chris Anderson, the editor of *Wired.* "It didn't pretend to know anything about the culture and conventions of advertising—it just assumed that better data, with better analytical tools, would win the day. And Google was right." Newspapers and other traditional media have complained from time to time about the arrogation of their content, but it is by absorbing the world's advertising that Google has become their most destructive competitor.

Like all forms of artificial intelligence, targeted advertising has hits and misses. Levy cites a classic miss: a gory *New York Post* story about a body dismembered and stuffed in a garbage bag, accompanied on the *Post* Web site by a Google ad for plastic bags. Nonetheless, anyone could now add a few lines of code to their Web site, automatically display Google ads, and start cashing monthly checks, however small. Vast tracts of the Web that had been free of advertising now became Google partners. Today Google's ad canvas is not just the search page but the entire Web, and beyond that, great volumes of e-mail and, potentially, all the world's books.

Search and advertising thus become the matched edges of a sharp sword. The perfect search engine, as Sergey and Larry imagine it, reads your mind and produces the answer you want. The perfect advertising engine does the same: It shows you the ads you want. Anything else wastes your attention, the advertiser's money, and the world's bandwidth. The dream is virtuous advertising, matching up buyers and sellers to the benefit of all. But virtuous advertising in this sense is a contradiction in terms. The advertiser is paying for a slice of our limited attention; our minds would otherwise be elsewhere. If our interests and the advertisers' were perfectly aligned, they would not need to pay. There is no information utopia. Google users are parties to a complex transaction, and if there is one lesson to be drawn from all these books it is that we are not always witting parties.

Seeing ads next to your e-mail (if you use Google's free e-mail service) can 30 provide reminders, sometimes startling, of how much the company knows about your inner self. Even without your e-mail, your search history reveals plenty—as Levy says, "your health problems, your commercial interests, your hobbies, and your dreams." Your response to advertising reveals even more, and with its advertising programs Google began tracking the behavior of individual users from one Internet site to the next. They observe our every click (where they can) and they measure in milliseconds how long it takes us to decide. If they didn't, their results wouldn't be so uncannily effective. They have no rival in the depth and breadth of their data mining. They make statistical models for everything they know, connecting the small scales with the large, from queries and clicks to trends in fashion and season, climate and disease.

It's for your own good—that is Google's cherished belief. If we want the best possible search results, and if we want advertisements suited to our needs and desires, we must let them into our souls.

The Google corporate motto is "Don't be evil." Simple as that is, it requires parsing.

It was first put forward in 2001 by an engineer, Paul Buchheit, at a jawboning session about corporate values. "People laughed," he recalled. "But I said, 'No, really.'" (At that time the booming tech world had its elephant-in-the-room, and many Googlers understood "Don't be evil" explicitly to mean "Don't be like Microsoft"; i.e., don't be a ruthless, take-no-prisoners monopolist.)

Often it is misquoted in stronger form: "Do no evil." That would be a harder standard to meet.

Now they're mocked for it, but the Googlers were surely sincere. They believed 35 a corporation should behave ethically, like a person. They brainstormed about their values. Taken at face value, "Don't be evil" has a finer ring than some of the other contenders: "Google will strive to honor all its commitments" or "Play hard but keep the puck down."

"Don't be evil" does not have to mean transparency. None of these books can tell you how many search queries Google fields, how much electricity it consumes, how much storage capacity it owns, how many streets it has photographed, how much e-mail it stores; nor can you Google the answers, because Google values its privacy.

It does not have to mean "Obey all the laws." When Google embarked on its program to digitize copyrighted books and copy them onto its servers, it did so in stealth, deceiving publishers with whom it was developing business relationships. Google knew that the copying bordered on illegal. It considered its intentions honorable and the law outmoded. "I think we knew that there would be a lot of interesting issues," Levy quotes Page as saying, "and the way the laws are structured isn't really sensible."

Who, then, judges what is evil? "Evil is what Sergey says is evil," explained Eric Schmidt, the chief executive officer, in 2002.

As for Sergey: "I feel like I shouldn't impose my beliefs on the world. It's a bad technology practice." But the founders seem sure enough of their own righteousness. ("'Bastards!' Larry would exclaim when a blogger raised concerns about user privacy," recalls Edwards. "'Bastards!' they would say about the press, the politicians, or the befuddled users who couldn't grasp the obvious superiority of the technology behind Google's products.")

Google did some evil in China. It collaborated in censorship. Beginning in   40
2004, it arranged to tweak and twist its algorithms and filter its results so that
the native-language Google.cn would omit results unwelcome to the government.
In the most notorious example, "Tiananmen Square" would produce sightseeing
guides but not history lessons. Google figured out what to censor by checking
China's approved search engine, Baidu, and by accepting the government's supple-
mentary guidance.

Yet it is also true that Google pushed back against the government as much
as any other American company. When results were blocked, Google insisted on
alerting users with a notice at the bottom of the search page. On balance Google
clearly believed (and I think it was right, despite the obvious self-interest) that its
presence benefited the people of China by increasing information flow and making clear the violation of transparency. The adventure took a sharp turn in January
2010, after organized hackers, perhaps with government involvement, breached
Google's servers and got access to the e-mail accounts of human rights activists.
The company shut down Google.cn and now serves China only from Hong Kong—
with results censored not by Google but by the government's own ongoing filters.

So is Google evil? The question is out there now; it nags, even as we blithely
rely on the company for answers—which now also means maps, translations, street
views, calendars, video, financial data, and pointers to goods and services. The
strong version of the case against Google is laid out starkly in *Search & Destroy*, by
a self-described "Google critic" named Scott Cleland. He wields a blunt club; the
book might as well have been titled *Google: Threat or Menace?*! "There is evidence
that Google is not all puppy dogs and rainbows," he writes.

> Google's corporate mascot is a replica of a Tyrannosaurus Rex skeleton on
> display outside the corporate headquarters. With its powerful jaws and teeth,
> T-Rex was a terrifying predator. And check out the B-52 bomber chair in
> Google Chairman Eric Schmidt's office. The B-52 was a long range bomber
> designed to deliver nuclear weapons.

Levy is more measured: "Google professed a sense of moral purity . . . but it
seemed to have a blind spot regarding the consequences of its own technology on
privacy and property rights." On all the evidence Google's founders began with an
unusually ethical vision for their unusual company. They believe in information—
"universally accessible"—as a force for good in and of itself. They have created and led
teams of technologists responsible for a golden decade of genuine innovation. They
are visionaries in a time when that word is too cheaply used. Now they are perhaps
disinclined to submit to other people's ethical standards, but that may be just a matter of personality. It is well to remember that the modern corporation is an amoral
creature by definition, obliged to its shareholder financiers, not to the public interest.

The Federal Trade Commission issued subpoenas in June in an antitrust investigation into Google's search and advertising practices; the European Commission
began a similar investigation last year. Governments are responding in part to organized complaints by Google's business competitors, including Microsoft, who charge,
among other things, that the company manipulates its search results to favor its

friends and punish its enemies. The company has always denied that. Certainly regulators are worried about its general "dominance"—Google seems to be everywhere and seems to know everything and offends against cherished notions of privacy.

The rise of social networking upends the equation again. Users of Facebook 45 choose to reveal—even to flaunt—aspects of their private lives, to at least some part of the public world. Which aspects, and which part? On Facebook the user options are notoriously obscure and subject to change, but most users share with "friends" (the word having been captured and drained bloodless). On Twitter, every remark can be seen by the whole world, except for the so-called "direct message," which former Representative Anthony Weiner tried and failed to employ. Also, the Library of Congress is archiving all tweets, presumably for eternity, a fact that should enter the awareness of teenagers, if not members of Congress.

Now Google is rolling out its second attempt at a social-networking platform, called Google+. The first attempt, eighteen months ago, was Google Buzz; it was an unusual stumble for the company. By default, it revealed lists of contacts with whom users had been chatting and e-mailing. Privacy advocates raised an alarm and the FTC began an investigation, quickly reaching a settlement in which Google agreed to regular privacy audits for the next twenty years. Google+ gives users finer control over what gets shared with whom. Still, one way or another, everything is shared with the company. All the social networks have access to our information and mean to use it. Are they our friends?

This much is clear: We need to decide what we want from Google. If only we can make up our collective minds. Then we still might not get it.

The company always says users can "opt out" of many of its forms of data collection, which is true, up to a point, for savvy computer users; and the company speaks of privacy in terms of "trade-offs," to which Vaidhyanathan objects:

> Privacy is not something that can be counted, divided, or "traded." It is not a substance or collection of data points. It's just a word that we clumsily use to stand in for a wide array of values and practices that influence how we manage our reputations in various contexts. There is no formula for assessing it: I can't give Google three of my privacy points in exchange for 10 percent better service.

This seems right to me, if we add that privacy involves not just managing our reputation but protecting the inner life we may not want to share. In any case, we continue to make precisely the kinds of trades that Vaidhyanathan says are impossible. Do we want to be addressed as individuals or as neurons in the world brain? We get better search results and we see more appropriate advertising when we let Google know who we are. And we save a few keystrokes.

QUESTIONS FOR DISCUSSION AND WRITING

1. Gleick begins by recounting a common phenomenon on Google: typing in a search term or expression and having Google try to finish it for you. What does this reveal about how Google's search engine operates? Does that bother you or not?

2. The use of Google to find information is so common that the word has become a verb. What are the advantages of using Google? The disadvantages? Be specific.

3. One of Google's founders, Sergey Brin, states, "Ultimately I view Google as a way to augment your brain with the knowledge of the world" (following paragraph 7). Does that statement bother you? Why or why not? Also following paragraph 7, the other founder, Larry Page, states, "Eventually you'll have an implant, where if you think about a fact, it will just tell you the answer." Does *that* bother you? Why or why not?

4. Much of the article sketches the history of Google, and its embrace of nontraditional business practices (such as showing up to meetings in skater attire). What advantages did that nontraditional approach give Google? Consider its approach to creating better searches, or its e-mail functions, or other Google products. What does this say about the Internet industry in general? Is being unconventional actually, to use the expression, being "crazy like a fox"? Explain your answer.

5. Part of the article addresses how Google applied advanced technology to advertising and, in particular, the targeting of ads to specific consumers, as well as the selling of advertising to business. A major aspect of that targeting also involves questions of privacy. Do you feel that you have a right to privacy? Does that right extend to the Internet? Should your Internet searches be considered private, or is Google (or any other search engine) justified in considering those searches information they can use for their own (profitable) purposes? Defend your answer.

6. Are you a Google user? If you are the rare person who is not, why not? If you are, have you noticed the advertisements that come to your screen when you conduct a Google search? How often do you click on an advertisement? How often have you purchased a good or service because of your exposure to an advertisement that came from a Google search? After reading this article, are you more likely or not to change how you use Google?

NEIL POSTMAN

The Judgment of Thamus

Neil Postman (1931–2003) was a writer and professor at New York University. He is perhaps best known for his 1985 book Amusing Ourselves to Death, *in which he argues that the avalanche of images and information that inundates society is not making us smarter or wiser; instead, we are reducing complex and sophisticated problems to simplistic and superficial ones. In other words, modernization is not making us better thinkers; it is actually dumbing us down. At the time, television was the big villain in this discussion (the Internet as it currently exists was years away).*

He also argued "the tie between information and action has been severed." In the end, what we ultimately want is to be entertained, not to think, and that will be our undoing. Besides Amusing Ourselves to Death, Postman also wrote numerous other books, including Conscientious Objection: Stirring Up Trouble about Language, Technology, and Education (1988; reprinted 1992), and Building a Bridge to the Eighteenth Century: How the Past Can Improve Our Future (1999). At NYU, he was appointed a University Professor, the only one in the School of Education. He died of lung cancer in 2003.

In this excerpt, taken from Technopoly: The Surrender of Culture to Technology (1992), Postman uses Plato's famous story about Thamus, a king in ancient Egypt who spoke with the god Theuth. Theuth was an inventor, and among his many accomplishments, he is credited with inventing writing. However, Thamus is not pleased with this particular invention, and sees in it that people's memories will weaken and they will not achieve true wisdom.

THE JUDGMENT OF THAMUS

You will find in Plato's Phaedrus a story about Thamus, the king of a great city of Upper Egypt. For people such as ourselves, who are inclined (in Thoreau's phrase) to be tools of our tools, few legends are more instructive than his. The story, as Socrates tells it to his friend Phaedrus, unfolds in the following way: Thamus once entertained the god Theuth, who was the inventor of many things, including number, calculation, geometry, astronomy, and writing. Theuth exhibited his inventions to King Thamus, claiming that they should be made widely known and available to Egyptians. Socrates continues:

> Thamus inquired into the use of each of them, and as Theuth went through them expressed approval or disapproval, according as he judged Theuth's claims to be well or ill founded. It would take too long to go through all that Thamus is reported to have said for and against each of Theuth's inventions. But when it came to writing, Theuth declared, "Here is an accomplishment, my lord the King,

which will improve both the wisdom and the memory of the Egyptians. I have discovered a sure receipt for memory and wisdom." To this, Thamus replied, "Theuth, my paragon of inventors, the discoverer of an art is not the best judge of the good or harm which will accrue to those who practice it. So it is in this; you, who are the father of writing, have out of fondness for your off-spring attributed to it quite the opposite of its real function. Those who acquire it will cease to exercise their memory and become forgetful; they will rely on writing to bring things to their remembrance by external signs instead of by their own internal resources. What you have discovered is a receipt for recollection, not for memory. And as for wisdom, your pupils will have the reputation for it without the reality: They will receive a quantity of information without proper instruction, and in consequence be thought very knowledgeable when they are for the most part quite ignorant.

And because they are filled with the conceit of wisdom instead of real wisdom they will be a burden to society."[1]

I begin my book with this legend because in Thamus' response there are several sound principles from which we may begin to learn how to think with wise circumspection about a technological society. In fact, there is even one error in the judgment of Thamus, from which we may also learn something of importance. The error is not in his claim that writing will damage memory and create false wisdom. It is demonstrable that writing has had such an effect. Thamus' error is in his believing that writing will be a burden to society and *nothing but a burden*. For all his wisdom, he fails to imagine what writing's benefits might be, which, as we know, have been considerable. We may learn from this that it is a mistake to suppose that any technological innovation has a one-sided effect. Every technology is both a burden and a blessing; not either-or, but this-and-that.

Nothing could be more obvious, of course, especially to those who have given more than two minutes of thought to the matter. Nonetheless, we are currently surrounded by throngs of zealous Theuths, one-eyed prophets who see only what new technologies can do and are incapable of imagining what they will *undo*. We might call such people Technophiles. They gaze on technology as a lover does on his beloved, seeing it as without blemish and entertaining no apprehension for the future. They are therefore dangerous and are to be approached cautiously. On the other hand, some one-eyed prophets, such as I (or so I am accused), are inclined to speak only of burdens (in the manner of Thamus) and are silent about the opportunities that new technologies make possible. The Technophiles must speak for themselves, and do so all over the place. My defense is that a dissenting voice is sometimes needed to moderate the din made by the enthusiastic multitudes. If one is to err, it is better to err on the side of Thamusian skepticism. But it is an error nonetheless. And I might note that, with the exception of his judgment on writing, Thamus does not repeat this error. You might notice on rereading the legend that he gives arguments *for* and *against* each of Theuth's inventions. For it is inescapable that every culture must negotiate with technology, whether it does so intelligently or not. A bargain is struck in which technology giveth and technology taketh away. The wise know this well, and are rarely impressed by dramatic technological changes, and never overjoyed. Here, for example, is Freud on the matter, from his doleful *Civilization and Its Discontents*:

> One would like to ask: is there, then, no positive gain in pleasure, no unequivocal increase in my feeling of happiness, if I can, as often as I please, hear the voice of a child of mine who is living hundreds of miles away or if I can learn in the shortest possible time after a friend has reached his destination that he has come through the long and difficult voyage unharmed? Does it mean nothing that medicine has succeeded in enormously reducing infant mortality and the danger of infection for women in childbirth, and, indeed, in considerably lengthening the average life of a civilized man?

---

[1]Plato, *Phaedrus and Letters VII and VIII* (New York: Penguin Classics, 1973), p. 96.

Freud knew full well that technical and scientific advances are not to be taken lightly, which is why he begins this passage by acknowledging them. But he ends it by reminding us of what they have undone:

> If there had been no railway to conquer distances, my child would never have left his native town and I should need no telephone to hear his voice; if traveling across the ocean by ship had not been introduced, my friend would not have embarked on his sea-voyage and I should not need a cable to relieve my anxiety about him. What is the use of reducing infantile mortality when it is precisely that reduction which imposes the greatest restraint on us in the begetting of children, so that, taken all round, we nevertheless rear no more children than in the days before the reign of hygiene, while at the same time we have created difficult conditions for our sexual life in marriage. . . . And, finally, what good to us is a long life if it is difficult and barren of joys, and if it is so full of misery that we can only welcome death as a deliverer?[2]

In tabulating the cost of technological progress, Freud takes a rather depressing line, that of a man who agrees with Thoreau's remark that our inventions are but improved means to an unimproved end. The Technophile would surely answer Freud by saying that life has always been barren of joys and full of misery but that the telephone, ocean liners, and especially the reign of hygiene have not only lengthened life but made it a more agreeable proposition. That is certainly an argument I would make (thus proving I am no one-eyed Technophobe), but it is not necessary at this point to pursue it. I have brought Freud into the conversation only to show that a wise man—even one of such a woeful countenance—must begin his critique of technology by acknowledging its successes. Had King Thamus been as wise as reputed, he would not have forgotten to include in his judgment a prophecy about the powers that writing would enlarge. There is a calculus of technological change that requires a measure of even-handedness.

So much for Thamus' error of omission. There is another omission worthy of note, but it is no error. Thamus simply takes for granted—and therefore does not feel it necessary to say—that writing is not a neutral technology whose good or harm depends on the uses made of it. He knows that the uses made of any technology are largely determined by the structure of the technology itself—that is, that its functions follow from its form. This is why Thamus is concerned not with *what* people will write; he is concerned *that* people will write. It is absurd to imagine Thamus advising, in the manner of today's standard-brand Technophiles, that, if only writing would be used for the production of certain kinds of texts and not others (let us say, for dramatic literature but not for history or philosophy), its disruptions could be minimized. He would regard such counsel as extreme naiveté. He would allow, I imagine, that a technology may be barred entry to a culture. But we may learn from Thamus the following: Once a technology is admitted, it plays out its hand; it does what it is designed to do. Our task is to understand what that

[2]Sigmund Freud, *Civilization and Its Discontents* (New York: W. W. Norton, 1961), pp. 38–39.

design is—that is to say, when we admit a new technology to the culture, we must do so with our eyes wide open.

All of this we may infer from Thamus' silence. But we may learn even more from what he does say than from what he doesn't. He points out, for example, that writing will change what is meant by the words "memory" and "wisdom." He fears that memory will be confused with what he disdainfully calls "recollection," and he worries that wisdom will become indistinguishable from mere knowledge. This judgment we must take to heart, for it is a certainty that radical technologies create new definitions of old terms, and that this process takes place without our being fully conscious of it. Thus, it is insidious and dangerous, quite different from the process whereby new technologies introduce new terms to the language. In our own time, we have consciously added to our language thousands of new words and phrases having to do with new technologies—"VCR," "binary digit," "software," "front-wheel drive," "window of opportunity," "Walkman," etc. We are not taken by surprise at this. New things require new words. But new things also modify old words, words that have deep-rooted meanings. The telegraph and the penny press changed what we once meant by "information." Television changes what we once meant by the terms "political debate," "news," and "public opinion." The computer changes "information" once again. Writing changed what we once meant by "truth" and "law"; printing changed them again, and now television and the computer change them once more. Such changes occur quickly, surely, and, in a sense, silently. Lexicographers hold no plebiscites on the matter. No manuals are written to explain what is happening, and the schools are oblivious to it. The old words still look the same, are still used in the same kinds of sentences. But they do not have the same meanings; in some cases, they have opposite meanings. And this is what Thamus wishes to teach us—that technology imperiously commandeers our most important terminology. It redefines "freedom," "truth," "intelligence," "fact," "wisdom," "memory," "history"—all the words we live by. And it does not pause to tell us. And we do not pause to ask.

This fact about technological change requires some elaboration, and I will return to the matter in a later chapter. Here, there are several more principles to be mined from the judgment of Thamus that require mentioning because they presage all I will write about. For instance, Thamus warns that the pupils of Theuth will develop an undeserved reputation for wisdom. He means to say that those who cultivate competence in the use of a new technology become an elite group that are granted undeserved authority and prestige by those who have no such competence. There are different ways of expressing the interesting implications of this fact. Harold Innis, the father of modern communication studies, repeatedly spoke of the "knowledge monopolies" created by important technologies. He meant precisely what Thamus had in mind: Those who have control over the workings of a particular technology accumulate power and inevitably form a kind of conspiracy against those who have no access to the specialized knowledge made available by the technology. In his book *The Bias of Communication,* Innis provides many historical examples of how a new technology "busted up" a traditional knowledge monopoly and created a new one presided over by a different group. Another way of saying this is that the benefits and deficits of a new technology are not distributed equally. There are, as it were, winners and losers. It is both puzzling and poignant that on many occasions the losers, out of ignorance, have actually cheered the winners, and some still do.

Let us take as an example the case of television. In the United States, where television has taken hold more deeply than anywhere else, many people find it a blessing, not least those who have achieved high-paying, gratifying careers in television as executives, technicians, newscasters, and entertainers. It should surprise no one that such people, forming as they do a new knowledge monopoly, should cheer themselves and defend and promote television technology. On the other hand and in the long run, television may bring a gradual end to the careers of schoolteachers, since school was an invention of the printing press and must stand or fall on the issue of how much importance the printed word has. For four hundred years, schoolteachers have been part of the knowledge monopoly created by printing, and they are now witnessing the breakup of that monopoly. It appears as if they can do little to prevent that breakup, but surely there is something perverse about schoolteachers' being enthusiastic about what is happening. Such enthusiasm always calls to my mind an image of some turn-of-the-century blacksmith who not only sings the praises of the automobile but also believes that his business will be enhanced by it. We know now that his business was not enhanced by it; it was rendered obsolete by it, as perhaps the clearheaded blacksmiths knew. What could they have done? Weep, if nothing else.

We have a similar situation in the development and spread of computer technology, for here too there are winners and losers. There can be no disputing that the computer has increased the power of large-scale organizations like the armed forces, or airline companies or banks or tax-collecting agencies. And it is equally clear that the computer is now indispensable to high-level researchers in physics and other natural sciences. But to what extent has computer technology been an advantage to the masses of people? To steelworkers, vegetable-store owners, teachers, garage mechanics, musicians, bricklayers, dentists, and most of the rest into whose lives the computer now intrudes? Their private matters have been made more accessible to powerful institutions. They are more easily tracked and controlled; are subjected to more examinations; are increasingly mystified by the decisions made about them; are often reduced to mere numerical objects. They are inundated by junk mail. They are easy targets for advertising agencies and political organizations. The schools teach their children to operate computerized systems instead of teaching things that are more valuable to children. In a word, almost nothing that they need happens to the losers. Which is why they are losers.

It is to be expected that the winners will encourage the losers to be enthusiastic about computer technology. That is the way of winners, and so they sometimes tell the losers that with personal computers the average person can balance a checkbook more neatly, keep better track of recipes, and make more logical shopping lists. They also tell them that their lives will be conducted more efficiently. But discreetly they neglect to say from whose point of view the efficiency is warranted or what might be its costs. Should the losers grow skeptical, the winners dazzle them with the wondrous feats of computers, almost all of which have only marginal relevance to the quality of the losers' lives but which are nonetheless impressive. Eventually, the losers succumb, in part because they believe, as Thamus prophesied, that the specialized knowledge of the masters of a new technology is a form of wisdom. The masters come to believe this as well, as Thamus also prophesied. The result is that certain questions do not arise. For example, to whom will the technology give greater power and freedom? And whose power and freedom will be reduced by it?

I have perhaps made all of this sound like a well-planned conspiracy, as if the winners know all too well what is being won and what lost. But this is not quite how it happens. For one thing, in cultures that have a democratic ethos, relatively weak traditions, and a high receptivity to new technologies, everyone is inclined to be enthusiastic about technological change, believing that its benefits will eventually spread evenly among the entire population. Especially in the United States, where the lust for what is new has no bounds, do we find this childlike conviction most widely held. Indeed, in America, social change of any kind is rarely seen as resulting in winners and losers, a condition that stems in part from Americans' much-documented optimism. As for change brought on by technology, this native optimism is exploited by entrepreneurs, who work hard to infuse the population with a unity of improbable hope, for they know that it is economically unwise to reveal the price to be paid for technological change. One might say, then, that, if there is a conspiracy of any kind, it is that of a culture conspiring against itself.

In addition to this, and more important, it is not always clear, at least in the early stages of a technology's intrusion into a culture, who will gain most by it and who will lose most. This is because the changes wrought by technology are subtle if not downright mysterious, one might even say wildly unpredictable. Among the most unpredictable are those that might be labeled ideological. This is the sort of change Thamus had in mind when he warned that writers will come to rely on external signs instead of their own internal resources, and that they will receive quantities of information without proper instruction. He meant that new technologies change what we mean by "knowing" and "truth"; they alter those deeply embedded habits of thought which give to a culture its sense of what the world is like—a sense of what is the natural order of things, of what is reasonable, of what is necessary, of what is inevitable, of what is real. Since such changes are expressed in changed meanings of old words, I will hold off until later discussing the massive ideological transformation now occurring in the United States. Here, I should like to give only one example of how technology creates new conceptions of what is real and, in the process, undermines older conceptions. I refer to the seemingly harmless practice of assigning marks or grades to the answers students give on examinations. This procedure seems so natural to most of us that we are hardly aware of its significance. We may even find it difficult to imagine that the number or letter is a tool or, if you will, a technology; still less that, when we use such a technology to judge someone's behavior, we have done something peculiar. In point of fact, the first instance of grading students' papers occurred at Cambridge University in 1792 at the suggestion of a tutor named William Farish.[3] No one knows much about William Farish; not more than a handful have ever heard of him. And yet his idea that a quantitative value should be assigned to human thoughts was a major step toward constructing a mathematical concept of reality. If a number can be given to the quality of a thought, then a number can be given to the qualities of mercy, love, hate, beauty, creativity, intelligence, even sanity itself. When Galileo said that the language of nature is written in mathematics, he did not mean to include human feeling or accomplishment or insight. But most of us are now inclined to make these inclusions. Our psychologists, sociologists, and educators find it quite impossible to do their work without numbers. They believe that without numbers they cannot acquire or express authentic knowledge.

I shall not argue here that this is a stupid or dangerous idea, only that it is peculiar. What is even more peculiar is that so many of us do not find the idea peculiar. To say that someone should be doing better work because he has an IQ of 134, or that someone is a 7.2 on a sensitivity scale, or that this man's essay on the rise of capitalism is an A− and that man's is a C+ would have sounded like gibberish to Galileo or Shakespeare or Thomas Jefferson. If it makes sense to us, that is because our minds have been conditioned by the technology of numbers so that we see the world differently than they did. Our understanding of what is real is different. Which is another way of saying that embedded in every tool is an ideological bias, a predisposition to construct the world as one thing rather than another, to value one thing over another, to amplify one sense or skill or attitude more loudly than another.

This is what Marshall McLuhan meant by his famous aphorism "The medium is the message." This is what Marx meant when he said, "Technology discloses man's mode of dealing with nature" and creates the "conditions of intercourse" by which we relate to each other. It is what Wittgenstein meant when, in referring to our most fundamental technology, he said that language is not merely a vehicle of thought but also the driver. And it is what Thamus wished the inventor Theuth to see. This is, in short, an ancient and persistent piece of wisdom, perhaps most simply expressed in the old adage that, to a man with a hammer, everything looks like a nail. Without being too literal, we may extend the truism: To a man with a pencil, everything looks like a list. To a man with a camera, everything looks like an image. To a man with a computer, everything looks like data. And to a man with a grade sheet, everything looks like a number.

But such prejudices are not always apparent at the start of a technology's 15 journey, which is why no one can safely conspire to be a winner in technological

---

[3]This fact is documented in Keith Hoskin's "The Examination, Disciplinary Power and Rational Schooling," in *History of Education,* vol. VIII, no. 2 (1979), pp. 135–46. Professor Hoskin provides the following story about Farish: Farish was a professor of engineering at Cambridge and designed and installed a movable partition wall in his Cambridge home. The wall moved on pulleys between downstairs and upstairs. One night, while working late downstairs and feeling cold, Farish pulled down the partition. This is not much of a story, and history fails to disclose what happened next. All of which shows how little is known of William Farish.

change. Who would have imagined, for example, whose interests and what world-view would be ultimately advanced by the invention of the mechanical clock? The clock had its origin in the Benedictine monasteries of the twelfth and thirteenth centuries. The impetus behind the invention was to provide a more or less precise regularity to the routines of the monasteries, which required, among other things, seven periods of devotion during the course of the day. The bells of the monastery were to be rung to signal the canonical hours; the mechanical clock was the technology that could provide precision to these rituals of devotion. And indeed it did. But what the monks did not foresee was that the clock is a means not merely of keeping track of the hours but also of synchronizing and controlling the actions of men. And thus, by the middle of the fourteenth century, the clock had moved outside the walls of the monastery, and brought a new and precise regularity to the life of the workman and the merchant. "The mechanical clock," as Lewis Mumford wrote, "made possible the idea of regular production, regular working hours, and a standardized product." In short, without the clock, capitalism would have been quite impossible.[4] The paradox, the surprise, and the wonder are that the clock was invented by men who wanted to devote themselves more rigorously to God; it ended as the technology of greatest use to men who wished to devote themselves to the accumulation of money. In the eternal struggle between God and Mammon, the clock quite unpredictably favored the latter.

Unforeseen consequences stand in the way of all those who think they see clearly the direction in which a new technology will take us. Not even those who invent a technology can be assumed to be reliable prophets, as Thamus warned. Gutenberg, for example, was by all accounts a devout Catholic who would have been horrified to hear that accursed heretic Luther describe printing as "God's highest act of grace, whereby the business of the Gospel is driven forward." Luther understood, as Gutenberg did not, that the mass-produced book, by placing the Word of God on every kitchen table, makes each Christian his own theologian—one might even say his own priest, or, better, from Luther's point of view, his own pope. In the struggle between unity and diversity of religious belief, the press favored the latter, and we can assume that this possibility never occurred to Gutenberg.

Thamus understood well the limitations of inventors in grasping the social and psychological—that is, ideological—bias of their own inventions. We can imagine him addressing Gutenberg in the following way: "Gutenberg, my paragon of inventors, the discoverer of an art is not the best judge of the good or harm which will accrue to those who practice it. So it is in this; you, who are the father of printing, have out of fondness for your off-spring come to believe it will advance the cause of the Holy Roman See, whereas in fact it will sow discord among believers; it will damage the authenticity of your beloved Church and destroy its monopoly."

We can imagine that Thamus would also have pointed out to Gutenberg, as he did to Theuth, that the new invention would create a vast population of readers

---

[4]For a detailed exposition of Mumford's position on the impact of the mechanical clock, see his *Technics and Civilization* (New York: Harcourt Brace, 1934).

who "will receive a quantity of information without proper instruction . . . [who will be] filled with the conceit of wisdom instead of real wisdom"; that reading, in other words, will compete with older forms of learning. This is yet another principle of technological change we may infer from the judgment of Thamus: New technologies compete with old ones—for time, for attention, for money, for prestige, but mostly for dominance of their world-view. This competition is implicit once we acknowledge that a medium contains an ideological bias. And it is a fierce competition, as only ideological competitions can be. It is not merely a matter of tool against tool—the alphabet attacking ideographic writing, the printing press attacking the illuminated manuscript, the photograph attacking the art of painting, television attacking the printed word. When media make war against each other, it is a case of world-views in collision.

In the United States, we can see such collisions everywhere—in politics, in religion, in commerce—but we see them most clearly in the schools, where two great technologies confront each other in uncompromising aspect for the control of students' minds. On the one hand, there is the world of the printed word with its emphasis on logic, sequence, history, exposition, objectivity, detachment, and discipline. On the other, there is the world of television with its emphasis on imagery, narrative, presentness, simultaneity, intimacy, immediate gratification, and quick emotional response. Children come to school having been deeply conditioned by the biases of television. There, they encounter the world of the printed word. A sort of psychic battle takes place, and there are many casualties—children who can't learn to read or won't, children who cannot organize their thought into logical structure even in a simple paragraph, children who cannot attend to lectures or oral explanations for more than a few minutes at a time. They are failures, but not because they are stupid. They are failures because there is a media war going on, and they are on the wrong side—at least for the moment. Who knows what schools will be like twenty-five years from now? Or fifty? In time, the type of student who is currently a failure may be considered a success. The type who is now successful may be regarded as a handicapped learner—slow to respond, far too detached, lacking in emotion, inadequate in creating mental pictures of reality. Consider: What Thamus called the "conceit of wisdom"—the unreal knowledge acquired through the written word—eventually became the pre-eminent form of knowledge valued by the schools. There is no reason to suppose that such a form of knowledge must always remain so highly valued.

To take another example: In introducing the personal computer to the class- 20 room, we shall be breaking a four-hundred-year-old truce between the gregariousness and openness fostered by orality and the introspection and isolation fostered by the printed word. Orality stresses group learning, cooperation, and a sense of social responsibility, which is the context within which Thamus believed proper instruction and real knowledge must be communicated. Print stresses individualized learning, competition, and personal autonomy. Over four centuries, teachers, while emphasizing print, have allowed orality its place in the classroom, and have therefore achieved a kind of pedagogical peace between these two forms of learning, so that what is valuable in each can be maximized. Now comes the computer, carrying anew the banner of private learning and individual problem-solving. Will the widespread use of computers in the classroom defeat once and for all the claims of communal speech? Will the computer raise egocentrism to the status of a virtue?

These are the kinds of questions that technological change brings to mind when one grasps, as Thamus did, that technological competition ignites total war, which means it is not possible to contain the effects of a new technology to a limited sphere of human activity. If this metaphor puts the matter too brutally, we may try a gentler, kinder one: Technological change is neither additive nor subtractive. It is ecological. I mean "ecological" in the same sense as the word is used by environmental scientists. One significant change generates total change. If you remove the caterpillars from a given habitat, you are not left with the same environment minus caterpillars: You have a new environment, and you have reconstituted the conditions of survival; the same is true if you add caterpillars to an environment that has had none. This is how the ecology of media works as well. A new technology does not add or subtract something. It changes everything. In the year 1500, fifty years after the printing press was invented, we did not have old Europe plus the printing press. We had a different Europe. After television, the United States was not America plus television; television gave a new coloration to every political campaign, to every home, to every school, to every church, to every industry. And that is why the competition among media is so fierce. Surrounding every technology are institutions whose organization—not to mention their reason for being—reflects the world-view promoted by the technology. Therefore, when an old technology is assaulted by a new one, institutions are threatened. When institutions are threatened, a culture finds itself in crisis. This is serious business, which is why we learn nothing when educators ask, Will students learn mathematics better by computers than by textbooks? Or when businessmen ask, Through which medium can we sell more products? Or when preachers ask, Can we reach more people through television than through radio? Or when politicians ask, How effective are messages sent through different media? Such questions have an immediate, practical value to those who ask them, but they are diversionary. They direct our attention away from the serious social, intellectual, and institutional crises that new media foster.

Perhaps an analogy here will help to underline the point. In speaking of the meaning of a poem, T. S. Eliot remarked that the chief use of the overt content of poetry is "to satisfy one habit of the reader, to keep his mind diverted and quiet, while the poem does its work upon him: much as the imaginary burglar is always provided with a bit of nice meat for the house-dog." In other words, in asking their practical questions, educators, entrepreneurs, preachers, and politicians are like the house-dog munching peacefully on the meat while the house is looted. Perhaps some of them know this and do not especially care. After all, a nice piece of meat, offered graciously, does take care of the problem of where the next meal will come from. But for the rest of us, it cannot be acceptable to have the house invaded without protest or at least awareness.

What we need to consider about the computer has nothing to do with its efficiency as a teaching tool. We need to know in what ways it is altering our conception of learning, and how, in conjunction with television, it undermines the old idea of school. Who cares how many boxes of cereal can be sold via television? We need to know if television changes our conception of reality, the relationship of the rich to the poor, the idea of happiness itself. A preacher who confines himself to considering how a medium can increase his audience will miss the significant question: In what sense do new media alter what is meant by religion, by church, even by God? And if the politician cannot think beyond the next election, then *we* must wonder about what new media do to the idea of political organization and to the conception of citizenship.

To help us do this, we have the judgment of Thamus, who, in the way of legends, teaches us what Harold Innis, in his way, tried to. New technologies alter the structure of our interests: the things we think *about*. They alter the character of our symbols: the things we think *with*. And they alter the nature of community: the arena in which thoughts develop. As Thamus spoke to Innis across the centuries, it is essential that we listen to their conversation, join in it, revitalize it. For something has happened in America that is strange and dangerous, and there is only a dull and even stupid awareness of what it is—in part because it has no name. I call it Technopoly.

QUESTIONS FOR DISCUSSION AND WRITING

1. In the story of Thamus and Theuth, as related by Plato, Thamus is not pleased with the invention of writing. He argues that people will "cease to exercise their memory and become forgetful" and people who can write "are filled with the conceit of wisdom instead of real wisdom" (paragraph 1). Why does Thamus feel this way about writing? Imagine a society in which writing does not exist: What, then, would be the function of memory? What would be real wisdom?

2. Postman interprets Thamus's rejection of writing in a few ways. First, he faults Thamus for failing to recognize the benefits of writing. However, Postman states that Thamus "knows that the uses made of any technology are largely determined by the structure of the technology itself" (paragraph 5). He says later that "wisdom will become indistinguishable from mere knowledge" (paragraph 6). Now consider not writing, but computer technology, including the Internet, smartphones, social media, and other more recent inventions. How do they apply to these objections? For example, has being able to "Google" any topic substituted mere knowledge for wisdom? Where does wisdom come from in today's world when answers to questions are seconds away from anyone holding a smartphone?

3. Postman speaks of "knowledge monopolies" (paragraph 7) and how new technologies create new winners and losers. How have recent advances in computer technologies done this? Who are today's winners? Who are today's losers? Be specific.

4. Postman makes a comparison to the creation of the printing press. He points out that Gutenberg was a "devout Catholic" who never intended to help an

"accursed heretic" like Martin Luther (paragraph 16). In other words, the law of unintended effects operates: No one can be sure about all of the consequences of an action. In the case of the creation of new media, this has been proven true as well. What have been some unintended effects of more recent new media? Think of television, the personal computer, the Internet, social media, smartphones, and other technological advances. What were they created for? What have been the actual effects?

5. In a deeper sense, these advances fundamentally alter the world. As Postman notes, Europe in 1500 was not the same one that existed fifty years before the printing press: It was an entirely new Europe (paragraph 21). By extension, in today's world, we're not the same as we were twenty-some years ago, only now with the Internet: It's a new world. Postman urges the audience to ask fundamental questions about the nature of these changes, what institutions are threatened, and how. What is your response to this? Is Postman overreacting, or do you agree? Be specific.

6. In paragraph 23, Postman states: "What we need to consider about the computer has nothing to do with its efficiency as a teaching tool. We need to know in what ways it is altering our conception of learning, and how, in conjunction with television, it undermines the old idea of school." Investigate and write about how education and learning are affected by new technologies. Are we moving away from print, and if so, what are the long-term implications of that move? What will need to happen for these changes to be positive and not negative? Be specific.

WILLIAM DERESIEWICZ

From "Faux Friendship"

William Deresiewicz (b. 1964) was an assistant professor, then associate professor of English at Yale from 1998 to 2008. His provocative essays and reviews have appeared in a variety of publications, including the Nation, *the* American Scholar, *the* London Review of Books, *and the* New York Times. *His book,* A Jane Austen Education: How Six Novels Taught Me about Love, Friendship, and the Things That Really Matter, *appeared in 2011.*

We live at a time when friendship has become both all and nothing at all. . . . What, in our brave new mediated world, is friendship becoming? The Facebook phenomenon, so sudden and forceful a distortion of social space, needs little elaboration. Having been relegated to our screens, are our friendships now anything more than a form of distraction? When they've shrunk to the size of a wall post, do they retain any content? If we have 768 "friends," in what sense do we have any? Facebook isn't the whole of contemporary friendship, but it sure looks a lot like its future. Yet Facebook . . . and Twitter, and whatever we're stampeding for next—are just the latest stages of a long attenuation. They've accelerated the fragmentation of consciousness, but they didn't initiate it. They have reified the idea of universal friendship, but they didn't invent it. In retrospect, it seems inevitable that once we decided to become friends with everyone, we would forget how to be friends with anyone. We may pride ourselves today on our aptitude for friendship—friends, after all, are the only people we have left—but it's not clear that we still even know what it means. . . .

With the social-networking sites of the new century—Friendster and MySpace were launched in 2003, Facebook in 2004—the friendship circle has expanded to engulf the whole of the social world, and in so doing, destroyed both its own nature and that of the individual friendship itself. Facebook's very premise—and promise—is that it makes our friendship circles visible. There they are, my friends, all in the same place. Except, of course, they're not in the same place, or, rather, they're not my friends. They're simulacra of my friends, little dehydrated packets of images and information, no more my friends than a set of baseball cards is the New York Mets.

I remember realizing a few years ago that most of the members of what I thought of as my "circle" didn't actually know one another. One I'd met in graduate school, another at a job, one in Boston, another in Brooklyn, one lived in Minneapolis now, another in Israel, so that I was ultimately able to enumerate some 14 people, none of whom had ever met any of the others. To imagine that they added up to a circle, an embracing and encircling structure, was a belief, I realized, that violated the laws of feeling as well as geometry. They were a set of points, and I was wandering somewhere among them. Facebook seduces us, however, into exactly that illusion, inviting us to believe that by assembling a list, we have conjured a group. Visual juxtaposition creates the mirage of emotional proximity. "It's like they're all having a conversation," a woman I know once said about her Facebook page, full of posts and comments from friends and friends of friends. "Except they're not."

Friendship is devolving, in other words, from a relationship to a feeling—from something people share to something each of us hugs privately to ourselves in the loneliness of our electronic caves, rearranging the tokens of connection like a lonely child playing with dolls. The same path was long ago trodden by community. As the traditional face-to-face community disappeared, we held on to what we had lost—the closeness, the rootedness—by clinging to the word, no matter how much we had to water down its meaning. Now we speak of the Jewish "community" and the medical "community" and the "community" of readers, even though none of them actually is one. What we have, instead of community, is, if we're lucky, a "sense" of community—the feeling without the structure; a private emotion, not a collective experience. And now friendship, which arose to its present importance as a replacement for community, is going the same way. We have "friends," just as we belong to "communities." Scanning my Facebook page gives me, precisely, a "sense" of connection. Not an actual connection, just a sense.

What purpose do all those wall posts and status updates serve? On the 5 first beautiful weekend of spring this year, a friend posted this update from

Central Park: "[So-and-so] is in the Park with the rest of the City." The first question that comes to mind is, if you're enjoying a beautiful day in the park, why don't you give your iPhone a rest? But the more important one is, why did you need to tell us that? We have always shared our little private observations and moments of feeling—it's part of what friendship's about, part of the way we remain present in one another's lives—but things are different now. Until a few years ago, you could share your thoughts with only one friend at a time (on the phone, say), or maybe with a small group, later, in person. And when you did, you were talking to specific people, and you tailored what you said, and how you said it, to who they were— their interests, their personalities, most of all, your degree of mutual intimacy. "Reach out and touch someone" meant someone in particular, someone you were actually thinking about. It meant having a conversation. Now we're just broadcasting our stream of consciousness, live from Central Park, to all 500 of our friends at once, hoping that someone, anyone, will confirm our existence by answering back. We haven't just stopped talking to our friends as individuals, at such moments, we have stopped thinking of them as individuals. We have turned them into an indiscriminate mass, a kind of audience or faceless public. We address ourselves not to a circle, but to a cloud. . . .

Perhaps I need to surrender the idea that the value of friendship lies precisely in the space of privacy it creates: not the secrets that two people exchange so much as the unique and inviolate world they build up between them, the spider web of shared discovery they spin out, slowly and carefully, together. There's something faintly obscene about performing that intimacy in front of everyone you know, as if its real purpose were to show what a deep person you are. Are we really so hungry for validation? So desperate to prove we have friends?

But surely Facebook has its benefits. Long-lost friends can reconnect, far-flung ones can stay in touch. I wonder, though. Having recently moved across the country, I thought that Facebook would help me feel connected to the friends I'd left behind. But now I find the opposite is true. Reading about the mundane details of their lives, a steady stream of trivia and ephemera, leaves me feeling both empty and unpleasantly full, as if I had just binged on junk food, and precisely because it reminds me of the real sustenance, the real knowledge, we exchange by e-mail or phone or face-to-face. And the whole theatrical quality of the business, the sense that my friends are doing their best to impersonate themselves, only makes it worse. The person I read about, I cannot help feeling, is not quite the person I know. . . .

Finally, the new social-networking Web sites have falsified our understanding of intimacy itself, and with it, our understanding of ourselves. The absurd idea, bruited about in the media, that [an online] profile or "25 Random Things About Me" can tell us more about someone than even a good friend might be aware of is based on desiccated notions about what knowing another person means: First, that intimacy is confessional—an idea both peculiarly American and peculiarly young, perhaps because both types of people tend to travel among strangers, and so believe in the instant disgorging of the self as the quickest route to familiarity. Second, that identity is reducible to information: the name of your cat, your favorite

Beatle, the stupid thing you did in seventh grade. Third, that it is reducible, in particular, to the kind of information that social-networking Web sites are most interested in eliciting, consumer preferences. Forget that we're all conducting market research on ourselves. Far worse is that Facebook amplifies our long-standing tendency to see ourselves ("I'm a Skin Bracer man!") in just those terms. We wear T-shirts that proclaim our brand loyalty, pique ourselves on owning a Mac, and now put up lists of our favorite songs. "15 movies in 15 minutes. Rule: Don't take too long to think about it."

So information replaces experience, as it has throughout our culture. But when I think about my friends, what makes them who they are, and why I love them, it is not the names of their siblings that come to mind, or their fear of spiders. It is their qualities of character. This one's emotional generosity, that one's moral seriousness, the dark humor of a third. Yet even those are just descriptions, and no more specify the individuals uniquely than to say that one has red hair, another is tall. To understand what they really look like, you would have to see a picture. And to understand who they really are, you would have to hear about the things they've done. Character, revealed through action: the two eternal elements of narrative. In order to know people, you have to listen to their stories.

But that is precisely what the Facebook page does not leave room for, or 10 500 friends, time for. Literally does not leave room for. E-mail, with its rapid-fire etiquette and scrolling format, already trimmed the letter down to a certain acceptable maximum, perhaps a thousand words. Now, with Facebook, the box is shrinking even more, leaving perhaps a third of that length as the conventional limit for a message, far less for a comment. (And we all know the deal on Twitter.) The 10-page missive has gone the way of the buggy whip, soon to be followed, it seems, by the three-hour conversation. Each evolved as a space for telling stories, an act that cannot usefully be accomplished in much less. Posting information is like pornography, a slick, impersonal exhibition. Exchanging stories is like making love: probing, questing, questioning, caressing. It is mutual. It is intimate. It takes patience, devotion, sensitivity, subtlety, skill—and it teaches them all, too.

They call them social-networking sites for a reason. Networking once meant something specific: climbing the jungle gym of professional contacts in order to advance your career. The truth is that Hume and Smith were not completely right. Commercial society did not eliminate the self-interested aspects of making friends and influencing people, it just changed the way we went about it. Now, in the age of the entrepreneurial self, even our closest relationships are being pressed onto this template. A recent book on the sociology of modern science describes a networking event at a West Coast university: "There do not seem to be any single-tons—disconsolately lurking at the margins—nor do dyads appear, except fleetingly." No solitude, no friendship, no space for refusal—the exact contemporary paradigm. At the same time, the author assures us, "face time" is valued in this "community" as a "high-bandwidth interaction," offering "unusual capacity for interruption, repair, feedback and learning." Actual human contact, rendered "unusual" and weighed by the values of a systems engineer. We have given our hearts to machines, and now we are turning into machines. The face of friendship in the new century.

optimistic, therapeutic culture of today's America rejects the notion that there are inherently bad people. As individuals, we seek insights into our failings so we can learn to overcome them and achieve a new start. From a sociological perspective, people are thrown off course by their social conditions—because they are poor, for instance, and subject to discrimination. But these conditions can be altered, and then these people will be able to lead good lives. Under the right conditions, criminals can pay their debt to society and be rehabilitated, sex offenders can be reformed, and others who have flunked out can pass another test. Just give them a second chance.

The latest chapter of this deeply entrenched narrative introduces a big bad wolf, the Internet. It stands charged with killing the opportunity for people to have that much-deserved second chance. By computerizing local public records, the Internet casts the shadow of people's past far and fast; like a curse they cannot undo, their records now follow them wherever they go. True, even in the good old days, arrest records, criminal sentences, bankruptcy filings, and even divorce records were public. Some were listed in blotters kept in police stations, others in courthouses; anyone who wished to take the trouble could go there and read them. But most people did not. Above all, there was no way for people in distant communities to find these damning facts without going to inordinate lengths.

The first sign of trouble due to technological changes came about in the late 19th century when newspapers started publishing this sort of information. In 1890, after newspapers printed social gossip about the family of Boston lawyer Samuel D. Warren, he and his law partner, the future Supreme Court Justice Louis D. Brandeis, published in the *Harvard Law Review* what is considered the most seminal law review article ever written, one that became the foundation of the American right to privacy. In it, they asserted that an individual has the right to keep certain information hidden from others. Warren and Brandeis were not trying to stop gossip. (Although people often find gossip annoying, sociologists view it as an important part of the informal social controls that nudge people to be better than they would otherwise be, thus minimizing the role for policing. Hence the great concern with the breakdown of communities—where people know each other and gossip—and the quest for new soft tools to advance social order.) But Warren and Brandeis correctly saw that a major change takes place once gossip is spread to a large community, as it is via the print media, to people who do not personally know those who are being gossiped about, and who are therefore unaware of the special circumstances, of the "whole story." This change was a harbinger of things to come.

In recent decades, online databases have dramatically increased the size of   5 the audience that has access to public information and the ease with which it can be examined. Several companies have started compiling criminal records, making them available to everyone in the country and indeed the world. For instance, PeopleFinders, a company based in Sacramento, recently introduced CriminalSearches.com, a free service to access public criminal records, which draws data from local courthouses. A similar thing is happening to many other types of public records, ranging from birth records to divorces.

These developments disturb privacy advocates and anyone who is keen on ensuring that people have the opportunity for a new start. Beth Givens, director of the Privacy Rights Clearinghouse, says that Internet databases cause a "loss of 'social forgiveness.'" For instance, a person's "conviction of graffiti vandalism at age 19 will still be there at age 29 when [he's] a solid citizen trying to get a job and raise a family"—and the conviction will be there for anyone to see. Furthermore, as companies "rely on background checks to screen workers, [they] risk imposing unfair barriers to rehabilitated criminals," wrote reporters Ann Zimmerman and Kortney Stringer in the *Wall Street Journal*. In short, as journalist Brad Stone wrote in the *New York Times,* by allowing the producers of databases to remove "the obstacles to getting criminal information," we are losing "a valuable, ignorance-fueled civil peace."

But hold on for just a minute. Is the Internet age really destroying second chances, making us less forgiving and hindering the possibility for rehabilitation and even redemption? The sad fact is that most convicted criminals in the pre-digital age did not use the second chance that their obscurity gave them, nor did they use their third or fourth chances. Convincing data show that most criminal offenders—especially those involved in violent crimes—are not rehabilitated; they commit new crimes. And many commit numerous crimes before they are caught again. Thus, while obscurity may well help a small percentage of criminals get a second chance, it helps a large percentage of them strike again.

Take the case of James Webb (not the U.S. Senator from Virginia of the same name). He had served 20 years in prison for raping six women when, on August 16, 1995, he was released on parole. But rather than look for a new start, he raped another woman the day after he was released. Then he raped three more women in the next few months. He was re-arrested in December 1995, after he committed the fourth rape. Or consider the case of James Richardson, a New York resident who served 20 years of a life term for raping and murdering a 10-year-old girl. After he was paroled in 1992, he committed three bank robberies before being re-incarcerated. Both cases happened before the advent of databanks of criminal convictions.

These two are typical cases. In its most recent study on recidivism in the United States, the Justice Department's Bureau of Justice Statistics tracked two-thirds of the prisoners released in 15 states in 1994. It found that within three years of their release, 67.5 percent of them were re-arrested for a new offense. In short, most people who commit crimes are more likely to commit crimes in the future than to make good use of a second chance. This was true long before the digitization of criminal data and the loss of obscurity.

Moreover, just because only two-thirds of the prisoners were re-arrested 10 does not mean that the other third did not commit any crimes. Many crimes are never solved and their perpetrators never caught. Studies found that the majority of rapists and child molesters had been convicted more than once for a sexual assault—and committed numerous offenses before they were caught again. On average, these offenders admitted to having committed *two to five times* as many sex crimes as were officially documented. That is, not only did they fail to use their second chances to start a new life, they used obscurity to their advantage.

In short, the image of a young person who goes astray, and who would return to the straight and narrow life if just given a second chance, does not fit most offenders. Indeed, prisons are considered colleges for crime; they harden those sentenced to spend time in them, making them *more* disposed to future criminal behavior upon release. Social scientists differ about whom to blame for the limited success of rehabilitation. Some fault "the system," or poor social conditions, or lack of job training. Others place more blame on the character of those involved. In any case, obscurity hardly serves to overcome strong factors that agitate against rehabilitation.

Online databases also display the records of physicians who do not live up to the Hippocratic oath; these doctors do harm, and plenty of it. The National Practitioner Data Bank allows state licensing boards, hospitals, and other health care entities to find out whether the license of a doctor has been revoked recently in another state or if the doctor has been disciplined. Doctors' licenses are generally revoked only if they commit very serious offenses, such as repeated gross negligence, criminal felonies, or practicing while under the influence of drugs or alcohol.

If these databases had been used as intended in the late 1990s and early 2000s, they could have tracked Pamela L. Johnson, a physician who was forced to leave Duke University Medical Center after many of her patients suffered from unusual complications. In response, Johnson moved to New Mexico and lied about her professional history in order to obtain a medical license there and continue practicing. After three patients in New Mexico filed lawsuits alleging that she was negligent or had botched surgical procedures, she moved again and set up shop in Michigan.

Similarly, Joseph S. Hayes, a medical doctor licensed in Tennessee, was convicted of drug abuse and assault, including choking a patient, actions which resulted in the revocation of his Tennessee license in 1991. But his license was reinstated in 1993. When he was charged with fondling a female patient in 1999, he simply moved to South Carolina to continue practicing medicine. Similar stories could be told about scores of other doctors. (The exploits of one of the most notorious of these doctors are laid out in a new book, *Charlatan*, by Pope Brock.)

Beyond assuming that Internet databases do little harm to those who are not 15 likely to reform themselves, we can show real benefits from the widespread dissemination of information about wrongdoers—for their potential victims. Few doctors are hired by hospitals these days without first being checked through the digitized data sources. Before you hire an accountant, such data makes it possible to discover whether he or she has a record of embezzlement. A community can find out if a new school nurse is a sex offender. Employers may direct ex-offenders to other jobs, or they may still hire them but provide extra oversight, or just decide that they are willing to take the risk. But they do so well informed—and thus warned—rather than ignorant of the sad facts.

Registration and notification laws for sex offenders provide a good case in point. The Washington State Institute for Public Policy conducted a study in 2005 that evaluated the effectiveness of the state's community notification laws. In 1990, Washington passed the Community Protection Act, a law that requires sex offenders to register with their county sheriff and authorizes law enforcement to release information to the public. The study found that by 1999 the recidivism rate among felony sex offenders in the state had dropped 70 percent from the pre-1990 level, in part due to communities' awareness of the sex offenders in their neighborhoods. In addition, offenders subject to community notification were arrested for new crimes much more quickly than offenders who were released without notification.

True, online databases increase the size of the community that has access to information, but these technological developments merely help communities catch up with other social developments. People do business over greater distances and move around much more, and much farther, than they did in earlier eras. Our travel and transactions are no longer limited to the county store and local diner. Our access to data needs to expand to match the new scope of our lives.

All of this is not to deny that we face a moral dilemma. Although most offenders are not rehabilitated, some are. It is incorrect to assume that "once a criminal, always a criminal." Take the case of Mike Kolomichuk, who in 1979 pleaded guilty to two counts of battery after having an altercation with an undercover police officer in a bar in Florida. As punishment, he received unsupervised probation, during which he conducted himself well. Kolomichuk eventually moved to Ohio, where almost 30 years later he ran as a write-in candidate for mayor of the village of Lakemore and won. His criminal past was not an issue in the election because his record was unknown in the village of 2,500 people. When his criminal history came out a few months later, there was talk of the need for a new election, but it soon subsided. Today, Kolomichuk remains mayor and is continuing his efforts to revitalize the community. In this case, obscurity may well have helped.

The argument can be made, then, that just as we believe it is better to let a hundred guilty people walk free than to condemn one innocent person, we should let a hundred criminals benefit from obscurity in order to provide a chance at rehabilitation for the few who put obscurity to good use. But there are ways, although imperfect, for allowing second chances for offenders while still allowing a community to protect itself by using online databases.

What is needed is a mixture of technological and legal means to replace the mea- 20 sures that were once naturally woven into the fabric of communities with measures that can satisfy the needs of a large, complex, and mobile society.

For example, where the inefficiency of paper records once ensured that information would not travel far, we now must introduce into the digitized world barriers for information that should not be spread. Formerly, in smaller communities, if a person was arrested, his neighbors would learn whether he had been exonerated or convicted. The community might even have had a sense of whether a person who was released had in fact committed the crime, or whether the arrest was unjustified. These days, an arrest record may travel across the globe in nanoseconds, but it is difficult to find out if it was justified. Either arrest records should not be made public (although they might be available to police in other jurisdictions) or they must be accompanied with information about the outcome of the case.

In addition, a criminal record could be sealed both locally and in online databases, say after seven years, if the person has not committed a new crime. There is considerable precedent for such a move. For instance, information about juvenile offenders and presentations to grand juries are often sealed.

Another measure could limit access to certain databanks to those who are trained to understand the limitations of these databanks. For instance, several states allow only police authorities and educational institutions to access databases on sex offenders.

One other major concern is that lawbreakers who have paid their debt to society will face discrimination in hiring and housing. Protections against such discrimination are already in place, but others might be added. For instance, employers cannot, as a general rule, legally maintain a policy of refusing to hire people merely because they are ex-cons, whether the employer gets this information from a police blotter or a computer.

Internet databases should be held accountable for the information they pro- 25 vide. If they rely on public records, then they should be required to keep up with the changes in these records. They should also provide mechanisms for filing complaints if the online data are erroneous, and they should make proper corrections in a timely fashion, the way those who keep tabs on credit records are expected to do.

These are a few examples of measures that provide obscurity equivalents in the digital age. Still, let's remember the importance of gossip fueled by public records. As a rule, we care deeply about the approval of others. In most communities, being arrested is a source of major humiliation, and people will go to great pains to avoid ending up in jail. In such cases, the social system does not work if the information is not publicly available. This holds true for the digitized world, where the need for a much wider-ranging "informal social communication," as sociologists call gossip, applies not merely to criminals, sexual predators, and disgraced physicians. It holds for people who trade on eBay, sell used books on Amazon, or distribute loans from e-banks. These people are also eager to maintain their reputation—not just locally but globally. If we cannot find ways to deal in cyberspace with those who deceive and cheat, then our ability to use the Internet for travel, trade, investment, and much else will be severely set back.

This need is served in part by user-generated feedback and ratings, which inform others who may do business via the Internet—much like traditional community gossip would. The ability of people to obscure their past in pre-Internet days made it all too easy for charlatans, quacks, and criminal offenders to hurt more people by simply switching locations. The new, digitized transparency is one major means of facilitating deals between people who do not know each other. With enough effort, its undesirable side effects can be curbed, and people can still gain a second chance.

QUESTIONS FOR DISCUSSION AND WRITING

1. Does everybody who has made a mistake, particularly one leading to a criminal conviction, deserve a second chance? Why is this opportunity such a pervasive and "important American value" in today's "progressive, optimistic, therapeutic culture" (paragraph 2)? Analyze the reasons Etzioni and Bhat offer in paragraph 2 for this culture of forgiveness. Should these always be operative?

2. What concepts of privacy discussed by Solove in the e-Pages at bedfordstmartins .com/arlington are applicable to people with criminal convictions?

3. Why is the Internet the "big bad wolf," capable of "killing the opportunity for people to have that much-deserved second chance" (paragraph 3)? In what ways does the Internet contribute to "the breakdown of communities—where people know each other and gossip" (paragraph 4) by spreading gossip "to people who do not personally know those who are being gossiped about, and who are therefore unaware of the . . . 'whole story'" (paragraph 4)?

4. "But hold on," say Etzioni and Bhat. "The sad fact is that most convicted criminals in the pre-digital age did not use the second chance that their obscurity gave them, nor did they use their third or fourth chances"—they committed new crimes (paragraph 7). Does the evidence concerning wrongdoers in paragraphs 7–17 convince you that "Internet databases do little harm to those who are not likely to reform themselves" and there are "real benefits from the widespread dissemination of information about wrongdoers—for their potential victims" (paragraph 15)? Why or why not? If you personally know of a criminal conviction, see what you can find out about the person and the case via an Internet search. How easy was it to find the information? How does the availability of the information affect your opinion?

5. Do Etzioni and Bhat offer any solutions to the possibility that, if convicted, you may run but you can't hide? Should access to "certain databanks" be limited "to those who are trained to understand the limitations of these databanks," thereby allowing "only police authorities and educational institutions to access databases on sex offenders" (paragraph 23)?

6. Discuss the impact of the availability on the Internet of any and all information about a person from a combination of perspectives—social, ethical, moral, legal, psychological. Formulate a policy statement that you believe should govern Internet dissemination of such information. What would it take to implement your proposed policy?

CHAPTER 10

Ethics: What Principles Do—and Should—We Live By?

JEFFREY WATTLES

The Golden Rule—One or Many, Gold or Glitter?

Jeffrey Wattles (b. 1945) received his bachelor's degree from Stanford University and his master's degree and doctorate from Northwestern. He is a professor of philosophy at Kent State University, where his research and teaching focus on ethics, comparative religious thought, and ways of integrating science, philosophy, and religion. He has written extensively about the golden rule in such journal articles as "Levels of Meaning in the Golden Rule" and "Plato's Brush with the Golden Rule." His book, The Golden Rule *(1996), is a detailed examination of the history, cultural variations, and interpretations of the classic moral dictum "Do to others as you want others to do to you."*

The following selection is from the opening chapter of The Golden Rule. *Here Wattles summarizes its themes, particularly his response to critics who argue that the golden rule fails to acknowledge differences among human beings, that it establishes a relatively low standard of morality, and that it encourages a simplistic moral outlook.*

Children are taught to respect parents and other authority figures. Adolescents are urged to control their impulses. Adults are told to conduct themselves in accord with certain moral and ethical standards. Morality, then, may seem to be just an affair of imposition, a cultural voice that says "no" in various ways to our desires. To be sure, there are times when the word "no" must be spoken and enforced. But, time and again, people have discovered something more to morality, something rooted in life itself. The "no" is but one word in the voice of life, a voice that has other words, including the golden rule: Do to others as you want others to do to you. This book is about the life in that principle.

THE UNITY OF THE RULE

What could be easier to grasp intuitively than the golden rule? It has such an immediate intelligibility that it serves as a ladder that anyone can step onto without a great stretch. I know how I like to be treated; and that is how I am to treat others. The rule asks me to be considerate of others rather than indulging in self-centeredness.

The study of the rule, however, leads beyond conventional interpretation, and the practice of the rule leads beyond conventional morality.

The rule is widely regarded as obvious and self-evident. Nearly everyone is familiar with it in some formulation or other. An angry parent uses it as a weapon: "Is that how you want others to treat you?" A defense attorney invites the members of the jury to put themselves in the shoes of his or her client. Noting that particular rules and interpretations do not cover every situation, a manual of professional ethics exhorts members to treat other professionals with the same consideration and respect that they would wish for themselves. Formulated in one way or another, the rule finds its way into countless speeches, sermons, documents, and books on the assumption that it has a single, clear sense that the listener or reader grasps and approves of. In an age where differences so often occasion violence, here, it seems, is something that everyone can agree on.

Promoting the notion that the golden rule is "taught by all the world's religions," advocates have collected maxims from various traditions, producing lists with entries like the following: "Hinduism: 'Let no man do to another that which would be repugnant to himself.'" "Islam: 'None of you [truly] believes until he wishes for his brother what he wishes for himself.'" The point of these lists is self-evident. Despite the differences in phrasing, all religions acknowledge the same basic, universal moral teaching. Moreover, this principle may be accepted as common ground by secular ethics as well.

Under the microscope of analysis, however, things are not so simple. Different formulations have different implications, and differences in context raise the question of whether the same concept is at work in passages where the wording is nearly identical. Is the meaning of the rule constant whenever one of these phrases is mentioned? There is a persistent debate, for example, about the relative merit of the positive formulation versus the negative one, "Do not do to others what you do not want others to do to you." Nor can the full meaning of a sentence be grasped in isolation. For example, to point to "the golden rule in Confucianism" by quoting a fifteen-word sentence from the *Analects* of Confucius does not convey the historical dynamism of the rule's evolving social, ethical, and spiritual connotations. What do the words mean in their original context? How prominent is the rule within that particular tradition? Finally, how does the rule function in a given interaction between the speaker or writer and the listener or reader? The rule may function as an authoritative reproach, a pious rehearsal of tradition, a specimen for analytic dissection, or a confession of personal commitment. Is the rule one or many? Can we even properly speak of *the* golden rule at all? Some Hindus interpret the injunction to treat others as oneself as an invitation to identify with the divine spirit within each person. Some Muslims take the golden rule to apply primarily to the brotherhood of Islam. Some Christians regard the rule as a shorthand summary of the morality of Jesus's religion. And countless people think of the rule without any religious associations at all.

Raising the question about the meanings of the golden rule in different contexts is not intended to reduce similarities to dust and ashes merely by appealing to the imponderable weight of cultural differences. Context is not the last word on meaning; the sentence expressing the golden rule contributes meaning of its own to its context. Meaning does involve context, but the fact that contexts differ does not prove that there is no commonality of meaning. Language and culture, moreover, are not reliable clues for identifying conceptual similarity and difference, since conceptual harmony is experienced across these boundaries.

The golden rule, happily, has more than a single sense. It is not a static, one-dimensional proposition with a single meaning to be accepted or rejected, defended or refuted. Nor is its multiplicity chaotic. There is enough continuity of meaning in its varied uses to justify speaking of *the* golden rule. My own thesis is that the rule's unity is best comprehended not in terms of a single meaning but as a symbol of a process of growth on emotional, intellectual, and spiritual levels.

THE QUALITY OF THE RULE

"Gold is where you find it" runs a proverb coined by miners who found what they were seeking in unexpected places. So what sort of ore or alloy or sculpture is the teaching that, since the seventeenth century, has been called "the golden rule"? Is it gold or glitter? Certain appreciative remarks on the golden rule seem to bear witness to a discovery. "Eureka!" they seem to say. "There is a supreme principle of living! It *can* be expressed in a single statement!"

By contrast, theologian Paul Tillich found the rule an inferior principle. For him, the biblical commandment to love and the assurance that God *is* love "infinitely transcend" the golden rule. The problem with the rule is that it "does not tell us what we *should* wish."

Is the rule *golden*? In other words, is it worthy to be cherished as a rule of living or even as *the* rule of living? The values of the rule are as much in dispute as its meanings. Most people, it seems, intuitively regard the golden rule as a good principle, and some have spoken as though there is within the rule a special kind of agency with the power to transform humankind. 10

It is understandable that the golden rule has been regarded as *the* supreme moral principle. I do not want to be murdered; therefore I should not murder another. I do not want my spouse to commit adultery, my property to be stolen, and so forth; therefore I should treat others with comparable consideration. Others have comparable interests, and the rule calls me to treat the other as someone akin to myself. Moreover, I realize that I sometimes have desires to be treated in ways that do not represent my considered best judgment, and this reflection makes it obvious that reason is required for the proper application of the golden rule. Finally, in personal relationships, I want to be loved, and, in consequence, the rule directs me to be loving. From the perspective of someone simply interested in living right rather than in the construction and critique of theories, the rule has much to recommend it.

Some writers have put the rule on a pedestal, giving the impression that the rule is *sufficient* for ethics in the sense that no one could ever go wrong by adhering to it or in the sense that all duties may be inferred from it. Others have claimed that the rule is a *necessary* criterion for right action; in other words, an action must be able to pass the test of the golden rule if it is to be validated as right, and any action that fails the test is wrong. Some philosophers have hoped for an ethical theory that would be self-sufficient (depending on no controversial axioms), perfectly good (invulnerable to counterexamples), and all-powerful (enabling the derivation of every correct moral judgment, given appropriate data about the situation). They have dreamed of sculpting ethics into an independent, rational, deductive system, on the model of geometry, with a single normative axiom. However much reason may hanker for such a system, once the golden rule is taken as a candidate for such an axiom, a minor flexing of the analytic bicep is enough to humiliate it. A single counterexample suffices to defeat a pretender to this throne.

Many scholars today regard the rule as an acceptable principle for popular use but as embarrassing if taken with philosophic seriousness. Most professional ethicists rely instead on other principles, since the rule seems vulnerable to counterexamples, such as the current favorite, "What if a sadomasochist goes forth to treat others as he wants to be treated?"

Technically, the golden rule can defend itself from objections, since it contains within itself the seed of its own self-correction. Any easily abused interpretation may be challenged: "Would you want to be treated according to a rule construed in this way?" The recursive use of the rule—applying it to the results of its own earlier application—is a lever that extricates it from many tangles. Close examination of the counterexample of the sadomasochist . . . shows that to use the rule properly requires a certain degree of maturity. The counterexample does not refute the golden rule, properly understood; rather, it serves to clarify the interpretation of the rule—that the golden rule functions appropriately in a *growing* personality; indeed, the practice of the rule itself promotes the required growth. Since the rule is such a compressed statement of morality, it takes for granted at least a minimum sincerity that refuses to manipulate the rule sophistically to "justify" patently immoral conduct. Where that prerequisite cannot be assumed, problems multiply.

The objections that have been raised against the rule are useful to illustrate   15 misinterpretations of the rule and to make clear assumptions that must be satisfied for the rule to function in moral theory.

It has been objected that the golden rule assumes that human beings are basically alike and thereby fails to do justice to the differences between people. In particular, the rule allegedly implies that what we want is what others want. As George Bernard Shaw quipped, "Don't do to others as you want them to do unto you. Their tastes may be different." The golden rule may also seem to imply that what we want for ourselves is good for ourselves and that what is good for ourselves is good for others. The positive formulation, in particular, is accused of harboring the potential for presumption; thus, the rule is suited for immediate application only among those whose beliefs and needs are similar. In fact, however, the rule calls for due consideration for any relevant difference between persons—just as the agent would want such consideration from others.

Another criticism is that the golden rule sets too low a standard because it makes ordinary wants and desires the criterion of morality. On one interpretation, the rule asks individuals to do whatever they imagine they might wish to have done to them in a given situation; thus a judge would be obliged by the golden rule to sentence a convicted criminal with extreme leniency. As a mere principle of sympathy, therefore, it is argued, the rule is incapable of guiding judgment in cases where the necessary action is unwelcome to its immediate recipient.

A related problem is that the rule, taken merely as a policy of sympathy, amounts to the advice "Treat others as they want you to treat them," as in a puzzle from the opening chapter of Herman Melville's *Moby-Dick*, where Ishmael is invited by his new friend, Queequeg, to join in pagan worship. Ishmael pauses to think it over:

> But what is worship?—to do the will of God—*that* is worship. And what is the will of God?—to do to my fellow man what I would have my fellow man to do to me—*that* is the will of God. Now, Queequeg is my fellow man. And what do I wish that this Queequeg would do to me? Why, unite with me in my particular Presbyterian form of worship. Consequently, I must then unite with him in his; ergo, I must turn idolator.

If the golden rule is taken to require the agent to identify with the other in a simplistic and uncritical way, the result is a loss of the higher perspective toward which the rule moves the thoughtful practitioner.

The next clusters of objections have a depth that a quick, initial reply would betray, so I defer my response until later. If the rule is not to be interpreted as setting up the agent's idiosyncratic desires—or those of the recipient—as a supreme standard of goodness, then problems arise because the rule does not specify what the agent ought to desire. The rule merely requires consistency of moral judgment: one must apply the same standards to one's treatment of others that one applies to others' treatment of oneself. The lack of specificity in the rule, its merely formal or merely procedural character, allegedly renders its guidance insubstantial.

The rule seems to exhibit the limitations of any general moral principle: it [20] does not carry sufficiently rich substantive implications to be helpful in the thicket of life's problems. Even though most people live with some allegiance to integrating principles, action guides, mottoes, proverbs, or commandments that serve to unify the mind, the deficiency of any principle is that it is merely a principle, merely a beginning; only the full exposition of a system of ethics can validate the place of an asserted principle. An appeal to a general principle, moreover, can function as a retreat and a refusal to think through issues in their concreteness.

There is also criticism of a practice widely associated with the rule—imagining oneself in the other person's situation. The charge is that this practice is an abstract, derivative, artificial, male, manipulative device, which can never compensate for the lack of human understanding and spontaneous goodness.

The rule has been criticized as a naïvely idealistic standard, unsuited to a world of rugged competition. The rule may seem to require that, if I am trustworthy and want to be trusted, I must treat everyone as being equally trustworthy. Furthermore, the broad humanitarianism of the golden rule allegedly makes unrealistic psychological demands; it is unfair to family and friends to embrace the universal concerns of the golden rule.

Last, some religious issues. The golden rule has been criticized for being a teaching that misleadingly lets people avoid confronting the higher teachings of religious ethics, for example, Jesus's commandment, "Love one another as I have loved you." Some find the rule of only intermediate usefulness, proposing that spiritual living moves beyond the standpoint of rules. Others have criticized the golden rule's traditional links to religion, arguing that moral intuition and moral reason can operate without reference to any religious foundation.

For responding to all these objections, there are three possible strategies: abandon the rule, reformulate it, or retain it as commonly worded, while taking advantage of objections to clarify its proper interpretation. I take the third way.

QUESTIONS FOR DISCUSSION AND WRITING

1. In paragraphs 4 and 5, Wattles offers variations on the golden rule from Hinduism and Islam as well as the rule in its negative formulation. Do these variations state essentially the same moral precept, or are there subtle differences among them? Why do you think so?

2. Wattles writes that it is "obvious that reason is required for the proper application of the golden rule" (paragraph 11). What does he mean? How does this idea fit in with his point that the rule "takes for granted at least a minimum sincerity that refuses to manipulate the rule sophistically to 'justify' patently immoral conduct" (paragraph 14)?

3. Wattles raises objections that have been made regarding the usefulness of the golden rule, some of which he briefly responds to. His point, however, is that considering these various objections is "useful to illustrate misinterpretations of the rule and to make clear assumptions that must be satisfied for the rule to function in moral theory" (paragraph 15). Might this kind of thinking tend to make what is essentially a straightforward statement of moral principle into something too complicated to put into practice? Given the objections Wattles mentions, how would you go about interpreting the golden rule?

4. In an essay, consider the principles that you live by and explain whether they help you "in the thicket of life's problems." Do you ever use your principles "as a retreat and a refusal to think through issues in their concreteness" (paragraph 20)? Or do they provide you with a positive, adaptable, and useful set of guidelines for moral behavior?

5. Read "Hate," Lynda Barry's graphic essay, in the e-Pages at bedfordstmartins .com/arlington. In what ways—if any—does Barry complicate Wattle's assertions in "The Golden Rule"? Be specific.

LYNDA BARRY

Hate   [GRAPHIC ESSAY]

The substitute teacher "was the first person to explain the difference between the kind of hate that has destructive intent and the kind that's a response to something destructive."

 In the e-Pages at bedfordstmartins.com/arlington

MICHAEL SANDEL

What Isn't for Sale?

The Anne T. and Robert M. Bass Professor of Government at Harvard University, Michael Sandel (b. 1953) has achieved wide acclaim as a writer and lecturer. His undergraduate course, Justice, has enrolled over fifteen thousand students, making it the most popular class ever at Harvard. A Rhodes scholar, Sandel is the recipient of the Harvard-Radcliffe Phi Beta Kappa Teaching Prize. He also served on the President's Council on Bioethics from 2002 to 2005, and he is a member of the American Academy of the Arts and the Council on Foreign Relations. His numerous publications include Liberalism and the Limits of Justice *(1982),* The Case Against Perfection: Ethics in the Age of Genetic Engineering *(2007), and, recently,* What Money Can't Buy: The Moral Limits of Markets *(2012).*

Sandel's article "What Isn't for Sale?" was first published in the Atlantic *in April 2012. Sandel argues that we have moved from being a market economy to a market society, in which everything is for sale. That word "everything" includes things that just thirty years ago most people would not have thought were appropriate to sell. Sandel argues that the market is not neutral or inert, but that putting things on the market affects them, and changes how society thinks of them. He looks at areas like education, health care, and criminal justice as having been deeply affected by bringing market forces to bear, to the point where, for example, inmates can purchase upgrades in jail facilities. The question then becomes, What limits should be placed on a market society? In what areas does the market no longer serve the public good?*

There are some things money can't buy—but these days, not many. Almost everything is up for sale. For example:

- *A prison-cell upgrade: $90 a night.* In Santa Ana, California, and some other cities, nonviolent offenders can pay for a clean, quiet jail cell, without any nonpaying prisoners to disturb them.

- *Access to the carpool lane while driving solo: $8.* Minneapolis, San Diego, Houston, Seattle, and other cities have sought to ease traffic congestion by letting solo drivers pay to drive in carpool lanes, at rates that vary according to traffic.

- *The services of an Indian surrogate mother: $8,000.* Western couples seeking surrogates increasingly outsource the job to India, and the price is less than one-third the going rate in the United States.

- *The right to shoot an endangered black rhino: $250,000.* South Africa has begun letting some ranchers sell hunters the right to kill a limited number of rhinos, to give the ranchers an incentive to raise and protect the endangered species.

- *Your doctor's cellphone number: $1,500 and up per year.* A growing number of "concierge" doctors offer cellphone access and same-day appointments for patients willing to pay annual fees ranging from $1,500 to $25,000.

- *The right to emit a metric ton of carbon dioxide into the atmosphere: $10.50.* The European Union runs a carbon-dioxide-emissions market that enables companies to buy and sell the right to pollute.

- *The right to immigrate to the United States: $500,000.* Foreigners who invest $500,000 and create at least 10 full-time jobs in an area of high unemployment are eligible for a green card that entitles them to permanent residency.

Not everyone can afford to buy these things. But today there are lots of new ways to make money. If you need to earn some extra cash, here are some novel possibilities:

- *Sell space on your forehead to display commercial advertising: $10,000.* A single mother in Utah who needed money for her son's education was paid $10,000 by an online casino to install a permanent tattoo of the casino's Web address on her forehead. Temporary tattoo ads earn less.

- *Serve as a human guinea pig in a drug-safety trial for a pharmaceutical company: $7,500.* The pay can be higher or lower, depending on the invasiveness of the procedure used to test the drug's effect and the discomfort involved.

- *Fight in Somalia or Afghanistan for a private military contractor: up to $1,000 a day.* The pay varies according to qualifications, experience, and nationality.

- *Stand in line overnight on Capitol Hill to hold a place for a lobbyist who wants to attend a congressional hearing: $15–$20 an hour.* Lobbyists pay line-standing companies, who hire homeless people and others to queue up.

- *If you are a second-grader in an underachieving Dallas school, read a book: $2.* To encourage reading, schools pay kids for each book they read.

We live in a time when almost everything can be bought and sold. Over the past three decades, markets—and market values—have come to govern our lives as never before. We did not arrive at this condition through any deliberate choice. It is almost as if it came upon us.

As the Cold War ended, markets and market thinking enjoyed unrivaled prestige, and understandably so. No other mechanism for organizing the production and distribution of goods had proved as successful at generating affluence and prosperity. And yet even as growing numbers of countries around the world embraced market mechanisms in the operation of their economies, something else was happening. Market values were coming to play a greater and greater role in social life. Economics was becoming an imperial domain. Today, the logic of buying and selling no longer applies to material goods alone. It increasingly governs the whole of life.

The years leading up to the financial crisis of 2008 were a heady time of market 5 faith and deregulation—an era of market triumphalism. The era began in the early 1980s, when Ronald Reagan and Margaret Thatcher proclaimed their conviction that markets, not government, held the key to prosperity and freedom. And it continued into the 1990s with the market-friendly liberalism of Bill Clinton and Tony Blair, who moderated but consolidated the faith that markets are the primary means for achieving the public good.

Today, that faith is in question. The financial crisis did more than cast doubt on the ability of markets to allocate risk efficiently. It also prompted a widespread sense that markets have become detached from morals, and that we need to somehow reconnect the two. But it's not obvious what this would mean, or how we should go about it.

Some say the moral failing at the heart of market triumphalism was greed, which led to irresponsible risk-taking. The solution, according to this view, is to rein in greed, insist on greater integrity and responsibility among bankers and Wall Street executives, and enact sensible regulations to prevent a similar crisis from happening again.

This is, at best, a partial diagnosis. While it is certainly true that greed played a role in the financial crisis, something bigger was and is at stake. The most fateful change that unfolded during the past three decades was not an increase in greed. It was the reach of markets, and of market values, into spheres of life traditionally governed by nonmarket norms. To contend with this condition, we need to do more than inveigh against greed; we need to have a public debate about where markets belong—and where they don't.

Consider, for example, the proliferation of for-profit schools, hospitals, and prisons, and the outsourcing of war to private military contractors. (In Iraq and Afghanistan, private contractors have actually outnumbered U.S. military troops.) Consider the eclipse of public police forces by private security firms—especially in the United States and the United Kingdom where the number of private guards is almost twice the number of public police officers.

Or consider the pharmaceutical companies' aggressive marketing of prescrip- 10 tion drugs directly to consumers, a practice now prevalent in the United States but prohibited in most other countries. (If you've ever seen the television commercials on the evening news, you could be forgiven for thinking that the greatest health crisis in the world is not malaria or river blindness or sleeping sickness but an epidemic of erectile dysfunction.)

Consider too the reach of commercial advertising into public schools, from buses to corridors to cafeterias; the sale of "naming rights" to parks and civic spaces; the blurred boundaries, within journalism, between news and advertising, likely to blur further as newspapers and magazines struggle to survive; the marketing of "designer" eggs and sperm for assisted reproduction; the buying and selling, by companies and countries, of the right to pollute; a system of campaign finance in the United States that comes close to permitting the buying and selling of elections.

These uses of markets to allocate health, education, public safety, national security, criminal justice, environmental protection, recreation, procreation, and other social goods were for the most part unheard-of 30 years ago. Today, we take them largely for granted.

Why worry that we are moving toward a society in which everything is up for sale?

For two reasons. One is about inequality, the other about corruption. First, consider inequality. In a society where everything is for sale, life is harder for those of modest means. The more money can buy, the more affluence—or the lack of it—matters. If the only advantage of affluence were the ability to afford yachts, sports cars, and fancy vacations, inequalities of income and wealth would matter less than they do today. But as money comes to buy more and more, the distribution of income and wealth looms larger.

The second reason we should hesitate to put everything up for sale is more   15 difficult to describe. It is not about inequality and fairness but about the corrosive tendency of markets. Putting a price on the good things in life can corrupt them. That's because markets don't only allocate goods; they express and promote certain attitudes toward the goods being exchanged. Paying kids to read books might get them to read more, but might also teach them to regard reading as a chore rather than a source of intrinsic satisfaction. Hiring foreign mercenaries to fight our wars might spare the lives of our citizens, but might also corrupt the meaning of citizenship.

Economists often assume that markets are inert, that they do not affect the goods being exchanged. But this is untrue. Markets leave their mark. Sometimes, market values crowd out nonmarket values worth caring about.

When we decide that certain goods may be bought and sold, we decide, at least implicitly, that it is appropriate to treat them as commodities, as instruments of profit and use. But not all goods are properly valued in this way. The most obvious example is human beings. Slavery was appalling because it treated human beings as a commodity, to be bought and sold at auction. Such treatment fails to value human beings as persons, worthy of dignity and respect; it sees them as instruments of gain and objects of use.

Something similar can be said of other cherished goods and practices. We don't allow children to be bought and sold, no matter how difficult the process of adoption can be or how willing impatient prospective parents might be. Even if the prospective buyers would treat the child responsibly, we worry that a market in children would express and promote the wrong way of valuing them. Children are properly regarded not as consumer goods but as beings worthy of love and care. Or consider the rights and obligations of citizenship. If you are called to jury duty, you can't hire a substitute to take your place. Nor do we allow citizens to sell their votes, even though others might be eager to buy them. Why not? Because we believe that civic duties are not private property but public responsibilities. To outsource them is to demean them, to value them in the wrong way.

These examples illustrate a broader point: Some of the good things in life are degraded if turned into commodities. So to decide where the market belongs, and where it should be kept at a distance, we have to decide how to value the goods in question—health, education, family life, nature, art, civic duties, and so on. These are moral and political questions, not merely economic ones. To resolve them, we have to debate, case by case, the moral meaning of these goods, and the proper way of valuing them.

This is a debate we didn't have during the era of market triumphalism. As a result, without quite realizing it—without ever deciding to do so—we drifted from having a market economy to being a market society. 20

The difference is this: A market economy is a tool—a valuable and effective tool—for organizing productive activity. A market society is a way of life in which market values seep into every aspect of human endeavor. It's a place where social relations are made over in the image of the market.

The great missing debate in contemporary politics is about the role and reach of markets. Do we want a market economy, or a market society? What role should markets play in public life and personal relations? How can we decide which goods should be bought and sold, and which should be governed by nonmarket values? Where should money's writ not run?

Even if you agree that we need to grapple with big questions about the morality of markets, you might doubt that our public discourse is up to the task. It's a legitimate worry. At a time when political argument consists mainly of shouting matches on cable television, partisan vitriol on talk radio, and ideological food fights on the floor of Congress, it's hard to imagine a reasoned public debate about such controversial moral questions as the right way to value procreation, children, education, health, the environment, citizenship, and other goods. I believe such a debate is possible, but only if we are willing to broaden the terms of our public discourse and grapple more explicitly with competing notions of the good life.

In hopes of avoiding sectarian strife, we often insist that citizens leave their moral and spiritual convictions behind when they enter the public square. But the reluctance to admit arguments about the good life into politics has had an unanticipated consequence. It has helped prepare the way for market triumphalism, and for the continuing hold of market reasoning.

In its own way, market reasoning also empties public life of moral argument. 25 Part of the appeal of markets is that they don't pass judgment on the preferences they satisfy. They don't ask whether some ways of valuing goods are higher, or worthier, than others. If someone is willing to pay for sex, or a kidney, and a consenting adult is willing to sell, the only question the economist asks is, "How much?" Markets don't wag fingers. They don't discriminate between worthy preferences and unworthy ones. Each party to a deal decides for him- or herself what value to place on the things being exchanged.

This nonjudgmental stance toward values lies at the heart of market reasoning, and explains much of its appeal. But our reluctance to engage in moral and spiritual argument, together with our embrace of markets, has exacted a heavy price: It has drained public discourse of moral and civic energy, and contributed to the technocratic, managerial politics afflicting many societies today.

A debate about the moral limits of markets would enable us to decide, as a society, where markets serve the public good and where they do not belong. Thinking through the appropriate place of markets requires that we reason together, in public, about the right way to value the social goods we prize. It would be folly to expect that a more morally robust public discourse, even at its best, would lead to agreement on every contested question. But it would make for a healthier public life. And it would make us more aware of the price we pay for living in a society where everything is up for sale.

QUESTIONS FOR DISCUSSION AND WRITING

1. Sandel begins his article with a list of things money can buy that didn't used to be for sale, and he follows that with a brief list of ways to make money that didn't exist before, either. His point is about the expansion of market economics into areas of life previously not touched by markets. Why is this expansion of market economics a bad thing? Is the sale of any particular items on the list morally offensive or reprehensible to you? Why? If nothing on the list bothered you, what are your own limits of market economics? What should not be for sale?

2. Sandel points to the 1980s, when leaders like Ronald Reagan and Margaret Thatcher pushed for less government control of the economy so that free markets could create not only economic wealth but also political freedom. He argues that the extension of this logic has been that "markets are the primary means for achieving the public good" (paragraph 5). But what is the public good? Is the public good simply what the market determines it to be? In paragraph 6, Sandel argues that in recent years, there has been a rise of doubt about whether, in fact, "markets have become detached from morals." Do you agree or disagree with this observation? Do you subscribe to the view that free markets are inherently connected to the public good, or do you think there is a separation of the two? Explain. Be specific in your response.

3. Sandel makes an argument of definition when he says that we have moved from a market economy to a market society, in which "market values [reached] into spheres of life traditionally governed by nonmarket norms" (paragraph 8). Sandel lists for-profit schools, hospitals, and prisons, as well as the use of private military contractors in war as examples of changes that occurred based on market triumphalism (paragraph 9). What are the advantages to having markets in these areas? What are some of the disadvantages? What areas of life would this include? How has the market changed those areas?

4. Sandel's two primary concerns about the movement of the market into traditionally nonmarket areas involve inequality and corruption. Explain what he means by both of these terms in relation to the market. Do you agree with his concerns? Why or why not?

5. In contrast to some economists, Sandel argues that the market does indeed have an effect on what it sells; Sandel states the markets "express and promote

certain attitudes toward the goods being exchanged" (paragraph 15). He cites the trading of human beings (i.e., slavery) as an obvious example of how the buying and selling of something affects our attitudes toward it. What examples can you think of, if any, of currently available goods and services that, in your opinion, should not be subject to the market? Defend your answers.

CHRISTINE OVERALL

Think before You Breed

Christine Overall (b. 1949) is a professor in the Department of Philosophy at Queen's University in Ontario, Canada. At Queen's University, she currently holds the position of University Research Chair. She has written numerous reviews, articles, and books, including Ethics and Human Reproduction: A Feminist Analysis, *originally published in 1987 and republished in 2012 by Routledge Library Editions. Her book* Aging, Death, and Human Longevity: A Philosophical Inquiry *(2003) won the Abbyann D. Lynch Medal in Bioethics awarded by the Royal Society of Canada. Her most recent book is* Why Have Children: The Ethical Debate *(2012).*

In this article, which initially appeared in the Opinionator, online commentary from the New York Times, *Overall discusses the ethical questions behind having children. She argues that while childless couples usually have to defend their decision not to procreate, seldom do people examine reasons for having children. Yet, Overall argues, the decision to have children has much greater impact and importance than a decision not to have children, not the least of which is the decision to create a "dependent, needy, and vulnerable human being." Overall asks the reader to think about the ethics of having children. She puts forth the example of Nadya Suleman, the "Octomom," who created, with the help of a doctor specializing in fertility treatment, fourteen children that she cannot support by herself. Of course, most babies are not created under such circumstances, but Overall urges the reader to consider that more thought should go into the decision to have a baby than typically happens.*

As a young woman in my twenties I pondered whether or not to have children. Is there a way, I wondered, to decide thoughtfully rather than carelessly about this most momentous of human choices?

Having children has impact far beyond the family circle.

It's a tough decision because you can't know ahead of time what sort of child you will have or what it will be like to be a parent. You can't understand what is good or what is hard about the process of creating and rearing until after you have the child. And the choice to have a child is a decision to change your life forever. It's irreversible, and therefore, compared to reversible life choices about education, work, geographical location, or romance, it has much greater ethical importance.

Choosing whether or not to procreate may not seem like the sort of decision that is deserving or even capable of analysis. The Canadian novelist Margaret Laurence wrote, "I don't really feel I have to analyze my own motives in wanting children. For my own reassurance? For fun? For ego-satisfaction? No matter. It's like (to me) asking why you want to write. Who cares? You have to, and that's that."

In fact, people are still expected to provide reasons *not* to have children, but no reasons are required to have them. It's assumed that if individuals do not have children it is because they are infertile, too selfish, or have just not yet gotten around to it. In any case, they owe their interlocutor an explanation. On the other hand, no one says to the proud parents of a newborn, Why did you choose to have that child? What are your reasons? The choice to procreate is not regarded as needing any thought or justification. 5

Nonetheless, I think Laurence's "Who cares?" attitude is mistaken.

We are fortunate that procreation is more and more a matter of choice. Not always, of course—not everyone has access to effective contraception and accessible abortion, and some women are subjected to enforced pregnancy. But the growing availability of reproductive choice makes it clear that procreation cannot be merely an expression of personal taste.

The question whether to have children is of course prudential in part; it's concerned about what is or is not in one's own interests. But it is *also* an ethical question, for it is about whether to bring a person (in some cases more than one person) into existence—and that person cannot, by the very nature of the situation, give consent to being brought into existence. Such a question also profoundly affects the well-being of existing people (the potential parents, siblings if any, and grandparents). And it has effects beyond the family on the broader society, which is inevitably changed by the cumulative impact—on things like education, health care, employment, agriculture, community growth and design, and the availability and distribution of resources—of individual decisions about whether to procreate.

There are self-help books on the market that purport to assist would-be parents in making a practical choice about whether or not to have children. There are also informal discussions on Web sites, in newspapers and magazines and in blogs. Yet the ethical nature of this choice is seldom recognized, even—or especially—by philosophers.

Perhaps people fail to see childbearing as an ethical choice because they think of it as the expression of an instinct or biological drive, like sexual attraction or "falling in love," that is not amenable to ethical evaluation. But whatever our biological inclinations may be, many human beings do take control over their fertility, thanks to contemporary means of contraception and abortion. The rapidly declining birthrate in most parts of the world is evidence of that fact. While choosing whether or not to have children may involve feelings, motives, impulses, memories, and emotions, it can and should also be a subject for careful reflection. 10

If we fail to acknowledge that the decision of whether to parent or not is a real choice that has ethical import, then we are treating childbearing as a mere expression of biological destiny. Instead of seeing having children as something that women *do*, we will continue to see it as something that simply *happens* to women, or as something that is merely "natural" and animal-like.

The decision to have children surely deserves at least as much thought as people devote to leasing a car or buying a house. Procreation decisions are about whether or not to assume complete responsibility, over a period of at least 18 years, for a new life or new lives. Because deciding whether to procreate has ethical dimensions, the reasons people give for their procreative choices deserve examination. Some reasons may be better—or worse—than others.

My aim, I hasten to add, is not to argue for policing people's procreative motives. I am simply arguing for the need to think systematically and deeply about a fundamental aspect of human life.

The burden of proof—or at least the burden of justification—should therefore rest primarily on those who choose to have children, not on those who choose to be childless. The choice to have children calls for more careful justification and thought than the choice not to have children because procreation creates a dependent, needy, and vulnerable human being whose future may be at risk. The individual who chooses childlessness takes the ethically less risky path. After all, nonexistent people can't suffer from not being created. They do not have an entitlement to come into existence, and we do not owe it to them to bring them into existence. But once children do exist, we incur serious responsibilities to them.

Because children are dependent, needy, and vulnerable, prospective parents 15 should consider how well they can love and care for the offspring they create, and the kind of relationship they can have with them. The genuinely unselfish life plan may at least sometimes be the choice not to have children, especially in the case of individuals who would otherwise procreate merely to adhere to tradition, to please others, to conform to gender conventions, or to benefit themselves out of the inappropriate expectation that children will fix their problems. Children are neither human pets nor little therapists.

Some people claim that the mere fact that our offspring will probably be happy gives us ample reason to procreate. The problem with this argument is, first, that there are no guarantees. The sheer unpredictability of children, the limits on our capacities as parents, and the instability of social conditions make it unwise to take for granted that our progeny will have good lives. But just as important, justifying having kids by claiming that our offspring will be happy provides no stopping point for procreative behavior. If two children are happy, perhaps four will be, or seven, or ten.

The unwillingness to stop is dramatized by the so-called Octomom, Nadya Suleman, who first had six children via in vitro fertilization, then ended up with eight more from just one pregnancy, aided by her reprehensible doctor, Michael Kamrava. Higher-order-multiple pregnancies often create long-term health problems for the children born of them. It's also unlikely that Suleman can provide adequate care for and attention to her fourteen children under the age of twelve, especially in light of her recent bankruptcy, her very public attempts to raise money, and the impending loss of their home. Was Suleman's desire for a big family fair to her helpless offspring?

Consider also reality television "stars" Michelle and Jim Bob Duggar, the parents of nineteen children. The Duggars claim to have religious motives for creating their large family. But it's not at all clear that God places such a high value on the Duggar genetic heritage. Unlike Suleman, the Duggars don't struggle to support their brood, but mere financial solvency is not a sufficient reason to birth more than a dozen and a half offspring, even if the kids seem reasonably content.

People like the Duggars and Suleman might respond that they have a right to reproduce. Certainly they are entitled to be free from state interference in their procreative behavior; compulsory contraception and abortion, or penalties for having babies, are abhorrent. But a right to noninterference does not, by itself, justify every decision to have a baby.

We should not regret the existence of the children in these very public families, now that they are here. My point is just that their parents' models of procreative decision making deserve skepticism. The parents appear to overlook what is ethically central: the possibility of forming a supportive, life-enhancing and close relationship with each of their offspring. 20

After struggling with our own decision about whether to procreate, in the end my spouse and I chose to have two children, whom we adore. The many rewards and challenges of raising kids have gradually revealed the far-reaching implications of procreative decision making. In choosing to become a parent, one seeks to create a relationship, and, uniquely, one also seeks to create the person with whom one has the relationship. Choosing whether or not to have children is therefore the most significant ethical debate of most people's lives.

QUESTIONS FOR DISCUSSION AND WRITING

1. In paragraph 2, Overall states that the decision to have children "has impact far beyond the family circle." What sort of impact is she referring to? Try to list as many effects of having children as possible. Then, consider the impact of not having children. What, if any, are the effects of that decision?

2. Overall notes that society assumes couples without children "are infertile, too selfish, or have just not gotten around to it" (paragraph 5). Do you agree or disagree with this statement? What other reasons might there be for a couple not to have children? Beyond this is another assumption: that healthy, heterosexual couples in a committed relationship will have children. Is this a fair or "natural" assumption to make? Why or why not?

3. Part of Overall's argument is about the idea of what is natural. She contrasts the idea of having children as something women *do* with what *happens* to women as something "'natural' and animal-like" (paragraph 11). Underpinning this is the argument that women, thanks to birth control and abortion, are no longer simply at the mercy of biology in terms of deciding to have a baby. Is Overall creating a separation between what is human and what is natural? Is such a separation helpful or does it obscure the issues? Defend your answer. Supply examples from other areas of life in your defense.

4. Overall states that sometimes the unselfish act is *not* to have children. What support does she give for this argument? Do you agree? Examine the statement, "Children are neither human pets nor little therapists" (paragraph 15). In your own realm of experience and observations, have you seen parents who have taken that position toward their children? Explain.

5. Overall mentions the Octomom, Nadya Suleman, who, with medical assistance, gave birth to six children first, and then octuplets, making for a total of fourteen children. Suleman since then has had well-documented financial difficulties. Overall also mentions the Duggar family, which has nineteen children, although without financial distress. What is Overall's argument against having such large families? Given that such large families are rare, is Overall making too much out of such examples? What larger point is she trying to illustrate?

PETER SINGER

The Singer Solution to World Poverty

When Princeton University appointed Peter Singer to a new chair in bioethics in 1998, a New Yorker *profile hailed him as "the most influential living philosopher," and the* New York Times *as "perhaps the world's most controversial ethicist." Born in Melbourne, Australia (1946), Singer attended the University of Melbourne (B.A., 1967; M.A., 1969) and Oxford (B. Phil., 1971). After teaching at Oxford and at New York University, he led the Centre for Human Bioethics at Monash University in Australia (1983–1998). A vegetarian since college, Singer has devoted his career to protecting animals from human "speciesism"—the valuing of human rights above those of other species. In* Animal Liberation: A New Ethics for Our Treatment of Animals *(1975), he argues against redundant experimentation, advocates humane food production, and recommends that we consume more vegetable protein and less meat. Singer's work as coauthor and editor includes* Making Babies: The New Science and Ethics of Conception *(1985), about ethical issues in human conception such as in vitro fertilization and surrogate motherhood;* Should the Baby Live? The Problem of Handicapped Infants *(1985); and* Rethinking Life and Death *(1995), about the quality-of-life issues raised by modern technology.*

In "The Singer Solution to World Poverty," originally published in the New York Times Magazine *(September 1999), Singer interrogates the ethics of affluence, arguing that because it is just as immoral to ignore the plight of sick and starving children overseas as it is to allow a child to be killed, we should willingly donate to charity the portion of our income not spent on necessities.*

In the Brazilian film *Central Station,* Dora is a retired schoolteacher who makes ends meet by sitting at the station writing letters for illiterate people. Suddenly she has an opportunity to pocket $1,000. All she has to do is persuade a homeless

9-year-old boy to follow her to an address she has been given. (She is told he will be adopted by wealthy foreigners.) She delivers the boy, gets the money, spends some of it on a television set and settles down to enjoy her new acquisition. Her neighbor spoils the fun, however, by telling her that the boy was too old to be adopted—he will be killed and his organs sold for transplantation. Perhaps Dora knew this all along, but after her neighbor's plain speaking, she spends a troubled night. In the morning Dora resolves to take the boy back.

Suppose Dora had told her neighbor that it is a tough world, other people have nice new TV's too, and if selling the kid is the only way she can get one, well, he was only a street kid. She would then have become, in the eyes of the audience, a monster. She redeems herself only by being prepared to bear considerable risks to save the boy.

At the end of the movie, in cinemas in the affluent nations of the world, people who would have been quick to condemn Dora if she had not rescued the boy go home to places far more comfortable than her apartment. In fact, the average family in the United States spends almost one-third of its income on things that are no more necessary to them than Dora's new TV was to her. Going out to nice restaurants, buying new clothes because the old ones are no longer stylish, vacationing at beach resorts—so much of our income is spent on things not essential to the preservation of our lives and health. Donated to one of a number of charitable agencies, that money could mean the difference between life and death for children in need.

All of which raises a question: In the end, what is the ethical distinction between a Brazilian who sells a homeless child to organ peddlers and an American who already has a TV and upgrades to a better one—knowing that the money could be donated to an organization that would use it to save the lives of kids in need?

Of course, there are several differences between the two situations that could 5 support different moral judgments about them. For one thing, to be able to consign a child to death when he is standing right in front of you takes a chilling kind of heartlessness; it is much easier to ignore an appeal for money to help children you will never meet. Yet for a utilitarian philosopher like myself—that is, one who judges whether acts are right or wrong by their consequences—if the upshot of the American's failure to donate the money is that one more kid dies on the streets of a Brazilian city, then it is, in some sense, just as bad as selling the kid to the organ peddlers. But one doesn't need to embrace my utilitarian ethic to see that, at the very least, there is a troubling incongruity in being so quick to condemn Dora for taking the child to the organ peddlers while, at the same time, not regarding the American consumer's behavior as raising a serious moral issue.

In his 1996 book, *Living High and Letting Die*, the New York University philosopher Peter Unger presented an ingenious series of imaginary examples designed to probe our intuitions about whether it is wrong to live well without giving substantial amounts of money to help people who are hungry, malnourished or dying from easily treatable illnesses like diarrhea. Here's my paraphrase of one of these examples:

Bob is close to retirement. He has invested most of his savings in a very rare and valuable old car, a Bugatti, which he has not been able to insure. The Bugatti is his pride and joy. In addition to the pleasure he gets from driving and caring for his car, Bob knows that its rising market value means that he will always be able to sell it and live comfortably after retirement. One day when Bob is out for a drive, he parks the Bugatti near the end of a railway siding and goes for a walk up the track. As he does so, he sees that a runaway train, with no one aboard, is running down the railway track. Looking farther down the track, he sees the small figure of a child very likely to be killed by the runaway train. He can't stop the train and the child is too far away to warn of the danger, but he can throw a switch that will divert the train down the siding where his Bugatti is parked. Then nobody will be killed—but the train will destroy his Bugatti. Thinking of his joy in owning the car and the financial security it represents, Bob decides not to throw the switch. The child is killed. For many years to come, Bob enjoys owning his Bugatti and the financial security it represents.

Bob's conduct, most of us will immediately respond, was gravely wrong. Unger agrees. But then he reminds us that we, too, have opportunities to save the lives of children. We can give to organizations like UNICEF or Oxfam America. How much would we have to give one of these organizations to have a high probability of saving the life of a child threatened by easily preventable diseases? (I do not believe that children are more worth saving than adults, but since no one can argue that children have brought their poverty on themselves, focusing on them simplifies the issues.) Unger called up some experts and used the information they provided to offer some plausible estimates that include the cost of raising money, administrative expenses and the cost of delivering aid where it is most needed. By his calculation, $200 in donations would help a sickly two-year-old transform into a healthy six-year-old—offering safe passage through childhood's most dangerous years. To show how practical philosophical argument can be, Unger even tells his readers that they can easily donate funds by using their credit card and calling one of these toll-free numbers: (800) 367-5437 for UNICEF; (800) 693-2687 for Oxfam America.

Now you, too, have the information you need to save a child's life. How should you judge yourself if you don't do it? Think again about Bob and his Bugatti. Unlike Dora, Bob did not have to look into the eyes of the child he was sacrificing for his own material comfort. The child was a complete stranger to him and too far away to relate to in an intimate, personal way. Unlike Dora, too, he did not mislead the child or initiate the chain of events imperiling him. In all these respects, Bob's situation resembles that of people able but unwilling to donate to overseas aid and differs from Dora's situation.

If you still think that it was very wrong of Bob not to throw the switch that would have diverted the train and saved the child's life, then it is hard to see how you could deny that it is also very wrong not to send money to one of the organizations listed above. Unless, that is, there is some morally important difference between the two situations that I have overlooked.

Is it the practical uncertainties about whether aid will really reach the people who need it? Nobody who knows the world of overseas aid can doubt that such uncertainties exist. But Unger's figure of $200 to save a child's life was reached after he had made conservative assumptions about the proportion of the money donated that will actually reach its target.

One genuine difference between Bob and those who can afford to donate to overseas aid organizations but don't is that only Bob can save the child on the tracks, whereas there are hundreds of millions of people who can give $200 to overseas aid organizations. The problem is that most of them aren't doing it. Does this mean that it is all right for you not to do it?

Suppose that there were more owners of priceless vintage cars—Carol, Dave, Emma, Fred and so on, down to Ziggy—all in exactly the same situation as Bob, with their own siding and their own switch, all sacrificing the child in order to pre-serve their own cherished car. Would that make it all right for Bob to do the same? To answer this question affirmatively is to endorse follow-the-crowd ethics—the kind of ethics that led many Germans to look away when the Nazi atrocities were being committed. We do not excuse them because others were behaving no better.

We seem to lack a sound basis for drawing a clear moral line between Bob's situation and that of any reader of this article with $200 to spare who does not donate it to an overseas aid agency. These readers seem to be acting at least as badly as Bob was acting when he chose to let the runaway train hurtle toward the unsuspecting child. In the light of this conclusion, I trust that many readers will reach for the phone and donate that $200. Perhaps you should do it before reading further.

Now that you have distinguished yourself morally from people who put their vintage cars ahead of a child's life, how about treating yourself and your partner to dinner at your favorite restaurant? But wait. The money you will spend at the restaurant could also help save the lives of children overseas! True, you weren't planning to blow $200 tonight, but if you were to give up dining out just for one month, you would easily save that amount. And what is one month's dining out, compared to a child's life? There's the rub. Since there are a lot of desperately needy children in the world, there will always be another child whose life you could save for another $200. Are you therefore obliged to keep giving until you have nothing left? At what point can you stop?

Hypothetical examples can easily become farcical. Consider Bob. How far past losing the Bugatti should he go? Imagine that Bob had got his foot stuck in the track of the siding, and if he diverted the train, then before it rammed the car it would also amputate his big toe. Should he still throw the switch? What if it would amputate his foot? His entire leg?

As absurd as the Bugatti scenario gets when pushed to extremes, the point it raises is a serious one: only when the sacrifices become very significant indeed would most people be prepared to say that Bob does nothing wrong when he decides not to throw the switch. Of course, most people could be wrong; we can't decide moral issues by taking opinion polls. But consider for yourself the level of sacrifice that you would demand of Bob, and then think about how much money you would have to give away in order to make a sacrifice that is roughly equal to that. It's almost certainly much, much more than $200. For most middle-class Americans, it could easily be more like $200,000.

Isn't it counterproductive to ask people to do so much? Don't we run the risk that many will shrug their shoulders and say that morality, so conceived, is fine for saints but not for them? I accept that we are unlikely to see, in the near or even medium-term future, a world in which it is normal for wealthy Americans to give the bulk of their wealth to strangers. When it comes to praising or blaming people for what they do, we tend to use a standard that is relative to some conception of normal behavior. Comfortably off Americans who give, say, 10 percent of their income to overseas aid organizations are so far ahead of most of their equally comfortable fellow citizens that I wouldn't go out of my way to chastise them for not doing more. Nevertheless, they should be doing much more, and they are in no position to criticize Bob for failing to make the much greater sacrifice of his Bugatti.

At this point various objections may crop up. Someone may say: "If every citizen living in the affluent nations contributed his or her share I wouldn't have to make such a drastic sacrifice, because long before such levels were reached, the resources would have been there to save the lives of all those children dying from lack of food or medical care. So why should I give more than my fair share?" Another, related, objection is that the Government ought to increase its overseas aid allocations, since that would spread the burden more equitably across all taxpayers.

Yet the question of how much we ought to give is a matter to be decided in the 20
real world—and that, sadly, is a world in which we know that most people do not, and in the immediate future will not, give substantial amounts to overseas aid agencies. We know, too, that at least in the next year, the United States Government is not going to meet even the very modest United Nations–recommended target of 0.7 percent of gross national product; at the moment it lags far below that, at 0.09 percent, not even half of Japan's 0.22 percent or a tenth of Denmark's 0.97 percent. Thus, we know that the money we can give beyond that theoretical "fair share" is still going to save lives that would otherwise be lost. While the idea that no one need do more than his or her fair share is a powerful one, should it prevail if we know that others are not doing their fair share and that children will die preventable deaths unless we do more than our fair share? That would be taking fairness too far.

Thus, this ground for limiting how much we ought to give also fails. In the world as it is now, I can see no escape from the conclusion that each one of us with wealth surplus to his or her essential needs should be giving most of it to help people suffering from poverty so dire as to be life-threatening. That's right: I'm saying that you shouldn't buy that new car, take that cruise, redecorate the house or get that pricey new suit. After all, a $1,000 suit could save five children's lives.

So how does my philosophy break down in dollars and cents? An American household with an income of $50,000 spends around $30,000 annually on necessities, according to the Conference Board, a nonprofit economic research organization. Therefore, for a household bringing in $50,000 a year, donations to help the world's poor should be as close as possible to $20,000. The $30,000 required for necessities holds for higher incomes as well. So a household making $100,000 could cut a yearly check for $70,000. Again, the formula is simple: Whatever money you're spending on luxuries, not necessities, should be given away.

Now, evolutionary psychologists tell us that human nature just isn't sufficiently altruistic to make it plausible that many people will sacrifice so much for strangers. On the facts of human nature, they might be right, but they would be wrong to draw a moral conclusion from those facts. If it is the case that we ought to do things that, predictably, most of us won't do, then let's face that fact head-on. Then, if we value the life of a child more than going to fancy restaurants, the next time we dine out we will know that we could have done something better with our money. If that makes living a morally decent life extremely arduous, well, then that is the way things are. If we don't do it, then we should at least know that we are failing to live a morally decent life—not because it is good to wallow in guilt but because knowing where we should be going is the first step toward heading in that direction.

When Bob first grasped the dilemma that faced him as he stood by that railway switch, he must have thought how extraordinarily unlucky he was to be placed in a situation in which he must choose between the life of an innocent child and the sacrifice of most of his savings. But he was not unlucky at all. We are all in that situation.

QUESTIONS FOR DISCUSSION AND WRITING

1. What types of charitable donations do you or people you know make? What are the reasons for supporting these particular causes? How do they stack up against Singer's cause?

2. Singer's article opens with reference to the film *Central Station*. Later he advocates that we avoid spending money on luxuries in order to donate it to save children's lives. Is going to the movies a luxury? To what extent is Singer being morally or logically inconsistent?

3. Singer considers some of the reasons people might give to justify their not reducing their consumption of "luxuries" in order to save poor children's lives. What are those reasons? What other reasons might you or people you know offer? Speculate on why Singer does not consider them. How does his neglect of those other reasons affect his ability to persuade you as a reader?

4. One critic, Peter Berkowitz, argues (in the *New Republic*, January 2000) that Singer's example of Bob is oversimplified through *either/or* reasoning (either Bob threw the switch or he did not), through "focusing on a single moral intuition" rather than "the clash between competing moral intuitions," and through neglecting such competing values as that of "perfecting [one's] own talents," which takes time and money. Write an essay that supports Berkowitz's charges or that defends Singer from them.

5. Learn about efforts to "save children's lives" in a particular situation abroad, such as in Darfur, Ethiopia, Somalia, Bangladesh, or elsewhere. In the situation you analyze, what are the meanings of the word *save*? Write an essay describing the relief agencies' goals and accomplishments as well as the factors that inhibit the agencies' effectiveness.

MARTIN LUTHER KING JR.

Letter from Birmingham Jail

Martin Luther King Jr. (1929–1968) grew up listening to his father's and grandfather's sermons at Ebenezer Baptist Church in Atlanta. He earned a bachelor's degree in sociology at Morehouse College in 1948, a divinity degree at Crozer Theological Seminary in 1951, and a doctorate in theology at Boston University in 1955. When in December 1955 Rosa Parks refused to give up a "white" seat on a segregated bus, King became the eloquent and forceful leader of the subsequent Montgomery bus boycott. In 1957 he founded the Southern Christian Leadership Conference (SCLC) to challenge racial segregation in schools and public accommodations nationwide. King taught civil rights protesters how to practice the Gandhian doctrine of passive resistance in support of civil disobedience, a means of nonviolently breaking an unjust law in order to enact social change. King also reminded civil rights workers to protest with dignity and steady purpose in the face of segregationists' intimidation and violence.

In a letter published in the Birmingham Post-Herald, *eight white clergymen admonished King, the SCLC, and civil rights workers to wait peacefully for better conditions rather than persist in defying unjust laws. On April 12, 1963, Public Safety Commissioner Eugene "Bull" Connor arrested Dr. King for the thirteenth time, this time for "parading without a permit." From his jail cell, King wrote his "Letter from Birmingham Jail," ostensibly replying to the* Post-Herald *letter but actually addressing a national audience.*

"Letter from Birmingham Jail," revised and reprinted in King's Why We Can't Wait *(1964), is now taught not only for its ideas but also for its moving sermonic style, its sentence rhythms recalling those of Cicero and Donne, and its allusions to ideas gleaned from many cultures.*

April 16, 1963[1]

My Dear Fellow Clergymen:

While confined here in the Birmingham city jail, I came across your recent statement calling my present activities "unwise and untimely." Seldom do I pause to answer criticism of my work and ideas. If I sought to answer all the criticisms that cross my desk, my secretaries would have little time for anything other than such correspondence in the course of the day, and I would have no time for constructive work. But since I feel that you are men of genuine good will and that your

---

[1]This response to a published statement by eight fellow clergymen from Alabama (Bishop C. C. J. Carpenter, Bishop Joseph A. Durick, Rabbi Hilton L. Grafman, Bishop Paul Hardin, Bishop Holan B. Harmon, the Reverend George M. Murray, the Reverend Edward V. Ramage, and the Reverend Earl Stallings) was composed under somewhat constricting circumstances. Begun on the margins of the newspaper in which the statement appeared while I was in jail, the letter was continued on scraps of writing paper supplied by a friendly Negro trusty, and concluded on a pad my attorneys were eventually permitted to leave me. Although the text remains in substance unaltered, I have indulged in the author's prerogative of polishing it for publication.

criticisms are sincerely set forth, I want to try to answer your statement in what I hope will be patient and reasonable terms.

I think I should indicate why I am here in Birmingham, since you have been influenced by the view which argues against "outsiders coming in." I have the honor of serving as president of the Southern Christian Leadership Conference, an organization operating in every southern state, with headquarters in Atlanta, Georgia. We have some eighty-five affiliated organizations across the South, and one of them is the Alabama Christian Movement for Human Rights. Frequently we share staff, educational and financial resources with our affiliates. Several months ago the affiliate here in Birmingham asked us to be on call to engage in a nonviolent direct-action program if such were deemed necessary. We readily consented, and when the hour came we lived up to our promise. So I, along with several members of my staff, am here because I was invited here. I am here because I have organizational ties here.

But more basically, I am in Birmingham because injustice is here. Just as the prophets of the eighth century B.C. left their villages and carried their "thus saith the Lord" far beyond the boundaries of their home towns, and, just as the Apostle Paul left his village of Tarsus and carried the gospel of Jesus Christ to the far corners of the Greco-Roman world, so am I compelled to carry the gospel of freedom beyond my own home town. Like Paul, I must constantly respond to the Macedonian call for aid.

Moreover, I am cognizant of the interrelatedness of all communities and states. I cannot sit idly by in Atlanta and not be concerned about what happens in Birmingham. Injustice anywhere is a threat to justice everywhere. We are caught in an inescapable network of mutuality, tied in a single garment of destiny. Whatever affects one directly, affects all indirectly. Never again can we afford to live with the narrow, provincial "outside agitator" idea. Anyone who lives inside the United States can never be considered an outsider anywhere within its bounds.

You deplore the demonstrations taking place in Birmingham. But your statement, I am sorry to say, fails to express a similar concern for the conditions that brought about the demonstrations. I am sure that none of you would want to rest content with the superficial kind of social analysis that deals merely with effects and does not grapple with underlying causes. It is unfortunate that demonstrations are taking place in Birmingham, but it is even more unfortunate that the city's white power structure left the Negro community with no alternative.

In any nonviolent campaign there are four basic steps: collection of the facts to determine whether injustices exist; negotiation; self-purification; and direct action. We have gone through all these steps in Birmingham. There can be no gainsaying the fact that racial injustice engulfs this community. Birmingham is probably the most thoroughly segregated city in the United States. An ugly record of brutality is widely known. Negroes have experienced grossly unjust treatment in the courts. There have been more unsolved bombings of Negro homes and churches in Birmingham than in any other city in the nation. These are the hard brutal facts of the case. On the basis of these conditions, Negro leaders sought to negotiate with the city fathers. But the latter consistently refused to engage in good-faith negotiation.

Then, last September, came the opportunity to talk with leaders of Birmingham's economic community. In the course of the negotiations, certain promises were made by the merchants—for example, to remove the stores' humiliating racial signs. On the basis of these promises, the Reverend Fred Shuttlesworth and the leaders of the Alabama Christian Movement for Human Rights agreed to a moratorium on all demonstrations. As the weeks and months went by, we realized that we were the victims of a broken promise. A few signs, briefly removed, returned; the others remained.

As in so many past experiences, our hopes had been blasted, and the shadow of deep disappointment settled upon us. We had no alternative except to prepare for direct action, whereby we would present our very bodies as a means of laying our case before the conscience of the local and the national community. Mindful of the difficulties involved, we decided to undertake a process of self-purification. We began a series of workshops on nonviolence, and we repeatedly asked ourselves: "Are you able to accept blows without retaliating?" "Are you able to endure the ordeal of jail?" We decided to schedule our direct-action program for the Easter season, realizing that except for Christmas, this is the main shopping period of the year. Knowing that a strong economic-withdrawal program would be the by-product of direct action, we felt that this would be the best time to bring pressure to bear on the merchants for the needed change.

Then it occurred to us that Birmingham's mayoral election was coming up in March, and we speedily decided to postpone action until after election day. When we discovered that the Commissioner of Public Safety, Eugene "Bull" Connor, had piled up enough votes to be in the run-off, we decided again to postpone action until the day after the run-off so that the demonstrations could not be used to cloud the issues. Like many others, we waited to see Mr. Connor defeated, and to this end we endured postponement after postponement. Having aided in this community need, we felt that our direct-action program could be delayed no longer.

You may well ask: "Why direct action? Why sit-ins, marches and so forth? Isn't 10 negotiation a better path?" You are quite right in calling for negotiation. Indeed this is the very purpose of direct action. Nonviolent direct action seeks to create such a crisis and foster such a tension that a community which has constantly refused to negotiate is forced to confront the issue. It seeks so to dramatize the issue that it can no longer be ignored. My citing the creation of tension as part of the work of the nonviolent-resister may sound rather shocking. But I must confess that I am not afraid of the word "tension." I have earnestly opposed violent tension, but there is a type of nonviolent tension which is necessary for growth. Just as Socrates felt that it was necessary to create a tension in the mind so that individuals could rise from the bondage of myths and half-truths to the unfettered realm of creative analysis and objective appraisal, so must we see the need for nonviolent gadflies to create the kind of tension in society that will help men rise from the dark depths of prejudice and racism to the majestic heights of understanding and brotherhood.

The purpose of our direct-action program is to create a situation so crisis-packed that it will inevitably open the door to negotiation. I therefore concur with you in your call for negotiation. Too long has our beloved Southland been bogged down in a tragic effort to live in monologue rather than dialogue.

One of the basic points in your statement is that the action that I and my associates have taken in Birmingham is untimely. Some have asked: "Why didn't you give the new city administration time to act?" The only answer that I can give to this query is that the new Birmingham administration must be prodded about as much as the outgoing one, before it will act. We are sadly mistaken if we feel that the election of Albert Boutwell as mayor will bring the millennium to Birmingham. While Mr. Boutwell is a much more gentle person than Mr. Connor, they are both segregationists, dedicated to maintenance of the status quo. I have hope that Mr. Boutwell will be reasonable enough to see the futility of massive resistance to desegregation. But he will not see this without pressure from devotees of civil rights. My friends, I must say to you that we have not made a single gain in civil rights without determined legal and nonviolent pressure. Lamentably, it is an historical fact that privileged groups seldom give up their privileges voluntarily. Individuals may see the moral light and voluntarily give up their unjust posture; but, as Reinhold Niebuhr has reminded us, groups tend to be more immoral than individuals.

We know through painful experience that freedom is never voluntarily given by the oppressor; it must be demanded by the oppressed. Frankly, I have yet to engage in a direct-action campaign that was "well-timed" in the view of those who have not suffered unduly from the disease of segregation. For years now I have heard the word "Wait!" It rings in the ear of every Negro with piercing familiarity. This "Wait" has almost always meant "Never." We must come to see, with one of our distinguished jurists, that "justice too long delayed is justice denied."

We have waited for more than 340 years for our constitutional and God-given rights. The nations of Asia and Africa are moving with jetlike speed toward gaining political independence, but we still creep at horse-and-buggy pace toward gaining a cup of coffee at a lunch counter. Perhaps it is easy for those who have never felt the stinging darts of segregation to say, "Wait." But when you have seen vicious mobs lynch your mothers and fathers at will and drown your sisters and brothers at whim; when you have seen hate-filled policemen curse, kick, and even kill your black brothers and sisters; when you see the vast majority of your twenty million Negro brothers smothering in an airtight cage of poverty in the midst of an affluent society; when you suddenly find your tongue twisted and your speech stammering as you seek to explain to your six-year-old daughter why she can't go to the public amusement park that has just been advertised on television, and see tears welling up in her eyes when she is told that Funtown is closed to colored children, and see ominous clouds of inferiority beginning to form in her little mental sky, and see her beginning to distort her personality by developing an unconscious bitterness toward white people; when you have to concoct an answer for a five-year-old son who is asking: "Daddy, why do white people treat colored people so mean?"; when you take a cross-country drive and find it necessary to sleep night after night in the uncomfortable corners of your automobile because no motel will accept you; when you are humiliated day in and day out by nagging signs reading "white" and "colored"; when your first name becomes "nigger," your middle name becomes "boy" (however old you are), and your last name becomes "John," and your wife and mother are never given the respected title "Mrs."; when you are harried by day and haunted by night by the fact that you are a Negro, living constantly at tiptoe stance, never quite knowing what to expect next, and are plagued with inner fears and outer resentments; when you are forever fighting a degenerating sense of "nobodiness"—then you will understand why we find it difficult to wait. There comes a time when the cup of endurance runs over, and men are no longer willing to be plunged into the abyss of despair. I hope, sirs, you can understand our legitimate and unavoidable impatience.

You express a great deal of anxiety over our willingness to break laws. This is certainly a legitimate concern. Since we so diligently urge people to obey the Supreme Court's decision of 1954 outlawing segregation in the public schools, at first glance it may seem rather paradoxical for us consciously to break laws. One may well ask: "How can you advocate breaking some laws and obeying others?" The answer lies in the fact that there are two types of laws: just and unjust. I would be the first to advocate obeying just laws. One has not only a legal but a moral responsibility to obey just laws. Conversely, one has a moral responsibility to disobey unjust laws. I would agree with St. Augustine that "an unjust law is no law at all." 15

Now, what is the difference between the two? How does one determine whether a law is just or unjust? A just law is a man-made code that squares with the moral law or the law of God. An unjust law is a code that is out of harmony with the moral law. To put it in the terms of St. Thomas Aquinas: An unjust law is a human law that is not rooted in eternal law and natural law. Any law that uplifts human personality is just. Any law that degrades human personality is unjust. All segregation statutes are unjust because segregation distorts the soul and damages the personality. It gives the segregator a false sense of superiority and the segregated a false sense of inferiority. Segregation, to use the terminology of the Jewish philosopher Martin Buber, substitutes an "I-it" relationship for an "I-thou" relationship and ends up relegating persons to the status of things. Hence segregation is not only politically, economically, and sociologically unsound, it is morally wrong and sinful. Paul Tillich has said that sin is separation. Is not segregation an existential expression of man's tragic separation, his awful estrangement, his terrible sinfulness? Thus it is that I can urge men to obey the 1954 decision of the Supreme Court, for it is morally right; and I can urge them to disobey segregation ordinances, for they are morally wrong.

Let us consider a more concrete example of just and unjust laws. An unjust law is a code that a numerical or power majority group compels a minority group to obey but does not make binding on itself. This is *difference* made legal. By the same token, a just law is a code that a majority compels a minority to follow and that it is willing to follow itself. This is *sameness* made legal.

Let me give another explanation. A law is unjust if it is inflicted on a minority that, as a result of being denied the right to vote, had no part in enacting or devising the law. Who can say that the legislature of Alabama which set up that state's segregation laws was democratically elected? Throughout Alabama all sorts of devious methods are used to prevent Negroes from becoming registered voters, and there are some counties in which even though Negroes constitute a majority of the population, not a single Negro is registered. Can any law enacted under such circumstances be considered democratically structured?

Sometimes a law is just on its face and unjust in its application. For instance, I have been arrested on a charge of parading without a permit. Now, there is nothing wrong in having an ordinance which requires a permit for a parade. But such an ordinance becomes unjust when it is used to maintain segregation and to deny citizens the First-Amendment privilege of peaceful assembly and protest.

I hope you are able to see the distinction I am trying to point out. In no sense do I advocate evading or defying the law, as would the rabid segregationist. That would lead to anarchy. One who breaks an unjust law must do so openly, lovingly, and with a willingness to accept the penalty. I submit that an individual who breaks a law that conscience tells him is unjust, and who willingly accepts the penalty of imprisonment in order to arouse the conscience of the community over its injustice, is in reality expressing the highest respect for the law. 20

Of course, there is nothing new about this kind of civil disobedience. It was evidenced sublimely in the refusal of Shadrach, Meshach, and Abednego to obey the laws of Nebuchadnezzar, on the ground that a higher moral law was at stake. It was practiced superbly by the early Christians, who were willing to face hungry lions and the excruciating pain of chopping blocks rather than submit to certain unjust laws of the Roman Empire. To a degree, academic freedom is a reality today because Socrates practiced civil disobedience. In our own nation, the Boston Tea Party represented a massive act of civil disobedience.

We should never forget that everything Adolf Hitler did in Germany was "legal" and everything the Hungarian freedom fighters did in Hungary was "illegal." It was "illegal" to aid and comfort a Jew in Hitler's Germany. Even so, I am sure that, had I lived in Germany at the time, I would have aided and comforted my Jewish brothers. If today I lived in a Communist country where certain principles dear to the Christian faith are suppressed, I would openly advocate disobeying that country's anti-religious laws.

I must make two honest confessions to you, my Christian and Jewish brothers. First, I must confess that over the past few years I have been gravely disappointed with the white moderate. I have almost reached the regrettable conclusion that the Negro's great stumbling block in his stride toward freedom is not the White Citizen's Counciler or the Ku Klux Klanner, but the white moderate, who is more devoted to "order" than to justice; who prefers a negative peace which is the absence of tension to a positive peace which is the presence of justice; who constantly says: "I agree with you in the goal you seek, but I cannot agree with your methods of direct action"; who paternalistically believes he can set the timetable for another man's freedom; who lives by a mythical concept of time and who constantly advises the Negro to wait for a "more convenient season." Shallow understanding from people of good will is more frustrating than absolute misunderstanding from people of ill will. Lukewarm acceptance is much more bewildering than outright rejection.

I had hoped that the white moderate would understand that law and order exist for the purpose of establishing justice and that when they fail in this purpose they become the dangerously structured dams that block the flow of social progress. I had hoped that the white moderate would understand that the present tension in the South is a necessary phase of the transition from an obnoxious negative peace, in which the Negro passively accepted his unjust plight, to a substantive and positive peace, in which all men will respect the dignity and worth of human personality. Actually, we who engage in nonviolent direct action are not the creators of tension. We merely bring to the surface the hidden tension that is already alive. We bring it out in the open, where it can be seen and dealt with. Like a boil that can never be cured so long as it is covered up but must be opened with all its ugliness to the natural medicines of air and light, injustice must be exposed, with all the tension its exposure creates, to the light of human conscience and the air of national opinion before it can be cured.

In your statement you assert that our actions, even though peaceful, must be 25 condemned because they precipitate violence. But is this a logical assertion? Isn't this like condemning a robbed man because his possession of money precipitated the evil act of robbery? Isn't this like condemning Socrates because his unswerving commitment to truth and his philosophical inquiries precipitated the act by the misguided populace in which they made him drink hemlock? Isn't this like condemning Jesus because his unique God-consciousness and never-ceasing devotion to God's will precipitated the evil act of crucifixion? We must come to see that, as the federal courts have consistently affirmed, it is wrong to urge an individual to cease his efforts to gain his basic constitutional rights because the quest may precipitate violence. Society must protect the robbed and punish the robber.

I had also hoped that the white moderate would reject the myth concerning time in relation to the struggle for freedom. I have just received a letter from a white brother in Texas. He writes: "All Christians know that the colored people will receive equal rights eventually, but it is possible that you are in too great a religious hurry. It has taken Christianity almost two thousand years to accomplish what it has. The teachings of Christ take time to come to earth." Such an attitude stems from a tragic misconception of time, from the strangely irrational notion that there is something in the very flow of time that will inevitably cure all ills. Actually, time itself is neutral; it can be used either destructively or constructively. More and more I feel that the people of ill will have used time much more effectively than have the people of good will. We will have to repent in this generation not merely for the hateful words and actions of the bad people but for the appalling silence of the good people. Human progress never rolls in on wheels of inevitability; it comes through the tireless efforts of men willing to be co-workers with God, and without this hard work, time itself becomes an ally of the forces of social stagnation. We must use time creatively, in the knowledge that the time is always ripe to do right. Now is the time to make real the promise of democracy and transform our pending national elegy into a creative psalm of brotherhood. Now is the time to lift our national policy from the quicksand of racial injustice to the solid rock of human dignity.

You speak of our activity in Birmingham as extreme. At first I was rather disappointed that fellow clergymen would see my nonviolent efforts as those of an extremist. I began thinking about the fact that I stand in the middle of two opposing forces in the Negro community. One is a force of complacency, made up in part of Negroes who, as a result of long years of oppression, are so drained of self-respect and a sense of "somebodiness" that they have adjusted to segregation; and in part of a few middle-class Negroes who, because of a degree of academic and economic security and because in some ways they profit by segregation, have become insensitive to the problems of the masses. The other force is one of bitterness and hatred, and it comes perilously close to advocating violence. It is expressed in the various black nationalist groups that are springing up across the nation, the largest and best-known being Elijah Muhammad's Muslim movement. Nourished by the Negro's frustration over the continued existence of racial discrimination, this movement is made up of people who have lost faith in America, who have absolutely repudiated Christianity, and who have concluded that the white man is an incorrigible "devil."

I have tried to stand between these two forces, saying that we need emulate neither the "do-nothingism" of the complacent nor the hatred and despair of the black nationalist. For there is the more excellent way of love and nonviolent protest. I am grateful to God that, through the influence of the Negro church, the way of nonviolence became an integral part of our struggle.

If this philosophy had not emerged, by now many streets of the South would, I am convinced, be flowing with blood. And I am further convinced that if our white brothers dismiss as "rabble-rousers" and "outside agitators" those of us who employ nonviolent direct action, and if they refuse to support our nonviolent efforts, millions of Negroes will, out of frustration and despair, seek solace and security in black-nationalist ideologies—a development that would inevitably lead to a frightening racial nightmare.

Oppressed people cannot remain oppressed forever. The yearning for freedom 30 eventually manifests itself, and that is what has happened to the American Negro. Something within has reminded him of his birthright of freedom, and something without has reminded him that it can be gained. Consciously or unconsciously, he has been caught up by the *Zeitgeist*, and with his black brothers of Africa and his brown and yellow brothers of Asia, South America, and the Caribbean, the United States Negro is moving with a sense of great urgency toward the promised land of racial justice. If one recognizes this vital urge that has engulfed the Negro community, one should readily understand why public demonstrations are taking place. The Negro has many pent-up resentments and latent frustrations, and he must release them. So let him march; let him make prayer pilgrimages to the city hall; let him go on freedom rides—and try to understand why he must do so. If his repressed emotions are not released in nonviolent ways, they will seek expression through violence; this is not a threat but a fact of history. So I have not said to my people: "Get rid of your discontent." Rather, I have tried to say that this normal and healthy discontent can be channeled into the creative outlet of nonviolent direct action. And now this approach is being termed extremist.

But though I was initially disappointed at being categorized as an extremist, as I continued to think about the matter I gradually gained a measure of satisfaction from the label. Was not Jesus an extremist for love: "Love your enemies, bless them that curse you, do good to them that hate you, and pray for them which despitefully use you, and persecute you." Was not Amos an extremist for justice: "Let justice roll down like waters and righteousness like an ever-flowing stream." Was not Paul an extremist for the Christian gospel: "I bear in my body the marks of the Lord Jesus." Was not Martin Luther an extremist: "Here I stand; I cannot do otherwise, so help me God." And John Bunyan: "I will stay in jail to the end of my days before I make a butchery of my conscience." And Abraham Lincoln: "This nation cannot survive half slave and half free." And Thomas Jefferson: "We hold these truths to be self-evident, that all men are created equal. . . ." So the question is not whether we will be extremists, but what kind of extremists we will be. Will we be extremists for hate or for love? Will we be extremists for the preservation of injustice or for the extension of justice? In that dramatic scene on Calvary's hill three men were crucified. We must never forget that all three were crucified for the same crime—the crime of extremism. Two were extremists for immorality, and thus fell below their environment. The other, Jesus Christ, was an extremist for love, truth, and goodness, and thereby rose above his environment. Perhaps the South, the nation, and the world are in dire need of creative extremists.

I had hoped that the white moderate would see this need. Perhaps I was too optimistic; perhaps I expected too much. I suppose I should have realized that few members of the oppressor race can understand the deep groans and passionate yearnings of the oppressed race, and still fewer have the vision to see that injustice must be rooted out by strong, persistent, and determined action. I am thankful, however, that some of our white brothers in the South have grasped the meaning of this social revolution and committed themselves to it. They are still all too few in quantity, but they are big in quality. Some—such as Ralph McGill, Lillian Smith, Harry Golden, James McBride Dabbs, Ann Braden, and Sarah Patton Boyle—have written about our struggle in eloquent and prophetic terms. Others have marched with us down nameless streets of the South. They have languished in filthy, roach-infested jails, suffering the abuse and brutality of policemen who view them as "dirty nigger-lovers." Unlike so many of their moderate brothers and sisters, they have recognized the urgency of the moment and sensed the need for powerful "action" antidotes to combat the disease of segregation.

Let me take note of my other major disappointment. I have been so greatly disappointed with the white church and its leadership. Of course, there are some notable exceptions. I am not unmindful of the fact that each of you has taken some significant stands on this issue. I commend you, Reverend Stallings, for your Christian stand on this past Sunday, in welcoming Negroes to your worship service on a nonsegregated basis. I commend the Catholic leaders of this state for integrating Spring Hill College several years ago.

But despite these notable exceptions, I must honestly reiterate that I have been disappointed with the church. I do not say this as one of those negative critics who can always find something wrong with the church. I say this as a minister of the gospel, who loves the church; who was nurtured in its bosom; who has been sustained by its spiritual blessings and who will remain true to it as long as the cord of life shall lengthen.

When I was suddenly catapulted into the leadership of the bus protest in   35 Montgomery, Alabama, a few years ago, I felt we would be supported by the white church. I felt that the white ministers, priests, and rabbis of the South would be among our strongest allies. Instead, some have been outright opponents, refusing to understand the freedom movement and misrepresenting its leaders; all too many others have been more cautious than courageous and have remained silent behind the anesthetizing security of stained-glass windows.

In spite of my shattered dreams, I came to Birmingham with the hope that the white religious leadership of this community would see the justice of our cause and, with deep moral concern, would serve as the channel through which our just grievances could reach the power structure. I had hoped that each of you would understand. But again I have been disappointed.

I have heard numerous southern religious leaders admonish their worshipers to comply with a desegregation decision because it is the law, but I have longed to hear white ministers declare: "Follow this decree because integration is morally right and because the Negro is your brother." In the midst of blatant injustices inflicted upon the Negro, I have watched white churchmen stand on the sideline and mouth pious irrelevancies and sanctimonious trivialities. In the midst of a mighty struggle to rid our nation of racial and economic injustice, I have heard many ministers say: "Those are social issues, with which the gospel has no real concern." And I have watched many churches commit themselves to a completely other-worldly religion which makes a strange, un-Biblical distinction between body and soul, between the sacred and the secular.

I have traveled the length and breadth of Alabama, Mississippi, and all the other southern states. On sweltering summer days and crisp autumn mornings I have looked at the South's beautiful churches with their lofty spires pointing heavenward. I have beheld the impressive outlines of her massive religious-education buildings. Over and over I have found myself asking: "What kind of people worship here? Who is their God? Where were their voices when the lips of Governor Barnett dripped with words of interposition and nullification? Where were they when Governor Wallace gave a clarion call for defiance and hatred? Where were their voices of support when bruised and weary Negro men and women decided to rise from the dark dungeons of complacency to the bright hills of creative protest?"

Yes, these questions are still in my mind. In deep disappointment I have wept over the laxity of the church. But be assured that my tears have been tears of love. There can be no deep disappointment where there is not deep love. Yes, I love the church. How could I do otherwise? I am in the rather unique position of being the son, the grandson, and the great-grandson of preachers. Yes, I see the church as the body of Christ. But, oh! How we have blemished and scarred that body through social neglect and through fear of being nonconformists.

There was a time when the church was very powerful—in the time when the 40 early Christians rejoiced at being deemed worthy to suffer for what they believed. In those days the church was not merely a thermometer that recorded the ideas and principles of popular opinion; it was a thermostat that transformed the mores of society. Whenever the early Christians entered a town, the people in power became disturbed and immediately sought to convict the Christians for being "disturbers of the peace" and "outside agitators." But the Christians pressed on, in the conviction that they were "a colony of heaven," called to obey God rather than man. Small in number, they were big in commitment. They were too God-intoxicated to be "astronomically intimidated." By their effort and example they brought an end to such ancient evils as infanticide and gladiatorial contests.

Things are different now. So often the contemporary church is a weak, ineffectual voice with an uncertain sound. So often it is an archdefender of the status quo. Far from being disturbed by the presence of the church, the power structure of the average community is consoled by the church's silent—and often even vocal— sanction of things as they are.

But the judgment of God is upon the church as never before. If today's church does not recapture the sacrificial spirit of the early church, it will lose its authenticity, forfeit the loyalty of millions, and be dismissed as an irrelevant social club with no meaning for the twentieth century. Every day I meet young people whose disappointment with the church has turned into outright disgust.

Perhaps I have once again been too optimistic. Is organized religion too inextricably bound to the status quo to save our nation and the world? Perhaps I must turn my faith to the inner spiritual church, the church within the church, as the true *ekklesia* and the hope of the world. But again I am thankful to God that some noble souls from the ranks of organized religion have broken loose from the paralyzing chains of conformity and joined us as active partners in the struggle for freedom. They have left their secure congregations and walked the streets of Albany, Georgia, with us. They have gone down the highways of the South on tortuous rides for freedom. Yes, they have gone to jail with us. Some have been dismissed from their churches, have lost the support of their bishops and fellow ministers. But they have acted in the faith that right defeated is stronger than evil triumphant. Their witness has been the spiritual salt that has preserved the true meaning of the gospel in these troubled times. They have carved a tunnel of hope through the dark mountain of disappointment.

I hope the church as a whole will meet the challenge of this decisive hour. But even if the church does not come to the aid of justice, I have no despair about the future. I have no fear about the outcome of our struggle in Birmingham, even if our motives are at present misunderstood. We will reach the goal of freedom in Birmingham and all over the nation, because the goal of America is freedom. Abused and scorned though we may be, our destiny is tied up with America's destiny. Before the pilgrims landed at Plymouth, we were here. Before the pen of Jefferson etched the majestic words of the Declaration of Independence across the pages of history, we were here. For more than two centuries our forebears labored in this country without wages; they made cotton king; they built the homes of their masters while suffering gross injustice and shameful humiliation—and yet out of a bottomless vitality they continued to thrive and develop.

If the inexpressible cruelties of slavery could not stop us, the opposition we now face will surely fail. We will win our freedom because the sacred heritage of our nation and the eternal will of God are embodied in our echoing demands.

Before closing I feel impelled to mention one other point in your statement 45 that has troubled me profoundly. You warmly commended the Birmingham police force for keeping "order" and "preventing violence." I doubt that you would have so warmly commended the police force if you had seen its dogs sinking their teeth into unarmed, nonviolent Negroes. I doubt that you would so quickly commend the policemen if you were to observe their ugly and inhumane treatment of Negroes here in the city jail; if you were to watch them push and curse old Negro women and young Negro girls; if you were to see them slap and kick old Negro men and young boys; if you were to observe them as they did on two occasions, refuse to give us food because we wanted to sing our grace together. I cannot join you in your praise of the Birmingham police department.

It is true that the police have exercised a degree of discipline in handling the demonstrators. In this sense they have conducted themselves rather "nonviolently" in public. But for what purpose? To preserve the evil system of segregation. Over the past few years I have consistently preached that nonviolence demands that the means we use must be as pure as the ends we seek. I have tried to make clear that it is wrong to use immoral means to attain moral ends. But now I must affirm that it is just as wrong, or perhaps even more so, to use moral means to preserve immoral ends. Perhaps Mr. Connor and his policemen have been rather nonviolent in public, as was Chief Pritchett in Albany, Georgia, but they have used the moral means of nonviolence to maintain the immoral end of racial injustice. As T. S. Eliot has said: "The last temptation is the greatest treason: To do the right deed for the wrong reason."

I wish you had commended the Negro sit-inners and demonstrators of Birmingham for their sublime courage, their willingness to suffer, and their amazing discipline in the midst of great provocation. One day the South will recognize its real heroes. They will be the James Merediths, with the noble sense of purpose that enables them to face jeering and hostile mobs, and with the agonizing loneliness that characterizes the life of the pioneer. They will be old, oppressed, battered Negro women, symbolized in a seventy-two-year-old woman in Montgomery, Alabama, who rose up with a sense of dignity and with her people decided not to ride segregated buses, and who responded with ungrammatical profundity to one who inquired about her weariness: "My feet is tired, but my soul is at rest." They will be the young high school and college students, the young ministers of the gospel and a host of their elders, courageously and nonviolently sitting in at lunch counters and willingly going to jail for conscience' sake. One day the South will know that when these disinherited children of God sat down at lunch counters, they were in reality standing up for what is best in the American dream and for the most sacred values in our Judaeo-Christian heritage, thereby bringing our nation back to those great wells of democracy which were dug deep by the founding fathers in their formulation of the Constitution and the Declaration of Independence.

Never before have I written so long a letter. I'm afraid it is much too long to take your precious time. I can assure you that it would have been much shorter if I had been writing from a comfortable desk, but what else can one do when he is alone in a narrow jail cell, other than write long letters, think long thoughts, and pray long prayers?

If I have said anything in this letter that overstates the truth and indicates an unreasonable impatience, I beg you to forgive me. If I have said anything that understates the truth and indicates my having a patience that allows me to settle for anything less than brotherhood, I beg God to forgive me.

I hope this letter finds you strong in faith. I also hope that circumstances will   50 soon make it possible for me to meet each of you, not as an integrationist or a civil-rights leader but as a fellow clergyman and a Christian brother. Let us all hope that the dark clouds of racial prejudice will soon pass away and the deep fog of misunderstanding will be lifted from our fear-drenched communities, and in some not too distant tomorrow the radiant stars of love and brotherhood will shine over our great nation with all their scintillating beauty.

Yours for the cause of Peace and Brotherhood,
Martin Luther King Jr.

QUESTIONS FOR DISCUSSION AND WRITING

1. In paragraphs 27–32 of "Letter from Birmingham Jail," King answers charges that his actions are "extreme." What does *extreme* mean for King in the context of civil rights demonstrations? Consider various contemporary connotations of *extreme*, as in extreme risk, extreme strength, extreme sports, extreme brutality. Is there a common core of the meaning of *extreme* in these contexts? Are there significant differences? In what ways do these definitions resemble or differ from Dr. King's usage?

2. On what grounds does King defend extremism (paragraphs 27–31), and how extreme does he think he actually is? Who is more radical than King, and in what ways?

3. What does King mean by "direct action" (paragraph 6)? Provide some examples of what this might mean.

4. King distinguishes between just laws and unjust laws. On what basis does he make this distinction? Do you agree with it? Can you cite examples of laws—in the United States or elsewhere—that you consider "unjust"?

UNITED NATIONS

The Universal Declaration of Human Rights

After the cataclysm of World War II ended in 1945, the United Nations was founded to promote world peace and international cooperation in dealing with not only the immediate aftermath of the war, but with humanitarian, social, and economic issues more generally. Planning began in 1939 during U.S. President Franklin D. Roosevelt's administration, and the first session of the General Assembly was held on October 24, 1945, with 51 member nations participating. That number has increased to 192 nations today, virtually every sovereign state in the world. The work of the UN's major administrative bodies—the General Assembly, the Security Council, the Economic and Social Council, the Secretariat, and the International Court of Justice—has, like the rest of international politics, been full of controversy and disagreement throughout its nearly seventy-year history. Nevertheless, the members embraced the principle that the UN had a strong commitment to preventing a repetition of World War II's atrocities and genocide, "barbarous acts which have outraged the conscience of mankind" (Preamble). This consensus led the General Assembly to adopt the Universal Declaration of Human Rights on December 10, 1948, a major statement affirming UN principles to promote "a world in which human beings shall enjoy freedom of speech and belief and freedom from fear and want." Although not legally binding for the member nations, this document, reprinted in full below, is a simple, eloquent statement of the ideal principles of human relations and human rights, the foundational basis of individual, family, and social life which transcends time, nationality, and culture for the betterment of all.

PREAMBLE

Whereas recognition of the inherent dignity and of the equal and inalienable rights of all members of the human family is the foundation of freedom, justice and peace in the world,

Whereas disregard and contempt for human rights have resulted in barbarous acts which have outraged the conscience of mankind, and the advent of a world in which human beings shall enjoy freedom of speech and belief and freedom from fear and want has been proclaimed as the highest aspiration of the common people,

Whereas it is essential, if man is not to be compelled to have recourse, as a last resort, to rebellion against tyranny and oppression, that human rights should be protected by the rule of law,

Whereas it is essential to promote the development of friendly relations between nations,

Whereas the peoples of the United Nations have in the Charter reaffirmed their faith in fundamental human rights, in the dignity and worth of the human person and in the equal rights of men and women and have determined to promote social progress and better standards of life in larger freedom,

Whereas Member States have pledged themselves to achieve, in co-operation with the United Nations, the promotion of universal respect for and observance of human rights and fundamental freedoms,

Whereas a common understanding of these rights and freedoms is of the greatest importance for the full realization of this pledge,

Now, Therefore THE GENERAL ASSEMBLY proclaims THIS UNIVERSAL DECLARATION OF HUMAN RIGHTS as a common standard of achievement for all peoples and all nations, to the end that every individual and every organ of society, keeping this Declaration constantly in mind, shall strive by teaching and education to promote respect for these rights and freedoms and by progressive measures, national and international, to secure their universal and effective recognition and observance, both among the peoples of Member States themselves and among the peoples of territories under their jurisdiction.

Article 1.
All human beings are born free and equal in dignity and rights. They are endowed with reason and conscience and should act towards one another in a spirit of brotherhood.

Article 2.
Everyone is entitled to all the rights and freedoms set forth in this Declaration, without distinction of any kind, such as race, colour, sex, language, religion, political or other opinion, national or social origin, property, birth or other status. Furthermore, no distinction shall be made on the basis of the political, jurisdictional or international status of the country or territory to which a person belongs, whether it be independent, trust, non-self-governing or under any other limitation of sovereignty.

Article 3.
Everyone has the right to life, liberty and security of person.

Article 4.
No one shall be held in slavery or servitude; slavery and the slave trade shall be prohibited in all their forms.

Article 5.
No one shall be subjected to torture or to cruel, inhuman or degrading treatment or punishment.

Article 6.
Everyone has the right to recognition everywhere as a person before the law.

Article 7.
All are equal before the law and are entitled without any discrimination to equal protection of the law. All are entitled to equal protection against any discrimination in violation of this Declaration and against any incitement to such discrimination.

Article 8.
Everyone has the right to an effective remedy by the competent national tribunals for acts violating the fundamental rights granted him by the constitution or by law.

Article 9.
No one shall be subjected to arbitrary arrest, detention or exile.

Article 10.
Everyone is entitled in full equality to a fair and public hearing by an independent and impartial tribunal, in the determination of his rights and obligations and of any criminal charge against him.

Article 11.
(1) Everyone charged with a penal offence has the right to be presumed innocent until proved guilty according to law in a public trial at which he has had all the guarantees necessary for his defence.
(2) No one shall be held guilty of any penal offence on account of any act or omission which did not constitute a penal offence, under national or international law, at the time when it was committed. Nor shall a heavier penalty be imposed than the one that was applicable at the time the penal offence was committed.

Article 12.
No one shall be subjected to arbitrary interference with his privacy, family, home or correspondence, nor to attacks upon his honour and reputation. Everyone has the right to the protection of the law against such interference or attacks.

Article 13.
(1) Everyone has the right to freedom of movement and residence within the borders of each state.
(2) Everyone has the right to leave any country, including his own, and to return to his country.

Article 14.
(1) Everyone has the right to seek and to enjoy in other countries asylum from persecution.
(2) This right may not be invoked in the case of prosecutions genuinely arising from non-political crimes or from acts contrary to the purposes and principles of the United Nations.

Article 15.
(1) Everyone has the right to a nationality.
(2) No one shall be arbitrarily deprived of his nationality nor denied the right to change his nationality.

Article 16.
(1) Men and women of full age, without any limitation due to race, nationality or religion, have the right to marry and to found a family. They are entitled to equal rights as to marriage, during marriage and at its dissolution.
(2) Marriage shall be entered into only with the free and full consent of the intending spouses.

(3) The family is the natural and fundamental group unit of society and is entitled to protection by society and the State.

Article 17.
(1) Everyone has the right to own property alone as well as in association with others.
(2) No one shall be arbitrarily deprived of his property.

Article 18.
Everyone has the right to freedom of thought, conscience and religion; this right includes freedom to change his religion or belief, and freedom, either alone or in community with others and in public or private, to manifest his religion or belief in teaching, practice, worship and observance.

Article 19.
Everyone has the right to freedom of opinion and expression; this right includes freedom to hold opinions without interference and to seek, receive and impart information and ideas through any media and regardless of frontiers.

Article 20.
(1) Everyone has the right to freedom of peaceful assembly and association.
(2) No one may be compelled to belong to an association.

Article 21.
(1) Everyone has the right to take part in the government of his country, directly or through freely chosen representatives.
(2) Everyone has the right of equal access to public service in his country.
(3) The will of the people shall be the basis of the authority of government; this will shall be expressed in periodic and genuine elections which shall be by universal and equal suffrage and shall be held by secret vote or by equivalent free voting procedures.

Article 22.
Everyone, as a member of society, has the right to social security and is entitled to realization, through national effort and international co-operation and in accordance with the organization and resources of each State, of the economic, social and cultural rights indispensable for his dignity and the free development of his personality.

Article 23.
(1) Everyone has the right to work, to free choice of employment, to just and favourable conditions of work and to protection against unemployment.

(2) Everyone, without any discrimination, has the right to equal pay for equal work.

(3) Everyone who works has the right to just and favourable remuneration ensuring for himself and his family an existence worthy of human dignity, and supplemented, if necessary, by other means of social protection.

(4) Everyone has the right to form and to join trade unions for the protection of his interests.

Article 24.
Everyone has the right to rest and leisure, including reasonable limitation of working hours and periodic holidays with pay.

Article 25.
(1) Everyone has the right to a standard of living adequate for the health and well-being of himself and of his family, including food, clothing, housing and medical care and necessary social services, and the right to security in the event of unemployment, sickness, disability, widowhood, old age or other lack of livelihood in circumstances beyond his control.

(2) Motherhood and childhood are entitled to special care and assistance. All children, whether born in or out of wedlock, shall enjoy the same social protection.

Article 26.
(1) Everyone has the right to education. Education shall be free, at least in the elementary and fundamental stages. Elementary education shall be compulsory. Technical and professional education shall be made generally available and higher education shall be equally accessible to all on the basis of merit.

(2) Education shall be directed to the full development of the human personality and to the strengthening of respect for human rights and fundamental freedoms. It shall promote understanding, tolerance and friendship among all nations, racial or religious groups, and shall further the activities of the United Nations for the maintenance of peace.

(3) Parents have a prior right to choose the kind of education that shall be given to their children.

Article 27.
(1) Everyone has the right freely to participate in the cultural life of the community, to enjoy the arts and to share in scientific advancement and its benefits.

(2) Everyone has the right to the protection of the moral and material interests resulting from any scientific, literary or artistic production of which he is the author.

Article 28.

Everyone is entitled to a social and international order in which the rights and freedoms set forth in this Declaration can be fully realized.

Article 29.

(1) Everyone has duties to the community in which alone the free and full development of his personality is possible.

(2) In the exercise of his rights and freedoms, everyone shall be subject only to such limitations as are determined by law solely for the purpose of securing due recognition and respect for the rights and freedoms of others and of meeting the just requirements of morality, public order and the general welfare in a democratic society.

(3) These rights and freedoms may in no case be exercised contrary to the purposes and principles of the United Nations.

Article 30.

Nothing in this Declaration may be interpreted as implying for any State, group or person any right to engage in any activity or to perform any act aimed at the destruction of any of the rights and freedoms set forth herein.

QUESTIONS FOR DISCUSSION AND WRITING

1. The Preamble opens with the assertion that "the recognition of the inherent dignity and of the equal and inalienable rights of all members of the human family is the foundation of freedom, justice and peace in the world." What are the connections between fundamental human rights and "freedom, justice, and peace"?

2. The first twenty-nine articles of the Universal Declaration assert, in simple language, a comprehensive list of human rights. Identify some of the most significant. Or are they all of equal significance? Why are those you have chosen so important?

3. What ethical principles does the Universal Declaration of Human Rights embody?

4. In discussion and perhaps a paper written by yourself or with a partner, analyze the gap between the ideal of a human right and the reality of its application in a particular part of the world with which you are familiar, for instance, Article 25.1: "Everyone has the right to a standard of living adequate for the health and well-being of himself and of his family, including food, clothing, housing and medical care and necessary social services, and the right to security in the event of unemployment, sickness, disability, widowhood, old age or other lack of livelihood in circumstances beyond his control."

5. Imagine a worst-case scenario in which one of the human rights in this Declaration was absent, as in fact is often the case worldwide. What are the likely consequences, in political, economic, ethical, human terms?

GEORGE ORWELL

Shooting an Elephant

George Orwell (1903–1950) is best known for his anti-totalitarian novels, Animal Farm *(1945) and* 1984 *(1949). He was born Eric Arthur Blair in Bengal (now Bihar), India, where his father worked in the colonial civil service. Orwell was educated at Eton and served with the Indian Imperial Police in Burma, now Myanmar. Orwell writes of his frustration with racial and social barriers there in his novel* Burmese Days *(1934) and in his essay "Shooting an Elephant" (1936). In 1928 he committed himself to a life of hardship among Europe's poor and wrote* Down and Out in Paris and London *(1933) about his drudgery and near-starvation as a restaurant kitchen worker and as a tramp. In* The Road to Wigan Pier *(1937), he describes the harrowing lives of unemployed coal miners in Lancashire; and in* Homage to Catalonia *(1938), he writes of his fighting in 1936–1937 against the Communists in the Spanish Civil War. Rejected for military service in World War II, Orwell worked as a war correspondent for the BBC and the* Observer *until his death from tuberculosis in 1950. Orwell's political liberalism and his precise language and ability to tell vivid stories have made his essays widely anthologized.*

In Moulmein, in lower Burma, I was hated by large numbers of people—the only time in my life that I have been important enough for this to happen to me. I was [a] sub-divisional police officer of the town, and in an aimless, petty kind of way anti-European feeling was very bitter. No one had the guts to raise a riot, but if a European woman went through the bazaars alone somebody would probably spit betel juice over her dress. As a police officer I was an obvious target and was baited whenever it seemed safe to do so. When a nimble Burman tripped me up on the football field and the referee (another Burman) looked the other way, the crowd yelled with hideous laughter. This happened more than once. In the end the sneering yellow faces of young men that met me everywhere, the insults hooted after me when I was at a safe distance, got badly on my nerves. The young Buddhist priests were the worst of all. There were several thousands of them in the town and none of them seemed to have anything to do except stand on street corners and jeer at Europeans.

All this was perplexing and upsetting. For at that time I had already made up my mind that imperialism was an evil thing and the sooner I chucked up my job and got out of it the better. Theoretically—and secretly, of course—I was all for the Burmese and all against their oppressors, the British. As for the job I was doing, I hated it more bitterly than I can perhaps make clear. In a job like that you see the dirty work of Empire at close quarters. The wretched prisoners huddling in the stinking cages of the lock-ups, the grey, cowed faces of the long-term convicts, the scarred buttocks of the men who had been flogged with bamboos—all these oppressed me with an intolerable sense of guilt. But I could get nothing into perspective. I was young and ill-educated and I had had to think out my problems in the utter silence that is imposed on every Englishman in the East. I did not even know that the British Empire is dying, still less did I know that it is a great deal better than the younger empires that are going to supplant it. All I knew was that I was stuck between my hatred of the empire I served and my rage against the evil-spirited little beasts who tried to make my job impossible. With one part of my mind I thought of the British Raj as an unbreakable tyranny, as something clamped down, *in saecula saeculorum*, upon the will of prostrate peoples; with another part I thought that the greatest joy in the world would be to drive a bayonet into a Buddhist priest's guts. Feelings like these are the normal by-products of imperialism; ask any Anglo-Indian official, if you can catch him off duty.

One day something happened which in a roundabout way was enlightening. It was a tiny incident in itself, but it gave me a better glimpse than I had had before of the real nature of imperialism—the real motives for which despotic governments act. Early one morning the sub-inspector at a police station the other end of the town rang me up on the 'phone and said that an elephant was ravaging the bazaar. Would I please come and do something about it? I did not know what I could do, but I wanted to see what was happening and I got on to a pony and started out. I took my rifle, an old .44 Winchester and much too small to kill an elephant, but I thought the noise might be useful *in terrorem*. Various Burmans stopped me on the way and told me about the elephant's doings. It was not, of course, a wild elephant, but a tame one which had gone "must." It had been chained up, as tame elephants always are when their attack of "must" is due, but on the previous night it had broken its chain and escaped. Its mahout, the only person who could manage it when it was in that state, had set out in pursuit, but had taken the wrong direction and was now twelve hours' journey away, and in the morning the elephant had suddenly reappeared in the town. The Burmese population had no weapons and were quite helpless against it. It had already destroyed somebody's bamboo hut, killed a cow and raided some fruit-stalls and devoured the stock; also it had met the municipal rubbish van and, when the driver jumped out and took to his heels, had turned the van over and inflicted violences upon it.

The Burmese sub-inspector and some Indian constables were waiting for me in the quarter where the elephant had been seen. It was a very poor quarter, a labyrinth of squalid bamboo huts, thatched with palm-leaf, winding all over a steep hillside. I remember that it was a cloudy, stuffy morning at the beginning of the rains. We began questioning the people as to where the elephant had gone and, as usual, failed to get any definite information. That is invariably the case in the East; a story always sounds clear enough at a distance, but the nearer you get to the scene of events the vaguer it becomes. Some of the people said that the elephant had gone in one direction, some said that he had gone in another, some professed not even to have heard of any elephant. I had almost made up my mind that the whole story was a pack of lies, when we heard yells a little distance away. There was a loud, scandalized cry of "Go away, child! Go away this instant!" and an old woman with a switch in her hand came round the corner of a hut, violently shooing away a crowd of naked children. Some more women followed, clicking their tongues and exclaiming; evidently there was something that the children ought not to have seen. I rounded the hut and saw a man's dead body sprawling in the mud. He was an Indian, a black Dravidian coolie, almost naked, and he could not have been dead many minutes. The people said that the elephant had come suddenly upon him round the corner of the hut, caught him with its trunk, put its foot on his back and ground him into the earth. This was the rainy season and the ground was soft, and his face had scored a trench a foot deep and a couple of yards long. He was lying on his belly with arms crucified and head sharply twisted to one side. His face was coated with mud, the eyes wide open, the teeth bared and grinning with an expression of unendurable agony. (Never tell me, by the way, that the dead look peaceful. Most of the corpses I have seen looked devilish.) The friction of the great beast's foot had stripped the skin from his back as neatly as one skins a rabbit. As soon as I saw the dead man I sent an orderly to a friend's house nearby to borrow an elephant rifle. I had already sent back the pony, not wanting it to go mad with fright and throw me if it smelt the elephant.

The orderly came back in a few minutes with a rifle and five cartridges, and 5 meanwhile some Burmans had arrived and told us that the elephant was in the paddy fields below, only a few hundred yards away. As I started forward practically the whole population of the quarter flocked out of the houses and followed me. They had seen the rifle and were all shouting excitedly that I was going to shoot the elephant. They had not shown much interest in the elephant when he was merely ravaging their homes, but it was different now that he was going to be shot. It was a bit of fun to them, as it would be to an English crowd; besides they wanted the meat. It made me vaguely uneasy. I had no intention of shooting the elephant—I had merely sent for the rifle to defend myself if necessary—and it is always unnerving to have a crowd following you. I marched down the hill, looking and feeling a fool, with the rifle over my shoulder and an ever-growing army of people jostling at my heels. At the bottom, when you got away from the huts, there was a metalled road and beyond that a miry waste of paddy fields a thousand yards across, not yet ploughed but soggy from the first rains and dotted with coarse grass. The elephant was standing eight yards from the road, his left side towards us. He took not the slightest notice of the crowd's approach. He was tearing up bunches of grass, beating them against his knees to clean them and stuffing them into his mouth.

I had halted on the road. As soon as I saw the elephant I knew with perfect certainty that I ought not to shoot him. It is a serious matter to shoot a working elephant—it is comparable to destroying a huge and costly piece of machinery—and obviously one ought not to do it if it can possibly be avoided. And at that distance, peacefully eating, the elephant looked no more dangerous than a cow. I thought then and I think now that his attack of "must" was already passing off; in which case he would merely wander harmlessly about until the mahout came back and caught him. Moreover, I did not in the least want to shoot him. I decided that I would watch him for a little while to make sure that he did not turn savage again, and then go home.

But at that moment I glanced round at the crowd that had followed me. It was an immense crowd, two thousand at the least and growing every minute. It blocked the road for a long distance on either side. I looked at the sea of yellow faces above the garish clothes—faces all happy and excited over this bit of fun, all certain that the elephant was going to be shot. They were watching me as they would watch a conjurer about to perform a trick. They did not like me, but with the magical rifle in my hands I was momentarily worth watching. And suddenly I realized that I should have to shoot the elephant after all. The people expected it of me and I had got to do it; I could feel their two thousand wills pressing me forward, irresistibly. And it was at this moment, as I stood there with the rifle in my hands, that I first grasped the hollowness, the futility of the white man's dominion in the East. Here was I, the white man with his gun, standing in front of the unarmed native crowd—seemingly the leading actor of the piece; but in reality I was only an absurd puppet pushed to and fro by the will of those yellow faces behind. I perceived in this moment that when the white man turns tyrant it is his own freedom that he destroys. He becomes a sort of hollow, posing dummy, the conventionalized figure of a sahib. For it is the condition of his rule that he shall spend his life in trying to impress the "natives," and so in every crisis he has got to do what the "natives" expect of him. He wears a mask, and his face grows to fit it. I had got to shoot the elephant. I had committed myself to doing it when I sent for the rifle. A sahib has got to act like a sahib; he has got to appear resolute, to know his own mind and do definite things. To come all that way, rifle in hand, with two thousand people marching at my heels, and then to trail feebly away, having done nothing—no, that was impossible. The crowd would laugh at me. And my whole life, every white man's life in the East, was one long struggle not to be laughed at.

But I did not want to shoot the elephant. I watched him beating his bunch of grass against his knees, with that preoccupied grandmotherly air that elephants have. It seemed to me that it would be murder to shoot him. At that age I was not squeamish about killing animals, but I had never shot an elephant and never wanted to. (Somehow it always seems worse to kill a *large* animal.) Besides, there was the beast's owner to be considered. Alive, the elephant was worth at least a hundred pounds; dead, he would only be worth the value of his tusks, five pounds, possibly. But I had got to act quickly. I turned to some experienced-looking Burmans who had been there when we arrived, and asked them how the elephant had been behaving. They all said the same thing: he took no notice of you if you left him alone, but he might charge if you went too close to him.

It was perfectly clear to me what I ought to do. I ought to walk up to within, say, twenty-five yards of the elephant and test his behavior. If he charged, I could shoot; if he took no notice of me, it would be safe to leave him until the mahout came back. But also I knew that I was going to do no such thing. I was a poor shot with a rifle and the ground was soft mud into which one would sink at every step. If the elephant charged and I missed him, I should have about as much chance as a toad under a steam-roller. But even then I was not thinking particularly of my own skin, only of the watchful yellow faces behind. For at that moment, with the crowd watching me, I was not afraid in the ordinary sense, as I would have been if I had been alone. A white man mustn't be frightened in front of "natives"; and so, in general, he isn't frightened. The sole thought in my mind was that if anything went wrong those two thousand Burmans would see me pursued, caught, trampled on and reduced to a grinning corpse like that Indian up the hill. And if that happened it was quite probable that some of them would laugh. That would never do. There was only one alternative. I shoved the cartridges into the magazine and lay down on the road to get a better aim.

The crowd grew very still, and a deep, low, happy sigh, as of people who see the theatre curtain go up at last, breathed from innumerable throats. They were going to have their bit of fun after all. The rifle was a beautiful German thing with cross-hair sights. I did not then know that in shooting an elephant one would shoot to cut an imaginary bar running from ear-hole to ear-hole. I ought, therefore, as the elephant was sideways on, to have aimed straight at his ear-hole; actually I aimed several inches in front of this, thinking the brain would be further forward.

When I pulled the trigger I did not hear the bang or feel the kick—one never does when a shot goes home—but I heard the devilish roar of glee that went up from the crowd. In that instant, in too short a time, one would have thought, even for the bullet to get there, a mysterious, terrible change had come over the elephant. He neither stirred nor fell, but every line of his body had altered. He looked suddenly stricken, shrunken, immensely old, as though the frightful impact of the bullet had paralyzed him without knocking him down. At last, after what seemed a long time—it might have been five seconds, I dare say—he sagged flabbily to his knees. His mouth slobbered. An enormous senility seemed to have settled upon him. One could have imagined him thousands of years old. I fired again into the same spot. At the second shot he did not collapse but climbed with desperate slowness to his feet and stood weakly upright, with legs sagging and head drooping. I fired a third time. That was the shot that did for him. You could see the agony of it jolt his whole body and knock the last remnant of strength from his legs. But in falling he seemed for a moment to rise, for as his hind legs collapsed beneath him he seemed to tower upward like a huge rock toppling, his trunk reaching skywards like a tree. He trumpeted, for the first and only time. And then down he came, his belly towards me, with a crash that seemed to shake the ground even where I lay.

I got up. The Burmans were already racing past me across the mud. It was obvious that the elephant would never rise again, but he was not dead. He was breathing very rhythmically with long rattling gasps, his great mound of a side painfully rising and falling. His mouth was wide open—I could see far down into caverns of pale pink throat. I waited a long time for him to die, but his breathing did not weaken. Finally I fired my two remaining shots into the spot where I thought his heart must be. The thick blood welled out of him like red velvet, but still he did not die. His body did not even jerk when the shots hit him, the tortured breathing continued without a pause. He was dying, very slowly and in great agony, but in some world remote from me where not even a bullet could damage him further. I felt that I had got to put an end to that dreadful noise. It seemed dreadful to see the great beast lying there, powerless to move and yet powerless to die, and not even to be able to finish him. I sent back for my small rifle and poured shot after shot into his heart and down his throat. They seemed to make no impression. The tortured gasps continued as steadily as the ticking of a clock.

In the end I could not stand it any longer and went away. I heard later that it took him half an hour to die. Burmans were bringing dahs and baskets even before I left, and I was told they had stripped his body almost to the bones by the afternoon.

Afterwards, of course, there were endless discussions about the shooting of the elephant. The owner was furious, but he was only an Indian and could do nothing. Besides, legally I had done the right thing, for a mad elephant has to be killed, like a mad dog, if its owner fails to control it. Among the Europeans opinion was divided. The older men said I was right, the younger men said it was a damn shame to shoot an elephant for killing a coolie, because an elephant was worth more than any damn Coringhee coolie. And afterwards I was very glad that the coolie had been killed; it put me legally in the right and it gave me a sufficient pretext for shooting the elephant. I often wondered whether any of the others grasped that I had done it solely to avoid looking a fool.

QUESTIONS FOR DISCUSSION AND WRITING

1. Why did Orwell shoot the elephant when in fact he "did not want to shoot the elephant" (paragraph 8)? Is the immediate cause of his action, crowd pressure (paragraphs 7–10), the *only* cause? Why was he receptive to this pressure? What did he come to believe, in retrospect, that he should have done with regard to the crowd? In regard to the elephant?

2. Why does Orwell devote so much space to the preparation for the shooting (paragraphs 7–9), and to the actual shooting (paragraphs 10–12)? And so little to the aftermath (paragraphs 13 and 14)?

3. If Orwell hadn't shot the elephant, what ethical principle would he have substituted for what pragmatic one? What might the ideal consequences have been? How likely would they have been to occur, given the tension between the Burmese and the British?

4. When Orwell wrote this essay he was a young, inexperienced British colonial officer in Burma (now Myanmar), a role he came to detest. "[W]hen the white man turns tyrant it is his own freedom that he destroys" (paragraph 7). Explain the meaning of this in terms of "Shooting an Elephant." Is this principle applicable only to "white men" as tyrants? Examine recent wars and genocidal activities worldwide in your answer.

5. Write an essay in which you analyze an incident, event, or series of events, in which you—or someone you know well—acted contrary to your better judgment. In the process of showing why you acted as you did, disclose your current attitude toward your action. Are you proud of it? Ashamed? Ambivalent? Explain why. If you had it to do over again, what would you do? Based on what principles?

6. Pick a political action or decision either in America's history or in the current political climate that has made you angry. Analyze why it has angered you and identify one or more ethical principles that could have been applied to resolve it to your satisfaction.

DAVID EAGLEMAN

The Brain on Trial

A neuroscientist at Baylor College of Medicine, David Eagleman (b. 1971) is also a New York Times *best-selling writer. His book* SUM: Forty Tales from the Afterlives *(2009) is work of fiction that has been published in twenty-seven languages. His non-fiction publications include* Why the Net Matters: How the Internet Will Save Civilization *(2010), which is available only as an iBook. More recently, he has published* Incognito: The Secret Lives of the Brain *(2011). Eagleman also directs The Initiative on Neuroscience and the Law. Eagleman majored in British and American literature at Rice University as an undergraduate before earning a doctorate in neuroscience at Baylor College of Medicine. Among his numerous awards and recognitions, Eagleman has been named a Guggenheim Fellow, a Next Generation Texas Fellow, and a Fellow for the Institute for Ethics and Emerging Technologies.*

In this article, initially published in the Atlantic, *Eagleman takes on the question of free will and crime. Arguing that the physiology of the brain, including physical abnormalities like tumors, may be at the root of much dysfunctional and even criminal behavior, Eagleman asks the reader to take a new look at criminal activities. Although not going so far as to eliminate free will entirely, Eagleman states that "the choices we make are inseparably yoked to our neural circuitry"; in other words, a direct connection exists between the physiology of our brains and our actions. He argues for a greater understanding of the biology of the brain and how it affects actions, and for the need to tailor our criminal justice system to that understanding, in terms of rehabilitation or incarceration.*

On the steamy first day of August 1966, Charles Whitman took an elevator to the top floor of the University of Texas Tower in Austin. The twenty-five-year-old climbed the stairs to the observation deck, lugging with him a footlocker full of guns and ammunition. At the top, he killed a receptionist with the butt of his rifle. Two families of tourists came up the stairwell; he shot at them at point-blank range. Then he began to fire indiscriminately from the deck at people below. The first woman he shot was pregnant. As her boyfriend knelt to help her, Whitman shot him as well. He shot pedestrians in the street and an ambulance driver who came to rescue them.

The evening before, Whitman had sat at his typewriter and composed a suicide note:

> I don't really understand myself these days. I am supposed to be an average reasonable and intelligent young man. However, lately (I can't recall when it started) I have been a victim of many unusual and irrational thoughts.

By the time the police shot him dead, Whitman had killed thirteen people and wounded thirty-two more. The story of his rampage dominated national headlines the next day. And when police went to investigate his home for clues, the story became even stranger: In the early hours of the morning on the day of the shooting, he had murdered his mother and stabbed his wife to death in her sleep.

> It was after much thought that I decided to kill my wife, Kathy, tonight . . . I love
> her dearly, and she has been as fine a wife to me as any man could ever hope to
> have. I cannot rationa[l]ly pinpoint any specific reason for doing this . . .

Along with the shock of the murders lay another, more hidden, surprise: the juxtaposition of his aberrant actions with his unremarkable personal life. Whitman was an Eagle Scout and a former marine, studied architectural engineering at the University of Texas, and briefly worked as a bank teller and volunteered as a scoutmaster for Austin's Boy Scout Troop 5. As a child, he'd scored 138 on the Stanford-Binet IQ test, placing him in the 99th percentile. So after his shooting spree from the University of Texas Tower, everyone wanted answers.

For that matter, so did Whitman. He requested in his suicide note that an autopsy be performed to determine if something had changed in his brain— because he suspected it had.

> I talked with a Doctor once for about two hours and tried to convey to him
> my fears that I felt [overcome by] overwhelming violent impulses. After one
> session I never saw the Doctor again, and since then I have been fighting my
> mental turmoil alone, and seemingly to no avail.

Whitman's body was taken to the morgue, his skull was put under the bone saw, and the medical examiner lifted the brain from its vault. He discovered that Whitman's brain harbored a tumor the diameter of a nickel. This tumor, called a glioblastoma, had blossomed from beneath a structure called the thalamus, impinged on the hypothalamus, and compressed a third region called the amygdala. The amygdala is involved in emotional regulation, especially of fear and aggression. By the late 1800s, researchers had discovered that damage to the amygdala caused emotional and social disturbances. In the 1930s, the researchers Heinrich Klüver and Paul Bucy demonstrated that damage to the amygdala in monkeys led to a constellation of symptoms, including lack of fear, blunting of emotion, and overreaction. Female monkeys with amygdala damage often neglected or physically abused their infants. In humans, activity in the amygdala increases when people are shown threatening faces, are put into frightening situations, or experience social phobias. Whitman's intuition about himself—that something in his brain was changing his behavior—was spot-on.

Stories like Whitman's are not uncommon: Legal cases involving brain damage crop up increasingly often. As we develop better technologies for probing the brain, we detect more problems, and link them more easily to aberrant behavior. Take the 2000 case of a forty-year-old man we'll call Alex, whose sexual preferences suddenly began to transform. He developed an interest in child pornography—and not just a little interest, but an overwhelming one. He poured his time into child-pornography Web sites and magazines. He also solicited prostitution at a massage parlor, something he said he had never previously done. He reported later that he'd wanted to stop, but "the pleasure principle overrode" his restraint. He worked to hide his acts, but subtle sexual advances toward his prepubescent stepdaughter alarmed his wife, who soon discovered his collection of child pornography. He was removed from his house, found guilty of child molestation, and sentenced to rehabilitation in lieu of prison. In the rehabilitation program, he made inappropriate sexual advances toward the staff and other clients, and was expelled and routed toward prison.

At the same time, Alex was complaining of worsening headaches. The night before he was to report for prison sentencing, he couldn't stand the pain anymore, and took himself to the emergency room. He underwent a brain scan, which revealed a massive tumor in his orbitofrontal cortex. Neurosurgeons removed the tumor. Alex's sexual appetite returned to normal.

The year after the brain surgery, his pedophilic behavior began to return. The neuroradiologist discovered that a portion of the tumor had been missed in the surgery and was regrowing—and Alex went back under the knife. After the removal of the remaining tumor, his behavior again returned to normal.

When your biology changes, so can your decision-making and your desires. 10 The drives you take for granted ("I'm a heterosexual/homosexual," "I'm attracted to children/adults," "I'm aggressive/not aggressive," and so on) depend on the intricate details of your neural machinery. Although acting on such drives is popularly thought to be a free choice, the most cursory examination of the evidence demonstrates the limits of that assumption.

Alex's sudden pedophilia illustrates that hidden drives and desires can lurk undetected behind the neural machinery of socialization. When the frontal lobes are compromised, people become disinhibited, and startling behaviors can emerge. Disinhibition is commonly seen in patients with frontotemporal dementia, a tragic disease in which the frontal and temporal lobes degenerate. With the loss of that brain tissue, patients lose the ability to control their hidden impulses. To the frustration of their loved ones, these patients violate social norms in endless ways: shoplifting in front of store managers, removing their clothes in public, running stop signs, breaking out in song at inappropriate times, eating food scraps found in public trash cans, being physically aggressive or sexually transgressive. Patients with frontotemporal dementia commonly end up in courtrooms, where their lawyers, doctors, and embarrassed adult children must explain to the judge that the violation was not the perpetrator's fault, exactly: much of the brain has degenerated, and medicine offers no remedy. Fifty-seven percent of frontotemporal-dementia patients violate social norms, as compared with only 27 percent of Alzheimer's patients.

Changes in the balance of brain chemistry, even small ones, can also cause large and unexpected changes in behavior. Victims of Parkinson's disease offer an example. In 2001, families and caretakers of Parkinson's patients began to notice something strange. When patients were given a drug called pramipexole, some of them turned into gamblers. And not just casual gamblers, but pathological gamblers. These were people who had never gambled much before, and now they were flying off to Vegas. One sixty-eight-year-old man amassed losses of more than $200,000 in six months at a series of casinos. Some patients became consumed with Internet poker, racking up unpayable credit-card bills. For several, the new addiction reached beyond gambling, to compulsive eating, excessive alcohol consumption, and hypersexuality.

What was going on? Parkinson's involves the loss of brain cells that produce a neurotransmitter known as dopamine. Pramipexole works by impersonating dopamine. But it turns out that dopamine is a chemical doing double duty in the brain. Along with its role in motor commands, it also mediates the reward systems, guiding a person toward food, drink, mates, and other things useful for survival. Because of dopamine's role in weighing the costs and benefits of decisions, imbalances in its levels can trigger gambling, overeating, and drug addiction—behaviors that result from a reward system gone awry. Physicians now watch for these behavioral changes as a possible side effect of drugs like pramipexole. Luckily, the negative effects of the drug are reversible—the physician simply lowers the dosage, and the compulsive gambling goes away.

The lesson from all these stories is the same: Human behavior cannot be separated from human biology. If we like to believe that people make free choices about their behavior (as in, "I don't gamble, because I'm strong-willed"), cases like Alex the pedophile, the frontotemporal shoplifters, and the gambling Parkinson's patients may encourage us to examine our views more carefully. Perhaps not everyone is equally "free" to make socially appropriate choices.

Does the discovery of Charles Whitman's brain tumor modify your feelings   15 about the senseless murders he committed? Does it affect the sentence you would find appropriate for him, had he survived that day? Does the tumor change the degree to which you consider the killings "his fault"? Couldn't you just as easily be unlucky enough to develop a tumor and lose control of your behavior?

On the other hand, wouldn't it be dangerous to conclude that people with a tumor are free of guilt, and that they should be let off the hook for their crimes?

As our understanding of the human brain improves, juries are increasingly challenged with these sorts of questions. When a criminal stands in front of the judge's bench today, the legal system wants to know whether he is blameworthy. Was it his fault, or his biology's fault?

I submit that this is the wrong question to be asking. The choices we make are inseparably yoked to our neural circuitry, and therefore we have no meaningful way to tease the two apart. The more we learn, the more the seemingly simple concept of blameworthiness becomes complicated, and the more the foundations of our legal system are strained.

If I seem to be heading in an uncomfortable direction—toward letting criminals off the hook—please read on, because I'm going to show the logic of a new argument, piece by piece. The upshot is that we can build a legal system more deeply informed by science, in which we will continue to take criminals off the streets, but we will customize sentencing, leverage new opportunities for rehabilitation, and structure better incentives for good behavior. Discoveries in neuroscience suggest a new way forward for law and order—one that will lead to a more cost-effective, humane, and flexible system than the one we have today. When modern brain science is laid out clearly, it is difficult to justify how our legal system can continue to function without taking what we've learned into account.

Many of us like to believe that all adults possess the same capacity to make 20 sound choices. It's a charitable idea, but demonstrably wrong. People's brains are vastly different.

Who you even have the possibility to be starts at conception. If you think genes don't affect how people behave, consider this fact: If you are a carrier of a particular set of genes, the probability that you will commit a violent crime is four times as high as it would be if you lacked those genes. You're three times as likely to commit robbery, five times as likely to commit aggravated assault, eight times as likely to be arrested for murder, and thirteen times as likely to be arrested for a sexual offense. The overwhelming majority of prisoners carry these genes; 98.1 percent of death-row inmates do. These statistics alone indicate that we cannot presume that everyone is coming to the table equally equipped in terms of drives and behaviors.

And this feeds into a larger lesson of biology: We are not the ones steering the boat of our behavior, at least not nearly as much as we believe. Who we are runs well below the surface of our conscious access, and the details reach back in time to before our birth, when the meeting of a sperm and an egg granted us certain attributes and not others. Who we can be starts with our molecular blueprints—a series of alien codes written in invisibly small strings of acids—well before we have anything to do with it. Each of us is, in part, a product of our inaccessible, microscopic history. By the way, as regards that dangerous set of genes, you've probably heard of them. They are summarized as the Y chromosome. If you're a carrier, we call you a male.

Genes are part of the story, but they're not the whole story. We are likewise influenced by the environments in which we grow up. Substance abuse by a mother during pregnancy, maternal stress, and low birth weight all can influence how a baby will turn out as an adult. As a child grows, neglect, physical abuse, and head injury can impede mental development, as can the physical environment. (For example, the major public-health movement to eliminate lead-based paint grew out of an understanding that ingesting lead can cause brain damage, making children less intelligent and, in some cases, more impulsive and aggressive.) And every experience throughout our lives can modify genetic expression—activating certain genes or switching others off—which in turn can inaugurate new behaviors. In this way, genes and environments intertwine.

When it comes to nature and nurture, the important point is that we choose neither one. We are each constructed from a genetic blueprint, and then born into a world of circumstances that we cannot control in our most-formative years. The complex interactions of genes and environment mean that all citizens—equal before the law—possess different perspectives, dissimilar personalities, and varied capacities for decision-making. The unique patterns of neurobiology inside each of our heads cannot qualify as choices; these are the cards we're dealt.

Because we did not choose the factors that affected the formation and structure 25 of our brain, the concepts of free will and personal responsibility begin to sprout question marks. Is it meaningful to say that Alex made bad choices, even though his brain tumor was not his fault? Is it justifiable to say that the patients with frontotemporal dementia or Parkinson's should be punished for their bad behavior?

It is problematic to imagine yourself in the shoes of someone breaking the law and conclude, "Well, I wouldn't have done that"—because if you weren't exposed to in utero cocaine, lead poisoning, and physical abuse, and he was, then you and he are not directly comparable. You cannot walk a mile in his shoes.

The legal system rests on the assumption that we are "practical reasoners," a term of art that presumes, at bottom, the existence of free will. The idea is that we use conscious deliberation when deciding how to act—that is, in the absence of external duress, we make free decisions. This concept of the practical reasoner is intuitive but problematic.

The existence of free will in human behavior is the subject of an ancient debate. Arguments in support of free will are typically based on direct subjective experience ("I feel like I made the decision to lift my finger just now"). But evaluating free will requires some nuance beyond our immediate intuitions.

Consider a decision to move or speak. It feels as though free will leads you to stick out your tongue, or scrunch up your face, or call someone a name. But free will is not required to play any role in these acts. People with Tourette's syndrome, for instance, suffer from involuntary movements and vocalizations. A typical Tourretter may stick out his tongue, scrunch up his face, or call someone a name—all without choosing to do so.

We immediately learn two things from the Tourette's patient. First, actions 30 can occur in the absence of free will. Second, the Tourette's patient has no free won't. He cannot use free will to override or control what subconscious parts of his brain have decided to do. What the lack of free will and the lack of free won't have in common is the lack of "free." Tourette's syndrome provides a case in which the underlying neural machinery does its thing, and we all agree that the person is not responsible.

This same phenomenon arises in people with a condition known as chorea, for whom actions of the hands, arms, legs, and face are involuntary, even though they certainly look voluntary: Ask such a patient why she is moving her fingers up and down, and she will explain that she has no control over her hand. She cannot not do it. Similarly, some split-brain patients (who have had the two hemispheres of the brain surgically disconnected) develop alien-hand syndrome: while one hand buttons up a shirt, the other hand works to unbutton it. When one hand reaches for a pencil, the other bats it away. No matter how hard the patient tries, he cannot make his alien hand not do what it's doing. The movements are not "his" to freely start or stop.

Unconscious acts are not limited to unintended shouts or wayward hands; they can be surprisingly sophisticated. Consider Kenneth Parks, a twenty-three-year-old Canadian with a wife, a five-month-old daughter, and a close relationship with his in-laws (his mother-in-law described him as a "gentle giant"). Suffering from financial difficulties, marital problems, and a gambling addiction, he made plans to go see his in-laws to talk about his troubles.

In the wee hours of May 23, 1987, Kenneth arose from the couch on which he had fallen asleep, but he did not awaken. Sleepwalking, he climbed into his car and drove the 14 miles to his in-laws' home. He broke in, stabbed his mother-in-law to death, and assaulted his father-in-law, who survived. Afterward, he drove himself to the police station. Once there, he said, "I think I have killed some people . . . My hands," realizing for the first time that his own hands were severely cut.

Over the next year, Kenneth's testimony was remarkably consistent, even in the face of attempts to lead him astray: He remembered nothing of the incident. Moreover, while all parties agreed that Kenneth had undoubtedly committed the murder, they also agreed that he had no motive. His defense attorneys argued that this was a case of killing while sleepwalking, known as homicidal somnambulism.

Although critics cried "Faker!" sleepwalking is a verifiable phenomenon. 35 On May 25, 1988, after lengthy consideration of electrical recordings from Kenneth's brain, the jury concluded that his actions had indeed been involuntary, and declared him not guilty.

As with Tourette's sufferers, split-brain patients, and those with choreic movements, Kenneth's case illustrates that high-level behaviors can take place in the absence of free will. Like your heartbeat, breathing, blinking, and swallowing, even your mental machinery can run on autopilot. The crux of the question is whether all of your actions are fundamentally on autopilot or whether some little bit of you is "free" to choose, independent of the rules of biology.

This has always been the sticking point for philosophers and scientists alike. After all, there is no spot in the brain that is not densely interconnected with—and driven by—other brain parts. And that suggests that no part is independent and therefore "free." In modern science, it is difficult to find the gap into which to slip free will—the uncaused causer—because there seems to be no part of the machinery that does not follow in a causal relationship from the other parts.

Free will may exist (it may simply be beyond our current science), but one thing seems clear: If free will does exist, it has little room in which to operate. It can at best be a small factor riding on top of vast neural networks shaped by genes and environment. In fact, free will may end up being so small that we eventually think about bad decision-making in the same way we think about any physical process, such as diabetes or lung disease.

The study of brains and behaviors is in the midst of a conceptual shift. Historically, clinicians and lawyers have agreed on an intuitive distinction between neurological disorders ("brain problems") and psychiatric disorders ("mind problems"). As recently as a century ago, a common approach was to get psychiatric patients to "toughen up," through deprivation, pleading, or torture. Not surprisingly, this approach was medically fruitless. After all, while psychiatric disorders tend to be the product of more-subtle forms of brain pathology, they, too, are based in the biological details of the brain.

What accounts for the shift from blame to biology? Perhaps the largest driv- 40 ing force is the effectiveness of pharmaceutical treatments. No amount of threatening will chase away depression, but a little pill called fluoxetine often does the trick. Schizophrenic symptoms cannot be overcome by exorcism, but they can be controlled by risperidone. Mania responds not to talk or to ostracism, but to lithium. These successes, most of them introduced in the past sixty years, have underscored the idea that calling some disorders "brain problems" while consigning others to the ineffable realm of "the psychic" does not make sense. Instead, we have begun to approach mental problems in the same way we might approach a broken leg. The neuroscientist Robert Sapolsky invites us to contemplate this conceptual shift with a series of questions:

> Is a loved one, sunk in a depression so severe that she cannot function, a case of a disease whose biochemical basis is as "real" as is the biochemistry of, say, diabetes, or is she merely indulging herself? Is a child doing poorly at school because he is unmotivated and slow, or because there is a neurobiologically based learning disability? Is a friend, edging toward a serious problem with substance abuse, displaying a simple lack of discipline, or suffering from problems with the neurochemistry of reward?

Acts cannot be understood separately from the biology of the actors—and this recognition has legal implications. Tom Bingham, Britain's former senior law lord, once put it this way:

> In the past, the law has tended to base its approach . . . on a series of rather crude working assumptions: adults of competent mental capacity are free to choose whether they will act in one way or another; they are presumed to act rationally, and in what they conceive to be their own best interests; they are credited with such foresight of the consequences of their actions as reasonable people in their position could ordinarily be expected to have; they are generally taken to mean what they say.
>
> Whatever the merits or demerits of working assumptions such as these in the ordinary range of cases, it is evident that they do not provide a uniformly accurate guide to human behavior.

The more we discover about the circuitry of the brain, the more we tip away from accusations of indulgence, lack of motivation, and poor discipline—and toward the details of biology. The shift from blame to science reflects our modern understanding that our perceptions and behaviors are steered by deeply embedded neural programs.

Imagine a spectrum of culpability. On one end, we find people like Alex the pedophile or a patient with frontotemporal dementia who exposes himself in public. In the eyes of the judge and jury, these are people who suffered brain damage at the hands of fate and did not choose their neural situation. On the other end of the spectrum—the blameworthy side of the "fault" line—we find the common criminal, whose brain receives little study, and about whom our current technology might be able to say little anyway. The overwhelming majority of lawbreakers are on this side of the line, because they don't have any obvious, measurable biological problems. They are simply thought of as freely choosing actors.

Such a spectrum captures the common intuition that juries hold regarding blameworthiness. But there is a deep problem with this intuition. Technology will continue to improve, and as we grow better at measuring problems in the brain, the fault line will drift into the territory of people we currently hold fully accountable for their crimes. Problems that are now opaque will open up to examination by new techniques, and we may someday find that many types of bad behavior have a basic biological explanation—as has happened with schizophrenia, epilepsy, depression, and mania.

Today, neuroimaging is a crude technology, unable to explain the details of 45 individual behavior. We can detect only large-scale problems, but within the coming decades, we will be able to detect patterns at unimaginably small levels of the microcircuitry that correlate with behavioral problems. Neuroscience will be better able to say why people are predisposed to act the way they do. As we become more skilled at specifying how behavior results from the microscopic details of the brain, more defense lawyers will point to biological mitigators of guilt, and more juries will place defendants on the not-blameworthy side of the line.

This puts us in a strange situation. After all, a just legal system cannot define culpability simply by the limitations of current technology. Expert medical testimony generally reflects only whether we yet have names and measurements for a problem, not whether a problem exists. A legal system that declares a person culpable at the beginning of a decade and not culpable at the end is one in which culpability carries no clear meaning.

The crux of the problem is that it no longer makes sense to ask, "To what extent was it his biology and to what extent was it him?" because we now understand that there is no meaningful distinction between a person's biology and his decision-making. They are inseparable.

While our current style of punishment rests on a bedrock of personal volition and blame, our modern understanding of the brain suggests a different approach. Blameworthiness should be removed from the legal argot. It is a backward-looking concept that demands the impossible task of untangling the hopelessly complex web of genetics and environment that constructs the trajectory of a human life.

Instead of debating culpability, we should focus on what to do, moving forward, with an accused lawbreaker. I suggest that the legal system has to become forward-looking, primarily because it can no longer hope to do otherwise. As science complicates the question of culpability, our legal and social policy will need to shift toward a different set of questions: How is a person likely to behave in the future? Are criminal actions likely to be repeated? Can this person be helped toward pro-social behavior? How can incentives be realistically structured to deter crime?

The important change will be in the way we respond to the vast range of 50 criminal acts. Biological explanation will not exculpate criminals; we will still remove from the streets lawbreakers who prove overaggressive, underempathetic, and poor at controlling their impulses. Consider, for example, that the majority of known serial killers were abused as children. Does this make them less blameworthy? Who cares? It's the wrong question. The knowledge that they were abused encourages us to support social programs to prevent child abuse, but it does nothing to change the way we deal with the particular serial murderer standing in front of the bench. We still need to keep him off the streets, irrespective of his past misfortunes. The child abuse cannot serve as an excuse to let him go; the judge must keep society safe.

Those who break social contracts need to be confined, but in this framework, the future is more important than the past. Deeper biological insight into behavior will foster a better understanding of recidivism—and this offers a basis for empirically based sentencing. Some people will need to be taken off the streets for a longer time (even a lifetime), because their likelihood of reoffense is high; others, because of differences in neural constitution, are less likely to recidivate, and so can be released sooner.

The law is already forward-looking in some respects: Consider the leniency afforded a crime of passion versus a premeditated murder. Those who commit the former are less likely to recidivate than those who commit the latter, and their sentences sensibly reflect that. Likewise, American law draws a bright line between criminal acts committed by minors and those by adults, punishing the latter more harshly. This approach may be crude, but the intuition behind it is sound: Adolescents command lesser skills in decision-making and impulse control than do adults; a teenager's brain is simply not like an adult's brain. Lighter sentences are appropriate for those whose impulse control is likely to improve naturally as adolescence gives way to adulthood.

Taking a more scientific approach to sentencing, case by case, could move us beyond these limited examples. For instance, important changes are happening in the sentencing of sex offenders. In the past, researchers have asked psychiatrists and parole-board members how likely specific sex offenders were to relapse when let out of prison. Both groups had experience with sex offenders, so predicting who was going straight and who was coming back seemed simple. But surprisingly, the expert guesses showed almost no correlation with the actual outcomes. The psychiatrists and parole-board members had only slightly better predictive accuracy than coin-flippers. This astounded the legal community.

So researchers tried a more actuarial approach. They set about recording dozens of characteristics of some 23,000 released sex offenders: whether the offender had unstable employment, had been sexually abused as a child, was addicted to drugs, showed remorse, had deviant sexual interests, and so on. Researchers then tracked the offenders for an average of five years after release to see who wound up back in prison. At the end of the study, they computed which factors best explained the reoffense rates, and from these and later data they were able to build actuarial tables to be used in sentencing.

Which factors mattered? Take, for instance, low remorse, denial of the crime, 55 and sexual abuse as a child. You might guess that these factors would correlate with sex offenders' recidivism. But you would be wrong: Those factors offer no predictive power. How about antisocial personality disorder and failure to complete treatment? These offer somewhat more predictive power. But among the strongest predictors of recidivism are prior sexual offenses and sexual interest in children.

When you compare the predictive power of the actuarial approach with that of the parole boards and psychiatrists, there is no contest: Numbers beat intuition. In courtrooms across the nation, these actuarial tests are now used in presentencing to modulate the length of prison terms.

We will never know with certainty what someone will do upon release from prison, because real life is complicated. But greater predictive power is hidden in the numbers than people generally expect. Statistically based sentencing is imperfect, but it nonetheless allows evidence to trump folk intuition, and it offers customization in place of the blunt guidelines that the legal system typically employs. The current actuarial approaches do not require a deep understanding of genes or brain chemistry, but as we introduce more science into these measures—for example, with neuroimaging studies—the predictive power will only improve. (To make such a system immune to government abuse, the data and equations that compose the sentencing guidelines must be transparent and available online for anyone to verify.)

Beyond customized sentencing, a forward-thinking legal system informed by scientific insights into the brain will enable us to stop treating prison as a one-size-fits-all solution. To be clear, I'm not opposed to incarceration, and its purpose is not limited to the removal of dangerous people from the streets. The prospect of incarceration deters many crimes, and time actually spent in prison can steer some people away from further criminal acts upon their release. But that works only for those whose brains function normally. The problem is that prisons have become our de facto mental-health care institutions—and inflicting punishment on the mentally ill usually has little influence on their future behavior. An encouraging trend is the establishment of mental-health courts around the nation: Through such courts, people with mental illnesses can be helped while confined in a tailored environment. Cities such as Richmond, Virginia, are moving in this direction, for reasons of justice as well as cost-effectiveness. Sheriff C. T. Woody, who estimates that nearly 20 percent of Richmond's prisoners are mentally ill, told CBS News, "The jail isn't a place for them. They should be in a mental-health facility." Similarly, many jurisdictions are opening drug courts and developing alternative sentences; they have realized that prisons are not as useful for solving addictions as are meaningful drug-rehabilitation programs.

A forward-thinking legal system will also parlay biological understanding into customized rehabilitation, viewing criminal behavior the way we understand other medical conditions such as epilepsy, schizophrenia, and depression—conditions that now allow the seeking and giving of help. These and other brain disorders find themselves on the not-blameworthy side of the fault line, where they are now recognized as biological, not demonic, issues.

Many people recognize the long-term cost-effectiveness of rehabilitating offenders instead of packing them into overcrowded prisons. The challenge has been the dearth of new ideas about how to rehabilitate them. A better understanding of the brain offers new ideas. For example, poor impulse control is characteristic of many prisoners. These people generally can express the difference between right and wrong actions, and they understand the disadvantages of punishment—

but they are handicapped by poor control of their impulses. Whether as a result of anger or temptation, their actions override reasoned consideration of the future.

If it seems difficult to empathize with people who have poor impulse control, 60 just think of all the things you succumb to against your better judgment. Alcohol? Chocolate cake? Television? It's not that we don't know what's best for us, it's simply that the frontal-lobe circuits representing long-term considerations can't always win against short-term desire when temptation is in front of us.

With this understanding in mind, we can modify the justice system in several ways. One approach, advocated by Mark A. R. Kleiman, a professor of public policy at UCLA, is to ramp up the certainty and swiftness of punishment—for instance, by requiring drug offenders to undergo twice-weekly drug testing, with automatic, immediate consequences for failure—thereby not relying on distant abstraction alone. Similarly, economists have suggested that the drop in crime since the early 1990s has been due, in part, to the increased presence of police on the streets: Their visibility shores up support for the parts of the brain that weigh long-term consequences.

We may be on the cusp of finding new rehabilitative strategies as well, affording people better control of their behavior, even in the absence of external authority. To help a citizen reintegrate into society, the ethical goal is to change him as little as possible while bringing his behavior into line with society's needs. My colleagues and I are proposing a new approach, one that grows from the understanding that the brain operates like a team of rivals, with different neural populations competing to control the single output channel of behavior. Because it's a competition, the outcome can be tipped. I call the approach "the prefrontal workout."

The basic idea is to give the frontal lobes practice in squelching the short-term brain circuits. To this end, my colleagues Stephen LaConte and Pearl Chiu have begun providing real-time feedback to people during brain scanning. Imagine that you'd like to quit smoking cigarettes. In this experiment, you look at pictures of cigarettes during brain imaging, and the experimenters measure which regions of your brain are involved in the craving. Then they show you the activity in those networks, represented by a vertical bar on a computer screen, while you look at more cigarette pictures. The bar acts as a thermometer for your craving: If your craving networks are revving high, the bar is high; if you're suppressing your craving, the bar is low. Your job is to make the bar go down. Perhaps you have insight into what you're doing to resist the craving; perhaps the mechanism is inaccessible. In any case, you try out different mental avenues until the bar begins to slowly sink. When it goes all the way down, that means you've successfully recruited frontal circuitry to squelch the activity in the networks involved in impulsive craving. The goal is for the long term to trump the short term. Still looking at pictures of cigarettes, you practice making the bar go down over and over, until you've strengthened those frontal circuits. By this method, you're able to visualize the activity in the parts of your brain that need modulation, and you can witness the effects of different mental approaches you might take.

If this sounds like biofeedback from the 1970s, it is—but this time with vastly more sophistication, monitoring specific networks inside the head rather than a single electrode on the skin. This research is just beginning, so the method's effi-cacy is not yet known—but if it works well, it will be a game changer. We will be able to take it to the incarcerated population, especially those approaching release, to try to help them avoid coming back through the revolving prison doors.

This prefrontal workout is designed to better balance the debate between the long- and short-term parties of the brain, giving the option of reflection before action to those who lack it. And really, that's all maturation is. The main differ-ence between teenage and adult brains is the development of the frontal lobes. The human prefrontal cortex does not fully develop until the early 20s, and this fact underlies the impulsive behavior of teenagers. The frontal lobes are sometimes called the organ of socialization, because becoming socialized largely involves developing the circuitry to squelch our first impulses.

This explains why damage to the frontal lobes unmasks unsocialized behav-ior that we would never have thought was hidden inside us. Recall the patients with frontotemporal dementia who shoplift, expose themselves, and burst into song at inappropriate times. The networks for those behaviors have been lurking under the surface all along, but they've been masked by normally functioning frontal lobes. The same sort of unmasking happens in people who go out and get rip-roaring drunk on a Saturday night: They're disinhibiting normal frontal-lobe function and letting more-impulsive networks climb onto the main stage. After training at the prefrontal gym, a person might still crave a cigarette, but he'll know how to beat the craving instead of letting it win. It's not that we don't want to enjoy our impulsive thoughts (Mmm, cake), it's merely that we want to endow the frontal cortex with some control over whether we act upon them (I'll pass). Similarly, if a person thinks about committing a criminal act, that's permissible as long as he doesn't take action.

For the pedophile, we cannot hope to control whether he is attracted to chil-dren. That he never acts on the attraction may be the best we can hope for, especially as a society that respects individual rights and freedom of thought. Social policy can hope only to prevent impulsive thoughts from tipping into behavior without reflection. The goal is to give more control to the neural populations that care about long-term consequences—to inhibit impulsivity, to encourage reflection. If a per-son thinks about long-term consequences and still decides to move forward with an illegal act, then we'll respond accordingly. The prefrontal workout leaves the brain intact—no drugs or surgery—and uses the natural mechanisms of brain plasticity to help the brain help itself. It's a tune-up rather than a product recall.

We have hope that this approach represents the correct model: It is grounded simultaneously in biology and in libertarian ethics, allowing a person to help him-self by improving his long-term decision-making. Like any scientific attempt, it could fail for any number of unforeseen reasons. But at least we have reached a point where we can develop new ideas rather than assuming that repeated incar-ceration is the single practical solution for deterring crime.

Along any axis that we use to measure human beings, we discover a wide-ranging distribution, whether in empathy, intelligence, impulse control, or aggres-sion. People are not created equal. Although this variability is often imagined to be best swept under the rug, it is in fact the engine of evolution. In each generation, nature tries out as many varieties as it can produce, along all available dimensions.

Variation gives rise to lushly diverse societies—but it serves as a source of   70
trouble for the legal system, which is largely built on the premise that humans are all equal before the law. This myth of human equality suggests that people are equally capable of controlling impulses, making decisions, and comprehending consequences. While admirable in spirit, the notion of neural equality is simply not true.

As brain science improves, we will better understand that people exist along continua of capabilities, rather than in simplistic categories. And we will be better able to tailor sentencing and rehabilitation for the individual, rather than maintain the pretense that all brains respond identically to complex challenges and that all people therefore deserve the same punishments. Some people wonder whether it's unfair to take a scientific approach to sentencing—after all, where's the humanity in that? But what's the alternative? As it stands now, ugly people receive longer sentences than attractive people; psychiatrists have no capacity to guess which sex offenders will reoffend; and our prisons are overcrowded with drug addicts and the mentally ill, both of whom could be better helped by rehabilitation. So is current sentencing really superior to a scientifically informed approach?

Neuroscience is beginning to touch on questions that were once only in the domain of philosophers and psychologists, questions about how people make decisions and the degree to which those decisions are truly "free." These are not idle questions. Ultimately, they will shape the future of legal theory and create a more biologically informed jurisprudence.

QUESTIONS FOR DISCUSSION AND WRITING

1. Eagleman begins the article by recounting the famous shooting at the University of Texas in 1966, an incident in which a total of sixteen people were killed and more than thirty wounded. How does that serve to introduce the relationship between the brain and individual actions?

2. Eagleman points out that the physiology of the brain—its circuitry, and any abnormalities such as tumors—has a direct impact on behavior. Which examples that Eagleman presents, other than the University of Texas Tower shooting, seem most convincing to you of this relationship? Given this relationship, Eagleman poses a new question: "Wouldn't it be dangerous to conclude that people with a tumor are free of guilt, and they should be let off the hook for their crimes?" (paragraph 16). What is his own response to that question, and do you find his response convincing? Why or why not?

3. In paragraph 19, Eagleman argues that "we can build a legal system that is deeply informed by science." What would this mean? What would such a system look like? Is such a system realistically possible? Defend your answer.

4. Consider Eagleman's discussion of free will, including his argument that "If free will does exist, it has little room [in the human brain] in which to operate"

(paragraph 38). Is Eagleman completely rejecting free will, and if so, what consequences would that mean for all of our actions, not just criminal ones? Explain.

5. Eagleman writes about what he calls a "spectrum of culpability" (paragraph 43). Rather than a simple yes/no idea of guilt (e.g., he did it or he didn't do it), Eagleman argues that we need to consider issues like brain damage, frontotemporal dementia, tumors, and other abnormalities in the human brain. What are the advantages of such an approach for public safety? What disadvantages? Defend your response.

6. Another issue is that of rehabilitation versus punishment. Although Eagleman does not entirely reject punishment—especially for those at the "blameworthy" end of the spectrum of culpability (paragraph 43), he is interested in biological determinations of recidivism—in other words, how likely it is for the person to commit that crime again. He argues that many people currently incarcerated, such as drug abusers and the mentally ill, can and should be released from prison into rehabilitation facilities. Do you agree or disagree with his argument? Defend your answer.

STANLEY FISH

Condemnation without Absolutes

Stanley Fish (b. 1938) is the former dean of the College of Liberal Arts and Sciences at the University of Illinois at Chicago, and is currently the Davidson-Kahn Distinguished University professor of Humanities and a law professor at Florida International University. He has also taught at the University of California at Berkeley, Duke University, and Johns Hopkins, and was the Floersheimer Distinguished Visiting Professor at the Benjamin A. Cardozo School of Law, part of the Yeshiva University in New York City. Fish is also a contributor to the New York Times *Opinionator blog.*

Writing just a few weeks after the shocking and devastating attacks of September 11, 2001, Fish strikes back at those who claim that postmodernist relativism put America in a position of being unable to fight back against the terrorists. Furthermore, they argued it was postmodernist thought itself that had weakened America, emboldening its enemies. The argument then followed that since America clearly would fight back against its attackers, this meant the death of postmodernism as a viable intellectual theory. Fish outlines a counterargument that addresses large-scale misconceptions about postmodernism, what it purports to say and what it does not.

During the interval between the terrorist attacks and the U.S. response, a reporter called to ask me if the events of September 11 meant the end of postmodernist relativism. It seemed bizarre that events so serious would be linked causally with a rarefied form of academic talk. But in the days that followed, a growing number of commentators played serious variations on the same theme: that the ideas foisted upon us by postmodern intellectuals have weakened the country's resolve. The problem, according to the critics, is that since postmodernists deny the possibility of describing matters of fact objectively, they leave us with no firm basis for either condemning the terrorist attacks or fighting back.

Not so. Postmodernism maintains only that there can be no independent standard for determining which of many rival interpretations of an event is the true one. The only thing postmodern thought argues against is the hope of justifying our response to the attacks in universal terms that would be persuasive to everyone, including our enemies. Invoking the abstract notions of justice and truth to support our cause wouldn't be effective anyway because our adversaries lay claim to the same language. (No one declares himself to be an apostle of injustice.)

Instead, we can and should invoke the particular lived values that unite us and inform the institutions we cherish and wish to defend.

At times like these, the nation rightly falls back on the record of aspiration and accomplishment that makes up our collective understanding of what we live for. That understanding is sufficient, and far from undermining its sufficiency, postmodern thought tells us that we have grounds enough for action and justified condemnation in the democratic ideals we embrace, without grasping for the empty rhetoric of universal absolutes to which all subscribe but which all define differently.

But of course it's not really postmodernism that people are bothered by. It's 5 the idea that our adversaries have emerged not from some primordial darkness, but from a history that has equipped them with reasons and motives and even with a perverted version of some virtues. Bill Maher, Dinesh D'Souza, and Susan Sontag have gotten into trouble by pointing out that "cowardly" is not the word to describe men who sacrifice themselves for a cause they believe in.

Ms. Sontag grants them courage, which she is careful to say is a "morally neutral" term, a quality someone can display in the performance of a bad act. (Milton's Satan is the best literary example.) You don't condone that act because you describe it accurately. In fact, you put yourself in a better position to respond to it by taking its true measure. Making the enemy smaller than he is blinds us to the danger he presents and gives him the advantage that comes along with having been underestimated.

That is why what Edward Said has called "false universals" should be rejected: They stand in the way of useful thinking. How many times have we heard these new mantras: "We have seen the face of evil"; "these are irrational madmen"; "we are at war against international terrorism." Each is at once inaccurate and unhelpful. We have not seen the face of evil; we have seen the face of an enemy who comes at us with a full roster of grievances, goals, and strategies. If we reduce that enemy to "evil," we conjure up a shape-shifting demon, a wild-card moral anarchist beyond our comprehension and therefore beyond the reach of any counterstrategies.

The same reduction occurs when we imagine the enemy as "irrational." Irrational actors are by definition without rhyme or reason, and there's no point in reasoning about them on the way to fighting them. The better course is to think of these men as bearers of a rationality we reject because its goal is our destruction. If we take the trouble to understand that rationality, we might have a better chance of figuring out what its adherents will do next and preventing it.

And "international terrorism" does not adequately describe what we are up against. Terrorism is the name of a style of warfare in service of a cause. It is the cause, and the passions informing it, that confront us. Focusing on something called international terrorism—detached from any specific purposeful agenda—only confuses matters. This should have been evident when President Vladimir Putin of Russia insisted that any war against international terrorism must have as one of its objectives victory against the rebels in Chechnya.

When Reuters decided to be careful about using the word "terrorism" because, according to its news director, one man's terrorist is another man's freedom fighter, Martin Kaplan, associate dean of the Annenberg School for Communication at the University of Southern California, castigated what he saw as one more instance of cultural relativism. But Reuters is simply recognizing how unhelpful the word is, because it prevents us from making distinctions that would allow us to get a better picture of where we are and what we might do. If you think of yourself as the target of terrorism with a capital T, your opponent is everywhere and nowhere. But if you think of yourself as the target of a terrorist who comes from somewhere, even if he operates internationally, you can at least try to anticipate his future assaults.

Is this the end of relativism? If by relativism one means a cast of mind that renders you unable to prefer your own convictions to those of your adversary, then relativism could hardly end because it never began. Our convictions are by definition preferred; that's what makes them our convictions. Relativizing them is neither an option nor a danger.

But if by relativism one means the practice of putting yourself in your adversary's shoes, not in order to wear them as your own but in order to have some understanding (far short of approval) of why someone else might want to wear them, then relativism will not and should not end, because it is simply another name for serious thought.

QUESTIONS FOR DISCUSSION AND WRITING

1. The context of the article, written slightly less than a month after the attacks of September 11, 2001, provides a crucial backdrop for the arguments in the essay. Why did critics believe that postmodernism had contributed to the weakening of the country's resolve (paragraph 1)? What is their definition of postmodernism? Why do they define the term in that way? How does Fish respond?

2. Much of Fish's article is in many ways an extended definition of the term "postmodernism" in an attempt to convey to a larger audience a concept often unfamiliar to the general public. In paragraph 2, Fish begins with a formal definition of the term. What are the implications of the term in regard to the events of 9/11 and America's response?

3. Part of the concept of postmodernism is the rejection of universal or objective truths. Instead, truths are seen as coming from a certain perspective; for example, "one man's terrorist is another man's freedom fighter" (paragraph 10). What does this mean, and what are its larger implications? Consider, for

example, that the term "freedom fighter" was coined during the Reagan era to denote unconventional soldiers who fought against an established government that America opposed. Is there an objective way to make such a distinction, or is the term subjective, as postmodernism says? Why?

4. Adding an appeal to the audience, Fish argues that our inability to understand our enemy will impede the nation's attempts to fight against terrorism. By focusing on terrorism—rather than its cause—we may be drawn to support other conflicts that we don't want to support (e.g., Chechnya) in the name of fighting terrorism. Instead, we must understand the thinking of the enemy to better reflect on what we can do and what they might do next. Do you agree or disagree with Fish's position? Defend your answer using specific examples and details.

5. Ultimately, Fish is arguing that relativism as an intellectual concept has been broadly misunderstood—that it doesn't mean not to hold any convictions, but to recognize that one's convictions are not the only convictions held, and that we need to better understand the convictions of others. He argues that understanding is not the same as approval (paragraph 12). Consider current political and social conflicts in the world. How can a postmodernist approach help (or hinder) resolutions to such conflicts? Be specific.

Acknowledgments

Sherman Alexie. "The Joy of Reading and Writing: Superman and Me" from *The Most Wonderful Books*. Copyright © 1997 by Sherman Alexie. Reproduced with permission of Nancy Stauffer Associates. "What Sacagawea Means to Me" from *Time,* July 8, 2002. Copyright © 2002 by Time, Inc. Reproduced from *Time* and published with the permission of Time, Inc. Reproduction in any manner in any language in whole or in part without written permission is prohibited. All rights reserved.

Natalie Angier. "Men, Women, Sex and Darwin" as appeared in *The New York Times,* February 1999, from *Woman: An Intimate Geography.* Copyright © 1999 by Natalie Angier. Adapted and reproduced with permission of Houghton Mifflin Harcourt Publishing Company. All rights reserved.

Gloria E. Anzaldúa. "Beyond Traditional Notions of Identity" from *The Chronicle of Higher Education,* October 11, 2002. A different version of this essay was originally published as "(Un)natural bridges, (Un)safe spaces" from *This Bridge We Call Home: Radical Visions for Transformation,* ed. Gloria E. Anzaldúa and AnaLouise Keating. Copyright © 2002 by Gloria E. Anzaldúa. Reproduced with permission of the Gloria E. Anzaldúa Trust. All rights reserved.

James Baldwin. "Stranger in the Village" from *Notes of a Native Son.* Copyright © 1955, renewed 1983 by James Baldwin. Reproduced with permission of Beacon Press, Boston. All rights reserved.

Nicholas Carr. "Is Google Making Us Stupid?" from *The Atlantic,* July/August 2008. Copyright © 2008 by Nicolas Carr. Reproduced with permission. All rights reserved.

Andrea Cornwall. "Boys and Men Must Be Included in the Conversation on Equality" from *The Guardian,* March 21, 2012. Copyright © 2012 by Guardian News & Media Ltd. Reproduced with permission. All rights reserved.

William Deresiewicz. "Faux Friendship" from *The Chronicle of Higher Education,* December 6, 2009. Copyright © 2009 by William Deresiewicz. Reproduced with permission of the author. All rights reserved.

Joan Didion. "On Keeping a Notebook" from *Slouching Towards Bethlehem.* Copyright © 1966, 1968, renewed 1996 by Joan Didion. Reproduced with permission of Farrar, Straus, and Giroux, LLC. All rights reserved.

Brian Doyle. "Joyas Voladoras" from *The American Scholar,* autumn 2004, Volume 73, No. 4. Copyright © 2004 by Brian Doyle. Reproduced with permission. All rights reserved.

David Eagleman. "The Brain on Trial" as adapted for *The Atlantic,* June 2, 2011, from *Incognito: The Secret Lives of the Brain.* Copyright © 2012 by David Eagleman. Reproduced with permission of Pantheon Books, an imprint of the Knopf Doubleday Publishing Group, a division of Random House, LLC and Penguin Canada Books, Inc. All rights reserved.

Barbara Ehrenreich. "Bonfire of the Disney Princesses" from *The Nation,* December 11, 2007. Copyright © 2007 by Barbara Ehrenreich. Reproduced

Picture Credit

Rhetorical Index

Autobiography

Cause and Effect

Description

Graphic Selection

Humor and Satire

Illustration

Process Analysis

Index

Missing something? To access the online material that accompanies this text, visit **bedfordstmartins.com/arlington**. Students who do not buy a new book can purchase access at this site.

Inside the Bedford Integrated Media for *The Arlington Reader*

- Amy Walker, "21 Accents" [video]

- T. M. Luhrmann and Kurt Anderson, *When God Talks Back: Understanding the American Evangelical Relationship with God* [audio interview]

- Michael Oatman, *Admittance to a Better Life* [audio essay]

- Colleen Kinder, *Blot Out* [text essay]

- Daniel J. Solove, *The End of Privacy?* [text essay]

- Linda Barry, *Hate* [graphic essay]